Nonfiction Classics
for Students

Nonfiction Classics
for Students

Presenting Analysis, Context, and Criticism on Nonfiction Works

Volume 1

Elizabeth Thomason, Editor

GALE GROUP

★

THOMSON LEARNING

Detroit • New York • San Diego • San Francisco
Boston • New Haven, Conn. • Waterville, Maine
London • Munich

Nonfiction Classics for Students

Staff

Editor: Elizabeth Thomason.

Contributing Editors: Reginald Carlton, Anne Marie Hacht, Michael L. LaBlanc, Ira Mark Milne, Jennifer Smith.

Managing Editor, Literature Content: Dwayne D. Hayes.

Managing Editor, Literature Product: David Galens.

Publisher, Literature Product: Mark Scott.

Content Capture: Joyce Nakamura, *Managing Editor*. Sara Constantakis, *Editor*.

Research: Victoria B. Cariappa, *Research Manager*. Cheryl Warnock, *Research Specialist*. Tamara Nott, Tracie A. Richardson, *Research Associates*. Nicodemus Ford, Sarah Genik, Timothy Lehnerer, Ron Morelli, *Research Assistants*.

Permissions: Maria Franklin, *Permissions Manager*. Shalice Shah-Caldwell, *Permissions Associate*. Jacqueline Jones, *Permissions Assistant*.

Manufacturing: Mary Beth Trimper, *Manager, Composition and Electronic Prepress*. Evi Seoud, *Assistant Manager, Composition Purchasing and Electronic Prepress*. Stacy Melson, *Buyer*.

Imaging and Multimedia Content Team: Barbara Yarrow, *Manager*. Randy Bassett, *Imaging Supervisor*. Robert Duncan, Dan Newell, *Imaging Specialists*. Pamela A. Reed, *Imaging Coordinator*. Leitha Etheridge-Sims, Mary Grimes, David G. Oblender, *Image Catalogers*. Robyn V. Young, *Project Manager*. Dean Dauphinais, *Senior Image Editor*. Kelly A. Quin, *Image Editor*.

Product Design Team: Kenn Zorn, *Product Design Manager*. Pamela A. E. Galbreath, *Senior Art Director*. Michael Logusz, *Graphic Artist*.

Copyright Notice

National Advisory Board

Table of Contents

Literature: Conversation, Communication, Idea, Emotion

The so-called information age of which we are all a part has given birth to the internet, and so literature—the written word in its many forms—now has vaster, faster avenues in which to circulate. The internet is the latest revolutionary development in communication media. Before the internet, the development of the printing press and the advent of radio and television were equally astonishing events. This great network of circulating words and images amongst persons and populations can be thought of as a vast human conversation.

In conversation, speech arises from the desire to communicate an idea or a feeling or else it follows from an address and is a reply of sorts. How quickly one can formulate a communication or a reply depends upon the nature of the problem or of the address. Does one wish to communicate something simple, such as a command? Or does one wish to meditate on a significant problem or issue in one's personal life? Or in history or science? Is the address a greeting, an email, a painting, a letter, or a novel? Nonfiction works, the subject of *Nonfiction Classics for Students*, are written literary communications of a sustained nature, unlike ephemeral written communications such as emails or memos which are concerned with the immediately occurring events of the day. The length and breadth of the novel form follows from the amount of learning and experience that goes into the making of each novel, and from the amount of information it can convey. Nonfiction works that have become classics are those which have been particularly moving or influential, or both. These works have changed the way people live, think and see.

Influential and admired nonfiction works can be thought of as significant events in the traditions in which they are working or to which they are related, traditions such as autobiography, biography, history, science, the essay, and so forth. For example, published diaries such as *Anne Frank: The Diary of a Young Girl* are related to the traditions of autobiography and history. If the diary of this child is so valued by readers it is because, besides being engagingly written, it vividly brings forth an era and a set of world-effecting political disasters and events. Through the words of Anne Frank, the reader enters the world of a bright, hopeful teenager who is, nevertheless, haunted by the fear of her imminent death as the world around her crumbles. To know that this child eventually was captured and died in a concentration camp moves us to be more assiduous and vigilant in our protection of innocents, and we lament this terrible suffering and senseless waste of life.

Yet, if we wish to learn how it was that World War II came about, or who Europe's leaders were and what these leaders' beliefs and ideologies were, then we must turn to the written works which are histories and not autobiographies, works whose subject is not the history of a single person but rather the reconstruction of the social, cultural, and political panorama of the period or age under study. Histories, in turn, are related to the traditions of political and social science. The more polemical or argumentative the history book, the more it is a work of political theory, where facts are important— though not as critical as ideas about how human society works or can be arranged. Through the written word, social and political thinkers and philosophers make their arguments, and societies, cultures, and ways of governing rise and fall.

In the form of nonfiction, scientists make their arguments and present their formulae, and technology and medical, and psychological treatments are changed. It is because of the printed, widely disseminated word that women and other minorities win equal opportunity in the world. Ideas change the world, they are a part of our history. Students of literature enter into this vast human conversation and have the opportunity to contribute to it. *Nonfiction Classics for Students* prepares and equips these students so that his or her entry into this conversation is meaningful.

Nonfiction Classics for Students also presents relevant information and discussion about major figures and ideas. As for what makes a particular autobiography or diary stand out, it is often because the story of the single person seems to speak for many or because it is powerfully and beautifully written. While we do not necessarily demand high artistry from some writers of nonfiction prose, we do expect some degree of fluency from those writers practicing the art of the essay, autobiography, or biography. The various reasons why a particular work has been or is admired, and its reputation past and current, is also discussed in the pages of *Nonfiction Classics for Students*. In presenting students with discussions of a work's artistry and reputation, as well as of relevant, related traditions, theories, and ideas, *Nonfiction Classics for Students* models a process of reading and systematic study that a student can apply to any work he or she reads.

What this study of and engagement with a work of literature can produce is either a research paper, which is a presentation of what has been learned, or else it can give rise to a reply, a counter-communication. In composing writing in response to a work, a student participates in and contributes to the vast human conversation. The entries in *Nonfiction Classics for Students* suggest relevant topics for classroom discussion. *Nonfiction Classics for Students* is an aid to students who set out to inform themselves responsibly about a particular nonfiction work. This series equips students to contribute meaningfully to the vast human conversation. Are a writer's ideas productive and useful? Does the book teach us important lessons or move us? Do we detect the circulation of heinous ideologies in our present times that remind us of destructive ideologies and beliefs from the past? In reading and learning and communicating, we engage with history; to the extent that we live by what we learn, we make history when we respond to and act on what we have read.

Carol Dell'Amico
Santa Monica College, Santa Monica, California

Introduction

Purpose of the Book

The purpose of *Nonfiction Classics for Students* (*NCfS*) is to provide readers with a guide to understanding, enjoying, and studying nonfiction works by giving them easy access to information about the work. Part of Gale's "For Students" literature line, *NCfS* is specifically designed to meet the curricular needs of high school and undergraduate college students and their teachers, as well as the interests of general readers and researchers considering specific works. While each volume contains entries on "classic" works frequently studied in classrooms, there are also entries containing hard-to-find information on contemporary pieces, including works by multicultural, international, and women authors.

The information covered in each entry includes an introduction to the work and the work's author; a summary, to help readers unravel and understand the events in a work; descriptions of key figures, including explanation of a given figure's role in the work as well as discussion about that figure's relationship to other figures in the work; analysis of important themes in the work; and an explanation of important literary techniques and movements as they are demonstrated in the work.

In addition to this material, which helps the readers analyze the work itself, students are also provided with important information on the literary and historical background informing each work. This includes a historical context essay, a box comparing the time or place the work was written to modern Western culture, a critical overview essay, and excerpts from critical essays on the work. A unique feature of *NCfS* is a specially commissioned overview essay on each work, targeted toward the student reader.

To further aid the student in studying and enjoying each work, information on media adaptations is provided, as well as reading suggestions for works of fiction and nonfiction on similar themes and topics. Classroom aids include ideas for research papers and lists of critical sources that provide additional material on each work.

Selection Criteria

The titles for each volume of *NCfS* were selected by surveying numerous sources on teaching literature and analyzing course curricula for various school districts. Some of the sources surveyed included: literature anthologies; *Reading Lists for College-Bound Students: The Books Most Recommended by America's Top Colleges;* a College Board survey of works commonly studied in high schools; a National Council of Teachers of English (NCTE) survey of works commonly studied in high schools; Arthur Applebee's 1993 study *Literature in the Secondary School: Studies of Curriculum and Instruction in the United States;* and the *Modern Library's* list of the one hundred best nonfiction works of the century.

Input was also solicited from our expert advisory board (experienced educators specializing in English), as well as educators from various areas. From these discussions, it was determined that each volume should have a mix of "classic" works (those works commonly taught in literature classes) and contemporary works for which information is often hard to find. Because of the interest in expanding the canon of literature, an emphasis was also placed on including works by international, multicultural, and women authors. Our advisory board members—current high school teachers—helped pare down the list for each volume. If a work was not selected for the present volume, it was often noted as a possibility for a future volume. As always, the editor welcomes suggestions for titles to be included in future volumes.

How Each Entry Is Organized

Each entry, or chapter, in *NCfS* focuses on one work. Each entry heading lists the full name of the work, the author's name, and the date of the work's publication. The following elements are contained in each entry:

- **Introduction:** a brief overview of the work which provides information about its initial publication, its literary standing, any controversies surrounding the work, and major conflicts or themes within the work.

- **Author Biography:** this section includes basic facts about the author's life, and focuses on events and times in the author's life that inspired the work in question.

- **Summary:** a description of the major events in the work, with interpretation of how these events help articulate the work's themes. Subheads demarcate the work's various chapters or sections.

- **Key Figures:** an alphabetical listing of major figures in the work. Each name is followed by a brief to an extensive description of the person's role in the works, as well as discussion of the figure's actions, relationships, and possible motivation. Figures are listed alphabetically by last name. If a figure is unnamed—for instance, the narrator in *Pilgrim at Tinker Creek*—the figure is listed as "The Narrator" and alphabetized as "Narrator." If a person's first name is the only one given, the name will appear alphabetically by the name. Variant names are also included for each person. Thus, the full name "Richard

Monckton Milnes" would head the listing for a figure in *The Education of Henry Adams*, but listed in a separate cross-reference would be his more formal name "Lord Houghton."

- **Themes:** a thorough overview of how the major topics, themes, and issues are addressed within the work. Each theme discussed appears in a separate subhead, and is easily accessed through the boldface entries in the Subject/Theme Index.

- **Style:** this section addresses important style elements of the work, such as setting, point of view, and narration; important literary devices used, such as imagery, foreshadowing, symbolism; and, if applicable, genres to which the work might have belonged, such as Gothicism or Romanticism. Literary terms are explained within the entry, but can also be found in the Glossary.

- **Historical and Cultural Context:** This section outlines the social, political, and cultural climate *in which the author lived and the work was created.* This section may include descriptions of related historical events, pertinent aspects of daily life in the culture, and the artistic and literary sensibilities of the time in which the work was written. If the piece is a historical work, information regarding the time in which the work is set is also included. Each section is broken down with helpful subheads.

- **Critical Overview:** this section provides background on the critical reputation of the work, including bannings or any other public controversies surrounding the work. For older works, this section includes a history of how the work was first received and how perceptions of it may have changed over the years; for more recent works, direct quotes from early reviews may also be included.

- **Criticism:** an essay commissioned by *NCfS* which specifically deals with work and is written specifically for the student audience, as well as excerpts from previously published criticism on the work.

- **Sources:** an alphabetical list of critical material quoted in the entry, with full bibliographical information.

- **For Further Study:** an alphabetical list of other critical sources which may prove useful for the student. Includes full bibliographical information and a brief annotation.

In addition, each entry contains the following highlighted sections, set separate from the main text:

- **Media Adaptations:** a list of important film and television adaptations of the work, including source information. The list may also include such variations on the work as audio recordings, musical adaptations, and other stage interpretations.

- **Compare and Contrast:** an ''at-a-glance'' comparison of the cultural and historical differences between the author's time and culture and late twentieth-century Western culture. This box includes pertinent parallels between the major scientific, political, and cultural movements of the time or place the work was written, the time or place the work was set (if a historical work), and modern Western culture. Works written after the 1990 may not have this box.

- **What Do I Read Next?:** a list of works that might complement the featured work or serve as a contrast to it. This includes works by the same author and others, works of fiction and nonfiction, and works from various genres, cultures, and eras.

- **Study Questions:** a list of potential study questions or research topics dealing with the work. This section includes questions related to other disciplines the student may be studying, such as American history, world history, science, math, government, business, geography, economics, psychology, etc.

Other Features

NCfS includes ''Literature: Conversation, Communication, Idea, Emotion,'' a foreword by Carol Dell'Amico, an educator and author. This essay examines the nonfiction as a lasting way for authors to communicate, as well as the influence these works can have. Dell'Amico also discusses how *Nonfiction Classics for Students* can help teachers show students how to enrich their own reading experiences and how the series is designed to aid students in their study of particular works.

A Cumulative Author/Title Index lists the authors and titles covered in each volume of the *NCfS* series.

A Cumulative Nationality/Ethnicity Index breaks down the authors and titles covered in each volume of the *NCfS* series by nationality and ethnicity.

A Subject/Theme Index, specific to each volume, provides easy reference for users who may be studying a particular subject or theme rather than a single work. Significant subjects from events to broad themes are included, and the entries pointing to the specific theme discussions in each entry are indicated in **boldface.**

Entries may include illustrations, including photos of the author, stills from stage productions, and stills from film adaptations.

Citing Nonfiction Classics for Students

When writing papers, students who quote directly from any volume of *Nonfiction Classics for Students* may use the following general forms. These examples are based on MLA style; teachers may request that students adhere to a different style, so the following examples may be adapted as needed.

When citing text from *NCfS* that is not attributed to a particular author (i.e., the Themes, Style, Historical Context sections, etc.), the following format should be used in the bibliography section:

''The Journalist and the Murderer.'' *Nonfiction Classics for Students.* Ed. Elizabeth Thomason. Vol. 1. Farmington Hills, MI: The Gale Group, 2001, pp. 8–9.

When quoting the specially commissioned essay from *NCfS* (usually the first piece under the ''Criticism'' subhead), the following format should be used:

Hart, Joyce. Essay on ''Silent Spring.'' *Nonfiction Classics for Students.* Ed. Elizabeth Thomason. Vol. 2. Farmington Hills, MI: The Gale Group, 2001, pp. 8–9.

When quoting a journal or newspaper essay that is reprinted in a volume of *NCfS,* the following form may be used:

Limon, John. ''*The Double Helix* as Literature.'' *Raritan* Vol. 5, No. 3 (Winter 1986), pp. 26–47; excerpted and reprinted in *Nonfiction Classics for Students,* Vol. 2, ed. Elizabeth Thomason (Farmington Hills, MI: The Gale Group, 2001), pp. 84–94.

When quoting material reprinted from a book that appears in a volume of *NCfS,* the following form may be used:

Gunnars, Kristjana. ''Life as Fiction: Narrative Appropriation in Isak Dinesen's *Out of Africa,*'' in *Isak Dinesen and Narrativity,* ed. Gurli A. Woods, (Carleton University Press, 1990), pp. 25–34; excerpted and reprinted in *Nonfiction Classics for Students,* Vol. 2, ed. Elizabeth Thomason (Farmington Hills, MI: The Gale Group, 2001), pp. 282–87.

We Welcome Your Suggestions

The editor of *Nonfiction Classics for Students* welcomes your comments and ideas. Readers who wish to suggest works to appear in future volumes, or who have other suggestions, are cordially invited to contact the editor. You may contact the editor via E-mail at: **ForStudentsEditors@galegroup.com.** Or write to the editor at:

Editor, *Nonfiction Classics for Students*
The Gale Group
27500 Drake Rd.
Farmington Hills, MI 48331–3535

Literary Chronology

1838: Henry Brooks Adams is born in Boston, Massachusetts, on February 16.

1868: William Edward Burghardt Du Bois is born on February 23, in Great Barrington, Massachusetts.

1879: Edward Morgan Forster is born on January 1, in London.

1889: Arnold Toynbee is born on April 14, in London.

1889: Walter Lippmann is born in New York City, on September 23.

1903: *The Souls of Black Folk* is published.

1907: Rachel Carson is born on May 27, in Springdale, Pennsylvania.

1907: *The Education of Henry Adams* is privately published and is not published for the public until 1918.

1908: Richard Nathaniel Wright is born on September 4, at Rucker's Plantation in Roxie, Mississippi.

1918: Adams dies on March 27, in Washington, D.C.

1919: *The Education of Henry Adams* wins the Pulitzer Prize for autobiography.

1925: William Styron is born on June 11, in Newport News, Virginia.

1927: *Aspects of the Novel* is published.

1929: *A Preface to Morals* is published.

1930: Frank McCourt is born on August 19, in Brooklyn, New York.

1930s: Janet Malcolm is born in Prague, Czechoslovakia. The exact date of her birth is unknown.

1934–1961: *A Study of History* is originally published over a span of almost thirty years.

1937: Richard Rhodes is born on July 4, in Kansas City, Kansas.

1942: Isabel Allende is born in Lima, Peru, on August 2, 1942.

1945: *Black Boy* is published.

1945: Meta Ann Doak, better known as Annie Dillard, is born on April 30, in Pittsburgh, Pennsylvania.

1949: Elaine Potter Richardson, later known as Jamaica Kincaid, is born on May 25, in St. John's, Antigua.

1949: Andrew Scott Berg is born in Norwalk, Connecticut.

1960: Wright dies of a heart attack on November 28, in Paris

1962: *Silent Spring* is published.

1963: Du Bois dies on August 27, in Accra, Ghana.

1964: Carson dies of cancer in Silver Springs, Maryland, on April 14.

1970: Forster dies on June 7, in Coventry, England.

1974: Lippmann dies in New York City, on December 14.

1974: *Pilgrim at Tinker Creek* is published.

1975: Dillard wins the Pulitzer Prize for general nonfiction for *Pilgrim at Tinker Creek*.

1975: Toynbee dies in York, England, on October 22.

1987: *The Making of the Atomic Bomb* is published and wins the National Book Award for nonfiction.

1988: *The Making of the Atomic Bomb* is awarded the Pulitzer Prize for general nonfiction.

1989: *The Journalist and the Murderer* appears in the *New Yorker*; it is published in book form in 1990.

1990: *Darkness Visible* is published.

1994: *Paula* is published in Spanish; it is translated into English in 1995.

1996: *Angela's Ashes* is published.

1997: *Angela's Ashes* wins the Pulitzer Prize for autobiography.

1997: *My Brother* is published.

1998: *Lindbergh* is published.

1999: *Lindbergh* wins the Pulitzer Prize for biography.

Acknowledgments

The editors wish to thank the copyright holders of the excerpted criticism included in this volume and the permissions managers of many book and magazine publishing companies for assisting us in securing reproduction rights. We are also grateful to the staffs of the Detroit Public Library, the Library of Congress, the University of Detroit Mercy Library, Wayne State University Purdy/Kresge Library Complex, and the University of Michigan Libraries for making their resources available to us. Following is a list of the copyright holders who have granted us permission to reproduce material in this volume of *Nonfiction Classics for Students (NCfS)*. Every effort has been made to trace copyright, but if omissions have been made, please let us know.

COPYRIGHTED MATERIAL IN *NCfS*, VOLUME 1, WERE REPRODUCED FROM THE FOLLOWING PERIODICALS:

Americas, v. 47, November-December, 1995. ©1995 Américas. Reprinted by permission of Américas, a bimonthly magazine published by the General Secretariat of the Organization of American States in English and Spanish.—*A Review of International English Literature*, v. 20, July, 1989 for "But We Argued About Novel-Writing: Virginia Woolf, E. M. Forster and the Art of Fiction," by Ann Henley. Copyright ©1989 The Board of Governors, The University of Calgary. Reproduced by permission of the publisher and the author.— *Commentary*, v. 90, November, 1990 for "Depression-as-Disease," by Carol Iannone./ v. 107, January, 1999 for "First in Flight," by Sam Tanenhaus. Copyright ©1990, 1999 by the American Jewish Committee. All rights reserved. Both reproduced by permission of the publisher and the author.—*Dissent*, Fall, 1995 for "Rachel Carson's Silent Spring" by Yaakov Garb. ©1995, by Dissent Publishing Corporation. Reprinted by permission of the publisher and the author.—*First Things*, n. 75, August-September, 1997. Reproduced by permission.— *Journal of American Folklore*, v. 104, Summer, 1991 for "The Failure of Folklore in Richard Wright's Black Boy," by Jay Mechling. Reproduced by permission of the American Folklore Society from Journal of American Folklore and the author.—*Journal of Feminist Studies in Religion*, v. 6, Spring, 1990. Reproduced by permission.— *MELUS: Society for the Study of the Multi-Ethnic Literature of the United States*, v. 22, Summer, 1997. Copyright, MELUS: The Society for the Study of Multi-Ethnic Literature of the United States, 1997. Reproduced by permission.—*The Nation (New York)*, v. 250, June 25, 1990; v. 265, November 3, 1997. ©1990, 1997 The Nation magazine/The Nation Company, Inc. Both reproduced by permission.— *National Review*, v. l, October 26, 1998. Copyright ©1988 by National Review, Inc, 215 Lexington Avenue. New York, NY 10016. Reproduced by permission.—*The New Republic*, v. 221, November 1, 1999. ©1999 The New Republic, Inc. Reproduced by permission of The New Republic.—*North*

Dakota Quarterly, v. 56, Summer, 1988. Copyright 1988 by The University of North Dakota. Reproduced by permission.—*South Atlantic Quarterly*, v. 82, Spring, 1983. Copyright ©1983 by Duke University Press. Reproduced by permission.—*Style*, v. 27, Summer, 1993 for "Richard Wrights and the African-American Autobiography Tradition" by William L. Andrews. Copyright ©Style, 1993. All rights reserved. Reproduced by permission of the publisher and the author.—*Technology and Culture*, v. 30, October, 1989. ©The Johns Hopkins University Press. Reproduced by permission.—Tulane Studies in English, v. 22, 1977. Copyright ©1977 by Tulane University. Reproduced by permission.—*Washington Monthly*, v. 22, May, 1990. Reproduced with permission from The Washington Monthly. Copyright by the Washington Monthly Company, 1611 Connecticut Ave., N.W., Washington, D.C. 20009 (202) 4462–0128.—*The Women's Review of Books*, v. xiii, November, 1995 for "In the House of Spirits" by Ruth Behar. Copyright ©1995. All rights reserved. Reproduced by permission of the author.

COPYRIGHTED MATERIAL IN *NCfS*, VOLUME 1, WERE REPRODUCED FROM THE FOLLOWING BOOKS:

Colmer, John. From *E.M. Forster: The Personal Voice*. Routledge & Kegan Paul. ©John Colmer 1975. Reproduced by permission.—Horowitz, Howard. From *New Essays on The Education of Henry Adams*. Edited by John Carlos Rowe. Cambridge University Press, 1996. ©Cambridge University Press 1996. Reproduced with permission of Cambridge University Press and the author.—Thompson, Kenneth W. From *Toynbee's Philosophy of World History and Politics*. Louisiana State University Press, 1985. Copyright ©1985 by Louisiana State University Press. All rights reserved. Reproduced by permission of Louisiana State University Press.

PHOTOGRAPHS AND ILLUSTRATIONS APPEARING IN *NCfS*, VOLUME 1, WERE RECEIVED FROM THE FOLLOWING SOURCES:

Adams, Henry, illustration by P. Ruller.—Allende, Isabel, photograph. Archive Photos. Reproduced by permission.—Allende, Salvador, photograph. UPI/Bettmann. Reproduced by permission.—Austen, Jane, engravings. Source unknown.—Bail, Horace, sitting on porch of former slave shack, photograph. Corbis. Reproduced by permission.—Berg, A. Scott, photograph. Aloma. Reproduced by permission.—Bohr, Niels, photograph. The Library of Congress.—Carson, Rachel L., photograph. UPI/Bettmann Newsphotos. Reproduced by permission.—"Colored Drinking Fountain," photograph. The Library of Congress.—Corliss Engine, illustration. The Library of Congress.—Cover of "Le Petit Journal," photograph by Leonard de Selva. Corbis. Reproduced by permission.—Depressed women, sitting in window, photograph. ©1992 Science Photo Lib. Custom Medical Stock Photo. Reproduced by permission.—Dillard, Annie, photograph. Jerry Bauer. Reproduced by permission.—DuBois, W.E.B., photograph. The Bettmann Archive. Reproduced by permission.—Forster, E. M., photograph. Archive Photos, Inc. Reproduced by permission.—Goldstein, Gee, with her son Robert, photograph. Bettmann/Corbis. Reproduced by permission.—Guy, George H., 1961, Mississippi, photograph. AP/Wide World Photos, Inc. Reproduced by permission.—Hardy, Thomas, photograph. Archive Photos, Inc. Reproduced by permission.—Interior of the British Museum of Egyptian antiquities, photograph by Peter Aprahamian. Corbis. Reproduced by permission.—Kincaid, Jamaica, photograph by Adam Riesner. The Liaison Agency Network. Reproduced by permission.—La Mondeda/Plaza dl. Libertad, photograph Susan D. Rock. Reproduced by permission.—Levi, Primo, photograph by Jerry Bauer. ©Jerry Bauer. Reproduced by permission.—Lindbergh, Anne Morrow, holding her baby Charles Jr., photograph. ©Bettmann/Corbis. Reproduced by permission.—Lindbergh, Charles, photograph. The Library of Congress.—Lippman, Walter, photograph. Archive Photos, Inc. Reproduced by permission.—MacDonald, Dr. Jeffrey, being interviewed after being released from prison, photograph. ©Bettmann/Corbis. Reproduced by permission.—Malcolm, Janet. ©Jerry Bauer. Reproduced by permission.—McCourt, Frank, photograph by Jerry Bauer. ©Jerry Bauer. Reproduced by permission.—McGinniss, Joe, photograph. AP/Wide World Photos. Reproduced by permission.—Merton, Thomas, photograph. The Library of Congress.—Mushroom cloud rising from Baker Day atomic bomb blast at Bikini Island, photograph. Corbis. Reproduced by permission.—Rastafarian man standing behind banner, photograph by Daniel Laine. Corbis. Reproduced by permission.—Rhodes, Richard, standing in front of the Atom Bomb Dome, photograph. Reproduced by permission.—Scene from the film "Angela's Ashes," photograph. The Kobal Collection. Reproduced by permission.—Scopes Trial, photograph. UPI/Corbis-Bettmann. Reproduced by permission.—St. Patrick's Roman Catholic Cathedral, photograph by Michael St. Maur Sheil. Corbis. Reproduced by permission.—Street scene, with volcano in the distance, Antigua, Guatemala, photograph by David Johnson. Reproduced by permission.—Styron, William, New York City, 1990, photograph. AP/Wide World Photos. Reproduced by permission.—Three white-tailed does, eating from shrubs in the Appalachian Trail, Shenandoah National Park, photograph by Raymond Gehman. Corbis. Reproduced by permission.—Thucydides, illustration. The Library of Congress.—Toynbee, Arnold J., photograph. Hulton-Deutsche Collection/Corbis. Reproduced by permission.—Washington, Booker T, photograph.—Worker in protective photograph by Ed Young. Corbis. Reproduced by permission.—Wright, Richard, photograph. AP/Wide World Photos, Inc. Reproduced by permission.

Contributors

Bryan Aubrey: Aubrey holds a Ph.D. in English literature from the University of Durham, England. He has worked as editor for Lynn C. Franklin Associates and as a freelance writer and editor. Entries on *Angela's Ashes* and *A Study of History*. Original essays on *Angela's Ashes* and *A Study of History*.

Cynthia Bily: Bily teaches writing and literature at Adrian College in Adrian, Michigan, and writes for various educational publishers. Entry on *Pilgrim at Tinker Creek*. Original essay on *Pilgrim at Tinker Creek*.

Adrian Blevins: Blevins, a poet and essayist who has taught at Hollins University, Sweet Briar College, and in the Virginia Community College System, is the author of *The Man Who Went Out for Cigarettes,* a chapbook of poems, and has published poems, stories, and essays in many magazines, journals, and anthologies. Original essay on *My Brother*.

Liz Brent: Brent has a Ph.D. in American culture, specializing in film studies, from the University of Michigan. She is a freelance writer and teaches courses in the history of American cinema. Entries on *Aspects of the Novel*, *The Making of the Atomic Bomb*, and *A Preface to Morals*. Original essays *Aspects of the Novel*, *The Making of the Atomic Bomb*, and *A Preface to Morals*.

Brian Collins: Collins has written on nineteenth- and early-twentieth-century American literature. Entry on *Silent Spring*.

Joyce Hart: Hart has degrees in English literature and in creative writing. She is a freelance editor and published writer. Original essays on *Silent Spring* and *A Preface to Morals*.

Jeremy W. Hubbell: Hubbell is a freelance writer and is currently a Ph.D. candidate in history at the State University of New York at Stony Brook. Entries on *The Education of Henry Adams* and *Paula*. Original essays on *The Education of Henry Adams* and *Paula*.

Elizabeth Judd: Judd is a freelance writer and book reviewer with a master's in English from the University of Michigan and a bachelor's degree from Yale. Entry on *My Brother*. Original essay on *My Brother*.

David Kelly: Kelly is an instructor of creative writing at several community colleges in Illinois, as well as a fiction writer and playwright. Entry on *Lindbergh*. Original essay on *Lindbergh*.

Rena Korb: Korb has a master's degree in English literature and creative writing and has written for a wide variety of educational publishers. Entry on *The Journalist and the Murderer*. Original essays on *Angela's Ashes*, *Darkness Visible*, and *The Journalist and the Murderer*.

Jennifer Lynch: Lynch teaches at the Potrero Hill After School Program and the Taos Literacy Program and also contributes to *Geronimo*, a journal of politics and culture. Entry on *The Souls of Black Folk*. Original essay on *The Souls of Black Folk*.

Mary Mahony: Mahony earned a master's degree in English from the University of Detroit and a master's degree in library science from Wayne State University. She is an instructor of English at Wayne County Community College in Detroit, Michigan. Original essay on *Black Boy*.

Ian Palmer: Palmer is a full-time freelance writer who runs his own consulting business and has a bachelor's degree in journalism. Original essay on *Lindbergh*.

Stephen Patnode: Patnode is an instructor of American history and the history of medicine. Original essay on *The Making of the Atomic Bomb*.

Chris Semansky: Semansky holds a Ph.D. in English from Stony Brook University and teaches writing and literature at Portland Community College in Portland, Oregon. Entry on *Darkness Visible*. Original essay on *Darkness Visible*.

Karen D. Thompson: Thompson has done graduate work at the University of North Carolina, Greensboro, and has taught English at Asheboro High School (North Carolina), Manor High School, Dripping Springs High School, and Dripping Springs Middle School (Texas). Original essays on *Angela's Ashes* and *Darkness Visible*.

Kelly Winters: Winters is a freelance writer and editor and has written for a wide variety of academic and educational publishers. Original essay on *A Preface to Morals*.

Angela's Ashes

Frank McCourt

1996

In *Angela's Ashes*, Frank McCourt tells the story of his impoverished childhood and adolescence in Limerick, Ireland, during the 1930s and 1940s. Written from the point of view of the young boy, it is a long catalogue of deprivation and hardship: the alcoholism of his father, the despair of his mother, the deaths of three of his younger siblings, the grinding poverty and unsanitary living conditions they all had to endure. The story takes place in a highly religious society in which the dogmas of Roman Catholicism are accepted without question. In addition to Catholicism, the people of Limerick exhibit a narrow provincialism, in which Protestants and anyone who comes from the north of Ireland are despised, and an Irish nationalism that is fueled by hatred of the English. And yet the effect of the story, although often poignant and sad, is not depressing. The young narrator describes the events without bitterness, anger, or blame. Poverty and hardship are treated simply as if they are a fact of life, like the weather. And in spite of the hard circumstances, many episodes are hilarious.

The combination of childhood innocence, riotous humor, and descriptions of a degree of poverty beyond anything that contemporary readers in the West could imagine made *Angela's Ashes* a huge commercial success. It is regarded as an outstanding contribution to the growing popularity of the genre of the memoir.

Author Biography

Frank McCourt was born on August 19, 1930, in Brooklyn, New York. He was the first of seven children born to Malachy and Angela McCourt. When he was four, his sister Margaret died. In that same year, the family decided to leave New York and return to their native Ireland. They settled in Limerick in southwest Ireland.

In Limerick during the 1930s, the McCourt family was desperately poor. Malachy McCourt was an alcoholic and was frequently unemployed. McCourt's twin brothers both died of pneumonia, probably due to the unhealthy living conditions. McCourt spent three months in the hospital with typhoid fever when he was ten. In the early 1940s, during World War II, McCourt's father went to England to work in a munitions factory in Coventry, but he never sent any money back to his family. By the age of eleven, McCourt was the family bread-winner. Several years later he quit school and got a job delivering telegrams. He eventually managed to save enough money to leave Ireland for the United States. In 1949, at the age of nineteen, he arrived in New York City and got a job at the Biltmore Hotel. He was eventually fired from the Biltmore and took a series of menial jobs.

McCourt was drafted into the army during the Korean War and served in West Germany. After military service, he attended New York University under the G. I. Bill, where he earned a bachelor's degree in English. He later earned a master's degree in English at Brooklyn College.

For twenty-eight years, beginning in 1959, McCourt taught in schools in New York City. For the last fifteen of those years, he taught English and creative writing at Stuyvesant High School in Manhattan, which was noted for the high quality of its students and where he was known as a popular teacher.

McCourt retired in 1987. In 1994, he began writing a memoir of his life in Ireland, *Angela's Ashes*, which was published in 1996 by Scribner. The book was a huge success and won many awards, including the Pulitzer Prize.

In 1999, McCourt published *'Tis*, a memoir that took up the story of his life where *Angela's Ashes* left off.

McCourt is married to his third wife, Ellen Frey, a publicist whom he married in 1994. They live in New York City.

Summary

Chapters 1 and 2

Frank McCourt, the narrator of *Angela's Ashes*, describes his family origins and his early years in Brooklyn. His Irish father fled to America after serving with the Irish Republican Army in their conflict with the British. There he married Angela Sheehan from Limerick. Within a few years, Angela gave birth to five children, one of whom died in infancy. Life is hard in Brooklyn, and relatives arrange for the McCourts to return to Ireland and settle in Limerick. In their one-room dwelling, the entire family sleeps in one flea-infested bed. Frank's father, who is an alcoholic, goes on the dole. Angela accepts charity from the St. Vincent de Paul Society, but her family is miserably poor. Both twins die of pneumonia.

Chapters 3 and 4

The McCourts move to a slum house, and Angela gives birth to another boy, Michael. Frank's father tells him the baby was brought by the Angel on the Seventh Step. Sometimes Frank sits on the seventh step of the staircase in case the angel visits. Malachy gets a job in a cement factory, but on payday he spends all his money in the pub. Frank is washed and scrubbed and dressed in a new suit for his First Communion. Afterwards, Grandma makes him a special breakfast, which, to Grandma's dismay, he vomits up. His day ends with a trip to the cinema.

Chapters 5 and 6

Frank gets into trouble with Grandma when, instead of taking dinner to the lodger, he eats it himself. In a prank, Frank's brother Malachy puts his father's false teeth in his own mouth and cannot get them out, resulting in a trip to the hospital. Frank takes dance lessons but soon skips them in favor of the cinema. He reluctantly joins the Arch Confraternity and becomes an altar boy. At school the masters are bullies. With his friend Paddy Clohessy, Frank visits the home of their classmate Fintan Slattery, after which they steal apples from an orchard and drink milk directly from a cow's udder.

Chapters 7 and 8

Frank earns money by helping Uncle Pat deliver newspapers. He meets Mr. Timoney, an old man with poor eyesight, who pays Frank to read to him. Angela gives birth to another baby boy, Alphie. A classmate offers to let Frank and his friends climb the drainpipe at his house to see his sisters taking their bath. The adventure is a fiasco and they are caught. Frank catches typhoid fever and spends three months in the hospital. He talks to a young girl, Patricia Morgan, who later dies. Frank is punished for talking to her, which is against the hospital rules, by being moved to an empty ward. A cleaner named Seamus befriends him.

Chapters 9 and 10

Frank's father gets a job in a munitions factory in England but sends no money home. Frank has conjunctivitis and spends another month in the hospital. Angela is forced to seek public assistance and is humiliated by the men who dispense it. Then she gets pneumonia, and the boys are sent to live with Aunt Aggie and Uncle Pa. Aggie is cruel to them. When Angela returns from hospital, she is forced to beg for food at the priest's home.

Chapters 11 and 12

Eleven-year-old Frank gets a job helping his neighbor John Hannon deliver coal. His friends envy him, but the coal dust hurts his weak eyes. Frank's father returns for Christmas but brings no money. After his departure, the family is threatened with eviction for nonpayment of rent. They burn some loose wood from one of the walls of the rooms for heat. Frank hacks at one of the beams while his mother is out and the ceiling falls in. They are evicted and go to live with Angela's cousin Laman Griffin.

Chapters 13 and 14

At thirteen, Frank excels in school. His mother wants him to continue his education, but he is turned away from the Christian Brothers school. Laman comes home drunk and punches Frank, bruising his face. Frank goes to stay with his uncle Pat and quits school.

Chapters 15 and 16

Frank works as a telegram boy and meets Theresa Carmody, a girl who is dying of consumption. They make love. Within a short while, Theresa dies and Frank is heartbroken. Frank delivers a telegram to Mr. Harrington, who complains un-

Frank McCourt

truthfully to Frank's employers that Frank stole whiskey and food. A priest intervenes to save Frank's job, but Frank decides to quit anyway and takes a job distributing newspapers. He has a second job writing letters for Mrs. Finucane.

Chapters 17 and 18

Uncle Pa takes Frank for his first beer in a pub. He gets drunk and after going home hits his mother. A compassionate priest hears his confession. Frank works all winter at his new job and dreams of immigrating to America. Finally he saves enough money to buy a ticket and sail to New York.

Key Figures

Mr. Benson

Mr. Benson is a master at Leamy's National School. Fierce and short-tempered, he browbeats the boys and hits them with his stick. As Frank puts it, "He roars and spits all over us all day."

Theresa Carmody

Theresa Carmody is a seventeen-year-old girl whom Frank meets when he is delivering telegrams.

Media Adaptations

- *Angela's Ashes* has been recorded on audiotape, read by McCourt, in abridged (1996) and unabridged (1997) versions published by Simon and Schuster.

- In 1999, *Angela's Ashes* was made into a film, directed by Alan Parker and starring Robert Carlyle and Emily Watson.

Theresa has red hair and green eyes; she is dying of consumption. She and Frank make love several times, but she dies within weeks. Frank is heartbroken.

Paddy Clohessy

Paddy Clohessy is Frank's friend when they are seven years old. Paddy has six brothers and one sister, and the family is extremely poor. He goes to school barefoot, dressed in rags. In one incident, he and Frank rob an orchard and drink milk directly from a cow. Later, Paddy moves to England and works in a pub.

Declan Collopy

Declan Collopy is four years older than Frank. According to Frank, ''He has lumps on his forehead that look like horns. He has thick ginger eyebrows that meet in the middle and hang over his eyes, and his arms hang down to his kneecaps.'' Declan is a bully who is in charge of enforcing attendance at the Confraternity that Frank joins.

Peter Dooley

Peter Dooley is known as Quasimodo because he has a hump on his back like the hunchback of Notre Dame. He is five years older than Frank. Frank says of his appearance, ''His red hair sticks up in all directions. He has green eyes and one rolls around in his head so much he's constantly tapping his temple to keep it where it's supposed to be.'' Quasimodo cultivates an English accent and wants

to be a newsreader with the BBC. He dies of consumption.

Mrs. Brigid Finucane

Mrs. Finucane employs Frank to write threatening letters to people who owe her money.

Philomena McNamara Flynn

Philomena is a cousin of Frank's mother. She is a large, intimidating woman who helps to arrange for the McCourt family to leave Brooklyn and return to Ireland.

Delia McNamara Fortune

Delia is Philomena Flynn's sister and a cousin of Frank's mother. Like Philomena, she is large, ''great breasted and fierce.'' With her sister, she arranges for the McCourts to return to Ireland.

Grandma

Grandma is Angela's mother and Frank's grandmother. She has ''white hair and sour eyes'' and is known for her religious devotion. She does her best to help the McCourts but spends much of her time complaining. She dies of pneumonia when Frank is thirteen.

Laman Griffin

Laman Griffin is Angela's cousin. She and her sons go to live at his house after their own is destroyed. Laman is a former officer in the Royal Navy who works as a laborer for the Electricity Supply Board. He spends much time in bed reading and smoking, and he and Angela become lovers. Sometimes he gets drunk, and in one incident he becomes angry with Frank and beats him up.

Bridey Hannon

Bridey Hannon is the McCourts' neighbor. She is unmarried and lives with her mother and father. She smokes a lot and chats with Angela by the fire for long periods.

John Hannon

John Hannon is Bridey Hannon's father. He makes a living from delivering coal, but his legs are diseased, and he has trouble continuing to work. Frank gets a job helping him.

Mr. Harrington

Mr. Harrington is an Englishman whose wife has just died. He gets angry with Frank when the boy delivers a telegram, and he tries to get Frank fired from his job.

Aunt Aggie Keating

Aggie is Frank's aunt. She is large and has flaming red hair; she works in a clothing factory. Unable to have children of her own, she is jealous of her sister Angela. When the McCourt boys stay at her house, she is abusive, calling Frank ''scabby eyes.''

Uncle Pa Keating

Pa Keating is Frank's uncle. His skin is black from shoveling coal into the furnaces at the Limerick Gas Works. He is a veteran of World War I, in which he was a victim of poison gas. He has a fine sense of humor, and Frank finds him amusing.

Alphie McCourt

Alphie McCourt is the youngest of Frank's brothers; he is nine years old when Frank leaves for America.

Angela McCourt

Angela McCourt is Frank's mother. Formerly Angela Sheehan, she grew up with her three siblings in a Limerick slum. She never knew her father, who deserted the family before she was born. Sent by her family to New York while in her teens, Angela meets Malachy McCourt at a party. When she becomes pregnant, they marry, but it is not a happy partnership. Angela's husband is a feckless drunkard. She loses three of her seven children in infancy, and she has to feed and clothe her family in desperately poor conditions. Throughout these ordeals, Angela shows toughness and an ability to endure the blows of fate, although she frequently complains about her misfortunes.

Eugene McCourt

Eugene McCourt is Frank's younger brother, Oliver's twin. He dies of pneumonia at age two.

Frank McCourt

Frank McCourt, the eldest child of Malachy and Angela McCourt, is the narrator of the story. He is raised in poverty, but this does not diminish his good spirits since he has never known life to be any different. When his twin brothers die in infancy, he is too young to understand what has happened. Attending Leamy's National School, he makes friends easily and gets involved in a number of schoolboy pranks, but he is also mocked by the other boys for his clumsily repaired shoes, which reveal his poverty. The boys make up contemptuous jingles about him. Frank also has health problems; he catches typhoid fever and nearly dies, and later he develops severe conjunctivitis. Despite these setbacks, he excels at school. On the advice of the headmaster, Frank's mother tries to have Frank enrolled in the Christian Brothers School in order to continue his education, but he is turned down; there are few educational opportunities for a boy from the ''lanes,'' the slum districts of Limerick. Frank is not disappointed because he wants to leave school and earn money. He is immensely proud of himself when he gets some odd jobs and brings home money for his mother. As Frank enters adolescence, he has a first love affair with a dying girl, and he learns more of the tragedies of his world when he sees his mother begging for food and also observes the pitiful condition of some of the people he encounters in his job delivering telegrams. Finally, he saves enough money to fulfill his long-held dream of emigrating to America.

Malachy McCourt

Malachy McCourt is Frank's father. He was born in Ireland and fought with the Irish Republican Army against the British. Then he became a fugitive and made his way to New York, where he married Angela Sheehan. Malachy has a weakness for drink and cannot hold a job for more than a few weeks. When unemployed, Malachy often spends his dole money at the pub, coming home late singing patriotic Irish songs. Malachy is fond of his children, however, and entertains them with colorful stories that he makes up on the spot. He tells them they must be prepared to die for Ireland. Eventually, Malachy departs for England to work in a factory during World War II, but he sends no money back to his family. He returns briefly one Christmas, promising presents for everyone, but when his wife opens the box of chocolates he brings, she finds that he has eaten half of them himself.

Malachy McCourt

Malachy McCourt is Frank's brother, one year younger than Frank. Malachy is the first brother to leave home. He enrolls in the Army School of Music and moves to Dublin. He gives that up and gets various jobs in England: a Catholic boarding school, a gas works, and, finally, the stockroom of a garage. He wants to follow Frank to America.

Margaret McCourt

Margaret McCourt is Frank's sister who dies in infancy in Brooklyn.

Michael McCourt

Michael McCourt is six years younger than his brother Frank. At age six he shows a compassionate nature, bringing home stray dogs and homeless old men.

Oliver McCourt

Oliver McCourt is Frank's youngest brother and Eugene's twin. He dies of pneumonia at age two.

Mikey Molloy

Mikey Molloy is the son of Peter and Nora Malloy and a friend of Frank's. He has epileptic fits and is known as Malloy the Fit. He is two years older than Frank and is known as "the expert in the lane on Girls' Bodies and Dirty Things in General."

Nora Molloy

Nora Molloy is Peter Molloy's wife and a friend of Frank's mother. She is sometimes so demented with worry over how she is going to feed her family that she is admitted to the lunatic asylum.

Peter Molloy

Peter Molloy is Nora Malloy's husband. He is a champion beer drinker, and he sometimes drinks away his dole money. According to Frank, Peter "doesn't give a fiddler's fart about what the world says."

Mr. O'Dea

Mr. O'Dea is a master at Frank's school. He is especially good at hurting and shaming the boys.

Mr. Thomas O'Halloran

Mr. O'Halloran is the headmaster of Leamy's National School. The boys call him Hoppy because he has a short leg and hops when he walks. He is the hardest master in the school because he makes the boys learn everything by heart.

Mr. O'Neill

Mr. O'Neill is a master at Frank's school. He is called Dotty by the boys because he is small, like a dot. He loves Euclidean geometry and teaches it even when he is not supposed to.

Brendan Quigley

Brendan Quigley is a classmate of Frank's. He is always asking questions, so he's known as Question Quigley.

Quasimodo

See Peter Dooley

Seamus

Seamus is a cleaner at the hospital where Frank recovers from typhoid fever. He befriends Frank and brings him books to read.

Uncle Pat Sheehan

Uncle Pat Sheehan is Frank's uncle. He was dropped on his head when he was a baby and, as a result, is simple-minded. He is also called Ab, short for The Abbot. He is illiterate but makes a living selling newspapers.

Fintan Slattery

Fintan Slattery is a classmate of Frank's. He and his mother are very pious Catholics. He says he wants to be a saint when he grows up.

Mr. Timony

Mr. Timony is an old man with poor eyesight who pays Frank to read to him. He claims to be a Buddhist.

Themes

Poverty

The theme of poverty is pervasive. In Limerick, poverty is accepted as a fact of life; although there is a charitable society and a rudimentary system of public assistance, neither does much to lift the poor out of their misery. For the McCourts, the dole money is never sufficient. When they first settle in Limerick, Malachy receives a mere nineteen shillings a week, for a family of six. "Just enough for all of us to starve on," says Angela. The family often goes hungry.

Not only is food scarce; living conditions are appalling. The McCourts must deal with fleas, rats, flies, and lice. There is only one lavatory for the whole lane of eleven families, and it is directly outside their door. In summer the stench is unbearable. Malnutrition and bad living conditions are probably responsible for the deaths of the twin boys.

The children often have to dress in rags. At Leamy's School, six or seven boys go barefoot. Frank's shoes are falling to pieces, which leads to a comical episode in which his father, after being told by his wife that he is useless, attempts to repair the shoes using on old bicycle tire.

The family's poverty worsens when Frank's father goes to work in England but fails to send any money home. The children sleep on piles of rags. The downward cycle reaches its lowest point when Angela is forced to beg for food at the door of the priest's house, an incident that makes clear the link between poverty and humiliation.

Alcoholism

Limerick is a town that is damp, not only from the incessant rain; it is also awash in alcohol. The evenings that the men spend at the pub drinking pints of beer—usually referred to as stout or porter—as well as whiskey, are almost like religious rituals. These evenings give the men a chance to enjoy male camaraderie and forget the hardness of their lives (as well as their wives).

The worship of beer is quickly passed from man to boy. When Frank is about six, he accompanies his father to a pub, and his uncle Pa Keating explains to him, "Frankie, this is the pint. This is the staff of life. This is the best thing for nursing mothers and for those who are long weaned." In what amounts to a rite of passage, boys in Limerick are initiated into beer drinking on their sixteenth birthday when their fathers take them to the pub for a pint.

Beer drinking is also a competitive activity in Limerick. Pa Keating boasts that he is the champion pint-drinker. He wins bets by drinking more than anyone else, a feat he accomplishes by making himself vomit in the restroom, which enables him to go back to the bar and drink more beer. His son Mikey longs to emulate him.

The destructive effects of alcohol are apparent in Frank's father, the stereotypical Irish drunk. He ruins his life, and the lives of his family, by his addiction. Another character whose drinking causes suffering for others is Angela's cousin Laman Griffin, who beats Frank up one night in a drunken rage.

Topics for Further Study

- Research the history of Ireland's relations with England. Why do some Irish feel such bitterness toward their larger neighbor? Why has the conflict in Northern Ireland been so difficult to end?

- Discuss the different kinds of relief available for the poor in the Limerick of McCourt's youth. How does that assistance differ from the help that is available to the poor in America today?

- Investigate the topic of alcoholism. What causes it? Is it on the increase? Why do some people who drink alcohol become alcoholics but others do not?

- If you were to write a memoir of your own childhood, how would it resemble or differ from McCourt's memoir?

After his first two pints on his sixteenth birthday, Frank himself argues with his mother and hits her.

Catholicism

The people of Limerick are steeped in the rites and dogmas of Roman Catholicism, which they accept without question. These beliefs reach Frank's youthful mind as he listens to grown-up conversation or tries to make sense of what he is told at home or at school. The results are often comical. For example, he looks forward to his First Communion for weeks because the masters at school tell him it will be the happiest day of his life. He thinks that is because after First Communion boys are allowed to go around collecting money from relatives and neighbors, which they can then use to buy sweets and go to the Lyric Cinema. When the big day arrives, the priest puts the wafer, which according to Catholic dogma is the body of Christ, on Frank's tongue. To Frank's dismay, it sticks: "I had God glued to the roof of my mouth. I could hear the master's voice, Don't let that host touch your teeth for if you bite God in two you'll roast in hell for eternity." However, the crisis passes. "God was good," Frank says. "He melted and I swallowed

Him and now, at last, I was a member of the True Church, an official sinner.''

When Frank is confused about religion, he simply connects the bits and pieces he has heard until he has something that makes sense to him. When his little brother Eugene dies, he wonders whether he is cold in his coffin in the graveyard, but then he remembers that angels come and open the coffin and take Eugene up to the sky where he joins his other dead siblings and they have plenty of fish and chips and toffee.

As for the adults, they seem content with a narrow faith in which only Catholics are saved. Protestants and others are doomed to hell, and even unbaptized children languish forever in Limbo. ''Otherwise,'' says Frank's grandmother, ''you'd have all kinds of babies clamorin' to get into heaven, Protestants an' everything, an' why should they get in after what they did to us for eight hundred years?''

Style

Style

Angela's Ashes is narrated in the first person, and apart from the first part of chapter one, it is told in the present tense. The present tense narration serves the author's purpose well as it conveys the immediacy of the child's experience and avoids giving the impression, as a past tense might, that the story is being told by an adult reflecting on his childhood.

The language used throughout is colloquial and earthy. Slang, Irishisms, and vulgar expressions are used frequently, and these convey the way people really talked in Limerick during the author's childhood. Having a ''fine fist,'' for example, means that a person has good handwriting. To go ''beyond the beyonds'' is to behave in an outrageous manner.

Some words will be unfamiliar to American ears: ''gob'' is slang for mouth and ''fags'' are cigarettes. To call someone an ''eejit'' is to insult them, and the expression ''diddering omadhaun,'' as used by a schoolmaster to describe a boy, is obviously not a compliment.

The Irish way of expressing themselves is apparent in such statements as ''That's a great leg for the dancing you have there, Frankie,'' a compliment to young Frankie on his dancing ability. Some expressions are saltier. Mrs. O'Connor, the dance teacher, tells Frankie to stop frowning ''or you'll have a puss on you like a pound of tripe.'' Irish pronunciation is reflected in ''fillum star'' (film star), and occasionally there is a glimpse of what Frankie's father calls Limerick slum-talk, as in Uncle Pat's words, ''That's me mug and don't be drinkin' your way oush of ish.'' The last three words mean ''out of it.''

In an unusual device, there are not any quotation marks used to mark direct speech anywhere in this book, even when two people are engaged in a conversation. The effect of this is perhaps to subtly remind the reader that everything in the memoir is being filtered through the consciousness of the child narrator. It is always Frank who is reporting the speech, whether direct or indirect.

Tone

The tone of the book is often humorous. It is only rarely angry, even though Frankie might have a lot to be angry about. The humor occurs not only in humorous situations and events but in the way young Frankie strives to understand the world and what happens in it. On one occasion, when he is eleven or twelve, he discovers his parents' marriage certificate and notes that they were married on March 28, 1930. But this mystifies him:

> I was born on the nineteenth of August and Billy Campbell told me the father and mother have to be married nine months before there's a sign of a child. Here I am born into the world in half the time. That means I must be a miracle and I might grow up to be a saint with people celebrating the feast of St. Francis of Limerick.

Toward the end of the book, as Frank matures, the tone becomes compassionate, as Frank becomes more aware of the suffering of others.

Historical Context

Memoir Genre

The 1990s witnessed a huge growth in the number of personal memoirs, and the genre itself underwent significant change. Traditionally, the memoir was an autobiographical narrative, usually by a prominent person, that focused not on the personal experiences of the author but on the significant people and events he had witnessed or been involved in. In the 1990s, however, personal mem-

Compare & Contrast

- **1930s:** Limerick, Ireland, is economically depressed, with pockets of extreme poverty. Unemployment is high.

  Today: Helped by a growth in tourism and high-tech industries, Limerick flourishes. "Combat poverty" groups have been set up, using funds from the European Union.

- **1930s:** A common cause of death in Limerick, and Ireland as a whole, is tuberculosis. Tuberculosis is prevalent because living conditions are unsanitary and malnutrition is rife.

  Today: Advances in medicine have made tuberculosis a curable, rather than a deadly, disease. In 1998, Ireland reported 424 cases of tuberculosis, down from 640 in 1991.

- **1930s:** Although independent, Ireland is a member of the British Commonwealth. Ireland remains neutral when war breaks out between Britain and Germany in 1939 and withdraws from the Commonwealth in 1948.

  Today: Relations between Britain and Ireland are cordial. The two governments work together to secure peace in Northern Ireland. Both countries are members of the European Union.

---

oirs came to be written not only by famous people but by unknown ones, too. Many focused on a certain period in a person's life (thus distinguishing them from the more comprehensive scope of the autobiography). Often the memoir was about the growth from childhood or adolescence to young adulthood. Frequently these memoirs detailed an environment in which some deprivation or vice, such as poverty, alcoholism or sexual abuse, played a large part.

One of the most popular memoirs from the early part of the decade was *Darkness Visible* (1992), the account by the writer William Styron of his descent into mental illness. Susanna Kaysen's *Girl Interrupted* (1994) was a bestselling memoir of Kaysen's life in a mental institution. In 1995, Mary Karr published the hugely successful *The Liars' Club,* a memoir of growing up in a dysfunctional Texas family. In that year, approximately two hundred memoirs were published. Commentators linked the startling growth of the genre to the vogue for confessional television programs and the "tell-it-all" nature of popular culture. James Atlas, in his article "The Age of the Literary Memoir Is Now," comments on the openness that characterized the 1990s:

> In an era when 'Oprah' reigns supreme and 12-step programs have been adopted as the new mantra, it's

perhaps only natural for literary confession to join the parade. We live in a time when the very notion of privacy, of a zone beyond the reach of public probing, has become an alien concept.

It was in this literary and cultural climate that McCourt began writing *Angela's Ashes* in 1994. The memoir, with its tale of a family ruined by an alcoholic father, anguished by bereavement, and living with the shame of almost unimaginable poverty, fit comfortably into the genre as it was being redefined during the decade. So when *Angela's Ashes* was published two years later, its runaway success was perhaps not surprising.

England, Protestantism, and Ireland

Even a casual reader of *Angela's Ashes* could hardly fail to notice that the Irish of Limerick reserve a special hatred for the English, and they also despise Protestants. The origins of this antipathy go far back in history.

The English first invaded Ireland in the twelfth century, which explains the recurring Irish complaint in the book about "what the English did to us for eight hundred long years."

The Protestants are associated with the English, since it was the Protestant forces of Oliver Cromwell in the seventeenth century, followed by the Protestant army of William of Orange in 1690, that subjugated the Catholic Irish.

After a long struggle, most of Ireland won its independence in 1922. This period of Irish history is associated with the name of Eamon de Valera, the first president of the Irish Free State. In *Angela's Ashes*, Frank's father believes that de Valera is the greatest man in the world.

After 1922, the six predominantly Protestant northern counties of Ireland remained under British rule. This is why in *Angela's Ashes* anyone from the north of Ireland, even a good Catholic and an Irish nationalist like Malachy McCourt, is regarded with suspicion.

Critical Overview

Angela's Ashes was a massive success, becoming one of the most highly acclaimed nonfiction works of the decade. The book won numerous awards, including the National Book Critics Circle Award and the Pulitzer Prize for biography. It was on the *New York Times* bestseller list for over two years.

Almost all reviewers praised the book generously. The vividness with which McCourt evoked his childhood was particularly appreciated, as was the hilarity of much of the book. Writing for the *New York Times,* Michiko Kakutani praised McCourt's skill as a storyteller:

> McCourt . . . waited more than four decades to tell the story of his childhood, and it's been well worth the wait. With *Angela's Ashes*, he has used the storytelling gifts he inherited from his father to write a book that redeems the pain of his early years with wit and compassion and grace.

Kakutani noted that the book contained little of the resentment or bitterness that a reader might expect to find in the memoirs of a man who had endured almost unimaginable poverty and deprivation in his early years. She also commented favorably on McCourt's descriptive skill:

> Writing in prose that's pictorial and tactile, lyrical but streetwise, Mr. McCourt does for the town of Limerick what the young Joyce did for Dublin: he conjures the place for us with such intimacy that we feel we've walked its streets and crawled its pubs.

The verdict of Malcolm Jones Jr., in *Newsweek,* was equally positive: "It is only the best storyteller who can so beguile his readers that he leaves them wanting more when he's done. With *Angela's Ashes*, McCourt proves himself one of the very best.''

In *Time,* John Elson described *Angela's Ashes* as a "spunky, bittersweet memoir,'' noting that in spite of the bleakness of the story, McCourt's humor leaves a deeper impression: "Like an unpredicted glimmer of midwinter sunshine, cheerfulness keeps breaking into this tale of Celtic woe.'' Elson picked out McCourt's descriptions of his First Communion and his adventures as a post-office messenger as "riotously funny.''

Neal Ascheron, in the *New York Review of Books,* called *Angela's Ashes* a "wonderful'' memoir and pointed out that the central figure is not the Angela of the title but Frank's father, Malachy, whom Ascheron saw as a poignant, almost tragic figure: "McCourt shows a man who is almost literally dissolving, physically and mentally, in a world which has no time or means to help him.''

One of the few dissenting voices in this chorus of praise was that of R. F. Foster, a professor of Irish history, writing in *New Republic*. Although he acknowledged that some of the images and events in the book were "marvelously realized,'' Foster pointed out what he believed to be obvious flaws:

> [I]t all goes on for too long . . . . its author lacks an internal editor, a sense of developing structure. The language is monotonous and the incidents are repetitive. The characterizations are perfunctory: people are identified by formulaic straplines, which are trundled out again and again each time they appear.

Foster also questioned whether all the incidents were as factual as McCourt claimed. He pointed out that when McCourt's father attempts to secure an IRA pension, he has to visit the back streets of a Dublin suburb, but in reality such pensions were administered by a government department.

Foster's skepticism, however, was not shared by readers, who bought the book in huge numbers. *Angela's Ashes* has been translated into nineteen languages and has sold more than four million copies worldwide.

Criticism

Bryan Aubrey

Aubrey holds a Ph.D. in English. In this essay, he discusses Angela's Ashes *as a coming-of-age story.*

Joe Breen (left) as young Frank McCourt, Robert Carlyle as Malachy Sr., Emily Watson as Angela, Sean (Oisin) Carney Daly as Baby Michael, and Shane Murray-Corcoran as young Malachy in the 1999 film version of Angela's Ashes

Angela's Ashes is a coming-of-age story. It records the growth of Frankie McCourt from an impoverished childhood to his maturity at the age of nineteen, when he is able to plot his own course in life. Through the difficult circumstances of his early years Frankie grows intellectually, spiritually, and morally.

One of Frankie's first coming-of-age experiences is a more practical one, however. It concerns earning money. Given the fact that desperate poverty is rampant in Limerick, it is not surprising that Frankie's ability to supplement the family income marks a significant stage of his growth. He gets his first job helping his uncle deliver newspapers when he is only eight or nine years old. More important is when at the age of eleven he helps his neighbor Mr. Hannon deliver coal. ''I'm a man now,'' he says, and starts to take on manly domestic tasks such as lighting the fire in the morning. When he is able to put a shilling in his pocket as a reward for his labors, he proudly says, ''I'm not a child anymore,'' even though he is taunted by other boys and girls because of his coal-blackened appearance. Eventually, however, Frankie wins their respect and envy as he climbs up each day on Mr. Hannon's float ''like any

workingman.'' On payday he takes another major step to maturity when he presents his mother with the money he has earned. He is now able to do what his father would not or could not: provide a modest amount of money for the family. It is not surprising that his mother breaks down in tears.

Maturity is about more than earning wages, however. As a very young boy, Frankie is raised in an atmosphere soaked with a narrow, dogmatic Catholicism and the nationalistic myths of a pure and heroic Ireland oppressed for eight hundred years by the English. Much of his intellectual and spiritual growth will involve punching holes in these twin pillars of his upbringing.

It is the one-dimensional concept of history that is the first to go. Frankie has been hearing about Ireland and its history virtually since his birth. His drunken father comes home singing patriotic songs about Irish martyrs and tells his children they must be ready to die for Ireland. The English are blamed for just about everything that has gone wrong in Irish history. This moral culpability of Ireland's neighbors sometimes takes on comic proportions. When Frankie's uncle Pa Keating sees Malachy

What Do I Read Next?

- *'Tis: A Memoir* (1999) is McCourt's sequel to *Angela's Ashes*. It takes up McCourt's life story from his arrival in America in 1949.

- *A Monk Swimming* (1998) is a memoir written by McCourt's younger brother, Malachy, about his life mainly in New York City from 1952 to 1963. It is full of amusing stories about his experiences and the people he met.

- *Reading in the Dark* (1998), by Seamus Deane, is a novel about an Irish boy growing up in the 1940s and 1950s in Derry, a town near the border of Northern Ireland, the Republic of Ireland, and a focal point for conflict between Catholics and Protestants.

- *A Dublin Girl: Growing Up in the 1930s* (1999), by Elaine Crowley, is a memoir of Crowley's childhood in a slum district of Dublin. Reviewers compared it to *Angela's Ashes*; it has humor and poignancy, although the atmosphere is not as bleak as in McCourt's memoir.

McCourt beating a mattress to get the fleas out, he remarks that ancient Ireland had no fleas; fleas were brought by the English for the purpose of driving the Irish out of their wits.

Frankie absorbs a similar version of history at school. He is told that whenever the Irish have been on the brink of a noble victory, they have either been betrayed by a traitor or an informer or have fallen victim to some despicable English trick.

When he is eleven years old, Frankie finally hears something different. In a history lesson given by Mr. O'Halloran, the headmaster, he hears the phrase "atrocities on both sides" to describe an ancient battle between the Irish and the English. He is incredulous. He asks O'Halloran if it was true that the Irish committed atrocities. O'Halloran replies that the Irish killed prisoners and were no better or worse than the English. This is a revelation for Frankie:

> Mr. O'Halloran can't lie. He's the headmaster. All those years we were told the Irish were always noble and they made brave speeches before the English hanged them. Now Hoppy O'Halloran is saying the Irish did bad things. Next he'll be saying the English did good things.

O'Halloran, who seems to have been a great exception at Leamy's National School, tells the boys that they must study and learn to make up their own minds. It is a lesson Frankie takes to heart.

Frankie's religious indoctrination, however, is not to be so easily thrown off. Since he was a child, he has accepted what he has been told. As a young boy, he lacks the intellectual maturity to question. His mind is filled with the religious platitudes he hears from the adults around him and the more systematic dogmas in which he is instructed at school. Much of the comic effect of *Angela's Ashes* comes when religious dogma, on its way into the child's mind, gets hopelessly garbled. For the most part, Frankie simply does not have any understanding of what he is being told. He grows up, for example, with the idea that everyone who is not a Catholic is doomed. The word *doom* fascinates him, and he is astute enough to observe that it is the favorite word of priests. When he sees a group of Protestants going to church, he feels sorry for them, especially the girls. He knows they are doomed and he wants to save them: "Protestant girl come with me to the True Church. You'll be saved and you won't have the doom." The inappropriate use of the definite article ("the doom") contributes to the odd way he uses the term, as if doom is something that one catches, like influenza. It shows that young Frankie does not have the slightest understanding of what he is talking about.

Understood or not, Catholic teachings sink deeply into Frankie's mind. His eventual liberation from the confines of Catholic theology is connected to his emerging awareness of his sexuality. The acquiring of sexual knowledge is central to most coming-of-age stories, and *Angela's Ashes* is no exception.

As he reaches puberty, Frankie discovers the pleasures of masturbation. But this is not a guilt-free pleasure. He and the other boys of his age have to endure a chilling denunciation of ''self-abuse'' hurled at them by a priest:

> Our Lady weeps over these abominations knowing that every time you interfere with yourself you nail to the cross her Beloved Son, that once more you hammer into His dear head the crown of thorns, that you reopen those ghastly wounds.

For a short while afterwards, Frankie allows himself to feel guilty about his acts of ''self-defilement''; he prays to the Virgin Mary and promises not to do it again. But then, only a few months later, he climbs to the top of an old castle on a hill, from where he has a panoramic view of the River Shannon and the surrounding countryside. There, ''in full view of Ireland'' he defiantly commits the same ''sin'' of masturbation. It is a moment of self-liberation. Although he knows that he still faces ''the doom,'' he no longer seems to care.

It is a different matter when he has his first experience of sex with a girl. When he makes love to Theresa Carmody, who later dies of consumption, he feels extremely guilty because he knows that their lovemaking was sinful and that Theresa is now in hell. And it is his fault. On this occasion he is saved from the torments of guilt not by his own independent thinking but by Father Gregory, a kindly Franciscan priest to whom he confesses. This priest, who seems to possess more humanity than many of the others who populate the pages of *Angela's Ashes*, assures him that Theresa ''is surely in heaven. She suffered like the martyrs in olden times and God knows that's penance enough. You can be sure the sisters in the hospital didn't let her die without a priest.'' This is enough to convince Frank. He frees himself from guilt and learns that there is more than one way of interpreting the dogmas of Catholicism.

Along with his spiritual growth, Frankie also exhibits moral growth. The latter is shown by several incidents that take place when he works as a telegram boy. He is fourteen and regards this as his first job ''as a man'' (his earlier work delivering coal notwithstanding). His employers tell him that he must do no favors for anyone; his job is to deliver the telegrams and leave. But Frankie is moved by the plight of many of the people he encounters on his rounds. He feels compassion for Mrs. Gertrude

> **Frank's eventual liberation from the confines of Catholic theology is connected to his emerging awareness of his sexuality. The acquiring of sexual knowledge is central to most coming-of-age stories, and *Angela's Ashes* is no exception.''**

Daly, an old woman who dresses in rags and is starving and very ill. He feels sympathy also for a veteran of the Boer War who can hardly walk and lives in a freezing house where there is little food. The plight of a woman named Mrs. Spillane, who is attempting to raise her two crippled children in direst poverty, also touches his heart. So moved is Frank by the suffering of these people that he agrees to run errands for them, such as cashing a money order at the post office and buying groceries, even though he knows that this could cost him his job if he is caught. He is prepared to defy authority and obey his conscience—a sign of integrity and maturity.

These experiences are significant because up to that point, the suffering of others has not seemed to have made much impression upon him. But now the presence of suffering raises questions that make him reflect and consider: ''What are you supposed to do?'' he asks himself. Although he is moved more by the promptings of his heart than his head, he makes a conscious decision to take action based on a moral imperative to help others. This is of great value because it is a position he has reached himself, rather than one he has merely accepted in the form of the religious platitudes that have swirled around him since the day he was born.

It has been a hard upbringing for Frankie McCourt in the slums of Limerick. He has experienced more than enough deprivation for one lifetime. He has known sickness and poverty and the deaths of siblings and his first lover. But he has also developed survival skills, learning how to be independent and how to earn a living. He has developed the ability to think for himself and has discovered a sympathy and compassion for others. All these qualities will stand him in good stead as he achieves his long-held ambition of immigrating to America, the land of promise.

Source: Bryan Aubrey, Critical Essay on *Angela's Ashes,* in *Nonfiction Classics for Students,* The Gale Group, 2001.

Rena Korb

Korb has a master's degree in English literature and creative writing and has written for a wide variety of educational publishers. In the following essay, she discusses the portrayal of McCourt's family in Angela's Ashes.

On the opening page of his riveting memoir, *Angela's Ashes,* Frank McCourt describes his "miserable Irish Catholic childhood":

> the poverty; the shiftless loquacious alcoholic father; the pious defeated mother moaning by the fire; pompous priests; bullying schoolmasters; the English and the terrible things they did to us for eight hundred long years.

The perils of Frankie's childhood read like a laundry list of stereotypical suffering; however, as Michiko Kakutani so correctly writes in her review for the *New York Times,* "There is not a trace of bitterness or resentment in *Angela's Ashes,* though there is plenty a less generous writer might well be judgmental about." Frankie and his brothers grow up in a circle of adults who fail to provide them life's basic essentials. A simple but touching example is the parents' enjoyment of cigarettes: "There may be a lack of tea or bread in the house but Mam and Dad always manage to get the fags," Frankie notes. Despite the rampant selfishness, stinginess, and even downright meanness that surround him, Frankie loves his family; even more remarkably, he often feels true compassion for them:

Frankie's father, Malachy McCourt, serves as the most obvious example of Kakutani's latter assertion. An alcoholic, Malachy has little inclination to support his family. The money he does get his hands on—whether earned, received from the dole, or in one hideous instance, given as a gift to the new baby—goes straight to the pub. He makes countless promises to his family of better times ahead, but his one consistency lies in disappointing them. Only eleven, Frankie already recognizes the challenge that loving his father poses:

> I know when Dad does the bad thing. I know when he drinks the dole money and Mam is desperate and has to beg at the St. Vincent de Paul Society and ask for credit at Kathleen O'Connell's shop but I don't want to back away from him and run to Mam. How can I do

that when I'm up with him early every morning with the whole world asleep? He lights the fire and makes the tea and sings to himself or reads the paper to me in a whisper that won't wake up the rest of the family.

Malachy's utter irresponsibility forces Frankie to grow up quickly. "I think my father is like the Holy Trinity," he explains, "with three people in him: the one in the morning with the paper, the one at night with the story and the prayers, and then the one who does the bad thing and comes home with the smell of whiskey and wants us to die for Ireland." Frankie's sophisticated analysis of his father, in which he likens his father to a schizophrenic, belies his chronological age. For a long time, Frankie manages to hold fast to the belief that "the one in the morning is my real father," but in the end, it is the father afflicted with the "Irish thing" (drinking) who gains prominence. Once Malachy leaves for England, ostensibly to earn money though "[he] didn't send us a penny in months," he only reappears in the pages of *Angela's Ashes* on two more occasions.

Before his desertion of the family, Malachy does teach Frankie some important values, such as politeness and piety and "to be good boys at school because God is watching every move." Malachy also presents Frankie a broader picture of the world outside Limerick, telling him all about Adolf Hitler and Benito Mussolini and "the great [Franklin D.] Roosevelt," which most likely inflames Frankie's desire to leave Ireland. Most importantly, Malachy offers young Frank a precious gift: a love of stories and storytelling. Malachy knows about Irish history and Kevin Barry and Roddy McCorley and "the old days in Ireland when the English wouldn't let the Catholics have schools." He also provides Frank a personal hero, Cuchulain, who is greater than "Hercules or Achilles . . . [or] King Arthur and all his knights." Cuchulain fought to the death against his enemies, and from him, Frankie draws much-needed strength over the years. Through the repetition of the story of Cuchulain, the impoverished boy also comes to feel that he has something of his own. "That's my story" is Frankie's refrain as he tries to prevent his father from telling the younger boys about Cuchulain.

The rest of Frankie's family cannot make up for Malachy's inability to support his children and, in truth, hardly attempt to do so. Angela McCourt, though caring, proves ineffectual at providing for her children. She willingly begs for the sake of her children from disdainful officials at the relief organizations, skeptical shopkeepers, and the condescending post office clerks (to get Frankie his job back). On more than one occasion, she is reduced to picking up bits of coal from the street, a measure that her husband feels is beneath him. However, her pervading sense of hopelessness greatly contributes to the spiritual impoverishment of Frankie's childhood; her downtrodden spirit often renders her unable to meet the challenge of her sons' emotional needs. This characteristic, combined with a lack of money, leads the deserted family into the home of an emotionally abusive cousin, Laman. Angela becomes Laman's lover, even though he treats her—''a great lump living free under his roof''—and her ''pack of brats'' no better than servants. When Angela shares Laman's bed after he reneges on a deal to lend Frankie his bicycle, Frankie feels utterly betrayed. At thirteen years old, he leaves home and moves in with his uncle. Only Frankie's success as a telegram boy inspires Angela to rise above her condition, leaving Laman and obtaining a job of her own in which she finds some measure of peace.

Frankie's extended family in America provides yet more sources of disappointment for the needy child. Never do they receive the McCourts with any love or affection. Aunt Aggie's pronouncement—''Ye are nothing but trouble since ye came from America''—sums up the general feeling that her relatives share. In almost all cases, the family resents helping out the McCourts and only does so begrudgingly. Still, as with his parents, Frankie never chastises his family for their actions—or lack of actions. In his silence and lack of judgment, he implicitly recognizes the complexity of familial love.

Upon their return to Ireland, the McCourts first go to Malachy McCourt's family. These relatives live in a nice home, offering sausage and ''all the eggs you can hold'' because it is Easter Sunday. However, they feel no fondness for their kin. The silence with which the relatives regard her children reduces Angela to tears. Frankie unfavorably compares his aunts to their neighbors in America as they ''nod their heads but they don't hug us or smile.'' The McCourts quickly send Malachy and his family away, to the south of Ireland, saying, ''No work here and, God knows, we don't have room in this house for six more people.''

Angela's family is no more welcoming. Frankie's first introduction to his grandmother is inauspicious: ''there she was on the platform, Grandma, with white hair, sour eyes, a black shawl, and no smile for my mother or any of us, even my brother, Malachy, who had the big smile and the sweet white

> **Whether it be a police officer in Dublin, the railroad worker, or Mr. Hannon, many a time, it is strangers or neighbors who take nurturing acts toward the McCourt children.''**

teeth.'' The status of the grandmother's finances is unknown. However, she has enough money to live in a small but clean home, cut thick slices of bread, set up her daughter's family in a furnished room, and pay for passage to and from America for relatives. Though the boys turn to their grandmother when they need help and she finds a way to provide some relief, her actions never demonstrate that she is giving because she wants to; instead, she acts out of obligation. Her obliviousness to the true circumstances in which her kin live is sharply revealed when the family is evicted. She tells Frankie to put on his coat before they can leave, never having realized that Frankie does not own a coat. She originally sent the unmarried Angela to America because she was ''pure useless,'' and she seems to have included Angela's children in that opinion as well.

Another relative the children meet for the first time is Aunt Aggie, Angela's sister. Aggie lives in comparative luxury in her warm, dry flat that has electricity. She has no children of her own, but she still has to be impinged upon to share any of her material goods, even the minimum of food, with the McCourts. ''I don't know why we have to pay for Angela's mistakes,'' she complains. She tells Frankie, whom she calls ''scabby eyes,'' and his brothers more than once that ''she can't stand the sight of us another minute.'' Forced to take in the boys while Angela is in the hospital, one day when Frankie's brother Malachy asks for a piece of bread, she hits him with a paper. Malachy doesn't come home from school the next day, and her only response is, ''Well, I suppose he ran away. Good riddance.'' However, it is Aggie who buys Frankie new clothes so he can start his job as a telegram boy without being humiliated by his appearance, an action that reduces him to private tears.

Frankie's uncle, the Abbott, begrudgingly allows the boy to live in his home instead of Laman's.

The Abbott forbids Frankie to turn on the light and threatens to keep track of the electric meter. He takes pains to hide his food from Frankie, even carrying his bread in his pocket to safeguard it. In one instance, he eats fish and chips in front of the hungry child, all the while telling him ''there's no food in the house.'' After the Abbott has gone to sleep, Frankie licks the newspaper for the grease. It is while living with the Abbott, before his job begins, that Frankie resorts to stealing food to survive. Despite his almost constant litany of complaints about Frankie—and the rest of the family, who eventually move into the house—the Abbot allows him to stay.

Only Uncle Pa, Aggie's husband and not a blood relative, shows any sort of genuine affection for Frankie and his brothers. He feeds them ham sandwiches behind his wife's back. Many times he takes on the paternal role that Malachy has forsaken. It is Uncle Pa who lays Eugene to his final rest in his small white coffin. It is Uncle Pa who buys Frankie his first pint to celebrate his sixteenth birthday. ''I know 'tis not the same without your father,'' Pa says, ''but I'll get you the first pint. 'Tis what I'd do if I had a son.'' Frankie, for his part, ''could easily have Uncle Pa for a father'' and share ''great times'' with him.

Frankie looks for a father figure in other men who treat him kindly as well. When a railroad worker helps them out, Frankie wishes he ''had a father like the man in the signal tower who gives you sandwiches and cocoa.'' In telling his troubles to a Franciscan priest, he feels like a ''child and I lean against him, little Frankie on his father's lap, tell me all about Cuchulain, Dad, my story that Malachy can't have or Freddie Leibowitz on the swings.'' Another special relationship Frankie develops is with the neighbor Mr. Hannon, to whom he ''gave . . . the feeling of a son.''

Whether it be a police officer in Dublin, the railroad worker, or Mr. Hannon, many a time it is strangers or neighbors who take nurturing acts toward the McCourt children. A barman along Classon Avenue fills the twins' bottles with milk instead of the water with ''maybe a little sugar'' that Frankie has requested. An Italian grocer in their Brooklyn neighborhood gives the boys a bag of fruit. A shoplady in Limerick gives the children an onion for their sick brother. Minnie MacAdorey and Mrs. Leibowitz feed the boys after Angela becomes incapacitated by Margaret's death. The neighbors in Brooklyn understand that family should be able to help the McCourt boys; the Italian grocer wonders where are the ''relations [that] can take care of you.'' However, when appealed to, the Brooklyn cousins refuse any responsibility, instead arranging for the return of the McCourts to Ireland.

In *Angela's Ashes*, the very concept of the nuclear family comes under constant attack. Margaret dies in infancy, and the twins, Oliver and Eugene, die when they are only toddlers. The younger Malachy first leaves home to be a soldier and later to work at an English boarding school. The older Malachy deserts his family, thus lowering their status and worsening their circumstances even further. Angela is forced to rely on the Dispensary, ''the place to apply for public assistance when a father is dead or disappeared,'' which means that ''you're . . . maybe one level above tinkers, knackers and street beggars in general.'' For some time, however, the McCourts attempt to create a caring environment. Michael has a habit of bringing home stray animals and old men. Mam brings home women and children; she has no money to give them, but she offers them a cup of tea, a bit of fried bread, and a place to sleep.

It is no surprise that Frankie dreams of moving to America, where he can start a new life. He believes that the United States holds out the promise of hope and better times, as he indicates by his choice of lines to open his memoir: ''My father and mother should have stayed in New York where they met and married and where I was born.'' Before he leaves, Angela holds a party for him. All of the relatives attend, and their level of sharing has been previously unmatched and unimagined. Aunt Aggie brings a homemade cake; the Abbot brings stout and says, ''That's all right, Frankie, ye can all drink it as long as I have a bottle or two for meself.'' At the last moment, Frankie feels strongly tied to the people he is leaving behind. ''I'm on the ship and there goes Ireland into the night . . . I want Ireland back at least I had Mam and my brothers and Aunt Aggie bad as she was and Uncle Pa, standing me my first pint.'' His connection to his family has remained, despite the almost constant string of disappointments they have provided him. Frank's accomplishments, such as earning the money to flee to America, getting his mother away from Laman's house, and providing a better quality of life for his younger brothers all are hard won and demonstrate amazing self-reliance and courage. The adult McCourt wonders ''how I managed to survive at all.'' As Thomas Deignan writes in *Commonweal,* ''by the time McCourt is nineteen, we appreciate the awesome desperation in this seemingly hackneyed statement.''

Source: Rena Korb, Critical Essay on *Angela's Ashes,* in *Nonfiction Classics for Students,* The Gale Group, 2001.

Karen D. Thompson

Thompson is a freelance writer who writes primarily in the education field. In this essay, she discusses McCourt's gifted use of some of the traditional elements of fiction and nonfiction.

Fiction and nonfiction seem unquestionably to be mutually exclusive categories. In a library, the figurative dividing line between the two becomes a literal division created by open space, shelves, or, at the very least, a printed sign. Despite the obvious division between the two genres, authors have perpetually married the two in a union that sometimes enhances its separate parts and sometimes diminishes them. Thus there is historical fiction, a full-fledged joining of fiction and nonfiction, along with a complete spectrum that ranges from fiction liberally sprinkled with fact to make it believable to nonfiction embellished by the traditional elements of fiction.

In *Angela's Ashes*, author Frank McCourt manages to create the perfect marriage of fiction and nonfiction elements. His skillful presentation of dialogue creates a three-dimensional portrait, richly textured. He manages to create an illusion of dialect without relying solely on phonetic or invented spellings. He uses a finely tuned sense of irony and a well-chosen title to give his book a literary quality not often found in works of nonfiction. Ultimately, his narrative voice is so pure that his readers cannot discern if *Angela's Ashes* is the result of a child telling a story with an adult's vocabulary and perception or the memoir of a man who has the remarkable ability to recollect his childhood with crystalline clarity.

Readers immediately notice a structural oddity in this volume: quotation marks do not appear in it. Yet after the first few pages, readers become aware that they have witnessed several conversations. Though some time might be necessary to adjust to the absence of quotation marks as a method of separating speakers, the effectiveness of their omission soon becomes apparent. Because no quotation marks appear, no visual barriers separate the different speakers. Voices sound over and around each other without the intrusive formality of punctuation marks. Two voices converse without the standard

St. Patrick's Roman Catholic Cathedral in Armagh, Northern Ireland

convention of taglines—''she interrupted,'' ''he paused mid-sentence'' —or dashes or ellipses to show breaks in dialogue. The lack of punctuation marks also allows the reader to see a mental picture of several characters simultaneously. With quotation marks, speakers are so clearly set apart that only two mental pictures are possible. In the first, the character speaking at any given time might appear in the imagination as a talking head, speaking in isolation or simply having words assigned to him or her as in a cartoon strip. In the second possibility, several characters may be present in the scene, but one speaks as the others stand or sit inanimately. The result is a fractured feeling that does not allow for the recreation of natural dialogue and multi-layered conversation.

Another aspect of dialogue, dialect, also becomes an effective storytelling tool in McCourt's hands. Authors tend to present dialect in different degrees. Some, as Mark Twain did in *The Adventures of Huckleberry Finn,* develop a complete yet specific vocabulary that, on the one hand, speaks for an entire region and, on the other hand, is as individual as each character. In that case, the dialectical spellings are carried throughout the book, and the eye as well as the ear became used to each

> **Some people may be quick to dismiss Frank McCourt's gift for narrative by saying that his strength is his story, not his storytelling.''**

character's unique voice. Some authors choose to begin a work by using particular spellings to indicate specific dialect and then taper off their use of it as the book continues. In this case, the author hopes that he or she has sufficiently drawn a character so that the character's unique dialect stays in the reader's mind either consciously or subconsciously.

McCourt uses the writer's rule of ''show don't tell'' to implant the sound of his characters—if ''characters'' is an appropriate designation for real people—in the mind. He and his family have Irish accents. The oldest brothers, Malachy and Frank, have accents that are enough Irish to make them distinct in New York and ''Yank'' enough to distinguish them from the native Irish. Frank's father has a strong North Ireland accent that marks him immediately an outsider whether in New York or in the southern parts of Ireland. McCourt establishes the weight of the Irish accents in different ways. Early on he sprinkles in such dialectical phrases as ''half five'' (half past five o'clock) in sentences whose context allows no room for misunderstanding. Later, he allows the stories themselves to impress the accents upon the reader's consciousness. When Malachy McCourt decided it was time to register Frank's birth, he took his infant son to the clerk for a birth certificate. The clerk was so confused by McCourt's alcoholic mumbling and ''North of Ireland accent'' that ''he simply entered the name Male on the certificate.''

If Frank McCourt had presented other accents in his book in the same manner he presented the Irish accents, he would have removed the one seam that is apparent in the whole cloth of the book. For some reason, however, he chose to portray thick New York accents by resorting to typical alterations of spelling. Thus, a New York bartender speaks of the ''history o' da woild'' and a shopkeeper exclaims, ''Jeez. Polite kid, eh? Where ja loin dat?'' Later, when the family returns to Ireland, McCourt continues this distracting, contrived method of

achieving the sound of the Dublin dialect. When the McCourt family, tired and penniless, is allowed to spend a night in the police station, they are subjected to the jibes and questions of the drunken prisoners: ''Jasus, will ye listen to them. They sound like bloody fillum stars. Did yez fall outa the sky or what?'' The effect of such manipulated language is equivalent to seeing the wires and machines on a stage that allow the players to fly. It is sad that McCourt did not realize his dialogue could fly on its own.

Tight, natural-sounding dialogue is not usually an element found in nonfiction. Nonfiction is often narrated in an objective voice that reports rather than recreates conversation and action. Other elements usually not apparent in nonfiction permeate *Angela's Ashes* and give it the sometimes magical quality of fiction. One of these conventions is a liberal use of irony—the difference between what is expected and what actually occurs. There is a difference in how irony presents itself in fiction and in how irony presents itself in this work of nonfiction. In fiction, irony can appear artificial, manufactured strictly to entertain or serve some function of plot. In those instances the stories become unbelievable. The same is not true of irony encountered in real life. Though we might be astonished or amazed by multiple ironies in a single person's life, we do not disbelieve what we have witnessed. For this reason we can accept at face value the many ironies in McCourt's life. When a fifth child is born to the already impoverished McCourts, the expectation is that the senior McCourt will have more motivation than ever to forget his responsibilities under the influence of alcohol and keep himself away from home more than ever. Yet the birth of his fifth child, a daughter, brings about just the opposite in him. He finds a job, keeps it, and brings home his pay regularly. One irony that presents itself as a theme (another element ascribed to works of fiction) is the irony of young Frank feeling proprietary about certain myths and stories. Since his birth, Frank had lived in squalid poverty and never owned anything, not even adequate clothing. Even so, he believes himself to be the owner of the great heroes of Ireland and their stories. He believes in his heart that he owns the story of Cuchulain.

Another area in which McCourt seems to use elements of fiction to his advantage is with his title. Often the title of a nonfiction work is functional and provides simply the topic of the work. In fiction, an author often achieves extra effect from the title choice. For example, Steinbeck used *East of Eden* to prepare readers for a vast Biblical metaphor. McCourt does not directly explain the source of his title, but one can make a reasonable guess. Frank's life was colored by his family's Catholicism, and his title hints at the ashes associated with Ash Wednesday and the self-denial and sacrifice that begin on the first day of the Lenten season. Additionally, the title brings to mind the "ashes to ashes and dust to dust" verses in the Old Testament of the Bible and could be meant to indicate the futility of trying to change the quality of life since eventually everything returns to its original state. Most probably the title points to the mythical phoenix and what ultimately became Frank McCourt's rise from the ruins, or ashes, of his mother's life. When Frank leaves Ireland for America, fortune has finally smiled on him, but fortune has not cast a smile upon Angela beyond what her son provides.

One final element of fiction, especially dramatic fiction, that McCourt appropriates is the element of comic relief. Some of Shakespeare's most memorable scenes are those provided for comic relief, a chance for the audience to take an emotional break from the intensity of the drama. McCourt is able to use comic relief to great benefit. When his family is faced with more death than should be any family's due, when the rent is unpaid, when his father has drunk the dole money, when rain and sewage has turned one half of their home into a cesspool, McCourt provides comic relief for readers. He does this not through invention or artifice. He does this by becoming a child and writing the scenes through a child's eyes. Accordingly, rather than being continually appalled by Frank's and his brothers' treatment at the hands of their alcoholic father who wakes them in the middle of the night and makes them swear to die for Ireland and incensed by the oppressive teachers who exhort them to die for the Faith, readers are encouraged to laugh at them all while laughing with young Frank who exclaims, "I wonder if there's anyone in the world who would like us to live."

Frank McCourt seems to use to his advantage many elements of fiction in his memoir, but he additionally uses the advantages inherent in nonfiction. For example, within the story, readers encounter several "mistakes" in McCourt's account. In one passage, McCourt describes how he earned the privilege of riding Laman Griffin's bicycle. His purpose for borrowing the bicycle was to accompany a group of boys from his school on a cycling trip to Killaloe. However, in a later passage, when Frank tries to secure a job as a telegram boy, the

supervisor asks if he knows how to cycle. Frank's reply is "I lie that I do." If this type of error were found in a piece of fiction, someone would bear the responsibility for shoddy work. Either the writer would be criticized for lack of attention to plot development, or the editor would be criticized for ineptly allowing such a mistake to slip through. In a nonfiction work of this kind, however, such oversights can be forgiven if the author has simply established trustworthiness at the beginning. If readers believe that the author is not engaged in intentionally trying to mislead them, mild anachronisms and misstatements will be forgiven. Readers realize that human memories are imperfect and somewhat subjective. Often, accurate family histories are compiled only after many family members make a concerted effort to fill in their pieces of the mosaic. Because McCourt establishes himself as honest and trustworthy early in the book, his lapses in recollection can be excused.

None of the preceding examples fully explain why *Angela's Ashes* is such a compelling work. The secret lies in a statement the young Frank McCourt makes when he witnesses his young brother Eugene trying in vain to understand that his twin, Oliver, has died. Young Frankie states that Eugene cannot understand because he "doesn't have the words and that's the worst thing in the whole world." Young McCourt realized even then the power and the gift of words.

Some people may be quick to dismiss Frank McCourt's gift for narrative by saying that his strength is his story, not his storytelling. Certainly his family's tragic history presented him with a unique, captivating story to tell, but it is his unique talent that makes this work a certain classic. If all that was needed to tell a good story were to be present while one unfolded, there would be thousands of books chronicling every event. But there aren't. Though some books written by untalented writers make it to publication, they do not endure.

Stories by themselves do not capture readers. If they did, readers would spend their time reading and rereading newspaper accounts and history texts. But they don't, of course. They read and reread and tell their friends only about the stories that move them somehow. When this happens, it is the result of a worthwhile story and a skillful narrator. True, Frank McCourt was given the raw material of a childhood filled with tragedy, pain, and poverty; but readers would never know, and thus they could never care, if he were not also given the gift of storytelling.

Source: Karen D. Thompson, Critical Essay on *Angela's Ashes,* in *Nonfiction Classics for Students,* The Gale Group, 2001.

R. F. Foster

In the following review, Foster examines the McCourt phenomenon, and casts doubt on the veracity of some parts of Angela's Ashes.

What makes a publishing phenomenon—not merely a "best-seller seller," but a million-seller, a prize-gatherer, a cult-former, a legend still ensconced in the hardback charts when it goes straight to the very top of the paperback charts? It seems clear that hitting the jackpot requires not so much that people read a book as that "readers" buy a book to satisfy a felt or perceived need. Actually finishing the book may not be necessary. One suspects that very few people know how Stephen Hawking's *A Brief History of Time,* or Jung Chang's *Wild Swans,* or Dava Sobel's *Longitude,* ends.

The jaw-dropping success of those books testifies to the eternal human sense of gratification through self-betterment; mingled, perhaps, with the equally eternal human tendency to console ourselves by reading about the efforts and the tribulations of others. The actual readability of the book, let alone its literary quality, seems comparatively irrelevant—even (or especially) to prize committees. Much of this applies, certainly, to the phenomenon of *Angela's Ashes,* though there are peculiar variation in this case: the traditional Irish readiness to commercialize the past, for example, and the complex attitude of the United States to what it expects the Irish to be, and the enduring pride and reassurance that Americans find in hot water and flush lavatories.

The paperback edition of *Angela's Ashes* comes garlanded with pages and pages of ecstatic reviewers' quotations. Connoisseurs of the genre may note that the heavyweight names are often there in the guise of kind friends rather than dispassionate critics, but those who nailed their colors to the mast of, say, the *Clarion-Ledger* or the *Detroit Free Press* are no less enthusiastic: "Frank McCourt has seen hell, but found angels in his heart," "Frank McCourt's life, and his searing telling of it, reveal all we need to know about being human," and so on. It may seem like party-pooping to ask what this kind of bilge actually means (which is less than nothing). It is perhaps fairer to look at the significance of the book itself, and its spin-offs. These now stretch to its sequel, *'Tis,* and the autobiography of Frank's brother Malachy, *A Monk Swimming,* and a forthcoming film, and the name of at least one pub in Limerick.

Angela's Ashes began it all. In the beginning it was alternately identified as fiction and as autobiography, but by the time of publication it had settled down as "a memoir." It is the sort of memoir in which the protagonist can—like Tristram Shandy—retain absolutely concrete memories from the time of his conception, and retail word-for-word conversations exchanged and letters written from the age of three. Clearly the conventions of magical realism and post-structuralist flannel have had a striking effect on the genre of autobiography. This may be presented as a liberation from the tyranny of the ascertainable fact, but it makes for some confusion as far as the reader is concerned.

Thus (according to *'Tis*) Frank McCourt is born into a poor but feel-good immigrant community in Brooklyn in 1931. There are kind Italian shopkeepers. There are wonderful Jewish neighbors. Father is a sentimental Northern Irish republican who sings rebel ballads, and Mother is the regulation-issue Irish mammy. Cliché is invoked on the very first page of *Angela's Ashes,* a way that apparently promises subversion:

> Worse than the ordinary miserable childhood is the miserable Irish childhood, and worse yet is the miserable Irish Catholic childhood.

> People everywhere brag and whimper about the woes of their early years, but nothing can compare with the Irish version: the poverty; the shiftless loquacious alcoholic father; the pious defeated mother moaning by the fire; pompous priests; bullying schoolmasters; the English and the terrible things they did to us for eight hundred long years.

But what we hear is exactly what we will get, from the moment the author's parents leave America. Both go slightly off the rails (drink, depression) when their daughter dies, and they return to Ireland and a cold welcome: first of all in the North, then to the slums of Limerick.

Angela's Ashes records (or at least reimagines) Frank's youth in a downward spiral of poverty and misery, until he escapes back to America in October 1949, shortly after his nineteenth birthday. (This would actually make him born in 1930: magical realism may have to be invoked again.) It appears from McCourt's new book that he started using the awful privations of his childhood quite early, in essays at night school at New York University. Certainly the vividness of certain images and events is marvelously realized: the fleas, the mother's miscarriage, the mentally unbalanced neighbor begging all over Limerick for flour to bake bread for her children before she is taken away to the asylum. The poor are not always mutually supportive.

The father's Northern background is held against him, Republican though he is: he drinks and comes and goes and eventually goes for good. With incessant rain and the rising river Shannon, the slum floods; and when this happens, the family withdraws to the upstairs room, which they call "Italy." There is a lot about sex, and even more about dirt, defecation, shared privies in the back lane, and the indignity of emptying chamber pots.

> Mam goes to the door and says, Why are you emptying your bucket in our lavatory? He raises his cap to her. Your lavatory, missus? Ah, no. You're making a bit of a mistake there, ha, ha. This is not your lavatory. Sure, isn't this the lavatory for the whole lane. You'll see passing your door here the buckets of eleven families and I can tell you it gets very powerful here in the warm weather, very powerful altogether.

Charity is cold, the kindness of strangers is almost non-existent, and the remnant of the family end up living with a repulsive cousin, with whom the passive and exhausted mother is forced to sleep: a step for which her writer sons do not forgive her, then or—apparently—later.

But it all goes on for too long. *Angela's Ashes* is not and will never be (*pace* the *New York Times*) "a classic memoir," because its author lacks an internal editor, a sense of developing structure. The language is monotonous and the incidents are repetitive. The characterizations are perfunctory: people are identified by formulaic straplines, which are trundled out again and again each time they appear. One uncle, a jovial cynic, is never introduced without declaring that he doesn't give "a fiddler's fart" for respectable opinion. Still, the level of intellectual give-and-take is reassuringly high, and there is usually someone at hand to descant on a Cuchulain or a Jonathan Swift:

> Next morning, Mr. Timoney says, Wait till we get to *Gulliver,* Francis. You'll know Jonathan Swift is the greatest Irish writer that ever lived, no, the greatest man to put pen to parchment. A giant of a man, Francis. He laughs all through *A Modest Proposal* and you'd wonder what he's laughing at when it's all about cooking Irish babies.

Yeats's invocation to Cuchulain's wife, "greatbladdered Emer," is also surprisingly common currency in the McCourt household.

Angela's Ashes goes on at relentless length, and is actually quite a job to finish. Laboring through it,

> **And this uncertain and fantastic element is compounded by an eerie sense that this 'memoir' has been recalled through the prism of subsequent reading."**

the reader also begins to feel certain nagging irritations and doubts. One concerns the relation of the text to fact. Frank McCourt has guaranteed in interviews that "all the facts are true," but some incidents surely stretch credulity. The father's claim of an IRA pension, for instance, is presented as a venture into a strange underworld, involving trips to back rooms in seedy suburbs. In Ireland in the mid-1930s, however, these pensions were a matter of strict and official record, done through a government department, now preserved (though not always accessible) in the National Archives.

Some doubt has also been expressed in Ireland at the likelihood of quite so many boys attending Leamy's School in Limerick in bare feet in midwinter, or of open sewers coursing down the streets; but this may simply be injured local pride. It is certainly hard to credit the urban slum boys, escaped into the countryside, being able to sustain themselves by milking cows in the fields. (The cows even thoughtfully stand still enough for a small child to lie underneath them, imbibing the milk directly from the udder.)

Our hero also talks regularly to an angel, just as prescribed by Hollywood. This being is strangely conjured up by Frank's father, a bewildering mixture of sensitive soul, good housekeeper, and drunken layabout. The angel materializes on the seventh step of the slum stairs and strengthens Frank's resolve to confess his sins at First Communion. This puts his father straight into self-help councilor mode:

> Isn't it better to be able to tell your father your troubles rather than an angel who is a light and a voice in your head?
>
> 'Tis, Dad.

And this uncertain and fantastic element is compounded by an eerie sense that this "memoir" has been recalled through the prism of subsequent reading. There is a fire-breathing priest's sermon to guilt-ridden boys that is straight out of *A Portrait of the Artist as Young Man.* There is a doomed love affair with a glamorous sixteen-year-old consumptive girl that is very reminiscent of Michael MacLiammoir's autobiography, *All for Hecuba* (where it was, given MacLiammoir's redoutably unabashed homosexuality, an even less likely incident). There is an aged female moneylender, for whom the young McCourt writes improbably high-flown dunning letters, who owes a large literary debt to Dostoevsky and Dickens.

Over it all, finally, hovers the inspiration—and the convention—of Sean O'Casey's autobiographies. O'Casey's memoirs are—as his biographers have pointed out—notoriously unreliable as records of his early life, but they were—as McCourt himself notes—the first Irish memoirs to exploit the full potential of childhood deprivation. Of course, O'Casey's background was the tenements of late Victorian Dublin rather than the Limerick of fifty years ago.

In *'Tis,* which follows, straight on from *Angela's Ashes,* McCourt describes his education in America. It is a classic subject, but it is disappointingly handled. McCourt does point out, revealingly, that as he began to read more and more omnivorously, situations encountered in great novels seemed to parallel his own experience. He epitomizes the Irish hunger for education, and the Irish reliance on self-supporting communities and aggressive camaraderie, which makes the story of Irish America so cheering. He is also honest—self-deprecatingly so—about the national predilection to seek solace and absolution in alcohol, and its effect on his own marriage, though his first wife remains among the most unreal characters in the book.

McCourt's rise from floor-sweeper and lavatory-cleaner, via a spell as a G.I. in Germany, to high-school teacher and night-school lecturer, is impressive in its own terms. But with the best will in the world, it is not very interesting, and the terrible weaknesses of *Angela's Ashes* also bedevil *'Tis.* The characterizations come straight from central casting: the pedophile priest, the angry-but-noble communist, the saintly and paternal black warehouseman. There are encounters that once again strike echoes of other autobiographies. (The inevitable meeting with Billie Holiday is strongly reminiscent of an incident in *The Autobiography of Malcolm X.*) And the chronological context wavers curiously: McCourt's night-school students in the early 1970s go home to watch Jane Fonda exercise videos, and Irish Americans ask each other in 1958

(eleven years before Northern Ireland erupted) why Catholics and Protestants are at war in "the old country."

McCourt's return visits to Ireland betray equally skewed powers of observation and a fuzzy air of anachronism. This is more important than it might seem, because there is some danger that America is ready to believe in Ireland, past and present, as interpreted through the memories of the McCourt family. Malachy McCourt has already got in on the act, with a book which—it is fair to suppose—would never have seen the light of day without his brother's precedent. This is the literary equivalent of the demographic phenomenon known as "chain migration."

From the awkward pun in the title—*Amongst Women,* get it?—to the slack, whoozy, flatulent style, the book is an embarrassment. It is a mediocre and self-adoring account of boozing and weeping and whoring and—intermittently—acting. McCourt himself ran a successful New York bar, after leaving Limerick unable (he says) "to do anything but tell lies." He also went on the stage, and fell an early victim of the curse of minor celebrity and major dipsomania. His tedious memoir is a much more unattractive performance than either of his brother's volumes, as well as a far less literate one. It is maniacally class-obsessed—the New York bourgeoisie show off by "yawning at incomprehensible operas" and "yelping over museums." bad cess to 'em—and violently anti-British. These predictable bigotries are by and large absent even from Frank's somewhat jaundiced worldview.

Still, one of the unintentionally interesting elements in *A Monk Swimming* concerns the author's relationship to the English language. The publishers have the temerity to declare that he "makes the English language do tricks the British never intended." (Hyperion's editors certainly carry the trick through, allowing a passage in which female lips are "ermined" rather than—presumably—"carmined," the legendary Fleet Street bar El Vino is Americanized as "Alvino's," and a bit from J. M. Synge is quoted in so garbled a form as to be senseless.) McCourt himself believes that the Irish "took a dull tongue, English, and made it roar." Here is a sample of his own roaring;

> I averred it was a sight to gladden the eyes, the heart, and the internal organs of any decent man walking the earth this day. "Stop the yap." sez the bould Mitchum, "and get it inside of you." He had done a few movies in Ireland, and therefore knew the lingo, and how it could interfere with the quaffing.

In *A Monk Swimming,* the quaffing has interfered drastically with the lingo. Stage-Irishry leans heavily on a catechism of the tiredest ersatz-English archaisms: almost everything is "ye olde," exchanges are "quoth," things happen "ere long," sex involves "dipping the wick" (though masturbation is "shaking hands with the unemployed"), the author "hies him off" (not often enough), beer is "the chilled amber beverage," Muhammad Ali is "Mr M. Ali of fisticuffs fame," and Jews are "of the Hebraic persuasion."

Malachy McCourt is a professed admirer of J. P. Donleavy and P. G. Wodehouse—neither of them a writer who should be imitated, for exactly opposite reasons. His literary, voice comes through as a misheard echo, looking for sympathy and a seat on the bandwagon. From time to time, though, Malachy McCourt's book does convey something of New York in the 1950s and 1960s, as it must have appeared to a healthy and hungry young immigrant: a Manhattan at once intimate and glamorous, pre-crack, pre-Giuliani, pre-Tribeca.

By contrast, one of the strange nullities at the heart of Frank McCourt's autobiographies is the lack of a sense of place—outside, that is, the recalled actuality of Limerick. Frank McCourt's Dublin is pure cardboard. There is, for instance, a very odd interlude in the Shelburne Hotel. This is actually an elegant and venerable Irish institution, with something of the atmosphere of the old Biltmore and the establishment cachet of the Plaza; but in Frank McCourt's memory it is transformed into a place where babies' prams are parked outside, and the bar is peopled by yelling Kerry farmers. Similarly, his time in Germany is never described in terms of the place itself.

In *'Tis,* there is not a single New York institution that is sharply realized, with the possible exception of the Staten Island Ferry. Despite wheeling out the odd mandatory jazzman or bum, this Village in these 1950s could be anywhere. McCourt's memoir carries off neither a Proustian recreation of the past through the writer's perfect internal absorption in it, nor the Isherwood trick of becoming an unblinking camera. The voice in the ear wavers, the focus is off-beam.

And yet it is what millions of people want to read (or at least to buy). It confirms the traditional and comforting belief that the Old World is a sow who devours her own farrow, and everything will eventually come right in America, along with creature comforts, blonde women, and hot running water. It fulfills the stereotype of the Irish as brawlers and boozers, excluded from the effete WASP world, at one with their fellow underdogs, with a tear and a smile always at the ready, and a miraculous way with words—as Malachy McCourt must put it, "warm words, serried words, glittering, poetic, harsh, and even blasphemous words."

In a moment of unwitting and damning confession, Malachy McCourt also remarks that "they're all mad in America—they pay you for talking." But they would probably not pay you very much for talking about the new Euro-Ireland. They probably would not pay you for apostrophizing the efficient, moneymaking, politically ruthless Irish-America that was already broaching the country clubs when the brothers McCourt were invading the saloons, and is by now firmly fixed in the yuppie hierarchy of the Upper East Side.

The true story of the Irish in contemporary America could provide just as inspiring a narrative in its own way, but it conforms less to the comfortable old straitjackets of the stories that have gone before. Evelyn Waugh once remarked that to the Irishman there are only two ultimate realities: hell and the United States. The McCourt version postulates that you have to suffer the first in order to be redeemed by the second. It may be a welcome parable for many, especially to the accountants at Simon and Schuster, but it is very, very far from the whole story.

Source: R. F. Foster, "The Million-Dollar Blarney of the McCourts," in *New Republic,* Vol. 221, No. 18, November 1, 1999, pp. 29–32.

Christopher Shannon

In the following review of Angela's Ashes, *Shannon calls it "the most refreshingly unsociological account of poverty I have ever read."*

Early last November, high in the Catskills, I attended a celebration of Irish music and dance, the Green Linnet Twentieth Anniversary Festival. Green Linnet is a surprisingly successful record company and organized the event to promote the sale of its tapes and CDs, advertising the weekend in the spirit of secular ecumenism that gladly welcomes the credit cards of every race, creed, and color. But they forgot, perhaps, that this was an Irish party, and nothing Irish ever happens without some kind of fight. The culture war that America has exported to Ireland played itself out quietly in two talks delivered on the margins of the music and dancing: one by the writer Frank McCourt, the other by the priest Father Charlie Coen.

A first-time author at the age of sixty-six, Frank McCourt earned a spot on the Green Linnet roster thanks to the astonishing success of *Angela's Ashes,* a memoir of his poverty-stricken childhood in Brooklyn and Limerick that has spent months on the bestseller lists and recently won the Pulitzer Prize for nonfiction. McCourt has spent most of his unpublished adult life living in the shadow of his brother Malachy, a New York celebrity known as a harddrinking, Irish literary raconteur, a modernist stage-Irish act of the type perfected by Brendan Behan. McCourt's own public statements, and the initial critical reception of the book, seemed to place it firmly within the tradition of Irish modernist anti-Catholicism. The Irish masses have traditionally not taken kindly to Irish modernism's take on Ireland: the plays of John Synge and Sean O'Casey occasionally met with public riots when they premiered at Dublin's Abbey Theater. In the spirit of riots past, a resident of Limerick is reported to have informed the McCourt brothers, ''There are people in this town who would joyfully slit yereffin' throats.''

In fact, despite the pious proclamations of the Irish Tourist Board, modern Irish writing remains where it has always been: a long, long way from the spirit of traditional Irish music. I was curious as to how McCourt's anti-Irish Irishman act would play at a weekend devoted to the celebration of Irish culture. McCourt's reading began with a laundry list of Irish pathologies: the drunken father, the helpless mother, the pompous priest, the bullying schoolmaster. As he continued, however, it oddly began to appear that the real blame for his miserable Irish Catholic childhood lay with the weather: ''Above all—we were wet.'' The rain ''created a cacophony of hacking coughs, bronchial rattles, asthmatic wheezes, consumptive croaks. It turned noses into fountains, lungs into bacterial sponges.'' I had not read the book, and nothing in the reviews prepared me for McCourt's reading. A friend who had read the book was equally surprised. What she, and many reviewers, had thought of as a serious expression of ''raw pain'' now sounded more like a comic defiance of death.

Having attended McCourt's reading, I can only conclude that the critical reception of *Angela's Ashes* says more about the expectations of ''serious'' Irish writing than about the book itself. Serious Irish writing must involve a solitary hero coming to self-consciousness, throwing off the dead weight of tradition (especially Catholicism), and having sex happily ever after. Critics have mistakenly read the book through the lenses of modernist sociology and psychology. Tough-guy New York newspaperman Pete Hamill praised the book as a scathing indictment of the ''culture of poverty'' (yes, he really uses this phrase) fostered by ''Eamon de Valera's Ireland,'' while the literary critic Denis Donoghue, writing in the *New York Times,* presented the book in much the same way (though he clearly lacks Hamill's enthusiasm for the story).

It is true that McCourt refuses no gruesome detail in his account of the poverty he experienced as a child in Limerick. But I nonetheless found *Angela's Ashes* to be the most refreshingly unsociological account of poverty I have ever read. Like premodern folk tales, McCourt's stories present extreme suffering more as a fact of life than a problem to be solved. The childlike voice of the narrator invests poverty with an almost natural quality akin to the weather. People certainly complain about the weather, but they do not criticize it.

I think Hamill, Donoghue, and nearly every other of the American critics who praised *Angela's Ashes* have equally misread the book as a chronicle of a young man's liberation from a ''smothering Irish parochialism.'' In what is ostensibly a coming-of-age story, the narrator never really shows psychological development. Young Frank discovers Swift and Shakespeare, but reading plays almost no part in the story. Young Frank discovers sex, but sexual awakening appears simply as an awakening to sex, not to some salvific knowledge. In a world where nothing is hidden, nothing can be revealed. The book does conclude with a pseudo-Joycean sexual epiphany, but it appears slapped on as a matter of convention—as that which is expected of an Irish writer. Refreshingly, the book offers not another Portrait of the Artist as a Young Man, but a fascinating and straightforward Portrait of the Young Man as a Young Man.

This strength is also its weakness. *Angela's Ashes* leaves one with a sense of the whole being less than the sum of its parts. The book offers a lively sampling of urban folk stories held together only by a sentimental rejection of all things Irish. In this way, it stands as a kind of evil twin to Green Linnet Records, which offers a lively sampling of great musical stories held together only by a sentimental affirmation of all things Irish. *Angela's Ashes* and Green Linnet Records both speak of a culture still alive with stories but lacking a *story.*

For most of the twentieth century, Ireland has had a story—a cultural story of tradition against modernity; a political story of nationalism and agrarian republicanism against colonialism; and above all a religious story of Catholicism against Protestantism. These three dimensions of Ireland's story came together in the symbolic politics of the Easter Rising of 1916, which offered to the Irish a link between Ireland's secular struggle for independence and the sacred story of Jesus Christ. I held little hope of hearing this story in the Catskills. And then I went to Mass on Sunday.

Even the most secular Irish festival has to have a Mass, if only for the old-timers. Presiding was Fr. Charlie Coen, a Galway native who has served as a parish priest in the greater New York area since his ordination in 1968. Fr. Coen also happens to be a world-class concertina player, with several recordings released through Green Linnet Records. As a Green Linnet artist, Fr. Coen was a natural choice to say the Mass. As a priest, he could not have been further from the spirit of Green Linnet Records.

Fr. Coen is an Irish storyteller who dares to tell the Story. He began his sermon with some good-natured sarcasm concerning the medieval kitsch of the Friar Tuck Inn in which the festival was held. He then placed himself in the role of court chaplain. In medieval times, he told us, a king would often have a personal chaplain for his court. The court chaplain had to be careful—if he said anything to offend the king, he might lose his job. Fr. Coen then proceeded to give a sermon that would have cost a court chaplain not only his job, but his life.

I cannot do justice to the grace and humor with which Fr. Coen delivered his hard message, I can only summarize the content of his sermon: "No one enjoys playing a tune or singing a song more than I. We should all be grateful to Green Linnet Records for providing the opportunity for us to come together in celebration of Irish music and dance. I fear, however, that Irish culture is in great danger. Irish people have turned away from the faith that sustained them through centuries of oppression. Yes, priests and nuns have done many bad things, but they have done much good as well. When I was a boy in Ireland, people were poor, but they were happy. Today's affluent generation in Ireland and America gloat over the scandals that have rocked the Church and boast of their new-found freedom. This freedom has not brought happiness, only broken families and broken lives. This freedom leads to

> **❝ Refreshingly, the book offers not another Portrait of the Artist as a Young Man, but a fascinating and straightforward Portrait of the Young Man as a Young Man.❞**

death, as witnessed most recently by President Clinton's veto of the ban on partial-birth abortions."

I have never heard the battle lines of today's culture war drawn so eloquently. Appropriately enough, Fr. Coen left the last word on this war to the language of song. In response to repeated requests, Fr. Coen consented to sing a song before he gave the final blessing at the end of the Mass. It began simply enough, a nice melody telling a story of lost love. It soon became clear, however, that the song was addressed from a father to a daughter: "One lovely year is all we had, until the sickness came. And stole the roses from her cheeks, my tears they fell like rain. For nine long months she carried you, but in the end she died. She chose to go that you might live. Long, long before your time."

The Irish-American press has been tripping all over itself with praise for Frank McCourt. I have not come across a single review of the Green Linnet weekend that even mentions Fr. Coen. For those who envision a brave new post-Christian Ireland, I offer the contrast of Coen and McCourt. Fr. Coen tells a story of death that affirms life; Frank McCourt tells a story of death that ultimately affirms only Frank McCourt.

Source: Christopher Shannon, "Rising from the Ashes," in *First Things,* No. 75, August/September 1997, pp. 68–70.

Sources

Ascheron, Neal, "Ceremony of Innocence," in *New York Review of Books,* Vol. XLIV, No. 12, July 17, 1997, pp. 24–26.

Atlas, James, "The Age of the Literary Memoir Is Now," in *New York Times Magazine,* May 12, 1996, pp. 25–27.

Elson, John, "Reliving His Bad Eire Days," in *Time,* Vol. 148, No. 15, September 23, 1996, p. 74.

Foster, R. F., "Tisn't: The Million-dollar Blarney of the McCourts," in *New Republic,* November 1, 1999, p. 29.

Jones, Malcolm, Jr., Review in *Newsweek,* Vol. 128, No. 10, September 2, 1996, pp. 68–69.

Kakutani, Michiko, "Generous Memories of a Poor, Painful Childhood," in *New York Times,* September 17, 1996.

Further Reading

Donoghue, Denis, "Some Day I'll Be in Out of the Rain," in *New York Times Book Review,* September 15, 1996, p. 13.
In this review of *Angela's Ashes*, Donoghue comments on his own experiences growing up in Ireland, which were similar to McCourt's.

"Fighting Irish," in *National Review,* October 26, 1998, p. 40.
This editorial describes how the publication of *Angela's Ashes* has contributed to an upsurge in America of interest in all things Irish.

Hughes, Carolyn T., "Looking Forward to the Past: A Profile of Frank McCourt," in *Poet and Writers Magazine,* Vol. 27, No. 5, September–October 1999, pp. 22–29.
This profile of McCourt describes the genesis of *Angela's Ashes* and McCourt's thoughts on writing and teaching.

Sullivan, Robert, "The Seanachie," in *New York Times Magazine,* September 1, 1996, pp. 24–27.
A seanachie is a storyteller, and this profile of McCourt emphasizes the wealth of personal stories that McCourt has at his disposal. He is presented as a man who finds humor in the darkest of places.

Aspects of the Novel

E. M. Forster

1927

Aspects of the Novel is the publication of a series of lectures on the English language novel, delivered by E. M. Forster at Trinity College, Cambridge, in 1927. Using examples of classic works by many of the world's greatest writers, he discusses seven aspects he deems universal to the novel: story, characters, plot, fantasy, prophecy, pattern, and rhythm.

Forster dismisses the method of examining the novel as a historical development, in preference to an image of all novelists throughout history writing simultaneously, side by side. He first establishes that, if nothing else, a novel is a story that takes place over a period of time. He stresses the importance of character, maintaining that both ''flat'' and ''round'' characters may be included in the successful novel. He regards the necessity of plot, which creates the effect of suspense, as a problem by which character is frequently sacrificed in the service of providing an ending to the novel. Fantasy and prophecy, which provide a sense of the ''universal,'' or spiritual, Forster regards as central aspects of the great novel. Finally, he dismisses the value of ''pattern,'' by which a narrative may be structured, as another aspect that frequently sacrifices the vitality of character. Drawing on the metaphor of music, Forster concludes that rhythm, which he defines as ''repetition plus variation,'' allows for an aesthetically pleasing structure to emerge from the novel, while maintaining the integrity of character and the

open-ended quality that gives novels a feeling of expansiveness.

Author Biography

Edward Morgan Forster was born in London on January 1, 1879, the only surviving son of Edward Morgan Llewellyn Forster, an architect, and Alice Clara Forster. Forster's father died of tuberculosis in 1880, and he was subsequently raised by several female family members, in addition to his mother, all of whom made a strong impression on his youth, and some of whom eventually turned up as characters in his novels. Marianne Thornton, his great-aunt on his father's side, died in 1886, leaving him an inheritance, which paid for his secondary and college education, as well as his subsequent world travels, and bought him the leisure to pursue the craft of writing. Forster recalled bitter memories of his time spent as a day attendant at Tonbridge School in Kent, from 1893 to 1897. In 1897, he enrolled in King's College, Cambridge, where he was grateful to be exposed to the liberal atmosphere and ideas lacking in his education up to that point.

Upon graduating with a bachelor of arts degree in classics and history, Forster went abroad and devoted himself to a writing career. He lived in Greece and Italy from 1901 to 1907, during which his first novel, *Where Angels Fear to Tread* (1905) was published. Upon returning to England, he lectured at Working Men's College. His second and third novels, *The Longest Journey* (1907), and *A Room With a View* (1908) appeared during this time. *Howard's End* (1910), his first major literary success, was a critique of the British upper class. In 1912, he made one of several trips to India. During a period including World War I, Forster worked as a Red Cross volunteer in Alexandria from 1915 to 1919. When the war ended, he returned to England, serving as literary editor of the Labor Party's *Daily Herald,* and contributing to journals such as *Nation* and *New Statesman.*

From 1921, Forster held various prestigious lectureships in England, and gave a lecture tour in the United States in 1941. He became associated with the London intellectual and literary salon known as the Bloomsbury Group, which included such celebrated modernist writers as Virginia Woolf. His second masterpiece, *A Passage to India*, was published in 1924, after which he published no more novels during his lifetime, devoting himself to non-fiction writing, such as essays, literary criticism, and biography. In addition to *Aspects of the Novel,* two important essay collections were *Abinger Harvest* (1936) and *Two Cheers for Democracy* (1951). After his death on June 7, 1970, in Coventry, England, his novel *Maurice* (1971) was published for the first time, apparently suppressed by the author because of its autobiographical content concerning a young homosexual man.

Summary

Introduction

In an introductory chapter, Forster establishes the ground rules for his discussion of the English novel. He defines the novel simply—according to M. Abel Chevalley in *Le Roman Anglais de notre temps,* as "a fiction in prose of a certain extent." He goes on to define English literature as literature written in the English language, regardless of the geographic location or origin of the author. Most importantly, Forster makes clear that this discussion will not be concerned with historical matters, such as chronology, periodization, or development of the novel. He makes clear that "time, all the way through, is to be our enemy." Rather, he wishes to imagine the world's great novelists from throughout history sitting side by side in a circle, in "a sort of British Museum reading room—all writing their novels simultaneously." Finally, he acknowledges the intended ambiguity of the phrase "aspects of the novel" to indicate an open-ended discussion in which he will cover seven of these "aspects": story, characters, plot, fantasy, prophecy, pattern, and rhythm.

The Story

In a chapter on "The Story," Forster begins with the assertion that the novel, in its most basic definition, tells a story. He goes on to say that a story must be built around suspense—the question of "what happens next?" He thus defines the story as "a narrative of events arranged in their time sequence." Forster adds that a good novel must include a sense of value in the story. He then discusses *The Antiquary,* by Sir Walter Scott, as an example of a novel that is built on a series of events that narrate "what happens next." However, he criticizes *The Antiquary* as a novel that adheres to a sequence of events but has no sense of value in the story. Forster refers to Russian novelist Tolstoy's *War and Peace* as an example that includes value in a narrative of events that unfold over time. He brings up the American writer Gertrude Stein as an example of a novelist who has attempted to abolish time from the novel, leaving only value. However, he declares this a failure that results in nonsense.

Characters

In two chapters entitled "People," Forster discusses characterization in the novel. He describes five "main facts of human life," which include "birth, food, sleep, love, and death," and then compares these five activities as experienced by real people (*homo sapiens*) to these activities as enacted by characters in novels (*homo fictus*). He goes on to discuss the character of Moll Flanders, in the novel by Defoe of the same title. Forster focuses on *Moll Flanders* as a novel in which the form is derived from the development of the main character. In a second lecture on characters, Forster distinguishes between flat characters, whose characterization is relatively simple and straightforward, and round characters, whose characterization is more complex and developed. Forster finds advantages in the use of both flat and round characters in the novel. He points to Charles Dickens as an example of a novelist nearly all of whose characters are flat but who nonetheless creates "a vision of humanity that is not shallow." He spends less time discussing round characters but provides the examples of Russian novelists Leo Tolstoy and Fyodor Dostoyevski, most of whose characters are round. Forster moves on to a brief mention of point of view, concluding that novels with a shifting or inconsistent point of view are not problematic if the author possesses the skill to integrate these shifts into the narrative whole.

Plot

In a chapter on plot, Forster defines plot as a narrative of events over time, with an emphasis on causality. He claims that the understanding of plot requires two traits in the reader: intelligence and memory. He discusses George Meredith who, he claims, though not a great novelist, is one of England's greatest masters of the plot. He then turns to Thomas Hardy as an example of a novelist whose plots are heavily structured at the expense of the characters; in other words, the characters are drawn to fit the measure of the plot and therefore lack a life of their own. He asserts that "nearly all novels are feeble at the end," because the dictates of plot require a resolution, which the novelists write at the expense of the characters. He adds that "death and marriage" are the most convenient recourse of the

E. M. Forster

novelist in formulating an ending. He provides the example of André Gide's *Les Faux monnayeurs* as a novel in which the author attempted to do away with plot completely, concluding that, though plot often threatens to suffocate the life out of characters, it is nonetheless an essential aspect of the novel.

Fantasy

In a chapter on fantasy, Forster asserts that two important aspects of the novel are fantasy and prophecy, both of which include an element of mythology. Using the novel *Tristram Shandy,* by Sterne, as an example, Forster claims even novels that do not include literal elements of the supernatural may include an implication that supernatural forces are at work. He lists some of the common devices of fantasy used by novelists, "such as the introduction of a god, ghost, angel, or monkey, monster, midget, witch into ordinary life." He adds to this list "the introduction of ordinary men into no-man's land, the future, the past, the interior of the earth, the fourth dimension; or divings into and dividings of personality. He goes on to discuss the devices of parody and adaptation as elements of fantasy, which, he says, are especially useful to talented authors who are not good at creating their own characters. He points to *Joseph Andrews,* by Henry Fielding, which began as a parody of *Pam-*

ela, by Richardson. He goes on to the example of *Ulysses,* by James Joyce, which is an adaptation from the ancient text the *Odyssey,* based on Greek myth.

Prophecy

Forster describes the aspect of prophecy in a novel as ''a tone of voice'' of the author, a ''song'' by which ''his theme is the universe,'' although his subject matter may be anything but universal. He notes that the aspect of prophecy demands of the reader both ''humility'' and ''the suspension of a sense of humor.'' He then compares Dostoevsky to George Eliot, concluding that, though both express a vision of the universal in their novels, Eliot ends up being preachy, whereas Dostoevsky successfully expresses a ''prophetic song'' without preaching. Forster confesses that there are only four writers who succeed in creating prophetic novels: Dostoevsky, Melville, D. H. Lawrence, and Emily Brontë. He discusses passages from *Moby Dick* and the short story ''Billy Budd'' in order to illustrate Melville's prophetic voice and from *Wuthering Heights* for a discussion of Brontë as ''a prophetess.'' He points to D. H. Lawrence as the only living novelist whose work is successfully prophetic.

Pattern and Rhythm

In a chapter on pattern and rhythm, Forster describes the aspect of pattern in the novel in terms of visual art. He describes the narrative pattern of *Thaïs,* by Anatole France, as that of an hourglass and the novel *Roman Pictures,* by Percy Lubbock, as that of a chain. He determines that pattern adds an aesthetic quality of beauty to a novel. Forster then discusses the novel *The Ambassadors,* by Henry James, which, he claims, sacrifices the liveliness of the characters to the rigid structure of an hourglass pattern. Forster concludes that the problem of pattern in novels is that it ''shuts the door on life.'' He then turns to the aspect of rhythm, which he describes as ''repetition plus variation,'' as better suited to the novel than is pattern. He describes the multi-volume novel *Remembrance of Things Past,* by Marcel Proust, as an example of the successful use of rhythm. Forster concludes that rhythm in the novel provides a more open-ended narrative structure without sacrificing character.

Conclusion

In a brief conclusion, Forster speculates as to the future of the novel, asserting that it will in fact not change at all because human nature does not change. He concludes that ''the development of the novel'' is no more than ''the development of humanity.''

Key Figures

Jane Austen

Jane Austen (1775–1817) was an English novelist whose works depicting the British middle class are a landmark in the development of the modern novel. She is best known for the novels *Sense and Sensibility* (1811), *Pride and Prejudice* (1813), *Mansfield Park* (1814), *Emma* (1815), and *Persuasion* (1817). Drawing examples from both *Emma* and *Persuasion,* Forster notes that all of the characters in Austen's novels are ''round.''

Sir Max Beerbohm

Sir Max Beerbohm (1872–1956) was a British journalist celebrated for his witty caricatures of the fashionable elite of his time. His publications include *The Works of Max Beerbohm; Caricatures of Twenty-Five Gentlemen* (both in 1896); *The Happy Hypocrite* (1897), a light-hearted fable; and *Seven Men* (1919), a short story collection. Forster discusses Beerbohm's only novel, *Zuleika Dobson,* a parody of Oxford University student life, as an example of the complex use of fantasy.

Arnold Bennett

Arnold Bennett (1867–1931) was a British novelist, critic, essayist, and playwright whose major works include a series of novels set in his native region of the ''five towns,'' then called the Potteries (now united into the single city of Stoke-on-Trent). The ''Five Towns'' novels include *Anna of the Five Towns* (1902), *The Old Wives' Tale* (1908), *Clayhanger* (1910), *Hilda Lessways* (1911), *These Twain* (1916), and *The Clayhanger Family* (1925). Forster discusses *The Old Wives' Tale* as an example of a novel in which time is ''celebrated'' as the ''real hero.'' He concludes that, while *The Old Wives' Tale* is ''very strong and sad,'' the conclusion is ''unsatisfactory,'' and it therefore ''misses greatness.''

Charlotte Brontë

Charlotte Brontë (1816–1855), the sister of Emily Brontë, was a British novelist of the Victorian era, celebrated for her masterpiece *Jane Eyre* (1847). Her other works include *Shirley* (1849) and *Villette* (1853). Forster uses *Villette* as an example of a novel in which the plot suffers due to an inconsistency in the narrative voice.

Emily Brontë

Emily Brontë (1818–1848), the sister of Charlotte Brontë, was a British writer whose only novel, *Wuthering Heights* (1847), is generally considered to be a greater achievement than any of her sister's novels. Forster asserts that Emily Brontë ''was a prophetess,'' in his literary sense of the word. He explains that, while *Wuthering Heights* makes no reference to mythology, and ''no book is more cut off from the Universals of Heaven and Hell,'' the prophetic voice of her novel gains its power from ''what is implied,'' rather than from what is explicitly stated.

Daniel Defoe

Daniel Defoe (1660–1731) was an English novelist and journalist, and author of the novels *Robinson Crusoe* (1719–1722) and *Moll Flanders* (1722). Forster discusses *Moll Flanders* as an example of a novel in which the plot and story are subordinate to the main character. Forster states that ''what interested Defoe was the heroine, and the form of his book proceeds naturally out of her character.''

Charles Dickens

Charles Dickens (1812–1870) is often considered the greatest English novelist of the Victorian era. His works, many of which remain popular classics, include *A Christmas Carol, Oliver Twist* (1837–1839), *David Copperfield* (1849–1850), *Bleak House* (1852–1853), *A Tale of Two Cities* (1859), *Great Expectations* (1860–1861), and *Our Mutual Friend* (1864–1865). (His novels were originally published in serial form, often spread out over a period of years.) Forster makes the point that most of the characters in Dickens novels are ''flat'' and can be summed up in one sentence. However, he asserts that these characters evoke ''a wonderful feeling of human depth,'' by which Dickens expresses ''a vision of humanity that is not shallow.'' In a discussion of narrative point-of-view, Forster uses the example of *Bleak House,* in which the narrative perspective shifts around inconsistently, yet does not alienate the reader, due to Dickens' stylistic skill.

Media Adaptations

- Forster's best known novels were adapted to film during the 1980s and 1990s. *A Passage to India* (1984), directed by David Lean, stars Judy Davis, Victor Bannerjee, and Alec Guinness. Merchant-Ivory productions adapted several of his novels, under the direction of James Ivory: *A Room With a View* (1986) stars Helena Bonham Carter, Daniel Day-Lewis, Judi Dench, Julian Sands, and Maggie Smith; *Maurice* (1987) stars James Wilby and Hugh Grant; *Howard's End* (1992) stars Helena Bonham Carter, Anthony Hopkins, Vanessa Redgrave, and Emma Thompson. *Where Angels Fear to Tread* (1991), directed by Charles Sturridge, stars Helena Bonham Carter, Judy Davis, and Rupert Graves.

Fyodor Dostoevsky

Fyodor Dostoevsky (1821–1882; also spelled Dostoevski) was a nineteenth-century Russian writer who remains one of the greatest novelists of all time. His most celebrated works include the novels *Crime and Punishment* (1866), *The Idiot* (1868–1869), *The Possessed* (1872), and *The Brothers Karamazov* (1879–1880), and the novella *Notes from the Underground* (1864). In a discussion of prophesy, Forster compares a passage from *The Brothers Karamazov* with a passage from a novel by George Eliot, concluding that in Dostoevsky's work can be heard the prophetic voice of the novelist.

Norman Douglas

Norman Douglas (1868–1952) was an Austrian writer of Scottish-German descent who traveled widely in India, Italy, and North Africa, and most of his works are set on the Island of Capri in southern Italy. Master of a conversational style of prose, he is best known for the novels *Siren Land* (1911), *South Wind* (1917), and *Old Calabria* (1915) and for the autobiography *Looking Back* (1933). Forster mentions Norman Douglas in a discussion of character.

He quotes an open letter written by Douglas to D. H. Lawrence, in which he criticizes the novelist for his undeveloped characters.

George Eliot

George Eliot (pseudonym of Mary Ann, or Marian, Evans; 1819–1880) was an English novelist celebrated for the realism of her novels. Her best known works include *Adam Bede* (1859), *The Mill on the Floss* (1860), *Silas Marner* (1861), and *Middlemarch* (1871–1872), her masterpiece. In a discussion of prophesy, Forster compares a passage from *Adam Bede* with a passage from *The Brothers Karamazov,* by Dostoevsky, concluding that, while both express a Christian vision, Dostoevsky's vision is that of a prophet, whereas Eliot's is merely preachy.

Henry Fielding

Henry Fielding (1701–1754) was a British writer, considered to be one of the inventors of the English novel. His best known works include the novels *Joseph Andrews* (1742) and *Tom Jones* (1749). Forster mentions Fielding as a novelist who successfully creates ''round'' characters. In a discussion of point of view, Forster criticizes Fielding for his intrusive narrative voice, which is no better than ''bar-room chattiness'' that deflates the narrative tension. In a discussion of fantasy, Forster mentions *Joseph Andrews* as an example of an ''abortive'' attempt at parody. He explains that Fielding started out with the intention of parodying the novel *Pamela,* by Samuel Richards, but, through the invention of his own ''round'' characters, ended up writing a completely original work.

Anatole France

Anatole France (1884–1924) was a French novelist and critic who was awarded the Nobel Prize for literature in 1921. In a discussion of pattern, Forster describes France's novel *Thaïs* (1890) as having a narrative structure in the shape of an hourglass.

David Garnett

David Garnett (1892–1981) was a British novelist best known for his satiric tales, such as *Lady into Fox* (1922) and *A Man in the Zoo* (1924). He also wrote several books based on his association with the Bloomsbury Group, including *The Golden Echo* (1953), *The Flowers of the Forest* (1955), *The Familiar Faces* (1962), and *Great Friends: Portraits of Seventeen Writers* (1980). In addition, he edited a 1938 edition of *The Letters of T. E. Lawrence* (1938). Forster discusses *Lady into Fox,* in which a woman is transformed into a fox, as an example of the fantastic in the novel.

André Gide

André Gide (1869–1951) was a French writer awarded the Nobel Prize for literature in 1947 and is best known today for his novel *L'Immoraliste* (1902; The Immoralist). In a discussion of plot, Forster discusses Gide's *Les Faux monnayeurs* as an example of a novel in which the story is entirely determined by the main character and contains almost no plot whatsoever.

Oliver Goldsmith

Oliver Goldsmith (1730–1774) was an English novelist, essayist, and playwright whose major works include the novel *The Vicar of Wakefield* (1766), the essay collection *The Citizen of the World, or Letters from a Chinese Philosopher* (1762), the poem *The Deserted Village* (1770), and the play *She Stoops to Conquer* (1773). In a discussion of plot, Forster describes *The Vicar of Wakefield* as a novel in which the formulation of the ending comes at the expense of the story and characters. Referring to Goldsmith as ''a lightweight,'' Forster notes that in *The Vicar of Wakefield,* as in many novels, the plot is ''clever and fresh'' at the beginning, yet ''wooden and imbecile'' by the ending.

Thomas Hardy

Thomas Hardy (1840–1928) was an English novelist and poet whose major works include the novels *Far from the Madding Crowd* (1874), *The Return of the Native* (1878), *The Mayor of Casterbridge* (1886), *Tess of the d'Urbervilles* (1891), and *Jude the Obscure* (1895). In a discussion of plot, Forster describes Hardy as a novelist whose plots are so overly structured that the characters are lifeless.

Henry James

Henry James (1843–1916) was an American-born novelist who lived much of his adult life in

England, creating characters who represent conflicts between American spirit and European tradition. His major works include the novels *Daisy Miller* (1879), *The Portrait of a Lady, Washington Square* (both 1881), *The Bostonians* (1886), *The Wings of a Dove* (1902), and *The Ambassadors* (1903). In a discussion of pattern, Forster describes *The Ambassadors* as a novel in which the narrative is structured in the pattern of an hourglass, stressing symmetry at the expense of character.

James Joyce

James Joyce (1882–1941) was an Irish novelist whose major works include the novels *A Portrait of the Artist as a Young Man* (1916), *Ulysses* (1922), and *Finnegans Wake* (1939), and the short story collection, *Dubliners* (1914). In a discussion of the fantastic, Forster describes the experimental novel *Ulysses* as an adaptation of the classic Greek mythology of the *Odyssey*. Although he refers to *Ulysses* as "perhaps the most remarkable literary experiment of our time," Forster concludes that it is not entirely successful as a novel, as it lacks the element of prophecy.

D. H. Lawrence

D. H. Lawrence (1885–1930) was an English novelist whose major works include *Sons and Lovers* (1913), *Women in Love* (1920), and the highly controversial *Lady Chatterley's Lover* (first published in 1928, though not readily available to the reading public until 1959). Drawing an example from *Women in Love,* Forster asserts that Lawrence is, to his knowledge "the only prophetic novelist writing today," (in 1927).

Percy Lubbock

Percy Lubbock was an author and critic whose book *The Craft of Fiction* (1921) contributed to the development of the theoretical study of the novel. In a discussion of character, Forster cites Lubbock as claiming that point of view is central to characterization. In a discussion of narrative pattern, Forster discusses Lubbock's *Roman Pictures,* a comedy of manners, as a narrative structured in the pattern of a chain. Forster asserts that this novel is successful, not simply because of this pattern, but because of the appropriateness of the pattern to the mood of the story.

Herman Melville

Herman Melville (1819–1891) was an American novelist whose masterpiece, *Moby Dick* (1851) is considered one of the greatest novels ever written. In a discussion of prophecy, Forster describes Melville as a profoundly prophetic writer, citing passages from both *Moby Dick* and the short story "Billy Budd."

George Meredith

George Meredith (1828–1929) was an English novelist and poet, known for his concern for women's equality and his mastery of the internal monologue. Meredith was highly influential among many of the great modern novelists of the early twentieth century. His major works include *The Ordeal of Richard Feverel* (1859), *Evan Harrington* (1860), *The Adventures of Harry Richmond* (1871), *Beauchamp's Career* (1876), *The Egoist* (1879), and *Diana of the Crossways* (1885). In a discussion of plot, Forster, drawing from the examples of *Harry Richmond* and *Beauchamp's Career,* explains that, while Meredith is no longer the towering figure of literary accomplishment he once was, he is, if nothing else, a master of plot in the novel.

Marcel Proust

Marcel Proust (1881–1922) was a French novelist whose masterpiece is the seven-volume, semi-autobiographical novel, *Á la recherche du temps perdu* (1913–27; Remembrance of Things Past). At the time of Forster's lectures, the final volume of *Remembrance of Things Past* had not yet been published. In a discussion of character, Forster refers to Proust as an example of a writer whose "flat" characters function to accent the "round" characters. In a discussion of rhythm in the novel, Forster praises the work of Proust as an example of a novel that, while chaotic in structure, is held together by rhythm, the literary equivalent of a musical motif.

Samuel Richardson

Samuel Richardson (1689–1761) was an English novelist credited with inventing the epistolary novel, in which the story is narrated through a series of letters between the characters. His major works are *Pamela* (1740) and *Clarissa* (1747–1748). In a discussion of parody and adaptation, Forster mentions *Pamela* as the work that Henry Fielding set out to parody in his novel *Joseph Andrews*.

Sir Walter Scott

Sir Walter Scott (1771–1832) was a Scottish novelist credited with the invention of the historical novel. *Ivanhoe* (1819) is the best known of his many novels and novel cycles. In a discussion of storytelling in the novel, Forster uses the examples of *The Bride of Lammermoor* (1819) and of *The Antiquary* (1816; the last of a trilogy, set in Scotland from 1740–1800, known as the ''Waverly'' novels). Forster, although admitting that he does not consider Scott a good novelist, does concede that he is a good storyteller, to the extent that he is able to narrate a sequence of events that occur over time. Forster concludes, however, that the result of Scott's perfunctory storytelling is a shallow and unemotional work, lacking the qualities which lend value to a novel.

Gertrude Stein

Gertrude Stein (1874–1946) was an American writer of experimental novels, stories, and essays, whose major works include *Three Lives* (1909), *Tender Buttons* (1914), *The Making of Americans* (1925), and *The Autobiography of Alice B. Toklas* (1933). In a discussion of story, Forster describes Stein as an example of a novelist who attempted to write stories without the element of time.

Laurence Sterne

Laurence Sterne (1713–1768) was an Irish-English writer whose masterpiece is the novel *Tristram Shandy* (1759–1767), in which narrative digression dominates the story line. In a discussion of fantasy and prophecy, Forster mentions Sterne among a number of novelists in whose works both fantasy and prophecy are essential.

Leo Tolstoy

Leo Tolstoy (1828–1910) was a Russian novelist whose major works, *War and Peace* (1865–1869) and *Anna Karenina* (1875–1877), are considered among the greatest novels ever written. In a discussion of character, Forster describes *War and Peace* as a novel in which the narrative point of view, while scattershot and inconsistent, is successfully rendered by the skill of the novelist. In a discussion

of rhythm, Forster celebrates *War and Peace* as a novel in which the author not only succeeds in creating rhythm but comes close to the equivalent of a musical symphony on a par with Beethoven's Fifth.

H. G. Wells

H. G. Wells (1866–1946) was an English novelist best known for his now-classic science fiction novels *The Time Machine* (1895), *The Island of Doctor Moreau* (1896), and *The War of the Worlds* (1898), as well as the comedic novels *Tono-Bungay* (1909) and *The History of Mr. Polly* (1910). In a discussion of character, Forster notes that Wells's characters, like those of Dickens, are almost all completely ''flat'' yet succeed in the context of his novels due to his great narrative skill.

Virginia Woolf

Virginia Woolf (1882–1941) was a British novelist and critic whose major works include the novels *Mrs. Dalloway* (1925), *To the Lighthouse* (1927), and *Orlando* (1928), as well as the early work of feminist criticism, *A Room of One's Own* (1929). In his introduction, Forster cites a passage written by Woolf in comparison with a passage by Sterne.

Themes

The Literary Critic

Throughout his lecture series, Forster includes commentary on the role he plays as a literary critic in relation to literature. He makes observations about his methodology as a critic, occasionally refers to the assertions of other critics, and sometimes questions the validity of the critic in the world of literature. In his introduction, Forster dismisses, for the purposes of his discussion, standard methods in literary criticism based in the tracing of historical development and the influence of earlier writers on those who come after them. Likewise, Forster mentions the notion of tradition put forth by T. S. Eliot, who asserted that it is the task of the critic to preserve the best of literary tradition. Forster immediately dismisses this as an impossible task. He does, however, agree with Eliot that the critic is

Topics for Further Study

- Forster discusses many of the major novelists of the English language, as well as several French and Russian writers. Pick one author from the list of Key Figures in this entry and learn more about that author and her or his major works.

- Forster discusses seven aspects he deems essential to the novel: story, plot, character, fantasy, prophesy, pattern, and rhythm . Pick a work of fiction not specifically mentioned by Forster and analyze it in terms of these seven elements. How well does it measure up to Forster's standards? Do you agree with this assessment?

- Although Forster discusses elements specific to the novel, they may also be applied to the short story. Try writing a short story which takes into account each of the seven aspects discussed by Forster.

- Two years after Forster's lecture series on *Aspects of the Novel*, Virginia Woolf, his contemporary and a fellow member of the Bloomsbury Group, wrote a very different critical work on literature and literary history, a book-length essay entitled *A Room of One's Own*. Read *A Room of One's Own*. What are the central points of Woolf's discussion of literature in this essay? To what extent do you agree or disagree with her arguments and conclusions?

---

required to see literature in its entirety and not as it may be determined by the constraints of a historical timeline. Throughout the book, Forster occasionally cites other literary critics, often in order to present a counterargument. He also continues to question the relationship of the critic to literature when he observes that perhaps his lectures have moved away from literature itself, in the pursuit of abstract theorizing about literature. Ultimately, however, Forster asserts that the most important measure by which literature ought to be judged is that of the "human heart," concluding that the most important "test" of a novel is "our affection for it."

Reading

Forster's series of lectures on the novel are concerned not just with analysis of the novel itself but with what he deems the requirements the novel demands of the reader. He asserts that the appreciation of plot requires of the reader both intelligence and memory. He explains that, while curiosity may be what leads the reader to take an interest in the story, it is, in itself, a rather basic and uninteresting trait in a reader. In order to grasp the plot, however, the reader must first possess intelligence. He observes that, though curiosity is the quality that

allows the reader to take an interest in individual pieces of information, intelligence makes it possible for the reader to appreciate the aura of mystery embedded in plot, allowing her or him to contemplate the relationships between pieces of information. He further notes that the reader requires memory in order to recall the relationship of information provided earlier in a novel to that which comes later; it is therefore the responsibility of the writer to satisfy the reader's memory by making sure each piece of information contributes to the whole. Forster further claims that the element of prophecy requires both humility and the "suspension of a sense of humor." He explains that humility is required of the reader in order to hear the voice of the prophetic in the novel and that "suspension of a sense of humor" is required in order to avoid the temptation to ridicule the universal, or spiritual, element that makes it great. In describing his requirements for the great novel, Forster thus makes clear his definition of the appropriate reader of great literature.

The Universal

In his discussion of prophecy, Forster touches upon the element of the universal as the most profound aspect of the novel. The universal, as

Forster uses it, could also be thought of as the spiritual, in the broadest sense of the term, although not necessarily in relation to a specific creed or religion. Forster explains that the universal in a novel may refer to specific religions or spiritual practices, or it may refer to profound human emotions such as love and hate. He notes that the element of the universal in a novel may be indicated directly, or it may be implied through subtle, indirect means. In order to illustrate what he means by the prophetic, Forster compares passages from George Eliot's *Adam Bede* and Fyodor Dostoevsky's *The Brother's Karamazov*. He observes that, though both authors are from a Christian background and both wish to express the idea of salvation as inspired in the sinner by love and pity, Eliot's direct reference to Christianity comes off as a heavy-handed sermon, whereas Dostoevsky's subtle and indirect reference to Christian spirituality succeeds in being prophetic. Forster goes on to observe that, though Eliot is sincere in her invocation of the spiritual, her references to Christianity remain in the realm of realism and fail to inspire in the reader a sensation of the spiritual. Dostoevsky, on the other hand, though also a master of realism, imbues his characters with the spirit of the infinite, or universal, so that, "one can apply to them the saying of St. Catherine of Siena that God is in the soul and the soul is in God as the sea is in the fish and the fish is in the sea."

Style

Tone and Structure

The narrative tone, or voice, of *Aspects of the Novel* is first and foremost determined by the fact that it is a printed version of a series of lectures, originally written and presented in verbal form by the author before an audience of college and university students and professors in the halls of Trinity College, Cambridge, Forster's alma mater, in the name of the distinguished Clark lecture series. An editor's note that opens the reprinted lectures observes that their tone is "informal, indeed talkative." Because of this informal, chatty tone, Forster's voice throughout this collection of lectures is relatively intimate and, on a surface level, appears to make unexpected digressions or include various asides, which one might not find in a work origi-

nally intended solely for the printed page. The overall structure of Forster's discussion, however, is not the least haphazard or off-the-cuff. Each chapter/lecture progresses through a clearly planned series of points to present a specific position on each of the seven aspects of the novel with which Forster is concerned. Thus, though informal in narrative tone, the underlying structure of *Aspects of the Novel* progresses through a well-developed argument, illustrated by carefully chosen examples.

Analogy

An analogy is a use of figurative language in which the writer draws a parallel between a concrete, familiar, or easily understandable object or concept and a more abstract, original, and complex idea for purposes of explanation and clarity. The central analogy with which Forster opens and concludes *Aspects of the Novel* is an image of all of the novelists from world literature throughout history writing simultaneously, side by side, in a great circular room, such as that of the library of the British Museum. Forster utilizes this analogy in order to make the point that the novel and the novelist are oblivious to variation in culture and history and that all novelists write in accordance with the same basic principals of creativity.

Forster employs this overarching analogy in order to make clear that, in his discussion of the novel, he is not interested in historical development or regional difference but in the universal qualities. The analogy of writers working side-by-side allows Forster to discuss the work of novelists who lived and worked in disparate centuries and continents, in order to demonstrate their commonalties as well as differences. He thus devotes a significant portion of the introduction to placing side-by-side passages from such far-flung origins as Samuel Richardson of the eighteenth century and Henry James of the early twentieth century or a Dickens novel from 1860 with an H. G. Wells novel from 1920. Forster thus utilizes the analogy of novelists writing side-by-side in order to illustrate his premise that "history develops, art stands still." In his concluding chapter, Forster comes back to this analogy in order to speculate about the direction of the novel in the future. He proposes that "we must visualize the novelists of the next two hundred years as also writing in the same room," asserting that the "mechanism of the human mind" remains essentially the same throughout history.

Compare & Contrast

- **1837–1901:** The reign of Queen Victoria lends its name to the Victorian era, a term that first comes into use in the 1850s.

  1901–1910: The reign of King Edward VII, referred to as the Edwardian age, marks a contrast with the national atmosphere of his austere mother.

  1914–1918: The horror and disillusionment experienced by the World War I era has a profound effect on English literature and the modernist movement.

  1924–1937: James Ramsay MacDonald is the first candidate of the Labour Party, with which Forster sympathized, to be elected prime minister. MacDonald, however, holds office for only nine months. MacDonald again holds the office from 1929–1935. However, during the 1920s and 1930s, English politics are dominated by Prime Minister Baldwin, who holds office from 1924 to 1929 and from 1935 to 1937, as a result of which the 1920s and 1930s come to be known as the Baldwin Era.

  1979–1997: British politics are dominated by the Conservative government of Prime Minister Margaret Thatcher, whose term of office is followed by that of the Conservative John Major.

  1997: The Labour Party, with which Forster had been associated during his lifetime, wins a landslide victory in the election of Tony Blair as prime minister.

- **1780s–1840s:** Romanticism, focusing on the imagination of the individual, is the predominant literary movement in England.

  1840s–1890s: Romanticism gives way to the Gothicism and realism of the Victorian era novelists.

  1901–1910: Novelists of the Edwardian era express a critical perspective on British society.

  1910s–1930s: The modernist movement in literature expresses a desire for doing away with older literary forms in extending the boundaries of the novel.

  1939–1945: During the World War II era, various factors cause poetry and the short story to gain prominence over the novel in English literature. A brief movement in poetry known as the New Apocalypse develops during the war years.

  1940s: The New Apocalypse gives way to a development known simply as the Movement in poetry.

  1950s: A group of novelists known as the Angry Young Men are known for their realistic, autobiographical works.

  Today: New developments in the novel are characterized by what is known as post-colonial and post-modern fiction, alongside the enduring form of the realist novel.

Historical Context

English History and Literature

Forster's discussion covers three centuries of the novel; his own life and work spanned the late nineteenth through the late twentieth centuries. His life was affected by such major events as World War I, in which he participated, and his novels bridge the historical transition from Victorian to Edwardian England, as well as the literary transition from romanticism to modernism.

Victorian and Edwardian England

The Victorian era is the name given to the period of English history during the long reign of Queen Victoria, from 1837 to 1901. While commonly associated with a culture of conventionality and prudishness, Victorian England witnessed major upheavals in economic, political, and technological structure. In the nineteenth century, England lead the way in the Industrial Revolution, ultimately followed by other European and non-European nations. Significant advances in wages and a significant population expansion were integral to a series of political reforms that gradually increased the rights of average citizens and decreased the power of the regency in the political realm. The Reform Act of 1832 began a trend that lead to the Reform Bill of 1867 and a series of economic and social reforms introduced in the 1870s. The requirements for voting rights were altered to vastly increase the proportion of the male population eligible to participate in elections to Parliament and local government offices. While the era of Queen Victoria was in part characterized by the conservative values associated with traditional family structure and social propriety, a strong strain of liberal thought characterized significant elements of nineteenth-century intellectual life. A major and controversial landmark was the biological theory of evolution put forth in Charles Darwin's 1859 *Origin of the Species*. The Victorian era ended upon the death of Queen Victoria in 1901, when her son ascended the throne as King Edward VII, thus initiating the much shorter era of Edwardian England. King Edward, unlike his mother, brought with him a freer, looser atmosphere that had its effect on the mood of the nation. Edward, who was already fifty-nine years of age when he became king, died in 1910 and was succeeded by King George V, whose reign lasted until his death in 1936.

World War I and the Post-War Era

The period of World War I, from 1914 to 1918, had a profound effect on Forster, who served as a Red Cross volunteer throughout the War, and many of the writers of his generation. A landmark in British politics of the post-War era was the People Act of 1918, which extended the right to vote to women over the age of thirty and to all men over the age of twenty-one, regardless of property holdings. In 1928, the right to vote was extended to women ages twenty-one to thirty. Forster was an active supporter of the Labour Party, which won its first major victory in 1924 when James Ramsay MacDonald was the first Labour Party leader elected to the position of prime minister of England. MacDonald, however, held this office only nine months before he was replaced by Stanley Baldwin, who remained prime minister until 1929, taking the office again in 1935, where he remained until 1937.

The 1920s and 1930s in England came to be known as the Baldwin Era, which encompassed the period in which Forster first wrote *Aspects of the Novel* in 1927. Although Forster was politically engaged, his lectures make little reference to political or historical events. His only direct reference to British politics is the mention of Prime Minister Asquith, who remained in power from 1908 until 1916.

English Literature

Though Forster explicitly avoids any discussion of historical development in the novel, it is helpful to have a basic understanding of the standard chronological periodization of English literature during the time periods in which the works discussed by Forster were produced.

In the course of his discussion, Forster mentions the four great novelists of the eighteenth century: Daniel Defoe, whose major works appeared in the 1720s; Samuel Richardson and Henry Fielding, both of whose major works appeared in the 1740s and 1750s; and Laurence Sterne, whose major works were published in the 1750s and 1760s. Major poets of the eighteenth century include Alexander Pope, Robert Burns, Oliver Goldsmith, and Samuel Johnson.

The literary era known as the romantic period spanned the 1780s to 1820s. Focusing on the imagination of the individual, the early romantic poets include William Blake, Samuel Taylor Coleridge, and William Wordsworth; the late romantic poets include Percy Bysshe Shelley, John Keats, and Lord Byron. The major English novels of the late eighteenth and early nineteenth centuries include the popular Gothic works of Ann Radcliffe and Mary Wollstonecraft Shelley (author of *Frankenstein: or, The Modern Prometheus,* 1818), the historical novels of Sir Walter Scott, and the masterpieces of Jane Austen.

The end of the romantic era in literature and the beginning of the Victorian era is generally dated around the mid-1840s, from which point numerous masterpieces of the English novel were produced. Charles Dickens, publishing from the 1830s through 1860s, was an early master of the Victorian age novel, contemporary with William Makepeace Thackeray whose masterpiece, *Vanity Fair,* was published in the 1840s, and Elizabeth Gaskell, publishing in the 1840s and 1950s. Among the greatest novelists of the age were the Brontë sisters, Emily and Charlotte, whose works, combining elements of Gothicism and realism, were published in the 1840s and 1950s. Later Victorian novelists working in the 1850s through 1890s include George Eliot, Anthony Trollope, George Meredith, and Thomas Hardy.

The literary period of the first decade of the twentieth century, associated with Edwardian England, was characterized by the novels of H. G. Wells, Arnold Bennett, Galsworthy, and Forster. The modernist movement in literature, with which Forster is also associated, began in the pre-World War I era and continued into the 1930s. Early modernism included the poets of the Georgian movement, who represented a transition from Victorian to modern literature, as well as the more forward-looking poetry of the imagist movement, made prominent by Anglo-American poet and critic Ezra Pound. The great modernist novelists wrote during and after World War I and included D. H. Lawrence, James Joyce, and Ford Madox Ford, as well as Forster. Modernist poets include T. S. Eliot and William Butler Yeats. Forster was a member of the informal group of modernist writers and intellectuals known as the Bloomsbury Group, which met regularly between 1907 and 1930 in private homes located in the Bloomsbury district of London to discuss literature and ideas and included such great modernist writers as Virginia Woolf. Most of the men belonging to the Bloomsbury Group, such as Forster himself, were graduates of King's College or Trinity College of Cambridge.

Critical Overview

Forster is best remembered as a master of the English novel. He published five novels between 1905 and 1924, including *Where Angels Fear to Tread* (1905), *The Longest Journey* (1907), *A Room with a View* (1908), *Howard's End* (1910), *A Passage to India* (1924), the last two being his undisputed masterpieces. He was to publish no more novels in his lifetime, although *Maurice*, originally written in 1914, was published posthumously in 1971. Norman Page, in *E. M. Forster* (1987), observing that Forster produced only six novels in his lifetime, notes, "Forster's impact on the twentieth century has gone far beyond what his modest output might lead one to expect." Of Forster's lifelong literary career, Claude J. Summers, in *E. M. Forster* (1983), notes that, at least since the 1950s, "he was

regularly . . . described as England's greatest living novelist." By the time of his death, "he had earned an international reputation as an incisive interpreter of the human heart and a champion of the liberal imagination."

Forster spent the last forty-five years of his life writing various forms of nonfiction, as well as a few short stories. While most agree that Forster cannot be considered a great literary critic, critics vary in their overall assessment of *Aspects of the Novel*. Lionel Trilling, in *E. M. Forster* (1943), an early and influential essay, claims that Forster is "not a great critic, not a great 'thinker.'" Trilling qualifies this statement, conceding that *Aspects of the Novel* "is full of the finest perceptions." He nonetheless observes, "Even if we grant Forster every possible virtue of his method—and it has virtues—he is never wholly satisfactory in criticism and frequently he is frustrating." However, Trilling suggests that "the laxness of the critical manner in which Forster sets forth his literary insights" is in fact a conscious protest against the Western over-valuation of rational thinking. Harry T. Moore, on the other hand, in *E. M. Forster* (1965), asserts that *Aspects of the Novel* "is valuable not only for what it tells of Forster's ways and means of writing, but it is also an important study of the art of fiction." Wilfred Stone, in *The Cave and the Mountain* (1966), claims that *Aspects of the Novel* is "Forster's most ambitious aesthetic statement." Moore, in *E. M. Forster* (1967), observes of both *Aspects of the Novel* and Forster's other works of literary criticism: "surprise and delight with unexpected insights, practical and impractical, casting light on Forster and his own fiction, obscuring both in order to illuminate some corner hitherto deprived of adequate light." Page assesses the significance and impact of *Aspects on the Novel* on literary criticism, as well as on Forster's career, in observing, "though informal in tone, [these lectures] were to have a wide influence in a period when the theory and criticism of fiction was relatively unsophisticated, and they increased Forster's reputation as a man of letters." Summers observes of *Aspects of the Novel* that it is "Forster's most sustained critical statement," in which the casual, conversational style of the writing masks an ambitious "ideological work" of criticism. Summers concludes, "*Aspects of the Novel* is extraordinarily well-written, amusing and lively as well as rueful in tone. Throughout, the book is enlivened by sharp judgments and original insights on particular works and individual authors." Finally, Summers asserts that "Forster's essays, criticism, and biogra-

One of the individual authors Forster examines is Thomas Hardy, whom he views as a writer "who conceives of his novels from an enormous height."

phies are a significant fraction of an important literary career."

Philip Gardner, in *Dictionary of Literary Biography,* points to Forster's humanism as the overriding theme throughout his essays:

> Through all his essays . . . one registers Forster as a man with an alert eye for the telling detail, who responds to what he sees, reads, and hears with emotions ranging from delight to indignation, but always with intelligence and personal concern. His voice is never that of a detached academic observer, but that of a human being reaching out to other human beings, on the one hand his readers, on the other the individuals, dead as well as living, about whom he writes.

Summers likewise assesses the corpus of Forster's eight books of nonfiction, *Aspects of the Novel* being among the "most completely successful" of these, in essentially glowing terms. He claims that these works "collectively chart a career remarkable for its breadth of interest and depth of commitment." He goes on to note, "In these books, Forster emerges as a sensitive and thoughtful critic, a charming yet unsentimental popular historian, a skillful biographer, and an essayist of rare power."

Criticism

Liz Brent

Brent has a Ph.D. in American culture, specializing in film studies, from the University of Michigan. She is a freelance writer and teaches courses in the history of American cinema. In the following essay, Brent discusses Forster's use of figurative language in Aspects of the Novel.

As explained in the above entry, an analogy is a use of figurative language in which the writer draws a parallel between a concrete, familiar, or easily understandable object or concept and a more abstract, original, and complex idea for purposes of explanation and clarity. Both metaphor and simile are types of analogies. In a metaphor, the subject under discussion is described in terms of the characteristics it shares with a more concrete image. In a simile, the writer states that his subject is similar to another object or concept. Throughout his series of lectures on seven aspects of the novel, Forster employs the figurative language of analogy, using both metaphor and simile, drawn from such disparate sources as nature, architecture, science, and music.

He often utilizes analogies drawn from nature in order to express his ideas about literature. In the introduction, he describes literature, "a formidable mass," as an "amorphous" body of water, "irrigated by a hundred rills and occasionally degenerating into a swamp," which he contrasts with the sturdy, solid, imposing image of a mountain. Forster is here explaining that the study of literature is made complicated by the fact that its exact definition and boundary lines are unclear, sometimes so much so that it resembles the murky water of a swamp. Claiming that, to his mind, there is no absolute definition of what does or does not constitute literature, Forster ventures, "All we can say of it is that it is bounded by two chains of mountains . . . Poetry and History" and, on a third side, by the sea. In other words, although it may not be possible to accurately define what literature *is,* one can at least say that it is not history and that it is not poetry. The sea, of course, is an image that continues the description of literature in terms of water. Forster uses water imagery in a different sense when employing the commonly used metaphor "the stream of time" in order to explain that his discussion of the novel will not be concerned with chronological development and thus will avoid viewing authors or works of literature as objects floating through the "stream

What Do I Read Next?

- *Wuthering Heights* (1847), by Charlotte Brontë, is an early Gothic novel by one of the four writers Forster deems truly prophetic. It concerns themes of inheritance and legitimacy among the upper classes of the English countryside and includes elements of the supernatural.

- *Moby Dick* (1851), by Herman Melville, is considered one of the greatest novels ever written. It narrates one man's obsession with the pursuit of Moby Dick, a great white whale that he is determined to kill. Forster deems this one of the truly prophetic novels ever written.

- The novel *The Brothers Karamazov* (1879–1880) is a masterpiece by the Russian writer Fyodor Dostoevsky, whom Forster deemed one of four truly prophetic novelists. It concerns a man accused of the murder of his own father.

- *Howard's End* (1910), a novel by Forster and his first major literary success, is concerned with divisions among upper and lower classes in Edwardian England, as expressed by the encounter between members of two different families.

- The novel *Women in Love* (1920) is one of the major works by D. H. Lawrence, whom Forster considered the only truly prophetic writer alive at the time of his lecture series in 1927. It concerns the romantic relationship of two sisters, both modern, independent, free-spirited women, in the post-World War I era of England. It is a continuation of the earlier novel *The Rainbow,* which chronicles three generations of a family from the 1960s up to the years preceding World War I.

- The novel *A Passage to India* (1924) is Forster's masterpiece, in which a young girl experiences the clash of cultures between the British and Indians in colonial India.

- *Abinger Harvest* (1936) is a collection of about fifty essays by Forster that originally appeared between 1919 and 1935. As in the later collection *Two Cheers for Democracy,* it includes biographical sketches of other writers, critical discussion of literature, and articulations of his political views as a liberal humanist. This collection includes ''Notes on the English Character,'' one of his best known essays.

- *Two Cheers for Democracy* (1951) is a collection of essays by Forster that, like the collection *Abinger Harvest,* includes biographical sketches of other writers, critical discussion of literature, reviews, and articulations of his liberal humanist political stance. It includes ''What I Believe,'' one of his best known essays.

- *Maurice* (1971), a novel finished by Forster in 1914, was published for the first time after Forster's death. It concerns a young man discovering his homosexuality and is generally believed to be autobiographical.

- *E. M. Forster: A Biography* (1994), by Nicola Beauman, is one of several recent biographies of Forster.

---

of time'' but will instead imagine them to have been writing simultaneously. Thus, in his use of metaphors drawn from nature, Forster distinguishes between his vision of literature as an amorphous body of water, whether it be a swamp or the sea, and an image of a stream of water, which implies a clearly-defined direction and flow of events.

Forster additionally employs metaphors drawn from nature when he discusses the use of adaptation in the novel. He describes the relationship between the twentieth-century novel *Ulysses,* by James Joyce, to the ancient Greek mythology of the *Odyssey* as that of ''a bat hanging to a cornice''—the novel, like the bat, has a life of its own yet clings to the original mythological text as an essential means of

> **Forster suggests that only one novel, Tolstoy's *War and Peace*, has successfully achieved the musical brilliance of Beethoven's Fifth Symphony, in which 'great chords of sound' can be heard to emerge from the narrative form."**

support. In a further metaphor drawn from the animal world, Forster, speaking again of *Ulysses,* adds that it is overrun with references to a variety of mythologies, to the extent that "smaller mythologies swarm and pullulate, like vermin between the scales of a poisonous snake." He further makes use of a simile drawn from images of nature in describing the relationship between the literary critic and the subject matter of criticism. Forster questions whether or not he may have gotten too far away from literature itself, in the course of his discussion of the novel, likening the flight of ideas generated by the critic to a bird in flight and the subject matter itself to the shadow of that bird:

> Perhaps our subject, namely the books we have read, has stolen away from us while we theorize, like a shadow from an ascending bird. The bird is all right—it climbs, it is consistent and eminent. The shadow is all right—it has flickered across roads and gardens. But the two things resemble one another less and less, they do not touch as they did when the bird rested its toes on the ground.

Forster extends this metaphor in suggesting that the literary critic, pursuing the route of theory, may find himself taking flights of thought into regions of ideas far removed from the works of literature with which he began.

In his discussion of story in the novel, Forster utilizes a curious set of metaphors drawn from biology. He interchangeably describes the function of the story in a novel as either a "backbone" or a "tape worm." He uses the image of a backbone to explain the role of the story as the internal structure that supports all other elements of the novel. However, he suggests the alternative image of a tapeworm in order to express the idea that the beginning and ending of the story in a novel is arbitrary, just as a tapeworm has no specified length and no discern-

ible head or tail. Yet, despite the arbitrary nature of the beginning and end of a story, Forster asserts that it must nonetheless be narrated over a span of time; thus, he states that the author must always "touch the interminable tapeworm." In other words, the novelist must, regardless of where he begins or ends, touch upon a series of events that unfold over a span of time. Forster continues to use metaphors drawn from biology in stating that the story "is the lowest and simplest of literary organisms, yet it is the highest factor common to all the very complicated organisms known as novels." He goes on to imagine the element of story as a "worm," held up for examination on the "forceps" of the literary critic. Through the image of the story and the novel as organisms, Forster puts forth the opinion that the element of story, fundamental to all novels, is, in itself, not especially interesting in comparison to the "very complicated" novel as a whole. He later notes that the plot is, however, a "higher" organism than the story, meaning that it is a more complex and interesting aspect of the novel. Forster observes that the story is a "lower," "simpler" organism also in the sense that it is primitive, a timeless human activity that originated in our primitive cultures.

Later in the introduction, Forster employs metaphors drawn from architecture in order to describe the magnitude of specific novels. He asserts that a number of English novels are "little mansions," meaning they are certainly impressive literary accomplishments but that they are by no means "mighty edifices," of grander significance. Forster compares these English novels to the "colonnades" and "vaults" of the great works of Russian novelists Leo Tolstoy and Fyodor Dostoevsky, thus implying that these authors have created majestic, imposing works of immense magnitude and enduring importance, well beyond that of many "great" English novels. Forster later employs a metaphor drawn from architecture when he describes Thomas Hardy's novels as stories in which the plot is the "ground plan," meaning that all other elements of the story are built upon the foundation of a highly structured plot.

In a discussion of the relationship between plot and character, Forster uses the metaphor of war. Critical of the overly schematic plot that deadens the life of the characters in a novel, he describes this tension as a "losing battle" at the end of which the novel is "feeble," due to the "cowardly revenge" of the plot upon the characters, as carried out by the inadequacy of most endings. He later uses the metaphor of war and battle in describing the attempts of some modernist writers to abolish the plot from their novels as a ''violent onslaught.'' Compared to the more benign metaphors drawn from nature and science, Forster employs imagery drawn from war in order to express the potentially destructive force of an overly structured plot on the very life of a novel's characters.

Another curious metaphor employed by Forster is that of the circus sideshow to describe the place of the ''fantastic'' in the novel. He explains that readers who enjoy the element of the fantastic are like the spectators who do not mind paying both the general price of admission to the circus and the additional ''sixpence'' to see the side show. Readers who do not care for the element of the fantastic in literature—and Forster does not fault these people—are not willing or able to pay the additional fee for the sideshow. Via this analogy, Forster suggests that some readers, while willing to use their imaginations in order to enter the story of a novel, do not possess the imaginative faculty for appreciating the element of the fantastic. Others, however, having entered into the relatively realistic world of the novel (the circus), are eager to make the extra imaginative leap (pay the extra fee) in order to enjoy the elements of the fantastic, which may stretch the boundaries of credibility.

In a very different type of metaphor, Forster describes the elements of fantasy and prophesy in the novel as a ''bar of light'' that ''illumines'' other aspects of the novel. In contrast to the more concrete analogies drawn from nature, architecture, and war, the analogy of a bar of light is appropriate to Forster's concern with fantasy and prophesy as more abstract, conceptual, universal, or spiritual elements of the novel. However, light is not in fact an abstract substance, and Forster later suggests that, as there are only a limited number of devices by which the novelist may express the fantastic, this ''beam of light can only be manipulated in certain ways.'' Forster thus implies that these literary devices, like light, have properties and laws of their own, according to which the author is limited in his ability to manipulate them to his will.

In his discussion of prophecy and rhythm in the novel, perhaps the elements that he most values in a great work, Forster makes use of analogies drawn from music. The element of prophecy he describes as a quality of the author's voice akin to that of a song—a song accompanied by ''the flutes and saxophones of fantasy.'' In contrast to the universal, or

spiritual (in the broadly defined sense of the term), elements of the novel, as expressed through fantasy and prophecy, Forster describes the element of realism, which he deems as essential to the novel as the interior structure and furnishings are to a house. Forster suggests that there is a degree of conflict between the abstract ''music'' of fantasy and ''song'' of prophecy and the concrete realism of dust and furniture in the rooms and hallways of a house; he observes the following regarding the prophetic novelist:

> [The prophetic novelist] proposes to sing, and the strangeness of song arising in the halls of fiction is bound to give us a shock. How will song combine with the furniture of common sense? We shall ask ourselves, and shall have to answer ''not too well'': the singer does not always have room for his gestures, the tables and chairs get broken, and the novel through which bardic influence has passed often has a wrecked air, like a drawing-room after an earthquake or a children's party.

Forster asserts, however, that the value of the chaotic and potentially disruptive nature of the prophetic voice in fiction is worth the risk of wrecking the furniture of realism. He then picks up the metaphor of the fantastic as a beam of light that cuts across the narrative, suggesting that the prophetic song of the novelist may also serve to light up a room, rather than, or in addition to, wrecking it a bit:

> Perhaps he will smash or distort, but perhaps he will illumine. . . . He manipulates a beam of light which occasionally touches the objects so sedulously dusted by the hand of common sense, and renders them more vivid than they can ever be in domesticity.

Having utilized the metaphor of song to illustrate the effect of the prophetic voice, Forster continues to describe another key aspect of the novel in terms of music. His final chapter, ''Pattern and Rhythm,'' dismisses the value of structuring a novel in accordance with the visual metaphor of pattern, such as in a woven fabric. Rather, he argues for the value of an open-ended structure akin to the musical motif in a symphony, or, in a novelistic masterpiece, a symphony in its entirety. Forster states that music is the best analogy for the novel. He uses the example of *Remembrance of Things Past,* by Marcel Proust, as a novel in which a recurring ''musical phrase'' provides internal unity throughout an otherwise structurally ''messy'' story. Unlike the pattern, which Forster deems ultimately too rigid and all encompassing to accommodate the best elements of the novel, the rhythm of a musical motif, which comes and goes throughout the story, can ''fill us with surprise and freshness and hope.'' Forster observes that the musical analogy of rhythm provides the novelist with a narrative form that is expansive and open-ended. Finally, Forster suggests that only one novel, Tolstoy's *War and Peace,* has successfully achieved the musical brilliance of Beethoven's Fifth Symphony, in which "great chords of sound" can be heard to emerge from the narrative form.

Throughout his lectures, Forster makes use of a variety of analogies in order to illustrate his central concerns with the novel. He draws imagery from the natural landscape, the animal kingdom, biology, architecture, interior design, war, properties of light, circus entertainments, and music. His use of analogy not only serves the practical purpose of clarifying his meaning but imbues his discussion with a playful, whimsical quality that captures his sense of joy in the creative act of reading and discussing, as well as writing, great literature.

Source: Liz Brent, Critical Essay on *Aspects of the Novel,* in *Nonfiction Classics for Students,* The Gale Group, 2001.

Ann Henley

In the following essay, Henley examines the debate over novel writing in general, and Aspects of the Novel *in particular, between E. M. Forster and Virginia Woolf*

In his "Introductory" to *Aspects of the Novel,* E. M. Forster invites his audience to imagine the glorious company of English novelists "seated together in a room, a circular room, a sort of British Museum reading-room—all writing their novels simultaneously." And so I invite you to adopt a similar stratagem and picture the two novelists who are the subject of this study—Forster and Virginia Woolf—seated, as they often were in fact, on either side of a smaller table in a more intimate room, a room in Forster's Cambridge lodgings, or at tea in a Bloomsbury townhouse or at Monk's House, the Woolfs' weekend residence in Sussex.

Woolf describes one such session in a letter to Vanessa Bell dated 19 May 1926: "Morgan came to tea yesterday," she says, "but we argued about novel writing, which I will not fret your ears with." This argument spills far beyond the edges of the 1926 tea table and permeates the novels and critical writings of both Woolf and Forster. One might say that chronologically the argument began in 1908— when, as a novice reviewer of books, Virginia Stephen applauded "the cleverness, the sheer fun, and the occasional beauty" of E. M. Forster's latest novel, *A Room with a View*—and ended in 1941

with Forster's Rede Lecture on Woolf at Cambridge just a few months before her death. In a larger sense, however, the dialogue continues today: not only does it mark off the fields of difference between the two most prominent literary figures in the Bloomsbury coterie and thus illuminate their novels as we read them, but it also isolates the aesthetic issues at stake in the first decades of the twentieth century. Many of the principles of modernism were forged, according to Michael H. Levenson, in the heat of active debate between certain of its fabricators—T. E. Hulme, Ezra Pound, Wyndham Lewis, Ford Madox Ford, and T. S. Eliot. Woolf and Forster's sparring was the same kind of formative dialogue: each forced the other to clarify his or her conception of the novel, to articulate the essential principles that, in their differing views, made fiction an art. In Forster's responses to Woolf's comments, we find a defence of the novel as a perpetuator of traditional values and a transmitter of belief; while Woolf, in her reactions to Forster's criticism, becomes increasingly the champion of an objective, self-sufficient, endlessly experimental art form.

The verbal duelling increases in interest when we see it in the context of the two novelists' long-standing but problematical friendship. Forster was one of the Cambridge graduates who gravitated to the Stephen siblings' Bloomsbury flat, but his somewhat sporadic association with the "Bloomsberries" was due primarily to his profound admiration for Leonard Woolf. Of Virginia herself Forster was wary: "One waited for her to snap," he said. He confided to Quentin Bell that "she was always very sweet to me, but I don't think she was particularly fond of me, if that's the word." If she was "sweet" to the skittish Forster publicly, privately she was often scathing: the letter to Vanessa Bell quoted earlier, for example, describes Forster as "limp and damp and milder than the breath of a cow." Nonetheless, throughout her twenty-five-year career as a novelist, Woolf's desire for Forster's critical approbation was ardent and undiminished. When he wrote in 1919 that he liked *Night and Day* far less than *The Voyage Out,* Woolf had to struggle to take the criticism philosophically: "This rubbed out all the pleasure of the rest," she says in her diary. The next week, however, she was able to comment, "I see it is not a criticism to discourage. . . . Morgan has the artist's mind; he says the simple things that clever people don't say; I find him the best of critics for that reason." And in 1940, when her fame as a novelist was undisputed, she all but held her breath as she waited for Forster's reaction to the Roger Fry biography: ''And I fear Morgan will say—just enough to show he doesn't like, but is kind.'' For his part Forster admired Woolf both as a novelist whose visionary quality corresponded to his wishes for his own fiction and as an authority on British literature. It was, in fact, in this latter capacity that he sought her advice at the contention-riddled tea table. Having been asked to deliver the Clark Lectures at Cambridge, the series subsequently published as *Aspects of the Novel,* Forster came to Woolf to find out how to lecture on novels and what novels he ought to include. She was to his mind the one member of an extraordinarily learned literary circle best equipped to give sound advice in both areas.

The teapot's lid was blown, in effect, by Woolf's two responses to *Aspects of the Novel*—a review, later entitled ''The Art of Fiction,'' in October 1927; and an essay in *Atlantic Monthly,* ''The Novels of E. M. Forster,'' the next month. These three works—plus Forster's ''The Early Novels of Virginia Woolf,'' his Rede Lecture, and Woolf's ''Modern Fiction'' and ''Mr. Bennett and Mrs. Brown''—comprise the ongoing debate. Taken together they abstract the two aspects of novel writing—character and artistic vision—which separate most emphatically the two teacups on the Bloomsbury table.

Having followed Forster's lead and dispensed altogether with chronology, we are free to begin tracing the Woolf-Forster disagreement at its conclusion, the 1941 Rede Lecture, for this is the document that divides the debate most neatly into two spheres. After discussing at some length Woolf's strengths as a novelist, Forster comes to what he calls ''her problem's center,'' that is, ''can she create character?'' Woolf had, Forster recognizes, some skill in creating characters who were not ''unreal . . . who lived well enough on the page''; her great flaw as a novelist was her inability to imbue her characters with ''life eternal'':

> She could seldom so portray a character that it was remembered afterward on its own account . . . Mr. and Mrs. Ramsay do remain with the reader afterwards and so perhaps do Rachel from *The Voyage Out* and Clarissa Dalloway. For the rest—it is impossible to maintain that here is an immortal portrait gallery . . .

Woolf's difficulty with character absorbs Forster here as it had sixteen years before in his essay ''The Early Novels of Virginia Woolf.'' Her first four novels had convinced Forster that here was a writer whose technical virtuosity clearly forecast a new era in the history of the novel. ''But,'' he objects, ''what of the subject that she regards as of the

❝❞ Thus the argument goes. Woolf's characters fail to live, says Forster, because they are too far removed from the flux of daily life; Forster's characters fail, says Woolf, because messages and material surroundings hamper their movement.❞

highest importance: human beings as a whole and as wholes?'' He continues: ''The problem that she has set herself and that certainly would inaugurate a new literature if solved—is to retain her own wonderful new method and form, and yet allow her readers to inhabit each character with Victorian thoroughness.'' Forster invites his readers to consider how difficult ''this problem'' is (and here he is speaking specifically of *Mrs. Dalloway*):

> If you work in a storm of atoms and seconds, if your highest joy is ''life; London; this moment in June'' and your deepest mystery ''here is one room; there another,'' then how can you construct your human beings so that each shall be not a movable monument but an abiding home, how can you build between them any permanent roads of love and hate?

The image of the novelist as architect or civil engineer is apposite when one considers the two chapters Forster devotes to character in *Aspects of the Novel,* for in this work he makes it clear that characters in a novel, whatever the depth and complexity of their inner lives, function to satisfy the demands of other aspects of the novel. ''We are concerned,'' he says, ''with the characters in their relation . . . to a plot, a moral, their fellow characters, atmosphere, etc. They will have to adapt themselves to other requirements of their creator.'' Again and again the utility of character is stressed. A novelist, Forster tells us, has two ''devices'' to help him cope with the trials which beset him: one device is point of view, and the other is the ''use'' of different kinds of characters.

Indeed, Forster's characters failed to convince Woolf precisely because they are so tightly hitched to their creator's intentions. Her review of *A Room with a View* expresses her disappointment with

Forster's treatment of his characters, their "belittlement," his "cramping of their souls." And while her discussion of *Howards End* in "The Novels of E. M. Forster" praises the reality with which the characters are presented, it also notes the distressing disjunction between the characters "as themselves" and the characters as they are forced to serve the ends of their maker. The reader, Woolf complains, must abandon "the enchanted world of imagination" where all the faculties operate in concert and enter "the twilight world of theory, where only our intellect functions dutifully." Occasionally Forster forgets his obligation to deliver his "message" and allows certain comic characters— Tibby and Mrs. Munt, for example—to range freely in the imaginary world unshepherded by the author. Such characters are, however, the exception in Forster's fiction; far more usual are characters pent by purpose. "Margaret, Helen, Leonard Bast, are closely tethered and vigilantly overlooked lest they may take matters into their own hands and upset the theory."

In her own treatise on character, "Mr. Bennett and Mrs. Brown," Woolf had already alluded to the damage done Forster's fiction by his subordination of character to theory. Forster's early work, like D. H. Lawrence's, Woolf says here, is "spoilt" because, instead of throwing away the tools of the Edwardians and their "enormous stress upon the fabric of things," he attempted to compromise with them. He "tried to combine [his] own direct sense of the oddity and significance of some character with Mr. Galsworthy's knowledge of the Factory Act, and Mr. Bennett's knowledge of the Five Towns." And though Woolf suggests that Forster has engaged to some extent in the general Georgian smashing and breaking of convention, she nonetheless finds him cementing his characters too firmly to their surroundings and to his own morals, struggles, and protests.

Nothing could contrast more sharply with Woolf's vision of character in the novel. Her comments on British and Continental novelists and her notes on her own novels attest to the fact that for her, character depends on no force outside the novel; rather it is the novel's moment of genesis, the vital centre from which the novel and all its various aspects radiate. All novelists write, she says in "Mr. Bennett and Mrs. Brown," because "they are lured on to create some character which has . . . imposed itself upon them." The realists fail to capture the will-o'-the-wisp of character because, in their fervour to express it in terms of surroundings or in terms of

some doctrine, they are blind to "character in itself." Laurence Sterne and Jane Austen, who alone among English writers receive unequivocal praise from Woolf, succeeded where her contemporaries fail because they "were interested in things in themselves; in character in itself; in the book in itself. Therefore everything was inside the book, nothing outside." Russian novelists, however, provided Woolf even sounder models of the proper relationship of character to the novel. Turgenev, for example, "did not see his books as a succession of events; he saw them as a succession of emotions radiating from some character at the centre." And it is thus that many of her own novels were conceived. About *To the Lighthouse* she says, "The centre is father's character, sitting in a boat, reciting We perished, each alone, while he crushes a dying mackerel." Writing a novel then requires dedication to the task of rendering that vision of character as accurately and suggestively as possible: "to try this sentence and that, referring each word to my vision, matching it as exactly as possible."

Thus the argument goes. Woolf's characters fail to live, says Forster, because they are too far removed from the flux of daily life; Forster's characters fail, says Woolf, because messages and material surroundings hamper their movement. Character, says Forster, is a device a novelist uses in the service of other aspects of the novel. Character, says Woolf, is the vital principle that calls the rest of the novel into being.

The second sphere of critical difference between Woolf and Forster is not so much an aspect of the novel as it is an aspect of the novelist—artistic vision, the faculty with which the writer selects and shapes the substance of his work. In describing Woolf in the opening paragraphs of the Rede Lecture, Forster mentions two qualities which apparently he feels were peculiarly hers: the first is her receptivity to sensual stimuli; the second is her singleness of vision. Most writers, he remarks,

> write with half an eye on their royalties, half an eye on their critics, and a third half-eye on improving the world, which leaves them with only half an eye for the task on which [Woolf] concentrated her entire vision. She would not look elsewhere . . .

But Forster is at best a grudging admirer of this singleness of purpose, for this fixed vision of Woolf's leads her toward that "dreadful hole" of aestheticism. "She has all the aesthete's characteristics," he complains: she "selects and manipulates her impressions . . . ; enforces patterns on her books; has no great cause at heart." Indeed Forster trips repeatedly over the fact that Woolf had no great cause at heart, that she felt no responsibility for improving the world. Her art suffered, in his estimation, because her feminism and her detachment from the working classes made her attitude to society "aloof and angular."

To take lack of sympathy with humankind as a basis for a literary judgment appears to be mistaking ethics for aesthetics, but or Forster the two amounted to very nearly the same thing. In *Aspects of the Novel* he insists that

> the intensely, stifling human quality of the novel is not to be avoided; the novel is sogged with humanity; there is no escaping the uplift or the downpour . . . We may hate humanity, but if it is exorcised or purified the novel wilts; little is left but a bunch of words.

The most valuable fiction, Forster feels, is produced not by the writer whose eye is single, trained exclusively upon what Woolf calls "the work itself," but by one whose eye is catholic, eclectic, capable of focusing at the same time upon the work and upon the human issues which surround it.

The conflict between the novel's intensely human quality and its aesthetic exigencies is the subject of the chapter of *Aspects of the Novel* entitled "Pattern," in which Forster recounts the debate between Henry James and H. G. Wells. The exchange figures importantly in our study because it mirrors the Woolf-Forster debate exactly and because Woolf responded to it so pointedly. Forster's objection to James's fiction is that "most of human life has to disappear before he can do us a novel." "There is," he protests,

> no philosophy in the novels, no religion . . . no prophecy, no benefit for the superhuman at all. It is for the sake of a particular aesthetic effect which is certainly gained, but at this heavy price.

Here in part is Woolf's rejoinder:

> For Henry James brought into the novel something besides human beings. He created patterns which, though beautiful in themselves, are hostile to humanity. And for his neglect of life, says Mr. Forster, he will perish.

> But at this point the pertinacious pupil may demand: "What is this 'Life' that keeps cropping up so mysteriously and so complacently in books about fiction? Why is it absent in a pattern and present in a tea party?"

Forster, of course, finds in favour of Wells, who asserts that life "'must hot be whittled or distended for a pattern's sake.'" And this same finding—that a novel must be imbued with its creator's eclectic double vision or it is finally "not worth doing"—is at the heart of Forster's criticism of Woolf.

Perhaps Forster denounced Woolf's singleness of vision in the Rede Lecture because years before in "The Novels of E. M. Forster" she had rather harshly attacked his doubleness. There is, she insists in this essay, "one gift more essential to a novelist than [any other], the power of combination—the single vision." But at the heart of Forster's novels she finds ambiguity supplanting this essential gift: "instead of seeing . . . one single whole we see two separate parts." She finds in *Howards End* all the elements necessary to a masterpiece but finds them in solution. "Elaboration, skill, wisdom, penetration, beauty—they are all there, but they lack fusion, they lack cohesion." *A Passage to India* too fails to live up to its readers' expectations, but it is at least beginning to approach "saturation": in this novel, Woolf says, "the double vision which troubled us in the earlier books was in process of becoming single."

The words "saturation," "fusion," "cohesion" are important critical terms for Woolf; a diary entry penned just a few months after her public responses to *Aspects of the Novel* explains them:

> The idea has come to me that what I want now to do is to saturate every atom. I mean to eliminate all waste, deadness, superfluity: to give the moment whole . . . Why admit anything to literature that is not poetry— by which I mean saturated? Is that not my grudge against novelists? that they select nothing?

And her entire career was a series of daring attempts to reproduce luminous moments of human consciousness no matter what conventional paraphernalia she had to eliminate in the process. Forster, like other novelists, fell far short of Woolf's exacting criteria because his double vision muddled his attempts to see and render the moment whole. Indeed the entire Woolf-Forster argument, about character as well as about the artist's vision, is largely an argument about whether a novel is the sum of various quantifiable parts dictated by material circumstances outside the novel—certainly Forster saw it thus—or whether it is what Woolf, influenced as she was by Coleridge and by G. E. Moore, felt it to be: an organic unit whose parts evolve spontaneously from an original conception of the whole.

As sincerely as Forster admired Woolf's technical achievement in the art of fiction, he nonetheless objected strongly to her apparent preference for the formal over the human elements of the novel. He was, as Mark Goldman points out, "too much the novelist of ideas; too involved, however skeptically, in the liberal tradition" to be completely receptive to Woolf's "novel of sensibility." Forster's comments on Woolf sound, in fact, remarkably like the importunate speaker's in Robert Frost's poem:

> O Star (the fairest one in sight),
> We grant your loftiness the right
> To some obscurity of cloud . . .
> But to be wholly taciturn
> In your reserve is not allowed.
> Say something to us we can learn
> By heart and when alone repeat.
> Say something! And it says, "I burn."

To Forster, observing the cultural confusion about him, the situation demanded literary communication of something which resembled, at any rate, the old verities and values. If, as David Daiches was to insist in 1938, the "community of belief" had vanished, if human relationships were forever altered, then the writer was obligated, these two critics felt, to offer something to stand in the place of those beliefs and relationships. Forster most clearly articulates his frustration with Woolf's refusal to "say something we can learn by heart" in his essay on her early novels: one novel is "not explanatory of the universe"; the style of another is so elusive that "it cannot say much or be sure of saying anything"; and another has no "message" save "'here is one room, there another.'" Woolf, he remarked after her death, had no great cause at heart; specifically, she declined to transport inherited beliefs and conventions through the post-World War I desert to whatever Promised Land lay on the other side.

But Woolf was no less sensitive to the seismic shocks of her time than Forster and Daiches. Observing in "Mr. Bennett and Mrs. Brown" that "on or about December, 1910, human nature changed," she goes on to acknowledge that such changes are always accompanied by radical changes in "religion, conduct, politics, and literature." She too, she says, cries out "for the old decorums, and envy the indolence of my ancestors who, instead of spinning madly through mid-air, dreamt quietly in the shade with a book." However, though she, like all novelists before and since, was preoccupied with the meaning of being human, she did not see that meaning threatened or obscured by the crashings going on about her. As a woman she had been at best a peripheral participant in the cultural and literary

tradition which had preceded the war; thus she saw in the splintering of convention freedom to fashion from "orts, scraps, and fragments" a fuller, more luminous, and finally more accurate rendering of the human condition than had previously been possible. Though convinced that Forster was "the best of critics," she nonetheless clung resolutely to her own evolving methods of reproducing vital experience. "We know," she says in "Modern Fiction," "that certain paths seem to lead to fertile land, others to the dust and the desert."

Forster was deeply stung by Woolf's reactions to *Aspects of the Novel;* her objection, to his dismissal of the claims of art in favour of the claims of "life" annoyed him especially, as this vexed letter to Woolf makes clear:

> Your article inspires me to the happiest repartee. This vague truth about life. Exactly. But what of the talk about art? Each sentence leads to an exquisitely fashioned casket of which the key has unfortunately been mislaid & until you can find your bunch I shall cease to hunt very anxiously for my own.

Woolf responded in an impersonal typewritten note that one ought to hunt more diligently than Forster had for the proper relationship of art to life before relegating art to an inferior realm. But then she added in her own hand a note apologizing for hurting or annoying him: "The article was cut down to fit The Nation, and the weight all fell in the same place. But I'm awfully sorry if I was annoying."

Thus ended the tempest in the 1927 teapot. However, despite admiration and conciliation, the debate between Woolf and Forster was inevitable. Because their verbal duel forced each to articulate critical theories and because it reflects two significant positions in the modernist dilemma, Woolf and Forster continue, in their essays as they once did across their tea tables, to argue about novel writing.

Source: Ann Henley, "'But We Argued about Novel-Writing': Virginia Woolf, E. M. Forster and the Art of Fiction," in *ARIEL,* Vol. 20, No. 3, July 1989, pp. 73–83.

Daniel R. Schwarz

In the following essay, Schwarz analyzes Aspects of the Novel *within the context of Forster's own novel writing and that of his peers.*

E. M. Forster's *Aspects of the Novel* (1927) remains a cornerstone of Anglo-American novel criticism. Forster's study helped define the values and questions with which we have approached novels for the past several decades. Moreover, today it still addresses the crucial questions that concern us about form, point of view, and the relationship between art and life. While acknowledging the importance of Percy Lubbock's *The Craft of Fiction* (1921) in extending the James aesthetic, the brilliance of Virginia Woolf's insights in her essays in *The Common Reader* (1925) and elsewhere, and the usefulness of Edwin Muir's *The Structure of the Novel* (1928), I believe that Forster's book is the one of those 1920's books on the novel to which we most frequently return to learn about *how* novels mean and *why* they matter to us. *Aspects of the Novel* is informed not merely by the living experience of Forster's having written novels throughout his adult life but more importantly by judgment, perspicacity, and erudition. To be sure, he does not articulate what we now think of as a theory, and he lacks the dialectical and polemical edge of recent criticism. Thus he disarmingly explains that he has chosen the term "aspects," "because it means both the different ways we can look at a novel and the different ways a novelist can look at his work." In the early chapters, Forster begins with such traditional aspects as story, people, and plot before turning in the later ones to less conventional ones such as fantasy, prophecy, pattern, and rhythm.

In the editor's introduction to the Abinger edition of E. M. Forster's *Aspects of the Novel,* Oliver Stallybrass rather patronizingly writes that Aspects *is* "a set of observations, somewhat arbitrarily arranged . . . of a man who is a novelist first, a slightly uncommon reader second, a friend third, and an analytical or theorizing critic fourth." Moreover, Stallybrass contends, "What most readers will cherish are the numerous particular judgments, instinctive rather than intellectual . . ." For Stallybrass, *Aspects* is merely "a useful adjunct to other, more sustained and consistent works of criticism"— although we are not told where we are to find these. That the editor of Forster's collected works makes such modest claims for such an historically significant study shows how far scholarship and theory have drifted apart. Because Forster defines aesthetic goals in terms of the values by which he wrote his own novels, it has been flippantly observed that *Aspects of the Novel* is Forster's *apologia.* Thus, Stallybrass quotes the narrator in Somerset Maugham's *Cakes and Ales:* "I read *The Craft of Fiction* by Mr. Percy Lubbock, from which I learned that the only way to write novels was like Henry James; after that I read *Aspects of the Novel* by E. M.

Forster regards Jane Austen as a major novelist because her "characters are ready for an extended life, for a life which the scheme of her books seldom require them to lead"

Forster, from which I learned that the only way to write novels was like Mr. E. M. Forster." Taking issue with this condescension, I shall argue that *Aspects of the Novel* is a seminal text in the criticism of fiction.

The key to understanding Forster is to realize that he writes in two traditions: the humanistic tradition, with its components of positivism, nominalism, and utilitarianism, and its admiration of realism; and the prophetic tradition, with Platonic and biblical origins, which sees art either as an alternative to, or an intensification of, this world. In this first tradition, we find Aristotle, Horace, Arnold, and usually James; in the second, we find Blake, Shelley, Pater, Wilde, Yeats, Lawrence, and Stevens. The first tradition strives to see life steadily and to see it whole. The second wants art to be superior in quality to life. Forster and, indeed, Woolf were drawn to both these traditions. In *Aspects,* we might imagine that Forster speaks in two voices, as he tries to do justice to the appeals of both these traditions. In the chapters "Story," "People," and "Plot," the voice of the first tradition

> **Despite Forster's lack of theoretical sophistication, his lucid, unpretentious discussion as the aesthetics of the novel challenges us to consider the necessary dialogue within fiction between art and life, between the imagined world created by the author and the real one in which we, like the author, live."**

dominates. But in the later chapters, beginning with "Fantasy" and becoming more pronounced in "Prophecy" and "Pattern and Rhythm," the voice of the second tradition becomes gradually more prominent. At times we feel, as in the chapter on fantasy, that he knows that he cannot resolve the contending claims of these two traditions.

Aspects of the Novel is not only a rough codification of the Bloomsbury aesthetic but also a specific response to Woolf's "Mr. Bennett and Mrs. Brown." Writing in 1924, Virginia Woolf insisted that the Georgian writers needed to abandon the "tools" and "conventions" of their Edwardian predecessors because the latter "have laid an enormous stress on the fabric of things":

> At the present moment we are suffering, not from decay, but from having no code of manners which writers and readers accept as a prelude to the more exciting intercourse of friendship . . . Grammar is violated; syntax disintegrated; . . . We must reflect that where so much strength is spent on finding a way of telling the truth, the truth itself is bound to reach us in rather an exhausted and chaotic condition.

In 1928, except for Conrad, the great modern British novelists—Lawrence, Joyce, Woolf—were at their peak even if their achievement and significance were far from clear. But while Lawrence, Joyce, Woolf, and Conrad sought new forms and syntax, Forster had shown in his novels—*Where Angels Fear to Tread* (1905). *The Longest Journey* (1907), *A Room With a View* (1908), *Howards End* (1910), and *A Passage to India* (1924)—that the English language and the novel genre already had

the resources to examine human life, including its instincts and passions; in *Aspects of the Novel* he sought to articulate that view.

Forster's own career as a novelist helps us to understand *Aspects*. His iconoclasm in part derives from his homosexuality and in part from his sense that he is an anachronism who belongs to a social and moral era that has been all but overwhelmed by modernism, progress, and utilitarianism. Forster wrote in "The Challenge of Our Time":

> I belong to the fag-end of Victorian liberalism, and can look back to an age whose challenges were moderate in their tone, and the cloud on whose horizons was no bigger than a man's hand. In many ways, it was an admirable age. It practised benevolence and philanthropy, was humane and intellectually curious, upheld free speech, had little colour-prejudice, believed that individuals are and should be different, and entertained a sincere faith in the progress of society.

In the guise of writing objective novels, he wrote personal, subjective ones. For Forster's novels, like those of the other great modern British novelists—Conrad, Lawrence, Joyce, and Woolf—are the history of his soul. His novels dramatize not only his characters' search for values but also his own—a quest that reflects his own doubt and uncertainty. As Wilfred Stones writes:

> His novels are not only chapters in a new gospel, they are dramatic installments in the story of his own struggle for selfhood—and for a myth to support it. They tell of a man coming out in the world, painfully emerging from an encysted state of loneliness, fear, and insecurity. Forster's evangelism springs as much from self-defense as from self-confidence, as much from weakness as from strength; but the style of his sermon always reflects those qualities about which there can be no compromise: tolerance and balance, sensitivity and common sense, and a loathing for everything dogmatic.

Put another way: what Stephen Dedalus says of Shakespeare in *Ulysses*—"He found in the world without as actual what was in his world within as possible"—is also true of Forster's novels and, as we shall see, of *Aspects*.

Like Forster's novels, particularly the later ones, *Aspects of the Novel* challenges the artistic and thematic conventions of the novel of manners. Indeed, the early chapters on story, people, and plot roughly correspond to the early period when he wrote *Where Angels Fear to Tread, The Longest Journey,* and *A Room With a View,* while the later sections discuss aspects that he tried to make more substantive use of in *Howards End* and, in particular, *A Passage to India*—the aspects of fantasy, prophecy, pattern, and rhythm. Not unlike his novels, *Aspects* enacts his quest for the inner life as well as his attempt to rescue himself from the curse of modernism. For *Aspects of the Novel* sometimes strikes an elegiac and nostalgic note when confronting contemporary avant-garde works, such as those of Gertrude Stein and James Joyce.

Forster's book originated as the 1927 Clark lectures given at Cambridge University. His conversational approach and lightness of touch, rather than dating the lectures, recreate the spontaneity of clear-headed, sensible, unpretentious talk. Forster is speaking in a tradition of manners that eschewed sharp conflicts and hyperbole on those occasions when a lowered voice and a tactful gesture would do. Although Forster's style is somewhat more informal in *Aspects,* it is marked by the same features as in his novels: leisurely pace, self-confidence, lucid diction, and poised syntax. As Lionel Trilling puts it, "The very relaxation of his style, its colloquial unpretentiousness, is a mark of his acceptance of the human fact as we know it now. . . . This, it seems to me, might well be called worldliness, this acceptance of man in the world without the sentimentality of cynicism and without the sentimentlaity of rationalism." As in his novels, Forster's style becomes his argument for the proportion, balance, and spontaneity that are essential to Forster's humanism.

Aspects enacts Forster's values. Like his novels, its tone and style are objective correlatives for the keen sensibility, the personal relationships, and the delicate discriminations of feeling that he sought. With its elegant phrasing, tact, balance, and sensibility, it is a protest against what he calls "the language of hurry on the mouths of London's inhabitants—clipped words, formless sentences, potted expressions of approval or disgust." Forster never forgets what he calls "the inner life" and the "unseen"—those aspects of life which resist language. By the "inner life," he means the passions and feelings that enable man to experience poetry and romance. For Forster, the "unseen" means not the traditional Christian God but a world beyond things that can be reached by passion, imagination, intelligence, and affection.

Aspects enacts Forster's values. Like his novels, its tone and style are objective correlatives for the keen sensibility, the personal relationships, including relatively abstract terms like "beauty," "curiosity," and "intelligence," refers to a shared cultural heritage and therefore conveys meaning.

Thus he can write: "Our easiest approach to a definition of any aspect of fiction is always by considering the sort of demand it makes on the reader. Curiosity for the story, human feelings and a sense of value for the characters, intelligence and memory for the plot." These are the "demands" that motivated Forster to write novels and the *values* that he felt must be central to a criticism of the novel. He is never afraid of being naive and expresses the full range of emotions from wonder and awe to impatience, chagrin, and dismay. He is, above all, a humanist. As Stone writes, "His art, and his belief in it, are his religion. . . . The religion *is* a coming together, of the seen and the unseen, public affairs and private decencies. Another name for this religion is humanism." With its carefully constructed patterns and symbolic scenes, the artificial order of the novel was for Forster an alternative to disbelief.

Forster's aesthetic values cannot be separated from his moral values. In an important 1925 essay, "Anonymity: An Enquiry," he wrote that "[a work of literature, such as *The Ancient Mariner*] only answers to its own laws, supports itself, internally coheres, and has a new standard of truth. Information is true if it is accurate. A poem is true if it hangs together. . . . The world created by words exists neither in space nor time though it has semblances of both, it is eternal and indestructible." For Forster, as for his Bloomsbury colleagues Roger Fry, Clive Bell, G. E. Moore, and, often, Virginia Woolf, art is a surrogate for religion. For those who, like himself, do not believe in the harmony of a divine plan or that a God directs human destiny, it provides "order" and "harmony" that the world lacks. At its best, art enables us to see life steadily and see it whole. Aesthetic order can provide a substitute for and an alternative to the frustrations and anxieties of life. in "Art for Art's Sake" (1949), he argued that what distinguished art from life is form, and that view, articulated by Bell and Fry well before *Aspects,* is implicit in much of Forster's book: "A work of art . . . is unique not because it is clever or noble or useful or beautiful or enlightened or original or sincere or idealistic or educational—it may embody any of those qualities—but because it is the only material object in the universe which may possess internal harmony." While life in action is fundamentally disorganized ("the past is really a series of *dis* orders"), creating and responding to art are ways of putting that disorder behind.

"Form" (which he does not discuss in its own chapter) is another name for the internal harmony achieved by the creative synthesis of other *aspects:* "[The artist] legislates through creating. And he creates through his sensitiveness and his power to impose form. . . . Form of some kind is imperative. It is the surface crust of the internal harmony, it is the outward evidence of order." But form is not merely the *significant* form of Bell and Fry; it includes—much more than for such a pure art as music—awareness of the complexity of life. Unlike music, the novel inevitably addresses how and for what human beings live. Responding to Lubbock, Forster eschews "principles and systems" as inappropriate to the novel. He insists on "the intensely, stifling human quality" as a critical focus, because the novel's subject is humanity: "Since the novelist is himself a human being, there is an affinity between him and his subject-matter which is absent in many other forms of art." By beginning with the chapters "Story" and "People," *Aspects of the Novel* shows that novels first and foremost depend on human life. Moreover, Forster does not use the formal term "character" in the title of the "People" chapters. And the centrality of people derives in part from Bloomsbury's stress on emotional and moral ties. Virginia Woolf asserted in "Mr. Bennett and Mrs. Brown": "I believe that all novels . . . deal with character, and that it is to express character . . . that the form of the novels, so clumsy, verbose, and undramatic, so rich, elastic, and alive, has been evolved."

Underlying *Aspects of the Novel* is a stress on the quality and intensity of novels' moral visions. Forster implies that a novel's ability to show us something we don't know about the people and the universe is important. Not only does penetrating the secret lives of characters help us as readers to become more perspicacious in life, but our aesthetic experience will enable us for a time to achieve internal harmony. As Forster wrote in "Anonymity: An Enquiry": "What is so wonderful about great literature is that it transforms the man who reads it towards the condition of the man who wrote, and brings to birth in us also the creative impulse. Lost in the beauty where he was lost, we find more than we ever threw away, we reach what seems to be our spiritual home, and remember that it was not the speaker who was in the beginning but the Word." On the one hand, Forster is speaking urgently in his prophetic voice, urging the religion of art that enables us to see beyond the real world, and we feel his kinship with Blake and Lawrence. On the other hand, despite his epiphanic language, Forster stresses the use of art in terms of the effects of art, and this stress is typical of Anglo-American criticism, which is influenced by a blend of Horatian *utile* and English utilitarianism.

II

Despite Forster's lack of theoretical sophistication, his lucid, unpretentious discussion as the aesthetics of the novel challenges us to consider the necessary dialogue within fiction between art and life, between the imagined world created by the author and the real one in which we, like the author, live. Forster defines the novel in terms of a dialectical relationship between fiction and reality: "there are in the novel two forces: human beings and a bundle of various things not human beings, and . . . it is the novelist's business to adjust these two forces and conciliate their claims." Forster taught us that interest in the novel as an art form is not incongruous with attention to content and that, paradoxically, the novels with the highest artistic values are the richest in insights about life. But Forster knew that *"homo fictus"* is not the same as *"homo sapiens."* What differentiates art from life is not only that the novel is a work of art, but that "the novelist knows everything about [a character in a book] . . . [I]n the novel we can know people perfectly, and, apart from the general pleasure of reading, we can find here a compensation for their dimness in life." Forster's assertion that we know the characters in a novel completely and that they contain, unlike characters in life, "no secrets" is belied by our experience that characters have secrets that even their creator or his own omniscient narrator does not recognize. (This is the point not only of Kermode's *The Genesis of Secrecy* [1979], but one implication of his own chapters on prophecy, pattern, and rhythm.

Forster's introductory chapter insists on a non-chronological approach which conceives of English novelists "writing their novels simultaneously" and turns away from questions of influence: "Literary tradition is the borderland between literature and history." Imagining a reader who encounters the total experience of the English novel enables him to take a quite different perspective from those who speak of influences and origins. His ahistorical approach—what we now call synchronic—appealed to the formalists of the next generation and probably, along with James and Lubbock, deterred thinking about the novel in terms of traditional literary history.

Forster's book was a response to James's critical legacy and Lubbock's codification and simplification of that legacy in *The Craft of Fiction,* which argued, following James, for the importance of point of view. Forster believes that critics have overstressed point of view. By speaking in compelling terms of the elements that he thinks are crucial, he rescued the novel from the dogmatism of James and Lubbock. Point of view is not the most important "aspect" but merely one of many secondary ones that do not deserve a separate chapter. The absence of a chapter on "point of view" probably affected the direction of novel criticism. With Lubbock (whom he has mentioned a few lines previously) in mind, he remarks that critics feel that the novel "ought to have its own technical troubles before it can be accepted as an independent art." For Forster, a novelist's "method" resolves "into the power of the writer to bounce the reader into accepting what he says." By discussing point of view in a few pages in the second chapter entitled "people," he is emphasizing that point of view, whether in the form of a persona or omniscient narrator, is significant only insofar as it expresses a human voice. Parting company with James and Lubbock, he writes, "the creator and narrator are one."

Forster's warning about self-conscious art is a deliberate attempt to separate himself from the James aesthetic: "The novelist who betrays too much interest in his own method can never be more than interesting; he has given up the creation of character and summoned us to help analyse his own mind, and a heavy drop in the emotional thermometer results." Unlike Lubbock, who questions Tolstoy's shifting point of view, he feels, "this power to expand and contract perception, . . . this right to intermittent knowledge" is not only "one of the great advantages of novel-form," but also "has a parallel in our perception of life." Finally, he holds, what is important is not the technique but the result. Unlike Lubbock, Forster never loses sight of the role of the reader and, like James on occasion, thinks of himself as the reader's surrogate. Stressing that novels must be convincing to readers, he writes: "All that matters to the reader is whether the shifting of attitude and the secret life are convincing . . ." Yet despite his avowed catholicity, he has his preferences and prejudices. While he believes that it is fine for an author "to draw back from his characters, as Hardy and Conrad do, and to generalize about the conditions under which he thinks life is carried on," he does not like the intimacy of Fielding and Thackeray, who take readers into confidence about their characters. Perhaps influenced by

James on this point, he implies that the artist should use his artistry to shape the reader's response rather than simply tell him what to think. *Aspects of the Novel* shows that Forster had a complicated oedipal love-hate attitude—an anxiety of influence—towards James, whose novels and criticism influenced him more than he acknowledged.

Forster's most important contribution to the aesthetic of the novel is the distinction between flat and round characters. While flat characters can be summarized in a single phrase and hence are often caricatures, round characters are as complex and multifaceted as real people: "The test of a round character is whether it is capable of surprising in a convincing way . . . It has the incalculability of life about it—life within the pages of a book." Forster demonstrates that characterization includes different kinds of mimesis in fiction, each with its own function, and that flat and round characters can coexist in the same novel. Although "It is only round people who are fit to perform tragically for any length of time and can move us to any feelings except humour and appropriateness," the "proper mixture of [flat and round] characters is crucial." The advantage of flat characters is that they are convenient for authors and easily recognized: moreover, they are easily controlled, "provide their own atmosphere," and "are easily remembered by the reader afterwards." Although they exaggerate one major factor at the expense of all others, they have a place in fiction.

The 1910–1912 Post-impressionist exhibits in London taught Forster and his contemporaries that different kinds of mimesis were possible in the same works; Forster is extending that principle to fiction and showing that the equation of "lifelike" and good is simplistic. Post-impressionists intentionally neglect some details, while they distort and exaggerate others. Their abrupt cutting of figures, elimination of traditional perspective, and foreshortening of figures and images influenced the quest of Lawrence, Joyce, Woolf, and Forster to move beyond realism. The concept of volume to describe character may derive from Charles Mauron, to whom *Aspects of the Novel* is dedicated. But it is also likely that Forster himself had learned from modern painting that objects occupying different places in space could be resolved on the same pictorial plane. It may even be that he has in mind the three-dimensionality of sculpture, particularly modern sculpture, which defines objects in relation to the space the work occupies in comparison to the inevitable two-dimensionality of painting.

With its focus on character in the novel in contrast to form, Muir's *The Structure of the Novel* was probably the most important of Forster's immediate offspring. Very much influenced by Forster, Muir has criticized him for depreciating and oversimplifying flat characters. Muir prefers to differentiate between "pure" characters, whom he generally equates with "flat" characters, and "dramatic developing" characters, whom he equates with "round" ones. His case for flat characters depends upon extending the concept to include all characters who remain relatively static: "All pure characters, formally, are in a sense artificial. They continue to repeat things *as if* they were true. . . . It is this accumulation of habits, dictated by their natures or imposed by convention, that makes every human being the potential object of humour." Thus, he concludes, "The co-existensive truth and congruity of its attributes, indeed, makes the flat character no less remarkable as an imaginative creation than the round; it is not less true, it is only different. It shows us the real just underneath the habitual." But Forster had in mind the differing function of characters, not simply their status within the imagined world. His distinction between flat and round characters is still influential because it showed us that the formal world of art functioned on different principles than the world of life. Subsequent critics, including Wayne Booth, Sheldon Sacks, and Northrop Frye, have focused on the rhetorical function of characterization.

Like the other major British modernists, Forster understood that human character is a continually changing flux of experience rather than, as depicted in the traditional realistic novel of manners, relatively fixed and static; consequently, in his novels he sought to dramatize states of mind at crucial moments. His emphasis on character helped to establish the respectability of the view that character (people) in fiction takes precedence over plot. By stressing the primacy of character over plot while rejecting their emphasis on point of view, Forster continued the movement of James and Lubbock away from the traditional stress on plot. The nineteenth century increasingly became more interested in character than plot; climaxing this trend was the interest in obsessions, compulsions, and dimly acknowledged needs and motives in the works of Browning and Hardy, and, indeed, in A. C. Bradley's *Shakespearean Tragedy* (1904).

Forster emphasized that novels depend on a complicated and, at times, messy dialogue between "life in time" and "life by values." It may appear that life by values is part of content or story, but it is clear that its presence in the novel depends upon what Forster calls the author's "devices" and what subsequent critics call his artistry or technique or discourse. While subsequent critics use different terms, Forster demonstrates that discussion of fiction must deal with the two variables—whether we call them life in time and life by values, life and pattern, content, and form, or story and discourse. (In his *Introduction to the English Novel,* Arnold Kettle borrows Forster's term "pattern" to define "the quality in a book which gives it wholeness and meaning," but his definition is much closer to what Forster means by "life by values" than to what he means by "pattern".)

Forster's distinction between story and plot is similar to the distinction in recent studies of narrative between story and discourse: "[Story] is a narrative of events arranged in their time sequence . . . [I]t can only have one merit: that of making the audience want to know what happens next. And conversely it can only have one fault: that of making the audience not want to know what happens next." By contrast plot is an aesthetic matter, the basic unit of form. Plot organizes story; it is "a narrative of events, the emphasis falling on causality. . . . The time-sequence is preserved, but the sense of causality overshadows it." Unlike drama, Forster contends, plots in novels rarely comply with Aristotle's "triple process of complication, crises, and solution." He sees plot as a series of circumstances, often arbitrarily selected and arranged, which enables the author to explore the major characters' personal lives and values: "In the novel, all human happiness and misery does not take the form of action, it seeks means of expression other than through plot, it must not be rigidly canalized." While Forster accepted the classical notion of an efficient plot, we should note that the terms "economical" and "organic" derive from the James influence: "[In the plot] every action or word ought to count; it ought to be economical and spare; even when complicated it should be organic and free from dead matter." But the meaning of plot depends on the active participation of a responsive reader: "[Over the plot] will hover the memory of the reader (that dull glow of the mind of which intelligence is the bright advancing edge) and will constantly rearrange and reconsider, seeing new clues, new chains of cause and effect, and the final sense (if the plot has been a fine one) will not be of clues or chains, but of something aesthetically compact, something which might have been shown by the novelist straight away, only if he had shown it straight away it would never have become beautiful.'' This is the very kind of active reader that R. S. Crane had in mind in his famous 1952 essay ''The Concept of Plot and the Plot of *Tom Jones*'' and upon whom recent theorists depend. Forster conceived of the structure of the novel as a continuous process by which values are presented, tested, preserved, or discarded, rather than the conclusion of a series which clarifies and reorders everything that precedes. He understood that the importance of a linear pattern within the imagined world relates to the temporal experience of reading the novel. He knew that, even if the greatest novels expand infinitely as if they were atemporal, ''It is never possible for a novelist to deny time inside the fabric of his novel.'' For when one ''emancipate[s] fiction from the tyranny of time . . . it cannot express anything at all'' because ''the sequence between the sentences'' is abolished, and then ''the order of the words,'' until there is no sense. Thus he pointed novel criticism away from James's spatial conception of form, a concept derived more from James's understanding of painting, sculpture, and architecture than from Coleridge's organic form. Forster helped keep alive temporality as a critical concept in the years when discussion of novel form in spatial terms predominated because of the influence of James and later Joseph Frank.

Forster's insights about endings influenced the work of Alan Friedman's *The Turn of the Novel* (1966) and anticipated Kermode's *The Sense of an Ending* (1967). Endings, Forster avows in the chapter on plot, are inherently defective: ''Nearly all novels are feeble at the end. This is because the plot requires to be wound up.'' According to Forster, death and love are ordering principles that end novels neatly but not in accordance with our own experience of life. The ending should be a part of a process, the last section chronologically in the narrative, but not a completion or a summary because, until death, life is a continuing process. We let authors urge us into thinking love is permanent, even though in reality we know the future would disconfirm this. Because, in his view, life is always open, problematic, and unresolved, Forster's own novels end on a deliberately inconclusive and ambiguous note. Characteristically, his ending does not resolve the social and moral problems dramatized by the plot. Rather it is another in a series of episodes in which man's limitations are exposed, rather than an apocalyptic climactic episode which resolves prior problems. As we shall see, in the following section on ''rhythm,'' he speaks of the possibility of novels, like symphony music, expanding and opening out for their audience; but he is speaking of the resonance of a work upon its audience after its reading is completed.

III

As *Aspects* progresses, Forster moves further away from the doctrine of nineteenth-century realism that novels must be imitations of life and begins to introduce categories that his classically trained lecture audience would have found innovative and exciting, if at times provocatively idiosyncratic, whimsical, and even bizarre. By introducing these categories and by refusing to restrict himself to what can be seen and analyzed within a novel, Forster reintroduced an imaginative and creative strain to criticism that Lubbock's more positivistic approach had denied. Such a strain was a dominant force in Pater, Wilde, and, at times, James.

Following the chapter on plot, Forster turns to fantasy. Forster's ''fantasy'' includes the kinds of extraordinary events that James called ''romance,'' but it also includes very different kinds of speculative, tonal, and stylistic departures from realism. Fantasy asks the reader to ''accept certain things'' that are unnatural. Fantasy ''implies the supernatural, but need not express it;'' like prophecy, it has a ''sense of mythology.'' According to Forster, the devices of a writer of fantasy include ''the introduction of a god, ghost, angel, monkey, monster, midget, witch into ordinary life; or the introduction of ordinary men into no man's land, the future, the past, the interior of the earth, the fourth dimension; or divings into and dividings of personality; or finally the device of parody or adaptation.'' As a parody of *Pamela,* Fielding's *Joseph Andrews* is an example of the last kind. Inspired by both ''an already existing book'' and a ''literary tradition.'' *Ulysses* is also a fantasy that depends on parody and adaptation.

If fantasy takes us to a linear world of diversity, difference, and idiosyncrasy, prophecy takes us to a vertical dimension where this world is a shadow of a more intense world. The truth of prophecy is the truth of vision. Thus in the subsequent chapter entitled ''Prophecy,'' Forster asks us to put aside our logic and reason and look elsewhere for insight and knowledge of the human plight. He wants the novel to move beyond local nominalistic insights toward unity and toward truth beyond itself. Stone aptly describes Forster's concept of prophecy as ''the seeing of the visible world as the living garment of God, the miracle of natural supernaturalism.'' When novels expand temporally and spatially, they displace the reader's awareness of the world in which he lives and give him a spiritual experience. Such experience is cognate to the moment when all will be one, except here the signified is not Christ but a sense of wholeness that derives from awareness of man's common plight and common psychological past.

Thus the theme of the chapter ''Prophecy'' is ''the universe, or something universal.'' Prophecy ''is a tone of voice''; ''What matters is the accent of [the prophet's] voice, his song.'' Forster's examples are Lawrence, Dostoevsky, Melville, and Emily Brontë. The prophetic impulse demands from the reader ''humility and the suspension of the sense of humour.'' While George Eliot is a preacher, Dostoevsky is a prophet:

> [Mitya] is the prophetic vision, and the novelist's creation also. . . . The extension, the melting, the unity though love and pity occur in a region which can only be implied and to which fiction is perhaps the wrong approach. . . . Mitya is a round character, but he is capable of extension. He does not conceal anything (mysticism), he does not mean anything (symbolism), he is merely Dmitri Karamazov, but to be merely a person in Dostoevsky is to join up with all the other people far back.

The prophetic dimension cannot be pinned down in particular sentences or patterns of language: ''The essential in *Moby Dick,* its prophetic song, flows athwart the action and the surface morality like an undercurrent. It lies outside words.'' But how, one might ask, can we agree on the presence of prophecy? Forster might respond that it is the truth that passes understanding, our epiphanic realization that transcends any single moment of narrative.

Chapter 8 is entitled ''Pattern and Rhythm,'' terms which are borrowed respectively from painting and from music. First, Forster discusses pattern: ''Whereas the story appeals to our curiosity and the plot to our intelligence, the pattern appeals to our aesthetic sense. It causes us to see the book as a whole.'' He dismisses as jargon the notion that we see a book as a physical shape: ''Pattern is an aesthetic aspect of the novel, and . . . though it may be nourished by anything in the novel—any character, scene, word—it draws most of its nourishment from the plot.'' Although Stallybrass thinks Forster is merely paying homage to a friend when he mentions Lubbock's novels, Forster is making a critical point by using a novel by Lubbock to illustrate pattern and by praising it for qualities quite remote from point of view. Pattern is whatever in plot is beautiful: ''Beauty is sometimes the shape of

the book, the book as a whole, the unity.'' Not only is James discussed in the section on pattern rather than in the brief section on point of view within the second ''People'' chapter, but Strether's role as an observer, as ''a rather too first-rate oculist'' is facetiously noted. Forster indicts James for giving preference to pattern over life: ''[Rigid pattern] may externalize the atmosphere, spring naturally from the plot, but it shuts the doors on life and leaves the novelist doing exercises, generally in the drawing-room. . . . To most readers of fiction the sensation from a pattern is not intense enough to justify the sacrifices that made it.'' Writing of Forster's concern with pattern and rhythm, Edwin Muir, his contemporary and admirer, made a trenchant remark that accurately establishes Forster's link to the James tradition, notwithstanding Forster's effort to separate himself from James's aesthetic: ''We do not really believe that a novel has a pattern like a carpet or a rhythm like a tune. . . . James is the father of most of those question-begging terms; he was an incurable impressionist; and he has infected criticism with his vocabulary of hints and nods.''

Rhythm is the relation between ''movements.'' Rhythm is a linear version of organic form, for it provides the concept of internal harmony for the temporal process of reading, whereas pattern seems to define internal harmony in more traditional formal and somewhat spatial terms borrowed from painting and sculpture. According to Forster, the function of rhythm in fiction is ''not to be there all the time like a pattern, but by its lovely waxing and waning to fill us with surprise and freshness and hope. . . . It has to depend on a local impulse when the right interval is reached. But the effect can be exquisite, it can be obtained without mutilating the characters, and it lessens our need of an external form. Of course, rhythm forms a pattern too, but a temporal one, not a spatial one. Perhaps Forster should have differentiated between ''spatial pattern'' and ''rhythmic pattern''—recurrence within a temporal framework which is both ineffable and everchanging; the latter is a dynamic concept that adjusts continually to the experience of reading and probably owes something to the substantial influence in the 1920s of Gestalt psychology, which sees human events as dynamic patterns that constantly move and shift into new fields of perception. He finds rhythm in ''the easy sense'' in Proust's *Remembrance of Things Past:* ''The book is chaotic, ill-constructed, it has and will have no external shape; and yet it hangs together because it is stitched internally, because it contains rhythms.'' E. K.

Brown's influential *Rhythm in the Novel* (1950) derives directly from this discussion, but it also anticipates the kind of order that Hillis Miller discusses in his recent *Fiction and Repetition* and that Gerard Genette speaks of in *Narrative Discourse* (1980), a book whose focus is *Remembrance of Things Past* and which cites Forster with approval.

He then turns to a more sophisticated and elusive kind of rhythm, which he finds only in *War and Peace:*

> Music, though it does not employ human beings, though it is governed by intricate laws, nevertheless does offer in its final expression a type of beauty which fiction might achieve in its own way. Expansion. That is the idea the novelist must cling to. Not completion. Not rounding off but opening out. When the symphony is over we feel that the notes and tunes composing it have been liberated, they have found in the rhythm of the whole their individual freedom. . . . As we read [*War and Peace*] do not great chords begin to sound behind us, and when we have finished does not every item—even the catalogue of strategies—lead a larger existence than was possible at the time?

In his novels and in *Aspects of the Novel,* Forster is trying to create this "expansion" for his audience, in part by trying to reach back to the sources of man's humanity. But isn't this passage extremely impressionistic? Do we know from this why *War and Peace* achieves its greatness? Aren't we being simply asked to endorse Forster's responses? Indeed as *Aspects* progresses, the argument becomes weaker and weaker and depends, beginning with the chapter "Fantasy," more on assertion and apt turns of phrase. It is as if he wishes the book to conclude with a prolonged lyric about the novel's potential to move its readers. Yet in the passage, does he not seek to join with those—Pater, Wilde, and usually Woolf—who see art as greater and more important than life and to participate in Yeats's urgent wish in "Sailing to Byzantium," to be a golden bird "to sing / To lords and ladies of Byzantium / Of what is past, or passing, or to come?"

The discussion of prophecy and rhythm (and, to a lesser extent, fantasy and pattern) is part of an effort to define something inexplicable, something spiritual and unseen, which might be an antidote to his own discovery and dramatization of evil in the Marabar caves in *A Passage to India.* Forster yearned for something beyond the pedestrian, disorganized, and sometimes banal stuff of novels. When he speaks of reaching back and "expansion," we must not forget the influence of Freud, Frazer, and Jung. *The Golden Bough* (1890) had extended the range of the past beyond biblical time and even beyond

historical time; later, Jung's emphasis on archetypes stressed that all cultures share common anthropological experience and psychological traits. And Forster believed that, despite differences in breeding, customs, and values, a common heritage united mankind. *Aspects,* like *A passage to India,* written only a few years before, is a quest for something beyond the diurnal life. But his tragedy was finally that he could not believe, with Stevens in "An Ordinary Evening in New Haven," that "the words of the world are the life of the world." At times Forster regretfully concedes that creating and perceiving art cannot compensate for the frustrations and anxieties of daily life, and that concession may be why he stopped writing novels.

IV

Before closing we should acknowledge what now seem as shortcomings of *Aspects of the Novel.* The book does not discuss precisely the means by which life is transformed into art and would benefit from separate chapters on form and narrative technique and more detailed discussion of style, the reader's role, and setting. Sometimes Forster provides us with little more than an impressionistic, gustatory statement of like and dislike. But lyricism is not the same as argument, and his credo that "the final test of a novel will be our affection for it" is a bit tautological. At times, his generalizations need more precise evidence and tauter supporting argument. Clearly, he is ambivalent about the critical enterprise and worried that it is too scientific, even mechanistic. For this reason, he speaks of holding up "story" with a "forceps" (as if it were a part of Tristram Shandy's anatomy.) Even if we attribute the lack of sustained analyses to the limitations of length imposed by the original lecture format, we have to admit that his own ratings of prior English novelists are at times quirky and reductive. For example, Scott, who has "a trivial mind and a heavy style," is a writer for a time when our brains "decay"; but "he could tell a story. He had the primitive power of keeping the reader in suspense and playing on his curiosity."

In the face of the bold and experimental, Forster's fastidious and conservative temper, which prefers order, proportion, clarity, and precision, sometimes leads him astray. Although he praises Lawrence for his "rapt bardic quality," he completely misunderstands *Ulysses,* of which he writes, "the aim . . . is to degrade all things and more particularly civilization and art, by turning them inside out and upside down." At times, he suppresses his prophetic strain and sees himself as a custodian of humanistic (some might facetiously say bourgeoise) principles in the face of challenges from the avant-garde.

Yet, while a contemporary reader, accustomed to either the critical nominalism of the New Criticism of the theorizing of recent European criticism, might find it at times lacking in rigor, *Aspects of the Novel* remains one of our seminal texts of novel criticism. We value it because Forster speaks to us not only as a major novelist and an incisive critic, but also as a reader who is concerned with how aspects of the novel relate to aspects of our lives.

Source: Daniel R. Schwarz, "The Importance of E. M. Forster's *Aspects of the Novel*," in *South Atlantic Quarterly,* Vol. 82, No. 2, Spring 1983, pp. 189–205.

John Colmer

In the following essay excerpt, Colmer gives an overview of Aspects of the Novel, *saying it is still popular because it "is alive on every page" and "communicates the author's own enthusiasms."*

The invitation to give the Clark Lectures at Cambridge in 1927 was a tribute to Forster's distinction as a novelist and his perception as a critic; moreover, it re-established his connection with Cambridge that was to remain close until his death in 1970. After he lost his house on his mother's death in 1945, King's College elected him an Honorary Fellow and later provided him with rooms in College. For the Clark Lectures in 1927, he chose as his topic the Novel; and when the lectures were published he gave them the title, *Aspects of the Novel,* a modest title totally in keeping with the personality of the lecturer and his general tone and approach. In view of Forster's frequent disclaimers to scholarship (he 'was not a scholar and refused to be a pseudo-scholar', said Virginia Woolf), it is worth considering what qualifications he did actually possess. He had knowledge of the novel from the inside, having written five novels, the last—*A Passage to India*—recognized as a masterpiece as soon as it appeared in 1924. He had an extensive knowledge of English, American, and European fiction. As a frequent book-reviewer, he had learnt to seize on essentials in any work, to be sensitive to nuances of meaning and style, to summarize imaginatively, to select quotations aptly, and to develop an attractive and flexible prose style for communicating his acute insights to a wide public. Moreover, he was already an accomplished lecturer and reader of scholarly papers, although not a professional academic. He had lectured on a variety of literary topics

to the Weybridge Literary Society, including 'Literature and the War'; he had addressed the Working Men's College 'On Pessimism in Modern Literature' and other subjects; he had given talks on literary topics to students in India. As the result of this very mixed experience, he had developed his own informal method of speaking about literature and saw no particular reason to change it for his Cambridge audience. This included A. E. Housman, who, much to Forster's disappointment, came to only two lectures, put off perhaps by the lecturer's informality and self-confessedly 'ramshackly course' of lectures. 'Housman came to two & I called on him on the strength of this, but he took no notice.'

Forster's approach to the novel was deliberately anti-historical, in marked contrast to his essay on the 'Novelists of the Eighteenth Century and their Influence on Those of the Nineteenth', submitted for an undergraduate prize in October 1899. When he came to give the Clark Lectures he knew that he lacked the range of knowledge and the 'rare gifts' necessary for 'genuine scholarship'. Despising the cataloguing and classifying absurdities of 'pseudo-scholarship', he therefore decided to abandon the historical approach altogether and to imagine all the great novelists of the world writing their masterpieces under the dome of the central reading room of the British Museum. A charming and whimsical fancy that does enable Forster to 'exorcise' the 'demon of chronology' and to concentrate on the novelist's common task of finding in art a mirror for reality—a common task because, unlike History which develops, 'Art stands still.'

Forster begins by presenting his audience with two passages of introspection, two funeral scenes, and two passages of fantasy about the muddle of life: the first pair are by Richardson and James; the second pair by Wells and Dickens; and the third by Virginia Woolf and Sterne. Forster deliberately withholds the names of the authors to bring out the idea that similarity of vision transcends chronology, yet any well-trained undergraduate today would have little difficulty in showing how deeply the language and sensibility of each passage is rooted in its historic period, and could indeed have been written at no other time. Any connection that the use of unseen passages, the withholding of authorship and the anti-historicism, suggests with the new Cambridge school of 'practical criticism' of the 1920s is utterly misleading. Indeed, Forster's neglect of close linguistic texture ('almost nothing is said about words', complained Virginia Woolf) and his neglect of social context, seriously limit his critical perspire. Of this, Forster was partly aware, regretting that his chosen method ruled out the discussion of literary tradition, especially as this affects a novelist's technique. Reference to tradition, he believed, could show that Virginia Woolf 'belonged to the same tradition' as Sterne, 'but to a later phase of it'. This is indeed a rather special conception of literary tradition. What Forster does not sufficiently appreciate is that the actual material of fiction and the consciousness of the artist are at least in part historically conditioned. It is illuminating to compare his remarks on Richardson with those of Ian Watt in *The Rise of the Novel* or with those of any other modern critic sensitive to the fact that the moral and social values embodied in a novel reflect the unique interaction of individual sensibility and the temper of an age.

Having—as it were—set his scene in the British Museum and having adopted a French critic's convenient definition of a novel as 'a fiction in prose of a certain extent', Forster focuses on seven formal properties of the novel. These he calls 'Aspects'. They are: 'The Story', 'People', 'The Plot', 'Fantasy', 'Prophecy', 'Pattern', and 'hythm'. This chatty updated Aristotelian approach gives the discussion an air of completeness while allowing Forster to speak about what happens to interest him most. The chosen framework might suggest an exclusive concern with form and technique, a concern shared by such novelists as James, Conrad, and Ford Madox Ford, exemplified also in Percy Lubbock's *The Craft of Fiction.* But, in fact, Forster avoids a strictly formalist approach; he maintains a pleasant balance between questions relating to technique and questions relating to truth and reality. At the beginning of the lecture on 'Fantasy', he indicates the principle that determines this balance; in the novel itself and in his own approach.

> The idea running through these lectures is by now plain enough: that there are in the novel two forces: human beings and a bundle of various things not human beings, and that it is the novelist's business to adjust these two forces and conciliate their claims.

Ultimately, however, Forster's supreme test is truth to life, an old-fashioned test certainly, but one that is susceptible of considerable refinement in application. But it did not satisfy Virginia Woolf, a close friend and admirer, who asked 'What is this ''Life'' that keeps on cropping up so mysteriously and so complacently in books about fiction?'. Here she was not only continuing the battle against the Edwardian realists, begun in *Mr Bennett and Mrs Brown,* and originally provoked by Bennett's claim that she had failed to create character or reality in

> **" Yet, with all its obvious limitations and weaknesses, it is a book one finds oneself returning to again and again and always with a sense of new discovery and fresh insight into some major novelist."**

Jacob's Room, but also remembering Forster's remarks about characters and life in his 1925 essay on her early fiction. 'Why', she asks pertinently of Forster, is reality 'absent in a pattern and present in a tea party?' From this it may be seen that, in spite of the chapter headings drawing attention to the formal properties of the novel, Virginia Woolf regarded *Aspects of the Novel* as typical of the 'unaesthetical' attitude that prevailed in English fiction and which would 'be thought strange in any of the other arts'. To understand her responses here we need to remember her admiration for the contribution made by Henry James and Turgenev to the 'art of the novel' and also her inordinate pride in Bloomsbury aesthetics. Bloomsbury, she believed, was a society 'alive as Cambridge had never been to the importance of the arts'. By contrast, Forster was altogether more sceptical towards Bloomsbury aesthetics and the art of the novel. 'This vague truth about life. Exactly. But what of the talk about art?', he asked Virginia Woolf in a letter. 'Each section leads to an exquisitely fashioned casket of which the key has unfortunately been mislaid and until you can find your bunch I shall cease to hunt very anxiously for my own'. Many years later he summed up his own sceptical pragmatic approach:

> The novel, in my view, has not any rules, and there is no such thing as the art of fiction. There is only the particular art that each novelist employs in the execution of his particular book.

The chief interest of the first chapter of *Aspects* is that it brings out Forster's comparative lack of interest in narrative: 'Yes—oh dear yes—the novel tells a story.' And yet, of course, Forster is himself a brilliant story-teller. But depreciation of this element leads him to reduce Scott's stature to that of a mere entertainer. 'He could tell a story. He had the primitive power of keeping the reader in suspense and playing on his curiosity.' If that summed up the whole of Scott he would certainly not enjoy the acclaim he enjoys today. That Forster allots two chapters to 'People' is an accurate indication of the importance he attributes to character in fiction. In the first chapter on People he breaks new ground by drawing attention to how little of our lives actually gets into fiction. The five main facts of life (birth, food, sleep, love, and death) appear selectively or hardly at all. The brief impressionistic notes on this topic prove that Forster's view of life was not the simple one ascribed to him by Virginia Woolf; they are products of a mind that has brooded long over the contrast between 'Art' and 'Life', that has seen that the novelist's function is 'to reveal the hidden life at its source'. Indeed Forster had recognized as clearly as Virginia Woolf or James Joyce that, by modifications of convention and technique, much more might be achieved to render our experience vivid as we 'move between two darknesses', birth and death. Forster returns to the same 'unavoidable termini', at the end of the essay, 'What I Believe': 'The memory of birth and the expectation of death always lurk within the human being, making him separate from his fellows and consequently capable of intercourse with them.'

In the second of the chapters on 'People', Forster draws a distinction between 'flat' and 'round' characters. By the first he means Jonsonian, 'humours' characters, 'constructed round a single idea or quality', like Mrs Micawber, for example, with her repeated 'I never will desert Mr Micawber.' These have the advantages that they are easily recognized and easily remembered. By the second, 'round' characters, he means characters that are so fully developed that we can imagine how they would behave in circumstances not actually presented in the novel (this is not quite the Bradley, 'How Many Children had Lady Macbeth?' approach applied to the novel). 'Round' characters also have the 'capacity of surprising us in a convincing way'. This distinction has caught on and become part of the language of twentieth-century criticism. But it lacks precision, is less illuminating than the distinction between 'life on the page' and 'life eternal' made in the Rede lecture on Virginia Woolf, and can at best be regarded as a convenient piece of critical shorthand. In *Aspects,* 'flat' and 'round' are sometimes used as neutral terms to describe differences in technique and sometimes as evaluative terms to award praise or blame. In the first case it is Forster the fellow-novelist speaking, in the second it is Forster the critic. Here is one place where the two do not quite coincide.

It is true that in literary criticism, as opposed to science, definitions can never be more than a rough and ready convenience to facilitate communication. Most readers of *Aspects* probably respond gratefully to the simplicity of Forster's definition of 'Plot' as distinct from 'Story'. 'The king died and then the queen died' is a story; but 'The king died, and then the queen died of grief' is a plot. The time sequence is preserved, Forster remarks, but 'the sense of causality overshadows it.' Beautifully simple. Yet the distinction leads ultimately to curious results. It leads, for example, to a further definition of the plot as 'the novel in its logical intellectual aspect'. But what about the aesthetic patterning function of plot? Forster has little to say about this under the heading of 'Plot'. The reason is that he wants later to make a clear distinction between 'Pattern' (something mechanical and external that determines the shape of Anatole France's *Thaïs* and James's *The Ambassadors*), and 'Rhythm' (something organic and internal, as in Proust, a process of 'repetition plus variation', and 'internal stitching'). Again, the definition of 'Fantasy' as a form of fiction that 'asks us to pay something extra', is too fanciful itself to take us very far, and the choice of Norman Matson's *Flecker's Magic* as a major exhibit marks a disastrous victory of fashion over sound judgment. It is in the sections on 'Prophecy' and 'Rhythm' that Forster rises to the height of his powers as a critic, combining lucid definitions with beautifully chosen examples. Here his sympathies were fully engaged and he was writing with half an eye on his own work, especially in developing his ideas on 'Rhythm'. The result is criticism of the very highest order. Three examples must suffice. The first comes from his account of Proust's use of rhythm

> . . . what we must admire is his use of rhythm in literature, and his use of something which is akin by nature to the effect it has to produce—namely a musical phrase. Heard by various people—first by Swann, then by the hero—the phrase of Vinteuil is not tethered: it is not a banner suck as we find George Meredith using—a double-blossomed cherry tree to accompany Clara Middleton, a yacht in smooth waters for Cecilia Halkett. A banner can only reappear, rhythm can develop, and the little phrase has a life of its own, unconnected with the lives of its auditors, as with the life of the man who composed it. It is almost an actor, but not quite, and that 'not quite' means that its power has gone towards stitching Proust's book together from the inside, and towards the establishment of beauty and the ravishing of the reader's memory. There are times when the little phrase-from its gloomy inception, through the sonata, into the sextet-means everything to the reader. There are times

when it means nothing and is forgotten, and this seems to me the function of rhythm in fiction; not to be there all the time like a pattern, but by its lovely waxing and waning to fill us with surprise and freshness and hope.

The second comes from his discussion of the 'prophetic' in Dostoevsky.

> Dostoevsky's characters ask us to share something deeper than their experiences. They convey to us a sensation that is partly physical—the sensation of sinking into a translucent globe and seeing our experience floating far above us on its surface, tiny, remote, yet ours. We have not ceased to be people, we have given nothing up, but 'the sea is in the fish and the fish is in the sea.'

The third example comes from his discussion of Melville. Here he points out the importance of evil in Melville's moral vision and its relative absence in English fiction, a theme brilliantly developed by Angus Wilson many years later in a series of unscripted radio talks.

> It is to his conception of evil that Melville's work owes much of its strength. As a rule evil has been feebly envisaged in fiction, which seldom soars above misconduct or avoids the clouds of mysteriousness. Evil to most novelists is either sexual and social, or something very vague for which a special style with implications of poetry is thought suitable.

Aspects of the Novel has survived remarkably well and continues to be read when more scholarly discourses on the novel gather dust on the shelves. The reasons are not difficult to discover. It is alive on every page; it communicates the author's own enthusiasms; it whets the reader's appetite through apt quotations and skilful commentary, while never doing the reader's work for him, the usual fault of popular literary handbooks. It is genuinely popular without being vulgar. In the simplest possible manner it throws new light on old problems, and it contains original insights into the art of many major novelists, especially Emily Brontë, Melville, Dostoevsky, and D. H. Lawrence. His discriminating praise of two novelists as unlike each other as Jane Austen and Herman Melville illustrates the range of his imaginative sympathies; it also reminds us of his own extraordinary feat in assimilating characteristic features of both into his own art. The pages on Melville repay the closest attention. Here was a writer, Forster realized, who had 'not got that tiresome little receptacle, a conscience', who was therefore able—unlike Hawthorne, or say, Mark Rutherford—to reach 'straight back into the universal, to a blackness and sadness so transcending our own that they are indistinguishable from glory'. Is this not what Forster achieves in *A Passage to India*

and in flashes in *The Longest Journey?* His continued admiration for Melville appears in his adaptation with Eric Crozier of Melville's short story *Billy Budd,* 'a remote unearthly episode', as a libretto for an opera by his friend and admirer Benjamin Britten. All three lived in the same house for a month; Forster and Crozier worked from a 'kind of skeleton synopsis', trying all the time to make the words flower into lyricism. 'I felt quite differently to what I have felt while writing other things,' remarked Forster, 'completely different. I was on a kind of voyage.' The idea of 'song' and a voyage into the unknown are the essential features of Forster's conception of Prophecy.

Aspects of the Novel is not without its faults. Forster brought to his task a mixed bag of likes and dislikes, of discriminating preferences and odd blind spots. His judgment of some major writers is consequently somewhat erratic. He is unfair to Scott, sees only the preacher in George Eliot, finds it difficult to be just to Meredith, his youthful idol, and he uses Henry James almost exclusively as an example of the sacrifice of 'Life' to 'Art', quoting Wells's brilliant but malicious account of the high altar of James's art ('and on the altar, very reverently placed, intensely there, is a dead kitten, an egg shell, a piece of string'), declaring that 'most of human life has to disappear' before James can do us a novel. Yet, notes for the lecture series in his Commonplace Book reveal a sympathetic insight into James's difficulties as a novelist—were they not his own? In these rough notes he considers evil in the English novel and claimants to 'Satanic intimacy', glances briefly at the 'Pan School', petering out in Hichens and E. F. Benson, and remarks perceptively that in *The Turn of the Screw,* Henry James 'is merely declining to think about homosex, and the knowledge that he is declining throws him into the necessary fluster.' It was a pity Forster's personal censor intervened before he actually gave the lectures, since this insight into James's creative psychology was startlingly original at the time.

There are two further weaknesses in *Aspects of the Novel.* Few of the definitions or distinctions, although they have passed into the language of criticism, will stand up to rigorous scrutiny. And ultimately the whole book throws as much light on Forster's own fiction as it does on the Art of the Novel, a point amply demonstrated by James McConkey in his application of the seven different 'Aspects' to Forster's own novels. Yet, with all its obvious limitations and weaknesses, it is a book one finds oneself returning to again and again and always with a sense of new discovery and fresh insight into some major novelist. This capacity to surprise and delight is the combined product of individual taste, personal integrity, and the inveterate habit of looking at life and art from unexpected angles. It is also the product of the crisp sensitive prose style. At a time when extravagant claims were being made in Cambridge for systematic and scientific criticism, *Aspects of the Novel* struck a minor blow for the more personal, informal approach.

Forster's earliest writings reveal his gift for recreating the lives of neglected characters from the past. He is obviously attracted to minor figures caught up in major events, to genuine seekers after truth however muddled, to interesting failures rather than to dull successes, to those who have left behind them at least one work that still lives or can be brought to life again. The two essays, 'Gemistus Pletho' and 'Cardan', both published in the *Independent Review* in 1905, illustrate Forster's youthful skill in combining history and biography in a highly entertaining fashion; they also foreshadow his later success in raising the biography of the obscure into a fine art, as in *Marianne Thornton* (1956), and, to a lesser extent, in *Goldsworthy Lowes Dickinson* (1934), although perhaps Dickinson could not be labelled 'obscure' in 1934, since, by then, he had become well known through his work for the League of Nations and through broadcasting.

The essay on Georgius Gemistus recounts the story of this little-known philosopher who was born at Constantinople in 1355 and who spent his life in Greece, but for one important visit to Italy when he helped to found the Neo-Platonic Academy in Florence. What attracts Forster to Gemistus and Cardan, an obscure scientist, is the strange but very human gap between their dreams of truth and the absurd form these dreams often take. Thus, writing of Gemistus' ideal of reviving the religion of Greece by invoking the names of the Greek gods, Forster writes:

> These names had for him a mysterious virtue: he attached them like labels to his uninspiring scheme, while he rejected all that makes the gods immortal— their radiant visible beauty, their wonderful adventures, their capacity for happiness and laughter. That was as much as his dim, troubled surrounding allowed to him. If he is absurd, it is in a very touching way; his dream of antiquity is grotesque and incongruous, but it has a dream's intensity, and something of a dream's imperishable value.

This was written when Forster himself was seeking to recapture the 'radiant visible beauty' of classical mythology, in his short stories and early novels. Throughout these two biographical vignettes, 'Gemistus Pletho' and 'Cardan', there is a delicate balance between sympathy and ironic detachment; a compassionate recognition, too, of the extent to which human beings are limited by their historical environment, by their 'troubled surroundings'. It is the quality of Forster's imaginative sympathy for human weakness and oddity and his refusal to extract easy laughter from the absurdities of the past that chiefly distinguish his biographical essays from those of Strachey. In this he is at one with Virginia Woolf in her biographical essays in *The Common Reader.* The ending of his account of the eccentric sixteenth-century Italian scientist, Cardan, brings out the essential difference between Forster's and Strachey's approach to biography.

> To raise up a skeleton, and make it dance, brings indeed little credit either to the skeleton or to us. But those ghosts who are still clothed with passion or thought are profitable companions. If we are to remember Cardan today let us not remember him as an oddity.

It is as an oddity that Dr Arnold appears, with his too short legs, in Strachey's brief biography, it is as an obsequious oddity that the poet Clough appears in his life of Florence Nightingale. What Forster looked for in biography and the study of the past were 'profitable companions' and not objects of ridicule or ironic contempt. In later years he certainly recognized that Strachey was 'much more than a debunker', that he did 'what no biographer had done before him: he managed to get inside his subject'. By comparison Forster's is a smaller achievement. He was not strongly drawn to biography as a literary form, and he made no startling innovations in technique; but he did write two fine biographies that reveal as much of their author as of their subject.

Source: John Colmer, "Life and Times," in *E. M. Forster: The Personal Voice,* Routledge & Kegan Paul, 1975, pp. 174–83.

Sources

Gardner, Philip, "E. M. Forster," in *Dictionary of Literary Biography,* Volume 98: *Modern British Essayists, First Series,* edited by Robert Beum, Gale Research, 1990, pp. 123–39.

Moore, Harry T., *E. M. Forster,* Columbia University Press, 1965, p. 14.

————, Preface to *E. M. Forster,* by Norman Kelvin, Southern Illinois University Press, 1967, p. 155.

Page, Norman, *E. M. Forster,* St. Martin's Press, 1987, pp. 1, 11.

Stone, Wilfred, *The Cave and the Mountain,* Stanford University Press, 1966, p. 110.

Summers, Claude J., *E. M. Forster,* Ungar, 1983, pp. 1, 295, 305–306, 311, 355.

Trilling, Lionel, *E. M. Forster,* New Directions, 1943, pp. 166, 168, 172, 181.

Further Reading

Bakshi, Parminder Kaur, *Distant Desire: Homoerotic Codes and the Subversion of the English Novel in E. M. Forster's Fiction,* P. Lang, 1995.
> This is a critical discussion of the homoerotic elements of Forster's novels.

Clarke, Peter, *Hope and Glory: Britain, 1900–1990,* Penguin, 1996.
> Clarke's book is a history of England in the twentieth century.

Ferguson, Niall, *The Pity of War: Explaining World War I,* Basic Books, 1999.
> This social-historical history of World War I, in which Forster served, had a profound affect on the post-War literature of his generation.

Lago, Mary, *E. M. Forster: A Literary Life,* St. Martin's Press, 1995.
> This biography of Forster focuses on the development of his literary career.

Lago, Mary, and P. N. Furbank, eds., *Selected Letters of E. M. Forster,* 2 Vols., Harvard University Press, 1983, 1985.
> This two-volume selection of Forster's correspondence includes the years 1879–1920 in Volume 1, and the years 1921 to the time of his death in 1970 in Volume 2.

Moynahan, Brian, Annabel Merullo, and Sarah Jackson, *The British Century: A Photographic History of the Last Hundred Years,* Random House, 1997.
> This work presents a history of Forster's native Britain in the twentieth century through documentary photographs and text.

Naylor, Gillian, ed., *Bloomsbury: Its Artists, Authors, and Designers,* Little Brown, 1990.
> This history of the Bloomsbury literary and intellectual salon in London, in which Forster was a participant, discusses key figures in the Bloomsbury Group.

Paterson, John, *Edwardians: London Life and Letters, 1901–1914,* I. R. Dee, 1996.
> This is a history of life, society, and culture during the reign of King Edward, during which era Forster was an active participant in the literary culture of London and in which many of his novels take place.

Pugh, Martin, *Britain Since 1789: A Concise History,* St. Martin's Press, 1999.
> This work is a broad-view history of Britain in the nineteenth and twentieth centuries, during which Forster lived and wrote.

Black Boy

Richard Wright

1945

Richard Wright's masterful recording of his own life in the form of the work *Black Boy: A Record of Childhood and Youth*, earned him the significance of "father" of the post-WWII black work and precursor of the Black Arts movements of the 1960s. Published in 1945 as a Book-of-the-Month Club selection, *Black Boy* was received enthusiastically by the reading public and topped the bestseller lists, with 400,000 copies sold. The commercial success of this work secured for Wright what his success of 1940, *Native Son*, had demanded. With these two works, Richard Wright is correctly said to be one of the most powerful forces in twentieth-century American literature. Without doubt, he is the most powerful influence on modern African-American writing due to his impact on James Baldwin (*Another Country,* 1962), and Ralph Ellison (*The Invisible Man,* 1953).

Black Boy is an autobiographical work in which Wright adapted formative episodes from his own life into a "coming of age" plot. In the work, Richard is a boy in the Jim Crow American South. This was a system of racial segregation practiced in some states of the United States, which treated blacks as second-class citizens. In his work, Wright emphasizes two environmental forces of this system: hunger and language. He shows how hunger drives the already oppressed to even more desperate acts, and his emphasis on language explains how he managed to survive Jim Crow, by developing an attention to language as a coping mechanism for the

surface world of life. Meanwhile, literature offered him internal release from the tensions of living without the freedom to express his dignity as a human being. Thus, Wright's work is a powerful story of the individual struggle for the freedom of expression.

Author Biography

Richard Nathaniel Wright was born on September 4, 1908, at Rucker's Plantation in Roxie, Mississippi. His parents were Ellen Wilson, a schoolteacher, and Nathan Wright, a sharecropper. His brother Leon was born in 1910 and one year later they moved to Ellen's parents house in Natchez. It is that house in which Wright's work *Black Boy* has its opening drama.

The family moved to Memphis in 1913 and soon thereafter Richard's father deserted them. For the next few years, Ellen did her best to feed and clothe the boys, but she suffered the first of many illnesses. At one point she moved her boys to the prosperous home of her sister Maggie and brother-in-law Silas Hoskins in Elaine, Arkansas. Unfortunately, Silas was murdered by a white mob, and Maggie, Ellen, and the boys fled to West Helena.

Over the next few years, Ellen's illness forced the extended family to shift Richard between them while she lay in bed at Grandma Wilson's. Richard eventually went to his grandmother's house to be near his mother. In 1920, Richard attended the Seventh-Day Adventist School taught by his Aunt Aggie. He later transferred to the Jim Hill School where he made friends and skipped the fifth grade. Next, he attended Smith-Robertson Junior High and published his first short story, "The Voodoo of Hell's Half-Acre," in the *Jackson Southern Register*.

After graduating as valedictorian in 1925, he moved to Memphis where he was joined by his mother and brother in 1927. One year later, Richard moved his family to Chicago.

Over the next decade, Richard published various stories in magazines, supervised a black youth program, and wrote for communist newspapers. He started his first novel in 1935, but *Cesspool* was not

Richard Wright

successful (posthumously published as *Lawd Today*). By 1938, with a $500 prize for *Fire and Cloud*, Wright had embarked on a career as an author. That year, *Uncle Tom's Children* appeared to good reviews.

Wright became established as a writer in 1940 with the publication of *Native Son*. Personally, reconciliation with his father failed and he ended his marriage with his first wife, Dhima Rose Meadman. Almost immediately, he married Ellen Poplar and had two daughters—Julia in 1942 and Rachel in 1949.

After *Native Son*, Wright published some articles and left the Communist Party. In 1945, *Black Boy* was published and received excellent reviews while topping bestseller charts. After this, Richard left the United States.

Wright refused to return to racist America and the risk of subpoena by anti-communist investigations. In 1953, he published the first American existentialist novel, *The Outsider*. In 1956, he published *The Color Curtain: A Report on the Bandung Conference*. He continued to write until he died of a heart attack on November 28, 1960, in Paris, but he never regained the acclaim awarded him by *Black Boy*.

Summary

Chapters I–IV

Richard Wright's autobiographical account in *Black Boy* opens with his earliest memory, standing before a fireplace as a four-year-old child on a rural Mississippi plantation. Warned repeatedly to "keep quiet," young Richard instead plays with fire and nearly burns his family's house down, then unsuccessfully tries to avoid being severely punished by hiding under the burning house. After the family moves to a new home in Memphis, Richard again challenges parental authority by taking literally his father's exaggerated demand that he kill a noisy kitten. Richard lynches the cat and then feels triumphant over his stern father who can not beat Richard because he was just following orders. However, when his mother forces him to bury the animal and pray for forgiveness for his cruel act, he feels crushing guilt. These two incidents set the stage for various attempts by young Richard to express his powerful feelings and to test the limits placed on him by his family and his environment.

Richard begins to explore the world around him early on, sneaking into saloons and begging for pennies and drinks, learning to read from neighborhood school children and learning to count from the coal man, and above all, asking questions of everyone he encounters. He is witness to several disturbing scenes and events that do not make sense to his young mind. He hears that a "'black' boy had been severely beaten by a 'white' man" and he can only assume that it is because the "boy" is the white man's son, since in Richard's world fathers are allowed to beat their children and Richard does not know what "black" and "white" means. He sees a black military regiment and asks his mother to explain the meaning of "soldiers," "rifles," "Germans," "enemies," and "wars." He sees a group of "strange, striped animals" and learns that it is a chain gang of black prisoners and white guards. Finally, after learning that white men have murdered his Uncle Hoskins for his thriving business, Richard and his family flee to yet another home, trying "to avoid looking into that white-hot face of terror that we knew loomed somewhere above us."

As he grows older, Richard's life at home with his family causes him as much distress as his experience with the larger world of the South. After his mother is deserted by his father and falls ill, Richard's life becomes a continual struggle with poverty and hunger. After some time in an orphan-age (from which he tries to run away), Richard and his family move from place to place, living in the cheapest lodgings they can find or with relatives. Richard begins to attend school and to develop friendships with other boys, but as his mother's health worsens, he feels more and more responsible for supporting the family by working. When his mother has a nearly-fatal stroke, Richard senses an end to his childhood. Over time, his mother's illness comes to represent all the pain and suffering of his life and shapes his outlook on the future.

> My mother's suffering grew into a symbol in my mind, gathering to itself all the poverty, the ignorance, the helplessness; the painful, baffling, hunger-ridden days and hours; the restless moving, the futile seeking, the uncertainty, the fear, the dread; the meaningless pain and the endless suffering. . . . A somberness of spirit that I was never to lose settled over me during the slow years of my mother's unrelieved suffering, a somberness that was to make me stand apart and look upon excessive joy with suspicion, that was to make me self-conscious, that was to make me keep forever on the move, as though to escape a nameless fate seeking to overtake me.

> At the age of twelve, before I had had one full year of formal schooling, I had a conception of life that no experience would ever erase, a predilection for what was real that no argument could ever gainsay, a sense of the world that was mine and mine alone, a notion as to what life meant that no education could ever alter, a conviction that the meaning of living came only when one was struggling to wring a meaning out of meaningless suffering.

After living with relatives for a short time after his mother's stroke, Richard returns to live with his mother at his grandparents' home in Jackson, Mississippi. Here the outlook on life that he has forged in response to his mother's suffering comes into conflict with his grandmother's religious belief. Although she "maintained a hard religious regime," Richard succeeds in resisting her attempts to make him "confess her God." After a more violent confrontation with his Aunt Addie, Richard finally promises his grandmother that he will try to pray to God, but try as he might, he fails: "I was convinced that if I ever succeeded in praying, my words would bound noiselessly against the ceiling and rain back down upon me like feathers." Instead, he begins to write, inventing stories full of "atmosphere and longing and death." Although he can find no one in his life who might appreciate what he has created, Richard senses that in his writing he has found a source of freedom from the pain of his life and a way of expressing himself, unhindered by the limitations of his environment or his family.

Chapters V–X

Richard's confrontations with his family over religion are reignited when his mother, recovered for a time, joins a Methodist church and pleads with him to be baptized. Forced into a position in which rejection of her Christian faith would constitute a visible and shameful rejection of his mother and the entire community, Richard relents and is baptized. Privately, however, he still finds his reading and writing of "pulp narrative" far more compelling than what the church, which he rejects as a "fraud," offers.

Having once again started school and in need of money for clothes and food, Richard confronts his grandmother about her religious refusal to allow him to work on Saturdays. When he finally threatens to leave her home if not allowed to work, she yields to his demand and Richard immediately begins to seek out employment. His first job, selling newspapers to black neighbors, not only provides him with an income but also a "gateway to the world" beyond his own. However, he soon learns that the newspaper he sells endorses the doctrines of the Ku Klux Klan, and he quits the job in shame. Various other jobs—including work at a farm, a brickyard, a sawmill, a clothing store, an optical company, and a movie theater—give Richard first-hand experience of the ways that white people live in the South and, more importantly, the ways that they expect blacks to live and behave. Finding himself unable to act out the roles expected of him, Richard fears that a wrong word or action will cost him his life, and he finally resolves to leave Mississippi for Memphis.

Chapters XI–XIV

Upon his arrival in Memphis, Richard quickly finds, to his surprise, a friendly family with whom he can lodge; but he is even more surprised when Mrs. Moss, the proprietor, pressures him to marry her daughter Bess. Richard comes to realize that the Mosses live by a "simple unaffected trust" that he knows to be "impossible" in his own life. Richard immediately begins looking for work and he finds it running errands for another optical company. While working there Richard meets several other black workers who discuss together "the ways of white folks toward Negroes," but he also recognizes that the ways of some blacks toward white folks—like Shorty, who acts like a degraded clown for money—fill him with "disgust and loathing." Against his own will, however, Richard is forced into playing a similar role when the white men he works with

coerce him into fighting another black boy. The psychological tension he feels around whites makes him reject the kindness of a "Yankee" white man who wants to help him.

To feed his growing hunger for books, Richard cautiously borrows a white man's library card—something forbidden to Southern blacks—and then begins to read voraciously. Reading writers whose names he can not even pronounce, Richard finds "new ways of looking and seeing" and feels "a vast sense of distance between me and the world in which I lived." Believing that he could no longer survive in the South and inspired by his reading to seek a life of meaning and possibility in the North, Richard finally flees the South for Chicago.

Chapters XV–XX

Originally deleted by Wright's publisher and finally restored in the Library of America's 1991 edition of *Black Boy*, this section details Wright's experiences after arriving in Chicago. Continuing his quest for a meaningful way to "live a human life," Wright realizes that the lives of blacks and whites are less segregated in the North but are separated nonetheless by a great "psychological distance." For a time Wright finds meaning in the work of the Communist party, but eventually he becomes disillusioned with the party's limited role for him. He closes Part Two with the decision to write, "determined to look squarely at my life" and to "build a bridge of words between me and that world outside."

Key Figures

Mrs. Bibbs

Mrs. Bibbs, like most white characters in the work, represents one facet of the oppressive society that confronts Richard from birth. In this case, she articulates the white assumption that blacks are inherently suited to menial labor. Therefore, when she hires Richard to do chores around her house, she is astounded to learn that Richard cannot milk a cow.

Mr. Crane

In the work, Mr. Crane stands for the liberal whites who are well-meaning, but ultimately too weak to stand up to the prevailing racism of their society. Mr. Crane is a Yankee business man who owns an optical company in Jackson and he wants to take on a black boy with the enlightened notion of

Media Adaptations

- A recording of *Black Boy* was made by Brock Peters. It was made available in 1989 by Caedmon/New York.

teaching him the trade of optics. Richard shows promise because of his algebraic skill so Crane hires him as a shop boy saying that he will gradually learn the trade. Unfortunately, Crane's other workers do not want to find themselves eventually equal to a black boy. Rather than risk bodily harm, Richard leaves the job. Mr. Crane is sorry to see him go and though he promises protection in the future, Richard refuses to divulge what happened because he knows what the repercussions will be outside the shop.

Ella (I)

Ella is a boarder at Grandma's house. A schoolteacher with a ''remote and dreamy and silent'' manner, Richard is attracted to her mystery, though afraid. She is always reading and Richard desires very much to ask her about what in the books is so fascinating. After increasing antagonism from Grandma, Ella is blamed for Richard's swearing and is asked to leave the house. In this clash of characters is summed up the essence of Richard's emerging consciousness—the struggle between the conflicting power of personal expression, narrative, and storytelling versus stricter religious and cultural demands.

Ella (II)

Richard's mother, also named Ella, tries her best to raise Richard after his father deserts the family. Unfortunately she falls ill and Grandma must care for her and the boys. Ella's illness forces the family to split up the boys but Richard eventually returns to Grandma's house to be near his ill mother. Her relationship with Richard is a difficult one since she is not well. At the end, she goes North because Richard sends for her.

Mr. Falk

Richard asks Mr. Falk if he might use his library card. This does not foster an alliance between them, only a light sympathy, but Mr. Falk does give Richard his library card without betraying him. Richard is then enabled to make regular trips to the ''whites only'' library.

Grandpa

See Richard Wilson

Griggs

Griggs is Richard's friend who repeatedly tries to convince Richard to take the ''easier'' route of conforming to white expectations of black behavior. For Richard he represents the self-enslaving nature of so many of his contemporaries, whose example he can never bring himself to follow.

Harrison

He is a shop boy who works across the street from Richard. He is beset by rumors that Richard wants to fight him while Richard is told that Harrison wants to fight him. Eventually they agree to fight, not because they have fallen for the rumors but because Harrison wants the $5. They fight once. In this episode, Wright sums up the ease with which blacks allow themselves to be pitted against other blacks for the entertainment of white society.

Mrs. Moss

Richard rents a room from Mrs. Moss and finds that she is offering more than just shelter. Mrs. Moss tries to tempt him to marry her daughter Bess. Richard doesn't want to, even if it means inheriting the house. He finds Bess too simple in her emotional outlook. Desperate to have them leave him alone he threatens to leave. They back off and he continues to rent his room.

Mr. Olin

Mr. Olin is Richard's foreman at the Memphis Optical Company. He tries to befriend Richard by telling him that Harrison wants to fight him. He is suspicious of Mr. Olin so he talks to Harrison. Mr. Olin eventually gets his fight by paying them.

Shorty

One of the black men that Richard meets working in Memphis is Shorty, who operates the elevator. Shorty is an intelligent man who would flee Jim Crow for the North if he could just save enough money. Richard thinks a great deal of Shorty because he is very conscious of racism as an environmental condition. However, one day Shorty says, "Just watch me get a quarter from the first white man I see." Shorty gets his quarter by letting the white man kick him. Richard is repulsed because Shorty knows the system too well and has allowed himself to be beaten by it.

Uncle Tom

As his name implies, Uncle Tom is an assimilationist who only seeks to get along with racist white society. From his entrance in the work, he views Richard as a fool by inferring that because Richard is not allowing himself to be brought up by the family in a "proper" manner he will end up at the mercy of a white mob, or a victim of the KKK. Richard refuses—with razors, no less—to learn this lesson.

Addie Wilson

Granny Wilson's youngest daughter Addie returns from her Seventh-Day Adventist religious school and immediately tries to rule Richard. First, she persuades Granny and Richard's mom that if Richard is to live in the house he ought to abide by religious guidance. He is enrolled in the new Seventh-Day Adventist school at which Addie is the only teacher. The showdown is quick in coming when Richard refuses to feel the pain of Addie's corporal punishment in front of the class. After school they fight again but Richard holds her off with a knife. Addie, like her mother, is in conflict with Richard because of her insistence on religious behavior.

Clarke Wilson

Richard chooses to live with Uncle Clarke when his mother becomes too ill to care for her children. His choice is based solely on Clarke's proximity to Richard's mother. However, Aunt Jody's dislike of Richard as the product of a "broken home," plus the fright caused by the knowledge that a boy died in his bed, forces Richard back to his Grandma's house. Once more, prejudice determines his choices in life.

Grandma Margaret Bolden Wilson

Richard opens his work with Granny's white, ill, face. This face disturbs Richard as a little boy because he fails to see how such a white-skinned person could be "black." The most important tension Richard holds with Grandma, however, is neatly summed up at the start of the fourth chapter: "Granny was an ardent member of the Seventh-Day Adventist Church and I was compelled to make a pretense of worshipping her God, which was her exaction for my keep." Ardent is not a strong enough word. Grandma is consumed by her belief in religion and its promise to reward her in the hereafter for the suffering of the Jim Crow now. Her zealotry, Richard claims, also means ruining his life. Grandma will not let him get a job that will mean his working on Saturday (their Sabbath) and thus Richard cannot buy food, clothes, and other things necessary amongst children his age. Grandma also prevents him from reading as he would like to or even hearing stories, like *Bluebeard,* because they are not the Bible. Indirectly, this teaches Richard all about the pretense and the hypocrisy of religion. More directly, due to a deal he makes with Grandma to pray every day, he writes his first short story when he should be quietly praying in his room and thus begins to harbor the idea of being a writer. Grandma sets the pace of the family as well as establishing its treatment of Richard. She tried to orchestrate his religious conversion but finally gives up, concluding that his inability to accept the religious view of things, the established view of things, will lead to his doom. For his questioning and intolerance of status quo, he is punished or ignored.

Richard Wilson

Grandpa was wounded while fighting for the Union Army in the Civil War. Due to his illiteracy, he asked a white officer for assistance with filling out the paperwork necessary to receive a disability pension. The officer misspelled his name as Richard Vinson. Not knowing of the mistake, Grandpa returned home. However, as time passed and he received no pension he applied to the War Department who had no trace of him. Eventually, the above story of the "mistake" formed but the War Department demanded proof that Grandpa was in fact deserving of the pension. In consequence, Grandpa spends the rest of his life trying to convince the government he is who he said he is. Grandpa, says Richard, is just "like 'K' in the Kafka novel, *The Castle.*" He tries desperately to persuade the authorities of his true identity right up to the day of his death, and fails.

Grandpa is a strong male influence in Richard's life who only proves to him that "manliness" is impossible for black men in the Jim Crow South. As a warrior, Grandpa has fought and been wounded for his country, yet the army never pays him the respect—or the disability pension—he has earned. In the home, Richard is also taught that men are "impotent": despite the fact that Grandma calls Grandpa in to administer punishment, it soon becomes apparent that it is she, not he, who rules the house.

Tom Wilson
See Uncle Tom

Leon Wright

Richard's brother plays a very minor role in *Black Boy*. He is a tag-along sibling when Richard sets fire to the house in the opening scene of the book, a witness to Richard hanging the cat, and present when the rest of the family shuns Richard once he is again back at Grandma's from Maggie's. At the close of the work though, Leon is brought north along with his mother.

Nathan Wright

Richard's father is his lawgiver and his exemplar. Nathan is the only character in the novel that Richard gives a future glimpse of. Furthermore, by granting this future view of his father, Richard also gives a view of his present, writing self. At the end of chapter 1 he defines his father and he defines his own conception of himself. Looking at his father twenty-five years after being deserted, Richard says:

"I forgave him and pitied him as my eyes looked past him to the unpainted wooden shack. From far beyond the horizons that bound this bleak plantation there had come to me through my living the knowledge that my father was a black peasant who had gone to the city seeking life, but who had failed in the city; a black peasant whose life had been hopelessly snarled in the city, and who had at last fled the city—that same city which had lifted my in its burning arms and borne me toward alien and undreamed-of shores of knowing."

Richard's father left the plantation hoping for a better life for his family, but being beaten by the city, he deserted his family, left them destitute, and fled back to the plantation. Richard is ultimately able to accomplish what his father failed by leaving the plantation clay behind.

Richard Wright

Richard is the protagonist of the story—he is the "black boy." He tells his own story as if he is a victim of his surroundings, almost as if he is an existentialist given limited choice in every circumstance. There is really only one thing he is ever sure of throughout the work and which drives him to leave the South and tell his story. That one thing is a conception of himself as a person who individually can conceive of the world. In addition to this, he knows that his awareness of having this conception of himself in the world marks him out as different. His certainty of this subjectivity is settled by the age of twelve. By then, he says at the end of chapter 3, he had a, "notion as to what life meant that no education could ever alter, a conviction that the meaning of living came only when one was struggling to wring a meaning out of meaningless suffering."

His father is a peasant who is little more than clay struggling to wrest a living out of the soil, whereas he, Richard, is aware of words, of the world, and insistent that it can be different if the difference is only that he not have to mop up after white people.

Ellen Wilson Wright
See Ella

Themes

Race and Racism

Racism is not as much a theme in this work as it is an environmental condition—an integral part of the setting. The work tries to expose the ethical effect that the Jim Crow system had on its subjects—both black and white. *Black Boy* is a work about individual positions within a racist mind-set. That is, the world in which Richard must live is racist, and within that world prejudice against blacks is all-pervasive. However, Richard occasionally meets with tolerant persons. Furthermore, Richard himself must be tolerant with those around him who do not have the intellect to see the world like he does. He must also endure the Jim Crow system until he has enough money to escape or else he will be killed.

Richard, having realized that his options are either to play along by being dumb or to be tolerant

Topics for Further Study

- Read a novel by Ann Petry or any other member of the "Wright School" (Chester Himes, Willard Savoy, Philip B. Kaye, etc.) and compare with *Black Boy*. In the case of Petry's *The Street*, address the difference in terms of gender and the world of the urban black in the cities of post-WWII America.

- What difference does it make whether one reads *Black Boy* or *American Hunger* to one's understanding of Wright's critical view of America? Does America "get off" easy in *Black Boy* because, after all, Wright does escape to the better life in the north?

- Research the issue of Jim Crow and then compare that environment to race relations today: do we live in a more tolerant, egalitarian, society? Discuss current issues such as: Californian challenges to affirmative action; the declaration of English as the one and only language in some states; the unequal distribution of minorities and the effects on busing, services, insurance, health care, or any other issue.

- Think about perceptions: Wright repeatedly remarks about his refusal at first to adopt proper Jim Crow mannerisms and then the necessity of his having to do so—are there roles that we play based on gender, class, or racial perceptions and are these influenced or based upon information gathered from television sitcoms? Further, what are the perceptions taught us by media on this issue of behavior (think for example about programs like *Cops* versus a network 10 o'clock news program or *Baywatch* versus *Martin*)?

- Find some images that were around during World War II and after; get a book of posters from the library showing the overt effort to get people behind the war effort. After viewing these images, consider the way in which Wright presents the same era. For example, the few white women he does encounter throughout the narrative (especially in the second part of "American Hunger") do not seem to fit the images you will find in the posters. Think about the aim of "urban realism" in light of these posters; think about Wright's struggle to write for people.

and escape, chooses the route of escape. However, while awaiting the chance, he spends his time trying to figure out Jim Crow in his own head at least. The novel is his retrospective exploration of the way in which he learned the values and drawbacks that constitute both prejudice and tolerance. Richard may find the coping mechanism of Shorty and Griggs repulsive but in his role as passive observer he only amounts to a chronicler of the facts of Jim Crow. To be sure, to have done more than balk at the easy manner with which a girl handles sexual harassment by a constable would have found Richard strung up like the cat or Uncle Silas. It is worth noting, therefore, that young Richard comes to understand prejudices as opinions that readers hold no matter how incorrect they are and tolerance as that degree of openness they have to a world that does not accord with their opinions.

Richard never learns the lesson of how to be "black." Part of this is due to the confusion aroused early in Richard's consciousness by his grandmother. Her white appearance implicates that the different treatment of blacks is a treatment based on something other than color. With this hint, Richard decides that blackness is a social decision, not a real fact. For the same reason, he decides that whiteness is not a reality—just an invisible fright like a ghost or bogey. After Uncle Silas is lynched, Richard has evidence of the consequences of being seen as black, but he has not witnessed it himself. Therefore, it was not until he himself is run off a job that Richard understand that whites can be oppressors.

Even after the incident with Pease and Reynolds, Richard fails to understand racism. He doesn't begin to gain an understanding of prejudice and tolerance until he begins to play the system by borrowing Mr. Falk's library card. To use it, he writes the note in which he calls himself a nigger. The librarian questions him but he claims to be illiterate. Having fooled her, he checks out H. L. Mencken who viewed the South as "hell" on earth. The title of Mencken's work was *Prejudices* and this causes Richard to pause and wonder if he hadn't made a mistake in reading Mencken. Certainly, Richard thought to himself "a man who had prejudices must be wrong." However, he discovers that prejudice is a word for a category of thought, rather than simply another word for racism. That is, racism is but one of many prejudices.

For Richard the mind blocks of prejudice and tolerance are also applicable to religion. This discovery brings him a great deal of grief with family members who are prejudiced toward a certain way of understanding and refuse to budge. An example comes as soon as the start of the fourth chapter where Richard listens to a fire and brimstone sermon that Granny, for one, believes. However, when Richard leaves the church and feels "the throbbing of life" then the sermon inside the church is placed in perspective—it is but one of many ways of seeing the world but a way of seeing best left inside the church. As for the Jim Crow system, Richard would like to leave it in the South.

Individualism

For Richard, a life's meaning is in the independence of the individual. That means that Richard sees life as a quest for truth. He stubbornly seeks answers where none—or no satisfactory ones—are given. Richard wants answers that will stand up to argument. Time and again, Richard finds himself at odds with the world: people beat him without justification; he has to be servile to whites; his love of words and stories that lead him to dream of writing brings him ridicule. Then there is religion that reveals to him how people amalgamate into groups driven by dogma—they give up, as in the case of Granny or Aunt Addie, their human rights in return for a heavenly inheritance.

Instead of certainty brought about by these beliefs, Richard finds he has something else by the end of the third chapter:

> I had a conception of life that no experience would ever erase, a predilection for what was real that no argument could ever gainsay, a sense of the world that was mine and mine alone, a notion as to what life meant that no education could ever alter, a conviction that the meaning of living came only when one was

struggling to wring a meaning out of meaningless suffering.

Richard goes on in the next paragraph to explain that this made him a good listener to any who would talk to him and it also made him the keen observer he needed to be in order to become the famous writer he would be. Armed with observations and experience, he relates the reality he has found in the form of words, and thus his identity is entwined with his search for the reason that people behave the way they do, especially why they behave so inhumanely. His conclusions are his novels.

Style

Narration

Taking liberty with his own life's story, Richard Wright created a masterpiece in the story of *Black Boy*, a first person narrative portraying a boy who grows up under the oppression of Southern racism. This narration demonstrated the principles of living within the Jim Crow system that Wright had previously laid out in "The Ethics of Living Jim Crow," published in *Uncle Tom's Children*. He represented these ethics through the didactic story of *Black Boy* with the intention of altering white America's racism. Wright believed that a well-developed protagonist in a successful novel would do more for race relations than any political speech or ruling. Therefore, by the use of his own experience re-enforced by a first person persona, *Black Boy* exposes the reality of life for the black American realistically but without offering solutions.

Wright used the first-person narrative to provide an objective viewpoint that borders on the style that would come to be known as existentialism. He did this by portraying his own development in the same way that French writers like Albert Camus and Jean-Paul Sartre presented their leading protagonists. Events and characters encountered by Richard are given only what depth is required to tell Richard's story, so that, in effect, Richard is the only character. The boy in the fourth chapter who wants to save Richard's soul is only an extension of Granny's "machinery," and Granny herself is but an incarnation of the repressive system of Christianity.

An example of how Richard glosses over every character, mentioning them only when they infringe on his consciousness, is the scene where he describes a confrontation amongst some unnamed boys in a school yard. He terms the associations of other black boys as a fraternity; not a conscious friendship, but a spontaneous gathering. The boys find themselves easily congregated together and are just as easily called away. No emotional links are described or maintained—not even with Griggs who behaves in such a brotherly manner to Richard. For Richard, the only important things are his own awakening consciousness, his telling of his awakening, and his escape to the North.

Structure

Black Boy is structured as a series of spliced-together episodes in the life of Richard. Thus, the work reads much like a movie, because in a very real way, Richard makes a documentary of himself. It is as if each chapter is a scene that is cut away from and moved into the next story. The finish of each chapter is punctuated with a sense of progress but not of ending. The work is very easily visualized by the reader, not only because it is written in a naturalistic style, but also because there are no intrusions by other voices. Key to this structuring is the awareness that Richard has a growing appreciation and use for words. The whole world is filtered through Richard's growing consciousness into an existential *Weltanschauung* (world view) understandable only through his assignation of meaning.

This can be explained by noting that Richard was not allowed free motion—running, shouting, questioning—but had to stay quiet, avoid beatings, and answer his own ceaseless quest for explanation. As a result, Richard was formed by his conscious alienation: he knew he was under restraint but had no concept of an alternative. In reaction, he is very interested in life around him for the clues it reveals about the real world. However, he maintains his interest objectively and from a distance, just like when he is hungry but pretends disinterest in food because the eating of it would remind him of his shameful hunger.

Historical Context

World War II

World War II was coming to an end when *Black Boy* was published in 1945. In fact, as the work topped the best-seller charts, the U.S. 9th Armored Division and the 1st Armored Division secured Ally control on the west bank of the Rhine, and U.S. B-24 bombers were bombing Tokyo. The war in Europe ended on May 8, 1945. In the Pacific, the war dragged on until August when an atomic bomb was dropped on Hiroshima and then another was dropped on Nagasaki, Japan. World War II ended, and the loss of life was estimated at 54.8 million.

The Cold War was still a few years away, and 1945 seemed to be a year of victory for the Allies and the ideology of democratic capitalism. The United States was approaching the zenith of its industrial-economic might due to trade imbalance caused by war. Hollywood was not shy to back up the tales of U.S. Army plenty with movies showing how rich and ideal life in America was. The reality, however, was quite different. Americans were wealthy as a nation, and had shown just how wealthy they were by the immensity of the resources they had thrown behind the Allied cause, but individually things were mediocre. For the minorities in America, it was just plain bad: blacks lived under Jim Crow in the South of the United States; the Dakotan, Navajo, Apache, and other tribal groups lived in reservations little better than concentration camps; and Japanese-Americans were being released from internment camps where they had been held under suspicion while the United States fought Japan. For these minority groups, there was no possibility of the Hollywood image being real, and in some sense members of these minority groups who had fought in the war had it worse. Like Richard Wright's grandfather, they fought for America but had little to show for it when they came home.

In some sense these problems were only dawning in 1945, because the transition to unemployment resulting from the demobilization of the war's industrial complex into a peacetime economy had not yet arrived. During the year there were signs of the upcoming struggle. Workers in car factories went on strike and despite those strikes, the American Gross National Product approached $211 billion. New agricultural procedures increased food production both within the United States and around the world, and food rationing in the United States ceased, although it remained a reality in Europe. It was not, and never had been, a problem of wealth in America but, as evidenced in Wright's work, a problem of distribution. America was rich in 1945 but its minorities were poor, very poor.

A societal revolution was beginning to evolve out of this economic inequality. As troops returned home throughout the year, America began a transition back to a peace time economy, thus shifting workers away from military complexes. To succeed at this transition, images changed from encourage-

Compare
&
Contrast

- **1940s:** Race relations are tense, at best, with Jim Crowism sanctioned in several states of the union as well as being practiced by the U.S. military.

  Today: Jim Crowism was killed by the Civil Rights movement. Anti-hate legislation and human rights laws are being instituted around the country and rendering the justice system intolerant of all forms of discrimination. Thus, legally things look very good, but, as a recent series of black church burnings and challenges in California to affirmative action show, race relations are still imperfect.

- **1940s:** In the South, $17 of tuition is spent per black student per year and $35 per white child. Richard is not obligated nor able to go beyond the ninth grade (which, he says, is really the eighth grade).

  Today: Cuts in tuition assistance put college almost beyond the reach of the poorest students. At the grade school level, no racial distinctions are made in public schools in the matter of spending. Instead, educational spending is decreasing due to congressional cuts. Furthermore, spending is not equally distributed; wealthy districts can afford to, and do, spend a lot more on their children's educations than less wealthy ones.

- **1940s:** America attempts to keep its people working and begins to build a safety net so that no person goes hungry, without care, or is unable to retire.

  Today: From Wisconsin to California, U.S. legislators are removing the threads that make up the American safety net.

---

ment of the war effort to encouragement of family and consumption. In the case of women, this meant the image not of a female in a factory, but a female at home, in a dress, with a baby. This coincided with a media revolution as America increased its private ownership of televisions from only 5,000 sets to the ubiquity it has today. The U.S. government began its most effective and profitable investment ever—the GI Bill—which allowed the returning soldiers to go back to school or buy a home. This had two effects. First, the already painful transition to a peacetime economy in the job market was not made worse by the soldiers because they instead filled the universities. Second, after a delay there was a tremendous increase in the available numbers of college educated workers.

The ideal of a peaceful world seemed closer than ever after World War II. Atomic power promised to deter large scale military aggression and the establishment of the United Nations in June of 1945 provided the forum for nonviolent resolutions and concerted action between the world governments. This was the hope, but the reality was being dis-

played in Palestine by Jewish settlers as they escalated their harassment of British forces in control of the region, and in China where the Russians and the Americans attempted to pick the right side of a battle just beginning between the revolting communists under Mao Tse-tung and Chiang Kai-shek and his followers.

Critical Overview

When considering the critical reputation of *Black Boy* it is important to note that the work was available only in a truncated version until 1977. In that year, the full text, *American Hunger*, was published. This work gives the reader a very different view of Richard because the hope granted by the escape to the North at the ''end'' of the first section is undercut by the broken American dream found in Chicago in the second part. However, *Black Boy* in its 1945 version was well received and remains a popular work to this day. Critically, the work has been viewed as Wright's masterpiece, a twentieth-century version of the slave narrative, and a work of protest against racism, censorship, and intolerance. More recently, criticism has been focused on the restored work (the version established by the Library of America) as cultural critique and a weapon against censorship. Such recent reviews have also looked more closely at the novel as pure sociology or, as Ellison previously suggested, at the Joycean quality of Wright's writing. This latter view sees Richard as a black version of Stephen Dedalus in *Portrait of the Artist as a Young Man.*

Ralph Ellison reviewed Wright's work for the *Antioch Review* in 1945 in an essay entitled "Richard Wright's Blues." To him the work was a "blues-tempered" lyric such as Bessie Smith might sing. Richard Wright, Ellison went on, had given himself a duplicitous role: "to discover and depict the meaning of Negro Experience; and to reveal to both Negroes and whites those problems of a psychological and emotional nature which arise between them when they strive for mutual understanding." This became the aim of the "Wright School of Urban Realism." They were a group of authors inspired by Wright to use writing, as Robert A. Bone put it in *The Negro Novel in America* (1965), as a "means of dispelling inner tensions of race . . . [and through a fictional protagonist] alter [white] attitude toward race."

In addition to Ellison, the work was reviewed by Lionel Trilling for *The Nation,* on April 7, 1945. Trilling applauded Wright's effort, saying, "He has the objectivity which comes from refusing to be an object." A few months later, in an article for *Esquire* (June 23, 1945), Sinclair Lewis took a more direct approach. His review took the opportunity not to be critical of Wright but of America. Lewis defended the book against those who were made uncomfortable by it. He said there could be no reason to doubt the veracity of the book's report on living conditions for blacks given the echo found in official reports made by the NAACP, the daughter of a white Navy officer (Ruth Donenhower Wilson) in a book on Jim Crow, the U.S. government itself, and others. All told, he said, the South does in fact practice Jim Crowism and the North is not much better. Why, Lewis wonders with the NAACP, should Jim Crowism exist even within the troops and the Red Cross in the European war—within the "Army of Democracy" itself?

In the 1950s, the reputation of Wright ebbed as Ellison and Baldwin came into popularity. However, in the 1960s, black militancy preferred the forthright attitude of Wright, and his popularity rose to new heights. Ronald Sanders, in "Richard Wright and the Sixties" (*Midstream* (1968)), had nothing but praise for Wright. Saunders called *Black Boy* Wright's masterpiece but also his swan song. Critically, the work was regarded for what it was doing as a sociological study. For example, in *The Art of Richard Wright,* Edward Margolies portrays Wright as a generalist who extrapolates a blanket statement about American minorities based on his life. Margolies goes so far as to criticize Wright for playing the innocent too much: "[Wright's] theme is freedom and he skillfully arranges and selects his scene in such a way that he is constantly made to appear the innocent victim of . . . tyranny." That may be, but in the 1970s, critics begin to make greater comparisons and even, as Martha Stephens does, place the pre-*Native Son* works ahead of the greater commercial successes. Stephens also returns to the questions of Ellison and Baldwin as to whether Wright has a picture of "real" negroes. The answer, she says, lies in the whole of his oeuvre.

Roger Whitlow, in his 1973 book entitled *Black American Literature,* shows Wright as a cultural mirror of blacks before the era of Civil Rights. Wright, for Whitlow, is a portrait of the blacks who made the same journey North making the same critical discoveries. *Black Boy*, according to Whitlow, echoes the theme of *Native Son*:

> A man must have enough control over his environment to feel that he can mold it, if only slightly, so that it can provide him with at least a part of the realization of his dreams. When he has no such control, he ceases to be a functioning member of that environment; and he thereby divorces himself from its mores and its legal restrictions.

Further, just as Richard discovered that neither the North nor South wanted the black man, he had to force his way in. Forcibly black writers, protesters, and speakers have hurled "words into darkness" though many assert that they are still waiting for the full echo of the dream of equality.

Recent views of Wright's work include an article by Maryemma Graham and Jerry W. Ward, Jr. written in 1993. There, in "*Black Boy (American Hunger):* Freedom to Remember" published in *Censored Books: Critical Viewpoints,* the authors says that *American Hunger* is a statement against censorship of all forms. The inclusiveness of Wright's stance can be seen in the novel itself where Richard reflects on how he prefers the Southerner's outright rejection of him to the Northerner's polite tolerance. This article places Wright with Ray Bradbury, George

A former slave shack on a Natchez, Mississippi, plantation in 1938

Orwell, and other writers of anti-censorship works by saying that "these books invite us to imaginatively recreate the experience of living within closed systems. It tells us much about social breakdown and disorder in American life with a vividness sociological writing cannot provide." In other words, Graham and Ward nicely tie together the artistic place of the writer with his responsibility (that responsibility that the "Wright school" focused on) to alter the consciousness of America for the better. In Wright's specific capacity as a survivor of Jim Crow and as a black man, they say, "*Black Boy (American Hunger)* is a critique of American optimism betrayed." The work is a display of how the American dream as product fails to live up to the claims of the advertisement. Such critique is noted but needs to be acted upon.

Criticism

Mary Mahony

Mahony is an English instructor at Wayne County Community College in Detroit, Michigan. In this essay, she discusses Wright's portrayal of the influence that language exerts on personal and societal roles.

Richard Wright's *Black Boy* contains two distinct yet interrelated themes. The first reveals the development of his literary and artistic skills, tracing their emergence from a set of fragile roots to the eventual fruition that Wright depicts in the second section of his autobiography, *American Hunger*. The second theme revolves around the difficulty of becoming a responsible and articulate black man in an oppressive and racist culture that has organized its social, political, and educational structure to prevent that from happening. These two themes are interwoven throughout both sections of Wright's autobiography in a chain of incidents that exposes the devastating consequences of racism.

One of the methods Wright uses to develop these themes involves focusing the attention of the reader on the enormous potential of language. Words, grammar, sentences, and the ideas that they contain are central to almost every episode in the autobiography. For Wright, language is a complex and multifaceted tool. He depicts it not only as a positive element that can enable an individual to transcend his environment but also as a dangerous and even a deadly one. This emphasis on language becomes apparent as early as the opening scene, which takes place when Wright is only four years old. After being told to keep quiet because his grandmother is

What Do I Read Next?

- Wright's first success was *Native Son* (1940). It is the tragic tale of Bigger Thomas and explores many of the same themes as *Black Boy*.

- The 1963 novel entitled *Lawd Today* is in many ways Richard Wright's best work, although it was never as successful as *Black Boy* or *Native Son*. This story began as "Cesspool" in 1935 and tells the story of the futile life of Jake Jackson, who lives in Chicago as a postal worker.

- A member of the "Wright School," Ann Petry wrote about the trials of life on 116th Street, Harlem, in *The Street.* In that 1946 novel, Petry explores the relationship of environment and a black woman's effort to live with self-respect in the ghetto. Written both by and about a woman, it is a nice companion to Richard Wright's work.

- *Invisible Man,* the 1953 novel by Ralph Ellison, has become a classic portrayal of black experience in America.

- For a nonfictional view of what actually constituted Jim Crow, see *Jim Crow Guide: The Way It Was* that has been recently re-published by Florida Atlantic University Press. In this work by Stetson Kennedy, the legal basis as well as the civic rules that created the system of legal discrimination are displayed. The book is highly informative and very readable.

- An account of black experience in the "democratic army" that fought in World War II has been recorded by Mary Patrick Motley in *The Invisible Soldier: The Experience of the Black Soldiers, WWII.* Motley's work is a collection of interviews with veterans of the war who told her about the fighting as well as the unfortunate existence of Jim Crow in the United States—a practice that other armies did not mirror.

- For further reading on race relations in the United States at the time of the novel, see R. Polenberg's *One Nation Divisible: Class, Race, and Ethnicity in the United States since 1938.*

---

ill, he reacts with resentment since he longs to shout and play. In his anger, he accidentally sets the house on fire. As a result, he is scolded and severely beaten.

Note that this incident foreshadows many others in the novel by setting a pattern of behavior. First Wright is forbidden to express himself. Sometimes it is the restrictions of the white-dominated society that force this restraint; at other times, members of his own family attempt to curb his speech. In either case, such denials only arouse his anger and resentment. His response to the situation is perceived as hostile, threatening, or inappropriate. The eventual result of these incidents is some sort of verbal or even physical assault; as Wright matures, he discovers that the threat of violence is at times more potent than an actual physical wound. Through these incidents, both Wright and the reader discover the controlling force that language serves in organizing family relationships, in defining an individual's

goals and dreams, and in determining one's role in the social order.

Several events in Wright's early childhood help to build his understanding of the power of words. At the age of six, he is taught to repeat obscenities by the drunks in the local bar. After a performance, they reward him with drinks. Later, after hearing these same words in the schoolyard, he writes them on the neighborhood windows with soap. In both of these cases, he learns that language may bring the reward of an attention that is frequently enticing enough to outweigh the unpleasantness of punishment.

In one of the most powerful of these early tales, Wright manipulates his father by deliberately acting on the literal meaning of his father's words rather than on the intended meaning. After his father is awakened by the crying of a small kitten, he orders

> " His first attempt at writing his own fiction, an adventure called *The Voodoo of Hell's Half-Acre*, springs up in three days out of his eighth-grade dreams and fantasies."

his sons, "Kill that damn thing! . . . Do anything, but get it away from here." Wright resents his father's yelling at him. In fact, he feels that his father's presence is little more than a brooding and tyrannical shadow over the entire household. Although he knows that his father does not really wish for his children to harm the animal, Wright deliberately strangles it with a noose since he sees this as an opportunity to retaliate against his father's continual demands. For the first time, he is able to undermine his father's oppressive dominance. Even though he is still a child, Wright intuits that his father will not punish him for obeying so specific a request. If his father does so, it will prove that his word is worthless. Although Wright correctly surmises that his father will be rendered impotent by this strategy, the boy is not held blameless for the incident, however. Interestingly, his chastisement is verbal rather than physical. His mother first describes the horrors of taking a life, which "spawned in my mind a horde of invisible demons bent on exacting vengeance." She later terrifies him with prayers over the kitten's grave. Continually throughout this passage, Wright uses imagery to reinforce the impact of his mother's speech. Her words are "calculating," her voice "floating" and "disembodied," her injunctions "paralyzing."

The previous incidents focus primarily on Wright's discovery of various methods through which language can influence behavior and roles within the family and in interpersonal relationships. A second series of tales deals with the social role of communication as he struggles to acquire the unique vocabulary that was required for African Americans to survive in the South in the first half of the twentieth century. Wright demonstrates that clear patterns of communication were demanded by the dominant white culture. This included rules not only about when to speak and when to remain silent, but which type of words were allowed as well. Body language was equally important; the proper response could be negated by an unacceptable look or gesture. These lessons were extremely important to survival, since failure to behave in an appropriately subservient manner could have potentially deadly consequences.

Wright's initial introduction to the social role of words occurs while he is a young child. He notes that he "stumbled" in his attempts to understand the difference between black and white. While he later recognizes that these terms determine almost every aspect of life in the United States, he is unable, as a child, to connect the societal definition of the word "white" with his own perceptions, since his grandmother "was as 'white' as any white person." From this point on, Wright becomes aware that much of the language around him contains a code—one that puzzles him. Since he senses that there is an entire realm of awareness that is being hidden from him, he continually questions his mother about this. However, her answers do not satisfy him. "She was not concealing facts, but feelings, attitudes, connections which she did not want me to know." Gradually, of course, Wright becomes fully aware of the dangers that may befall a young black male in the world in which he lives. As a series of racial conflicts erupts throughout the United States in the years following World War I, he is necessarily exposed to many stories of the atrocities that have taken place. Eventually, as a result of this, he notes that an uncomfortable tension would set in at the mere mention of "whites."

This reaction occurs even when Wright's activities are relatively remote from daily contact with white society. Once he begins to work, he discovers that he is in constant turmoil trying to behave in the expected manner. He is quickly fired from one of his first jobs, at a clothing store, because he can't "laugh and talk like the other niggers." He continually has to move on to a new job because his employers are threatened by his speech and by his way of looking at them. While his words are "innocent" by themselves, they indicate an awareness that continually infuriates the white people he encounters. Wright describes this inability to conform to the stereotype demanded by the world around him, saying that while he recognizes that white people are expecting him to behave in what is a clearly established manner, he finds that their speech and behaviors are "baffling signs to me. . . . Misreading the reactions of whites around me made me say and do the wrong things . . . I could not make subservience an automatic part of my behavior."

This meant that he was forced to carefully analyze every word and every action. Even then he frequently found himself saying one sentence too few or one too many.

Wright then becomes aware that most of the blacks he knows operate on two different levels. In actuality, they have learned two different vocabularies. They adopt the role in which society forces them into using one set of words and gestures, while at the same time they enjoy a private and often completely contrasting life and language among other blacks. Wright's friend Griggs reminds him that he will get killed if he doesn't learn to adapt to these rules of life in the South. Griggs continues by saying that he, also, hates white people, but he has learned never to let it be seen. While Wright understands the wisdom of this advice, he continually forgets to follow it. More importantly, he rebels against the limits that this type of life automatically sets, realizing that to accept these boundaries means that any aspirations to a richer and more unified existence would have to be abandoned.

A third group of incidents details the steps through which Wright develops a recognition of the power of language, not simply to convey emotions and feelings but to become a transforming element into a new way of thinking and living, a "gateway to a forbidden and enchanting land." As early as six, he describes himself as fascinated by words and stories. Although he is not yet in school, he borrows the books of children in the neighborhood. During this period, he demands that his mother read to him from newspapers and any other available source. Even at this age, his hunger for words has begun. However, it is not until he meets Ella, the schoolteacher who is living with his grandmother, that he first gets a sense of the enormous potential for fiction to enrich his life. In spite of the fact that his grandmother views secular books as sinful, he eventually convinces Ella to read one of her novels to him. The tale of *Bluebeard and His Seven Wives* immediately enthralls him. Wright vividly describes how the story grasped his imagination, as "reality changed" and "my sense of life deepened." Even when his grandmother interrupts the session and forbids him to have anything more to do with books, he is unable to stop, sensing that somehow reading is essential to his spirit.

Several other events also reveal Wright's growing sensitivity to words and ideas. He tells of his emotional response to the symbolism of the religion that his grandmother pushes upon him, although he is unable to adhere to its teachings intellectually. His first attempt at writing his own fiction, an adventure called *The Voodoo of Hell's Half-Acre*, springs up in three days out of his eighth-grade dreams and fantasies. While the story is interesting enough to be published in the neighborhood newspaper, Wright does not receive any encouragement from his family or his friends. Instead, his grandmother calls it the devil's work, while his classmates view him with suspicion for behavior that is inexplicable to them. Later, when he is selected as valedictorian for his ninth-grade graduation, he refuses to deliver the speech that the principal has written for him. Although he agrees that his own manuscript is more poorly composed, he resists all threats and pleas to change his mind because, for all its weaknesses, his speech contains a message while the principal's is made up of pretty but empty words. The accumulation of these incidents begins to stimulate his dreams of going north and becoming a writer.

It is not until the end of the first part of the autobiography, however, that Wright fully recognizes the power of language. When he reads a virulent denunciation of the writer H. L. Mencken in the newspaper, he contrives an elaborate scheme to get access to Mencken's work. It is a revelation to him when he discovers that Mencken is attacking society with "words as a weapon." This experience reminds him of the passion he had previously experienced when he was reading and writing. His hunger for literature is reborn and he begins reading as frequently as he can; in fact, he refers to reading as a drug. The revelations he receives are as often devastating as they are informative or pleasurable. While he becomes more fully aware of the possibilities the world might hold, he is also made even more conscious of the barriers around him. He begins to fully realize the hostility of the Southern culture, recognizing now that his goals have set him in direct conflict with the expectations of the society around him.

> "I was building up a dream in me which the entire educational system in the South has been rigged to stifle. I was feeling the very thing that the state of Mississippi has spent millions of dollars to make sure that I never would feel; I was becoming aware of the thing that the Jim Crow laws had been drafted and passed to keep out of my consciousness."

The first section of the autobiography ends with Wright returning his borrowed library card and beginning his trip to Chicago. However, once he is there, he discovers no promised land. Instead, his struggle continues as he searches to develop his potential as a writer while adjusting to the confusing and contradictory demands of both family and society.

Source: Mary Mahony, Critical Essay on *Black Boy*, in *Nonfiction Classics for Students,* The Gale Group, 2001.

Anthony Dykema-VanderArk

Dykema-VanderArk is a doctoral candidate at Michigan State University. In the following essay, he examines the autobiographical nature of Wright's Black Boy *and how it shows Wright's belief in "the influence of environment on a person's actions and attitudes."*

Richard Wright's reputation as one of the most influential figures in the tradition of African-American literature rests on two works in particular, his best-selling novel, *Native Son* (1940), and his autobiography, *Black Boy* (1945). In *Native Son*, Wright depicts in graphic physical and psychological detail the realities of a young black man's life under the pressures of a racist environment. In *Black Boy*, one might say that Wright turns the novelist's gaze to his own life, providing (as his subtitle indicates) "A Record of Childhood and Youth" that is at once informative as a historical account and gripping in the way a novel can be. Blurring the boundaries between fiction and nonfiction, Wright dramatizes various scenes from his early life, recreates dialogue that he could not possibly recall, and incorporates sections of poetic rumination that resemble haiku—but none of these inventions challenges the force and eloquence of Wright's truth-telling in *Black Boy*. Wright uses his autobiography not only to recount significant experiences in his life but also to record his emotional and psychological reactions to those experiences, his intellectual awakening, his "hunger" for a meaningful life, and his condemnation of American racism. In his attempt to capture the significance of his own life, both for himself and for the reader, Wright creates in *Black Boy* a profoundly moving "record" of his remarkable life.

Because one of Richard Wright's primary interests in all of his writing is the influence of environment on a person's actions and attitudes, it is not surprising that he begins his own story by portraying the family environment of his childhood. His mother's injunction in the opening scene that Richard "keep quiet" and his father's similar demand in a following scene suggest, in one small way, the limits that were placed on his life within the family. His response in both cases—first, "accidentally" starting the house on fire, and second, killing a noisy kitten—attest to Richard's desire, even as a young child, to express his feelings and assert his presence in his family in strong terms. Richard's responses unsettle the reader because they seem excessive, out of proportion to the situations he is in. But the scene establishes two themes that run through the whole of *Black Boy*: First, that many things in Richard's Southern environment are in fact excessive, often dangerously and violently so; and second, that Richard will go to great lengths to resist limitations placed on him and to find some means of self-expression.

These opening scenes also portray the tensions that Richard feels within his family, the psychological distance that exists between them even when living close together in cramped quarters. Richard sees his father as "the lawgiver in our family," someone whose very presence stifles his voice and laughter, and someone who remains "a stranger . . . always somehow alien and remote." After his father deserts the family, Richard associates him with the "pangs of hunger" he feels, hating him with "a deep biological bitterness." Richard's distance from his mother results not from abandonment but from her illness. It is because of his mother's sickness that Richard must stay in the orphanage and later with various relatives, and after she suffers a severe stroke he feels absolutely alone in the world, unable any longer to "feel" or "react as a child." Eventually, his mother's affliction becomes a powerful symbol in Richard's mind, producing a "somberness of spirit" that sets him apart from other people and inspiring "a conviction that the meaning of living came only when one was struggling to wring a meaning out of meaningless suffering."

This outlook shapes Richard's view of his Grandmother's religious belief, which he finds a poor substitute for his own rootedness in the hard realities of life. Although he responds to the drama and the emotion of the church service and its religious symbols, he rejects entirely its "cosmic threats" of damnation and develops "a callousness toward all metaphysical preachments." Richard rejects religion in part because it finds otherworldly causes and solutions for the real-world suffering that he cannot escape. He believes that the religion of his Aunt Addie and Granny leads people to ignore or accept passively the pain of their lives. Even the schoolkids he meets at his Aunt's religious school seem to live flattened-out lives, almost as if they were mentally and emotionally impaired by their religion: "These boys and girls were will-less, their speech flat, their gestures vague, their personalities devoid of anger, hope, laughter, enthusiasm, passion, or despair.'' Religion can also be coercive, Richard realizes, as when he is ''trapped'' by his mother and the entire community of her church into joining the church—or, as he puts it, into giving ''the sign of allegiance'' to the ''tribe.''

Richard understands the desire behind religious belief—as he puts it, ''the hunger of the human heart for that which is not and can never be''—but his grandmother's religion offers nothing to satisfy his own ''hunger,'' just as her sparse fare at home leaves him physically hungry to the point of sickness. What he doesn't find in religion Richard seeks elsewhere, and his ''hunger'' for something beyond mere food becomes a dominant motif throughout *Black Boy*. Of course, real, painful physical hunger haunts Richard at every turn, and six-year-old Richard's innocent thought—''Why could I not eat when I was hungry?''—lingers as an unanswered question throughout his narrative. Wright clearly wants the reader of *Black Boy* to *feel* Richard's ''biting hunger, hunger that made my body aimlessly restless, hunger that kept me on edge,'' and to ask ''why?'' along with him. Physical hunger also causes considerable psychic suffering in Richard's life, as a sign of punishment at the orphanage, as a symbol of his father's desertion, and as a barrier between him and friends at school. But Richard also depicts ways in which deeper longings, more significant to him than physical need, define his experience of life.

At times these longings point to something healthy and positive in Richard's character, as when he senses ''a new hunger'' before he leaves the South for Chicago. This hunger inspires Richard's strong sense of self-reliance, his unwillingness to betray his deepest feelings, and his refusal to ''surrender to what seemed wrong.'' But Richard also describes the longing he feels as hurtful and damaging to his personality. ''Again and again,'' he writes, ''I vowed that someday I would end this hunger of mine, this apartness, this eternal difference.'' Here and elsewhere Richard's hunger becomes a symbol not of his positive yearning but of his isolation and loneliness, his sense of exclusion from the world around him.

Richard doesn't always understand his sense of ''eternal difference'' from those around him, and clearly his temperament, his learning, and his willful separation from community institutions such as the church all play a part in his ''apartness.'' But as he grows up, Richard increasingly sees that the racist environment of the South creates and sustains

> **In a racist society that wants him to be content with his spiritual as well as his physical hunger, Richard finally finds 'vague glimpses of life's possibilities' only in literacy, reading, and writing.''**

his feeling of exclusion. Richard's attitudes toward white people begin to form early on, when, for example, he watches from the kitchen as a white family eats from a ''loaded table'' while he and his brother wait for whatever food is leftover. Though at the time he feels only ''vaguely angry'' and decidedly hungry, such experiences eventually convince Richard that ''white folks'' are in some way responsible for his exclusion from literacy and education, from knowledge of the wider world, from justice and equality, from possibilities in life, even from meaningful relationships with other people. In his fight with Harrison, Richard realizes that the power of white people to limit his life even extends to his relationships with his black peers. He fights Harrison against his will, beating up another oppressed ''black boy''—and himself—because he cannot express his shame, anger, and hatred directly to the white men responsible for his feelings.

In a racist society that wants him to be content with his spiritual as well as his physical hunger, Richard finally finds ''vague glimpses of life's possibilities'' only in literacy, reading, and writing. He realizes at a young age that in order to lay bare the secrets of the world around him, he must understand ''the baffling black print'' that he sees in the school children's books. When he does learn to read, Richard uses his ability to probe into ''every happening in the neighborhood,'' and this includes the realities of racial prejudice and hatred. When he hears that ''a 'black' boy had been severely beaten by a 'white' man,'' he interrogates his mother about the difference between ''black'' and ''white,'' words whose full significance he cannot yet grasp. At the same time, reading stories of ''outlandish exploits of outlandish men in faraway, outlandish cities'' gives Richard access to an imaginary world beyond his own. When he is older, Richard's reading opens his eyes to ''new ways of looking and seeing'' that "made the look of the world different" and let him imagine his life under different circumstances. Richard eventually recognizes that the social system of the South strives to keep black Americans from just such ways of thinking. Thus, Richard must lie about being able to read in order to check out books with a white man's library card, and he carries his new-found knowledge with him like "a secret, criminal burden." In the end, Richard's reading and his writing do not merely open his eyes to the realities of his life in the South but also create "a vast sense of distance" between him and that world, motivating him to leave it forever.

Wright's record of his experiences after his move to the North did not appear in the initial publication of *Black Boy*, though it was part of his original manuscript. (In order to see his work published by the Book of the Month Club, Wright had to agree to print a shortened version that concludes with his flight from the South.) What Richard finds in Chicago is not, by any means, an environment free from the racism of the South but rather a more "perplexing" situation in certain ways. Wright discovers that while whites and blacks in the North may view each other as merely "part of the city landscape," this nonchalance only masks a great "psychological distance" between the races. Many of the themes he develops in the first part of his narrative reemerge in the latter part, including his feelings of emotional isolation from other people, his sense of the psychological damage caused by race—prejudice and hatred, and his hunger for knowledge and understanding of the world and of himself. But more importantly, just as reading and writing alone offer Richard both a source information about his environment and a means of escape from it, Wright seeks meaning and purpose in the North by way of books and the pen. He concludes his original version of *Black Boy*, significantly, not with the resolution of his deep hungers or the healing of his psychic wounds but with a vow to write—to "look squarely" at his life, to "build a bridge of words" between him and the world, to "hurl words into this darkness" that surrounds him. This, in a sense, is what Wright does in *Black Boy*, creating from words a "Record of Childhood and Youth" that speaks to all readers of that which is "inexpressibly human," "the hunger for life that gnaws in us all."

Source: Anthony Dykema-VanderArk, Critical Essay on *Black Boy*, in *Nonfiction Classics for Students,* The Gale Group, 2001.

William L. Andrews

In the following essay, Andrews examines Black Boy *within the context of African-American autobiography, comparing it with W. E. B. Du Bois's* Dusk of Dawn *and other notable works.*

To tell the whole truth in the name of complete honesty or to conceal part of the truth out of deference to white readers' sensibilities—this dilemma and the anxiety it spawned have haunted African-American autobiography since its beginnings. The earliest black American autobiographers frequently commented on their unique dilemma: speak forthrightly and be thought a liar or censor oneself in the hope of being believed. Antebellum slave narrators introduced what Robert Stepto has called "distrust of the reader" into African-American autobiographical discourse by admitting, in the classic formulation of Harriet Jacobs, "I have not exaggerated the wrongs inflicted by Slavery; on the contrary, my descriptions fall far short of the facts." By assuring her white reader that she has not told the whole truth, Jacobs paradoxically seeks to confirm the first and most important statement she makes in her autobiography: "Reader, be assured this narrative is no fiction."

One way to chart the development of African-American autobiography is to track the gradual replacement of a discourse of distrust and self-restraint that relies on white-authored prefaces and appendices to authenticate and authorize black writing by a discourse that avows frank self-expression as a sign of authenticity and independent self-authorization. We know, of course, that much nineteenth-century black autobiography was structured and to some extent governed by internal rhetorical strategies and external documents designed to confirm the sincerity (i.e., the genuineness and good character) of the narrator and the sincerity (i.e., the truthfulness) of her or his story. What is not so well understood, perhaps, is the role that discourses of sincerity and autobiographical acts of authentication have played in the evolution of black-American autobiography into the modern era. My purpose is to situate Richard Wright's *Black Boy (American Hunger)* in the context of African-American autobiography's long-standing concern with sincerity and authenticity in order to show how *Black Boy (American Hunger)* redefined these crucial parameters and thus signaled the arrival of a new kind of discourse in the history of black autobiography in the United States.

A young African-American girl drinks at a colored drinking fountain

Most antebellum slave narrators were sufficiently distrustful of, or deferential to, the sensibilities of whites that they and/or the whites who introduced their texts felt obliged to assure their readers that credibility, not self-expression, was their watchword in narrating their stories. Frederick Douglass's 1845 *Narrative* carries a preface by William Lloyd Garrison, promising the reader that while "essentially true in all its statements," Douglass's story "comes short of the reality, rather than overstate a single fact in regard to SLAVERY AS IT IS." Douglass also understood how useful the discourse of sincerity could be, as is clear when he professed not to care whether some might consider him egotistical in judging his boyhood removal to Baltimore "a special interposition of divine Providence in my favor." "I prefer to be true to myself, even at the hazard of incurring the ridicule of others, rather than to be false, and incur my own abhorrence," Douglass claimed. Yet in stating that he cared less about the ridicule of others than about telling the truth, Douglass indirectly promised that his reader could believe him because he had openly declared his dedication to truth, regardless of whether it placed him in a less than admirable light. By stating that he would rather be true than credible, Douglass subtly bears witness to how seriously he takes his own credibility. Only a writer who wants

very much to be believed will claim to be more sincerely dedicated to truth than to credibility. A further indication of Douglass's espousal of the discourse of sincerity comes up in the appendix to his *Narrative,* where he announces that, despite all appearances to the contrary in his autobiography, he is not "an opponent of all religion." He wants his reader to understand that he means to denounce only "the hypocritical Christianity of this land" so that it will not be confused with "the pure, peaceable, and impartial Christianity of Christ," which "I love." In this instance Douglass is sufficiently worried about white "misapprehensions" of his religious views that he feels obliged to declare himself a sincere Christian so that the hard truths he has told will not be dismissed by those whom he believes are still capable of moral reform.

During the crisis decade of the 1850s, occasionally a black autobiographer, most notably Harriet Jacobs, would hint at or complain of the tension between a sense of obligation to self and to the white reader's expectations. This attempt to be honest about what it meant not to be fully honest in telling one's story was fairly short-lived, however. Post-Reconstruction autobiographies such as the *Life and Times of Frederick Douglass* (1881), John Mercer Langston's *From the Virginia Plantation to the*

> "The hallmark of Wright's personal authenticity in *Black Boy* is not his refusal to conform to social demands; rather, it is his constitutional *inability* to conform though he is told repeatedly by blacks and whites who he is to be and how he is to act in order to get along."

National Capitol (1894), and Booker T. Washington's *Up from Slavery* (1901) had nothing to say about the question of sincerity versus credibility in black-American autobiography. By implication, this postbellum breed of successful, progressive black autobiographer had little difficulty following Polonius's advice to Hamlet: "to thine own self be true / And it doth follow, as the night the day, / Thou canst not then be false to any man." In these lines, which represent the epitome of the traditional idea of sincerity according to Lionel Trilling, we learn that truth to self naturally and inevitably leads one to do right by everyone else, an idea that Washington espoused in *Up from Slavery* not only for himself but for all progressive-minded people, black and white. Like Washington, the most famous turn-of-the-century black autobiographers represented themselves as so much in agreement with what white Americans already believed that the old anxieties about truth to self versus believability to others seemed no longer an issue.

With the rise of the so-called "New Negro" in the 1920s, the problem of self-expressiveness versus self-restraint returned to center stage in the well-known battles that black artists and intellectuals fought over what blacks should write about in general and how they should represent themselves in particular. To those, white as well as black, who prescribed any agenda, any standard of discrimination and value other than that emanating from within the artist, Langston Hughes retorted defiantly: "We younger Negro artists who create now intend to express our individual dark-skinned selves without fear or shame." Despite his black critics'

shame or his white critics' fears, Hughes defended himself and his frankly "racial" jazz poetry by stating: "I am sincere as I know how to be in these poems." Hughes's New Negro supporters, such as Wallace Thurman and Claude McKay, championed a similar creed of artistic sincerity that granted any black writer the right, in effect, to call them as he saw them as long as he did not pander blatantly to white prejudices.

Yet while New Negro critics egged on their fellow novelists, dramatists, and poets toward greater self-expressiveness, the question of how much an autobiographer should feel free to expose about himself or herself or about the relationships of actual blacks and whites in the recent past or immediate present did not get much attention. In part this is attributable to the fact that few critics in the 1920s, black or white, are likely to have thought of autobiography at all when they considered the kinds of African-American literary "art" that needed policing or protecting. The New Negro era was a time of comparatively few noteworthy autobiographies. Those that did get a hearing were mostly by men of traditional values and outlook: successful members of the black clergy, such as Bishop William Henry Heard, author of *From Slavery to the Bishopric in the A. M. E. Church* (1924), or protégés of Washington, such as Robert Russa Moton, whose *Finding a Way Out* (1920) preached the message of the great Tuskegeean in a manner calculated to leave an image of the African-American leader as a man of "unemotional business-like self-control."

During the 1920s almost all the literary New Negroes were too busy working in the more traditional belletristic genres to take the time to write personal reminiscences. One significant exception, William Pickens, who published his autobiography, *Bursting Bonds,* in the same year as *Cane,* evoked the familiar parameters of nineteenth-century narrative when he stated in his preface: "If I am frank, it is only to be true." For Pickens, though very much the New Negro with the New Negro's determination to speak his mind, the traditional Shakespearian formulation of sincerity was still applicable: frankness about oneself was a necessary condition to telling white people the truth. Frankness was in fact the sign of truthfulness rather than, as it had often seemed to whites reading blacks, a warning flag that something unpleasantly "bitter" was about to come up. Nevertheless, even Pickens acknowledged that aspects of his experience as a New Negro in the South would defy his white reader's credibility. Thus, when recounting a year he spent in east Texas just before the outbreak of World War I, Pickens prefaced his remarks by stating that he would "not strain credulity too far by endeavoring to tell the whole truth" about the "savage treatment of colored people in this section of the civilized world," but would instead "relate only some of the believable things."

Some white readers of the 1920s, particularly the more "liberal" and trendy of the white literati, seem to have been prompted by the cult of primitivism to embrace and indeed assume that black personal narratives would bare the soul of their authors. Muriel Draper's introduction to Taylor Gordon's *Born to Be* (1929) promised the white reader that this celebrated black entertainer had composed his story "with rare candor," attributable, she suggests, to his inherent "honesty, humor and complete freedom from vulgarity" as well as to his lack of both "racial self-consciousness" and "literary self-consciousness." In Draper's assessment of Gordon, we find a curious resolution of the conflict between candor and truthfulness: only let the black autobiographer be "unfettered" from consciousness of himself as a black person writing, and the result will be a prodigy at liberty simply to be himself, which in fact, Draper implies, is what this Negro was "born to be." Draper's notion that an identification of selfhood with race must inhibit a black autobiographer's ability to speak fully and fairly gives us an early instance of a presumption invoked by many white critics during the first half of the twentieth century: namely, that if blacks would start writing as "people" rather than as Negroes, their (white) readers would find them more interesting and more believable. Ironically, however, in his foreword to Draper's introduction to Taylor Gordon's autobiography, Carl Van Vechten could not help raising doubts about Draper's reading of Gordon as an unself-conscious, freely expressive black autobiographer. Van Vechten applauded Gordon for his writing especially "frankly" about blacks, but of Gordon's recollections of his dealings with whites Van Vechten warned: "constantly you suspect him of concealing the most monstrous facts." Thus even the "new kind of personality" that Van Vechten saw in this remarkable New Negro could not be fully trusted. Van Vechten could not believe that the traditional mask of the black autobiographer had been abandoned.

The decade and a half after the New Negro Renaissance saw the publication of a number of important autobiographies by James Weldon Johnson (*Along This Way,* 1933), Claude McKay (*A Long Way from Home,* 1937), Angelo Herndon (*Let Me Live,* 1937), Mary Church Terrell (*A Colored Woman in a White World,* 1940), Langston Hughes (*The Big Sea,* 1940), W. E. B. Du Bois (*Dusk of Dawn,* 1940), Zora Neale Hurston (*Dust Tracks on a Road,* 1942), J. Saunders Redding (*No Day of Triumph,* 1942), and of course, Richard Wright (*Black Boy,* 1945). Significantly, only four of these autobiographies—Terrell's, Du Bois's, Redding's, and Wright's—have prefaces at all. Those by Johnson, McKay, Herndon, Hughes, and Hurston enter directly into the narration without so much as a hint of whether their authors have negotiated or simply ignored the old problem of self-expressiveness versus self-restraint. One might think from reading the majority of these remarkable life stories that the old problem had been rendered passé by virtue of the liberation of consciousness and expression enacted by the New Negro Renaissance. Only Terrell harked back to the hesitancy of the past when she introduced her life story with the caveat: "In relating the story of my life I shall simply tell the truth and nothing but the truth—but not the whole truth, for that would be impossible. And even if I tried to tell the whole truth few people would believe me." In the "apology" that prefaces *Dusk of Dawn* Du Bois depreciated what he called "mere autobiography," but he did not attribute to black autobiography the "reticences, repressions and distortions which come because men do not dare to be absolutely frank." He implied instead that selective truthfulness and lack of candor were inherent in autobiography as a form, regardless of the ethnicity of the author. For Du Bois, the solution to this problem lay in writing the sort of narrative that transcended personality altogether. His autobiography would subsume the whole vexed question of the individual's obligation to the truth under a larger, historically verifiable rubric: the Truth of a race's experience. Hence the subtitle of *Dusk of Dawn* is *An Essay toward an Autobiography of a Race Concept.* By making himself a spokesman and exemplar of a supposedly desubjectivized Truth of history rather than of the self, Du Bois tried, in effect, to claim for his autobiography the ultimate sincerity of which he felt himself and his form capable: the sincerity of the historian-sociologist impartially dedicated to recovering the Truth of his era.

Du Bois's bid for ultimate sincerity did not, however, turn the tradition of African-American autobiography in a new direction with regard to the relationship of narrator, narratee, and narrative. Most of Du Bois's contemporaries in black autobiography in the 1930s and '40s showed little interest in modeling themselves on any historically verifiable idea of representativeness or typicalness. Instead of this traditional, nineteenth-century way of conceiving selfhood, the likes of Hurston, Hughes, McKay, and Redding argue that they were sufficiently different—that is, temperamentally resistant to the models of their predecessors and atypical of their peers as well—that they could appeal to nothing more valid than the example of their own individuality as a standard for judging the credibility of what they said about themselves.

In *Dust Tracks on a Road,* for instance, Hurston describes herself as having felt impelled from her earliest school days "to talk back at established authority." Yet even Hurston admitted that she concealed her "feeling of difference from my fellow men" out of fear that telling the truth about what she saw and felt would bring her ridicule as well as the reputation of being "a story-teller": that is, a liar. Similarly, when McKay recalled his decision not to follow the example of William Stanley Braithwaite, the most successful African-American poet of his time, the West Indian claimed with pride that his own poetic expression was "too subjective, personal and tell-tale" to suit the expectations of traditionalists. Yet McKay, in the spirit of Hurston, confessed later in *A Long Way from Home* that there had been limits to his often-professed creed of full romantic self-expression. He had deliberately omitted "If We Must Die," a poem of revolutionary candor, from his first widely read volume of poetry, *Spring in New Hampshire* (1920), and it had taken a white man, Frank Harris, to sting him into full recognition of the sort of betrayal this act of self-censorship had entailed. Harris had called McKay "a traitor to [his] race" for implicitly disavowing "If We Must Die." But, wrote McKay in his autobiography, "I felt worse for being a traitor to myself. For if a man is not faithful to his own individuality, he cannot be loyal to anything."

In this statement, McKay iterates once again the sentiments of Shakespeare's Polonius, affirming the long-standing Euro-American ideal of sincerity as a truth to, and of, self that ensures inevitably a communal bond of right dealing with the other. As I have tried to show, Douglass, Washington, Pickens, and Du Bois gave McKay ample precedent for believing that a black autobiographer could find a way to reconcile truth to self with a credible, socially constructive relationship to the white reader. On the other hand, as I have also tried to illustrate, from Jacobs to Hurston to Terrell,

important African-American women autobiographers called attention to the gender-specific problems that arose whenever a black woman tried to speak frankly in order to expand her white reader's horizon of belief with regard to the realities of the color line. I do not want to make too much of this gendered distinction in African-American autobiography; one could easily point to black women autobiographers who do not allude in any way to the problem of sincerity as I have tried to outline it here, for instance. What is more significant for the history of this tradition is the way that Richard Wright in *Black Boy (American Hunger)* tried to dispose of the whole question of whether or at what cost a black autobiographer could or should adopt the discourse of sincerity in addressing whites.

In her "Introductory Note" recommending the 1945 edition of *Black Boy* to all "morally responsible Americans," Dorothy Canfield Fisher characterizes with only three adjectives Wright's "story of a Negro childhood and youth." Fisher labels the story "honest," "dreadful," and "heart-breaking." Like many white liberals before her, Fisher was proud to put her name on the line in testimony to a black autobiographer's honesty. But refusing to claim more for *Black Boy* than that it was "dreadful" and "heart-breaking" and in particular refusing to speak of how the book could enlighten the reader or help to change the social order—this failure, in other words, to attest to any desire in Wright to have an ameliorative effect on the world that his autobiography describes constitutes a significant change in the purpose to which prefaces by whites had been traditionally put in the tradition of black American autobiography. In this sense, Fisher's preface hints at a move away from sincerity in Wright's discourse and toward a new kind of self-authentication.

We find Wright articulating this new standard of selfhood most explicitly in chapter 9 of his autobiography, wherein he discusses his last months in Jackson, Mississippi, before he left for Memphis at the age of seventeen. The aloof, defensive, and yet unyielding teenager who refused to give in to his principal over the content of his ninth-grade valedictory speech has to begin his first sustained dealings with whites in order to get a job. He plays the part of black supplicant so awkwardly that his friend Griggs takes him aside to explain the rules of the game. "Dick, look, you're black, black, *black,* see? . . . You act around white people as if you didn't know that they were white. And they *see* it." Wright retorts, "I can't be a slave." But Griggs reminds him, "[Y]ou've got to eat." Therefore, he continues, "When you're in front of white people, *think* before you act, *think* before you speak. Your way of doing things is all right among *our* people, but not for *white* people." Wright's response to this advice has often been quoted by scholars as a key to the mind of the man.

> What Griggs was saying was true, but it was simply utterly impossible for me to calculate, to scheme, to act, to plot all the time. I would remember to dissemble for short periods, then I would forget and act straight and human again, not with the desire to harm anybody, but merely forgetting the artificial status of race and class. It was the same with whites as with blacks; it was my way with everybody.

Wright's "way," put simply, was that of personal authenticity, not sincerity. From Douglass forward, the way of sincerity required representing oneself in such a way as to try quite deliberately not to offend whites but rather to try to show them how sincere discourse from a black autobiographer could give the white reader a truth that would set him or her free. Autobiographers like Jacobs foregrounded the calculatedness, the insincerity, of adopting a discourse of sincerity in African-American autobiography, but neither Jacobs nor Hurston nor any other black autobiographer before Wright would claim that he or she simply could not adopt that autobiographical act even though it seemed the only way to keep from alienating whites predisposed to be distrustful. What Wright suggests in his analysis of his inability to conform to Griggs's advice is that by the time he was ready to go out on his own, he was constitutionally incapable of being anyone or anything other than himself. He was, and could not help but be, authentically and inescapably himself, regardless of whom he was around, regardless of what would seem to be in his best interest or anyone else's.

The hallmark of Wright's personal authenticity in *Black Boy* is not his refusal to conform to social demands; rather, it is his constitutional *inability* to conform though he is told repeatedly by blacks and whites who he is to be and how he is to act in order to get along. The more people, black as well as white, judge him strange, intractable, offensive, and threatening, the more Wright encourages his reader to conclude that he was the only truly authentic person in the oppressive world in which he grew up. Every time the black boy is told to shut up or is slapped on the mouth, every time he shocks someone with his writing or is punished by someone in power for refusing to censor himself, Wright, in effect, authenticates himself as the quintessentially authentic

modern writer, devoted absolutely to expression of self, indifferent to any external standard, especially that of pleasing or improving the reader. Instead of arguing that being true to himself was for the good of others and indeed made community possible, the usual justification of the discourse of sincerity, Wright's autobiography shows how truth to the self led to ruptures with every community the black writer tried to join.

Cast out by southern blacks and northern whites, hated by Dixie rednecks and Yankee reds, Wright turns his alienation from community into a badge of his intellectual and ultimately his artistic integrity. To identify himself as the supremely authentic man, he must render the entirety of society, black as well as white, profoundly inauthentic, pervasively false. This tactic, it seems to me, is why from the outset of *Black Boy (American Hunger)* Wright is at such pains to condemn the black southern community, to deny that black people even had a community or had the capacity for community, as is evidenced in his famous denunciation of "the cultural barrenness of black life" and his complaints about "how lacking we were in those intangible sentiments that bind man to man." Individual authenticity is not measured in the modern era by the degree to which the social order recognizes and endows one with authenticity but by the extent to which one can claim to have asserted one's self in direct opposition to that which the social order recognizes and respects. Thus from his struggles with the Seventh-Day Adventists through his disillusionment with the Communist Party, Wright fashions an image of himself as uniquely and authentically "human" by showing how every community had failed him, how "my country had shown me no examples of how to live a human life," how in the end he would have to go on alone with nothing but his inner "hunger for life" to guide him.

The discourse of authenticity pioneered in Wright's autobiography introduced a new mode of authentication for African-American autobiography in the post-World-War-II era. Not until the 1960s, however, did Wright's call provoke a response in the writings of an unprecedentedly bold group of black autobiographers who not only regarded autobiography as an important means of telling white America the truth about itself but also portrayed themselves as messengers unmuzzled by past forms of racial etiquette, as tribunes whose militant dedication to telling it like it is constituted vocal confirmation of the authority and authenticity of the selfhood they claimed. Eldridge Cleaver's opening proclamation in *Soul on Ice* (1968) about the necessity of "speaking frankly and directly" about the most volatile of personal topics—such as the attraction and repulsion of black men for white women—was designed to demonstrate the black man's commitment to "individuality" and the "salvation" of his manhood, two hallmarks of authenticity in Wright's autobiography. One of the central themes of *Coming of Age in Mississippi* (1968) is Anne Moody's accelerating alienation from family in general and her mother's expectations in particular because of an awakening of "discontent" and "rebelliousness" that cause her to behave "as if I should please myself doing whatever pleased me." Others in her family may be able to stifle their sense of oppression, but as Moody comes of age, she takes pride in her inability to suppress her "discontent" with the status quo. "It had always been there. Sometimes I used to try to suppress it and it didn't show. Now it showed all the time." Autobiographical writings of the 1960s by people like Cleaver and Moody testify to a process of self-discovery very much reminiscent of Wright's search for personal authenticity, except that in the 1960s the expression of such authenticity often finds its fulfillment in a sociopolitical radicalization about which Wright at the end of his autobiography seems distinctly ambivalent. While personal authenticity and radical politics dovetail in many "revolutionary" black autobiographies of the 1960s, in the Wright model the authentic man is cast out by his fellow radicals for being, in effect, too radically committed to telling everyone (even the radicals) the truth as he sees it. In considering this difference between Wright and his 1960s successors, one should remember that the second half of Wright's autobiography *(American Hunger)*, which records the author's disillusionment with radical politics, did not get into print until 1977, well after the heyday of the militant black autobiographer of the 1960s.

On the verge of his death in 1963, Du Bois, the archradical among twentieth-century African-American intellectuals, would not deceive himself or his reader with the claim of having achieved full truthfulness in his final *Autobiography* (1968). The author of *Dusk of Dawn* still thought autobiography was "always incomplete, and often unreliable." His last book, therefore, would be at best "the Soliloquy of an old man on what he dreams his life has been as he sees it slowly drifting away; and what he would like others to believe." But Du Bois's skepticism about what a black autobiographer, even with the most authentic of intentions, could say did

not cause the readers of *The Autobiography of Malcolm X* (1965) to doubt Malcolm when he insisted, "I'm telling it like it *is!*." A man who went through as many name changes and revisions of identity and political persuasions as had Malcolm had great need of the discourse of authentication, which he invoked without qualification throughout his autobiography in such statements as, "You *never* have to worry about me biting my tongue if something I know as truth is on my mind. Raw, naked truth exchanged between the black man and the white man is what a whole lot more of is needed in this country." Even more explicitly than Wright, Malcolm predicates his authenticity as a black man on the fear he instills in whites every time he tells them the "raw, naked truth" about the racial scene in the United States. Those he labels contemptuously as "ultra-proper-talking Negroes" betray their racial inauthenticity, their lack of genuine solidarity with black people, in every word of integrationist reconciliation they utter. Only by working separately toward the eradication of racism and defeatism in their separate racial groups, Malcolm concludes in the last chapter of his autobiography, can "sincere white people and sincere black people . . . show a road to the salvation of America's very soul." The implication of Malcolm's words is that only authentic black and white people have a chance to become sincerely socially redemptive. While the pursuit of integration would abet more role playing and pretense, racial separatism dedicated toward a common antiracist goal could foster an unprecedented "mutual sincerity" between the races. In light of Polonius's classic formulation of sincerity, Malcolm might be read as applying Polonius's advice to a racial group, rather than an individual self, and promising that truth to one's race is the only way to guarantee an end to falseness to those of any other race.

The Autobiography of Malcolm X is one of the last African-American autobiographies to be introduced by a white person, in this case the journalist M. S. Handler, who, very much in the spirit of such introductions, represents Malcolm among the ranks of those "remarkable men who pulled themselves to the summit by their bootstraps" and championed "Negroes as an integral part of the American community." Such a testimonial, with its concluding image of Malcolm as a disillusioned separatist and a protointegrationist, calls attention to a crucial disjunction between Handler's notion of what ultimately qualified Malcolm as a sincere black writer (a perception of Malcolm's emerging acceptance of integration) and what Malcolm himself implied was the basis of a black writer's sincerity (his rejection of integration as inevitably inauthentic and self-abnegating). Like abolitionist introducers and reviewers of slave narratives, Handler betrays a lingering desire to measure a black autobiographer's sincerity according to the palatability of his or her politics and personal style; hence Handler attempts to rehabilitate Malcolm X by promising that the private Malcolm of the autobiography had outgrown the "diabolic dialectic" of his public persona and was moving toward a more revealing and less polarizing style of self-representation. Maybe Handler's well-meaning but unthinking recapitulation of the traditional role of the white introducer as "handler" in effect, as manager and manipulator of first impressions, as character reference for the sincerity of the black autobiographer—especially when contrasted with Malcolm's own powerful rhetoric of self-authentication—crystallized in an unprecedented and unmistakable way the problematic function of the white introducer and his or her discourse of sincerity. In any event, after *The Autobiography of Malcolm X,* the few whites who were asked to introduce African-American autobiographies made little attempt to adduce the sincerity of the autobiographer in question. Instead these introductions, usually written by academics, concentrate on matters of authenticity relating to the text (not the autobiographer), such as how the text came into being, how it has been edited, and what its value is to a reliable understanding of literary, cultural, or social history.

In surveying the evolution of discourses of sincerity and authenticity in African-American autobiography, we need to be careful in gauging the impact of Wright's mode of self-authentication on black autobiography of the last forty years. Wright was virtually unique in predicating authenticity on the alienation of the individual from any community, black as well as white. When we celebrate Wright's contribution to African-American autobiography, we should remember that his myth of the individual could not have given us narratives of self-discovery through, rather than in spite of, community, narratives such as Maya Angelou's *I Know Why the Caged Bird Sings* (1969), Ned Cobb's *All God's Dangers* (1974), or John Wideman's *Brothers and Keepers* (1984). Wright's example of personal authenticity was sufficiently magnetic to draw the pendulum of tradition toward the polar opposition he represented, but his significance may ultimately depend more on the force that he exerted on the pendulum's swing than on the arc it has followed since his death.

If recent African-American autobiographers have felt little need to authenticate themselves in Wright's manner, the fact that they (and their publishers) have felt little need of an introducer (white or black) to testify to their sincerity or credibility may evince sufficiently their debt to Wright's conviction that an African-American autobiography could be, and had to be, self-authenticating in every sense of the term. Nowadays it is not impossible to find an African-American autobiographer invoking the old conventions of sincerity and authentication, but when such discourse turns up, as in Itabari Njeri's *Every Good-Bye Ain't Gone* (1990), we ought not be surprised to see the terms of that discourse ironically exploited. "What follows on these pages," Njeri writes in her preface to her autobiography, "began as a novel and ends up the literal truth; many might not have believed the portrayals otherwise. . . . But the characters in my family only seem made up. At times both comical and tragic, they *have* been too large for life." In acknowledging that her African-American reality may seem "too large for life" and hence for life story as well as too incredible for fiction, Njeri takes her reader back to Jacobs's dilemma in which neither telling "the literal truth" nor resorting to the subterfuge of fiction could satisfy a black woman autobiographer's need to be read as sincere and credible. Like Jacobs, Njeri wants her reader to "be assured this narrative is no fiction," but the changing status of the discourses of sincerity and authenticity enables Njeri to escape Jacobs's trap, the trap of promising to be credible by not telling the whole truth. Njeri has come to realize that fiction, for so long the bogeyman of the black autobiographer, the presumed refuge of the insincere black narrator, need not be a diversion from the truth, but may serve as the means to her ultimate autobiographical end, the telling of "literal truth."

Since this is so, Njeri need not try to prove her sincerity or demonstrate her credibility by rejecting fiction or by subscribing to the simple oppositions of fact versus fiction, authenticity versus credibility that have bedeviled African-American autobiographers for so long. Njeri can simply point out that her attempt to encompass her African-American reality in fiction brought her to the outer boundaries of probability. To break through those limits she had to make a commitment to a radical concept of autobiography. She had to reject the anxieties of African-American autobiographers who felt that their form, more than anything else, had to read credibly in order for them to be regarded as sincere. Once Njeri realized that the only way to *seem* sincere or credible was to write "the literal truth" of autobiography, acknowledging that such truth was almost inevitably "too large for life," she had in effect got the monkey of sincerity off her back and thrust it into her reader's lap. Is her reader prepared to accept autobiography as the closest thing to an adequate means of reconstructing a personal and family history inherently "too large" for the house of fiction or any other narrative model except autobiography itself? If so, then we as readers can join Njeri as autobiographer and put anxieties about sincerity and authenticity far enough behind us when we read texts like *Every Good-Bye Ain't Gone* so as to confront African-American life first and fully before trying to decide how to accommodate our sense of truth to it.

Source: William L. Andrews, "Richard Wright and the African-American Autobiography Tradition," in *Style,* Vol. 27, No. 2, Summer 1993, pp. 271–82.

Jay Mechling

In the following essay, Mechling examines how Wright both uses folklore and exposes its limitations in Black Boy.

We are so accustomed to talking and writing about folklore as a human strength, as a personal and community resource for enduring, connecting, and celebrating, that we sometimes overlook those instances when folklore fails. Perhaps it is the streak of romanticism in folklorists that leads them to celebrate humanity and folklore. Perhaps it is the functional bias of most folklore theories that leads to the expectation that traditions persisting across generations must be working somehow. Whatever the cause, our elation at the successes of folklore can use a sobering antidote now and then, for in examining the failures of folklore, we might be able to see dynamics and processes invisible to us when folklore succeeds.

Richard Wright's *Black Boy* (1945), the first of his two autobiographical volumes, provides the folklorist with an elaborate, fixed text for exploring some of the ways folklore can fail the individual. My aim in this essay is to approach this text with the usual stock of the folklorist's questions about folklore in literature and then to pose the questions not often asked: how does folklore fail the protagonist of this autobiography, and why does this failure occur? I believe the answers to these queries draw our attention to the double bind as a structural

instrument of cultural hegemony. Understanding the double bind and the limitations of folklore as a resource for resisting the double bind will teach us something about the workings of folklore as a communications strategy.

Black Boy tells the story of Wright's growing up in the segregationist American South of the early 20th century, from his earliest memories (age four, in 1912) to his decision at age 19 (1927) to flee north (as the closing sentence of the book explains),

> full of a hazy notion that life could be lived with dignity, that the personalities of others should not be violated, that men should be able to confront other men without fear or shame, and that if men were lucky in their living on earth they might win some redeeming meaning for their having struggled and suffered here beneath the stars.

In between, Wright chronicles an unstable life, including his abusive father's desertion, his mother's stoic pragmatism and wrenching death, his upbringing with an assortment of relatives, his discovery of the power of words in books, his troubles with white teachers and employers, the consequences of transgressing the society structured by Jim Crow laws, and more. *Black Boy* resembles Wright's fiction in its realism, in its unflinching portrayal of the numbing violence, brutality, cruelty, and deprivation (especially hunger, a reigning trope in the book) Wright experienced in his youth.

The present moment in both literary criticism and interpretive anthropology reminds us that all narrative texts are "fictions" and that many fictions have ethnographic insight. Although there is plenty of truth in *Black Boy,* there is also plenty of evidence that Wright fashioned a fictionalized biography, an artistic memory for his own purposes. Even so, a fictionalized autobiography by Wright serves our purpose here. Richard Dorson (1957) and Alan Dundes (1965) laid out the initial terms for the conversation about the relationships between folklore and literature, and since then, folklorists and literary critics pretty much have worked out the practice of the paradigm. We know that demonstrating folklore in American literature, for example, should consist of more than mere lists of items or motifs; that we must look to the details of the artist's uses of the folk texts in context; and that in the finest examples of literature, the author uses folklore not merely for familiarity's sake but also for clear, artistic purposes that advance the fictive world created in the story.

The traditional approach to folklore in *Black Boy* discovers soon enough a wealth of items and genres. At times, Wright's book reads like a folklorist's ethnography. In a letter advising his friend Joe C. Brown to record the black idiom of the South, Wright wrote:

> I wonder if you are not walking each day pass [*sic*] some damn good stuff. I heard a record recently called the Dirty Dozens. It consisted of a recital of the little jingles with which you and I heard in our childhood set to boogie woogie music; the dumb folks around New York are eating it up. Boy, why don't you take pencil and paper and hang around the black boys and put on paper what they say, their tall tales, their words, their folk tales, their songs, their jokes? That stuff is some of the best real stuff this country has produced. . . . The life of the Negro in America is right where you are, on the black lips of men, women, and children.

Wright followed his own advice. *Black Boy* devotes two pages to a catalog of folk beliefs he learned as a child, listed in parallel construction:

> If I pulled a hair from a horse's tail and sealed it in a jar of my own urine, the hair would turn overnight into a snake.
>
> If I passed a Catholic sister or mother dressed in black and smiled and allowed her to see my teeth, I would surely die.
>
> If I walked under a leaning ladder, I would certainly have bad luck.
>
> If I kissed my elbow, I would certainly turn into a girl.

And so on. He tells of six taunts he recalls using with his seven- to nine-year-old friends to torment the Jewish owner of the small grocery store in the small Mississippi town where he lived, taunts such as

> Jew, Jew,
> Two for five
> That's what keeps
> Jews alive.
>
> and
>
> Bloody Christ killers
> Never trust a Jew
> Bloody Christ killers
> What won't a Jew do?

A little older, Wright hangs out with a group of boys and learns from them the lessons of "the talk of black boys who met at the crossroads." Again, he offers something like an ethnography of the black boys' folk group, including their verbal dueling, riddle-jokes, games, and parodies of Sunday school hymns and stories. "And the talk," observes Wright,

> would weave, roll, surge, spurt, veer, swell, having no specific aim or direction, touching vast areas of life, expressing the tentative impulses of childhood. . . . The culture of one black household was thus transmitted to another black household, and folk tradition was handed from group to group. Our attitudes were made,

> **Whereas language works *within* a folk community and learning the language games may be an important element in socialization of members of the community, *those same language games may fail in the intellectual encounter.*"**

defined, set, or corrected; our ideas were discovered, discarded, enlarged, torn apart, and accepted.

One evening Wright hears a legend that has a powerful impact on him, a legend about a black woman who, given permission by the four white men who killed her husband to take her husband's body for burial, used a shotgun hidden in the burial sheets to shoot dead her husband's murderers. "I did not know if the story was factually true or not, but it was emotionally true," recalls Wright, "because I had already grown to feel that there existed men against whom I was powerless, men who could violate my life at will. I resolved that I would emulate the black woman if I were ever faced with a white mob. . . . The story of the woman's deception gave form and meaning to confused defensive feelings that had long been sleeping in me." Wright clearly understands the expressive and instrumental functions of this talk, showing how he and the boys used the verbal dueling and stories to construct and sustain meanings in their lives as young black men in the South.

But Wright's autobiography has the structure and texture of a folklore performance far beyond the mere inventory of genres. On one level, *Black Boy* shares with slave narratives a number of motifs listed by Robert Stepto: "the violence and gnawing hunger, the skeptical view of Christianity, the portrait of a black family valiantly attempting to maintain a degree of unity, the impregnable isolation, the longing and scheming to follow the North Star resolved by boarding the 'freedom train'." But most of all, argues Stepto, *Black Boy* resembles slave narratives in "the narrator's quest for literacy."

Apart from this decades-old critical approach that looks at traditional texts and formulae in new contexts, some black critics of African-American literature have been pursuing ways to talk about the continuities between ordinary, vernacular African-American discourse and artistic African-American discourse. Houston Baker, for example, criticizes both Stepto and Henry Louis Gates, Jr., for their "reconstructionist" theories that privilege literary discourse and adopt a semiotic view of African-American literature as a closed system of signs. Baker advocates an interdisciplinary, anthropological approach to African-American art, redesigning the approach of Stephen Henderson and other representatives of the "Black Aesthetic" movement of the 1960s and early 1970s. Baker aims "to establish a verbal and musical *continuum of expressive behavior* in Afro-American culture as an analytical category." He argues for a performance theory of literature that requires the critic to "have at least some theoretically adequate notions of the entire array of cultural forces which shape the performer's cognition, allowing him to actualize a 'text' as one instance of a distinct cultural semantics." Criticism in this mode—which Baker calls the "tropological mode," borrowing Hayden White's (1978) neologism—should resemble the blues, as do the African-American texts themselves, such that the "improvisational dynamism" of the criticism matches that of the texts. His guiding model for understanding the *continuities* of African-American expressive culture—continuities between vernacular and high art—is the blues matrix, blues as both code and force in the culture. Baker looks to the ways in which African-American writers tap "blues energies" to write, as he puts it, "blues books most excellent."

Other critics have tried to talk about African-American literature as blues performances. Wright himself provided early fuel for this approach in a lecture on "The Literature of the Negro in the United States," which he had given in the mid-1940s but which was not published until the appearance of *White Man, Listen!* in 1956. Wright identifies two different traditions of African-American expression in literature. The first is the Narcissistic Level, a formal, self-conscious writing that speaks of the alienation of the black middle class and pleads for the recognition of the humanity of blacks. The other tradition, which Wright calls Forms of Things Unknown, is the realm of the oral folk culture of lower-class blacks, and it amounts to a vernacular repertoire from which African-American literature can draw. John McClusky (1983) shows us Wright's ongoing interest in the blues idiom and Ralph Ellison (1945) goes so far as to call

Black Boy a blues in prose. Henderson revived this notion of the Forms of Things Unknown as he attempted in 1973 to provide a theory for the Black Aesthetic movement, especially within poetry. For Henderson, "blackness" in expressive culture must exist in the structures of the expressive object, structures that reflect the "interior dynamism" or "inner life" of African-American folk. Theme and structure contribute to blackness, but so does what Henderson calls "saturation," a semantic category. "Certain words and constructions," writes Henderson, "seem to carry an inordinate charge of emotional and psychological weight, so that whenever they are used they set all kinds of bells ringing, all kinds of synapses snapping, on all kinds of levels." He calls these "mascon words," words that carry "a massive concentration of Black experiential energy which powerfully affects the meaning of Black speech, Black song, and Black poetry—if one, indeed, has to make such distinctions."

Baker faults the Black Aesthetic movement for its "romantic Marxism," but he builds upon its interdisciplinary anthropology-of-art approach to the continuities and discontinuities between nonliterary and literary forms of African-American expressive culture. Baker takes seriously the attempt to go beyond the thematic similarity between *Black Boy* and a blues song to seek thicker ways to talk about books as blues performances.

Baker proposes a tropological perspective on Wright, the suggestive trope being the physical phenomenon, the black hole. This perspective leads him to read *Black Boy* as a tale of desire, with the narrator as a "black hole" of blues energy consuming books and experiences to "feed" the "hunger" of the black hole for energy. "In the autobiography," writes Baker, "the mother's suffering absence becomes a figure gathering to itself all lineaments of a black 'blues life'." And just as a black hole "squeezes" matter to a zero sum, so Wright "as voracious center of desire—seeking desire's trace as 'point of view'—reduces literary language to zero sum. *Black Boy* is utterly relentless in its representations of what might be termed a 'code of desire' that reduces conventional discourse to zero." Baker cites several examples of Wright's zero-sum reduction of conventional discourse in the autobiography, citing as an example the black boys' parodies of the preacher's sacred hymns:

When the preacher intoned:
Amazing grace, how sweet it sounds
we would wink at one another and hum under
our breath:

A bulldog ran my grandma down

For Baker, this folk discourse amounts to Wright's adopting what Julia Kristeva calls "carnivalesque discourse" as the ultimate linguistic strategy for challenging the social order.

On a different level, Wright's use of African-American vernacular language connects in interesting ways with Gertrude Stein's uses in "Melanctha," the centerpiece of *Three Lives* (1909), and in her poetry. It is well known that Wright was terribly excited about "Melanctha," even to the extreme of taking the book to the workplaces of laboring blacks in order to read to them aloud from the story. One critic, Eugene Miller, has explored the Wright-Stein-blues triangle in a reading of a relatively obscure Wright short story, "The Man Who killed a Shadow." Miller draws upon an unpublished Wright manuscript, "Memories of My Grandmother," to show Wright's linking of black folk expression, including the blues, with surrealism.

These attempts to talk about *Black Boy* as a blues performance are, in my view, still tentative and incomplete. Baker has not yet exploited fully the aesthetic anthropology of Robert Plant Armstrong or Robert Farris Thompson, nor has he exploited fully the ethnographically informed work of folklorists on African-American performance style. Some of the more obvious poetic elements of blues lyrics, such as repetition, are clear enough in the autobiography. Wright often renders pages of single sentences in parallel construction, and even the list of folk beliefs I cited earlier has this quality; surely these are the passages critics have in mind when they are moved to call *Black Boy* a blues poem.

But there is more to be said about this structure. Critics have likened the structure of *Black Boy* other well-known formula genres, such as the slave narrative or *Bildungsroman,* the story of a boy's quest and character formation. This suggests, erroneously, I believe, that the aesthetic principle underlying the structure of *Black Boy* is *synthesis*—the familiar Western literary formula in which thesis and antithesis are resolved by synthesis. In contrast, Armstrong identifies an aesthetic principle, *syndesis,* which he finds in Yoruba art and, by extension, in folk arts generally. Whereas *synthesis* "apprehends and enacts the world and the self—through a process of oppositions and eventuations," *syndesis* works "through a process of accretion." "The synthetic work," continues Armstrong,

> owns inherent principles of *development.* It proceeds through the execution and resolution of opposites. Its

successive units are different from one another; and insofar as successive phases grow out of prior ones, the synthetic work is linear. The syndetic work, on the other hand, grows in accordance with extrinsic principles; its *growth* is through repetition of the same or of a small inventory of similar units. It does not *develop;* there is no entailment of the subsequent to be found in the prior.

Notwithstanding the illusion of linear synthesis that an autobiography creates, *Black Boy* is far more a syndetic than a synthetic work of art, and it is on this structural principle that it resembles a blues performance. Although Wright presents his dozens of small stories in roughly chronological order, the meaning of the entire autobiography would change little if the stories were rearranged in random order. The stories are variations on the same theme, and there is no logical order to them other than the chronological.

This syndetic aesthetic governing the structure of *Black Boy* is a prime instance of "intertextuality" between oral and written expression, and critics of African-American literature recognize intertextuality as a primary feature both of African-American expression and of so-called postmodern expression. Walter Ong's notion of the "residual orality" in printed and, finally, in electronic forms of communication is relevant here, as oral traditions of all sorts provide form and content for cultural texts thought to be far from folklore. This is not to say that *Black Boy* is a "postmodern text"; rather, the important point is that the intertextuality between folklore and high cultural forms may be a feature linking most 20th-century African-American texts.

Thus far I have discussed, in effect, the ways in which folklore "succeeds" in *Black Boy*. Wright documents in a thick description of texts and contexts the ways in which traditional African-American talk served socialization, bonding, and tendentious functions for black men growing up in the South. Moreover, the very structures of the book, from the sentence level to the paragraph to the chapter, seem to establish a continuity between African-American vernacular discourse and African-American literary discourse. What, then, of the claim of "failure" announced in the title of this essay?

One way to read *Black Boy* as a literary performance continuous with folk performances is to focus on the uses of folklore as a way out of double binds and other paradoxes of communication that fill our everyday lives. This everyday communications approach alerts the reader to the tentative, incomplete, and possibly disastrous character of every face-to-face encounter. Every folk encounter has the possibility of failure.

Folklore is one of those classes of healthy human behavior, along with play, humor, and art, that makes it possible to survive communication paradoxes. And examining in detail African-American strategies reminds us how much folklore is about surviving in asymmetical power relations. The notion of paradoxical communication is central to the ideas that Gregory Bateson was developing in the mid-1950s. His 1954 essay, "A Theory of Play and Fantasy" (published in 1972), established his use of the Theory of Logical Types to distinguish between logical types of communication, such as between a message and a metamessage (i.e., a message about messages). This, of course, is the key to Bateson's "frame" analysis, which has contributed importantly to symbolic interactionist theories in sociology and to performance theory in folklore. The discontinuity between messages and meta-messages makes paradoxical communication inevitable in our everyday lives, as in Epimenides's familiar case of the Cretan liar. Humans learn to cope with these paradoxical communications involving multiple logical types by invoking ritual, art, humor, play, and related genres of metaphorical behavior.

Bateson developed his ideas about frames and play while working with a team of psychologists interested in developing a communication-based theory of schizophrenia. Bateson later regretted that his ideas about paradoxical communication and double binds became linked so solidly with the schizophrenia research because, for him, the idea of the double bind explained a broad range of "transcontextual phenomena" and did not have to rest on changing ideas about schizophrenia. According to the theory of the double bind, the schizophrenic lacks the normal person's ability to discriminate between levels of messages. Indeed, schizophrenia becomes the actor's primary defense mechanism against the paradox created by the double bind. The elements of the double bind include:

> 1. Two or more persons. . . . 2. Repeated experience . . . . 3. A primary negative injunction. This may have either of two forms: (a) "Do not do so and so, or I will punish you," or (b) "If you do not do so and so, I will punish you." . . . 4. A secondary injunction conflicting with the first at a more abstract level, and like the first enforced by punishments or signals which threaten survival. . . . 5. A tertiary injunction prohibiting the victim from escaping the field.

P. Watzlawick, J. H. Beavin and D. D. Jackson have used these ideas to define an entire field, the pragmatics of communication. Drawing on Bateson, they show how pervasive paradoxical communications are in our interpersonal interactions. They call these "pragmatic paradoxes" and include the category called "paradoxical injunctions," of which the barber paradox is the most famous example. In Hans Reichenbach's (1947) version of this paradox, "the barber is a soldier who is ordered by his captain to shave all the soldiers of the company who do not shave themselves, but no others." Does the barber shave himself? Such a barber cannot logically exist, but in the real world of barbers and military officers the order *can* exist. "A person caught in such a situation," write Watzlawick, Beavin and Jackson,

> is in an untenable position. . . . As soon as we begin to look at paradox in interaction contexts, the phenomenon ceases to be merely a fascinating pursuit of the logician and the philosopher of science and becomes a matter of stark practical importance for the sanity of the communicants, be they individuals, families, societies, or nations.

Such is the condition of any person forced to interact with others while assuming the inferior power position in that interaction. In *Black Boy* Wright tells the story of how a child learns to cope with daily pragmatic paradoxes without going crazy. The answer, of course, is that the child learns to distinguish between levels of communication and further learns to use those distinctions as both a defense mechanism and as a tool for taking power whenever possible in the paradoxical situation. Because play, humor, art, ritual, and the entire range of metaphoric behavior are the processes the child learns for coping with pragmatic paradoxes, and because these are recognizable folkloric processes, we are justified in looking at Wright's *Black Boy* as a primer in folklore as communication strategy for the relatively powerless. Let me offer a few salient examples from the autobiography to make my point.

Wright's earliest lesson in the paradoxes of communication involved his father, who worked as a night porter and was barely part of Wright's childhood even before leaving the family. Wright's primary memory was of having to be quiet during the daytime, when his father slept. "He was the lawgiver in our family," says Richard, "and I never laughed in his presence. . . . He was always a stranger to me, always somehow alien and remote."

The episode that was seared in Wright's memory had to do with a stray kitten he and his brother found and befriended. But the kitten's meowing was loud and persistent, which awakened his father.

Richard and his brother were ordered to keep the kitten quiet.

> "Kill that damn thing!" my father exploded. "Do anything, but get it away from here!"

> He went inside, grumbling. I resented his shouting and it irked me that I could never make him feel my resentment. How could I hit back at him? Oh, yes . . . He had said to kill the kitten and I would kill it! I knew that he had not really meant for me to kill the kitten, but my deep hate of him urged me toward a literal acceptance of his word.

And so, much to the horror of his brother, Richard hangs the cat. Upon discovering this, his mother drags him before the father.

> "You know better than that!" my father stormed.

> "You told me to kill'im," I said.

> "I told you to drive him away," he said.

> "You told me to kill'im," I countered positively.

> "You get out of my eyes before I smack you down!" my father bellowed in disgust, then turned over in bed.

> I had had my first triumph over my father. I had made him believe that I had taken his words literally. He could not punish me now without risking his authority. I was happy because I had at last found a way to throw my criticism of him into his face. I had made him feel that, if he whipped me for killing the kitten, I would never give serious weight to his words again. I had made him know that I felt he was cruel and I had done it without his punishing me.

This was Wright's first lesson in the power of words, but he also saw that the power he had over his father was the power to move between levels of logical types in his messages. His father had spoken figuratively and counted on Richard's correctly interpreting the message. Richard reversed the power relationship by literally interpreting a figurative message, just as in other circumstances he takes power by interpreting figuratively a literal message. Schizophrenics, according to the double-bind theory, confuse the literal and metaphorical and are victimized by the confusion. The normal person, on the other hand, finds power and creativity in mixing the literal and metaphorical. Humor often works out of that mix, just as play and ritual depend on it. By taking power in his interactions with his father and by willfully mixing the literal and the metaphorical, Richard marks the early stages of his expressive creativity, a sort of protofolklore. Word games with his peers were a lesson of one sort; word games with his father were far more dangerous, but the games paralleled and anticipated the asymmetry of power that Richard would encounter when dealing with white people.

Elsewhere in the autobiography there are clearcut examples of paradoxical injunctions and other pragmatic paradoxes, and the strategies Wright employs for surviving them. But some of the paradoxes prove not to be susceptible to language games, and in those instances Richard sees how the paradoxes themselves work not only to trap their black victims but also to induce the victims into cooperating with their own victimization. One such paradox arises when Richard turns out to be valedictorian of his class. Richard, who had already written a story, "The Voodoo of Hell's Half-Acre," that had been published in a newspaper, looks forward to writing his valedictorian's speech. But the black principal hands Richard a speech to read, and when Richard balks, insisting on writing and reading his own speech, the principal warns him that he "can't afford to just say *anything* before those white people that night." Richard keeps insisting that he should be able to write his own speech, and the principal finally issues the ultimatum:

> "You know, I'm glad I talked to you," he said. "I was seriously thinking of placing you in the school system, teaching. But, now, I don't think that you'll fit."

> He was tempting me, baiting me; this was the technique that snared black young minds into supporting the southern way of life.

Richard realizes that this black principal is just as trapped in the system as he is. "I had been talking to a 'bought man'," muses Richard on the way home, "and he had tried to 'buy' me. I felt that I had been dealing with something unclean." His friend Griggs advises him to go along with the principal, and his uncle Tom reads both speeches and advises Richard to read the principal's—"the better speech." "The principal's speech was simpler and clearer than mine," observes Richard as his uncle departs, "but it did not say anything; mine was cloudy, but it said what I wanted to say." Richard does deliver his own speech and walks away from that world: "The hell with it! With almost seventeen years of baffled living behind me, I faced the world in 1925."

In this episode Richard faces a paradoxical injunction: speak! but don't speak your own words. Your own words are too dangerous. As the culmination of childhood socialization that aimed at teaching Richard the power of words (in the word games with his peers, in the standoff language game with his father), Richard faces a warning that words are dangerous, at least in the presence of white people. Speak, but say nothing. Silence yourself. It made Richard feel "unclean."

A second paradoxical injunction Richard perceives in the South is the prohibition against dishonesty. As opposed to the previous injunction to speak but to say nothing, this injunction asks the black boy to speak, but always speak truthfully. Searching for a job while in school, Richard is interviewed by a ''dour white woman'' who needs ''an honest boy'' to do chores around the house.

> ''Now, boy, I want to ask you one question and I
>   want you to tell me the truth,'' she said.
> ''Yes, ma'am,'' I said, all attention.
> ''Do you steal?'' she asked me seriously.
> I burst into a laugh, then checked myself.
> ''What's so damn funny about that?'' she asked.
> ''Lady, if I was a thief, I'd never tell anybody.''
> I had made a mistake during my first five minutes
>   in the white world. I hung my head,
> ''No, ma'am,'' I mumbled. ''I don't steal.''
> She stared at me, trying to make up her mind.
> ''Now, look, we don't want a sassy nigger around
>   here,'' she said.
> ''No, ma'am,'' I assured her. ''I'm not sassy.''

Later, after graduation, Richard works in a hotel as part of his effort to earn enough money to flee the South and become a writer. All around him in the hotel, ''Negroes were stealing'' and urging him to do the same. Richard observes that the white employers seemed not at all threatened by the theft. ''But I,'' he realizes, ''who stole nothing, who wanted to look them straight in the face, who wanted to talk and act like a man, inspired fear in them. The southern whites would rather have had Negroes who stole, work for them than Negroes who knew, however dimly, the worth of their own humanity. Hence, whites placed a premium upon black deceit. . . .'' The paradoxical injunction was as clear as could be. Be honest, but don't speak the truth. Be honest, even though your stealing helps confirm your nature.

A third, even more complex example of the paradoxical injunction that becomes a double bind is the fistfight Richard is induced to enter with another black boy, Harrison. Both work for the same optical company and one day Richard's young white foreman, Mr. Olin, sidles up beside Richard for some unexpected conversation: '''Say, Richard, do you believe that I'm your friend?' he asked me. The question was so loaded with danger that I could not reply at once.'' Richard cautiously acknowledges that he'd like to think Mr. Olin is his friend, and Olin then warns Richard to be careful of ''that nigger Harrison,'' telling him that Harrison is waiting for Richard with a knife. Olin warns Richard not to talk with Harrison, but at lunchtime Richard seeks out Harrison, and the two warily discover that

Olin has told each of them the same story. And has given each of them a knife for ''protection.'' The two agree that they have no grudge against one another and that they'll not tell the white foreman they know the truth.

But the white provocation continues for a week until Olin proposes a boxing match to settle the alleged grudge between Richard and Harrison. At first both resist, but on the promise of five dollars Harrison begins to urge Richard to box with him. Each begins to suspect the motives of the other. Harrison thinks they should do it, just for the money.

> ''Look, let's fool them white men,'' Harrison said.
> ''We won't hurt each other. We'll just pretend, see?
> We'll show 'em we ain't dumb as they think, see?'' ''I
> don't know.'' ''It's just exercise. Four rounds for five
> dollars. You scared?'' ''No.'' ''Then come on and
> fight.'' ''All right,'' I said. ''It's just exercise. I'll fight.''

Of course, the fight turns out to be more than just exercise. ''We squared off,'' recalls Wright, ''and at once I knew that I had not thought sufficiently about what I had bargained for. I could not pretend to fight.'' The feigned punches soon become real enough. Richard fights hard, condensing his shame and his hate into each blow. Finally, the white men pull apart the two young men. ''I clutched my five dollars in my fist and walked home,'' Wright admits. ''Harrison and I avoided each other after that and we rarely spoke. . . . I felt that I had done something unclean, something for which I could never properly atone.''

By far the most striking example of a double bind in the autobiography is also the one that shows most clearly how folklore ultimately fails Wright. Richard finds work in an optical factory where he is befriended by a white man who wants to teach him that trade. But his fellow white workers, Misters Reynolds and Pease, do not like the idea. At first they simply harass Richard, warning him that he ought not try to act white and saying things like ''If I was a nigger, I'd kill myself.'' But soon Richard faces a genuine double bind. Pease asks Richard if, as Reynolds said, Richard had called him ''Pease,'' meaning that he had failed to call him ''Mr. Pease,'' as a black person ought. While Richard is grasping the question, Reynolds warns him to tell the truth because Reynolds had heard him:

> If I had said: No sir, Mr. Pease, I never called you
> *Pease,* I would by inference have been calling Reynolds a liar, and if I had said: Yes, sir, Mr. Pease, I
> called you *Pease,* I would have been pleading guilty
> to the worst insult that a Negro can offer to a southern
> white man. I stood trying to think of a neutral course

that would resolve this quickly risen nightmare, but my tongue would not move.

Later, when the white shop owner, Mr. Crane, tries to help Richard and asks what went on between him, Pease, and Reynolds, Richard is once more speechless:

> An impulse to speak rose in me and died with the realization that I was facing a wall that I would never breech. I tried to speak several times and could make no sounds. I grew tense and tears burnt my cheeks.

Richard solves this double bind by escaping— that is, by quitting his job. So in this quintessential example of a pragmatic paradox, Richard is unable to summon artistic—that is, folkloric—resources to help him resolve the situation.

The episode warrants closer scrutiny. Actually a version of a formula found in African-American verbal games, the episode helps us to understand how folklore fails some individuals. Gates puts the folklore figure of ''the Signifying Monkey'' and the language games of ''Signifyin(g)'' at the center of his understanding of African-American literature. While acknowledging that folklorists have long recognized ''the Signifying Monkey'' as a key black rhetorical trope, Gates gently chides previous critics for interpreting the monkey tales ''against the binary opposition between black and white in American society'' and for ignoring ''the *trinary* forces of the Monkey, the Lion, and the Elephant.'' ''In the narrative poems,'' explains Gates,

> the Signifying Monkey invariably repeats to his friend, the Lion, some insult purportedly generated by their mutual friend, the Elephant. The Monkey, however, speaks figuratively. The Lion, indignant and outraged, demands an apology of the Elephant, who refuses and then trounces the Lion. The Lion, realizing that his mistake was to take the Monkey literally, returns to trounce the Monkey. It is this relationship between the literal and the figurative, and the dire consequences of their confusion, which is the most striking repeated element of these tales. The Monkey's trick depends on the Lion's inability to mediate between those two poles of signification, of meaning.

The language game in these poems, therefore, relies on the relationships between the three stock characters. The Monkey is the trickster figure and a ''rhetorical genius.'' Unable to match the Lion's physical power, the Monkey bests the Lion by ''lyin(g),'' that is, by telling a tale with figurative discourse.

Wright presents a perversely transformed version of this Signifyin(g) triangle in both the episode between himself, Pease, and Reynolds and the ear-lier episode of his arranged fight with Harrison. In these versions the white men have turned this African-American language game back on Wright. They have the power to assign roles in the triangle. Pease and Reynolds are the Lion and the Monkey, respectively, casting Richard in the role of the Elephant. But Richard, of course, has none of the real power of the Elephant. Richard cannot stomp Pease to Reynolds's delight. Richard is the victim of a rhetorical device traditionally used by African-Americans to assert power by setting rivals against one another. He is rendered speechless by this episode, a condition uncharacteristic of him when he is among his adolescent peers. Richard may be familiar with the game, but not as the victim.

What are we to make of this reversal? It is unlikely that Wright unconsciously created this strangely transformed version of a traditional African-American oral formula. He was plenty familiar with this rhetorical strategy and, as Gates shows, used Signifyin(g) in several of his stories, including *Lawd Today* and ''Big Boy Leaves Home.'' Why did Richard Wright, the artist, choose to take an African-American rhetorical formula and transform it thus?

Wright, I believe, is recording here the failure of folklore. Richard's speechlessness in the face of this circumstance stands in stark contrast to the empowering speech elsewhere in the autobiography. Whereas language works *within* a folk community and learning the language games may be an important element in socialization of members of the community, *those same language games may fail in the intellectual encounter.* Gates acknowledges this as Roger Abraham's point that ''intergroup'' Signifyin(g) generally fails except as the Signifyin(g) is used by the African-Americans as a form of ''masking behavior.'' But this is Gates's only mention of the extreme difficulty of Signifyin(g) in the intercultural encounter.

Wright's episodes in the optical shop clarify the difference between the double bind and language games, and the difference lies in the power relations between the participants. Bateson recognized that the double bind is no mere language game. It resembles language games in that both rely on the difference between messages and metamessages, but the double bind is possible only when there is a real asymmetry of power between the participants. The paradox of the double bind can lead in the direction of either creativity or madness, with a thin line separating the two.

Richard's language game worked on his father in the kitten episode. Although Richard was in the inferior power position in that encounter, he was able to resist his father's authority by taking a figurative message literally. But things could have turned out otherwise. Richard could have received a beating from his father for killing the kitten; indeed, he did get a beating from his mother. And certainly one cannot imagine the language game working on a white schoolteacher or employer, for in those situations the double bind is a structural, institutional reality for African-Americans.

True, Richard and Harrison first tried to handle the double bind by stepping outside the frame provided by the white men. Richard and Harrison negotiated an alternative frame for the events and communications they were receiving from the white foreman; in Bateson's terms, they metacommunicated about the frame. They planned a false performance, playing at the white man's frame while preserving their own understanding of the situation. But their plan was undone by three things. First, as Wright says, he knew too little about such things to create a persuasive performance. More important, Richard and Harrison harbored the mutual suspicion that Richard found elsewhere in relations between black people in the South. Creating and sustaining an interpretive frame for an event as delicate and tentative as a play fight requires a strong metarelationship of trust between the participants, and it is this trust that the segregationist system destroys. Third, the planned-for play fight is undone by the real power advantage the white men held in the contest between interpretive frames. They were there to see two "niggers" fight, and it is doubtful that any performance short of "the real thing" would have satisfied them. The result for Richard, again, is shame, an unclean feeling, and speechlessness.

Striking in all these examples of paradoxical injunctions and full double binds in *Black Boy* is the central role of *speech* and *speechlessness* as tropes governing the episode. Wright learned early the power of words and the dangers lurking in that power. In each case, however, all of his training in language games proved useless in dealing with the language games played on him. "Why could I not learn to keep my mouth shut at the right time?" Wright asks himself at the conclusion of one more unsuccessful attempt to work for a white boss:

> I had said just one short sentence too many. My words were innocent enough, but they indicated, it seemed, a consciousness on my part that infuriated white people. . . .
>
> I knew what was wrong with me, but I could not correct it. The words and actions of white people were baffling signs to me. . . .
>
> I had begun coping with the white world too late. I could never make subservience an automatic part of my behavior . . . While standing before a white man I had to figure out how to perform each act and how to say each word. I could not help it. I could not grin. In the past I had always said too much, now I found it was difficult to say anything at all. I could not react as the world in which I lived expected me to; that world was too baffling, too uncertain.

The Jim Crow South posed a fundamental double bind: either Richard could continue to resist the white's definition of him and likely suffer a physical death, or he could accept that definition and suffer, as Orlando Patterson puts it, the "social death" of the slave, the living death of the nonperson. Of the options available to the potential victim of the double bind, from madness through humor, Wright chooses escape.

Wright's ultimate act in *Black Boy* is to turn his back on orality and to flee to the written word, to literature. Using a forged note to check books out of the library, Richard finds in the essays of Mencken and in the realist novels of Dreiser and Lewis and other writers a way of "fighting with words", but with written words. He resolves to flee north and become a writer. "It had been only through books," he realizes, "that I had managed to keep myself alive in a negatively vital way. Whenever my environment had failed to support or nourish me, I had clutched at books. . . ." For Wright, as for other African-Americans, learning to read and learning to write were political acts. Through writing, Wright again took the power of words, a power he more often felt as victim in the oral realm.

Readers and critics naturally wonder why Richard Wright, as depicted in *Black Boy,* was unable to muster the resources of folklore to help him resist the double-bind situations that ensnared him. Doubtless there are biographical facts that contributed to the failure of folklore for him at crucial times. For one thing, Wright's socialization in the African-American community was sporadic and disjointed. Mary Helen Washington observes in her introduction to an anthology of the writings of Zora Neale Hurston that Zora grew up in the unusually sheltered environment of Eatonville, Florida, without experiencing racial prejudice. Wright, on the other hand, grew up observing the routine brutality of racial oppression. Most biographies emphasize the "childhood trauma" that must have set the tone for the realism, violence, and brutality of Wright's adult fiction. His father's violence, then desertion; the strict religious expectations of his grandmother and aunt; his mother's suffering and death; the Jim Crow violence visited upon family members and acquaintances—all these doubtless had their effects on Wright.

But I believe there is a simpler, better view of why folklore failed Wright. Put simply, his mother actively discouraged conversations of the sort black children must learn in order to acquire Signifyin(g) as a skill for living. Her approach to child rearing and her advice could be called pragmatic, literal. It was his mother who beat Richard for killing the kitten; it was his mother who insisted he fight the gang of boys that waylaid him for his money on the way to the market to buy groceries; it was his mother who called him "foolish" for being unwilling to sell his dog to a white girl for a dollar to buy food. (When the dog was crushed a week later under the wheels of a coal wagon, his mother said coldly: "You could have had a dollar. But you can't eat a dead dog, can you?" And it was his mother who responded angrily and slapped him when, on a train ride that was his first experience with the segregation dictated by Jim Crow laws, he questioned her about the race of his grandmother (who had very light skin) and his father:

> "Then what am I?"
>
> "They'll call you a colored man when you grow up," she said. Then she turned to me and smiled mockingly and asked: "Do you mind, Mr. Wright?"
>
> I was angry and I did not answer. I did not object to being called colored, but I knew that there was something my mother was holding back. She was not concealing facts, but feelings, attitudes, convictions which she did not want me to know; and she became angry when I prodded her.

In Bateson's terms, Wright's mother was unwilling to communicate with Richard about communication. She entertained no language games. Nor did she entertain the sort of "indirection" in communication that another autobiographer, Maya Angelou, learned from her Momma, the grandmother who raised her. The child deprived of language games is deprived of metacommunication, and that child may never learn to acquire "normal" defenses against the double bind.

Of course, Wright had his male peer groups for learning, practice, and perfecting Signifyin(g) and other oral language games, and these may have mitigated somewhat the primary socialization in Wright's home. At least Wright recognized a language game when he heard it. Still, we ought to trust Wright's testimony that he was not like others, that he could not behave as other blacks and as whites wanted him to behave. His reaction to having the tables turned on him in double binds was not that of the adept player who sees he has been outmaneuvered; rather, he reacted consistently with shock and silence. African-American folklore was available to him for motifs and stylistic elements in his later writing, but they were not available to him in his everyday, oral repertoire, as they ought to have been. African-American writers who rely heavily on folklore tend to emphasize community; perhaps Wright's sense of alienation meant he could never find in African-American folklore more than perfunctory material. Certainly in *Black Boy* there is no sense of African-American folklore as a resource for living.

Blaming the failure of folklore in *Black Boy* upon the eccentricities of Richard Wright's life, however, may mean missing a more general point for folklorists and other culture critics to ponder. Perhaps the source of the failure lies more in the dynamics of folklore in the intercultural encounter. The example of *Black Boy* invites us to consider the following possibilities.

First, we notice in the book that folklore fails an *individual.* We tend to focus our folklore inquiry so much on the group that we often lose the individual in our analysis. Intracultural variation ought to temper our generalizations in any case, but we ought to allow for the individual who is simply not served well by the group's folk culture.

Second, we notice in *Black Boy* that folklore succeeds and works as we expect it should within the folk community, but that it *fails in the intercultural encounter.* Abrahams (1981) is one of the few folklorists who have paid attention to what happens to folklore in the intercultural encounter. (It is Abrahams, recall, who observes that Signifyin(g) across cultural borders is extremely difficult.) Abrahams draws our attention to "display events" at the borders where cultures meet, those planned-for occasions when "private antipathies explode into open antagonism and threaten to become public events." The folklorist's work at this border is politically "'engaged,' because it brings to the fore the antagonisms and inequities of everyday life as perceived by the performance community and as played out within the larger society."

Abrahams is exactly right in observing that to "analyze lore in terms of how the group projects and plays upon its own image, in relation to stereotypes of other groups within a complex society and a pluralistic cultural situation, is to alter significantly the very study of folklore." But Abrahams overemphasizes successful versions of such encounters. "If one wishes to find a successful model for cultural pluralism in operation," he writes, "let him or her look to these fairs and festivals—as the folk have for millennia." Fair enough; but what does the folklorist find in looking at a race riot, a "display event" not far removed (analytically) from the fair and festival? And Abrahams's analysis still works at the level of the group as an "ethnosemiotics" of encounters between groups. I would urge, as above, that we not lose the individual in our attention to the "successes" and the "failures" of folklore in the intercultural encounter.

Third, folklore may not be an effective source of resistance against the hegemony enjoyed by the dominant culture. If the double bind is a structural mode of maintaining hegemony, then language games will have no effect on the dominant culture or even in the intercultural encounter with other marginalized groups. "Masking" may be a form of resistance, but it is a form unlikely to change the situation. Folklore, in short, may be a force for *pacification* rather than *resistance,* a prospect that should not come as good news to those inclined to romanticize the folklore of underclasses.

This is an open question, one not often addressed by folklorists but deserving their immediate attention. Abrahams sees display events as ultimately subversive, as having "maintained a counter-culture of far more revolutionary potential than the radical tactics that brought life to a halt and the authorities to their knees in the sixties." And Abdul JanMohamed may be right in arguing that the key moment in resisting hegemony comes when one asserts control over one's own subjectivity, as Richard Wright did. Still, the role of folklore in the collective and individual resistance against cultural hegemony needs further clarification.

An autobiography is not an ethnographic monograph, but *Black Boy* tells more than just "emotionally true" stories about Richard Wright's youth. Folklorists and other culture critics can read his vignettes as rich, "thick descriptions" of the dynamics of the interactions between the individual, the folk group, and "cultural others." In reading the book, as in living a life, perhaps there is more to be learned from the mistakes and failures of folklore than from the successes that we take so much for granted.

Source: Jay Mechling, "The Failure of Folklore in Richard Wright's *Black Boy,*" in *Journal of American Folklore,* Vol. 104, No. 413, Summer 1991, pp. 275–92.

Sources

Bone, Robert A., *The Negro Novel in America,* rev. ed., Yale University Press, 1965, pp. 141–52.

Ellison, Ralph, "Richard Wright's Blues," in *The Collected Essays of Ralph Ellison,* edited by John F. Callahan, Modern Library, 1995, pp. 128–44.

Graham, Maryemma, and Jerry W. Ward Jr., "*Black Boy (American Hunger):* Freedom to Remember," in *Censored Books: Critical Viewpoints,* edited by Nicholas J. Karolides, Less Burress, and John M. Kean, Scarecrow Press, 1993, pp. 109–16.

Lewis, Sinclair, Review in *Esquire,* June 23, 1945.

Margolies, Edward, *The Art of Richard Wright,* 1969.

Sanders, Ronald, "Richard Wright and the Sixties," in *Midstream,* Vol. XIV, No. 7, August/September 1968, pp. 28–40.

Stephens, Martha, "Richard Wright's Fiction: A Reassessment," in *Georgia Review,* 1971, pp. 450–70.

Trilling, Lionel, Review in *Nation,* April 7, 1945.

Whitlow, Roger, "Chapter 4: 1940–1960: Urban Realism and Beyond" in *Black American Literature: A Critical History,* Nelson Hall, 1973, pp. 107–46.

Further Reading

Bloom, Harold, ed., *Richard Wright,* Modern Critical Views, Chelsea, 1987.
    This collection of essays on all of Wright's work includes an analysis of *Black Boy*'s place in the black literary tradition.

Clark, Edward D., "Richard Wright," in *Dictionary of Literary Biography,* Volume 76: *Afro-American Writers, 1940–1955,* Gale Research, 1988, pp. 199–221.
    Clark describes Wright's position in the history of American literature as that of a father to the post-World War II black novel.

Ellison, Ralph, "The World and the Jug," in *The Collected Essays of Ralph Ellison,* edited by John F. Callahan, Modern Library, 1995, pp. 155–88.
    In this essay, Ellison makes a powerful rejoinder to Irving Howe's commentary in "Black Boys and Native Sons."

Fabre, Michel, *The Unfinished Quest of Richard Wright,* William Morrow, 1973.
>   This lengthy biography, translated from French, evaluates Wright as a "representative man" and an important spokesperson of his age.

Gates, Henry Louis, Jr., and K. A. Appiah, eds., *Richard Wright: Critical Perspectives Past and Present,* Amistad, 1993.
>   This collection of critical essays on Wright's work, written with knowledge of the untruncated version, includes an essay by Horace A. Porter exploring in greater depth the similarity of Richard and Stephen Dedalus.

Gibson, Donald B., "Richard Wright: Aspects of His Afro-American Literary Relations," in *Critical Essays on Richard Wright,* edited by Yoshinobu Hakutani, G. K. Hall, 1982.
>   Gibson examines why Wright's work is "so clearly distinguished" from other literature by black authors, comparing Wright in particular to Charles Chesnutt and Paul Laurence Dunbar.

Howe, Irving, "Black Boys and Native Sons," in *A World More Attractive,* Horizon, 1963.
>   Howe's well-known essay examines and compares the element of "protest" in the works of Wright, James Baldwin, and Ralph Ellison.

Ray, David, and Robert M. Farnsworth, *Richard Wright: Impressions and Perspectives,* University of Michigan Press, 1971.
>   This unique collection of writings by and about Wright includes personal impressions, reminiscences, and correspondence.

Reilly, John M., ed., *Richard Wright: The Critical Reception,* Burt Franklin, 1978.
>   This overview of original critical responses to Wright's work includes excerpts of more than sixty early reviews of *Black Boy.*

Smith, Sidonie Ann, "Richard Wright's *Black Boy:* The Creative Impulse as Rebellion," in *Southern Literary Journal,* Vol. V, No. 1, Fall 1972, pp. 123–36.
>   In this essay, Smith presents Wright's autobiography as a slave narrative because of the commonalities of themes that the novel has with such pre-Civil War accounts.

Wright, Ellen, and Michel Fabre, eds., *Richard Wright Reader,* Harper and Row, 1978.
>   This collection of some of Wright's best writings includes excerpts from his fiction, poetry, essays, and criticism.

Darkness Visible

William Styron

1990

Developed from a lecture William Styron gave at a symposium on affective disorders at Johns Hopkins University, *Darkness Visible* was first published as an essay in the December 1989 issue of *Vanity Fair*. The title derives from Milton's description of hell in *Paradise Lost*. The slim book chronicles Styron's battle with depression, which consumes him shortly after his sixtieth birthday. Styron begins his story in October 1985 when he flies to Paris to receive the prestigious *Prix Mondial Cino del Duca*. During this trip the writer's mental state begins to deteriorate rapidly. Using a mix of anecdotes, speculation, and reportage, Styron reflects on the causes and effects of depression, drawing links between his own illness and that of celebrities and writers such as Virginia Woolf, Randall Jarrell, Albert Camus, Romain Gary, Primo Levi, Ernest Hemingway, and Abbie Hoffman. Critically acclaimed for its honesty and Styron's unflinching examination of his condition, *Darkness Visible* helped to de-mystify depression at a time when the disease was gaining more visibility in the media. The early 1990s saw the popularization of Prozac, a radically new kind of antidepressant, which was released in 1987 and is now the most widely prescribed antidepressant in the world. Styron's reputation as an internationally-acclaimed writer, and an older one, also helped the book gain a wide readership.

Author Biography

Born June 11, 1925, to engineer William Clark Styron and Pauline Margaret Abraham Styron, William Styron grew up in the port town of Newport News, Virginia. His grandparents and great-grandparents came from North Carolina and were deeply enmeshed in southern culture, running a cotton plantation and owning slaves. Styron's traditional southern education consisted of a heavy dose of the liberal arts and religious discipline. After studying at Presbyterian Davidson College, Styron enlisted in the Marine Corps, training to be an officer. His experience in the military became fodder for his books, especially *The Long March* (1956), a novel about a forced stateside road march of Marine reservists. After his stint in the Marines, Styron returned to the states to finish his degree at Duke University in North Carolina.

Thinking that he was feeding his dream of becoming a writer, Styron took a job at McGraw-Hill publishers but resigned shortly afterwards, returning to school. At New York City's New School for Social Research, Styron began writing his first novel *Lie Down in Darkness*, which, when published in 1951, would establish his reputation as one of America's most promising young writers. Disillusioned with the United States government and searching for a more satisfying way to live, Styron moved to France. There he founded *The Paris Review* with Peter Matthiessen and George Plimpton. *The Paris Review* remains one of the most influential and widely read literary journals published today. Styron is best known, however, for his novel about a slave's uprising. *The Confessions of Nat Turner* (1967) received the 1967 Pulitzer Prize and cemented Styron's standing as a leading American novelist. His 1979 novel, *Sophie's Choice*, the tale of an Auschwitz survivor who cannot escape her past, was made into a popular motion picture starring Meryl Streep and Kevin Kline.

Styron's writing has always been more popular in France than in the United States, his doomed characters and gloomy settings appealing to the French sensibility. In 1985, Styron was awarded the Prix Mondial Cino del Duca, a prestigious award given annually to an artist or scientist whose work embodies the principles of humanism. While in Paris to receive the award, Styron first became fully conscious of the debilitating depression that he would later chronicle in *Darkness Visible: A Memoir of Madness*(1990). Styron recovered from his

William Styron

depression and has gone on to write *A Tidewater Morning: Three Tales from Youth* (1993).

Styron lives in Connecticut and is married to Rose Burgunder.

Summary

Chapter One

In the first chapter of *Darkness Visible*, Styron locates his narrative in place and time, writing that he first became fully aware of his illness in October 1985 while in Paris to receive the *Prix Mondial Cino del Duca,* an award given each year to a writer or scientist whose work reflects the values of humanism. Styron employs a flashback to discuss the eeriness of returning to the city thirty-three years after first visiting it in 1952. By examining his own strange behavior in Paris, Styron illustrates the chaos into which the human mind sinks during an episode of deep depression. He discusses how enigmatic the disease is and how difficult it is to come up with an adequate definition of depression.

Chapter Two

In this chapter Styron reminisces about Albert Camus and Romain Gary. Camus was a well-known French writer and existentialist whose philosophy influenced Styron's novels. Existentialism, a philosophical position emphasizing humanity's aloneness in a godless world, was in large part popularized by Camus and Jean-Paul Sartre, another midcentury French writer. Camus died in an automobile accident in 1960, before Styron had the opportunity to meet him. Gary was a writer and a friend of Styron's, who committed suicide in 1980. Styron speculates on the relationship between suicide and depression, making connections between these two writers and his own situation.

Chapter Three

Styron continues reflecting on the connection between suicide and depression, pointing out artistic people are often more prone to the disease than others. He reflects on the deaths of political activist Abbie Hoffman, Italian writer and Auschwitz survivor Primo Levi, and American poet and writer Randall Jarrell, all of whom died under mysterious circumstances. Styron suggests that their deaths were probably suicides and attempts to explain their deaths as a consequence of their battles with depression.

Chapter Four

In this chapter Styron examines the history of the word *depression*, suggesting that a better word for the disease it signifies is *brainstorm*, for the latter more accurately portrays the tumult of the human brain when impaired. Styron speculates as to reasons for his own illness, considering his sixtieth birthday as one possible cause, and the fact that he has stopped drinking alcohol. He also notes that he had become addicted to Halcion, a powerful sleeping aid, in dosages dangerous for someone his age. He describes the chemical changes in the brain during depression and likens the symptoms to madness itself. He discusses admitting himself to the hospital in December 1985 and a few of the symptoms of his depression, including the loss of his libido and the waning of his voice.

Chapter Five

In this chapter Styron introduces his psychiatrist, the Yale-trained Dr. Gold. Styron presents Gold as largely ineffectual, whose attempt to help the author consisted primarily of prescribing medication. At this point in his illness, Styron writes that he is consumed with a sense of loss and has given up hope.

Chapter Six

Styron continues to deteriorate. He can no longer drive and has taken on the countenance of a much older man. Dr. Gold prescribes Nardil, an older antidepressant. Styron writes that he feels as if a "second self" is following him around, watching him as he prepares to die, rewriting his will, preparing a letter of farewell. The chapter is suffused with the writer's sense of nostalgia, of gloom and impending death. Styron details the events of the night before he checks into the hospital during which, on the brink of suicide, he destroys his diary.

Chapter Seven

In this chapter, the shortest in the book, Styron points out the irony of Dr. Gold helping him get admitted to the hospital. It is ironic because, earlier, Gold had told Styron to avoid the hospital "at all costs." For Styron, this is further evidence of Gold's ineffectuality.

Chapter Eight

Styron describes his seven weeks in the hospital, writing that his fantasies of self-destruction ended once he was taken off Halcion. He details his time spent in group therapy, during which he and others are infantalized, asked to participate in activities such as drawing a picture of his house and using colored modeling clay to make something that represents his condition. Nonetheless, during his stay in the hospital, Styron begins the process of recovery.

Chapter Nine

The author reflects on the genetic roots of depression and refers to a book by Howard Kushner, *Self Destruction in the Promised Land,* which argues that depression is in part caused by incomplete mourning. Styron notices the theme of suicide in most of his books and considers how a kind of low-level depression has been with him for most of his life.

Chapter Ten

In the last chapter of the book, Styron recapitulates the fact that so many people have suffered and continue to suffer from depression, especially those involved in the arts. He emphasizes, however, that there is an end to the suffering and offers hope to those who suffer. He uses figures and phrases from literature to emphasize this hope.

Key Figures

Albert Camus

Albert Camus (1913–1960) was a well-known French writer and philosopher who greatly influenced Styron's writing and thinking about the human condition. Camus ran a theater company during the 1930s and was a leading voice of the French Resistance. His books include *The Plague, The Fall, The Rebel,* and *A Happy Death.* He was awarded the Nobel Prize for literature in 1957. Styron writes that Camus' novel *The Stranger* influenced his approach to *The Confessions of Nat Turner,* Styron's psychological portrait of an American slave. Styron also mentions Camus' book, *The Myth of Sisyphus,* saying that it gave him great courage to continue in the face of his own struggles. Styron sums up the book's message: ''In the absence of hope, we must struggle to survive—by the skin of our teeth.'' Romain Gary had planned to arrange a dinner to introduce Styron to Camus, but Camus died in an automobile accident before that could happen.

Simone del Duca

Simone del Duca is the wife of Cino del Duca, a wealthy Italian immigrant, after whom the Prix Mondial Cino del Duca is named. Styron describes her as ''a large dark-haired woman of queenly manner.'' She is at the center of Styron's emotional breakdown while the writer is in Paris to receive the Prix Mondial Cino del Duca. His state of mind deteriorating at the time, Styron refused, then accepted, to appear at a luncheon with del Duca.

Francoise Gallimard

Gallimard is Styron's publisher in France. Styron makes a luncheon date with Gallimard instead of appearing at a luncheon in his honor with Simone del Duca.

Romain Gary

Romain Gary, a Russian Jew born in Lithuania, was a writer and close friend of Styron and Camus. Gary's works include *The Life Before Us, Promise at Dawn, European Education, Goodbye Gary Cooper,* and *Lady L.* He was married to the actress Jean Seberg. Styron describes Gary's life, his bat-

Media Adaptations

- Styron's novel *Sophie's Choice* was made into a motion picture in 1982, starring Meryl Streep as the survivor of Nazi concentration camps and Kevin Kline as an American Jew obsessed with the Holocaust.

- Styron has a bit part as an actor in the 1994 comedy *Naked in New York.*

- Styron's daughter, Susanna Styron, directed the 1999 film *Shadrach,* adapted from one of her father's short stories. The film stars Andie MacDowell and Harvey Keitel and was released by Columbia Pictures.

- Dick Cavett interviewed William Styron on PBS in 1979. The tape is available from the Public Broadcasting System.

tles with depression, and his suicide as a way of thinking through his own depression.

Dr. Gold

Dr. Gold is Styron's Yale-trained psychiatrist, introduced in chapter five. Styron compares his relationship to Dr. Gold with Emma Bovary's relationship to the village priest in Flaubert's novel *Madame Bovary.* Just as the priest had no cure for Madame Bovary's malaise, Dr. Gold could offer only platitudes to Styron. Gold met with Styron twice a week but was largely ineffectual in his treatment of the writer. Gold's primary attempts to help him were through the prescription of antidepressants, especially Nardil. Gold is symbolic of contemporary medicine's de-humanizing approach to depression, which considers the ailment almost exclusively in physical terms.

Abbie Hoffman

Hoffman was a counter-culture figure and one of the founders of the Yippies, a group of pranksters and political activists who wreaked havoc at the 1968 Democratic convention in Chicago. Styron testified on his behalf in 1970. In 1989 Hoffman died after taking more than 150 phenobarbitals. Styron thinks that Hoffman's death, like the death of many other celebrities and famous writers he mentions, was the result of depression and could have been prevented with the proper treatment and attention.

William James

James is the author of *The Varieties of Religious Experience,* which Styron cites as an example of a book that tries unsuccessfully to describe depression.

Randall Jarrell

Jarrell was an American poet and critic who battled depression and mental illness for most of his life. He died after being hit by a car in 1965. Styron uses Jarrell, like Hoffman, as an example of someone who committed suicide because the pain of living with debilitating depression was too much. Styron discusses the stigma of suicide and how those close to suicide victims often attempt to represent their deaths otherwise.

Howard Kushner

Kushner is the author of the book *Destruction in the Promised Land.* In the book, Kushner, a social historian, holds that incomplete mourning is a contributing cause of depression and suicide. Styron uses Kushner's theory as a way to think about his own childhood and the difficulty he had mourning the loss of his mother, which may have contributed to his depression as an adult.

Primo Levi

Primo Levi was an Italian writer and Auschwitz survivor who died after a fall down a stairwell in Turin in 1987. Levi had been ill and was said to have been depressed. Styron, who himself wrote about Holocaust survival in his novel *Sophie's Choice,* speculates that Levi committed suicide as a result of his depression. He wrote a letter to the *New York Times* saying that suicide will never fully be prevented until people understand the intense pain of those who suffer from depression. Styron details the intellectual community's refusal to acknowledge Levi's depression as a legitimate cause of his suicide, suggesting that others cannot possibly understand the torment of one experiencing depression.

Jean Seberg

Seberg was Romain Gary's wife. She was an Iowa-born actress who committed suicide after battling depression. Styron describes her during her depression: "All her once fragile and luminous blond beauty had disappeared into a puffy mask. She moved like a sleepwalker, said little, and had the blank gaze of someone tranquilized . . . nearly to the point of catalepsy." Her description is important, for Styron uses it to illustrate how an outsider can never know at the time what someone experiencing severe depression is going through. His awareness of Seberg's suffering comes to light only after Styron tries to make sense of his own depression.

Rose Styron

Rose Styron is the author's long-suffering wife who accompanies the author to Paris and is always at his side. The author describes her as, "The endlessly patient soul who had become nanny, mommy, comforter, priestess, and, most important, confidant–a counselor or rocklike centrality to my existence whose wisdom far exceeded that of Dr. Gold." Styron never describes her appearance.

William Styron

William Styron is the central character in his own story about his battles with depression. He chronicles the major events of his depression, from the onset of a major episode in October 1985 to the beginning of his recovery in February 1986. Styron is sixty years old when the full force of his depression hits him, and he details his battles with it and the effects it has on his body and his relationships with other people, including his wife, Rose, and his friends. He describes his gradual withdrawal from his friends and the life he had known, his inability to work, the loss of his voice and his libido. Everything readers learn about other characters is through Styron's responses to them. He is alternately meditative and nostalgic, wistful and indignant, as he reflects on the illness of depression and how it sapped all life and hope from him.

Therapist

The unnamed hospital therapist is well-intentioned yet almost comical in her behavior. Styron describes her as "a delirious young woman with a fixed, indefatigable smile, who was plainly trained at a school offering courses in Teaching Art to the mentally ill." She is relentless in her praise of those in group therapy, almost to the point of idiocy. Her therapy consists of having group members draw pictures and make clay models of themes in which they were interested. Styron felt infantalized by many of the activities but nonetheless grew to "become fond" of the woman.

Virginia Woolf

Woolf is a well-known British feminist and writer who also suffered from depression and extreme mood swings. Her novels include *To The Lighthouse, Mrs. Dalloway, A Wave,* and *A Room of One's Own.* She committed suicide by drowning herself in the River Ouse. Woolf appears in Styron's list of famous writers and artists who have committed suicide because of their depression.

Themes

Medicine

Darkness Visible illustrates the controversies at the heart of treating depression. On the one hand, many of those afflicted do not want to be treated with drugs, believing that the root of their illness is not necessarily in their bodies but either in the world in which they live or in their spirit or mind. People in this camp often seek psychotherapy for treatment. On the other hand, a large part of the medical community itself staunchly defends the use of pharmaceuticals, arguing that depression is a result of faulty brain chemistry and that drugs are the most effective form of treatment for sufferers. Styron himself weighs both of these positions, writing:

> The intense and sometimes comically strident factionalism that exists in present-day psychiatry—the schism between the believers in psychotherapy and the adherents of pharmacology—resembles the medical quarrels of the eighteenth century (to bleed or not to bleed) and almost defines in itself the inexplicable nature of depression and the difficulty of its treatment.

Styron never resolves the conflict for himself, partaking of both psychotherapy and antidepressants at various points. Although he "conquers" the disease by the end of his story, his claim that "the disease of depression remains a great mystery" remains his final word on depression. Depression, for Styron, is as much an affliction of the soul as it is of the brain, and he compares those who have endured the "despair beyond despair" to poets who have trudged up from hell into the daylight of emotional health.

Meaning

In a way, *Darkness Visible* is a meditation on loss and meaning. When his depression hits, he writes that he feels his "mind dissolving" and that his brain is full of "anarchic disconnections." He loses his voice, his sexual desire, his physical energy, his ability to work, to communicate, to love. He has even lost the capacity to dream. All of the elements that conventionally define human behavior and identity are compromised. He describes himself as existing in a trance, unable to participate in the world in any meaningful way. The relentless whittling away of his world leads Styron at one point to contemplate suicide, the ultimate loss of self. Styron reflects on the relation between suicide and depression, making connections between the deaths of friends and acquaintances and their own struggles with depression or mood disorders. Such reflection, however, at least in retrospect, strengthens his conviction that many of these deaths could have been prevented if the victims (for example, Abbie Hoffman, Primo Levi, Albert Camus) had sought treatment for their depression. Meaning, Styron suggests, comes from the very act of surviving, of human courage in the face of a possibly meaningless universe. And cultivating meaning is more an act of human will than anything else. Styron recoups a degree of his own losses during his recovery from his writing about the disease. In the act of attempting to understand the experience of his depression, he reflects on the loss of his own mother during his childhood and speculates that his inability to mourn her death adequately may have contributed to his illness as an adult.

Style

Style

Darkness Visible is written from the first-person point of view and is a type of memoir. Memoirs are autobiographical accounts of a particular part of the writer's life. They entail the narrator looking back on an experience or period of time and trying to make sense of it. The narrator is Styron himself, who recounts six months of his life when he battled severe depression, writing from the vantage point of four years later. All of the characters have relevance to the theme of the story, which is the ability of the

Topics for Further Study

- Styron suggests that the onset of his severe depression came after he stopped drinking alcohol. Research the links between alcoholism and depression and discuss the ways in which the former may contribute to the latter.

- Write an essay exploring common psychological or physical diseases commonly associated with artists and writers.

- After interviewing people afflicted with emotional illness, write a short essay comparing their pain to the pain of those afflicted with physical illness. Draw on your own experience or that of people you know, if possible.

- Research the lives of Virginia Woolf, Randall Jarrell, and Vincent Van Gogh, then discuss what you see as the relationships between their emotional illnesses and their creative lives. In what ways do they influence each other?

- Read one of Styron's novels such as *Lie Down in Darkness* or *The Confessions of Nat Turner*. Describe the tone of these novels. What, if any, connections can you make between Styron's depression and the novels themselves. Keep in mind that Styron wrote that a dark mood has accompanied him through most of his life.

human spirit to endure and triumph in the face of severe adversity. The story is of *his* depression, and all other characters and their stories have relevance to Styron's own. Styron tells his story in a straightforward, literal manner with very little figurative language. This approach befits a nonfiction account of a medical illness.

Flashback

Flashbacks are frequently used to present action or fill in information that occurred before a story begins. Styron begins *Darkness Visible* by ''flashing back'' to the time when he first visited Paris, some thirty-three years before in 1952. By comparing his attitude when he first visited Paris to his mood when he is visiting the city in 1985, Styron dramatizes the change in his emotional state. Whereas once he was young, curious, full of possibility and hope, now he is old, exhausted, and consumed with despair.

Tone

Tone is the attitude of the speaker toward the subject matter. Styron's tone in *Darkness Visible* befits the very title of the book. As he recounts his

experience with depression, his language embodies the very nature of the disease. His sentences are languid, often sterile, and he repeats himself at times, as if struggling to get his mind around the very experience he is attempting to describe. But readers trust Styron's voice because he is at a distance from the experience. Though his prose is at times sluggish, it is also measured, rational, and—as much as he can be—objective.

Setting

The setting of a story refers to the when and where of the narrative's action. Most frequently, the setting is physical; for example, Mark Twain's *Huck Finn* takes place on and along the Mississippi River in the middle of the nineteenth century. Although Styron describes a few different physical places and geographical locations, the primary setting of his story is the author's mind itself. He describes Paris, his home in Connecticut, Martha's Vineyard, and the hospital to which he admits himself, but these descriptions are sketchy and not important to the story's development. What *is* important is Styron's emotional health, the interplay between his behavior and the trajectory of his depression and his cure.

Historical Context

The 1980s and Drugs in America

Styron's mental breakdown in 1985 preceded by two years the release of Prozac, the most popular antidepressant in the history of the world. Before pharmaceutical giant Eli Lilly developed Prozac, people with depressive disorders were treated with monoamine oxidase inhibitors and tricyclics such as Nardil, which Styron was prescribed. These drugs, however, often had debilitating side effects. Prozac, the brand name for fluoxetine hydrochloride, acts in a different way on the brain than the previous generation of antidepressants, regulating the action of serotonin. It needs to be taken only once daily, and its side effects, Lilly claims, are minimal. In its first ten years, Prozac was prescribed to more than ten million Americans for everything from depression and anxiety to personality disorders. Since its arrival on the market, Prozac has been a media phenomenon appearing on the cover of major magazines such as *Newsweek*. The drug's continued popularity and widespread use has also been the source of much controversy rooted in issues of human identity and money. Many opponents of the drug claim that it is being overprescribed, that increasingly doctors are using it to treat personality quirks, making it the equivalent of a designer drug. They argue that, though many may recover their emotional health, they often lose their sense of self in the process. Other Prozac naysayers, such as Peter Breggin, author of *Talking Back to Prozac,* claim that Eli Lilly rushed the product to market even though tests were inconclusive. Breggin suggests that Lilly is more concerned with profits than human health and that adverse side effects, such as decreased libido, nausea, and insomnia, are more common than has been reported.

The 1980s and 1990s witnessed an increase not only in the use of new antidepressants such as Prozac but also in the use of other so-called prescription designer drugs such as Halcion, a sleeping aid, which Styron himself used and for which he in part blames his depression; the diet drug phen-fen; and, in the late 1990s, Viagara, a drug also from Eli Lilly, which treats male impotence. While Americans were flocking to prescription drugs in record numbers to improve their lifestyle, the United States government was waging a war on illicit non-prescription drugs. Cocaine, much of it smuggled in from Latin American countries such as Colombia and Peru, became the recreational drug of choice for many middle- and upper-class Americans. Crack, a smokable and very potent form of cocaine, was often used by poorer people, who became easily addicted to the drug. Ronald Reagan's administration emphasized the danger of drug use to the family and to the moral fabric of society, as well as the cost to business. Attempting to influence consumption patterns before they happened, Nancy Reagan's "Just say No" campaign targeted children. Seeking to continue where his predecessor Ronald Reagan left off, President George Bush initiated his own "war on drugs" in 1989 when he outlined the federal government's strategy for ending drug use. The bulk of Bush's $8 billion plan went toward law enforcement, whereas only 30 percent went to prevention, education, and treatment. Such emphasis has resulted in a record number of people being incarcerated for drug-related crimes, most of them victimless.

Critical Overview

Styron penned *Darkness Visible* when he was sixty-four years old, after a successful career in which he had gained a reputation as a prose stylist who wrote engaging stories that emphasized enduring human themes. Its critical reception is to a large degree based on Styron's established reputation and the respect it affords him. With few exceptions the book was praised for its insight and candor. Reviewing the book for *Newsweek,* Peter Prescott wrote that "*Darkness Visible* . . . is an essay of great gravity and resonance. Never has Styron used so few words so effectively." Jon Saari of *Antioch Review* agreed, writing: "[Styron's] memoir should become a valuable addition to the understanding of depression, confirming again the role the literary artist plays in bringing light to the darkest secrets of the human psyche." Writing for *Magill Reviews,* R. Baird Shuman concurs: "His account of this struggle is candid and balanced. As an anatomy of the kind of severe depression that often culminates in suicide, *Darkness Visible* is a deeply personal statement."

Not all critics praised the book, however. R. Z. Sheppard writes in *Time* magazine that "by Styronian standards, [*Darkness Visible*] is a mote of a book. It began as a speech at Johns Hopkins University and was expanded to an article. . . . Adding 5,000 words to the magazine piece, the author manages to fill eighty-four pages of generously spaced type." Although Sheppard thinks the provocative content of the book makes it worth its price, he says, "There

Darkness Visible is Styron's meditation on his 1985 descent into suicidal depression and his reflection on possible causes and cures

is little literary justification for . . . [making the article into a book]. The loose narrative suggests the dangers of stretching one form to do the work of another.''

Criticism

Chris Semansky

Semansky is an instructor of English literature and composition at Chemeketa Community College. His fiction, poetry, and essays appear regularly in literary magazines and journals. In this essay, he examines Darkness Visible *in relation to themes of existentialism.*

The contradictions inherent in understanding the phenomenon of human depression parallel the contradictions inherent in understanding human existence itself. It is no surprise that Styron claims that Albert Camus, more than any other writer, has influenced his writing and his life. Camus' existentialism is rooted in the idea of the absurdity of human existence and the inscrutability of the world in which humans live. Comparing existentialist themes to themes of depression will show that the latter is an appropriate, if not necessary, condition for the former. After all, it is seldom that one hears about a happy existentialist.

The cornerstone of existentialist thought is that existence precedes essence. This position emphasizes human beings' material nature, their place apart from any system of predetermined behavior or nature. Human beings make choices, and their lives are the result of those choices. This idea is particularly evident in Camus' novel *The Stranger,* which tells the story of a man who commits murder for reasons he cannot fathom but who ultimately takes responsibility for the act. Styron's own refusal to see his depression as the result of any one cause *and* his admission that he himself might have brought on his condition (through his years of alcohol abuse) show his awareness that his own choices helped bring about the illness.

But if systems of thought, morality, and meaning are themselves bankrupt, to what does the individual anchor himself? For existentialists such as Camus, what remains is the void, an absence of meaning and meaning-making structures. Emptiness itself forms the background against which life is lived. Styron's own life in the wake of his depression mirrors this emptiness. It's as if the onslaught of full-blown depression enables him to realize the emptiness of his existence. Again and again in *Darkness Visible* he writes of the losses in his life during his depression, his inability to see beauty in the world, to make love to his wife, to write, even to hold a conversation. All of these things become impossible because of his depression. What remains is the feeling of loss itself, the emptiness at the root of his despair. Often accompanying this feeling of loss, for existentialists, is the feeling of alienation from one's own self. Karl Marx has described alienation as resulting from contradictions inherent in society. Human beings' desires are created by societal structures, which themselves are not capable of fulfilling those desires. Styron describes his own alienation from himself when he says that he often felt haunted, as if a ''wraithlike observer . . . not sharing the dementia of his double, is able to watch with dispassionate curiosity as his companion struggles against the oncoming disaster, or decides to embrace it.'' Styron's relentless self-conscious only adds to his pain, as he watches himself sink further and further into the bleakness, without the ability to halt it.

What Do I Read Next?

- *The Stranger* (1942), Albert Camus' classic existentialist novel, illustrates the terrors of human decision-making in a godless world. Styron names this book as a major influence on his own writing.

- Marty Jezer's 1992 biography of 1960s' rebel and Styron's friend Abbie Hoffman, *Abbie Hoffman: American Rebel,* attempts to reconcile Hoffman's public persona with his personal life. Styron speculates that Hoffman's death was a suicide linked to mental illness.

- Howard Kushner's 1991 study, *American Suicide: A Psychocultural Exploration,* explores the cultural fabric of American life and speculates on its relationship to the phenomenon of suicide in the United States.

- Hermione Lee's exhaustive 1999 biography, *Virginia Woolf,* provides theories and accounts of Woolf's bouts with depression.

- William Styron's *Lie Down in Darkness* (1951) chronicles the lives of a southern family and describes the events that culminate in the suicide of Peyton Loftis. This is Styron's first published novel.

- Elizabeth Wurtzel's 1997 memoir, *Prozac Nation: Young and Depressed in America,* chronicles the life of a young and privileged woman suffering from depression who is treated with Prozac, an antidepressant.

- Psychiatrist Peter Kramer's book *Listening to Prozac* (1997) explores the status of the antidepressant Prozac in America. Kramer examines the use of Prozac to "cure" personality problems as well as depression.

Accompanying Styron's feeling of loss and alienation are anxiety and dread, the overriding emotions that color existentialist thought. In existentialism, anxiety and dread undergird life itself. Human beings are anxious because they're aware that life has no meaning, that nothingness, non-being, is the ultimate reality. Systems of thought that posit happiness or salvation as the goal of human activity are naive because they give people false hope. Styron describes his own anxiety as a "brainstorm," saying that he could rarely sleep and that he was frequently overcome with a "positive and active anguish." Such anxiety is common in those diagnosed with depression, but it is almost always attributed to a neuro-chemical imbalance and treated with drugs. For "professionals," who themselves are a part of the system that attempts to give meaning to the lives of others, to admit that anxiety is a universal human condition is to admit defeat. (It would also put them out of a job.)

For existentialists, what can be more empty than death itself, the final nothingness that hovers over all life? Death, the absence of consciousness and continuity of the self is something that most human beings do not think about often. Yet existentialism, especially that strain put forth by German thinkers such as Martin Heidegger and Friedrich Nietszche, holds that it is only when contemplating one's own death that one can achieve authentic existence. However, taking one's own life, the ultimate existential act, is taboo for most and, in many societies, a crime. The very absurdity of that law underscores the (unspoken) anxiety that society has about life's meaning(lessness). Styron spends a great many words reflecting on suicide, particularly the suicide of others, suggesting that the deaths of many writers and artists, such as Virginia Woolf, Primo Levi, Romain Gary, and Abbie Hoffman, among others, might have been prevented if only these people had been aware of and sought help for their depression. But this very attitude by Styron contradicts another strain in his writing, which sympathizes with the choice that those very people made in taking their lives. In discussing Camus' *The Myth of Sisyphus,* which asks whether life is worth

> But if systems of thought, morality, and meaning are themselves bankrupt, to what does the individual anchor himself?"

living, Styron himself asks whether Camus' statement about suicide, "and his general preoccupation with the subject, might have sprung at least as strongly from some persistent disturbance of mood as from his concerns with ethics and epistemology." Styron himself contemplated suicide and indeed went so far as to destroy his diary, speak with his lawyer, and begin to compose a farewell letter when, at the last minute, he chose to check himself into a hospital.

Styron's inability to name his state of mind, his constant refrain that depression is "indescribable" and "beyond words," mirrors the ways in which existential philosophers have approached the idea of existence. Just as language cannot adequately represent depression, it also cannot represent the experience of existence itself. However, the difference between Styron's story of illness and recovery and the human condition as seen from an existential point of view is that he *has* found the language to represent depression. It is a language rooted in simple faith that there is meaning in the world. The meaning-producing system from which he finds the language to describe his experience is the discourse of art and artists. Just as Styron draws on a legion of artists and writers to illustrate the links among creativity, depression, and self-destruction, so too does he draw on the same figures to illustrate the redemption that comes from enduring suffering. These are Styron's words for those who have been healed of depression by time: "For those who have dwelt in depression's dark wood, and known its inexplicable agony, their return from the abyss is not unlike the ascent of the poet, trudging upward and upward out of hell's black depths and at last emerging into what he saw as 'the shining world.'" Such a description, drawn from Dante, does not attempt to explain the nature of the illness or even to offer strategies for surviving it. Indeed, nowhere in his narrative does Styron provide a real reason to refute existentialism's claim that the universe is inherently meaningless and that life is not worth

living. His only solace for those suffering from depression is that "depression is not the soul's annihilation . . . it is conquerable." The world that the sufferer returns to may not be more meaningful, or more rational, but it is, for Styron, more tolerable. Faced with a world in which meaning is not evident and in which communication often seems impossible, existentialists are often consumed with trying to find reasons to live, to justify *not* taking one's own life. For Styron, who endured an illness that surely magnified the absurdity of the human condition many times over, these reasons, like depression and existence itself, are beyond language.

Source: Chris Semansky, Critical Essay on *Darkness Visible*, in *Nonfiction Classics for Students*, The Gale Group, 2001.

Rena Korb

Korb has a master's degree in English literature and creative writing and has written for a wide variety of educational publishers. In the following essay, she discusses the contributions that Darkness Visible *makes to the layperson's understanding of depression, particularly as the illness is experienced by the sufferer.*

In 1985, author William Styron suffered a bout of depression so severe that after months of misery, barely able to sleep, engulfed by a "gray drizzle of horror," convinced there was "no escape" from his devastating situation, he stood on the brink of taking his own life. Although Styron managed to withdraw from the abyss and commit himself to a psychiatric ward where he regained his mental health, questions remained for him. What had caused the depression? How was he able to recover from it? How does society, including the medical community, react to its depressed members? Styron explores these issues through the deeply personal chronicle of his experience, *Darkness Visible*.

With remarkable candor, Styron shows that the depressed person lacks any belief that circumstances will get better. His close brush with suicide came when he had "reached the phase of the disorder where all sense of hope had vanished, along with the idea of a futurity." By December 1985, Styron was certain that "no remedy will come—not in a day, an hour, a month, or a minute." Any "mild relief" he might feel was "only temporary," leading him to the state of hopelessness that "crushes the soul." However, on the eve that Styron prepared for his suicide, he heard a snippet of Brahms, which "pierced my heart like a dagger." Although he had been "numbly unresponsive for months" to any form of pleasure, Styron reacted unexpectedly to the music as it made him recall "all the joys the house had known"—the children, the love, the hard work. "All this I realized was more than I could ever abandon," Styron remarked. "And just as powerfully I realized I could not commit this desecration on myself."

After battling back to health, Styron openly discussed his illness. In *Darkness Visible*, he shares a stark and truthful account of the downward journey from which many other gifted but troubled authors have been unable to emerge. Perhaps his main accomplishment is to help people who have not suffered from depression get some inkling about how the debilitating disease feels to its victims. Drawing on his own experiences, Styron provides several compelling and convincing examples of the healthy person's inability to comprehend depression. A devotee of the French novelist and philosopher Albert Camus, Styron strongly responded to "the cosmic loneliness" of the hero of Camus' *The Stranger;* when he read Camus' *The Fall,* however, he only "admired it with reservation" because "the guilt and self-condemnation of the lawyer-narrator, gloomily spinning out his monologue in an Amsterdam bar, seemed a touch clamorous and excessive." Having read the book before his own illness, Styron did not recognize that Camus had drawn an accurate if distressing portrayal of a man suffering from clinical depression. "Such was my innocence of the very existence of the disease," the post-sickness Styron acknowledges.

Even coming face-to-face with severe depression did not bring about any greater comprehension in Styron. He recalls a visit with a close friend, the novelist Romain Gary, and Gary's ex-wife, actress Jean Seberg, which took place only a few years before his own lapse into depression. Styron was "shocked and saddened" to see Seberg who "moved like a sleepwalker, said little, and had the blank gaze of someone tranquilized (or drugged, or both)." Despite this grim picture and despite Gary's mention of "something about antidepressant medications," Styron failed to realize the seriousness of the situation. "This memory of my relative indifference is important," he writes, "because such indifference demonstrates powerfully the outsider's inability to grasp the essence of the illness." Seberg committed suicide the following year, and when Styron subsequently visited with Gary in Paris, he noticed that his friend manifested physical symptoms of a malady—trembling hands and a voice that sounded prematurely aged. The culprit was re-

vealed when Gary bluntly stated that "his loss of Jean had so deepened his depression that from time to time he had been rendered nearly helpless." Recalls Styron of the encounter and his reaction, "But even then I was unable to comprehend the nature of his anguish." Shortly thereafter, Gary shot himself through the head. The implications of Gary's suicide still did not truly reach Styron; not until he neared helplessness himself, when "the pain descended," did Styron finally begin to grasp what Gary and Seberg had experienced—the certainty that "on some not-too-distant tomorrow—I would be forced to judge that life was not worth living."

Styron occupies a unique perspective; he has seen close friends undergo the torture of severe depression and has undergone it himself—and lived to tell. Because of these credentials, Styron can be trusted when he explains that the illness of depression is "a sensation close to . . . actual pain." The adjectives he continuously comes back to in repeated attempts to explain depression to healthy people are such words or phrases as "incomprehensible," "beyond description," and "unimaginable." Healthy people, he writes, have a "basic inability . . . to imagine a form of torment so alien to everyday experience."

As Styron's own case of depression further illustrates, it takes time even for the sufferer himself to develop self-awareness of the disease's manifestation. Styron's onset of depression was heralded only by a "subtle" change. His "surroundings took on a different tone at certain times," and he experienced "a moment during my working hours in the late afternoon when a kind of panic and anxiety overtook me, just for a few minutes." Though in hindsight he believes that "it should have been plain to me that I was already in the grip of the beginning of a mood disorder," at the time, he only felt "unfocused stirrings." Not until October 1985, while he was in Paris to accept an illustrious literary prize—one "which should have sparklingly restored my ego"—did Styron finally realize the seriousness of his situation.

The general lack of understanding of depression on the part of laypeople often results in others' refusal to accept the reality of depression-induced suicide. People close to a suicide victim who deny the truth about this death make the sufferer "unjustly . . . appear a wrongdoer." Suicide victims are viewed as acting out of cowardice, personal weakness, or "moral feebleness"; in truth, the individual most likely was "afflicted with a depression that was so devastating that he could no longer endure the pain of it." When the well-known 1960s radical Abbie Hoffman died from a major overdose of sedatives, Hoffman's brother still appeared on television "to deflect the idea of suicide, insisting that Abbie, after all, had always been careless with pills." Italian writer Primo Levi poses another striking example of a suicide casualty that others did not want to accept. After living through, and writing about, the horrors of the death camp at Auschwitz, years later the sixty-seven-year-old Levi threw himself down a flight of stairs. Styron notes that many participants at a conference on Levi "seemed mystified and disappointed" by the author's actions:

> It was as if this man whom they had all so greatly admired, and who had endured so much at the hands of the Nazis—had by his suicide demonstrated a frailty, a crumbling of character they were loath to accept. In the face of a terrible absolute—self-destruction—their reaction was helplessness and . . . a touch of shame.

Styron strongly disagreed; it was not weakness that killed Levi but an "anguish [that] can no longer be borne."

"[T]he disease of depression remains a great mystery," writes Styron. Significantly, it remains this way to many people, including those who suffer from it, those who witness it, and those who attempt to cure it. For instance, until becoming ill, Styron was unaware that "in its major stages [depression] possesses no quickly available remedy." He originally thought that his new doctor "would whisk my malaise away with his miraculous medications." Such naivete later shocked Styron: "I . . . am hardly able to believe that I possessed such ingenuous hope, or that I could have been so unaware of the trouble and peril that lay ahead."

Unfortunately, Styron's psychiatrist, whom he calls Doctor Gold, turns out to be little more than a quack. The only help he offered Styron, aside from

"ineffective" platitudes, was an antidepressant that made Styron "edgy" and "disagreeably hyperactive." When informed of these and other medical problems, Doctor Gold then prescribed Styron a new medication, one that did not actually take effect for several more weeks. He also prescribed a dosage that was three times the normal amount and particularly dangerous to someone Styron's age. (Styron later came to believe that this medication, taken in such large dosages, led him to become suicidal.) Perhaps even more shocking, when Styron broached the suggestion of checking into a hospital, Doctor Gold discouraged him from doing so, merely "owing to the stigma I might suffer." With this action, Doctor Gold obliquely but firmly upholds the erroneous idea that the depressed person is to blame for his problems. In the end, Styron had to rely on some hidden quality within himself to draw back from suicide. Like the "austere message" that Camus held out in *The Myth of Sisyphus,* Styron knew that "in the absence of hope we must still struggle to survive, and so we do—by the skin of our teeth."

After his recovery, in an effort to better understand depression, Styron hypothesizes as to the incipient cause of his condition. Though he categorizes his depression as "atypical," Styron nonetheless attributes it to standard causes, ones that are generally supported by research and science—primarily a genetic predisposition and an unresolved childhood trauma:

> The morbid condition proceeded, I have come to believe, from my beginning years—from my father, who battled the gorgon for much of his lifetime, and had been hospitalized in my boyhood after a despondent spiraling downward that in retrospect I saw greatly resembled mine. . . . But I'm persuaded that an even more significant factor was the death of my mother when I was thirteen; this disorder and early sorrow . . . appears repeatedly in the literature on depression as a trauma sometimes likely to create nearly irreparable emotional havoc.

"Loss," Styron writes, "in all of its manifestations is the touchstone of depression—in the progress of the disease and, most likely, in its origin."

Despite the many positive attributes of *Darkness Visible,* some readers will take issue with certain of Styron's assertions, namely his depiction of psychiatrists, therapists, and therapy; Styron seems to attack the state and practice of psychiatry in the United States. Though Doctor Gold certainly acts both immorally and hazardously, many readers will have a hard time accepting that he is representative of the American psychiatrist; countless people who have suffered from depression—both in its major and minor forms—have been greatly helped through psychiatric therapy as well as through medication. Though Styron boldly states that ''many psychiatrists . . . do not seem to be able to comprehend the nature and depth of the anguish their patients are undergoing,'' he provides no proof aside from his own experiences—he neither cites other people who have suffered from depression nor these maligned psychiatrists themselves. A hospital psychiatrist with whom Styron has some sessions also comes under attack. Styron finds this doctor, who ran group therapy, to be ''an odiously smug young *shrink* [emphasis mine].'' Both ''condescending and bullying,'' he seems to draw perverse personal satisfaction from making his patients cry. Further, the hospital's art therapist is described as ''a delirious young woman,'' one who was ''plainly trained at a school offering courses in Teaching Art to the Mentally Ill.'' Only in a brief, parenthetical aside does Styron acknowledge that he found most of the hospital's psychiatric staff ''exemplary in their tact and compassion.''

Styron's evocation of therapy is similarly dismissive. ''Group Therapy, I am told, has some value,'' he writes; ''I would never want to derogate any concept shown to be effective for certain individuals.'' However, he goes on to offer his own impression of it: ''Group Therapy did nothing for me except make me seethe . . . Time hangs heavy in the hospital, and the best I can say for Group Therapy is that it was a way to occupy the hours.'' Styron also was made to attend classes in art therapy, which he characterized as ''organized infantilism.'' Feeling ''humiliated rage'' at having to participate in this activity, Styron deliberately and successfully mimicked the ''intermediate stages of recuperation'' through his artwork, culminating in his creation of ''a rosy and cherubic head with a 'Have-a-Nice-Day' smile.'' His gulled therapist was ''overjoyed'' at the supposed ''example of the triumph over disease by Art Therapy.''

Styron credits the ''real healers'' of his illness as ''seclusion and time.'' If the depressed person can ''survive the storm itself,'' as Styron did, ''its fury almost always fades and then disappears. . . . Mysterious in its coming, mysterious in its going, the affliction runs its course, and one finds peace.'' The hospital merely served to facilitate this process, because in the institution ''one's only duty is to try and get well.'' Styron seems to claim that his recovery stemmed completely from his own efforts and his ability to hold on to life in the face of despair.

Still, Styron's final chapter is a testament to the sense of hope that he and other sufferers may yet find within themselves. Like Styron, many of those afflicted with this grave disease have recovered, conquering this despondency of the soul. Further, Styron believes that many of these people have also been ''restored to the capacity for serenity and joy.'' He ends his essay with a quote from Dante's *Inferno:* ''And so we came forth, and once again beheld the stars.'' Writes John Bemrose in *Maclean's,* ''That note of hope is *Darkness Visible*'s final, moving gift.''

Source: Rena Korb, Critical Essay on *Darkness Visible* in *Nonfiction Classics for Students,* The Gale Group, 2001.

Karen D. Thompson

Thompson is a freelance writer who writes primarily in the education field. In this essay, she explains how Styron creates for readers a vicarious journey into insanity through the style of his memoir.

Traffic snarls as motorists crane their necks toward an automobile accident, movies continually surpass each other in the amount and nature of graphic violence they depict, and real-life crime sells well in books and on television. Why is that so? Psychologists do not agree on the motivation behind such macabre interest. Many individuals cannot explain themselves the force that makes them look at things they would rather not see. But the answer as to *why* they look is not preeminent. What is important is that they *do* look. Reading William Styron's slim volume *Darkness Visible* is the literary equivalent of witnessing an indescribable act of violence. Whether readers devour it in amazement because they find within it the gruesomely accurate record of their own sufferings, or they endure it in thankful relief that their own situation does not approach the depth of despair voiced within it, they read it. When they have finished, they have in their minds a surprisingly accurate presentation of one man's descent into the abyss of a depressive disorder.

The book is not remarkable in that Styron found a way to describe the mental illness that is depression. He admits early on that there are no words for what he endured. His choice of title alone should be enough to convince potential readers that he does not have the words to describe his mental demise. The oxymoron ''visible darkness'' describes nothing at all. Styron reiterates in the final pages of this book that ''since antiquity . . . chroniclers of the human spirit have been wrestling with a vocabulary that might give proper expression to the desolation

According to an interview in the New York Times Book Review, *the catalyst for Styron's account of his depression was his defense of the writer Primo Levi, who committed suicide in 1987*

of melancholia.'' He acknowledges that to those who live with it, ''the horror of depression is so overwhelming as to be quite beyond expression, hence the frustrated sense of inadequacy found in the work of even the greatest artists.'' Though he attempts to describe certain symptoms of his disease, his description of the symptoms should not be equated with a description of the disease any more than a description of fever and aching joints should be equated with the description of a particular malady. The way this book succeeds in sharing an intimate experience with depression is not through a description of depression; it is through its form. The book's stark prose, fixation on death, and egocentric viewpoint that underscores the isolation of depression combine to create a hellish metaphor—a simulation rather than a snapshot.

The book is written in a style that mimics the starkness of being trapped in a depressed state. Stark in one sense can mean lifeless (as in lacking animation or vividness), and the prose in this work is definitely lifeless in that sense. The book begins with a scene remembered from a dark, rainy Octo-

ber evening. Styron was in France to receive a prestigious award and under normal circumstances would have relished the award, the vacation, and the company of his wife in one of the world's most romanticized cities, Paris. But the beauty, both real and mythical, of Paris was lost on Styron. He describes the ''damp, plain'' hotel where he first stayed as a young man visiting Paris thirty-five years earlier and remembers its ''drab bedroom'' and ''ill-lit hallway.'' As the book progresses, Styron stays in Paris and dines at a pair of exceptional restaurants. Yet in keeping with the stark nature of his depression, he describes neither ambiance nor cuisine. There is no color and no flavor in this writing.

The starkness of the book's tone is further developed in Styron's conscious or subconscious use of particular words. In the first sentence of the book he uses the word ''fatal'' in the sense of meaning ''deadly.'' He admits that his depression gradually reached a point at which he realized the outcome might be deadly. Almost immediately, he uses the word again, this time to describe a feeling of coming full circle, of literally ending his experience of Paris where he had begun it, at the Washington Hotel. His meaning of the word in context is quite clear; he means ''fatally'' as in ''fatefully'' or ''a fulfilling of fate.'' Yet he ends the paragraph with the statement that he feels he will never see Paris again, that when he leaves it will be ''a matter of forever.'' In other words, he has modulated into the initially used meaning of fatal as in ''deadly.''

Styron's use of the various meanings of the word *fatal* supports the statement that the book's language and thus its tone is stark, but it also prepares the reader for another characteristic of this book: It dwells largely on death. Primarily, Styron dwells on suicide in the book. From his first pages there can be no doubt that Styron believes his mental state to be grave. He is haunted by the continual specter of death: ''thoughts of death had long been common during my siege, blowing through my mind like icy gusts of wind.'' Very soon the rather general preoccupation with death becomes a preoccupation with suicide. He wrote that, at one point, ''many of the artifacts of my house had become potential devices for my own destruction.'' Included in his list are ''the attic rafters (and an outside maple or two) a means to hang myself, the garage a place to inhale carbon monoxide, the bathtub a vessel to receive the flow from my opened arteries. The kitchen knives in their drawers had but one purpose for me.'' Styron did seem to make, as far as this book is concerned, a rare attempt at humor by adding, almost in the way a comedian would, an aside about "an outside maple or two." However, this attempt serves only to highlight the total absence of any humorous or light-hearted elements in the rest of the book.

In addition to being overwhelmed by Styron's pervasive thoughts of death, readers are subjected to a ponderously long list of Who's Who among suicides. Additionally, numerous suicides are chronicled in detail. In those cases readers learn about possible motivating factors leading to the suicide, the observable signs of the deceased's irreversible slide into depression, and even the means by which the suicide was carried out. The effect is to leave the reader, once he or she has finished the book, crushed under the weight of the Grim Reaper as surely as if the black-cloaked figure was sitting upon the reader's chest.

A third way that this book manages to convey the experience of mental disorder is in its total egocentricity and the isolation represented by egocentricity. Saying that a person suffering from mental illness is egocentric is not to criticize that person for being vain or selfish. It is simply to say that a deeply depressed person loses the capacity to think of anyone or anything else. This may explain why hypochondria often accompanies depression. Styron explains this phenomenon quite deftly by explaining that it is part of "the psyche's apparatus of defense: unwilling to accept its own gathering deterioration, the mind announces to its indwelling consciousness that it is the body with its perhaps correctable defects—not the precious and irreplaceable mind—that is going haywire." Thus a depressed person's attention becomes consumed by the depressed person's mental and physical health. Each symptom elicits either paralyzing fear because it is a symptom of mental illness or joyous welcome— no matter how serious—because it is an identifiable symptom of a physical illness.

Another element of this work that suggests the self-centered nature and therefore isolating nature of depression is the way in which secondary figures in the book appear as no more than one-dimensional caricatures. This book was written as a memoir, after the fact of Styron's depressive episode. The reason none of the secondary people in the book achieve more than a cutout status is that Styron has no information about them on which to draw for his memoir. During his depression he was completely focused on himself. Thus Madame del Duca, who according to Styron plays a pivotal role in the

> **The effect is to leave the reader, once he or she has finished the book, crushed under the weight of the Grim Reaper as surely as if the black-cloaked figure was sitting upon the reader's chest."**

story's pivotal scene, never becomes a three-dimensional figure. Rather she is as flat as the Queen of Hearts in Alice's Wonderland. Styron's wife, Rose, whom he clearly loves, never achieves more than a marginal status. She is a disembodied voice that encourages him on his road to recovery and never an identifiable individual. Dr. Gold (one has to wonder if his made-up name was the result of Styron's attempt to discredit him even more by tying him to the crazed alchemists) is a comic book figure. A casting director would wish to resurrect Groucho Marx complete with cigar to play the much-maligned psychiatrist. Styron was attended in the hospital by a Barbie doll art therapist and a Machiavellian group facilitator. The only human who emerges from this book as a complete character is Styron. Clearly he felt, during the worst periods of his depression, that no person in the world could provide relief from his torture. He was completely isolated in a dark world.

All this having been said about the way a certain degree of self-fixation is understandable in a depressed individual, Styron cannot be completely absolved of his egocentricity. Certainly he should be excused to a great extent because this is, after all, an autobiographical work. By definition a writer must be the hero in his or her autobiography. But here it must be reiterated that this is a memoir, written after Styron's worst depression. Styron's preoccupation with self that results from his condition often gives way to sheer egotism. This happens in much the same way it happens in Robert Browning's dramatic monologues in which an unsuspecting narrator reveals quite unintentionally undesirable aspects of his or her own personality. Frequently, Styron draws attention away from his subject, depressive disorder, and onto himself. For example, when he relates the story of a piece he wrote for the *New York Times* concerning suicidal impulse and the unfairness of reproving posthumously those who commit suicide, he makes a sophomoric mistake: "It had taken, I speculated, no particular originality or boldness on my part to speak out frankly about suicide and the impulse toward it. . . ." Young writers learn early on that essays need not contain references to the self. Writers should state their opinions without announcing that they are their opinions. Readers can understand for themselves that the opinions expressed in the essay are, in fact, the opinions of the essay's author. To continually refer to the self as in "I believe" or "It is my opinion" is to pull attention away from the thought and place it upon the thinker.

In addition to constant and unnecessary references to himself, Styron reveals a great deal of egotism concerning his own accomplishments. He says in one paragraph (in which he used the pronoun "I" more than fifteen times) that

> throughout much of my life I have been compelled . . . to become an autodidact in medicine, and have accumulated a better-than-average amateur's knowledge about medical matters (to which many of my friends, surely unwisely, have often deferred) and so it came as an astonishment to me that I was close to a total ignoramus about depression.

As an isolated incident, a description of his own attainments in such straightforward terms would be seen as simple honesty. But once readers are subjected over and over to Styron's special attainments, whether they are literary awards, exceptional knowledge, or famous acquaintances, readers become impatient with Styron's constant waving of his own banner. His parenthetical mention that his friends may have deferred to his medical advice unwisely does not have the effect of downplaying his amateur medical knowledge or his intellectual attainment. It is a failed attempt to lower himself to the plain of the ordinary individual and it smacks of false modesty.

Despite this annoying egotism, *Darkness Visible* presents a fascinating vicarious journey through the spiraling depths of depression. Had Styron simply presented a case study of himself as a victim of uni-polar depression, the result would have been one more well meaning but ineffectual attempt to explain the vice grip of depression to those who have not been afflicted. What he ultimately produced was not a work of explanation but rather of inundation. Readers are enshrouded, much as victims of depression are, in the stark, lifeless existence of a person in the throes of a clinical depression. They are assaulted by the constant specter of Death in its most paradoxical form, suicide. Finally, they

are aware of the isolation imposed upon the depressed person by his or her own mind—a mind that cannot feel beyond its own pain, see beyond its own suffering, or hope for freedom from its self-imposed prison.

Source: Karen D. Thompson, Critical Essay on *Darkness Visible,* in *Nonfiction Classics for Students,* The Gale Group, 2001.

Carol Iannone

In the following review, Iannone questions Styron's depiction of depression as a disease over which sufferers have little control.

When an individual suffers the honors of Auschwitz, survives to write inspiringly about man's ability to endure in extreme circumstances, but years later takes his own life over what many would deem no more than the ordinary unhappiness of the human condition, the event seems bound to become at the very least a source of sorrowful wonder. Such was the death of the Italian Jewish writer Primo Levi in 1987, and such was the mixture of shock, dismay, disappointment, puzzlement, and confusion expressed by admiring writers and critics at a conference held some months after his suicide.

But the response of the American novelist William Styron was quite different. When he read a report in the New York *Times* on the Levi conference. Styron was offended to learn that the participants seemed to feel that

> this man whom they had all so greatly admired, and who had endured so much at the hands of the Nazis— a man of exemplary resilience and courage—had by his suicide demonstrated a frailty, a crumbling of character they were loath to accept. In the face of a terrible absolute—self-destruction—their reaction was helplessness and (the reader could not avoid it) a touch of shame.

Styron countered this "touch of shame" by writing an op-ed article for the *Times* setting out an argument that is further substantiated in his latest, very slim, book, in which he also tells of his own battle with severe depression and suicidal behavior. "The argument I put forth was fairly straightforward," Styron now writes of his op-ed piece:

> The pain of severe depression is quite unimaginable to those who have not suffered it, and it kills in many instances because its anguish can no longer be borne. The prevention of many suicides will continue to be hindered until there is a general awareness of the nature of this pain. Through the healing process of time—and through medical intervention or hospitali-

zation in many cases—most people survive depression, which may be its only blessing; but to the tragic legion who are compelled to destroy themselves there should be no more reproof attached than to the victims of terminal cancer.

Styron has made something of an avocation out of promulgating this view of depression-as-disease, and he sees his new book, combined with lectures and television appearances, as an effort both to help others similarly troubled and to help change social attitudes. But of course the "disease model" is nothing new in today's discourse; in fact, it has become the major means of characterizing numerous problems, like drug addiction and alcoholism, that were once seen as lapses in character or morality. So far from being new revelations, such characterizations may be passing their prime of acceptance; facing Kitty Dukakis's recent tell-all *Now You Know,* even a New York *Times* reviewer could write with a trace of weary condescension that "the sins and nasty habits of old are now labeled diseases . . . beyond the control of [their] victims. The idea of taking the moral blame and responsibility for failings has become passé." On the other hand, the fact that Styron's book has rocketed to the very top of the bestseller list seems to indicate that the disease model is still very much alive and well.

Behind the disease model, and behind the reverse moral righteousness of its purveyors, is a presumption that this approach lessens suffering, helps effect cures more readily, and alleviates the burden of inner worthlessness borne by depressives and others with similar disorders. But is it really such a liberation to adopt this model? Is it truly more helpful? Styron's own book offers plenty of grounds for doubt.

Take, to begin with, the book's tone. Significantly, Styron says that at one time he attempted to write a novel about his ordeal, but "the work ended up feeling artificial, and I abandoned it." The reader of *Darkness Visible* can easily see why. A lot of the time, Styron sounds like a second-rate Poe or Coleridge as he attempts, sensationalistically, melodramatically, to conjure up the horrors he experienced: "Doubtless depression had hovered near me for years, waiting to swoop down. Now I was in the first stage—premonitory, like a flicker of sheet lightning barely perceived—of depression's black tempest." Or: "Then, after dinner, sitting in the living room, I experienced a curious inner convulsion that I can describe only as despair beyond despair." Although Styron regrets the "indescribability" of depression, he seems actually

> **Before we heed the prophets who try to comfort us with assurances that our fate is entirely out of our hands, we should at least become aware of the alternatives."**

to be relying for effect on the awe and sympathy that can accompany "the basic inability of healthy people to imagine a form of torment so alien to everyday experience." As with the Dukakis book and other celebrity tell-alls, one begins to feel uncomfortably that by writing about the experience the author is satisfying the very craving for attention and pity that was part of the problem to begin with.

But what about the physical elements which to a great extent form the basis of the disease model? Styron reports: "It has been established with reasonable certainty" that depression "results from an aberrant biochemical process" in the brain, a complex chain reaction among neurotransmitters, chemicals, and hormones. But this does not stop him from pronouncing as well that "the disease of depression remains a great mystery," on that "strident factionalism . . . exists in present-day psychiatry—the schism between the believers in psychotherapy and the adherents of pharmacology." It has not stopped him from disbelieving in the efficacy of either psychiatric school in advanced cases. And it has not stopped him from conjecturing inconclusively about a host of other factors as possible components of his own trouble—from turning sixty, to childhood loss, to alcoholic withdrawal, to tranquilizer overdose, to dissatisfaction with his work.

No more, one might add, has it stopped the proliferation of theories about the etiology of depression in the medical profession, where heredity, temperament, childhood deprivations, and life experiences in addition to hormonal imbalance are all invoked a contributors to the disease. With such a combination of elements, it seems that we know everything and nothing. In other words, to say the cause is physical seems ultimately to be saying very little. Styron's own greatest hope lies in the passage of time and "the passing of the storm. . . . Mysterious in its coming, mysterious in its going, the affliction runs its course, and one finds peace."

But the course of Styron's own emergence from depression and suicidal behavior makes us wonder, not only at this characterization of time as the main healer, but at his confident insistence that to understand and deal with depression, we must abandon the moral dimension. Two key scenes stand out in the drama of his recovery.

The columnist Art Buchwald was a close friend who kept in contact with Styron during his trouble. Among the ways Buchwald helped was in continually ''admonishing me that suicide was unacceptable.'' Now, ''unacceptable'' may not be quite the equivalent of the ''Everlasting'' having ''fixed his canon 'gainst self-slaughter'' (*Hamlet*), but it's something. Thus, Styron's own resistance to suicide may have been strengthened by the very sort of moral consideration—however attenuated in the word ''unacceptable''—he takes pains to decry in his book. Suppose Buchwald had counseled him—as Styron would have us all be counseled—that, given the situation, suicide was entirely understandable?

At another moment, at the very crisis of his ordeal, actually on the verge of suicide, Styron hears the Brahms *Alto Rhapsody.* The sound ''pierced my heart like a dagger,'' he writes in one of the book's few animated passages,

> and in a flood of swift recollection I thought of all the joys the house had known: the children who had rushed through its rooms, the festivals, the love and work, the honestly earned slumber, the voices and the nimble commotion, the perennial tribe of cats and dogs and birds. . . . All this I realized was more than I could ever abandon, even as what I had set out so deliberately to do was more than I could inflict on those memories, and upon those, so close to me, with whom the memories were bound. And just as powerfully I realized I could not commit this desecration on myself. I drew upon some last gleam of sanity to perceive the terrifying dimensions of the mortal predicament I had fallen into.

What was happening here? Did not this flow of thoughts and impressions bring Styron to a choice in favor of life over death? What, then, at this point, were all his neurotransmitters and chemicals and hormones up to? Did those merciless gods turn their heads at the fatal moment? Clearly what happened was that Styron's self-absorption was suddenly broken, permitting the entrance of healing thoughts, and, importantly, of concern for others. Similarly, Buchwald, himself a recovering depressive, had reported that helping Styron was ''a continuing therapy for him,'' but from this Styron draws entirely the wrong lesson—that ''the disease engen-

ders lasting fellowship.'' What helped Buchwald was getting out of himself, feeling the blessedness of being useful to another. This release from self is the process at work in Tolstoy's Levin in *Anna Karenina,* who loses his morbid preoccupations when a peasant tells him that he must not live for himself but for God, or in a woman I know whose long depression was lifted when she heeded the admonition of an aunt to think of her children instead of herself.

Thinking in terms of choice, responsibility, or even ''sin'' is not a means of self-condemnation, which is after all another sin, but of liberation and redemption. Though the idea of sinfulness seems to make people furious nowadays—we are supposed to be wonderful in all points—really sin is simply a way of describing the essential flawedness of human nature and the human condition, reparable by recourse to the transcendent, or by opening oneself to an order of experience larger than the self. Thousands of years ago the Psalmist sang of this experience, while also incidentally evincing an awareness of the very physical symptoms of depression Styron writes about:

> . . . When I kept silence, my bones waxed old through my roaring all the day long. / For day and night Thy hand was heavy upon me: my moisture is turned into the drought of summer. / I acknowledged my sin unto Thee, and mine iniquity have I not hid. I said, I will confess my transgressions unto the Lord; and Thou forgavest the iniquity of my sin . . . / Many sorrows shall be to the wicked: but he that trusteth in the Lord, mercy shall compass him about. / Be glad in the Lord, and rejoice, ye righteous: and shout for joy, all ye that are upright in heart.

Another basis for the disease model—not invoked by Styron—may be Alcoholics Anonymous, but the AA program shows a deep understanding of the human character that much current discourse does not. It is true that AA calls alcoholism a disease—the term has been applied as well to the many other disorders, including depression, treated through the AA twelve-step program—but it does so mainly for the purposes of relieving the alcoholic of useless self-condemnation, of any tendency to blame others for his drinking, or of the temptation to spend fruitless energy searching for the cause. It is not meant to relieve him of responsibility for his plight. Once the ''disease'' has been acknowledged, the individual then embarks on a program of recovery in which he must ''take his inventory,'' or, as it would have been called in another age, examine his conscience, a process that can be demanding enough to satisfy a puritan saint. The individual must also make amends for past behavior that has been hurtful to others. Behind all this is the notion that faulty moral and characterological habits do indeed lead to the confusions and messes that can make a person escape into drink or drugs or depression.

Another apparently neglected aspect of these programs is the requirement of anonymity. It may be thought that this requirement was originally designed to protect the alcoholic from the glare of a disapproving society, and that now, in our radically altered social climate, it is no longer necessary. But there is yet another important reason for anonymity, and that is the need for humility, something severely compromised when one draws widescale attention to one's problems. The celebrity revolving-door-clinic, book-tour, and media-appearance approach seems to show little awareness of these aspects of the twelve-step program, concentrating exclusively on the disease concept which, by itself, can be efficacious only to a limited point.

It is really quite amazing how Styron manages to protect himself from any awareness along these lines. To describe his depression he boldly uses the famous opening stanza of the *Inferno* ("In the middle of the journey of our life / I found myself in a dark wood, / For I had lost the right path") and closes his book with the hopeful closing line of that same canticle ("And so we came forth, and once again beheld the stars") while studiously managing to ignore completely what comes in between.

The "sullen," as they are called in John Ciardi's translation of the *Inferno,* are Dante's version of the depressive, and they float beneath the surface of a muddy ditch in one of the upper circles of hell, gurgling: "Sullen were we in the air made sweet by the Sun; / in the glory of his shining our hearts poured / a bitter smoke." At a much lower circle Dante comes upon the wood of the suicides. There he experiences deep compassion with the poignant plight of Pier delle Vigne, and is overcome by emotion (as often happens when he is more in sympathy with the sinner than with divine justice). But ultimately Dante will not revoke the moral law which represents his own salvation and the salva-

tion of all, and which he knows is intricately connected to the sufferings men endure and inflict. After *this* knowledge, there *is* forgiveness.

Before we heed the prophets who try to comfort us with assurances that our fate is entirely out of our hands, we should at least become aware of the alternatives.

Source: Carol Iannone, "Depression-as-Disease," in *Commentary,* Vol. 90, No. 5, November 1990, pp. 54–57.

Sources

Breggin, Peter, and Ginger Breggin, *Talking Back to Prozac: What Doctors Aren't Telling You about Today's Most Controversial Drug,* St. Martin's Press, 1994.

Prescott, Peter S., "Journey to the End of Despair," in *Newsweek,* Vol. 116, No. 9, August 27, 1990, p. 60.

Saari, Jon, Review in *Antioch Review,* Vol. 49, Issue 1, Winter 1991, p. 146.

Sheffield, Anne, *How Can You Survive When They're Depressed,* Harmony, 1998.

Sheppard, R. Z., "Page Fright," in *Time,* Vol. 136, Issue 10, Sept. 3, 1990, p. 73.

Shuman, R. Baird, "Darkness Visible: A Memoir of Madness," in *Magill Book Reviews,* Salem Press, 1990.

Styron, William, *Darkness Visible*, Vintage, 1990.

Further Reading

Ross, Daniel William, ed., *The Critical Response to William Styron,* Greenwood, 1995.
    This collection of criticism offers essays from the 1950s to 1995 on novels such as *Lie Down In Darkness*, *The Long March*, and *Darkness Visible.* The essays treat themes such as Styron's place in the literary canon and the influences on his work.

West, James L. W., *William Styron: A Life,* Random House, 1998.
    In this definitive biography of Styron, West details the creative process behind each of Styron's novels. The attention to Styron's life outside of writing, however, is lacking.

The Education of Henry Adams

Henry Brooks Adams

1907

The Education of Henry Adams had been an important and influential text for a decade before Henry Adams was awarded the Pulitzer Prize in autobiography in 1918. The import of the text begins with its author, the weight of its influence with its first audience; its continued appreciation has as much to do with the first two factors as the fact that it was brilliantly constructed by a man of letters at the height of his powers.

Descended from one of America's most famous political families, Adams contributed a classic work of American historiography and one of the most famous autobiographies of American literature instead of making a great political contribution to the country. Adams does provide insight into the Adams family, a source of fascination not unlike the Kennedys, but he is curiously silent on two areas of his own life. Adams discusses his experience as private secretary to his father, minister to England during the American Civil War. However, he says almost nothing on his role as advisor and confidante to John Hay, secretary of state to President William McKinley and President Theodore Roosevelt, while the United States became a world power. The other deafening silence concerns the absence of the lessons he must have learned from his wife's suicide.

Adams' release of one hundred self-published folios of *The Education of Henry Adams* to some of the most powerful people on earth—from writers to heads of state—guaranteed interest. Those who

were not among the first one hundred went to extraordinary lengths to glean any information about the contents. These one hundred copies had a preface authored by Adams. The second text was released to the general public after Adams died. This edition contained a preface penned by Adams but signed by Henry Cabot Lodge in 1918.

Author Biography

The fourth child of statesman and diplomat Charles Francis and Abigail Brown, Henry Adams was born in Boston, Massachusetts, on February 16, 1838. At the age of four, having survived a bout with scarlet fever, Adams joined the rest of the family at their new home on Mount Vernon Street in Quincy, a suburb of Boston. Along with receiving an education appropriate to his class, Adams absorbed current political ideas from his father and those who visited the house, particularly Charles Sumner. Adams grew up believing himself to be a member of the ruling class destined to be involved in politics.

Adams attended Harvard College, receiving a bachelor of arts in 1858. Due to the influence of his tutor, James Russell Lowell, Adams pursued two years of graduate study at the University of Berlin. Due to his birth rank, the family had lower expectations for Adams, although he saw his role as private secretary to his father, during service as America's minister to Britain from 1861 to 1868, as a stepping stone to a career in politics. On the way to London, Adams met John Hay, Abraham Lincoln's private secretary, and they became lifelong friends.

Returning to Washington, D.C., from London in 1868, Adams used journalism to remain involved in politics. His time as a journalist ended when he accepted an invitation from Charles Eliot, president of Harvard College, to serve as assistant professor in medieval history and the editor of the *North American Review* in 1870. As an established man, Adams married Marian "Clover" Cooper in June of 1872. He gave up the Cambridge career in 1877, and the couple moved to Washington, D.C., where Adams began work on *History of the United States during the Administrations of Jefferson and Madison.*

Henry Adams

Adams kept his domestic affairs to himself and as a result speculation surrounded his years of married life. Tragically, Clover ingested a photochemical solution and died in December 1885. In response, Adams withdrew from society. He completed his nine-volume history (1889–1891) that won the Loubat Prize from Columbia University. In 1894, he became president of the American Historical Association.

Until a stroke in 1912 curtailed his activities, Adams traveled, reflected, and advised John Hay. Adams' journey to the South Pacific, where he visited with the people of Samoa and Tahiti, inspired a reconsideration of civilization. Adams saw the people of the South Pacific as still living in a unified culture. In response, Adams felt that unity was precisely the element eluding the America of the nineteenth century. His search for that lost unity led him to revisit the Gothic cathedrals of Normandy and inspired him to write *Mont-Saint-Michel and Chartres* (1905). By 1906, the companion volume, *The Education of Henry Adams* existed but only circulated privately in 1907. Though he wrote several thousand letters and a couple essays more, Adams' work of 1906 was his swan song. He died on March 27, 1918, in Washington, D.C.

Summary

Early Years

Beginning at his birth, Adams' describes himself as being at the mercy of historical forces. He was born into a family with a founding father and second president of the nation, the sixth president, and the historical inertia of Boston's seat of the War for Independence against Great Britain. Adams comments on these forces and the way in which they display themselves while his earliest years are divided between the Brooks' home in Boston and the Adams' house in Quincy. After relating a remarkable lesson in discipline, taught to him by his grandfather, John Quincy Adams, Adams discusses his development in the shadow of his father's character. Adams molds himself after Charles Francis by observing him in comparison with other political figures that frequent the house, namely Charles Sumner. Throughout his childhood in Quincy and Boston, Henry Adams is "free to turn with the world." Washington, D.C., would change that.

School Years

In 1850, Adams travels with his father to Washington, D.C., to visit his grandmother, Louisa. While there, Adams' belief in his destiny becomes bolstered while he tours the Senate Chamber and visits President Taylor in the White House, a home he views as that of his family. He and his father tour Mount Vernon where the paradox of George Washington, symbol of freedom and slave owner, do not phase Adams. Back in Boston, Adams lost Sumner to a Congressional term in Washington, D.C.

Adams attends Harvard College where disillusionment sets in. Except for a few quirky Virginians, Adams finds his classmates unremarkable. Although Adams ranked near the bottom of his class, he was elected Class Orator and delivered the commencement address. From Harvard College, Adams headed to the University of Berlin for two years. He had thought it was the place to study Civil Law but his enthusiasm was stymied by "the lecture system in its deadliest form as it flourished in the thirteenth century." His other excuse for not studying was the city. A change to Dresden improved his scenery but not his study. He finds that the Germany he loved was a romanticized eighteenth-century Germany, not the militarized Germany of Bismarck. Fortunately, his sister—now married to Charles Kuhn—lures him to Switzerland and then Italy. Adams heads home after an accident causes his sister's death.

The Civil War

Since Adams had not embarked on any career, he accompanied his father to Washington, D.C., in the capacity of a private secretary. Adams intended to continue his law studies by reading Blackstone. Instead, the excitement of secession and possible war stopped progress on those lines as he joined the rest of the nation in the education of war. The first events came in the congressional battle to keep Virginia in the Union. Seward in the Senate and Charles Francis in the House led these efforts. As Lincoln's term in office opened, Adams meets John Hay but loses Sumner's friendship during the emergency wrangling.

Lincoln wisely sent Charles Francis to London as the American minister. There the legation's chief function was to maintain America's dignity at the seat of the British Empire while diffusing the British intent of illegally aiding the Confederates. With his few friends and his own social standing, Charles Francis played his role in British domestic politics and he played for time. Political success remained impossible while the Union Army suffered defeat but Charles' constancy paid large dividends in 1863 during "The Battle of the Rams," the ironclads *Monitor* and *Merrimac*. His use of British society and British law were now supported by Union victories and Britain was forced to dry-dock several ironclads that they had hoped to send to the Confederacy. Meanwhile, Adams discerned many lessons about the way British power works and how British minds operate. However, while an American politician might master the ecology of London utilizing family and social connection as well as brains, such an education exactly disabled him for service anywhere else.

A Career Despite Himself

Adams has a career in journalism, which begins with the publication of some of his letters home in Boston. Persuaded by his success and his family, he decides to take advantage of his connections and pursue writing to the extent of his powers. He begins writing while still working for his father and mostly out of boredom. He has several scoops published anonymously, which luckily do not create a scandal for his father. Attracted by the latest scientific theories disrupting the natural sciences, Adams successfully aids in their popularization through his magazine articles. This period of almost normal professionalism leads to a position as assistant professor at Harvard as well as a magazine editor. His career ends in 1877 when he decides that institutional education is useless.

Man as a Force

Remarking from the vantage point of 1892, Adams finished his education in 1871 when he began to apply it; this marked the beginning of his last section of his work. In this section, Adams reflects on the acceleration of change in American society wrought by technology and a shift to a "banker's world." His venues for reflection include the World's Fairs and the careers of his closest friends. In Chicago and again in Paris, he dwells on the power of the new machines at the heart of societal change. In response, he positions Hay and Clarence King as representatives of the new ideal American. In contrast to his own failure to attain a position of power, his best friends sit at the height of politics and science, respectively. Hay's accomplishments, as secretary of state, reveal a hope for the future and show that power does not always corrupt but, with some men, leads to a better world. King's accomplishments in the West promise to yield an even more prosperous, larger, America.

Throughout this last section, Adams discusses the current state of scientific history and poses guiding principles for further study. His prognostications have the appearance of prophecy but they are the result of a careful analysis and employment of a grammar. Realizing through Hay that the problems of the Atlantic World were being resolved, Adams notes that the future challenge will be a greatly expanded and powerful Russia. Finally, Adams believes that history will become a hard science complete with algorithms and laws.

Key Figures

Mrs. Louisa Catherine Adams

Despite Abigail's disapproval, Louisa was an ideal wife for John Quincy while they lived within the circle of European and American elite; as a wife of a Bostonian, Louisa fails miserably.

Mrs. Abigail Adams

Abigail Adams, wife of John Adams, is the ideal eighteenth-century woman. Abigail's disapproval of Louisa (Johnson) as a suitable match for her son, John Quincy, provides insight into Adams' idea of women. He says that this moment of disapproval teaches the correctness of women's judgment.

Brooks Adams

While Adams teaches at Harvard, he rooms in the same house as his brother, Brooks, who was attending law school. Brooks, younger by a decade, influences Adams' thinking about history. Brooks "taught [Adams] that the relation between civilizations was that of trade." Due to Brooks' influence, Adams searches the ancient trading routes for "a city of thought" but does not find one.

Henry Brooks Adams

The main character of the story attempts to discuss what parts of education are useful according to his own experiences. His search for knowledge also imitates other spiritual odysseys like Dante's or that of John Bunyan's Christian. He gained little from structured educational experiences. Whether grade school or Harvard College, education by discipline is a large waste of time in his mind. Stubbornly, Adams sticks to the idea that four tools are necessary to any successful education. They are knowledge of German, Spanish, French, and a facility with mathematics. Those are the building blocks. Otherwise, he highlights certain lessons in his own life but does not come up with any kind of educational program.

Mrs. Abigail Brown Adams

Abigail Brown, daughter of Peter Brooks and wife of Charles Francis, proved to be a great asset to the American legation in London because she excelled in British custom. Adams realizes that his mother's success stems from her ability to assimilate.

Mr. Charles Francis Adams

Adams' father, Charles Francis, served as America's minister to the Court of St. James during the American Civil War. His diplomatic success in preventing the British from openly siding with the Southern Confederacy is a highpoint of Adams' education, though it disqualified him for a political career. Adams looks to his father as his first role model.

Adams realizes that his father's concern with national politics stems from a principled refusal to take part in the corruption of state politics. He also admires his father's mind as it interacts with allies in the parlor of the Quincy home. Adams judges his father's mind to be "the only perfectly balanced mind that ever existed in the name." This did not mean it was a brilliant mind but that it "worked with singular perfection'' so that Charles Francis ''stood alone''—without master. A motivating force for this mind was a staunch conviction of Puritan thought that prevented Charles Francis from compromising his abolitionist stance.

President John Quincy Adams

Adams holds up his grandfather, John Quincy, as an exemplar man of power who can coerce others into following a proper path. While a boy, Adams once attempted to avoid going to school by throwing a tantrum against his mother. This ended when ''the President'' silently ushered him all the way to his school desk. ''The President . . . had shown no temper, no irritation, no personal feeling, and had made no display of force. Above all, he had held his tongue.'' The remarkable thing for Adams about this experience was the impact; the president acted so correctly that Adams felt no ''rancor'' but just the opposite, he admired where before he had been ''paralyzed by awe.'' The episode is just one of many moments in the book when Adams reflects on the proper use of power.

George Sewall Boutwell

Boutwell's appointment to secretary of the treasury by President Grant suggests that the Grant administration, in Adams' terms, will be victimized by ''inertia.'' Boutwell's incompetence encouraged the notorious robber baron, Jay Gould, to attempt to corner the gold market. A nationwide panic ensued. Sadly, Boutwell represents the type of politician ''pathetic in their helplessness to do anything with power when it came to them.''

John Bright

Orators like John Bright, one of the most eloquent orators of nineteenth-century Britain, succeed in politics not only as a result of having ''the courage of a prize-fighter'' but because ''Bright knew his Englishmen better than England did.'' Consequently, Bright ''knew what amount of violence in language was necessary to drive an idea into a Lancashire or Yorkshire head.'' Bright's professional success bolsters Adams repertoire of lessons in national difference. Adams knows that Bright's methods would not work anywhere but amongst the English. Adams also sees that Bright's verbal violence combines with other qualities. Bright ''betrayed no one, and he never advanced an opinion in practical matters that did not prove to be practical.''

Peter Chardon Brooks

Adams' ''other grandfather,'' Peter Brooks, was a wealthy banker whose fortune at his death was the largest in Boston. Brooks' estate was divided amongst the children and thus the Adams family increased in wealth through Abigail Brown's share.

Senator James Donald Cameron

Senator Cameron of Pennsylvania ''had shipwrecked his career in the person of President Grant.'' Adams sees Cameron as a Pennsylvanian in the mold of Benjamin Franklin. For Adams, the Pennsylvanian puts aside his prejudices against the world once his interests are allied with those of others. Accordingly, Cameron was a member of Adams' circle as he was an ally of Hay, Lodge, and Roosevelt.

George Douglas Campbell

See Duke of Argyll

Duke of Argyll

One of Charles Francis' most valuable friends during his service at the Court of St. James was the duke of Argyll. The duke believed in Russell's honesty and Charles Francis follows him. Their gullibility amazes Adams.

Charles William Eliot

Adams had a brief career as a professor at the request of the president of Harvard College, Charles Eliot. After seven years, Adams views collegiate education, even under Eliot's reformed system, as costly and wasteful. Eliot ''hinted that Adams's services merited recognition.''

William Maxwell Evarts

Upon his return from London, Adams found welcome in the home of William Evarts, President Johnson's attorney general. They had long discussions about legal tender as Evarts sought to defend the president's position, although, Evarts had opposed it in the past.

William Edward Forster

One of the British statesmen who helps Charles Francis and the cause of the Union was the talented young radical, William Edward Forster. According to Adams, Forster was ''pure gold'' even when he eventually became part of the establishment as he rose to the rank of cabinet minister.

William Evart Gladstone

Gladstone's confession of 1896 causes Adams to rethink his education as private secretary to his father. In 1905, Adams learns that Gladstone considered it a mistake on his part to have thought that Jefferson Davis had actually formed a nation—a gross mistake that nearly led to war—but still a mistake. Dumbfounded by the passage, Adams reflects that "he had seen nothing correctly at the time. His whole theory of conspiracy . . . resolved itself into [Gladstone's] 'incredible grossness.'" However, as with his grandfather, Adams feels no rancor because he believes that nothing about an individual's psychology can impact an historical event.

John Hay

As a reward for his support of McKinley's Republican campaign for the presidency, Hay was appointed the American ambassador to England. However, when William R. Day left to finalize the outcome of the Spanish-American War in Paris, Hay was recalled to serve as secretary of state. He stayed in this position.

Hay is the ideal American for Adams in part because he brings to fruition the political machinations of Adams' forebears. Hay studies John Quincy's work closely and he seeks advice from Adams on a regular basis. In Hay's successful foreign policy, Adams sees "the family work of a hundred and fifty years fell at once into the grand perspective of true empire building."

Ebenezer Rockwood Hoar

Adams' continuing hopes for a political position are dashed when he finds himself in disagreement with his friend, Ebenezer Hoar, President Grant's attorney general. Adams writes an article in favor of the Supreme Court in the matter of the Legal Tender Cases. Hoar, as Grant's point man, favors the government's right to print paper specie. The Supreme Court decided against this in 1870 but after Grant appointed two more justices, the Court found in favor of the government when it revisited the question. As a result of the political fights, Hoar was driven from office.

Lord Houghton

See Richard Monckton Milnes

Clarence King

As the first head of the Geological Survey, Clarence King was a remarkable combination of hardy adventurer and scientist. The occupation and exploitation of the continent was made possible due to men like King. For Adams, King is larger than life—a scientist but also a man who can survive in the wilderness. However, King's abilities do not prevent his tragic end. Losing his fortune in the crash of 1893, King dies alone and forgotten in a hotel in the Southwest.

Mrs. Louisa Catherine Kuhn

Firstborn child to Charles Francis and Abigail Brown, Louisa "was one of the most sparkling creatures [Adams] met in a long and varied experience of bright women." Louisa married Charles Kuhn and invited Adams to join them on a European tour. Adams happily accepts an excuse to leave Germany. This experience reminds Adams of the superiority of nineteenth-century American women—especially those of the Adams family—and his preference for being in their control.

Though Italy proved to be a wonderful influence on Adams, the death of Louisa becomes a powerful lesson; "he had never seen Nature—only her surface—the sugar-coating that she shows to youth." This was the first time Adams had watched someone die. Louisa had been thrown from a cab and bruised her foot. Tetanus had set in and "hour by hour the muscles grew rigid, while the mind remained bright, until after ten days of fiendish torture she died in convulsions." The "harsh brutality of chance" was not soon forgotten.

Mrs. Anna Cabot Mills Lodge

Along with Mrs. Cameron, Anna Lodge was a "dispenser of sunshine over Washington." Adams views Anna in a light usually reserved only for the women of his family. Mirroring the role of Louisa, Anna takes command of Adams. In 1895, when all the world seemed just simply too confusing to Adams, Anna gives him the busy task of serving as traveling companion and tutor to the Lodges and their two sons.

Henry Cabot Lodge

One of Adam's students at Harvard was Henry Lodge. Adams regarded Lodge as a younger brother or nephew and a source of solace toward the end of his life.

James Russell Lowell

Adams finds classes at Harvard a bore until he begins to take advantage of the German method of private readings used by James Russell Lowell. ''Education was not serious'' but Adams found Lowell to be a good conversationalist.

Richard Monckton Milnes

Richard Milnes epitomizes the ''gargantuan type,'' the sort of man who is larger than life and whose grasp seems universal. Milnes was a member of the upper class whose breakfasts were so famous that nobody dared turn down an invitation but died to attend. He knew everyone and excelled in his literary and artistic tastes. As one of the pro-Union faction, he often provided refuge to Charles Francis at his home in Fryston.

Viscount Palmerston

When the Adams family journeys to the Court of St. James on behalf of the United States government in 1861, they find the British prime minister to be Palmerston. Known for his fiery defense of ''British Interest,'' Adams likens his family to Christians showing up in Rome during the time of Emperor Tiberius when martyring Christians was good sport. Palmerston represents the despotic ruler who sacrifices others on a whim.

Earl John Russell

A study in British politicians is found in Palmerson's *betise,* John Russell. Of all the pro-Confederacy members of the British government, Russell's call for recognition of the American rebels is the loudest. In the end, his scheming falls apart and he must bow to Charles Francis and international law by finding new buyers for the deadly ironclads that he wanted to send against the Union Navy.

Governor William Henry Seward

William Seward was secretary of state to President Lincoln and friend of the Adams family since the days of the Free Soil Party.

Augustus St. Gaudens

Throughout the text, Adams lists Augustus St. Gaudens among the great artists of his day. In passing, Adams comments on his aesthetic reaction to the memorial Adams commissioned for Mrs. Henry Adams at Rock Creek Cemetery in Washington, D.C. The statue, in the text, is simply the virgin, the symbol of femininity, opposing the dynamo.

Charles Sumner

Until he disapproves of Charles Francis' appointment to head the legation to St. James Court in London, Charles Sumner stood fast as a friend of the family and a role model to young Adams. While still pursuing their unpopular abolitionist crusade as members of the Free Soil Party in Boston, Sumner stood out amongst Charles Francis' friends as ''heroic.'' Sumner stood alone—he was without family and his political position made many doors closed to him. His lack of Boston allies outside the Adams' circle caused Sumner to cultivate his European connections. For this reason, he is one of the few American leaders during the Civil War of which the British think well.

Henry John Temple

See Viscount Palmerston

Themes

Education

Adams presents himself as a scientist who will sample and test various methods of education so that he may offer some wisdom for a man facing the twentieth century. As he says in the preface, ''no one has discussed what part of education has, in his personal experience, turned out to be useful, and what not. This volume attempts to discuss it.'' Traditional systems of education are soundly rejected; a schoolmaster is ''a man employed to tell lies to little boys.'' The lecture system found in colleges does not fair much better nor does scientific education: ''the theory of scientific education failed where most theory fails—for want of money.''

In the rejection of standard educational systems, Adams formulates an alternative understanding of education. The acquisition of knowledge should not be the mastery of the schoolmaster's unity or the complete embrace of all possible scientific facts. Instead, education ''required conflict, competition, contradiction'' and ''accidental education'' in order to see the ''world exactly as it is.'' For this reason, he emphasizes those moments in life when he learned by accident. His experience with men, from his grandfather to his students, teaches him about power and the benefit of a balanced mind. His experience with women teaches the profound problem of multiplicity. Accidental education causes Adams to realize that society does not educate itself ''or aimed at a conscious pur-

Topics for Further Study

- Imagine that *The Education of Henry Adams* will be published in 2007. What technological symbols could be used to interpret the twentieth century and prepare for the twenty-first century? Imitating the style Adams uses in his work, discuss those symbols in terms of their historical force through a description of an imagined event, like a World's Fair of the year 2005.

- Compare the use of evolutionary theory in intellectual discourse of the late nineteenth century with the genetic explanations offered today. What are the dangers of popular usage of scientific theories? What are the benefits of making science transparent and accessible?

- Explain the attraction that railroads have for Adams. What has happened over the last century to that rail network? What sort of analysis might Adams make of this change?

- Coal is still our number one source for energy. What other sources of energy have been developed over the last century? Are those energy technologies sufficient to meet current and future needs? Discuss the challenges of energy policy in a particular country with reference to that country's historical development.

- Select one of the many utopian novels written between Edward Bellamy's *Looking Backward* (1888) and the general publication of *The Education of Henry Adams* (1918). Compare the idea of the new human Adams puts forth to inhabit a technologically complex world to the ideal put forth by Utopian Socialists.

- Jared Diamond, in his "Epilogue" to *Guns, Germs, and Steel,* discusses how history might become just as scientific as some natural sciences in which experimentation is impossible (like astronomy). Compare Diamond's reasoning with Adams' ideas on a scientific history. What future does history have as a science?

---

pose.'' Consequently, Adams notes that successful minds are those that react to the capriciousness of reality.

While Adams hints throughout the work that education amounts to self-knowledge, his formulation of self-knowledge involves an understanding of the journey he has been through. Toward the end of the text, Adams says:

> Every man with self-respect enough to become effective, if only as a machine, has had to account to himself for himself somehow, and to invent a formula of his own for his universe, if the standard formulas failed, there, whether finished or not, education stopped.

Though a man may "invent a formula," his success is not assured. To prove this, Adams compares the fate of Clarence King and John Hay, two men who were able to formulate their universe and be effective. Hay masters the instruments of state in order to guide the foreign policy of the country through two administrations. King also has a formula—literally, he has an ingenious one for surveying the 40th parallel. However, King's story proves that science cannot exist independently of money, which King loses in the economic downturn of 1893.

Technology

For Adams, technology is intrinsic to an understanding of the great difference between the late nineteenth and the thirteenth century. Moreover, technology holds the key to a bright future so long as a new mind will emerge within society that will not be overawed by it. Adams' inability to react appropriately to science and technology exacerbates his propensity for failure. This is presented early in the work through Adams' preference for a non-technological Boston to which the Boston and Albany Railroad has come regardless of his wishes. To his credit, Adams stubbornly faces the source of his discomfort with technology, especially with coal.

Adams constantly watches out for the extent to which a society, starting with his own, is burning coal. He knows that coal fuels industry, which fuels the economy. The cost to a society is the illness of its workers and of sections of the country. Still, Adams feels everyone must face up to coal in all its forms. For this reason, Adams describes coal production as a "Black District, another lesson, which needed much more to be rightly felt." Facing coal and its lesson becomes a rite of passage. Coal "made a boy uncomfortable. . . . The boy ran away from it, as he ran away from everything he disliked." But a man of education will face coal and its meaning. Within his scientific observation of societies, "Coal-power alone asserted evolution—of power—and only by violence could be forced to assert selection of type." Thus, the country that makes the best use of their coal will, eventually, be the greatest industrial might. The other technology Adams celebrates is the railway. The train engine burns coal and, therefore, the miles of track are another indicator of a country's coal-power.

History

Throughout *The Education of Henry Adams*, Adams formulates a new idea about scientific history wherein historical events emerge out of chaos or from nowhere, like the *Pteraspis*. The only thing that events prove, for Adams, is the ever-changing nature of society. Adams' notion of history invalidates any attempt to assume a grand narrative of history like the "Anglo-Saxon Chronicle and the Venerable Bede." History, in this view, becomes a dynamic and ever-changing record of life. Narrative approaches, meanwhile, indicate the specific feature of society Adams loathes, inertia.

Through the experience of actually teaching history from this viewpoint, Adams realizes the difficulty. His approach encourages students to think independently but without mastery of a body of knowledge that could be examined or displayed in a measurable way. Thus, while his approach approximates a more accurate understanding of historical dynamism, ironically it fails to be useful.

Style

Autobiography

Adams uses his life story to illustrate his views of society, history, and education. However, his employment of the third person point of view serves to distance himself and the reader from the intimacy normally associated with the autobiographical form. As he confesses in his preface, the character of Henry Adams is a manikin—a figure adapted to the author's wants. In this case, the character of Adams becomes adapted to the larger purpose of exploring the theme of education that is a series of disillusionment with his "real" life, the promises of education, the United States as a nation, and women.

Other clues in the Preface and allusions scattered throughout the text technically support the conscientious illusion of autobiography and the admitted attempt at spiritual autobiography. In the preface, the figures of Jean-Jacques Rousseau and St. Augustine are invoked. Adams imitates their works to some extent in that he attempts to embody the fate of the nation. Later he will conjure Rasselas, Odysseus, and Dante. Like their works, his is a story of a journey toward knowledge. The fact that he never arrives at knowledge displays the impossibility of the quest. In other words, Adams' narrative device supports his theme of failure in order to operate as a reality check on those grandiose narratives of Western man.

Symbolism and Metaphor

Adams marks the break up of unity into chaos with various signs. Adams identifies these symbols and metaphors as such in the text. Due to the self-conscious discussion of symbols, they act as rational signposts for the larger theory of the work instead of romantic allusions. Adams consistently interrupts unified pictures with inhuman forces. One of the ways in which these two techniques work is exemplified in the death of his sister. His sister, symbolizing the unity of femininity and youth, has an accident that leads to an excruciating death. As Adams witnesses this, he identifies the entrance of nature into his text as a force of chaos that will forever disrupt attempts by humans to form unity.

Every time Adams mentions Quincy, the eighteenth century, or Boston, he evokes a string of nostalgia for a happier, quiet, almost Edenic time. Simultaneously, technologic representatives enter to ensure disruption and multiplicity. For Adams, a garden of bliss and rest is impossible for whenever a woman makes it likely, technology or other forces like a capricious nature, interrupt. The event of his sister's death encapsulates this construction, but the formula presents itself very early in the work. For example:

> he and his eighteenth-century troglodytic Boston were suddenly cut apart—separated forever—in act if not

in sentiment, by the opening of the Boston and Albany Railroad; the appearance of the first Cunard steamers in the bay; and the telegraphic messages which carried [news] from Baltimore to Washington.

Motif

Thinking that a number of perplexing problems with a scientific approach to history can be cleared up through an understanding of evolution, Adams seeks out the ultimate parent. Sir Charles Lyell introduces him to the *Pteraspis*. The fish happens to be the first vertebrate but its existence clarifies nothing about evolution. The fish simply enables him to prove change. In terms of the evolutionary chart, before the fish is nothing and after the fish is everything. From this point on, *Pteraspis* serves as a shorthand for those men or machines that appear in history with profound effect but no obvious ancestry.

Another motif is Adams' actual or virtual sitting on the steps of the Church of Santa Maria di Ara Coeli in Rome. The first time he sits there, he explains the significance of his act; his guidebook told him it was the place where Edward Gibbon had sat when he conceived the idea of writing *Decline and Fall of the Roman Empire*. Mention, therefore, of the Ara Coeli invokes Gibbon, Rome, and the historiographic fact that despite Gibbon's monumental history on Rome, the mystery of the fall of Roman Civilization remains just as provocative. Both Ara Coeli and *Pteraspis* repeatedly show Adams the futility of his quest for ultimate education. The motifs declare that Adams will fail in his attempt to clearly trace a line of progress from the Middle Ages to the present

Obfuscation

The Education of Henry Adams does not faithfully represent historical events. Rather, Adams selects episodes when it suits his purpose for exploring themes. Certain events left out of the narrative lend support to the idea that part of the intent of the work was to mystify the elite of the United States. For example, Adams glosses over the fact that as capitalist industrialists moved toward full mass production, the skills of their workers dwindled, as one worker would insert a pin, another tighten a bolt, etc. Trained craftsmen were being replaced by unskilled laborers as technology became more prevalent. Adams does not hint at the embarrassing fate that befell his hero, Charles Sumner on the floor of the U.S. Senate Chamber when he was beaten with a cane. Violent outbursts with canes on the Senate floor were not unknown but Sumner spent the next

three years recovering from the assault. Nor does Adams mention that Clarence King, under the name John Todd, had maintained a family with Ada Copeland, an African American—despite his proud recollection of his family's anti-slavery position.

Historical Context

Reform Era

A new spirit of civic awareness by members of the middle class who identified themselves as Progressives launched the Reform Era in the 1890s. Progressives believed that the rampant development of the economy had led to wasted resources, lives, and health. In response, Progressives applied a belief in maximum efficiency to every facet of life. Their goal was to make America a more efficient society and, in the end, more prosperous. The Progressives also applied new ideas about the individual. They replaced social Darwinism with environmentalism: good environments made good citizens. Thus, an improvement of society's environment (namely cities) would improve the citizenry. Both tenants were mixed with a fervent belief in the "Social Gospel" or a secularizing of the Christian gospels. Progressives, in other words, sought to make real the messages of "love of neighbor" that they believed Christ taught.

During the Reform Era, slums were cleared, houses built, and municipal services begun: sewage and water systems were installed and garbage pickup became customary. Political reform also made some headway as the corrupt political machines fell to the onslaught of Progressives and Populists. Labor movements seemed ascendant in the same era that Robber Barons ruled corporations whose annual profits dwarfed those of the entire U.S. tax revenue. Socialist parties were viable entities and would soon count mayors and governors. At the same time, the federal government regularly leant its troops to corporations engaged in battles with striking workers.

Progressives gradually looked to the federal government to increase its powers and control the reign of the Robber Barons. To this end, the Roosevelt administration began utilizing the Sherman Antitrust Act (1890) that led to the dissolution of the Northern Securities Company under order of the Supreme Court in 1904. Real progress against monopolies would not be made, however, until the Taft

Compare & Contrast

- **1907:** Reginald Aubrey Fessenden ushers in the year with the second broadcasted radio program on New Year's Eve, 1906. Due to atmospheric conditions, the broadcast reaches the West Indies from its origination at Brant Rock, Massachusetts.

  Today: The internet continues to accelerate communications and media dissemination through worldwide fiber optic and satellite networks.

- **1907:** Robert Baden-Powell returns from leading a camping trip of twenty-five boys on Brownsea Island to establish the Boy Scouts.

  Today: The proud tradition of the Boy Scouts of America is under a cloud today due to its intolerance of openly gay scout masters.

- **1907:** Utilizing a right recently given by the U.S. Congress to bar non-U.S.-passport bearing people from the country, President Roosevelt refuses entry of Japanese workers to the United States from Canada, Hawaii, and Mexico.

  Today: The United States remains reluctant to welcome immigrants except in the case of Cubans or high-tech professionals.

- **1907:** President Roosevelt withheld antitrust action against U.S. Steel so that J. P. Morgan could prop up the American market.

  Today: The U.S. economy's incredible market pivots on one man, secretary of the Federal Reserve Board, Alan Greenspan.

- **1900s:** Department stores exist several decades before the first shopping centers are built. In 1907, one of the first such centers opens outside Baltimore, Roland Park Shopping Center. It lacks the intense planning and rationalization that would come to mark shopping center development. The first integrated mall is built outside Kansas City, Missouri, in 1922. It is called the Country Club Plaza.

  Today: Minnesota, which hosted the first two-story mall in 1956 (Southdale Mall), has become home to the mother of all shopping malls—the Mall of America (1992). The gigantism, which marks malls today, testifies to their central place in American culture.

Administration's victory over the American Tobacco Company and the Standard Oil Company (both in 1911). The Reform Era ended with World War I.

Panic of 1907

The gross national product (GNP) in the United States increased from $18.7 billion in 1900 to $35.3 billion in 1910. Along the way, serious doubts were cast on the economy by the crisis of 1907, and the stock market collapse of 1893 (which affected the Adams family fortunes negatively) was never far from the minds of investors. Early warning signs accompanied the dawn of the new century: runaway global economic growth combined with an increase in government security issues fueled stock speculation that met a credit supply that had been decreasing since 1900. Countries responded by increasing their interest rates. Banks in Tokyo began to fail in early 1907 and were soon followed by banks in Europe and South America. Stock prices began to fall as a consequence but F. Augustus Heinze's attempt to corner the copper market almost destroyed the American financial market.

America Becomes a World Power

Responsibility for the emergence of the United States as a world power, normally attributed to Roosevelt, lies with Secretary of State John Hay. The most precious advantage Hay gained for this coming out was the roping in of European powers into an American system of peace in the Atlantic. Guided by conversations with Henry Adams, Hay made the United States appear benevolent toward other nations in the name of open markets and free trade. This rule set the pace for American Foreign Policy of the twentieth century.

Hay's diplomacy had the backing of American victories. A military defeat of Spain in the Spanish-American War thrust America onto the world stage. This was accompanied by a display of force and technical ability through a circumnavigation of the globe by the U.S. Navy. Furthermore, successful construction of the long dreamed of Panama Canal, where the French had failed, crowned America's claim as an industrial power. These successes were unambiguous. However, the accomplishment of the "Open Door Policy" in China, paternalism in Latin America and the Philippines were less admirable.

The United States appeared to be a non-aggressor in the European race for colonies. Appearances aside, the United States agreed to allow European aggression so long as it respected the Monroe Doctrine (allowing the United States governance of the American hemisphere). This arrangement allowed the United States to violently put down the Filipino revolt and annex Hawaii. In all matters concerning the hemisphere, the American government took a stance favorable to multinational corporations.

This May 20, 1893, edition of Le Petit Journal *depicts the Government Pavilion at the 1893 Chicago Exhibition*

Critical Overview

A discussion of the reception of the *The Education of Henry Adams* must first consider its route of dissemination. Adams first distributed his swan song to what amounts to a list of the one hundred most powerful and influential people of his time. He asked, in a rather tricky fashion, that each person correct their text and return it to him. Few were bold enough to do so and of those who did, Charles Eliot—who brought Adams to Harvard as professor of history and who created the famous Harvard Classics Series—returned his copy without comment.

Considering that the work won a Pulitzer for autobiography, biographers have found the text a tantalizing source for insight into the mind of Adams. Within this biographical criticism there are different points of emphasis. For example, Richard P. Blackmur, in *The Expense of Greatness,* focuses on the *The Education of Henry Adams* as Adams' reflection on his contribution to society. Gerrit H. Roelofs' "Henry Adams: Pessimism and the Intelli-

gent Use of Doom" disagrees with Blackmur. For Roelof, Adams is challenging the twentieth century to live up to the greatness of the nineteenth century.

Another emphasis of scholars discussing Adams' work focuses on those moments in the text that predict America's development. Granville Hickes concludes his review, "Struggle and Flight," with "it is little exaggeration to say that *The Education of Henry Adams* carries us from the adolescence of American industrial capitalism to its senility." Nearly fifty years later, William Wassertrom echoed Hicks, in *The Ironies of Progress,* saying, "it was indeed Henry Adams who first insisted that America itself belied progress, that these states did in fact symbolize the hope and despair of advanced industrial order in the world." Adams' obvious perspicuity in all matters of American industrial triumph made *The Education of Henry Adams* an inspirational text during the first decade of the Cold War. In *The Scientific Thought of Henry Adams,* Henry Wasser appreciates Adams' rationalization of historical thought and its use as a point of reflection. Wasser writes, "Adams is scientific in his history in the sense that he tries to deduce the laws of history from the laws of science wherein laws applicable to human society are a special case of the laws applicable to the entire universe.''

Recent criticism is applying gender and postcolonial theory to show that Adams veils the patriarchal and imperial operations of his friends and peers. Martha Banta, in ''Being a 'Begonia' in a Man's World,'' exposes how Adams manipulates the period's notions of masculinity. Banta raises the idea that ''whether [Adams] viewed himself as living up to his credentials as a male within the masculine society through which he moved'' matters in a consideration of the text. John Carlos Rowe investigates another area of mystique. In ''*The Education of Henry Adams* and the American Empire,'' Rowe zeroes in on the avowed purpose of the text to explain ''Twentieth-Century Multiplicity'' with the complete absence of any mention of ''the political forces clearly reshaping the globe at the turn of the century.'' All of the critics mentioned here and those left out do agree with current assessments that *The Education of Henry Adams* belongs in the list of the greatest nonfiction works of the twentieth century.

Criticism

Jeremy W. Hubbell

Hubbell seeks a Ph.D. in history with an emphasis on technological development at the State University of New York at Stony Brook, where he is a member of the Technoscience Research Group. In the following essay, he examines the relevance of Adams' work in the contemporary American philosophy of technology.

Long before the digital age caused headlines about digital divides and the rapidity of innovation, thinkers reflected upon human adaptation to accelerated technological innovation. *The Education of Henry Adams*, written as a reflection on the so-called second industrial revolution, was welcomed as such a reflection when it was published but has since become simply an autobiography. Adam's text explores the interaction between humans and technology, making note of generational tensions surrounding innovation. The idea of a child operating the VCR better than the parent enjoys the status of cliché now, but the concept of technology requiring new minds was not common knowledge at the time

of Adams' writing. Yet, Adams foresaw that innovation would demand new types of people and personalities who in turn required greater technological complexity. In his work, Adams does not simply praise science or display the way in which technology awes the elderly; he also reveals the American pattern for embracing and adopting technology. The way in which Adams formulates his reflections early in the twentieth century has a similarity to the work of American philosopher of technology, Don Ihde, at the end of the century. Ihde, author of *Technology and the Lifeworld: From Garden to Earth*, without having read Adams uses the metaphoric device, the Garden of Eden, which is repeatedly used in *The Education of Henry Adams* to expose society's philosophy of technology.

Adams encapsulates this concern by tracing the trajectory of civilization as it evolved from the unity of Christendom (1200 A.D.) to multiplicity (1900 A.D.) through the heuristic device of the Garden of Eden. By way of contrast, Ihde uses the Garden of Eden motif to trace technological adaptation in different but contemporary cultures. He shows that even supposedly primitive tribes who, by definition, exist without the other worries of civilization live by virtue of technology exactly developed for their environment. Further, Adams shows that people are naturally quick to implement new technologies into an existing regime: ''human activity from immemorial time and across the diversity of cultures has always been technologically embedded.'' This happens, according to Ihde, because technologies are multi-stable. By this term, he sums up the idea that while ''technologies transform experience and its variations'' for humans, the way in which this happens is without intent, or determinism. In other words, humans select technologies and utilize them for their specific purposes; they are not victimized by technology. Each accelerated stage of this process at once disturbs humans in their supposedly nontechnological garden until the technology withdraws into the background. When humans grow accustomed to riding trains, for example, then train travel becomes a ''normal'' part of life, part of society's garden. While Adams would agree with this analysis, he would focus on the process by which a technological device becomes disturbing and then accepted by people. With wariness, Adams considers the ability of the human mind to react quickly enough to innovation, a concern Ihde does not share.

While ''The Dynamo and the Virgin,'' chapter XXV of *The Education of Henry Adams*, is one of

What Do I Read Next?

- Adams described the unity of the medieval worldview as being reflected through its cathedrals in *Mont-Saint-Michel and Chartres*. The work was published privately in 1904.

- In *A Letter to American Teachers of History* (1910), Adams calls upon his fellow historians to make whatever changes necessary to the curriculum in order to prepare students for the technology of the twentieth century. In his letter, Adams expresses a fear that if education is not reformed, the consequences may be dire.

- Adams refers to Jean-Jacques Rousseau's *Confessions* as a model for his work. Rousseau wrote his autobiography as a justification for his actions in hope that he might regain his friends and country. The work was posthumously published beginning in 1782.

- An experimental novel by Laurence Sterne, entitled *The Life and Opinions of Tristram Shandy, Gentleman,* was a surprising success from the moment of its release in 1759. Full of eighteenth-century British humor, this supposed autobiography shows some striking similarities to Adams' autobiography.

- From Frederick Jackson Turner's 1893 Frontier Thesis—which still holds sway amongst conservatives in America—to Charles Austin Beard's 1913 work *An Economic Interpretation of the Constitution,* the writing of history in America became more scientific. Richard Hofstadter explores this transition in his 1968 work, *The Progressive Historians: Turner, Beard, Parrington.*

- Historians of the early twentieth century rediscovered periods of history that had been defamed during the nineteenth century. Specifically, historians, like Adams, reappraised the Dark Ages. C. W. David discusses this reconsideration in "American Historiography of the Middle Ages, 1884–1934," in the April 1935 issue of *Speculum.*

---

the most often quoted chapters in the theoretical writings on technology, the rest of the book is often neglected. Many theorists have discussed Adams' arguments on science, but rarely has he been taken seriously as a philosopher of technology. Certainly, Adams helped popularize science and technology and he desired to examine history in scientific terms. But scientific elements in the course of historical reflection or moments of awe before dynamos do not begin to make a philosophy of technology. What proves that Adams is a philosopher of technology is his contention that technology always exists in relation to human society, represented by the metaphoric garden; through the garden motif he simulates the cultural process of technological adaptation. His formula shows that as technology grows more complex and prevalent, human society becomes a technologically embedded garden—a technical ecology that supports human interaction.

Throughout Adams' text, a form of technology, whether Faraday's magnet, Curie's radiation, or Lyell's Pteraspis, presents "evidence of growing complexity, and multiplicity, and even contradiction." This leads him to surmise that he was "still Adam in the Garden of Eden between God who was unity, Satan who was complexity, with no means of deciding which was truth." This self-reflection is part of Adams' problem: he wants to be in the position of making the choice. Adams wants to introduce technology to himself and to his world, his garden, and not be imposed upon. Thus, Adams tries to experience the entire rail network in America and see how it makes the great space of America a garden viewed comfortably from a window. However, technology arrives too quickly for Adams to adapt to it and he cannot help but grow angry, feel cheated, and attribute a consciousness or magic to it. When Adams is not deluding himself, he knows he exists in a multi-stable universe where he can re-

> **The main idea in Adams' work, further articulated by Ihde, is that technology always exists in relation to human society, to a garden.''**

ceive telegraphed reports from his friends back in Washington, D.C., even while exploring the primitive land of the Laps: ''the electro-dynamo-social universe worked better even than the sun.'' Adams does not hide from technology or fear it; rather, he wants to comprehend leisurely the import of technological arrivals. He wishes to appreciate the telegraph at his own pace, no matter how much it complicates his life. He desires to control technological introduction and use of technology, which is why he likes the automobile.

The human garden, for Adams, grows increasingly complex as humans develop their technology. Knowing that the past was simpler causes Adams to feel nostalgic. However, his nostalgia is ironic since Adams owes his awareness of the garden to which he attributes the most human balance, the Middle Ages, to a form of technology. The ultimate Garden of the Gothic Cathedrals of Normandy was made possible by the automobile:

> the automobile alone could unite them in any reasonable sequence, and although the force of the automobile, for the purposes of a commercial traveler, seemed to have no relation whatever to the force that inspired a Gothic cathedral, the Virgin in the twelfth century would have guided and controlled both bag-man and architect, as she controlled the seeker of history.

Adams knows that every human activity has been embedded with technology, but as a historian, he carefully denotes the arrival of each technology and the way it changes his garden. The number one machine disturbing his gardens is the railroad, but the steamer and the telegraph are worthy assistants while the automobile has not yet begun to alter the landscape. Adams begins this pattern of disruption of the old by the new early in the book, stating that ''he and his eighteenth-century troglodytic Boston were suddenly cut apart—separated forever—in act if not in sentiment, by the opening of the Boston and Albany Railroad.''

Understanding the formulation of past gardens, like Eden or his beloved eighteenth-century Boston, questions the view that this is Adams' professed discomfort with the technological development of society. Rather, Adams—far from being a failure— successfully outlines the garden as the space of societal change where the interaction between humans and their technology plays out. Adams views the human mind as deftly integrating technology and nature in order to renew the garden. Consider again the definition that Adams puts forth of the ideal man, one who has a ''formula of his own for his universe'' that makes him capable of reacting to and with societal change. Place that man in the following context:

> The movement from unity into multiplicity, between 1200 and 1900, was unbroken in sequence, and rapid in acceleration. Prolonged one generation longer, it would require a new social mind . . . [that can] enter a new phase subject to new laws. Thus far, since five or ten thousand years, the mind had successfully reacted, and nothing yet proved that it would fail to react—but it would need to jump.

Now the Garden, whether eighteenth-century Boston always presented by Adams as literally disrupted by the arrival of the Boston-Albany Railroad, or primitive Lapland disturbed by the telegraph, is a natural and healthy indicator of the acceleration in societal complexity in place from the beginning. Like Ihde, Adams does not believe in a non-technological Garden, even though his religious predilection leads him to long for one.

Usually, in literature, the Garden of Eden motif conjures the notion of unspoiled nature created by God and untouched by human innovation; knowledge and changes created by it come with Satan's influence and, therefore, technology is automatically coded as evil. Showing that Adams plays with this motif out of a concern with technology and not simply with the theme of science, involves returning to *The Education of Henry Adams* to take seriously his consistent disruption of the Garden of Eden motif with a technological device. As a historian who desires time for reflection and introduction of new technology, Adams allows technology to appear as an evil disturbance in a calm scene, a traditional use of the image of the garden. However, he always writes about the same technology elsewhere as he uses it or as he reflects on how a device, say a telegraph, facilitates a positive aspect of human society—communication. Upsetting as the technology is at first, it eventually becomes essential to human society so much so that it becomes a natural part of living: it withdraws and embeds itself within the garden.

Adams' employment of this formula is not a means of predicting future dystopias, but of creating a system of education—a philosophy—wherein the human mind remains reactive to technology. The idea that people might be paralyzed in the face of a new technology and shy away from it frightens Adams. For this reason, Adams' formula presents a series of gardens in time or in space to show how human society, humanity's garden, has already been disrupted by technological innovation. Such gardens include his visit to the Laps in Scandinavia, the cathedrals of Normandy, or eighteenth-century Boston. Each idyllic and calm setting is disrupted by a train, a telegraphed message, or made possible only because of the automobile. In other words, technology is never absent from the garden; Adam's idea of education demands that people always be quick to integrate technology into their conceptualization of the ''garden'' of America.

Utopian writers, like Edward Bellamy, pinned their hopes for deliverance of utopia on the advancement of technology. Technology historians, like Lewis Mumford, or urban planners, like Patrick Geddes, also assumed that technology would eventually realize a more healthy and prosperous human environment. Thus, at the time of turn-of-the-century doom and gloom, optimism flowed concerning the future; yet all agreed a new citizen was necessary. Adams partook of this utopian discussion as the sober, patrician voice. He reveals a consciousness of a technologically embedded world—a more complex, multi-stable lifeworld—and the consequent problems associated therein. Adams earnestly desired to expose, for the benefit of Americans, the ways in which they might educate themselves to live within an industrialized America. Today, Ihde hopes to do the same thing using the heuristic device originated by Adams, the Garden of Eden, because Americans continue to cling to the notion of an unspoiled nature.

Source: Jeremy W. Hubbell, Critical Essay on *The Education of Henry Adams,* in *Nonfiction Classics for Students,* The Gale Group, 2001.

Howard Horwitz

In the following essay excerpt, Horwitz discusses Adams' ideas on history writing as found in The Education of Henry Adams.

Adams's parody of the autobiographical self resonates in his parallel genre of history-writing, and it is not accidental that the Adams persona defines the self as mistake while deciding to accept the post at Harvard. Adams's persona is a clear diminution of what E. R. A. Seligman and Charles A. Beard (both of Columbia University) called ''the great man theory'' of history-writing, which, along with a teleological idea of progress and a methodological confidence about identifying causes and their effects, was one of the three central premises of historical discourse at the time.

The great-man theory of history is familiar to us from traditional political history. In this model of historiography, as James Harvey Robinson (also of Columbia) wrote, the historian compiles ''striking events of the past'' and identifies them with ''the achievements and fate of conspicuous persons.'' We ''string our narrative upon a line of kings,'' Robinson sneered. The result is an annals of statesmenship, with, Seligman wrote, events ''ascribed to great men'' like Caesar, Napoleon, and Washington. This tendency is manifest in the major histories of the period (especially textbooks), like John W. Burgess's *Reconstruction and the Constitution* (1911) George Burton Adams's *European History* (1899) or *Civilization during the Middle Ages* (1894), and Woodrow Wilson's five-volume *History of the American People* (1901–1903), and including as well Robinson's own *An Introduction to the History of Western Europe* (1903), his colleague Beard's *Contemporary American History* (1914), and Beard and Robinson's *Outlines of European History* (1916). Henry Adams's own histories of the early republic, culminating in the monumental, nine-volume *History of the United States of America during the Administrations of Jefferson and Madison* (1889–91), were focused through the activities of people like these two early Presidents and also *Albert Gallatin* (1879) and *John Randolph* (1882).

Almost despite their practice, prominent historians like the authors just listed objected that the great man theory, while it may fulfill our desire for the dramatic, as far too theatrical and arbitrary. As an alternative, the revisionists, who came to be known as the progressive historians, sought to ''raise history to the rank of a science,'' as Adams wrote in *''The Tendency of History''* (1894), an open letter he wrote to the American Historical Association when his tenure as its president expired. By scientific, these scholars meant a history that discovered

Adams's parody of the autobiographical self resonates in his parallel genre of history-writing, and it is not accidental that the Adams persona defines the self as mistake while deciding to accept the post at Harvard."

laws of historical action and development that were analogous if not equivalent to natural (meaning physical) laws. Ideally, these laws would, Frederick Teggart of the University of California wrote, "express the constant relations among phenomena." These constant relations amounted to the "continuity or unity of history," as Robinson phrased the principle for the Congress of Arts and Science at the 1904 St. Louis Exposition. I cite Robinson's formulation among myriad others because its typical conflation of "continuity" with "unity" so nicely suggests the assumptions driving the doctrine, assumptions that *The Education* often ridicules. "Continuity" and "unity" are not, of course, synonyms. The successiveness or even progression denoted by "continuity" connotes less coordination than does "unity." Nevertheless, the terms were used interchangeably, with the phrase "the unity of history" frequently used to stand for history's continuity.

Before the nineteenth century, the human species was thought to be discontinuous with other species, a special creature unrelated to so-called lower orders, divinely made out of nothing or out of dust. This idea was one element of the prevalent account of temporal alterations among species, called catastrophism. Catastrophism held that biological changes were sudden and wholesale, with later species, like humans, having no antecedents in earlier ones. Although portions of this idea survived to contest evolutionism, Jean Lamarck, Charles Lyell, and Charles Darwin—whatever the conflicts in their understanding of the mechanism of physiological change—generally established that humans had developed *from* other species. In their view, alterations from species to species and within species were not catastrophic, as Albion W. Small put it with reference to historical change, but incremental

stages in the sequential modification that all species continually undergo.

The great-man theory suited the catastrophic model of historical narrative, positing that changes occur by the chance appearance of exceptional individuals. In contrast, the evolutionists, as Henry Adams called them in "Letter to American Teachers," believed that these conspicuous individuals must be understood as manifestations of particular historical conditions and confluences. For the evolutionists, the greatness of the great man was both function and emblem of historical context, which is to say of evolving historical forces. So understood, history could become an inquiry into the development of human phenomena. This reorientation led many historians to demand that their colleagues pursue "obscure" incidents, as Wilson wrote in his Chairman's Address to the Division of Historical Sciences at the Congress of Arts and Sciences convened at the 1904 St. Louis Universal Exposition. This willingness to entertain the importance of apparently insignificant matters was one of the hallmarks of the so-called New Historians, whose best known figure became James Harvey Robinson after he issued a collection of his essays entitled *The New History* (1912). Robinson forcefully opposed studying "conspicuous events and striking crises" and advocated examining "the small, the common, and the obscure," the "homely elements in human life."

In practice, historians did not heed this charge in any sustained way; nevertheless, the progressives' theoretical interest in the obscure detail and homely element exemplifies their evolutionary bent. Small details were the key antecedents in a progression—not merely succession—of events, with later events evolving from (not just following) series of preceding events. Hence, these historians' commitment to evolution (continuity) was also a commitment to a narrative of progression in the root sense of the word. Antecedents did not merely precede their successors but prepared the way for them.

The continuity discoverable in the phenomenon of history became unity for these historians because they assumed that the progression they observed amounted to a teleological pattern that they called progress. Like continuity and unity, the terms progression and progress are surely not synonymous, but historians conflated them: as a narrative of progression, history was also, therefore, a narrative of progress, of what Adams called "elevation," and Adams was a rare voice criticizing historians' elevation of progression into progress. Thinking of the phenomenon of history as progress and of history-writing as both the commemoration and continuation of that progress involves two related assumptions. First, it presumes the moral superiority of later to earlier forms of social organization and human conduct; second, it assumes that later stages of development are fulfilling the possibilities of earlier stages, and that some ultimate, even perfect form of social organization and human conduct is immanent in present conditions.

Students of the development of the historical discipline, like David Noble and Dorothy Ross, have noted what they call the millennialism of turn-of-the-century American historians, for whom Western civilization and especially American society were fulfilling a divine plan for the perfection of man. This teleological enthusiasm suffuses everything historians wrote. A concise example of millennialism appears in the contribution of Columbia's William Sloane to the 1904 St. Louis Congress of Arts and Science. Sloane celebrates Giambattista Vico as the first "historical evolutionist. To him the story of a nation was the record of an ever complete realization in fact of certain remnants of a pre-natal revelation." This realization reveals a "law of moral progress" through which "all human faculties . . . perfect themselves."

Frederick Jackson Turner extolled history in similarly exalted terms. "History [both the phenomenon and its study] has a unity and a continuity" because it is, "in truth, the self-consciousness of humanity," a self-consciousness acquired by understanding its development from the past, "the undeveloped present." Because history is the "becoming" of the present in the past and of both the past and future in the present, the study of history can "enable us to behold our own time and place as a part of the stupendous progress of the ages"; it can "enable us to realize the richness of our [unconscious] inheritance, the possibility of our lives, the grandeur of the present." In Turner's most famous essay, the frontier is a receding border where past—the "inherited ways" of Europe—and inchoate present—the coarse, practical, and individualistic—cross-fertilize to provide "a gate of escape from the bondage of the past." At the frontier, then, the Enlightenment past is at once continued and purified, and the present is an ever more perfect realization of democratic ideals.

Charles A. Beard, best known for criticizing the American Constitution as an expression of mon-

eyed interests, is a supreme example of the progressive historians' teleological bent. In *The Industrial Revolution,* Beard bemoans the misery unleashed by industrialism, with its mechanization of individual action and subordination of the human "desire for freedom . . . to the production of marketable commodities." Having made individualism possible in the first place, industrialism then compromised it. But ultimately industrialism redeems individualism. "The hope of the future," Beard urges in an idealistic Hegelian mode, is the very "corporate society" that evolved to sustain industrialism. For Beard, the individual is reempowered by being transfigured in the highest form of corporate organization, the trust. Without denying the trusts' dislocation of and at times violence against workers, Beard—like most Americans who contemplated it, labor leaders like Eugene Debs no less than John D. Rockefeller—considered the trust the latest manifestation and intimation of progress. Progress, Beard reflects, consists of the substitution of "organization for chaos and anarchy," and "the trusts are merely pointing the way to higher forms of industrial methods in which the people, instead of a few capitalists, reap the benefits." As the frontier does for Turner, for Beard the trust represents a higher freedom than common individual freedom, creating "unity in diversity" by "increasing intercommunication of all parts of the world." Therefore, the trust induces "education from the lowest to the highest form," "training . . . the individual, so that in seeking the fullest satisfaction of his own nature he will harmoniously perform his function as a member of a corporate society." Through the trust, individualism is redeemed by being "elevated to social service," and therefore the trust is the fulfillment of both antecedent forms of organization and an innate human desire for freedom.

Beard is typical in transforming the identification of continuity in development into a celebration of progress toward a teleological order consolidated in the term unity. Some historians criticized their colleagues' millennial spirit. In 1916, Frederick Teggart urged historians to distinguish Darwinian evolution from their incurably teleological ideas of progress and unity. If Darwinian evolution speaks of "an orderly process" by which new forms of life emerge from old ones, nevertheless evolution manifests no intrinsic direction and seeks no goal or final shape. It effects, as David J. Hill put it, "variations" rather than linear development in human conduct and social organization. In a similar spirit, Adams wryly submitted that "evolutionists might be said to consider not the descent but the ascent of man." But Adams further, and uniquely, spurned the assumptions behind the Darwinian model of scientific history.

Source: Howard Horwitz, "*The Education* and the Salvation of History," in *New Essays on "The Education of Henry Adams,"* edited by John Carlos Rowe, Cambridge University Press, 1996, pp. 125–30.

Earl N. Harbert

In the following essay, Harbert examines Adams' intentions in The Education of Henry Adams, *autobiographical and otherwise.*

For readers who have been fascinated by *The Education Henry Adams,* the most significant event of recent years was the appearance in 1973 of a carefully revised edition, corrected according to the author's final intentions and edited by Adams's chief biographer, Ernest Samuels. At long last, and for the first time since the book was put on sale in 1918, the title page of the *Education* appears without the infamous and misleading subtitle, "An autobiography." Those two words, added to the 1918 version without authorization from Adams himself, who died before that printing appeared, have been largely responsible for a general confusion about the author's intentions, and, in turn, for a profusion of conflicting opinions, comments, and judgments concerning the final success or failure of Adams's achievement. Yet, all together this almost uncollectable critical response to the book forms at best a partial truth; for by any conventional definition, at least, the *Education* must be seen to offer us something much larger than the usual understanding of "autobiography" allows. How the shade of Henry Adams, at his sardonic best, must relish the last of his many jokes—this one played unintentionally on the three generations of readers who have helped to keep the *Education* alive.

All this is not to say that the book is free of autobiographical influences. Quite the contrary: many scholars have noted the author's debts to Rousseau and Augustine, to the private literature of the Adams family, especially the diaries of John and John Quincy Adams; and to that peculiarly American strain of personal narrative which can be traced, with some variations, from the Puritans, through Jonathan Edwards and Benjamin Franklin, to Henry James and Henry Adams. And convincing evidence of indebtedness to an autobiographical tradition is provided by Adams himself in his "Preface" to the *Education,* where he acknowledges a familiarity with a variety of personal narratives in the various forms of confessions, autobiographies, and memoirs, mentioning their authors by name. From the perspective of our usual interest in admitted and implied influences, then, Adams's reliance on a great autobiographical tradition is well established. So a sound case can be made—for treating his book as an impressive extension of that older tradition into the twentieth century. But, in fact, the *Education* should also be thought of, at least in part, as the first modern American autobiography, a seminal volume, as important in its way as was T. S. Eliot's announcements of modernity in his best poetry of the same period. To realize just how modern the *Education* really is, a reader need only compare it with the *Autobiography* of Henry's older brother, Charles Francis Adams II, published in 1916. Charles's book shows what the mere conjunction of the well-established family writing habit, with a prosaic tradition of memoir-writing, and a pedestrian historical outlook could be expected to produce in the work of an almost exact contemporary. Nowhere in Charles's *Autobiography* does one find the play of artistic imagination that stamps Henry's *Education* as a unique work of genius, an account that is at once both traditional and highly experimental. For the *Education* is an American classic, and readers must take it on its own terms or fail to comprehend its full meaning.

Nor was this uniqueness lost to T. S. Eliot himself. In one of the earliest reviews of Adams's book, titled "A Sceptical Patrician" and printed in the *Athenaeum* in 1919, the poet warned: "It is doubtful whether the book ought to be called an autobiography, for there is too little of the author in it." Unfortunately, while most readers of the very popular *Education* have recognized its autobiographical possibilities, few have taken Eliot's warning seriously enough.

* * *

Aside from Eliot's cautionary advice, which Adams had no opportunity to read, any more than he had a chance to strike the misleading subtitle from later reprintings, there is abundant external evidence that the author did not plan his work as simply yet another contribution to the tradition of American autobiography. Here, Adams's personal correspondence is extremely useful in putting us on the track of his thoughts concerning the autobiographical form in literature, even before he began the *Education.* Writing to Henry James in 1903 about the latter's biography of William Wetmore Story, Adams said:

> The painful truth is that all of my New England generation, counting the half-century, 1820–1879, were in actual fact only one mind and nature; the individual was a facet of Boston . . . Type Bourgeois bostonian [*sic*]! A type quite as good as another but more uniform. . . . God knows that we knew our want of knowledge! the [*sic*] self-distrust became introspection—nervous self-consciousness—irritable dislike of America, and antipathy to Boston.
>
> So you have written not Story's life, but your own and mine—pure autobiography. . . .

Later, after he had completed the *Education,* Adams sent a copy of the private printing to James in 1908, together with a letter that explained: ''The volume is a mere shield of protection in the grave. I advise you to take your own life in the same way, in order to prevent biographers from taking it in theirs.'' The truth found by biographers and autobiographers could prove to be ''painful truth'' indeed. As a biographer himself, Henry Adams knew this firsthand, having written the lives of Albert Gallatin, John Randolph, and Aaron Burr before he began the *Education.* Certainly the possibilities for using some version of autobiography as a ''shield of protection'' had occurred to Adams as early as 1891, when he wrote to his English friend, Charles Milnes Gaskell: ''The moral seems to be that every man should write his life, to prevent some other fellow from taking it.'' So Adams determined to take his own life in literature but in a unique way, as he turned a chronological narrative of personal experience into an autobiographical literary experiment.

In the *Education* itself, perhaps the most obvious signal of the author's extraordinary intentions may be found on the ''Contents'' page. Surely a superb historian like Adams could do better than to leave such a hiatus as that between Chapter XX, entitled ''Failure (1871)'' and Chapter XXI, entitled ''Twenty Years After (1892).'' For ''protection,'' of course, he had seen fit to leave this period in his life blank—a gap that excluded every detail of his relationship with Marion Hooper Adams, the wife who is never mentioned in the *Education.* Gone too, along with the personal version of his marriage, is all pretense to confessional sincerity or historical accuracy and completeness. Instead, as Adams makes clear, the reading game must be played by the author's own rules.

Nowhere is this made so clear as in the ''Preface'' to the *Education.* From that point onward in the book, the introduction of a ''manikin'' figure

One of the most famous sections of the work, ''The Dynamo and the Virgin,'' reflects Adams' fascination with the Corliss engine he saw at the Great Exposition in Paris in 1900

called ''Henry Adams'' serves to protect the real author from excessive self-revelation, by offering the disguise of personal experience as a covering for didactic art. From almost the first word, the reader is warned that he should not expect another confessional in the tradition of Rousseau or of the American Puritans. For Adams, the *Confessions,* although written like the *Education* ''in the manner of the eighteenth century,'' can be instructive in the twentieth century only when correctly viewed or read. Timely interpretation emphasizes personal limitations rather than accomplishments, and makes the *Confessions* useful as a warning and not as a model.

> As educator, Jean Jacques was in one respect, easily first; he erected a monument of warning against the Ego. Since his time, and largely thanks to him, the Ego has steadily tended to efface itself, and, for purposes of model, to become a manikin on which the toilet of education is to be draped in order to show the fit or misfit of the clothes. The object of study is the garment, not the figure. The tailor adapts the manikin as well as the clothes to his patron's wants. The tailor's object, in this volume, is to fit young men, in universities or elsewhere, to be men of the world, equipped for any emergency; and the garment offered

> **But, in fact, the *Education* should also be thought of, at least in part, as the first modern American autobiography, a seminal volume, as important in its way as was T. S. Eliot's announcements of modernity in his best poetry of the same period."**

to them is meant to show the faults of the patchwork fitted on their fathers. . . .

The manikin, therefore, has the same value as any other geometrical figure of three or more dimensions, which is used for the study of relation. For that purpose it cannot be spared; it is the only measure of motion, of proportion, of human condition; it must have the air of reality; must be taken for real; must be treated as though it had life. Who knows? Possibly it had!

Enter the manikin "Henry Adams" and exit all pretense of conscious self-revelation. As the author tells us 432 pages later,

Of all studies, the one he would rather have avoided was that of his own mind. He knew no tragedy so heart-rending as introspection, and the more, because—as Mephistopheles said of Marguerite—he was not the first. Nearly all the highest intelligence known to history had drowned itself in the reflection of its own thought, and the bovine survivors had rudely told the truth about it, without affecting the intelligent.

Here, the "painful truth" Adams first had described to James emerged more painful still. The source was not simply personal revelation of the usual kind—the embarrassing details of an outward life—but rather the traditional autobiographical practice of looking inward, and of telling truthfully what one has found. Far better to spare the pain and turn away from self, to teach, instead, in the words of the "Preface," ". . . young men, in universities or elsewhere, to be men of the world equipped for any emergency." And teach, Adams did in the pages of his book.

* * *

This is not the place to trace in detail the many lessons in politics, religion, philosophy, science, and art—which measure the author's didactic intention in the *Education*. These main lines of educative force also provide themes for the narrative; while the manikin's example demonstrates over and over the repeated "failure" of the subject ever to learn enough. Gradually, by accretion, this "failure" grows to seem conclusive—just as certain as the failure, in Adams's mind, of Rousseau in his *Confessions* to provide any effective guidance for modern man. Yet the larger, more general lesson here is one of change and not of failure alone; and to give it force, the author concentrates his attention on a central human figure, the persona Henry Adams, who grows from child to man as he tries out, for the reader's benefit, a variety of possibly educational experiences.

But finally the life of "Henry Adams" by itself does not teach enough to satisfy the author, who tells us why:

Truly the animal that is to be trained to unity must be caught young. Unity is vision; it must have been part of the process of learning to see. The older the mind, the older its complexities, and the further it looks, the more it sees, until even the stars resolve themselves into multiples; yet the child will always see but one.

Experience has led the manikin away from unity and instinct, and time has played him false, even while it pretended to educate.

In the face of such change, man must seek to recapture a sense of instinctive unity in art, as Adams hoped to do in his *Education*. For him, art was the only possible alternative to chaos, although for others who may be better educated than he, the author holds out another possibility of scientific unity, especially in the final chapters of his book and in his later essays. But the *Education* tells Henry Adams's story, beginning with his origins in "Quincy" (Chapter I) and "Boston" (Chapter II), and ending with the futuristic speculations that radiated from his mature mind. Put together in his way, the whole story is an experiment in didactic art—taking up in the twentieth century where Rousseau and Franklin left off. For, much as when he was a classroom instructor at Harvard College, the author of the *Education* still kept his faith in the timeless value of the teacher, who could shape human thought into worldly force, and effectively link the past and present with an uncertain future. As Adams wrote in the *Education,* "A teacher affects eternity; he can never tell where his influence stops." By reaching out to the "one [mind] in ten" that "sensibly reacts" to such teaching, the writer hoped to have his autobiographical lessons accepted by his readers in the same way that, in the "Preface," he claimed to use Rousseau's *Confessions,* as "a monument of warning against the Ego."

Finally, only the vigorously reacting mind, Adams believed, could benefit fully from lessons which otherwise became surface polish for the merely passive manikin:

> The object of education for that mind should be the teaching itself how to react with vigor and economy. No doubt the world at large will always lag so far behind the active mind as to make a soft cushion of inertia to drop upon, as it did for Henry Adams; but education should try to lessen the obstacles, diminish the friction, invigorate the energy, and should train minds to react, not at haphazard, but by choice, on the lines of force that attract their world. What one knows is, in youth, of little moment; they know enough who know how to learn.

That rare tenth mind alone knows how to learn: it follows out Adams's lines of force and interest only to react against the egoistic example of the manikin. For that mind only, Adams holds out the hope of being prepared "by choice" to "jump" and stay ahead of the other expanding forces in the universe. Just such a mind might well succeed where the author knew himself to have failed; it might complete a patterning of life and experience with a mastery that would turn chaos into orderly design. Yet, so far as Adams could see in the *Education,* all education based on example—at least human example—was already obsolete. Traditional autobiography, like other forms of human experience, seemed to have reached the end of its usefulness, as education and as art.

What was left to Adams and to modern literature was experiment. So he attempted to turn his narrative of personal experience into something both artistic and useful. Alongside the warnings provided by the chronological gap in the narrative and by the manikin subject, the author developed a vocabulary of symbols, used to tie past experience to future possibility by drawing on instinct rather than reason. The most famous example, of course, is Chapter XXV, "The Dynamo and the Virgin," perhaps the best evidence that the *Education* can be read as modern art, as many anthologies testify.

I do not pretend in this brief survey to judge the *Education* either a failure or a success as art. Still it should be useful to point out that the overall effect of Adams's symbolic treatment—like the picture of the titular character in the book who is both manikin and tailor, and the impression created by the before-and-after organization—is once again to underscore division or contradiction in human experience, and to deny the possibility of unity in the "vision" of the aging author. Perhaps the "child will always see but one"; yet the reader of the *Education,* on the other hand, is left to yearn for such childish unity—in subject matter, organization, and conclusion. The book lacks even an imposed authorial unity, in the form of a single symbolic pattern; and the reader cannot order the various lines of force and thought by reference to some convenient symbol, like the pond in *Walden.*

For Adams, "Chaos was the law of nature; Order was the dream of man." By telling us only what he wanted to about his own life, Henry Adams played the part of a natural man who yet remained always something of a dreamer. While he was a teacher, he was also an artist, who sought to make his own story into didactic art of a high order, still leaving all judgments about his ultimate success to his readers. Meanwhile, the lessons of his life became theirs to use as they saw fit. Properly, the final words about the didactic value of an autobiography might be expected to belong to the author, who could best summarize the meaning of his own life. But in Adams's case, the authorial strategy was different. At the time that he was writing his life story, the author of the *Education* showed that he was too nimble or too evasive to be caught without "protection" and a "shield" for the future. In a letter to E. D. Shaw, the artist managed to shift the burden of interpretation from intention to response, as he showed how he had made the substance of his own experience into a heuristic experiment, designed to test his audience rather than to reveal himself:

> All considerable artists make a point of compelling the public to think for itself, and their rule is to require each observer to see what he can, and this will be what the artist meant. To the artist the meaning is indifferent. Every man is his own artist before a work of art.

Taken as autobiography, then, the *Education* is most of all "a work of art." The genius of Adams's experiment in modernity lies in his dramatic conversion of the narrative and didactic conventions he has inherited—the stuff of traditional autobiography—to his own unique purposes. For, while he kept the surface appearance of the narrative of personal experience, perhaps to convince the public that they knew exactly what he was doing, Adams also offered his readers full artistic license to make every one of them his own autobiographer.

Source: Earl N. Harbert, "Henry Adams's *Education* and the Autobiographical Tradition," in *Tulane Studies in English,* Tulane University, Vol. 22, 1977, pp. 133–42.

Herbert F. Hahn

In the following essay, Hahn asserts that Adams' portrayal of his life as a failure was a literary device used for dramatic effect.

Anyone beginning to read Henry Adams' *Education* for the first time gets the impression from the very first chapters that Adams thought his life had been a failure, and that he considered it a failure because his education had not fitted him to play a useful part in the new and different world that was coming into being in the nineteenth century. The book can therefore be taken—so it seems—as a protest, based on one man's experience, against the effect of technology and industrialism on the personal values of the social system which they displaced.

Throughout the book Henry Adams gives the impression of a man who wished to participate actively in affairs but always missed the chance to function effectively. There is a certain poignancy in his desire to understand why a man like himself, who started with every apparent advantage and set out with such faith and eagerness, should have ended with so little accomplished. His antecedents and his personal attainments had indicated a career in the Adams tradition; yet he never found an opportunity to make a contribution to his time comparable with what his forebears had accomplished.

This presentation of himself as a failure has usually been accepted by Adams' readers at face value. In the 1920's a whole "generation of futilitarians" (Louis Kronenberger's phrase) found that Adams' theme of maladjustment between a cultivated personality and an increasingly mechanized civilization presented exactly the predicament which they were experiencing. His book became the Bible of the younger generation struggling with the frustrations of a world they neither made nor understood.

Could it be, on the other hand, that the dominant theme of Henry Adams' book was a literary device of the author's rather than a reflection of the facts? One recent critic has advanced the theory that Henry Adams fancied himself as the "heroic failure" of a modern epic. From this point of view, the dramatic irony inherent in the repeated assertions that Adams never felt at home in the world and despaired of ever playing a significant part in it was a consciously cultivated irony. If true, this view of Adams' intention helps to explain some things about the book which otherwise strike the reader as puzzling. There is, for example, in the chapters devoted to Adams' travel-years after graduation a certain tone of insouciance—a pose of naiveté—which leaves the reader with a very inadequate sense of how Adams reacted to the things he saw in Europe. He seems to be trying to emphasize the *lack* of "education" to be gained from the experiences available to a young man of his background in his day. And yet we know from the famous letters Adams wrote on subsequent travels that he was capable of responding richly to experience. In the *Education,* however, he gives the impression of making the grand tour without zest and of finding most things rather empty of meaning for him. This impression does not accord with what is otherwise known of his temperament. His attitude becomes understandable, however, if it can be regarded as a consciously planned device for emphasizing his "failure" to find an acceptable place in a civilization with which he felt himself out of tune.

Actually, the burden of Henry Adams' complaint was not his own "failure" to adjust to the world but the realization that the world in which he lived as an adult had changed so much from the world in which he grew up as a child that the traditional values of his upbringing had become meaningless and inapplicable. A relatively uncomplicated agrarian America, operating on the basis of stern but comprehensible Puritan principles, was rapidly being transformed into a highly complex industrialized state, with a bewildering shift in the principles on which it operated and an apparent exclusion of morality from the political means for achieving its goals. The disappearance of the sort of world in which an Adams could have functioned and its displacement by a new world which required a type of "education" such as no previous Adams had ever had—that is the real theme of Henry Adams' long book. He took pleasure, it is true, in presenting himself as an anachronism from a former age and indulged his tragic feeling of having been born too late. But behind the mask of "the tragic failure" was another Henry Adams who was not lamenting his fate so much as making a genuine effort to understand the times that were out of joint.

Henry Adams knew that a man must thoroughly understand the world in which he finds himself in order to be able to grapple with it. He sensed that his "education" in the ways of the new world would require him, first of all, to unlearn everything that he had been taught. However, he *believed* in the values of his grandfather's world; it was the rejection of those values by the new world, rather than his own failure to accommodate himself to it, that represented for him the real tragedy he was writing about. Nevertheless, he felt it was important to get beyond the perspectives of his traditional background and to make the attempt to understand the contemporary world. Lacking the opportunity to participate in affairs, he became an observer and commentator, writing detailed accounts of the political events he was living through, frequently with penetrating remarks on the personalities of the chief participants. His political chapters served the purpose of underlining the corruption, vulgarity, and cynicism of the modern world from which he felt himself alienated. Until Lincoln Steffens painted the same picture in more vivid colors and with much greater detail, Adams' account of the unprincipled dealings in American public life was the classic portrayal of a burgeoning business civilization creating a chaos in which self-interest was the sole guiding principle.

But political events and economic developments were only the surface features, after all. Henry Adams' education in the nature of the modern world would not be complete—at least, he would never be satisfied—until he had fathomed the driving forces and motivations that accounted for the surface phenomena. He understood in a general way that modern science with its practical achievements was responsible for the transformations which had changed the easy-going world of his forebears into a totally different, enigmatic world, that nevertheless seemed amazingly alive. But he doubted the correctness of the common point of view which regarded progress as inevitable and the American brand of material achievement as the climax of all progress. What Henry Adams really sought from his "education" was a standard or principle of interpretation by which he could estimate the truth of the world-view which made a virtue of chaos as long as it seemed to further "progress." As one who had been brought up in a tradition that gave great satisfaction through the unity and consistency of meaning it assigned to life, he was genuinely concerned to discover how it was possible to find a comparable satisfaction in a world that had become so complex and contradictory as to lose all unity and consistency of meaning.

" Critics are mistaken to emphasize the tragedy implicit in the *Education* a personal one for Henry Adams. Adams would have insisted that he was describing a situation that constituted a tragedy for all thoughtful and sensitive souls."

Adams failed to solve the problem, at first, because he assumed from the start that satisfaction in life would be found only by those who learned to *control* the complicated, multiple forces dominant in the world in their time. When he saw politicians and business men who were not "educated," in his sense, doing *just that* with phenomenal success, and when he saw men like his friend Clarence King failing miserably even though trained (educated) for exercising such control, he became pessimistic about the value of "education" as a means of finding satisfaction in life. For him, satisfaction meant understanding as well as controlling. He observed, however, that the successful men of his day controlled the forces operating in the world without understanding them, or even being conscious of a need to understand them. Adams, therefore, despaired of the possibility of finding any principle of action in modern life that gave unity of meaning to the diverse activities it engendered.

Adams, however, was not prepared to accept "multiplicity" as any more than a descriptive term for the modern situation: it could not be made, his whole temperament told him, into a philosophical justification for the situation. And so, he continued to study, to observe, and to weigh, in a constant search for the meaning of his contemporary environment. He gave up, for the time being, the attempt to identify a unifying principle in the world as he knew it; and turning to the world of the Middle Ages, where unity and significance had permeated all of life, he proceeded to study it thoroughly in order to find out its secret. It has been customary to regard Henry Adams' love affair with the Middle Ages as a nostalgic search for the very things he missed in modern civilization. The contrast between the two ages is striking enough: on the one hand, chaos without meaning; on the other, a unifying principle that gave significance to all the parts. But when Henry Adams immersed himself in the medieval outlook on life, it was not to ''go home'' to a world for which he felt an instinctive sympathy—actually he had been unaware of such a world before his tour of Normandy with the Henry Cabot Lodges. It was rather to gain perspective on his *own* world that he sought to understand medieval ''unity'' in contrast to nineteenth-century ''multiplicity.''

So satisfying did Henry Adams find the assurance and confidence reflected in the medieval point of view that he almost surrendered to it, and bowing himself before the Virgin of Chartres he asked for the peace that would come from understanding himself and his world as clearly as the Virgin's followers understood theirs. Significantly, he did not ask for ''the peace which *passeth* understanding''; he insisted on *having* understanding; as a child of the scientific age, he *had to know*. So, wistfully, he started ''once more'' his search for ''education'' (enlightenment).

The real significance of Henry Adams' *Education* is not the story of maladjustment that it tells, nor yet the contrast between two civilizations that it makes, but the explanation which the author eventually worked out for the trend of civilization from medieval unity to modern multiplicity. In a series of brilliant though still ironic chapters (31–34), Adams summed up what he had learned from his lifelong search for understanding of the world in which he lived. These philosophical chapters have seldom been taken quite seriously; they have sometimes been brushed aside as derivative: the chief idea in them came from the author's brother, Brooks Adams. But there is a philosophy of history in them, seemingly artificial because applied too mechanically, yet containing an explanation of modern ''chaos'' and the ''multiplicity'' of modern civilization which has proved to be so appropriate and so illuminating that it deserves reconsideration.

Henry Adams had learned, first of all, that modern science (itself an attempt to discover the immutable ''laws of nature'') had ended by discovering, in modern physical theory, that there were no simple, immutable laws of nature which gave unity, consistency, and order to the universe; that, rather, the laws of the physical world seemed to be infinitely complex, not always consistently predictable in their application, and hence undependable as a basis for finding order in the universe. In a word,

Henry Adams came to the realization that such a system of order and unity as the medieval synthesis was the creation of the mind of man imposing its desire for simplicity and significance on the phenomena of the world at large. As he said himself, ''Chaos was the law of nature; Order was the dream of man.''

Henry Adams had learned, in the second place, that the discoveries of modern science, destructive as they were to philosophical conceptions of the universe, were nevertheless making constructive contributions to the material comfort of mankind in the universe, by increasing man's knowledge of the number and kinds of physical energies available for application to his needs. As man's knowledge of the physical forces of nature became more complex (less unified even in theory), man's opportunities for bending them to his purposes increased proportionately. The ''multiplicity'' or complexity of modern industrialized life, in other words, corresponded to the actual ''chaos'' of forces existing in the physical universe.

In the light of these insights, it had been pointless as well as fruitless for Henry Adams to look for a unifying principle to explain the modern world. Multiplicity of conflicting forces was its chief characteristic, and inevitably so. Man might try to impose his control over the physical forces of nature and upon the human energies of society, but the resulting ''order'' was not inherent in either nature or society, and it lasted only as long as the mind of man thought the one and willed the other. Philosophically speaking, there was no ''God'' to give significance to the universe of forces and the world of energies. Logically, therefore, there was nothing wrong with the modern tendency to establish control of these forces and energies without understanding them. In relation to the universe and the world, men had become ''as gods''—without the divine capacity, of course, to give real significance to what they were doing with their new powers. The significant fact, for Henry Adams, was that the tendency was irreversible. He had come to realize that there was no going back, that a world of meaningful unity had never really existed (outside the human mind), that a world of chaotic, conflicting forces corresponded more nearly to the reality than all the orderly worlds created by man's imagination and reason.

The most famous part of Henry Adams' philosophy of history was what he called ''the law of acceleration'' (unconsciously demonstrating within himself his view that, though there be no actual laws, even in history, the mind will impose law as a device to help itself understand what it is talking about). He thought he saw in history a consistent trend toward *increasing* control over the forces of nature. Starting in a small way with the discovery and exploitation of the power of a water wheel and the power in a windmill, man had then, with smaller and smaller gaps of time between discoveries, but larger and larger amounts of power at his disposal, proceeded to find and use steam power, electric power, and so on. Henry Adams was convinced that this ''acceleration'' in man's control of nature's forces would continue in geometric proportion, until (he predicted) man would have discovered within fifty years of Adams' time the ultimate source of power locked in the atom.

In his own generation, the symbol of modern man's control of force was the dynamo, which Henry Adams found to be the most fascinating embodiment of ultimate power under complete control yet devised. Fascinating he found it to watch in operation—but apalling to think about in its implications. As a symbol of force under control, it helped to explain to him the nature of the civilization in which he lived. As a prophecy of the trend of civilization, it suggested increasing efficiency in man's control of ultimate force until the human race reached the point where it could even destroy itself with atomic energy. This eventuality Henry Adams could not regard with complacency. He could not accept the view of his contemporaries that the history of mankind in modern times was a story of inevitable progress upwards. ''Complexity, Multiplicity, even a step towards Anarchy, it might suggest, but what step towards perfection?''

It was not the ultimate denouement, however, that troubled Henry Adams in his innermost depths. That denouement, after all, remained only a logical possibility; it was not inevitably a foregone conclusion. He saw another already taking place which appalled him more specifically. As man's control of the forces of nature increased in efficiency, his will to dominate the social energies of mankind also increased, with a resulting tendency to *concentrate* the power inherent in the forces of society, again for the sake of efficiency. In other words, the technological advance of mankind was inexorably accompanied by a trend to regimentation and the collectivization of man's social relationships. It was the progressive destruction of human values in the

accelerating trend towards a power civilization that appalled Henry Adams the most.

Here was the real tragedy of living modern times. Critics are mistaken to emphasize the tragedy implicit in the *Education* a personal one for Henry Adams. Adams would have insisted that he was describing a situation that constituted a tragedy for all thoughtful and sensitive souls. With the increase in the means of control over energy and power, all that was distinctively human in human life was gradually being supplanted by all that was mechanical and impersonal. Adams' book was not simply a protest against an intolerable situation by one who had been most uncomfortable in it; it was an attempt to instruct a whole new generation in the conditions under which life in modern times was being lived, and to emphasize that no other conditions were possible under the circumstances.

Henry Adams made all this sound very pessimistic. But behind the pessimistic tone of his discussion it is possible to discern a positive note of emphasis on continuing human values, particularly the human capacity for thought. It is true that, in its context, his quotation from Karl Pearson: ''Order and reason, beauty and benevolence, are characteristics and conceptions which we find solely associated with the mind of man,'' sounds like a pessimistic acknowledgement of the fact that the universe does *not* contain order and reason but is essentially meaningless. On the other hand, like several ironic passages in Adams' last chapters, the quotation conceals his faith that, though the universe be meaningless, the very attempt of the human mind to create meaning from its diverse phenomena is the source of all truth and beauty and value in the *human* world. The meaningless chaos of the universe, though eternal, was as nothing compared with the ephemeral, but significant, flash of a human mind in the cosmic darkness.

Again, Henry Adams' parable of the young oyster, in which he compared the human mind to that little animal ''secreting its universe to suit its conditions until it had built up a shell of nacre that embodied all its notions of the perfect,'' but ''perishing in the face of the cyclonic hurricane or the volcanic upheaval of its bed,'' sounds like a realistic recognition of the fact that the universe has no interest in the existence of man and offers him only complete annihilation (death) as his ultimate fate. Few writers have described more pitilessly how completely indifferent the universe seems to be to the aspirations and strivings of the human race. Yet, behind the irony of the parable was the implication that it was precisely the aspiration and the striving that gave meaning, if only temporarily, to all that was human in an otherwise impersonal universe.

What Henry Adams accomplished in his *Education* was not only to describe remorselessly what kind of a world the modern world had become—philosophically, as well as politically and economically; he also provided a point of view with which to face that world without despair.

Source: Herbert F. Hahn, *"The Education of Henry Adams* Reconsidered," in *College English,* Vol. 24, No. 6, March 1963, pp. 444–49.

Sources

Banta, Martha, "Being a 'Begonia' in a Man's World," in *New Essays on "The Education of Henry Adams,"* edited by John Carlos Rowe, Cambridge University Press, 1996, pp. 49–86.

Blackmur, Richard P., *The Expense of Greatness,* Arrow Editions, 1942.

Diamond, Jared, *Guns, Germs, and Steel: The Fates of Human Societies,* W. W. Norton & Company, 1997.

Hicks, Granville, "Struggle and Flight," in *The Great Tradition: An Interpretation of American Literature Since the Civil War,* rev. ed., Macmillan Publishing Company, 1935, pp. 131–63.

Ihde, Don, *Technology and the Lifeworld: From Garden to Earth,* Indiana Series in the Philosophy of Technology, Indiana University Press, 1990.

Jordy, William H., *Henry Adams, Scientific Historian,* Yale University Press, 1952.

Mitcham, Carl, *Thinking through Technology: The Path between Engineering and Philosopher,* University of Chicago Press, 1994.

Roelofs, Gerrit H., "Henry Adams: Pessimism and the Intelligent Use of Doom," in *Journal of English Literary History,* Vol. 17, 1950, pp. 214–39.

Rowe, John Carlos, *"The Education of Henry Adams* and the American Empire," in *Literary Culture and U.S. Imperialism,* Oxford University Press, 2000, pp. 165–94.

Wasser, Henry, *The Scientific Thought of Henry Adams,* Thessaloniki, 1956.

Wasserstrom, William, *The Ironies of Progress: Henry Adams and the American Dream,* Southern Illinois University Press, 1984.

Further Reading

Geddes, Patrick, *Cities in Evolution: An Introduction to the Town Planning Movement and to the Study of Civics,* Benn, 1968.
    Beginning with an application of recent developments in cell theory, Geddes applies the notions of biology to urban planning. In this framework, the entire city with its people and industry form an organism within an ecology. Proper care of this system will evolve healthy, happy people.

Hays, Samuel P., *The Response to Industrialism: 1885–1914,* University of Chicago Press, 1957.
    Hays briefly delineates the events and ideas composing the Reform Era in the United States.

Highman, John, "Anti-Semitism in the Gilded Age: A Reinterpretation," in *Mississippi Valley Historical Review,* Vol. 43, No. 4, March 1957, 559–78.
    Highman's look at anti-Semitic themes of late nineteenth-century literature includes a discussion of Adams' work.

Lyon, Melvin, *Symbol and Idea in Henry Adams,* University of Nebraska Press, 1970.
    Lyon's book is a schematic breakdown of the themes and techniques Adams uses throughout his writing. The intent of the work is to show how those themes and techniques reveal Adams's "program for improving society."

Mumford, Lewis, "The Nucleation of Power," in *The Myth of the Machine: the Pentagon of Power,* Columbia University Press, 1964, pp. 230–62.
    Lewis Mumford argues that the advance of civilization depends upon the organization of humans into veritable construction machines. For Mumford, the complexity of human organization is more important than technological innovation.

Spring, Joel, *Education and the Rise of the Global Economy,* Lawrence Erlbaum Associates, 1998.
    Spring's work serves as a starting point for reflecting on the inadequacies of twentieth-century education systems to prepare people for the demands of a digital age.

The Journalist and the Murderer

Janet Malcolm

1989

Over the decades, Janet Malcolm has built a reputation for herself as a journalist who does not shy away from raising unpleasant topics. Whether tackling psychology, literature, or the criminal justice system, Malcolm's frankness and controversial opinions have often placed her outside the journalistic community. In an article in *Salon,* Craig Seligman, an admirer of her work, readily acknowledged that ''Malcolm is hard on her subjects.''

Malcolm's *The Journalist and the Murderer* first appeared as an article in the *New Yorker* in 1989 and the following year, along with an appended afterword, it was published as a book. This extended essay dealt with journalistic ethics by focusing on the libel suit that a convicted murderer brought against writer Joe McGinniss for breach of faith. It sent shockwaves among members of the press. While Seligman asserted that *The Journalist and the Murderer* is ''the masterpiece that permanently tied the noose around her neck.'' He maintained that she had a higher calling: ''the service of the truth.'' While many critics accused Malcolm of attacking journalistic ethics, Malcolm's work is rather an exploration of the responsibility the journalist has to both the subject and the reader. Though the ultimate commitment the journalist has is to the ''reader's interests,'' Malcolm concludes that the journalist should not ignore the ''moral impasse'' or employ ''crude and gratuitous two-facedness,'' both of which, she tries to prove, McGinniss did.

Author Biography

Malcolm was born in the 1930s to a Jewish family in pre-World War II Prague, Czechoslovakia. Her father was a psychiatrist. Because of rising anti-Semitism, the family left Europe in 1939 and settled in New York. Malcolm attended the High School of Music and Art in Manhattan and went on to the University of Michigan. Malcolm wrote reviews for the student paper and worked as an editor for the university's humor magazine.

In the 1960s, Malcolm became a staff writer for the *New Yorker,* focusing primarily on interior decoration and design. By the 1970s she had branched out into writing about photography for the magazine. She published her first book, *Diana and Nikon: Essays on the Aesthetic of Photography*, in 1980. Ten of the eleven essays had originally appeared in the *New Yorker,* and many of her later books would also have their first publication in the magazine.

With her next book, Malcolm delved into the psychoanalytical world. *Psychoanalysis: The Impossible Profession* presented a history of the psychoanalytical profession and community. Her next book was the first of many that would cause great controversy. In 1983, Malcolm published a pair of articles in the *New Yorker,* ''In the Freud Archives,'' which was published by Knopf the following year. It concerned the fight for control of Sigmund Freud's archives. Malcolm met one of the central figures, psychoanalyst Jeffrey Moussaieff Masson, won his trust, and then proceeded to write what Craig Seligman called in *Salon,* ''a masterwork of character assassination.'' Masson quickly sued Malcolm for libel, basing his case on five quotations that he claimed she had made up. The suit was not wholly resolved until 1994, when a jury found that although Malcolm had falsified two quotes, she had not done so with ''reckless disregard.''

While undergoing this trial, Malcolm took on the subject of journalist freedom. ''Reflections: The Journalist and the Murderer'' appeared in two installments in the *New Yorker* in 1989, and it was published as the book *The Journalist and the Murderer* the following year. In it, Malcolm explored the relationship between the journalist and the subject, but her assertions as to the inherent dishonesty that all reporters practice disturbed many readers.

Malcolm's 1994 *The Silent Woman: Sylvia Plath and Ted Hughes* (which also first appeared as a *New Yorker* article) generated controversy as she took an unorthodox view of Hughes. In *The Crime of Sheila McGough* (1999), Malcolm chronicles the trial of Virginia attorney McGough, who served two and a half years in federal prison after her 1990 felony conviction for defending a con artist and having financial involvement in his business dealings. Malcolm steadfastly believed in McGough's innocence, and her book examines the legal system.

Summary

In *The Journalist and the Murderer* (originally published almost in its entirety in the *New Yorker*), Malcolm explores the relationship between the journalist and the subject. Declaring that this relationship is always rife with seduction and betrayal, Malcolm focuses her argument around the example of MacDonald and McGinniss. MacDonald was the former Green Beret doctor convicted of murdering his wife and two young children. McGinniss was the writer who gained exclusive access to MacDonald and his lawyers, and, while professing to be a friend and supporter of MacDonald, wrote and published *Fatal Vision,* a nonfiction book that portrayed the doctor as a pathological liar and cold-blooded killer. MacDonald sued McGinniss for fraud and breach of contract.

McGinniss was already an award-winning nonfiction writer when he first met MacDonald in 1979. MacDonald's wife and children had been murdered in 1970, he alleged, by a group of hippies who broke into the family's apartment. Although an army tribunal cleared MacDonald, several years later more evidence was disclosed, and he was indicted for murder. About to face trial, MacDonald asked McGinniss if he would like to write a book about the case from the point of view of the defense team. McGinniss was drawn to the insider position. He accompanied the MacDonald team to North Carolina for the trial, lived in their rented fraternity house and eventually was made a member in order to guard lawyer-client privilege. In return for this exclusive access, MacDonald would receive a share of the royalties. He also signed a contract promising not to sue McGinniss for libel if he did not like McGinniss's finished product.

After a seven-week trial, MacDonald was convicted and sent to prison. McGinniss spent the next four years working on his book. Despite continuous contact with MacDonald, McGinniss never revealed that he believed MacDonald was guilty and that the book would clearly demonstrate this sentiment.

After *Fatal Vision* was published in 1983, MacDonald sued his former confidante. At the trial, cross-examination forced McGinniss to reveal his disingenuous behavior toward MacDonald. Trial excerpts included in Malcolm's book make him appear, simply, an opportunist. Rebuttal witnesses, fellow writers who attempted to justify being dishonest with subjects in order to get information, only hindered his case. Three months after the trial ended in a hung jury—a 6–1 split—an agreement was made under which McGinniss admitted to no wrongdoing but paid MacDonald $325,000.

Malcolm became interested in the case after receiving a letter from McGinniss's lawyer, Daniel Kornstein, in which he spoke of the threat the lawsuit posed to journalistic freedom. Malcolm responded by getting in touch with and subsequently interviewing McGinniss. Though McGinniss canceled all future interviews, Malcolm continued to investigate the story. She read the transcript of the MacDonald-McGinniss trial and interviewed other key participants. Malcolm met with lawyers, witnesses, private investigators, and jurists involved in the case. She used this research to draw numerous conclusions about the inherent uneasiness of the journalist-subject relationship.

One piece of information Malcolm did not include in the main body of the book was that she herself had been sued for libel by one of her own subjects; that libel suit had ended in its dismissal. Many of Malcolm's fellow journalists responded critically to her work, charging that she used McGinniss's ordeal to expatiate her own guilt. In an afterword, Malcolm denied these charges. She maintained that the problem of the journalist-subject relationship had long disturbed her, but she also acknowledged that the writer always finds some part of herself in her characters.

Key Figures

Gary Bostwick

Bostwick was the lawyer who represented MacDonald in his libel suit against McGinniss.

William F. Buckley, Jr.

Buckley, a writer, was a witness for the defense at McGinniss's libel trial. He testified that it was

Janet Malcolm

acceptable for a writer to falsely agree to something a subject says in order to acquire more information.

Lucille Dillon

Dillion was the one jurist serving on the McGinniss-MacDonald trial who did not find McGinniss guilty. Her refusal to deliberate forced the judge to declare a mistrial.

Dr. Jeffrey Eliot

Dr. Eliot was a writer and a professor who taught at North Carolina Central University. He was working on a book about MacDonald and served as a witness at the libel trial. He believed that MacDonald did not receive a fair trial and that a new one could result in his acquittal.

Bob Keeler

Keeler was a reporter from *Newsday* who had covered the MacDonald trial. He hoped to publish his own book about the crime but was unable to get a contract. He interviewed McGinniss, questioning him closely about his relationship to MacDonald.

Daniel Kornstein

Kornstein was the lawyer who defended McGinniss in his libel trial. He drew Malcolm's interest in the case in 1987 when he sent a letter to thirty journalists around the country, inviting them to talk to McGinniss and begin an investigation of this perceived threat to the freedom of journalistic expression.

Jeffrey MacDonald

MacDonald was a physician for a U.S. Army Green Beret unit in 1970 when his pregnant wife and two young daughters were stabbed to death in the family's home at Fort Bragg, North Carolina. MacDonald claimed four hippies had broken into the house and committed the crime. MacDonald moved to California and started a new life. Several years later, MacDonald was charged with the crime. The trial took place in 1979, and MacDonald was found guilty.

McGinniss's *Fatal Vision* supported this position. MacDonald sued McGinniss for breach of faith in 1987. The two parties' lawyers agreed to settle; McGinniss admitted to no wrongdoing but paid MacDonald $325,000. In the years since both of these trials, MacDonald has maintained his innocence.

Janet Malcolm

Malcolm is one of the key characters in her book. She narrates the book from the first-person point of view (though she maintains in the afterword that the ''I'' is merely a dispassionate narrator and not really Malcolm at all). As a journalist, Malcolm has undertaken the investigation of the relationship that exists between the journalist and his or her subject. As she tells the reader, this is an issue that has long troubled her. She has genuine experience in the difficulties this relationship poses, for she previously was the defendant in a lawsuit in which one of her subjects accused her of misquoting him. Her book is an extended musing on the ethics and responsibilities of the journalist, both to the subject and to the reader. She castigates any journalists who do not acknowledge the inherent problem that exists but readily admits that there is no easy solution to balancing the desires of all the parties involved. As she points out, a writer always transfers part of herself or himself onto the subject. ''The characters of nonfiction, no less than those of fiction,'' she writes, ''derive from the writer's most idiosyncratic desires and deepest anxieties; they are what the writer wishes he was and worries that he is.'' With her host of inflammatory statements, Malcolm opened herself up for the harsh criticism of her colleagues.

Michael Malley

Malley was a lawyer who had been MacDonald's college roommate. He had taken part in the army hearings that dismissed the charges against him in 1970, and he also took a leave from his law firm to work for his friend's defense in the murder trial. He was not happy that McGinniss was given such easy access to MacDonald's defense team. He played a key role in MacDonald's libel suit, testifying about the relationship that developed between MacDonald and McGinniss.

Joe McGinniss

McGinnis was a well-known nonfiction writer. At the time Malcolm wrote *The Journalist and the Murderer*, he had published six books. He first met MacDonald in 1979, right before his murder trial commenced. He contracted with MacDonald to write about MacDonald's experience and received complete and exclusive access to MacDonald and his lawyers. McGinniss seemed to become close friends with MacDonald, and after MacDonald was found guilty, McGinniss corresponded with him for almost four years. Though he actually believed that MacDonald was guilty, he kept this truth hidden while he was working on his book.

The book McGinniss published about the case, *Fatal Vision*, came out in 1983. Upon reading it, MacDonald discovered for the first time that McGinniss believed him to be guilty of the crime. Furthermore, the book also helped convince numerous readers of MacDonald's guilt.

Bernard Segal

Segal defended MacDonald before the Army tribunal—which found him uninvolved in the murders—and remained his lawyer until 1982. Getting a writer involved in MacDonald's story was originally Segal's idea.

Dr. Michael Stone

Dr. Stone was a witness for the defense at McGinniss' libel trial. He had diagnosed MacDonald as having a pathological illness after reading *Fatal Vision*.

Joseph Wambaugh

Wambaugh, a true crime writer, was a witness for the defense at McGinniss's libel trial. He maintained that there was a crucial difference between a lie and an untruth. He believed that it was acceptable for a journalist to deceive a subject in order to get at the actual truth, thus rendering it an "untruth."

Themes

Ethics and Truth

The exploration of journalistic ethics is at the core of *The Journalist and the Murderer.* At its outset, Malcolm asserts that every reporter is "a kind of confidence man, preying on people's vanity, ignorance or loneliness, gaining their trust and betraying them without remorse." To prove her thesis, Malcolm relates the narrative of the MacDonald-McGinniss lawsuit, which has at its heart MacDonald's contention that McGinniss had not maintained the "essential integrity" of his life story. By contrast, in an interview he gave after the publication of *Fatal Vision,* McGinniss said that his "only obligation . . . was to the truth." By that, he means the truth as he (and the MacDonald trial jury) saw it: MacDonald's guilt—not the truth that he presented to MacDonald: a belief in his innocence.

McGinniss claimed no wrongdoing. At his trial his lawyers brought in other journalists and nonfiction authors to defend his actions. William F. Buckley, Jr., admitted that he would "tell [a subject] something you don't really believe in order to get more information from him." Joseph Wambaugh, author of the true crime book *The Onion Field,* attempted to draw a distinction between a lie and an untruth: "A lie is something that's told with ill will or in bad faith," but an untruth is "part of a device wherein one can get at the actual truth." Such defense, however, failed to convince many spectators, including the jury.

Trust

MacDonald's suit of McGinniss stemmed from what MacDonald viewed as a colossal betrayal of trust. McGinniss asserted a false belief in MacDonald's innocence in order to gain access to his story. MacDonald's trust in McGinniss is readily apparent. After MacDonald was convicted and imprisoned, the correspondence between the two men reveals a closer connection than merely author-subject. On numerous occasions, McGinniss wrote of the unfairness of MacDonald's conviction and assured MacDonald of his friendship. MacDonald gave McGinniss permission to use his empty apartment and even to remove documents from them— documents that McGinniss would later use to vilify

MacDonald. Malcolm also points out that even after the experience with McGinniss, MacDonald continued to trust journalists, for instance, granting interviews and giving materials to them. Malcolm finds such behavior—which she believes manifests a "childish trust" in journalists—common among subjects.

Malcolm also explores the guilt that reporters feel about deluding their subjects from a personal point of view. Clearly finding McGinniss's actions toward MacDonald reprehensible, Malcolm still wanted to speak with McGinniss. However, McGinniss opted to end a series of projected interviews. While this crippled her endeavor to an extent, she also wrote that it freed her from the guilt she would have felt at talking to a man she thought had acted unethically, because "you can't betray someone you barely know."

Psychoanalysis and Psychology

Throughout her work, Malcolm uses language and knowledge gleaned from her previous work on psychoanalysis and psychology. On numerous occasions, she compares the journalist's subject to a therapy patient. For instance, in her opening pages, she likens the journalist's subject's discovery of his or her manipulation to a famous psychological experiment conducted in the 1960s. As another example, in discussing the trust that many subjects willingly place in journalists, Malcolm writes, "The journalistic encounter seems to have the same regressive effect on a subject as the psychoanalytic encounter." Malcolm draws further parallels between the journalist-subject relationship and the analyst-patient. The subject, like the patient, will tell his or her story to anyone who will listen and always plays the dominant role. Malcolm's journey to uncover these truths also resembles the therapeutic process. As the journalist, she has learned how the subject acts, as the analyst learns how the patient will act. However, Malcolm is not the only person who relies on the language of psychoanalysis. The wife of MacDonald's lawyer, herself a therapist, likens McGinniss's conflict that arose from pretending to be MacDonald's friend to therapy.

Psychology is also important to McGinniss's work *Fatal Vision.* In this book he labeled MacDonald a psychopath and a pathological narcissist and quoted several texts that described such deviants. Though the psychiatrist Michael Stone, who was a witness for the McGinniss defense, concurred with this diagnosis, he admitted that he had never met MacDonald; he had actually drawn this conclusion

Topics for Further Study

- Imagine that a dialogue took place between MacDonald and McGinniss after the publication of *Fatal Vision*. Write what you think that conversation might have been like.

- Read *Fatal Vision*. Keeping in mind the contradictory opinions you have read in *The Journalist and the Murderer*, write an essay about the role that McGinniss played in influencing the reader's opinion.

- If you had the opportunity to interview Malcolm about her own feelings about McGinniss and MacDonald, what would you want to know? Write a series of questions that you would pose to Malcolm, and then attempt to answer as you think Malcolm would.

- What opinion do you draw of Malcolm's own ethics though your study of *The Journalist and the Murderer*? Write an essay exploring this topic.

- Analyze Malcolm's use of language in *The Journalist and the Murderer*. Is it matter-of-fact? Exaggerated? Convincing?

- Do you agree with Malcolm's contentions about the relationship between the journalist and the subject? Write a review of *The Journalist and the Murderer*. You may want to read reviews that appeared when the work was first published.

- Seligman wrote in *Salon* of Malcolm, "What journalist of her caliber is so widely disliked or as often accused of bad faith? . . . In the animus toward her there is something almost personal." What opinion do you draw from *The Journalist and the Murderer* of Malcolm as a person (not as a journalist)?

---

years before, upon reading McGinniss's book. Malcolm concludes that the labeling of MacDonald as a psychopath was so important to McGinniss because it allowed him to feel that he was betraying an "it," not a real person.

Style

Point of View

Malcolm uses the first-person point of view throughout the book, which renders her a constant presence in the book. However, she complicates her position at the end of the book. In the afterword, Malcolm states that the journalist's—and her own— "I" character is "almost pure invention." She considers the "I" to function as a dispassionate narrator, one that can be as impartial as the third-person voice, which is much more widely used in nonfiction texts. Despite her claims, it is difficult at times to distinguish the narrative "I" from the Malcolm "I"; at one point she even makes certain to distinguish the two by referring to "(the actual) I." The "I" puts forth strong assertions, such as the one that opens her work, but is this "I" simply expressing a narrative opinion or Malcolm's opinion? When Malcolm admits to long being troubled by the "unhealthiness of the journalist-subject relationship," this only lends further credence to the blending of the two "I's."

The prominence of Malcolm's voice in developing her argument poses another potential problem, that of personal ethics. Many critics attacked Malcolm upon the article's original *New Yorker* publication because she never mentioned that, like McGinniss, she had been sued for libel by a subject. Some of these attacks suggested that she was simply projecting her own guilty conscience onto the text of her work. Malcolm felt compelled to respond in an article, which was included as the book's afterword, that this was not the case. However, Malcolm does not deny that even in nonfiction writing, a writer puts a great deal of himself or herself into the "characters." Malcolm's specific language here is revealing: in referring to real people as characters, she is expressing her belief that these people have a fictive function.

Essay

The Journalist and the Murderer is an extended essay. Malcolm builds her essay based on personal experience, knowledge, research, and philosophies, but she also draws on actual events, interviews, and other matters of the public record. Though she casts her ideas authoritatively, Malcolm is essentially writing a persuasive essay. She opens her work with a premise—that any decent journalist knows that he or she is acting immorally—and then provides evidence to prove this thesis to the reader. She relies on facts, interviews, and detailed research, as well as on what she perceives to be a solid understanding of human nature. She also attempts to assert her credibility by showing the mistakes she makes but quickly moves to correct. For example, she writes of her surprise at learning that her subtle and sensitive questioning elicited the identical responses from MacDonald as another reporter's more businesslike technique; however, she turns a blatantly elitist and self-important error into a positive by using it to reach the conclusion that subjects merely want someone who will listen to their story, their truth.

Quotations and Interviews

Malcolm employs several methods of supplying testimony to the reader. She quotes from the McGinniss trial transcript, correspondence, and nonfiction material, as well as from *Fatal Vision*. In these cases, it appears that she quotes from her sources word-for-word. During the course of working on this book, Malcolm also conducted numerous interviews with many people, including MacDonald, McGinniss, trial witnesses, other journalists, jurists, and friends of MacDonald. Malcolm reports on her interviews and quotes extensively from the dialogue that took place. In her afterword, she points out that readers assume that when they read a quotation in a newspaper, they are reading what the speaker actually said, not what the speaker probably said. However, she also acknowledges that "when a journalist undertakes to quote a subject he has interviewed on tape, he owes it to the subject, no less than to the reader, to translate his speech into prose." While Malcolm maintains that the journalist is merely performing the sort of "rewriting that, in life, our ear automatically and instantaneously performs," her revelation calls into

some question the exact veracity of the interviews that Malcolm chronicles.

Historical Context

The Reagan Revolution

The 1980s is known as the Reagan era. Conservative former California governor Ronald Reagan was elected to the first of two terms in 1980. His vice president, George Bush, succeeded Reagan in 1988. Reagan took a hard line against communism and a tough stance in foreign affairs in general. Scandals such as the Iran-Contra affair rocked the nation in the 1980s. In the Iran-Contra affair, members of Reagan's administration illegally sold missiles to Iran and then used the profits to pay for weapons and supplies for Nicaraguan Contras, who were fighting a civil war against the country's communist-supported government. Many Americans approved of Reagan because the economy improved during the decade. The 1980s had opened with the United States still mired in recession and stagflation. Reagan supported an economic theory called supply-side economics, in which taxes are cut for wealthy individuals in the hope that these people will invest these savings in businesses, thereby creating jobs and increasing consumer spending. Although the U.S. economy turned around, many critics charged that not all Americans benefited. In fact, during the Reagan years, a growing divide developed between the upper classes and the lower classes.

Crime

Crime rates in the United States had dipped in the early 1980s but were on the rise again by the middle of the decade. During the 1980s, public focus turned on the crimes of mass murderers and serial killers. Increased media attention contributed to this trend, as did a rise in "true crime" books. The FBI began to use psychological profiling to identify and arrest unknown killers. Several television programs, including *COPS, Unsolved Mysteries,* and *America's Most Wanted* (hosted by the father of a murdered child), also focused on the apprehension of criminals. These programs all highlighted real-life crimes and entreated the public to help capture the criminals.

White-collar crime also abounded. Two high-profile, white-collar crimes drew the attention of the nation. Ivan Boesky and Michael Milken, both

Compare & Contrast

- **1980s:** In several cases heard in the 1980s and 1990s, the U.S. Supreme Court rules that in order to find a defendant guilty of libel, reckless disregard and deliberate falsity must have taken place; a reporter must not only publish false information but do so recklessly, maliciously, and without trying to determine the information's accuracy.

  Today: At least one proposal has been made for a new set of libel laws that would make it easier for plaintiffs to prove their cases. The proposal also would eliminate large financial awards.

- **1980s:** At the beginning of the 1980s, there are 612,000 lawyers and 204,000 editors and reporters. By the end of the 1980s, there are 741,000 lawyers and 274,000 editors and reporters.

  Today: In 1998, there are 912,000 lawyers and 253,000 editors and reporters.

- **1970s:** At the end of the decade, about 20,000 murders are committed in a year in the United States.

1980s: In 1989, about 21,500 murders are committed in the United States.

Today: In 1998, about 18,200 murders are committed in the United States.

- **1980s:** At the beginning of the 1980s, 168,800 cases commence in U.S. district courts, of which only 6.5 percent reach trial. At the end of the 1980s, in 1990, 217,900 civil cases have commenced, of which 4.3 percent reach trial.

  Today: In 1997, 265,200 civil cases commence in U.S. district courts. Of these, only 3 percent reach trial.

- **1980s:** In 1980, 1,716 magazines are published every week. There are a total of 10,236 magazines, including weeklies, being published.

  1990s: In 1998, there are 364 magazines that are published weekly, but there are a total of 12,036 magazines, including weeklies, being published.

---

financiers, were convicted of illegal business activities. Milken was convicted for having sold junk bonds, and Boesky for having practiced insider trading.

The World of Words

Noted author Phillip Roth estimated that in the 1980s, there were only 120,000 readers of serious literature in the United States. Publishers were less likely to bring out quality literary books. Focusing on turning a larger profit instead of enhancing their reputation, many publishers awarded million-dollar advances to writers of would-be bestsellers, which were often, creatively, merely mediocre. Bestsellers spanned a range of topics, from Stephen Hawking's study of the universe, *A Brief History of Time,* to Oliver Sacks' examination of brain-injured patients, *The Man Who Mistook His Wife for a Hat,* to business and cartoon books. Horror-fiction writer

Stephen King was probably the most widely read novelist of the 1980s. By the middle of the decade, fifty million copies of his books were in print. Throughout the decade, the gap between bestsellers and great books continued to widen. Some important literary writers included Raymond Carver, Larry McMurtry, Alice Walker, and Toni Morrison.

The Media

While media flourished in the 1980s, the field of journalism worsened overall, with the careful journalistic probing that had dominated past endeavors all but disappearing. Instead, the media delivered what it believed the public wanted: lurid stories and events. The 1980s also saw a large increase in tabloid journalism and the number of talk shows.

Magazine publishing, however, experienced a boom. More new titles emerged that were aimed at increasingly specialized audiences. Magazines catered to almost all audiences from computer users, to parents, to sports fans and exercise fanatics. Many of these new publications closed down after only a few years in business, however.

Critical Overview

"Reflections: The Journalist and the Murderer" first appeared as a two-part article in the pages of the *New Yorker* in 1989. The book, with its added afterword (initially published in the *New York Review of Books*), was published the following year. Malcolm's article stunned the journalistic community in its portrayal of the journalist as "a kind of confidence man, preying on people's vanity, ignorance, or loneliness, gaining their trust and betraying them without remorse." Craig Seligman, who later wrote in his article "Brilliant Careers" in *Salon* about the experience of reading the article for the first time, held a distinctly minority opinion:

> Reading Malcolm's cool, considered, perfect prose, I knew I was in the presence of genius, and the weeklong wait for the second installment was a torment that only picking up the phone and calling friends who were going through the same thing could relieve.

But Seligman is aware that he is in the minority: "This was not, however, the reaction of Malcolm's fellow journalists—to put it mildly."

Even before publication in book form, the article drew immediate criticism from reviewers. In Seligman's words, they were split "between puzzled indignation and defensive fury." Faultfinders pointed out that, despite an incident at the heart of the issue—the MacDonald-McGinniss lawsuit— Malcolm never mentioned the libel suit lodged against her by Jeffrey Masson. Malcolm responded to such criticism in the book's afterword. In this short essay, Malcolm denied that the work was "a thinly veiled account of my own experiences," but she also alluded to the transference of feelings between the writer and the subject. "The characters of nonfiction . . . derive from the writer's most idiosyncratic desires and deepest anxieties; they are what the writer wishes he was and worries that he is."

Malcolm's declarations, however, did little to appease her critics. As Catharine R. Stimpson pointed out in the *Nation,* this experience must have given her "some expertise and authority," at a bare minimum, enough to realize that ignoring her own

libel suit left her open to greater scrutiny. Even Malcolm's supporter, Seligman, fully believed that *The Journalist and the Murderer* was a "brilliant solution to [Malcolm's] obvious impulse toward autobiography: Talking about McGinniss and MacDonald was an oblique and tactful way of talking about Malcolm and Masson." Upon reading the afterword in the published book, Seligman dubbed it "self-deceiving."

Fred Bruning, writing in *Maclean's,* further objected to the "shared guilt" that Malcolm inflicts on all journalists. There is a difference, he maintained, between practicing reporters and "celebrity writers," like McGinniss and Malcolm. Bruning contended that Malcolm's argument was unrealistic; reporters simply did not have the time to indulge in such elaborate "high-stakes games" as those described in *The Journalist and the Murderer.* Stimpson lodged another complaint against Malcolm: "Malcolm masculinizes the act of writing. . . . her tone-deafness about gender blunts her ability to hear and tell a story."

J. Anthony Lukas, a writer for *Washington Monthly* was one of Malcolm's most forceful critics. He called *The Journalist and the Murderer* "a work of inspired quackery." In his article Lukas examined Malcolm's background as a reporter and concluded that "for her, the relationship between reporter and subject is another version of therapist and patient." Lukas also mocked Malcolm's defense in the afterword as weak and unconvincing. Like Bruning, he rebelled against Malcolm's equation of all reporters as masters of "seduction and betrayal." (Lukas, it must be pointed out, was a long-time friend of the Malcolm-maligned McGinniss.)

Aside from Seligman, who lauded the book as "a masterpiece," other journalists did have praise for Malcolm's work. Stimpson called it a "spare, lucid, clever book." Fred Friendly of the *New York Times Book Review* acknowledged that although Malcolm's work would offend anyone who believed that criticism of journalistic freedom is an attack on the First Amendment, her inquiry "no matter if exaggerated, should force all of us in the news business to re-examine our methods and manners." Even Lukas conceded that the book and Malcolm both have their strengths. Malcolm's "outsider perspective enables [her] to plumb ironies that might be missed by workaday reporters." Her work, he wrote, "bristles with acute intelligence" and includes "some fine glancing insights."

Criticism

Rena Korb

Korb has a master's degree in English literature and creative writing and has written for a wide variety of educational publishers. In the following essay, she discusses the author's exploration of subject and reader manipulation.

Malcolm opens her work *The Journalist and the Murderer* with an extremely provocative premise: "Every journalist who is not too stupid or too full of himself to notice what is going on knows that what he does is morally indefensible. He is a kind of confidence man, preying on people's vanity, ignorance, or loneliness, gaining their trust and betraying them without remorse."

Malcolm uses the difficult relationship between convicted murderer Jeffrey MacDonald and the nonfiction writer Joe McGinniss to explore this weighty hypothesis. MacDonald sued McGinniss for a breach of good faith after the publication of *Fatal Vision,* which depicted the former Green Beret doctor as a psychopathic killer. Five of six jurists agreed with MacDonald that McGinniss had acted in a deceptive manner, and, clearly, so does Malcolm.

In *The Journalist and the Murderer*, Malcolm explores the manipulative tactics used by reporters and writers to draw out their subjects and influence their readers. At the same time, however, Malcolm—a journalist—cannot help but implicate herself to a very real degree. At times she does so obliquely, for instance, using descriptions to bolster her opinions about certain personages. She also implicates herself with several forthright statements in which she admits the power a journalist holds over the subject. In speaking of one person who appeared in the book, she writes, "I always knew I had the option of writing something about him that would cause him distress. . . . He was completely at my mercy. I held all the cards."

Concerning the MacDonald-McGinniss case, the facts are hardly in dispute. Malcolm presents a great deal of evidence to prove that McGinniss deliberately and deceitfully pretended to be a friend and supporter of MacDonald. In September 1979, less than one month after MacDonald's conviction, McGinniss wrote to him in jail, "Total strangers can recognize within five minutes that you did not receive a fair trial." In another letter written that same month, McGinniss shows greater emotion:

Jeff, one of the worst things about all this is how suddenly and totally all your friends—myself included—have been deprived of the pleasure of your company. . . . What the f— were those people thinking of? How could 12 people [the jury] . . . agree to believe such a horrendous proposition?

However, in a later interview with *Newsday* reporter Bob Keeler, McGinniss asserted that he concurred wholeheartedly with MacDonald's conviction. "I knew he had done it—no question." He subsequently dated his belief in MacDonald's guilt as occurring during the trial.

McGinniss's letters also show that throughout the period of writing *Fatal Vision,* the author was not opposed to making his beliefs about MacDonald's guilt known to others, only to the convicted man himself. McGinniss wrote to his book editor as early as 1981 about his concerns that MacDonald seemed "too loathsome too soon." He wanted to reveal "the worst revelations" at the end, "when we draw closer and closer to him, seeing the layers of the mask melt away and gazing . . . at the essence of the horror which lurks beneath." As further proof of his deliberate deceitfulness, the following year, McGinniss wrote to MacDonald that he hoped to be able to call him at home soon, instead of at prison.

In the one meeting between McGinniss and Malcolm, he attempted to justify his actions by pointing out that a journalist has no responsibility to tell a subject that he is creating a negative portrait. In the discussion of MacDonald's treatment of him, McGinniss reaches the crux of the matter:

MacDonald was clearly trying to manipulate me, and I was aware of it from the beginning. But did I have an obligation to say, 'Wait a minute. I think you are trying to manipulate me, and I have to call your attention to the fact that I'm aware of this, just so you'll understand you are not succeeding?'

McGinniss repeated several times that he felt his only responsibility was "to the book and this truth"—that is, the truth as he saw it.

MacDonald's lawyer, Gary Bostwick, strongly disagreed. At the trial he characterized the issue at hand as "a case about a false friend." MacDonald told Malcolm that "McGinniss has *no* excuse for his false portrayal. He wasn't watching a distant subject through a haze—he was deeply involved, as 'best friend,' for four years—and still managed to miss the entire core of my being." McGinniss might argue that he had a different view of MacDonald's core—seeing there the soul of a psychopathic murderer—but it remains infinitely troubling that McGinniss never intimated it.

What Do I Read Next?

- Malcolm's *The Silent Woman: Sylvia Plath and Ted Hughes* (1994) raises issues of biographical integrity and also posits a controversial position on the famous literary couple.

- Henry James's satiric novel *The Bostonians* (1886) includes a character who is a reporter who holds little regard for his interviewees.

- Carl Bernstein and Bob Woodward's *All the President's Men*, a book about the unearthing of the Watergate scandal, also raises the journalistic issue of telling lies in order to learn the truth.

- Sissela Bok's essay "Lying" (1978) examines the use of lies by journalists and police investigators in order to obtain greater knowledge. In this meditation, Bok takes on the role of philosophical investigator.

- *Fatal Vision* is a true-crime account written by Joe McGinniss, a firm believer in MacDonald's guilt.

- Jeffrey Allen Potter and Fred Bost argue for MacDonald's innocence in *Fatal Justice,* reporting the existence of suppressed evidence that would confirm this belief.

At McGinniss's trial, two well-known writers attempted to defend his actions as "standard operating procedure." William F. Buckley, Jr., presented the following analogy in his attempt to justify McGinnis' methods:

> If, for instance you were writing a book on somebody who was a renowned philanderer and he said, "I mean, you do think my wife is impossible, don't you?," you might say, "Yeah, I think she's very hard to get along with," simply for the purpose of lubricating the discussion in order to learn more information.

Joseph Wambaugh displayed even greater hypocrisy. In Malcolm's words, he "testified that misleading subjects was a kind of sacred duty among writers." However, Malcolm knows that reporters will act as Wambaugh described. She judges, "When Buckley and Wambaugh said bluntly that it's all right to deceive subjects, they breached the contract whereby you never come right out and admit you have stretched the rules for your own benefit."

In acknowledging the deceit inherent in journalism, however, Malcolm opens herself up for scrutiny. If allowing one's own ideas about a subject to infiltrate one's work is a journalistic sin, Malcolm also seems to be guilty. In the afterword, she raises doubts about her portrayal of the key figures who appear in her book when she asserts that

the "I" who speaks throughout *The Journalist and the Murderer* is not Malcolm but merely the voice of journalistic opinion:

> a journalistic "I" . . . an overreliable narrator, a functionary to whom crucial tasks of narration and argument and tone have been entrusted, an ad hoc creation, . . . which exists only for the occasion it has been summoned for and has no history or life of its own.

However, Malcolm's assertion—which she recognizes may be difficult for some readers to accept—may trouble a reader, who can extrapolate from it a crucial question: If we can't trust that Malcolm is Malcolm, how can we trust that the other characters are who she creates them to be?

In certain instances, Malcolm provides factual evidence to back up her allegations. When she quotes McGinniss's letters and transcripts from his trial, it seems reasonable that these words are the truth—though, of course, a reader does not have access to the *entire* set of McGinniss's letters or to the *complete* transcript. More potentially troublesome is that she relates, and has control of, many conversations with key players. This is true for two reasons. First, before writing *The Journalist and the Murderer*, Malcolm had been sued by one of her subjects for misquoting him. The case was eventually decided in her favor, but it is interesting to note that Malcolm no longer had the tape recordings of

> **In acknowledging the deceit inherent in journalism, Malcolm opens herself up for scrutiny. If allowing one's own ideas about a subject to infiltrate one's work is a journalistic sin, Malcolm also seems to be guilty.''**

the conversations, including the quotes in question. Second, Malcolm readily asserts in *The Journalist and the Murderer* that ''none of the quotations in this book . . . are, of course, identical to their speech counterparts.'' In essence, Malcolm's impression is really what matters.

Malcolm undercuts her own authority by doing what she accuses McGinniss of doing: manipulating the audience. She clearly shows her own dislike for the way McGinniss treated MacDonald. One telling example is her discussion of McGinniss's refusal to allow MacDonald to read an advance copy of the book. Though MacDonald was disappointed, he agreed to appear on *60 Minutes* prior to reading the book and there learned of its startling contents:

> [He] enthusiastically lent himself to the pre-publication publicity campaign for the book. His assignment was an appearance on the television show *60 Minutes,* and it was during the taping of the show in prison that the fact of McGinniss's duplicity was brought home to him. . . . Mike Wallace—who had received an advance copy of *Fatal Vision—without difficulty or lecture* [emphasis mine]—read out loud to MacDonald passages in which he was portrayed as a psychopathic killer.

Malcolm also attempts to sway the reader's opinion of MacDonald through specific narration. Because MacDonald was ''not suitable for a work of nonfiction, not a member of the wonderful race of auto-fictionalizers,'' she relies on description and direct statements to a much greater extent than she does with any other figures. She contends that she only saw one sign of ''anything disturbing and uncanny about MacDonald, of anything that isn't blandly 'normal.''' She also notes that she is ''struck by the physical grace of the man.'' In one visit, she rhapsodizes on his eating of doughnuts: ''He handled the doughnuts—breaking off pieces and un-

accountably keeping the powdered sugar under control—with the delicate dexterity of a veterinarian fixing a broken wing.'' With this description, Malcolm attempts to counter the image that McGinniss presented of MacDonald—that of a brutal killer.

In the afterword that Malcolm wrote after being criticized for the piece, she acknowledges more clearly than she had previously the difficult nature of the reporter-subject relationship:

> There is an infinite variety of ways in which journalists struggle with the moral impasse that is the subject of this book. The wisest know that the best they can do . . . is still not good enough.

Despite her lengthy investigation, Malcolm finds there is no easy remedy to the problem.

Source: Rena Korb, Critical Essay on *The Journalist and the Murderer,* in *Nonfiction Classics for Students,* The Gale Group, 2001.

Catharine R. Stimpson

In the following review, Stimpson discusses the thesis of The Journalist and the Murderer *and some of the cases presented within, finding Malcolm ''smartly aware of the impurities of nonfiction.''*

The Journalist and the Murderer is a slim book that has raised a hefty ruckus because of its chilly thesis: ''The journalist must do his work in a . . . deliberately induced state of moral anarchy . . . [an] unfortunate occupational hazard.'' To get information, a journalist must gain access to people. To write up this information, he must betray their faith in him as a good buddy and sympathetic publicist. Journalism is a rough trade that trades off human solidarity for the chance to craft a powerful likeness of reality. *Trado, ergo sum,* not *Cogito, ergo sum* or even *Scribo, ergo sum,* is its existential slogan. In brief, the journalist must become a kind of murderer.

Journalists have endured harsher opprobrium than this. Think of Matthias Pardon in Henry James's novel *The Bostonians* (1886), a giddy lightweight of an interviewer for whom a person is but ''food for newsboys.'' In 1978 the argument of Sissela Bok's ethical meditation, *Lying,* anticipated the worst of *The Journalist and the Murderer.* ''Journalists, police investigators, and so-called intelligence operators,'' Bok wrote, ''often have little compunction in using false-hoods to gain the knowledge they seek.'' Though a polite iconoclast, Bok found Carl Bernstein and Bob Woodward remiss for not acknowledging in *All the President's Men* the moral dilemma of telling lies in order to get at truths.

James was being satiric, while Bok was a philosophical investigator. Ironic, watchful, canny, Janet Malcolm assumes both those judgeships. She also serves as self-appointed diagnostician and therapist. "This book," the jacket flap promises, "examines the psychopathology of journalism." Malcolm believes in freedom of the press but not in its innocence. She deploys demystifying metaphors for the relationship between journalist and subject. In one, a figure of eros gone wrong, the journalist is a seductive confidence man who fleeces a "credulous widow." In another, a figure of family life gone wrong, during an interview the subject regresses to the blissful condition of a child with an all-forgiving mother. But then, at his desk, the writer becomes the "strict, all-noticing, unforgiving father."

Malcolm focuses on an aristocratic form of journalism, the long nonfiction essay. Her journalist is that anguished modern figure, the private detective stuck with reality; Malcolm specializes in the realities of an encounter between reader/text and interviewer/subject. Not for this book the bump and grind between the media and publicity offices; nor the sweat and flap of the daily deadline, be it for print or television; nor, on another level, the heroic crusades of an I.F. Stone or an Ida B. Wells. Nevertheless, Malcolm calls for the profession as a whole to achieve a stoical self-awareness about the impossibility of the profession, an intelligence that *The Journalist and the Murderer* displays and that its controversial first sentence extols: "Every journalist who is not too stupid or too full of himself to notice what is going on knows that what he does is morally indefensible."

None of this would guarantee a jolly ride on the press bus or a drink at the bar in the Holiday Inn of professional popularity. Moreover, Malcolm's investigation is a case study of epistemological difficulties. Like many vivid narratives about the travails of knowing, it involves the courts, an institution that the gods and the devils must have invented together during a wild, let's-really-get-the-humans night of revelry. For the courts are the arena of zero-sum games in which adversaries tell bitterly competitive stories to unpredictable judges and juries about a dramatic but enigmatic world. Those stories are simultaneously cognitive (Did X thrust a knife into Y?), moral (If so, is X a bad person?), legal (Which laws might cover X's alleged action?) and medical (Was X sane?).

Malcolm focuses her argument on the nature of the relationship between the journalist and the subject on a case involving Joe McGinniss, author of the true-crime novel Fatal Vision

Malcolm originally published *The Journalist and the Murderer* in *The New Yorker*. There she explored two interlocking trials. In 1979 Jeffrey MacDonald, a handsome doctor, was found guilty of the 1970 murder of his pregnant wife and two little daughters. Before the trial, MacDonald had hired Joe McGinniss, a celebrity journalist, as a member of his defense team in order to write a book about the ordeal. For the next four years, McGinniss led MacDonald to believe that this journalist was a friend who would exonerate him. To MacDonald's horror the book, *Fatal Vision*, as well as its film version sustained the jury's guilty verdict. In 1984 MacDonald sued McGinniss for fraud and breach of contract. A 1987 trial ended in a hung jury and a settlement.

On the basis of the 1979 trial material, Malcolm neither accepts nor rejects the "truth" of MacDonald as murderer. As agnostic about the belief in Nature as the Book of God, she writes, "It is like looking for proof or disproof of the existence of God in a flower—it all depends on how you read the evidence." With some interest she quotes Gary

> It suspects any commentator who cites human nature without self-interrogation. It offers little consolation to writers of some integrity who devise 'counterparts to real life.' Such writers do what they must, but some blood will fleck the keyboards of even wisest among them."

Bostwick, MacDonald's lawyer in the suit against McGinniss, who carefully distinguishes between "knowing" whether or not a MacDonald is a murderer and "believing" that he is not. His trial then is less a "search for truth" than a "cathartic" release of tensions and differences. Indeed, our major trials are rituals that re-enact deep social patterns of guilt and punishment, innocence and release.

Malcolm's fastidious professional skepticism leads to portraits of the intellectually and morally self-assured that are as edged and edgy as the Avedon photographs in which subjects posed in front of blank white paper: a writer and political scientist who testified against McGinniss; a psychiatrist who testified against MacDonald. Malcolm is even more sardonic about the certainties of psychiatric discourse: "Our standard psychiatric diagnostic nomenclature has all the explanatory power of the nomenclature of medieval physiology involving the four humors."

However, Malcolm can abandon the multivoiced statements of the agnostic in order to deliver an unequivocal judgment. Exploring her tense relationship with McGinniss, who emerges as less than ethically and psychologically kempt, she admits to the parallels between this relationship and his to MacDonald. Both journalists began to see increasingly unlovable subjects through the rude eyes of their legal opponents. Yet she finds McGinniss guilty of "crude and gratuitous two-facedness."

Next, in an "Afterword" that did not appear in *The New Yorker,* Malcolm admits to still another parallel between her career and that of McGinniss.

In 1984 she too was sued—by Jeffrey Masson, the central character in her book *In the Freud Archives.* The well-known libel case, *Jeffrey M. Masson v. The New Yorker Magazine Inc., Alfred A. Knopf, Inc. and Janet Malcolm,* is usually abbreviated to Masson-Malcolm or "The Malcolm Case." In a variation on the theme of doubled and reversed identities, the hunting journalist became the hunted defendant; the writer of one text became a character in another, the legal document; and the powerless subject became the powerful plaintiff.

Retaining her poise during her self-xdefense, Malcolm describes such suits as therapy, a gratifying "law cure" for narcissistically wounded subjects that is healthier for writers than assassination on an ayatollah's order. More icily, Malcolm denies that she took up *MacDonald v. McGinniss* as a screened confession that she had wronged Masson. She is too sophisticated to note the vulgar coincidence of writing about two Jeffreys (MacDonald and Masson) and four names with the initials "J.M.," but that very sophistication should have instructed her to warn her *New Yorker* readers that their guide to *MacDonald v. McGinniss* had been the defendant in *Masson v. Malcolm.* For surely this experience gave her some expertise and authority. Such a warning would also have saved her a pack of trouble. With uncharacteristic vehemence, Malcolm refutes both Masson's accusations that she "fabricated notes and invented quotations" and the *New York Times* account of the case by Albert Scardino, now David Dinkins's press secretary. Yet she wearily recognizes that the same power of the press that she exercises as a journalist has branded her an erring journalist. She is "tainted—a kind of fallen woman of journalism."

The tale of the three caskets has attracted mythmakers, fictioneers, folklorists, Shakespeare and Freud. In *The Merchant of Venice,* a different drama about suitors and lawsuits, Portia's would-be husbands must choose among the caskets of gold, silver and lead. Perhaps in *The Journalist and the Murderer* trials have become a substitute for the caskets, a journalist for the suitors, the winning of "truth" for the winning of a wife. In the MacDonald case, equivalent to the casket of gold, Malcolm finds death—MacDonald's wife and children and his reputation. In the McGinniss case, equivalent to the casket of silver, Malcolm finds a fool, Shakespeare's "blinking idiot": McGinniss himself. In the Malcolm case, equivalent to the casket of lead, she finds her own portrait, though no gallant Bassanio has claimed that it is spun of sugar and gold.

The picture is that of a writer. To analyze it, Malcolm juxtaposes the overlapping genres of fiction, nonfiction, the letter, psychotherapy and law. With shrewdness and style, if without desperate originality, she asks about the ontological status of their respective characters and authors. So doing, she reiterates the modern romance of the novelist as hero. He "fearlessly plunges into the water of self-exposure [while] the journalist stands trembling on the shore in his beach robe." The shivers of the journalist, I might add, are akin to the goose bumps of the critic.

Malcolm is smartly aware of the impurities of nonfiction. Only naïve-readers are not. Yes, nonfiction is also covert autobiography, a projection of "the writer's most idiosyncratic desires and deepest anxieties." "*Masson,*" she writes with a small, ironic flourish, "*c'est moi.*" Yes, nonfiction has a fictive character, the "I," its "overreliable narrator:" The uniqueness of McGinniss was not the discrepancy between the "I" of *Fatal Vision* and the McGinniss who signed a book contract but the fact that this discrepancy provoked a lawsuit. And yes, the journalist can touch up a subject's tape-recorded comments in order to convey their truth. Accurate prose is more shapely than a raw transcript.

Yet Malcolm will not collapse nonfiction into fiction. Adapting Henry James's figure of the "House of Fiction," she plays with the conceit of the "House of Actuality." The writer of nonfiction only rents this house and must live by the terms of his lease. He can bring in his own furniture, but he must leave the place the way he found it. The writer of fiction has "more privileges." "Master" of the house, he can rampage around, even tear the old manse down.

The passages about the "House of Actuality" are paths that lead to some difficult copses in this spare, lucid, clever book. Malcolm accepts an adulterated relationship between the writer of nonfiction and the techniques of fiction—for a reason. This coupling renders nonfiction more virtual and therefore more virtuous. However, Malcolm's argument retains the illusion of the existence of "the actual," an uncontaminated referent, a pure realm that exists *out there* and that our discourse has not already interpreted for us.

A metaphor for my meaning: I own a copy of *The House of Fiction,* Leon Edel's 1957 collection of James's literary criticism. A scalawag friend once wrapped it in the jacket of an edition of Vicki Baum's novel *Grand Hotel* that was issued af-

ter the film version. I gaze at the image of the gaze of Joan Crawford, John Barrymore, Greta Garbo, Lionel Barrymore and Wallace Beery. The jacket copy blares out, "Reader! Treat yourself to a glowing evening packed with moments of romance and excitement. Here is the story that has thrilled the theatre-goers, movie fans and readers of two continents."

I live in a house with new gutters and old moldings that need repair. However actual this house might be, however actual my life within it, I cannot sense and interpret them *for themselves.* Instead, I sense and interpret my homestead through acts of language that cover acts of language that cover acts of language: such legal documents as my deed and mortgage agreement, such metaphors' as the House of Fiction and the House of Actuality, such cross-media narratives as *Grand Hotel* and such drastic accounts as that of the MacDonald family in their apartment on the night of a triple murder.

Obviously, postmodernism has been the voice box for this quaver. Feminism is the voice box for my next: Malcolm masculinizes the act of writing. All writers are "he." A "master" throws his weight around the house of actuality. Malcolm might shrug and call me persnickety, but her tone-deafness about gender blunts her ability to hear and tell her story.

Two examples. Malcolm describes the friendship between McGinniss and MacDonald as "of a particularly American cast, whose emblems of intimacy are watching sports on television, drinking beer, running, and classifying women according to looks." This is not particularly American, but particularly male American. How masculine was the world of the MacDonald defense team? How might this have influenced MacDonald's sense of betrayal? Malcolm tells of a male interviewer who asked McGinniss if he was going to treat Jeffrey MacDonald as he had Richard Nixon in an earlier book, to "be . . . in his confidence . . . and then run it up his butt sideways." In theory the metaphor of the anal rapist might be applied to bullies of both sexes, but fear of the homosexual anal rapist is particularly male. How masculine is the world of journalism? How does this shape reports about the House of Actuality? And responses to responses to these reports?

Emily Dickinson's "Poem 1400" is a mordant lyric about epistemology. "But nature is a stranger yet," she writes. "The ones that cite her most/Have never passed her haunted house." A modernist text,

The Journalist and the Murderer finds human nature both strange and a stranger. It suspects any commentator who cites human nature without self-interrogation. It offers little consolation to writers of some integrity who devise ''counterparts to real life.'' Such writers do what they must, but some blood will fleck the keyboards of even wisest among them.

Source: Catharine R. Stimpson, ''The Haunted House,'' in *The Nation,* Vol. 250, No. 25, June 25, 1990, pp. 899–902.

J. Anthony Lukas

In the following review, Lukas calls The Journalist and the Murderer *''a work of inspired quackery,'' and asserts that Malcolm projects her own interests onto all journalists.*

Every reader of this magazine who isn't a moron or a pompous ass knows that his literary taste is utterly depraved.

There. Have I got your attention?

A year ago, writing in The *New Yorker,* Janet Malcolm fashioned a lead of comparable authority: ''Every journalist who is not too stupid or too full of himself to notice what is going on knows that what he does is morally indefensible.''

The ensuing articles were particularly arresting because they purported to be not just another haymaker thrown from the disaffected ranks of Middle America but sophisticated critiques by a practitioner of the very craft under attack.

But a rereading of these articles and a new ''afterword,'' now collected between hard covers, convinces me that Malcolm is writing from well outside the journalistic tradition—which accounts for both the strengths and weaknesses of this book.

The outsider's perspective enables Malcolm to plumb ironies that might be missed by workaday reporters. And there are some fine glancing insights: ''The subject is Scheherazade. He lives in fear of being found uninteresting, and many of the strange things that subjects say to writers—things of almost suicidal rashness—they say out of their desperate need to keep the writer's attention riveted.''

But Malcolm is rather like a clever chiropractor examining the practice of medicine. Finally, *The Journalist and the Murderer* is a work of inspired quackery.

Now a disclaimer. Since Malcolm has been widely accused of disguising a secret agenda, let me concede that I have long been a friend of Joe McGinniss, the target of her attack. On the other hand, for nearly 10 years, until he became editor of The *New Yorker,* my book editor was Robert Gottlieb, who is Malcolm's greatest patron and defender. With a foot in each camp, I'll try to walk a straight line.

Just who is this person who claims to have unveiled the dirty little secret of American journalism? She presents herself here as a reporter, explaining, ''I have been writing long pieces of reportage for a little over a decade.'' But there is reason to suspect this appellation. For, as Malcolm herself warns us, ''the 'I' character in journalism is almost pure invention.'' In her case, I think it is.

Malcolm has been a staff writer at The *New Yorker* since 1965, exploring a limited range of subjects—food, Shaker furniture, photography, and psychoanalysis among them. So far as I can determine, she has never been on the staff of another publication—since the days that she reviewed for the student paper and helped edit the humor magazine at the University of Michigan. She never went through the apprenticeship—general assignments off a city desk—that has shaped the work habits of so many American reporters of my generation.

To be sure, her work bristles with acute intelligence and a certain showy erudition: Proust and Chekhov, Kokoshka and Gurdjiev, Grandcourt and Osmond, Beethoven bagatelles and Cellini bronzes, Raymond de Saussure and Frieda Fromm-Reichman. But her learning smells of the lamp, of long hours in a mittel-Europa study, abstracted from the street and the workplace.

No, it seems to me that the woman who lurks behind the ''I'' in *The Journalist and the Murderer* is less reporter than analysand.

Seasoned Professional

We all know the professional student, the fellow with the green book bag over his shoulder who hangs around a university year after year, accumulating credits and even degrees, unwilling to let go of the academic experience. There is also the professional analysand, the patient who has gone through years of psychotherapy, but who, even after the analysis has been ''terminated,'' can't quite bring himself to let it go. Over and over, in his friendships, his marriage, his professional encounters, he goes on playing out the unresolved themes of his analysis.

Janet Malcolm is the daughter of a psychiatrist. She has undergone analysis. Two of her four books deal with psychoanalysis, and, as I reread them, it struck me that, for her, the relationship between reporter and subject is another version of therapist and patient.

If Malcolm is a professional analysand, she is one who seems to fantasize about reversing roles, about becoming the therapist. *In Psychoanalysis: The Impossible Profession,* she drew a portrait of a pseudonymous analyst she calls "Aaron Green." In her first interview/session with Green, Malcolm detects a curious phenomenon. "He subtly deferred to me, he tried to impress me. He was the patient and I was the doctor; he was the student and I was the teacher. To put it in psychoanalytic language, the transference valence of the journalist was here greater than that of the analyst."

Over and over in *The Journalist and the Murderer,* Malcolm sounds the same equation between subject and patient, e.g.: "The journalistic encounter seems to have the same regressive effect on a subject as the psychoanalytic encounter."

If Malcolm dreams about playing therapist, she often seems to drift into what analysts call "counter-transference," the projection onto the patient of characteristics of significant people from the therapist's own past.

Thus, Malcolm's assault on Joe McGinniss for the seduction and betrayal of his subject, Jeffrey MacDonald, struck many people as a reflection of her own concern about similar accusations leveled against her by Jeffrey Masson, the subject of her third book, *In the Freud Archives.* Both Jeffreys sued, claiming that they had been betrayed by the author in question, in MacDonald's case because McGinniss had allegedly misled him about his view of MacDonald's guilt in the murder of his wife and two daughters; in Masson's, because Malcolm allegedly misquoted and doctored material to show Masson, the onetime projects director of the Freud Archives, in a bad light.

What strikes me on this rereading is how Malcolm seems determined to universalize her own shortcomings, turning each into the journalistic equivalent of original sin. The first two McGinniss pieces seemed to be saying something like this: Look, if Masson accuses me of seduction and betrayal, doesn't he realize that's what all reporters do, and here's case far more egregious than mine to illustrate the point.

Jeffrey McDonald, convicted in 1980 of the 1970 murder of his wife and daughters, sued author Joe McGinniss for fraud and breach of contract, claiming that McGinniss's novel about the crime portrayed McDonald as a pathological liar and cold-blooded killer

Then when commentators—notably John Taylor in *New York* magazine—pointed out the parallels of the Masson case (she hadn't mentioned it), Malcolm fired back in the afterword, first published in The *New York Review of Books.*

Although she denied that her McGinniss pieces were merely a "thinly veiled account of my own experiences," she also wrote: "The characters of nonfiction, no less than those of fiction, derive from the writer's most idiosyncratic desires and deepest anxieties; they are what the writer wishes he was and worries that he is. Masson, c'est moi."

One waits in vain for the corollary: McGinniss, c'est moi. But Malcolm goes on to ridicule her journalistic critics for their thunderous discovery "that I had not 'made up' my story—that is, had not acted in good faith in presenting it as a new story. . ."

Fools, she seems to be saying, are you so psychonalytically illiterate that you don't see that all nonfiction writers project their desires and anxie-

> **If she often reveals a fundamental misunderstanding of the reporter's craft, Malcolm has nonetheless written a quirky, provocative outsider's book."**

ties on their subjects just as we all carry around with us for life the emotional luggage of our infancy?

Malcolm is surely no fool; she knows the weakness of this argument. Indeed, in the first McGinniss piece, she ridiculed the testimony of William Buckley and Joseph Wambaugh about the legitimacy of telling "untruths" to a source. The "debacle" of their testimony, she wrote, "illustrates a truth that many of us learn as children: the invariable inefficacy of the 'Don't blame me—everybody does it' defense." It doesn't work for Malcolm any better than it did for Buckley and Wambaugh.

Even if her famous lead sentence is premeditated hyperbole, it represents a profound misunderstanding of American journalism. The principal failings of the craft are not seduction and betrayal, but laziness and coziness.

Straight from the source's mouth

In the early sixties, when I was the city hall reporter for the *Sun* in Baltimore, all local news ran on the back page. Each morning as assistant city editor would scrawl "city" on column one of the back page dummy and "state" on column eight, signifying that, absent some typhoon or tidal wave, the state house reporter and I were responsible for supplying the day's two major stories.

This meant that, at all costs, we had to cultivate our sources in hopes that a steady stream of zoning board appointments and updates on the tax rate would feed that voracious back page. And that meant that betrayal was the very last impulse we could afford to indulge. For in the rococo corridors of city hall a reputation for betrayal was a sure guarantee that the supply of news would dry up—and with it our professional aspirations.

No, the premium was on keeping those channels of information open, even at the risk of unseemly coziness with our sources. And, notwithstanding the pyrotechnics of Vietnam and Watergate, that, I fear, is still the priority of most American journalism.

If Malcolm's sweeping generalization usually misses the target, it may have a limited application to a tiny swatch of the journalistic battleground: investigative magazine pieces and books, one-time ventures in which the reporter knows he will never have to deal with his source or subject again.

In a fit of frankness, Drew Pearson once commented, "We will give immunity to a very good source as long as the information he offers us is better than what we have on him." If a source is himself so deeply implicated in the story that he threatens to become the story, he may be in jeopardy. For some reporters, it comes down to a calculus of whether they have more to gain by cultivating the source or "burning" him. Critics will charge that the reporter has betrayed his source in pursuit of self-interest; the reporter will say he has gone after the more important story. Often the reporter does both.

But in a journalistic sea awash with mindless puffery and boundless gullibility, sharks like these, prowling a roiled but tiny pool, are scarcely representative of the species.

Moving to Malcolm's second universal rule, the tendency of all nonfiction writers to imbue their subjects with their own desires and anxieties, I would concede that some reporters may be inclined to play out their own preoccupations in the dramas they cover. But reporters raised in the discipline of the city desk learn rather early to struggle against that temptation, and they usually prevail.

With the writers of long nonfiction books, the struggle is a bit harder. The process of writing a Best and the Brightest or a Bright Shining Lie is so consuming that, not suprisingly, the author is tempted to color his protagonists with some of his own obsessions. But, again, the best of our non- fiction writers struggle to separate the interior and exterior worlds.

Not only does Malcolm almost willfully refuse to distinguish these realms, but she displays a lofty, indeed elitist, disdain for the plodding reporters who do. Joe Keeler, a reporter for *Newsday* who covered the MacDonald case, is characterized as "the unsubtle Keeler," with his "prepared questions and his newspaper-reporter's directness," and

Malcolm doubts that his straightforward approach would draw from his subjects "the kind of authentic responses that I try to elicit from mine with a more Japanese technique."

Keeler is treated kindly in comparison to Joseph Wambaugh, the kind of blunt nonfiction writer Malcolm clearly regards as a vulgarian ("I'm not an intellectual," she elicits from him with her sushi-slicing technique, "I write from the guts"). His prose style is described as "like that of the charmless writing in small print on a baggage-claim check."

Malcolm's distance from the constraints of normal journalistic practice is most evident in her statement that McGinniss's decision to halt their projected series of interviews "freed me from the guilt" she might have felt for what she was about to do to him.

Step into my parlor. . .

Most reporters know the hot pulse of anger when somebody refuses to talk with you. Don't they know who I am, you say? I'll show them. You go to bed determined to wreak vengeance. But, most of the time, you wake the next morning and say: Nah, it's not worth it. If the impulse survives the night, then your editor is bound to remind you that people have a right not to talk with you and a professional doesn't punish them for it. Indeed, at every journalistic institution where I have worked, the tradition—not always lived up to—was that you leaned over backwards to be fair to the people who wouldn't talk to you, for fear that you could be accused of exactly what Malcolm now proudly admits. Since she was published by one of her best friends and edited by her husband, she wasn't restrained as she might have been by a less collaborative hand.

(Malcolm's pique at McGinniss's failure to continue their talks is all the more peculiar because she is not renowned for openness herself. By all reports, she does not give interviews. And when a fact-checker from this magazine called to ask whether her father was an "analyst," she said, "That's not true," neglecting to add that his job description, "psychiatrist," was one that most laymen would be hard-pressed to distinguish from "analyst," and one indeed that many analysts share.)

For just one moment, let us consider the McGinniss matter drained of the punitive spirit Malcolm brings to her task.

At Jeffrey MacDonald's explicit invitation, McGinniss entered into a contract to tell the truth about the case and to divide the proceeds of the resulting book, with MacDonald's share earmarked to pay his huge defense costs. McGinniss has been criticized for so-called "checkbook journalism," but I'm not sure that I find anything inherently wrong with such a deal.

Imagine if you will the hypothetical, but not unrealistic, case of a reporter who writes a book about a black man accused of raping a white woman during the civil rights struggle. If the reporter believed the man was unjustly accused, how many of us would condemn him for sharing the book's proceeds with the defendant in order to pay court costs? If one believed that Jeffrey MacDonald was innocent—as Joe McGinniss plainly did when he entered into the deal—is this instance so terribly different?

But if McGinniss subsequently discovered that, despite his contract to tell the truth, MacDonald had systematically lied to him and indeed cynically used him to spread a false version of the events, then who has seduced and betrayed whom?

The answer, I suggest, hinges on whether you think MacDonald lied to McGinniss and thus on whether you believe that he was guilty of murdering his wife and children or not. But curiously, although she slyly hints that she has doubts about his guilt, Malcolm explicitly refuses to make the hard march through the evidence in which the answer ultimately may lie.

MacDonald sends her mounds of such material—"trial transcripts, motions, declarations, affidavits, reports." Malcolm can't read such stuff. She sees words like "'bloody syringe,' 'blue threads,' 'left chest puncture,' 'unidentified fingerprints,' 'Kimberly's urine,'" and she adds the document to the unread pile. "I know I cannot learn anything about MacDonald's guilt or innocense from this material."

Slogging through this gritty minutiae is all right for cloddish reporters like Keeler and McGinniss—and the judge, attorneys and jurors in the trial that found MacDonald guilty—but not for a woman of letters like Malcolm, adept at intuiting the inner life of her subjects.

Once McGinniss became convinced that MacDonald had both murdered his wife and children and lied to him about it, he confronted a difficult dilemma: how to hold his subject's confidence long enough for him to complete the research.

Some have argued with Malcolm that McGinniss simply made a self-interested calculation that he had more to gain by deceiving MacDonald than by "keeping faith" with him (which, in this case, I suppose would have meant informing him rather early on that he believed him to be guilty).

Knowing, liking, and respecting Joe McGinniss as I do, I regard his quandary as much more complicated: Whether MacDonald's betrayal in effect abrogated the spirit of their agreement, or whether he was still bound by some sort of obligation to his faithless "partner," and if so, what it was. Each of us would parse that problem differently.

I don't always recognize my friend in some of the supportive letters he wrote MacDonald, even as his views were shifting. I don't believe he had an obligation to inform MacDonald that he believed him guilty, but he might have been less ebullient in his letters of reassurance. McGinniss's mistake, I think, was in ever allowing himself to be drawn into a "friendship" with his subject, even when he still believed MacDonald to be innocent and saw him as under siege. Had he established a more detached stance from the beginning, he would never have had to worry about MacDonald discerning a shift in tone.

But what we are talking about here, I think, is not a defect in character but a matter of judgment. Whatever you believe McGinniss's mistakes to be, can they possibly justify Malcolm's scorched-earth expedition?

If she often reveals a fundamental misunderstanding of the reporter's craft, Malcolm has nonetheless written a quirky, provocative outsider's book. Even when her grandiloquent airs drive one to distraction, Malcolm's sheer intelligence makes her worth attending to. Her ruminations about the reporter-subject relationship are well-timed, because they coincide with some self-criticism from within the craft about the reigning orthodoxy of nonfiction, the third-person narrative in vogue ever since John Hersey's *Hiroshima* and Capote's *In Cold Blood.*

We are witnessing an interesting return to the first person—in autobiography, memoir, travel writing, and much other nonfiction. This reflects, in part, a suspicion that the third person disguises too many hidden sources and secret agendas. The first person appeals to some because it seems to promise greater frankness and authenticity. But, bearing in mind the memoirs of certain generals and politicians, a friend of mine warns, "The greatest lies are told in the confessional." Malcolm's book may be another case in point.

Source: J. Anthony Lukas, "*The Journalist:* A Source's Captive or Betrayer?" in *Washington Monthly,* Vol. 22, No. 4, May 1990, pp. 44–49.

Sources

Bruning, Fred, "Are Journalists Basically Liars?" in *Maclean's,* Vol. 102, No. 17, April 24, 1989, p. 11.

Friendly, Fred, Review in *New York Times Book Review,* February 25, 1990, Section 7, p. 1.

Lukas, J. Anthony, "*The Journalist :* A Source's Captive or Betrayer?" in *Washington Monthly,* Vol. 22, No. 44, May 1990, p. 44.

Seligman, Craig, "Brilliant Careers," salon.com (February 29, 2000).

Stimpson, Catherine R., Review in *Nation,* Vol. 250, No. 25, June 25, 1990.

Further Reading

Lakoff, Robin Tolmach, and Mandy Aftel, "In the Malcolm Archives," in *Nation,* December 16, 1996, p. 32.
    The authors discuss Malcolm's body of work, finding common themes, issues, and approaches.

Shalit, Ruth, "Fatal Revision," in *New Republic,* May 26, 1997, p. 18.
    This article provides more up-to-date information about the MacDonald murder case and enumerates suppressed evidence pointing to MacDonald's possible innocence.

Lindbergh

A. Scott Berg
1998

Lindbergh is A. Scott Berg's third biography. The first was his 1978 book about Maxwell Perkins, the editor who worked with such literary giants as F. Scott Fitzgerald, Ernest Hemingway, and Marjorie Kinnan Rawlings. Berg followed this with a 1989 book about legendary Hollywood producer Samuel Goldwyn. Berg's reputation as a meticulous researcher earned him an advance of over a million dollars for his third book, even before he had started writing it. In researching Charles A. Lindbergh, he was given full cooperation from Anne Morrow Lindbergh, the famous aviator's widow, who gave him exclusive interviews and access to private papers that previous biographers had sought to read, with no luck. The resulting 562-page book is considered to be the definitive work regarding Lindbergh's life and personality. It won the 1999 Pulitzer Prize for biography, and Stephen Spielberg has optioned the movie rights.

Berg's book includes all of the minute details about Lindbergh's background and his later life. The bulk of the story is spent, however, examining the events surrounding the three most remarkable occurrences in his life. His unprecedented solo flight over the Atlantic is covered in great detail, of course, from the first time he conceived of the idea, while flying a mail plane, to the ticker-tape parades he experienced that welcomed him around the globe. Berg also writes extensively about Lindbergh's second brush with fame; public interest surrounding the kidnapping of his son, the famous "Lindbergh

baby,'' led to what is still called the Trial of the Century. The book also explains, as well as it can be explained, how public opinion turned against Lindbergh because of his pro-Germany stance in the years before World War II and how the man who had been surprised to find himself a sudden hero was just as surprised to find himself the object of public scorn. From 1941 to his death in 1974, Lindbergh was out of the public eye but pivotal to the development of commercial aviation and the space program.

Author Biography

Andrew Scott Berg was born in Norwalk, Connecticut, in 1949 and raised in Los Angeles, where his father worked as a film producer. In high school, he became so interested in the writings of F. Scott Fitzgerald that he decided to study English at Fitzgerald's alma mater, Princeton University. There, his studies about Fitzgerald led him to an obscure yet important figure in modern American literature, Maxwell Perkins, who edited not only Fitzgerald's works but also works by Thomas Wolfe, Ring Lardner, Ernest Hemingway, Marjorie Kinnan Rawlings, and James Jones. Berg's senior thesis on Perkins won him an English department award. After graduation, he set about expanding his thesis into a full-length book. *Max Perkins: Editor of Genius*, published in 1978, was hailed by critics and won the National Book Award for that year.

In 1989, Berg published his second book, entitled *Goldwyn: a Biography*, about the legendary Hollywood movie producer Samuel Goldwyn. Although the subject was remotely related to his interest in the early days of the studio system that Fitzgerald had worked for, it was not one that he had gone looking for. Goldwyn's son had approached him and offered the family's cooperation if Berg would write it, and the offer was too rich in possibility for a biographer to pass up. As with the Perkins book, Berg's research was meticulous, but for various reasons, ranging from Goldwyn's personal shallowness to Berg's lesser degree of commitment, the resultant biography was met with mixed reviews and is considered to be the weakest of Berg's three books.

Berg's most recent biography, concerning aviation pioneer Charles A. Lindbergh, was met with immediate success when it was published in 1998, earning Berg the Pulitzer Prize for biography and a spot on the best-seller lists. Like his other books, Berg researched *Lindbergh* meticulously, reading hundreds of previously unpublished letters to and from his subject and working closely with a Lindbergh family member, in this case Colonel Lindbergh's widow, Anne Morrow Lindbergh, a respected writer. Berg currently lives in California.

Summary

Part One

Berg starts *Lindbergh* with a brief chapter about the high point of the aviator's life, his arrival in Paris on May 21, 1927, using this moment in his story to summarize many of the important events that are to come. The statement that Lindbergh believed that this flight had started long before its takeoff thirty-three hours earlier, that it began generations earlier ''with some Norsemen—infused with the Viking spirit—'' is used to catapult the story back to the time of Lindbergh's grandfather and to follow, thereafter, chronologically from Norway in 1859. Lindbergh's grandfather was a swindler named Ola Månsson who, when it was time to flee Sweden, offered to take his wife and children. When they refused, he took his mistress and their illegitimate son. During their passage to America, he changed his name to August Lindbergh and the baby's name to Charles.

Lindbergh's father, Charles, grew up on a farm in Minnesota, earned a law degree, lost his first wife while she was giving birth to a daughter, and married a woman from the wealthy, aristocratic Lodge family. Their son, also named Charles, is born in February of 1902. Lindbergh's father becomes a politician, is elected to Congress, and leaves the family with his wife's relatives in Detroit while he takes off for Washington, D.C., an event that leaves Charles feeling abandoned and embittered. Though politics is what first creates a rift in his family, Lindbergh's father proves spectacularly unsuccessful at it, losing several elections, including one for governor of Minnesota and one for his old house seat before leaving politics to invest in real estate.

Charles, who had been involved with his father in several of his campaigns and schemes, graduates high school and enrolls in the engineering college at the University of Wisconsin. He finds himself failing, unable to concentrate on his studies, and drops out to attend aviation school. The country is in the middle of an aviation boom, with hundreds of biplanes available that were originally commissioned for use during World War I and were later sold to private companies to put on stunt shows and spray pesticides on crops. By 1923, Charles is able to buy his first plane, and after a few years as a stunt pilot he moves to St. Louis, where opportunities have recently opened for flyers to deliver the U.S. Mail. His success increases public interest in airmail delivery—his handsome face appears on posters, and he speaks at business luncheons on the topic—but he finds the work too confining. Thinking about the full abilities of the new Wright-Bellanca aircraft, he comes across a contest offering $25,000 to the first aviator to cross the Atlantic alone.

He leaves Roosevelt Field in New York on the morning of May 20, 1927, in a small, open plane, the *Spirit of St. Louis.* Alone, over the dark ocean, with no contact with any person, he conserves the food he has brought and, throughout the thirty-three hour flight, only allows himself a few sips of water. Arriving in Paris, he finds the streets mobbed, as 150,000 people have come out to see the man who single-handedly made the world smaller.

A. Scott Berg

Part Two

As news of his feat travels around the globe, Lindbergh becomes an international hero. He is mobbed by reporters wanting interviews and invited to visit with the world's greatest leaders and royalty. He finds his personal life slipping away from him, as he has become, the moment the plane's wheels landed on French soil, one of the most famous people in the world. There are huge ticker-tape parades for him wherever he goes, and songs and dances are named after him. Within a month of returning to New York, he receives five million dollars worth of endorsement opportunities.

After some of the excitement dies down, Lindbergh expresses interest in helping commercial aviation, which at the time is just beginning. He becomes an advisor to the army and a partner with Henry Ford and some railroad officials in a commercial airline. He marries Anne Morrow, the daughter of the ambassador to Mexico. The couple travels the world for more than a year before having a house built just outside of Princeton, New Jersey. It is there that, on the night of March 1, 1932, their two-year-old son disappears from his nursery on the second floor of the Lindbergh house. Once again, the world's attention centers on the aviator as ransom notes are delivered, leads to the kidnappers'

identities are released, and negotiations go on with strangers who may or may not know those involved. On May 10, the boy's body is found buried in the woods near the house, having apparently been put there the night he disappeared.

A suspect, Bruno Richard Hauptmann, is arrested two years later, and his trial brings international attention. He is convicted and sentenced to death although many people, including famous celebrities of the time, object that he is being framed by the authorities. In time, the public comes to distrust Hauptmann's conviction, and some of their anger at the judicial system extends to include Lindbergh.

Part Three

To escape the public's curiosity, the Lindberghs move to England, where they end up renting a house and staying for years. While in England, Lindbergh is a guest in other countries. At the invitation of the American Embassy in Berlin, he goes to Germany, inspecting the German air force and offering advice. While not many people anticipated the Second World War in 1936, his friendliness toward Germany raises some concern, especially among American relatives of persecuted Jews. The situation is made worse when, as war in Europe approaches,

Lindbergh makes public statements discouraging American involvement, even if that means leaving Germany to overthrow Czechoslovakia, Poland, and Russia. As German aggression against its Jewish citizens and neighboring countries grows, newspapers and politicians denounce Lindbergh. When war actually begins in Europe, Lindbergh is writing articles for American magazines, urging the country to stay uninvolved. He becomes a spokesman for a grassroots movement, America First, giving speeches on behalf of nonintervention, even as the country is heading toward war.

Lindbergh is called a Nazi sympathizer and becomes one of the most hated men in America. His reputation is somewhat rehabilitated by his working for the United States Air Force during the war, testing experimental jets and helping design assaults in the Pacific.

Part Four

After the war, Lindbergh's work for the government in developing aerial defense systems continues. His noninterventionist attitude toward Germany is reversed because of the spread of communism, which he feels will almost certainly lead to nuclear war. As he spends more and more time away from home, he becomes estranged from his wife. He becomes a best-selling author, and the United States government, which had shunned him during the war, gives him the honorary title of general. A movie about his life is made, starring James Stewart. He becomes a board member for several airlines and is involved with several wildlife conservation groups. In 1969, he has a house built on Maui. When he becomes deathly ill in New York in 1974, he has friends in the airline industry arrange a flight for him so that he can return one last time to his Hawaiian home, where he dies on August 26.

Key Figures

Dr. Alexis Carrel

Dr. Carrel became a figure of major importance in Lindbergh's life. Berg presents him as a father figure, stating that ''in Dr. Carrel, the hero found a hero—the first since his father; and Carrel found a son.'' Lindbergh is introduced to Carrel in 1930, when Lindbergh inquires about why an artificial pump could not be used to circulate blood during an operation on his sister-in-law's heart and is told that

the doctor is working on just such a thing. Carrel was the first surgeon awarded the Nobel Prize, in 1912, for work on the grafting of blood vessels and organs. He was researching the artificial heart question for the Rockefeller Institute of Medical Research, where he was well respected but also considered somewhat of an oddball for his interest in holistic medicine and the occult. Like Lindbergh, Carrel was a man of broad interests, who sought to connect the physical and spiritual worlds. It was greatly due to the influence of Dr. Carrel that Lindbergh began to take more interest in the human body, and the doctor's death in 1944 raised spiritual concerns for Lindbergh.

John F. Condon

When Charles Lindbergh III was thought to be in the hands of kidnappers, Dr. Condon, a former school teacher and local eccentric from the Bronx, offered his services as an intermediary, an offer that the kidnappers accepted. The kidnappers gave Condon instructions on how to contact them through newspaper ads, using the pseudonym ''Jafsie'' (a form of his initials, J. F. C.). The police sent Condon to meet with a representative of the kidnappers, and they had an hour-long conversation. When he did deliver the money to the kidnappers, he talked them into taking $20,000 less than had been arranged, thinking that he was saving the Lindberghs some money. By doing this, he actually made the case more complex, because the $50 bills that were in the package that he held back would have been the easiest to trace, because the police gave him specially selected ransom money for this purpose. Condon's eccentricities gave the defense a chance to discredit his testimony against Hauptmann, one of the kidnappers on trial.

Robert Hutchings Goddard

Goddard is the father of rocket engineering, a man whose dream of sending a ship through outer space was routinely mocked in the press as a lunatic fantasy until Lindbergh took an interest in him, convincing wealthy investors to support his work. He was the chairman of the Physics Department at Clark University, when Lindbergh read an article about his work concerning the use of gasoline and liquid nitrogen to power vessels that could reach as far as the moon. The press wrote him off as a dreamer who wanted to reach the moon, but Lindbergh realized the practical application of rocket science to aviation and urged Henry DuPont, of DuPont Chemical, to support Goddard's research.

Media Adaptations

- An abridged audiocassette version of *Lindbergh*, read by Eric Stoltz, is available from Random House Audio.

- Susan Hertog's biography of Anne Morrow Lindbergh is available on audiocassette from Blackstone Audiobooks. It is read by Marguerite Gavin.

- The Arts and Entertainment Network has produced a video as part of their "Biography" series called *Charles and Anne Lindbergh,* available in 2000 on A&E Home Video.

- An older, less complete biography called *Lindbergh,* by Leonard Mosley and James Cunningham, is available on cassette from Books on Tape, Inc.

- Newsreel footage from the time of Lindbergh's flight can be seen on Time-Life Video's *The Century of Flight: Epic Flights, 1919–1939,* released in 1999.

- California Newsreel Corporation of San Francisco has released a videocassette called *Legacy of a Kidnapping: Lindbergh and the Triumph of the Tabloids.* This documentary, with journalist Lewis Lapham, traces the decline of journalistic standards, from the Lindbergh baby to the O. J. Simpson trial, the death of Princess Diana, and the Monica Lewinsky scandal.

- Brendon Gill's 1985 book *Lindbergh Alone* is available on audiocassette, read by John MacDonald.

- The story of Lindbergh's flight was told in the 1957 film *Spirit of St. Louis,* which was directed by Billy Wilder and starred James Stewart, Patricia Smith, and Arthur Space.

- Public Broadcasting System has produced, as part of their American Experience series, a video of the show *Lindbergh,* produced by Ken Burns and directed by Stephen Ives. It was originally broadcast in 1990.

When DuPont proved uninterested, Lindbergh went to the Carnegie Institution and finally to Daniel Guggenheim. Goddard and Lindbergh kept up a lifetime of correspondence.

Hermann Goering

General Goering was one of the most important men in Hitler's Third Reich. He was a man of many interests; not only was he the German Air Minister, but he also served as commissioner of the four-year plan for economic recovery, director of the state theater in Prussia, minister of forests, and presiding minister of the Reichstag. At a luncheon given for Lindbergh in 1936, Goering and his wife served as courteous hosts to Charles and Anne. Two years later, in 1938, Goering surprised Lindbergh during a dinner of international diplomats by presenting him with the Service Cross of the German Eagle. During the war, Lindbergh's detractors pointed to his close-

ness with Goering and his acceptance of the medal, as well as his refusal to return it, as a sign that he was a Nazi sympathizer.

Betty Gow

Gow was the nurse that the Lindberghs hired to watch young Charles III. When the baby disappeared, she was suspected of being an accomplice with the kidnappers, and her suitor, "Red" Johnston, was the first person arrested for suspicion because of the access that his relationship with Betty gave him to the house.

Bruno Richard Hauptmann

Hauptmann was the German-born carpenter who was accused and convicted of the kidnapping and death of the Lindbergh baby. He came to the attention of the authorities in 1933, more than a year after the boy's body was found, when he spent one of the bills from the ransom at a gas station. There was substantial evidence against Hauptmann: a large amount of the ransom money was found in his garage; a sketch of a ladder like the one used in the kidnapping was found in his sketchbook; a board from the ladder was identified as having come from his attic; he spelled some words in a certain way that was similar to the ransom note. Upon investigation, it was discovered that Hauptmann had been arrested several times before leaving Germany and had spent four years in jail there. He was so mysterious about his past that his own wife did not know until after his arrest that his real first name was Bruno. Hauptmann asserted his innocence throughout the trial, raising enough suspicion in the eyes of the public that there are people who, to this day, feel that the police persecuted an innocent man. After appeals, he was put to death on April 3, 1936.

Ambassador Myron T. Herrick

Herrick, the American ambassador to France in 1927, was the one to take Lindbergh home the night that he landed in Paris after his famous flight, giving him a place to rest, away from the mobs of people that suddenly wanted his attention. Ambassador Herrick arranged the young aviator's social schedule, guiding him into public life, taking him to embassy parties, government ministries, and meetings of influential organizations, all the while guarding him from the pressures caused by the hundreds of people who wanted to meet him, touch him, and get his autograph.

Arthur Koehler

Koehler was the wood technologist who examined the ladder that had been used in the kidnapping of the Lindbergh baby, tracing it to a particular lumberyard in the Bronx before other evidence lead to Hauptmann.

Anne Morrow Lindbergh

Anne first met Lindbergh when she was visiting her parents during Christmas break, 1927, the year of his flight to Paris. She became infatuated with him but assumed that he must be interested in her older sister Elisabeth. Later, Anne and Charles' romance received international press coverage, as did their marriage in 1929. For several years, Anne joined Lindbergh in travelling the world, settling down in 1930, when their son, Charles III was born. When the baby was kidnapped and later found dead, Anne retreated into herself, staying away from the Hauptmann trial. Throughout their marriage, Anne worked as a writer, producing novels, memoirs, and magazine articles. Her most successful book, personally and financially, was *Gift From the Sea*, published in 1955. Despite its commercial success, critics lambasted the book.

From the late 1950s on, as their children grew old enough to develop their own lives, Anne and Charles grew increasingly apart. He was often on trips so they spent most of their time in different cities, a situation that she came to realize she did not mind. She had her own career and a brief affair with her doctor, Dana Atchley. In the late 1960s, the Lindberghs reconciled, but they were never really close and still did not spend much time together.

Charles August Lindbergh Jr.

Lindbergh is the subject of this book and appears on every page of it. He was born in the Midwest and raised, for the most part, by his mother while his father was away tending to politics or business. In his childhood, young Charles showed a disposition for understanding mechanical things and a curiosity to find out what made things run. After graduating from high school, he showed little affinity for any particular field of work. He went to college to study engineering but eventually dropped out when he saw a brochure offering courses in a subject that he was really interested in: airplane flight. Lindbergh learned to fly and bought a small plane, which he used to make money putting on shows at fairs. While working for the earliest airmail service in St. Louis, he became interested in a contest offering money to the first person to fly across the Atlantic Ocean. He found financial backers, bought a suitable plane, calculated the necessary adjustments to be made, and in 1927 became the first person to fly across the ocean. The public reaction was enormous, making him one of the most recognized and revered people on the planet.

The other two defining events in Lindbergh's life were the kidnapping of his eighteen-month-old son, Charles III, in 1932, and his amicable relations with high-ranking members of Hitler's government at the beginning of World War II. The first event brought Lindbergh and his wife, Anne, an outpouring of sympathy from all over the world, but the second made many Americans reconsider the man they had called a hero, changing admiration into scorn.

After his history-making flight, much of Lindbergh's life was spent using his fame to promote worthy causes and investigate scientific subjects that concerned him. His involvement was one of the most important elements in the growth of commercial aviation in the early 1930s, and, with Dr. Alex Carrel, he helped to devise a pump to keep blood flowing during heart surgery. He was a sponsor of Robert Goddard, who was the man most responsible for the development of rocket science. He was active in the World Wildlife Fund and was an unofficial goodwill ambassador to countries all over the world. His many achievements came at the expense of his family life: like his father, Lindbergh was seldom home with his family, spending his time travelling and pursuing one mission after another.

Charles August Lindbergh Sr.

The father of the great aviator, Charles August Lindbergh Sr. was a man of principles; however, he was not well suited to be a father. He did not treat his son poorly, but, on the contrary, he treated him like a peer, which meant the boy was left to his own devices while growing up. C. A. was a poor businessman but passionate about politics. His greatest achievement came in 1907, when he was elected in Minnesota to the U.S. House of Representatives. He was insistent about the existence of conspiracies within the government and, like his son, was a strident isolationist who felt that the United States should remain out of the affairs of Europe. He did not get along with Lindbergh's mother and had affairs with other women but was careful not to bring his son into the middle of their disagreements. When the younger Lindbergh grew up, C. A. tried to bring him into his business deals, but the young aviator was uninterested; still, his effect on Lindbergh's personality is undeniable.

Dwight Morrow

Lindbergh first met Morrow when he was the senior partner at J. P. Morgan & Co. Morrow took on the responsibility to advise Lindbergh on how to invest the windfall of money that he had suddenly come into after the flight to Paris. Soon after, Morrow left the financial world when President Coolidge asked him to become America's ambassador to Mexico. While staying with Morrow and his family in Mexico City, Lindbergh developed a romantic interest in the ambassador's daughter, Anne, whom he later married.

H. Norman Schwarzkopf

The first superintendent of the New Jersey State Police, Schwarzkopf took over the investigation into the kidnapping of the Lindbergh baby almost immediately. Trained in military tactics (he is the father of the man with the same name, who gained national prominence during the 1991 Persian Gulf War), he coordinated the investigations into the various leads that, for the most part, turned out to be pointless.

"Shorty George" Snowden

Snowden was a harlem musician who coined the name of a popular dance after Lindbergh. On the night Lindbergh landed in Paris, Snowden looked out at the crowd at the Savoy Theater jumping up and down with excitement: "I guess they're doing the Lindy Hop," he observed. The dance caught on and, like Lindbergh himself, became a national craze.

Themes

Heroes and Heroism

For a generation of Americans, Charles A. Lindbergh defined what heroism was all about. While traditional understandings of heroism generally imply victory over some sort of enemy, Lindbergh's heroic action entailed braving the elements and the laws of physics and making his airplane stay aloft for thirty-three hours. His was a type of heroism that was particular to his day, which was a time when technology was new enough to be fascinating and not comprehensive enough to be frightening. From the time of the Wright Brothers' first flight in 1903 to Lindbergh's flight in 1927, the idea of airplane travel had become common, but it was always associated with short distances. The amount of time it took to travel between America and Europe, which had been measured in months at the start of the 1800s and in weeks at the start of the 1900s, was suddenly measured in hours, and making this mind-boggling feat conceivable to average people was not accomplished by an abstract corporation but by a single, handsome individual.

It is Lindbergh's individuality, as much as anything, that made him a hero in the eyes of the world. The cockpit of an aircraft was much more complex than anything most people had ever experienced, but imaginations could grasp the idea of his being isolated in a small, dark space, with no connection to the world at large. As more and more machines imposed themselves upon civilization, there was something almost primitive about the idea of his flight, with the wind blowing in his face and the bright stars above. And at the same time, he was

Topics for Further Study

- Parallels have been drawn between the kidnapping of the Lindbergh baby and the murder of JonBenet Ramsey, a child who died during an alleged kidnapping in 1996. Read about the Ramsey case and report on the similarities.

- Examine the significance of Lindbergh's contribution to heart surgery, the Lindbergh Pump, and compare it to the most recent techniques.

- America has always had groups like America First that oppose military involvement in the affairs of other countries. Find a web page from a group that is critical of the current government's foreign involvements and compare their arguments to those used by Lindbergh during the Second World War.

- Make a tape of songs that might have played at celebrations in America when news came that Lindbergh had landed safely in Paris.

- Report on what has happened to the Tasaday people of the Philippines since Lindbergh brought them into the modern world.

- Write a report on Amelia Earhart, who was the first woman to fly solo across both the Atlantic and the Pacific oceans, explaining the details of her journeys and the hardships she faced.

---

in control of his machine, making it achieve what no machine ever had. According to Berg's account, Lindbergh had the perfect blend of brains, charm, and self-assurance to fit the role of a hero for his time.

Helplessness

One of the things that made the kidnapping of the Lindbergh baby such a huge news story was the way that it presented such an extreme reversal from all that the public knew about their hero. If the 1929 flight was taken as a sign of one individual's ability to triumph over natural forces, the kidnapping drama showed how vulnerable anyone, even the most celebrated man on the planet, could be. An attack on Lindbergh's person could be fought off with the macho strength that the public had come to expect from its heroes. Even an attack on Anne Morrow Lindbergh, who as an adult had her own life and responsibilities, would not be as horrifying as the threat to the couple's child. While the flight across the Atlantic was considered a triumph over impossible conditions, the kidnapping episode was a true test of Lindbergh's character, an impossible situation of which he could not gain control.

The public, though sympathetic, could not see how controlled Lindbergh was during this ordeal.

Although the kidnappers had the upper hand and could not be provoked without putting young Charlie in danger, Lindbergh still kept a cool head and did what little he could to create a favorable situation. While he did not interfere with the police investigation, he did act efficiently and quickly to make sure that all possible leads were explored and that ransom money was available as soon as it was requested. Although obviously disturbed, Lindbergh had too much self-control to allow his feelings of helplessness gain control over him, but that coolness meant staying out of the public eye and saying little to the press, which fostered concern that the pressure had gotten to him. When a drop of the ransom money was arranged, Lindbergh was ready to go to the site and confront the kidnappers himself. For a man accustomed to acting alone, the proven police procedure was as crippling as the kidnapping itself, adding to his sense of helplessness. When the baby was found dead, and the months of patience proved to be worthless, Lindbergh briefly lost faith, but his own natural curiosity kept him from shrinking away from public view for long.

Isolationism

While Lindbergh's flight across the Atlantic will always be one of humanity's great feats, many

Americans will remember Lindbergh the man with scorn for his isolationist policies concerning the Second World War. Berg does much to show the factors that led to this isolationism, presenting it as a fairly reasonable reaction to the times and not, as Lindbergh's detractors would have it, a sign of sympathy for the policies of the Nazi regime. Lindbergh's father took a strong stand on isolationism, suffering in his political career because of it. Although they were not very close, it would make sense that the son would at least pick up some of the political theories of the father who raised him. Lindbergh had a fiercely independent spirit that enabled him to distinguish himself with his solo flight, an act which brought him public attention in the first place. Also, his travels to other countries, from 1927 on, gave him a perspective on international politics that many Americans lacked, gaining their information about such matters from the media.

Berg portrays Lindbergh's isolationism as being nothing too unusual for its time, an impression that he supports with ample evidence. The very fact that the America First party, which Lindbergh headed, became so popular in the late 1930s shows that the idea was fairly common. Berg reminds readers that Franklin Roosevelt won reelection in 1940 by promising to keep America out of the war in Europe and that the isolationist cause had many influential supporters. Still, Berg does acknowledge that Lindbergh was an apologist for Hitler after the invasion of Czechoslovakia, and he does chronicle the aviator's views on Jews, which many suspected to be at the root of his drive to keep America from fighting Germany. Although many Americans were unable to forgive Lindbergh for his isolationist policies, the federal government forgave him after the war was over and Roosevelt, who hated him, was dead. The next generation brought a massive popular struggle against America's involvement in another overseas war, in Vietnam.

Search for Knowledge

Having become internationally famous at a young age, Lindbergh spent most of his life working on intellectual pursuits, a fact that is made abundantly clear in this biography. He becomes personally involved in a number of experimental programs, showing equal degrees of curiosity about them all. His weeks of work in the laboratory of Dr. Alex Carrel forced him to learn about blood, tissue, and microorganisms, with the end result contributing to the development of an artificial heart pump. He supported Robert Goddard's work with rockets,

realizing the potential this had in the field of weaponry and in eventually breaking out of the Earth's orbit. During the Second World War, he worked with military specialists on assault strategies, and, when the United States Government refused to accept his assistance in any official capacity, he worked quietly with government scientists, test-flying bombers and allowing himself to be, as Berg puts it, a "guinea pig" for tests on high-altitude pressurization. In his later years, understanding the complex balance of ecology, he took up the environmental cause before it became popular. In his seventies, he often visited the Philippines, a country that Berg says "was one great test laboratory for Lindbergh, where the laws of human nature could be tested." On one visit there, he lead the first expedition from civilization to the land of the Tasaday, a cave-dwelling, primitive people. While another person may have rested securely with his fame established, Lindbergh was driven to know more, to build his mind, and to not take the respect accorded to him for granted. He was a scientist at heart, having learned from his grandfather that "science is the key to all mystery."

Style

Archetype

An archetype is a recurring image that is recognized throughout society, meaning practically the same thing to all people. The concept comes from the psychological concept of a collective unconscious, which theorizes that people all have deep within them similar memories, leading back to one common source. A mother holding a child, for instance, is an archetypal image that is universally recognized, as is an extended hand or a clenched fist. Usually, archetypes are thought to be images or ideas that date back thousands, if not millions, of years, to a time before different cultures developed out of one common source.

Charles Lindbergh's flight across the Atlantic is an archetype for the mechanical age. Spectators across the world, in all corners of the globe, marveled at the news of the aviator's accomplishment, indicating that there is something in humans of all societies that recognize what an incredible thing it is for a person to be able to fly. For the first twenty-five years of aviation history, the world saw airplanes as crude machines, chugging and puffing to pull themselves above the ground. Lindbergh's flight, though, imbued air travel with the magic and grace that earlier civilizations must have imagined when they speculated whether humans could ever fly. Because of who he was, with his good looks and refined personality, Lindbergh focused attention on the pilot, not the machine, tapping into dreams as old as the ancient Greek myth of Icarus, who made wings of wax that melted when he flew too close to the sun. In Lindbergh's case, however, a single man was triumphant over nature, and people throughout the world recognized him as the model of a new age of technological wonder.

In medias res

In medias res is a Latin term meaning "in the middle of things." It refers to the technique of beginning a story at its midpoint and then using various flashback devices to reveal previous action. *Lindbergh* does not use this technique throughout, but it does apply it in a small sense. The first chapter, "Karma," drops readers into the middle of Lindbergh's life, at the moment of his greatest triumph, in fact. Berg gives the facts about the crowds of people lining the streets of Paris, waiting for *The Spirit of St. Louis* to appear. By using this technique, Berg starts his story of Lindbergh's life on a lively note, whetting readers' appetites for the background of this event, buying attention that might otherwise dwindle as readers slog through the standard biographical fare of the subject's ancestors, his childhood, and the first signs that he is bound for greatness. The book, in fact, does slip back almost immediately to the earliest chronological point of the Lindbergh saga, picking it up in the year 1859 at the beginning of Chapter Two. After starting in the middle of the action for one introductory chapter, the rest of this autobiography follows in standard time sequence, with the scene described in the first chapter occurring about a quarter of the way through the story.

Style

Many things are involved in understanding the style of a written work. Writers make choices about which words to use, which scenes belong where, and which perspective to view the events from. Usually, readers can also get a sense of a writer's personality by noticing which information she or he chooses to give and which information is left out. What makes A. Scott Berg so well respected as a biographer is that his writing style does not overpower his subjects. He lets the story tell itself, with only the slightest indication of how the writer feels about the events he is describing. Because of the nature of biography, this can be an extremely difficult feat: there is seldom enough recorded information to know all of the facts of a situation that is being reported, and some writers are tempted to fill in by speculating about what their subject might have felt or how things might have seemed. Berg is able to fill in the minute details because of his exhaustive research on any subject. He can speak of any particular situation from Lindbergh's life from different perspectives because he has dug up the memoirs, letters, and public statements of other participants. He knows his subject thoroughly and so is able to give each moment in his book a feel of truth without having to draw attention to the facts, which he presents to speak for themselves. The fact that readers seldom take note of his writing style is proof that his knowledge of his material is thorough and authoritative.

Historical Context

Early Aviation

The idea flight goes back as long as humanity has existed with humans taking note of the ways that bird and human physiognomy resemble one another, except for birds' wings. History has kept no record of most of the small-time dreamers who have tried to make false wings that would give humans flight. One of the earliest recorded flights occurred in England, circa 1100 A.D., when an unnamed monk attached wings to his hands, jumped off a tower, and glided almost six hundred feet before breaking both legs upon landing. Most attempts to fly were of a similar vein: optimistic, ambitious, and futile. Leonardo da Vinci, the great Renaissance inventor and artist, was one of the first to approach the subject of flight from a scientific perspective. In 1500, he drew in his notebook a sketch of a flying contraption that had broad hinged wings that flapped by the power of a man attached to them in a harness. Although da Vinci's flying machine was never practical, some of his ideas about flight were useful to George Cayley, who, in 1804, designed a glider that was based on the ideas of propulsion, or forward motion, and the lift that could be achieved with the proper propulsion. These are the basic ideas that guide modern aviation.

The next pioneer in the advance of aviation was a German engineer, Otto Lilienthal, who realized

Compare & Contrast

- **1920s:** In the prosperous postwar economy, people look for diversions to keep themselves entertained. The tremendous celebration after Lindbergh's arrival in Paris is considered another reason to have a party.

  Today: For entertainment, broadcasters have found that people like "reality" shows with danger involved, such as *Survivor* and *When Animals Attack*.

- **1927:** The first federal agency for regulating airplane transportation is just a year old.

  Today: The air travel industry is crucial to the nation's economy, with many companies vulnerable to any disruption in business.

- **1927:** The world is astounded that a person could be walking around in America one day and be in France thirty-three hours later.

  Today: Airfreight companies routinely deliver letters between the two continents on a daily basis. The need for this has dropped since people are now sending information over the internet.

- **1930s:** An enthusiastic amateur like Lindbergh could work with a Nobel Prize-winning scientist on a major medical development like the heart pump.

  Today: Medical and technical training is so common and specific that there is little room for amateurs to become involved.

---

that wing design was crucial to transferring propulsion into lift. Lilienthal made over 2,500 glider flights with wings attached to his arms, experimenting with variables in balance and shape. His designs resembled hang gliders of today. He died during one of his flights, but he left behind extensive notes, which future generations of aviators drew upon. By Lilienthal's time, the idea of gliding in the air was fairly well established, but no one could find a way for a flying machine to propel itself without having so much equipment that it would be too heavy to lift off the ground.

In the early twentieth century, there were a number of inventors experimenting with the idea of a self-propelled airplane. One notable one was Samuel Langley, the curator of the Smithsonian Museum in Washington, D.C. Langley was fascinated with airplane theory, and he wrote an influential book on the subject, *Experiments in Aerodynamics*. In 1903, Langley thought that he had a working airplane, and he called members of the press to witness his initial flight, but as soon as the wires holding the plane down were cut, it rolled to the edge of the houseboat it was launching from and dropped into the ocean. A second attempt in December of that same year ended just as disastrously.

Nine days later, the Wright Brothers, Orville and Wilbur, launched a plane at Kitty Hawk, North Carolina. It stayed in the air on its own power for twelve seconds, confirming the Wrights' theories and ushering in the modern age of aviation.

Airplanes were still for hobbyists and scientists for the most part of the following decade. It was not until World War I, which started in 1914, that their true practicality became apparent. Originally, they were used by both sides for scouting enemy positions until the Germans thought to equip their planes with machine guns, leading to "dog fights" between enemy planes. This quickly advanced the mobility of airplanes and the number of trained, skilled pilots. After the war, many of these pilots had flying in their blood and continued to show off their talent at barnstorming shows across the country. The growth of the airmail industry, as outlined in *Lindbergh*, kept many ex-army pilots employed, doing what they loved.

Isolationism

Isolationism refers to a political theory which suggests that keeping the United States away from involvement in events in Europe and in the Western

Hemisphere is best. The United States has a history of isolationism going back to the early days of the republic. George Washington advised the country, in his farewell address, to stay out of alliances with other countries that might drag the United States into war. Thomas Jefferson expressed similar views. Throughout the nineteenth century, America followed the events in Europe, but there was always a strong, vocal segment of the population who held a high standard for what should be considered in the "national interest," particularly something worth becoming involved in a war.

In the twentieth century, the pull to become involved in European affairs became even stronger. Newer forms of transportation, such as the steamship and transcontinental air flight (which Lindbergh helped pioneer) cut the distance that naturally isolated America. At the same time, the European wars became more complex, involving more and more countries through treaties and obligations. At one time, thirty-two nations were involved in World War I.

Woodrow Wilson was reelected to the presidency in 1916 with the promise that he would keep the United States out of the war that had been raging in Europe for two years. In April 1917, after a coded message was intercepted regarding a German request for Mexico's help in attacking the United States, Wilson asked Congress to declare war. In 1940, Franklin Delano Roosevelt was reelected by promising to stay out of the European war, but that neutral stance was shoved aside when the naval base at Pearl Harbor, Hawaii, was attacked by the Japanese in December of 1941. One of the most powerful isolationist groups in the country's history was the America First Committee, founded in 1941, and of which Lindbergh was an active member. Once the country was at war, the general belief that World War II was "The Good War" (a nickname that continues to this day) doomed the cause of isolationism, making its adherents, including Lindbergh, seem cowardly and unpatriotic.

Critical Overview

The thoroughness of his research has led all three of the biographies written by A. Scott Berg to be respected by critics. As the *Library Journal* puts it

in a summary review in 1999, Berg's first two books have become "central texts in their fields," and *Lindbergh*, his most recent effort, is a "big, thoroughly researched book [that] is a fine work of restorative storytelling." Since its publication in 1998, critics have been impressed with the amount of work that went into producing *Lindbergh*. Some reviews have emphasized the exhaustive amount of detail about the aviator's life that A. Scott Berg sifted through in his nine years of research, focusing on the facts he presents instead of the way they are presented. Lance Morrow in *Time* magazine, for instance, calls the book a "superb biography," but that is the extent of his evaluation: the rest of the review talks about the aviator, not Berg's writing style. A brief review in *Booklist* does talk about the quality of the work, in the glowing praise that most reviewers use when writing about the book for mass-circulation magazines: "Masterfully written and extensively researched, this beautifully balanced biography depicts one of the twentieth century's most controversial, famous, and yet private of men."

More extensive reviews tend, after giving the book careful consideration, to find more to be critical about. For all of the mass of information that Berg presents, some reviewers are left wanting more. "There are no new insights into the boy flyer," wrote *Publishers Weekly*, "no new theories about the kidnapping, but there is a chilling portrait of a man who did not seem to enjoy many of the most basic human emotions. Perhaps more attention to Lindbergh's near-worship of the Nobel Prize-winning doctor, Alexis Carrel, would have explained more about his enigmatic character." Mark Stricherz, writing in *America*, finds the book's weaknesses to stem from the source of its strength: the very reason that Berg was able to work so many years with Lindbergh's story was an infatuation with the man that, in the end, proves to limit his range as a biographer. "The temptation is to become so enamoured of what you found or whom you know," he writes, referring to the many Lindbergh associates that Berg worked with, "that you lose sight of the subject's real story. . . . *Lindbergh* is marred by Anne Morrow Lindbergh's influence, to the point that the book avoids the most vital aspects of his life." Stricherz notes that the book's ample praise for Lindbergh's better qualities only draws greater attention to his shortcomings. "Lindbergh's life, therefore, must also be reckoned in philosophical and moral terms. The Holocaust did not occur in a vacuum."

One extensive mixed review, with much good and bad to say about this huge book, is by Sam Tanenhaus, in the January 1999 issue of *Commentary*. He notes that Berg "relates this remarkable story with energy and competence, unfolding his themes with a naturalness possible only because he has mastered vast quantities of detail." That said, however, he notes that the book becomes less interesting when the section about the Atlantic crossing is over. Tanenhaus does not believe that Berg understands the "complex social and political currents of the 1930's." Tanenhaus believes that Berg seems "unnerved" by this time period so crucial to Lindbergh's story. Even worse, he feels that Berg lacks insight into what motivated Lindbergh during what he calls his "misadventures in isolationism." "Lindbergh's political activities come at us as a string of regrettable incidents, not as the crisis of character they plainly were," Tanenhaus writes. "Important questions hide murkily below the smooth surface of the narrative, and Berg seems afraid of touching of them." Some readers might find it to be greedy of reviewers to want any more of Berg, given the thoroughness of his work that is universally agreed upon; others might blame the book for being this extensive and yet still leaving curious reviewers unsatisfied.

Criticism

David Kelly

Kelly is an instructor of creative writing and literature at Oakton Community College in Illinois. In the following essay, he examines how Berg's apparent hesitance to address Lindbergh's Nazi controversy leaves this biographical work incomplete.

One can hardly help being impressed with A. Scott Berg's recent biography of Charles Lindbergh, the famous aviator, inventor, and amateur statesman. As with Berg's previous books, this one is meticulously researched and rendered with a fluent biographical style that does not force readers to be aware of how much information is being handed to them or of the lengths to which the author must have gone when assembling it. Most Americans, familiar with Colonel Lindbergh only for his flight across the Atlantic, the tragedy involving his infant son, and his unpopular political views during the war,

Lindbergh in front of his plane, the "Spirit of St. Louis"

will find something new on each of the book's pages. In addition to the details of his life that any competent, diligent researcher could root out, there is also the mass of information that was made available to Berg alone, through an exclusive agreement with the Lindbergh estate. It would be futile to start listing the bits of knowledge about Lindbergh's life that are packed into the book, because they certainly number into the millions.

Yet, for all of this thoroughness, some reviewers have complained that Berg's biography does not let readers really know what the man thought of himself or of the world around him. There are things that can easily be assumed from his life—for instance, the fact that the Lindbergh's move to Europe after their son's murder was motivated by disgust with the United States. But there are other issues that reviewers have found even more problematic. The most obvious of these involve Lindbergh's ties to Nazi Germany. Berg presents this segment of the aviator's life as a huge misunderstanding, during which those favoring America's entry into the war for their own selfish interests made a scapegoat of him, presenting his isolationism as sympathy for Hitler's government. In fact, Berg does give one piece of evidence after another, including nu-

What Do I Read Next?

- A. Scott Berg's first book, *Max Perkins: Editor of Genius*, was met with critical acclaim. It is about the editor at Charles Scribner's Sons publishing company who worked with Ernest Hemingway, Thomas Wolfe, F. Scott Fitzgerald, James Jones, and others. This winner of the 1978 National Book Award was reissued in paperback in 1997.

- Berg's only other book is *Goldwyn: A Biography* (1998), concerning the legendary Hollywood producer Samuel Goldwyn. Berg's usual thoroughness is applied to a segment of American popular culture, the studio system that produced movies in the first half of the twentieth century.

- Antoine de Saint-Exupery, the author of *The Little Prince,* was a friend of the Lindberghs. His book *An Airman's Odyssey* (1984) covers his early days as a pilot.

- After the enormous press coverage of the kidnapping of the Lindbergh's first child, public attention to their home life waned. In 1998, their youngest child, Reeve Lindbergh, published her memoir of what it was like growing up in the famous family. Her story, entitled *Under A Wing,* gives an insider's perspective of her parents.

- Many books have been written questioning whether Bruno Hauptmann was indeed the kidnapper of the Lindbergh baby. One of the best, and most frequently cited, is Ludovic Kennedy's *The Airman and the Carpenter,* published in 1985. Kennedy, a British journalist, claims that the real kidnapper confessed his crime to him.

- The other half of Lindbergh's marriage is the focus of Susan Hertog's book *Anne Morrow Lindbergh: Her Life,* based on a series of interviews with the aviator's widow. Published in 2000, this is a useful companion piece to Berg's book.

- Lindbergh's first account of his flight across the Atlantic, *We,* was published soon after the flight occurred. It is flawed but still makes for a quick, easy-to-read, engrossing tale. He wrote a more detailed account of the same material in *The Spirit of St. Louis,* which was reissued in 1998.

- Anne Morrow Lindbergh's most personal and best-loved book, *Gift From the Sea* (1986), is currently available in paperback. Also available is *Return to the Sea: Reflections on Anne Morrow Lindbergh's "Gift From the Sea"* (1998), by Anne M. Johnson.

- Lindbergh's thoughts on nature and spiritual issues, from his perspective later in his life, are presented in his book *Autobiography of Values* (1992).

---

merous quotes from journals, clearly indicating that Lindbergh actually was sympathetic with the Germans.

There may seem to be overwhelming evidence, but the biographer can always prove such a simplistic assumption wrong. There is room for discussion about how Lindbergh felt about the policies of the German government in the middle 1930s, especially so if, like Berg, one spent months immersed in the complexity of his personality, his thoughts, and his humanitarian behavior. The casual observer may want to give in to the temptation to find that

final clue that settles the question of Lindbergh's beliefs once and for all. Common observers should not rush to judgement; the biographer must not rush to judgment. Still, even with that in mind, there is a lot of information in *Lindbergh* that suggests Lindbergh's comfort with the Nazi regime and little to refute the charges of these leanings except for Berg's unwillingness to believe the facts are damning.

One point of a biography is to free its subject from any gossip or innuendo that he might have labored under in his life. Berg is clear that this is his goal regarding Lindbergh's political leanings during the pre-war years. One way that he does this is to show how common it was, in 1936, for an American to be enthusiastic about the Third Reich. ''In the afterglow of the Berlin Olympics,'' he writes, ''Lindbergh's feelings toward Germany were hardly unique.'' Berg goes on to name a few others who were ''swayed by Hitler's magnetism,'' including Arnold Toynbee and Lloyd George. In a sense, effective biography writing is all about making today's readers understand actions in terms of their times. People can only act with the knowledge available to them. For instance, some people may look at the writings of former civilizations that accepted narrow definitions of ''citizenship'' and try to accept that they excluded people. Some of history's most revered literary figures were racist, misogynistic, and anti-Semitic. Is it or is it not fair to think they should have known better? There must be a point at which, if people were to condemn their ancestors for antiquated views, there would be no one left uncondemned, rendering the process of condemnation useless. But there is also a point at which even a man of his times can be taken to task for his beliefs.

Unfortunately for Lindbergh and his supporters, the Nazi regime has come, since the beginning of World War II, to represent the apex of absolute evil. One might look at Thomas Jefferson and James Madison arguing the rights of slaves and think that they were both honest and possibly even decent men, but since the Holocaust came to light, it has been nearly impossible to think of supporting the Nazis as just a case of youthful indiscretion. Berg nearly excuses Lindbergh's feelings for the Third Reich as part of the great wave of support for Germany that followed the Olympics. Careful readers will remember to see the subjects of a biography through their own words, not with the attitude the author projects. A few sentences after describing the Lindberghs' pro-German enthusiasm, Berg presents a quote that seems full of earnestness and innocence, relating Anne Morrow Lindbergh's shock over ''the strictly puritanical view at home that dictatorships are of necessity wrong, evil, unstable and that no good can come of them—combined with our funny-paper view of Hitler as a clown—combined with the very strong (naturally) Jewish propaganda in the Jewish owned papers.'' Yes, it is the biographer's place to take his subjects on their own terms, but it is also the writer's job to be clear on his stance toward his subject. If Berg truly believes that the Lindberghs were unfairly castigated by the American public for holding ideas that were reasonable,

> **There seems a direct relationship between Lindbergh's early friendship with the Nazis and his wish to keep America out of the war, but the book falls into some kind of thin moral chasm from there: it is as if Berg would rather not call Lindbergh a Nazi sympathizer even as his own evidence proves overwhelmingly that he was.''**

given their experience, then Mrs. Lindbergh's idea of what is excessively ''puritanical'' must be reasonable, in which case Berg does more harm by casting doubt on his own senses than he does good for the Lindberghs' reputation.

It is not likely that Berg approves of the Lindberghs' pro-Hitler beliefs. More likely, it is that he feels his position as biographer limits him to being impartial and staying out of the controversy. There may be merits to such an approach, but they do not really apply here because Berg spends so much effort trying to make Lindbergh seem reasonable that he cannot claim to be uninvolved. For the most part, he positions Lindbergh's detractors in an unflattering way, as bullies and schemers. He does not print reasonable, measured responses to Lindbergh that would show why, even in the light of the knowledge of the Holocaust, the Nazi persecution of Jews was just bad business for humanity. Instead, Berg quotes one carefully worded letter, chastising Lindbergh for consorting with the Nazis, but then makes a mockery of it by linking its author with Cornelius Vanderbilt Jr.'s telegram that grunts, ''WHAT AN UNPATRIOTIC DUMB BELL YOU ARE.'' He cites the outrage of millions of Americans but follows that with the House and Senate votes on the Lend-Lease bill to help Europe, as if the opposition to Lindbergh were only a segment of a larger political scheme.

Perhaps it was. Certainly, as Berg suggests, the opposition of Franklin D. Roosevelt's administration to Lindbergh served a greater political plan by giving a face to the war's opponents. Whether the administration's rebuke of Lindbergh was sincere anger, as F. D. R. certainly wished it to be seen as, or was just political posturing, making him a scapegoat for the problems the Nazis caused, is less relevant than the fact that Lindbergh, once the unflattering light was on him, refused to step away from it. It was his own supporter, Billy Rose, who offered him a public forum to do away with the Iron Cross that Nazi General Hermann Goering gave him—to melt it down in front of an audience at Madison Square Garden. Much is made by Berg of the fact that the medal was an unexpected surprise and that Lindbergh courageously refused to buckle under pressure from those who wanted him to show that while he may once have thought that the Nazi plan was acceptable, he did not any more. Where *Lindbergh* fails is that it wants readers to see the aviator as being courageous for standing up to public criticism, but it never really shows why he did it.

Reviewers have accused Berg of being too close to his subject, too immersed in Lindbergh's life to be able to address the man's weaknesses clearly. This may be so; otherwise, how could anyone walk away from this huge book feeling that there are crucial facts about the man's thinking that they do not understand? If Lindbergh had associated with any other organization, it might just be regretable as a personal, if controversial, choice, but since it was the Nazi party, explanations are in order. Whether Berg likes it or not, the Holocaust is one of the defining events of the modern age, even more significant than Lindbergh's solo flight across the Atlantic. Yes, readers have a right to know what he was thinking. He seemed to approve of evil, and Berg does not provide enough evidence to prove that assumption wrong.

Source: David Kelly, Critical Essay on *Lindbergh,* in *Nonfiction Classics for Students,* The Gale Group, 2001.

Ian Palmer

Palmer is a full-time freelance writer who runs his own consulting business. He has earned an undergraduate degree in journalism. In this essay, he considers Berg's book with regard to the double-edged sword of success and the ways in which the recipients of success sometimes react to the spotlight's constant glow.

Throughout modern history, certain individuals have captured the hearts and minds of vast populations. For whatever reason, the minutest of details pertaining to persons such as Princess Diana, John F. Kennedy, and Tupac Shakur have been fodder for newspaper articles, magazine features, radio clips, and television documentaries. Not even death has robbed these demigods of their cult status. Indeed, their lights still burn as when they were among the living. These were human beings with inherent failings and shortcomings, prejudices and preconceptions, hang ups and pet peeves. But obvious faults and blemishes of character seldom deter the legions from admiring and deifying the fallen. A. Scott Berg's *Lindbergh*, which represents a social commentary on the weight of success, tackles society's obsession with the rich and famous. Berg considers just how swiftly the cheers from the crowd can be transformed into the jeers from the mob, and he comes upon a discovery sure to confound Charles Lindbergh's staunchest critics and puzzle his most ardent supporters: he was indeed only human.

Hero worship, in and of itself, might be deemed a form of revisionism, whereby those given to hero worship esteem and emulate the positive qualities of their heroes while simultaneously ignoring or dismissing obvious character flaws. Diana, Kennedy, and Shakur were imperfect, and so was Lindbergh. Yet, for whatever reason, he has been praised and condemned, cheered and jeered, built up and torn down. Anne Morrow, Lindbergh's wife and the daughter of a U.S. ambassador, granted Berg complete access to 2,000 boxes containing Lindbergh's personal notes. In embarking upon this literary project, Berg's express purpose in taking eight years to research and write the biography was to sketch a more realistic and thorough portrait of a man he believes was grossly misunderstood. Doing so involved digging deeper than any biographer had done previously. It also meant attempting to look at the world through the eyes of a protagonist who kept everything bottled up inside.

Berg essentially performs a delicate operation, with a pen as his tool, to remove the cancerous misconceptions surrounding Lindbergh's true self. Doing so necessitates delving into the mind of an intensely private man, attempting to look at the world through the eyes of the man himself. While it might not be entirely possible to see through another person's eyes, it can be argued that Berg does a commendable job at providing more information on the enigma that was Lindbergh than any biographer prior or since. Through his words, Berg is able to reveal a man who was at odds with society's demands upon its heroes. Berg also shows that Lindbergh was set in his ways and never wavered when it came to giving up his right to privacy. *Lindbergh* provides a more intimate glimpse of the protagonist and gives some explanations as to why he was the way he was. His own little world is trekked through, and the findings do help to flesh out the particulars of his personality. To Lindbergh, the weight of success was akin to an albatross hanging around his neck. It might be argued that he hated the price of success to the same degree that his fans loved the very ground he walked on. Berg emphasizes that only by looking at the world as the protagonist was prone to do is it possible to see just how uncomfortable he was with fame and everything that came with it.

Rather than going with the rosy picture of celebrity life entertained by many a fan, Berg situates Lindbergh in the reality of his times. This is important in as much that some of his political views, as questionable as they were, stand out less prominently in the context of some of the anti-Semitic and isolationist views expressed during his era. For the purposes of this essay, the term "isolationist" is used to describe a school of thought advocating that America should only involve itself in the affairs of other sovereign nations if America's interests are somehow involved. One complaint leveled against Lindbergh by his critics is that he made several anti-Semitic statements over the course of his lifetime. As true as this is, some writers have demonized him as though he were the only one in history with bigoted ideologies. In *A Short History of Canada*, Desmond Morton writes that not only were there frequent outbursts of isolationist views aired in Congress during the war effort, but that "[r]efugees fleeing Hitler's concentration camps were rejected by Canada." In light of the status quo among the political elite in North America, it hardly seems just to expect Lindbergh to play the role of sacrificial lamb.

Charles Lindbergh's solo flight from New York to Paris in 1927 was a major event for those of the postwar era who were, as Berg states, desperate for heroes. When a 25-year-old pilot from Minnesota boarded his small plane and made possible what was previously thought to be impossible, Americans found the hero they so dearly craved. Berg, who was interviewed by Jamie Allen as part of a book review for *CNN Interactive*, called Lindbergh "the great hero of the century, and then the great victim, and then he became the great villain." Throughout the biography, furthermore, Berg paints a

> " When a 25-year-old pilot from Minnesota boarded his small plane and made possible what was previously thought to be impossible, Americans found the hero they so dearly craved."

picture that suggests that Lindbergh was greatly put off by the unrelenting demands of an enthralled public. He clung tenaciously to his privacy and continued doing so until his death. In a way, celebrity was not really something he was in a position to accept or reject. It was simply something that society bestowed upon him because of a feat he had accomplished. Society determined that Lindbergh was worthy of being placed on a pedestal, and his own feelings toward this were moot points. In fact, his anti-hero inclinations had the effect of endearing him more to a public enthralled by role models with an edge. Only when he was later perceived as a traitor for not wanting to fight in World War II did the media begin the process of deconstructing the myth they had helped to create. Berg explains how suddenly Lindbergh fell out of public favor and argues that many of these problems have been blown out of proportion. Despite the public campaign to discredit him, the myth had been perpetuated to the point of becoming undistinguishable from the actual man. It is this problem that Berg's biography was designed to remedy

Berg provides a comprehensive sketch of the protagonist's background that reveals clues as to why he simply was not up to the task of being a hero. At six years of age, his bickering parents parted ways. By the time they split up, the damage had been done. The stormy relationship between his parents simply pushed him further inward. Both his parents were emotionally distant from him while he was growing up, and this personal reality was a contributing factor to his resolve to keep the inner most longings of his heart to himself. Lindbergh was already a bit antisocial by nature, but his difficult childhood simply served to further refine this character trait. His mannerisms as a youth were but a prelude to the introverted qualities he would exude as a grown man. Berg wipes away at the gloss of celebrity and gives a more realistic picture of Lindbergh the man. He points out how his emotional dysfunction impacted upon his marriage, and how his emotional distance played a role in his wife's decision to have an affair early in their marriage. Despite the imperfections, society insisted on foisting the robe of royalty upon his unwilling shoulders. Geoffrey C. Ward of the *New York Times* takes a look at Lindbergh's life and times and says that "through it all, he remained taciturn, aloof, without apparent emotion . . . and something of a mystery even to his own children."

Another event in Lindbergh's life helps to shed some light on his enigmatic personality. In 1932, the world took notice when it was announced that the Lindbergh baby had been kidnapped. Though Lindbergh did reportedly pay the ransom required, the baby was found dead in close proximity to the family's home. The media attention this event attracted was distressing to the couple, but the trial for the suspect attracted even more widespread media attention. Perhaps the only fitting comparison would be the infamous O. J. fiasco. The subsequent trial ended in a verdict to execute the convicted party, Bruno Richard Hauptmann. Even the convicted killer's death did not stop the rumor mill, as some conspiracy theorists claimed that Lindbergh might have been involved in the murder of his own baby. In response to the media attention and the lack of privacy, both Lindbergh and his wife fled the country for some time alone. As Berg points out, this was not the first time that the couple had disappeared from the public eye. Neither of them much cared for the trimmings that came with being a high-profile couple.

There are, as Berg attests, aspects to Lindbergh's character that cannot simply be ignored or shrugged off. While an early section of this essay suggested Lindbergh should not be made a scapegoat, there is no excuse for attempting to attribute his outbursts to cases of unintentional ignorance. Berg's admitted admiration for the famed aviator seems to have clouded his judgement somewhat in this regard. He seems to make light of some of Lindbergh's questionable beliefs and utterances. Though Lindbergh left little doubt that he was enthralled by certain aspects of the Nazi regime, for example, and though Lindbergh did go on the record with some of his anti-Semitic comments, none of which he ever retracted, Berg appears intent on disassociating Lindbergh from the Nazis. He does so at the ex-

pense of his credibility as an objective scribe. Other critics have also noticed Berg's downplaying of some of the protagonist's political views. Geoffrey C. Ward of *New York Post* writes that Berg "argues persuasively that his stubbornly misguided subject was never a Nazi, never a would-be dictator, as Franklin Roosevelt for one believed he was." However, Ward takes issue that Berg suggests that Lindbergh was ignorant only in as much as he did not understand that his comments were anti-Semitic. Ward argues that Lindbergh was fully aware of what it is he said.

Though Berg does a commendable job in giving a much clearer picture of Lindbergh than was previously available, he often comes across as a cheerleader of sorts. For example, in an article that appeared on *CNN Interactive*, he raved about the importance of Lindbergh's exploits in aviation by drawing a parallel to Neil Armstrong's landmark excursion to the moon. "He really did become the first modern media superstar. He's the most celebrated living person ever to walk the earth . . . It's almost as if Neil Armstrong decided to go to the moon . . . decided to go by himself, just built his rocket ship and did it." Despite these criticisms, however, the biography represents a solid thrust forward in terms of understanding Lindbergh and in terms of understanding success and society's obsession with its celebrities.

Lindbergh clearly tells the story of how one man shirked the accolades many in society covet. It is the story of a man who saw the price of success and decided to go the other way. It tells the story of the double-edged sword of success and how it attaches itself to whomever it will. While the debate as to the true Lindbergh is far from over, Berg does provide the most comprehensive volume to date. The biography tells the story of an aviator who never had the slightest idea of how his landmark flight would change his life so completely. It also shows the anguish Lindbergh felt at being accosted by media hounds and the inquisitive public. Most importantly, *Lindbergh* drives home the point that even heroes have faults, that sometimes their humanity overshadows their celebrity. The story of Lindbergh's life is of a man who upon running into success while flying through the sky spent the rest of his life trying to escape it. Yet not even in death has he been able to achieve this goal.

Source: Ian Palmer, Critical Essay on *Lindbergh,* in *Nonfiction Classics for Students,* The Gale Group, 2001.

Sam Tanenhaus

In the following review, Tanenhaus finds Berg "relates this remarkable story with energy and competence," but is disappointed by Berg's insufficient attention to the darker aspects of Lindbergh's life.

In an era of staged events and planned spectacles, it is almost impossible to imagine what so many millions felt on May 21, 1927, when the news came that a tiny silver aircraft had broken through the morning fog west of Ireland and was pushing on toward Paris. Since Charles A. Lindbergh's takeoff from New York City in the *Spirit of St. Louis* the day before, there had been no word of the plane and its pilot. "While Lindbergh later said that no man before him had commanded such freedom of movement over earth," A. Scott Berg writes in his new biography, "he failed to note that no man before him had ever been so much alone in the cosmos."

Of course, the instant Lindbergh landed at Le Bourget airfield outside Paris, the sublime solitude ended. The twenty-five-year-old aviator was swept up in a wave of public adoration. When he returned home, courtesy of the U.S. Navy, the entire nation seemed to be waiting at dockside. In Manhattan, more than four million people lined the streets to see him, and within three weeks, Berg reports, "an estimated 7,430,000 feet of newsreel had recorded his movements." Lindbergh had become "the most celebrated living person ever to walk the earth."

Like so many of his generation's great figures, he came from the Midwest. His father, Charles A. Lindbergh, Sr.—"C.A.," as he was called—was a Swede raised in rural Minnesota, a self-made man who put himself through law school and then started a thriving practice in the town of Little Falls. After C.A. won election to Congress as a Republican in 1907, Charles, then aged two, joined his mother in seasonal migrations between Washington and the heartland. It was a haphazard existence. By the age of eighteen, Lindbergh had attended no fewer than ten schools, passing through them as an indifferent pupil and avid daydreamer, too much the nomad to collect enduring friends.

After flunking out of the University of Wisconsin, Lindbergh found his home—in the sky. "Sharp-sighted and coordinated, with quick reflexes, [he] proved to be a natural pilot," Berg writes. He soon

Lindbergh's wife, Anne Morrow Lindbergh, with their son, Charles III

developed a missionary devotion to aviation, applying himself diligently to problems of aeronautics and design.

Through a relative novice when he decided to join the select handful of "flying fools" competing to make the first nonstop trans-Atlantic flight, Lindbergh was surreally confident. Experts said the trip would require two pilots, as no single man could possibly remain alert over the day and a half needed to complete it. Lindbergh, however, preferred to fly solo: a second pilot would mean added weight, and every available ounce was needed for fuel. Thus, his

> His pages on the kidnapping trial—expert but businesslike, in the manner of a prosecutor hurrying to convict—skimp on the atmospherics that might help us see why this was the most gripping of Depression-era dramas. . ."

plane—built from scratch to his deeply pondered specifications—was little more than an aerial gas tank. He declined even to install a radio since the primitive equipment always seemed to break down when needed most.

The silly nickname he acquired, "Lucky Lindy," was completely wrong, Lindbergh left nothing to chance. He "compiled endless lists," writes Berg: "equipment he would need; maps he would have to study; landmarks he would have to learn; and information he would need from the Weather Bureau and the State Department." He plotted the 3,000-mile route himself, then recalculated it trigonometrically. So precise were these figurings, and so skilled a pilot was he, that when, after twenty hours in the air, he leaned out of the cockpit to yell to fishing boats 50 feet below, "Which way is Ireland?," he was less than three miles off course. For food he packed five sandwiches, explaining laconically, "If I get to Paris I won't need any more, and if I don't get to Paris, I won't need any more, either."

Of the many sobriquets applied to him, "Lone Eagle" was the most apt. The first modern celebrity, he resisted the cheap trappings of success, spurning offers worth over $1 million from Hollywood, vaudeville, and hucksters of every kind. He learned early to avoid the press, which he loathed, remaining incorruptibly private, his own man.

Still, Lindbergh could not escape his fame, and it exacted a singular price. The public's insatiable appetite for gossip, cynically fed by newspapers, was to blame, he was sure, for the most terrible event in his life—the 1932 kidnapping and murder of his twenty-month-old son, quickly dubbed the "crime of the century." Almost as shocking as the act itself was the grisly media spectacle of the

trial. The ordeal for Lindberg and his young wife, Anne Morrow, ended only with the conviction and execution of the dour German immigrant Bruno Hauptmann, who had steadfastly maintained he had been framed, giving rise to conspiracy theories still widely believed today.

In the wake of the kidnapping, Lindbergh withdrew emotionally. Never shedding a tear himself over his lost son, he forbade his wife to cry as well. After the birth of each of their five other children, he would insist that she accompany him on distant journeys, so as to wean her from the newborn. In later years, her husband's unyielding reticence and rigid self-discipline would leave her repeatedly on the verge of breaking down. These episodes disclosed an especially frigid aspect of what his biographer calls Lindbergh's "Nordic *sang-froid.*"

Convinced that America had descended into barbarism, the Lindberghs fled the country in 1935, settling for a time in England. They returned four years later, but Charles's disillusionment with the U.S. had not abated. As World War II approached, he plunged into the isolationist America First movement. To many it seemed he was lending his prestige to the nascent American fascism espoused by Father Charles Coughlin and Senator Huey Long. In nationwide radio addresses, Lindbergh darkly inveighed against the "Jewish" media; his letters and diary entries from the period abound with musings about "the pressing sea of Yellow, Black, and Brown" and "the infiltration of inferior blood."

Nor did Lindbergh disguise his admiration for Germany's industrial and military revival under the Nazis. In richly publicized trips, he toured the new Reich's airplane factories and allowed himself to be feted and decorated. He refused to denounce Nazi atrocities—he would continue in this refusal even after the war—and became for a time as mistrusted in the United States as he had once been adored.

After Pearl Harbor, Lindbergh sought redemption. Denied a military commission by Franklin Roosevelt, who had always disliked him, he volunteered his services to the burgeoning Army air force and won praise for his courage and effectiveness flying missions in the Pacific. In peacetime, he spent years developing the fresh, evocative prose that earned him a Pulitzer prize for *The Spirit of St. Louis* (1953), his splendid memoir of his flight. And there was a final surprise: by the time of his death in 1974, Lindbergh had repudiated the very technology he had done so much to romanticize. Reborn as a conservationist, he proclaimed himself at one with birds rather than airplanes.

A. Scott Berg relates this remarkable story with energy and competence, unfolding his themes with a naturalness possible only because he has mastered vast quantities of detail. The highlight of the book, fittingly, is Lindbergh's historic flight to Paris. Berg makes us see just how grand a feat it was, fully the equal of the moon landing 42 years later. Indeed, for all the courage of the Apollo astronauts, their success was a coronation of large-scale technological wizardry. Lindbergh's achievement, by contrast, was swashbucklingly human. In a *tour de force* of narration, Berg evokes the eerie otherworldliness of the trans-Atlantic flight, and the mysterious power it conferred on Lindbergh as *ur*-aviator.

But in the instant Lindbergh's life begins its descent, so too does Berg's biography. After the landing at Le Bourget, the action flags, the drama wanes. For the remainder of the book, Berg's attention is captured by the emotional travails of Anne Lindbergh during her 45-year marriage to a trying, distant husband.

More problematically, Berg—whose previous subjects were the literary editor Maxwell Perkins and the movie mogul Samuel Goldwyn—seems unnerved by the complex social and political currents of the 1930's. His pages on the kidnapping trial—expert but businesslike, in the manner of a prosecutor hurrying to convict—skimp on the atmospherics that might help us see why this was the most gripping of Depression-era dramas, a cathartic public spectacle, and why it belongs in the sequence of politically-charged trials that includes the Sacco-Vanzetti case and the confrontation between Alger Hiss and Whittaker Chambers.

Even more disappointing is the book's cursory treatment of Lindbergh's misadventures in isolationism. Berg forgoes any deep exploration of the America First movement or of the kindred malign forces abroad in the U.S. as late as 1941. Lindbergh's political activities come at us as a string of regrettable incidents, not as the crisis of character they plainly were. Important questions hide murkily below the smooth surface of the narrative, and Berg seems afraid of touching them. Did Lindbergh, with his matchless celebrity, really see himself as an unelected tribune destined to keep the nation out of war? Was he motivated by a lingering hatred of the public? Was he following the doomed example of his father, whose own political career ended catastrophically when he became a vocal opponent of American entry into World War I?

The irony is that in his peak years, no other man succeeded so well as Lindbergh in binding the Old World to the New, not only because of his great transoceanic flight but also because he effortlessly embodied traits that seemed uniquely American: modesty, courage, plain-spokenness, innocence, and invincible youth. But the darker side of Lindbergh was of course no less American and no less integral to his being. It is this conjunction of light and dark, of heroism and folly, that continues to make Lindbergh so intriguing, even as his claim to our interest steadily weakens.

Source: Sam Tanenhaus, "First in Flight," in *Commentary*, Vol. 107, No. 1, January 1999, pp. 61–63.

John J. Miller

In the following review, Miller discusses Lindbergh's life and commends Berg for "his outstanding biography."

When Charles Lindbergh landed *The Spirit of St. Louis* in darkness at France's Le Bourget airfield on May 21, 1927, all he wanted to do was sleep. His nonstop journey of 3,614 miles from New York to Paris, which made him the first pilot to fly alone across the Atlantic Ocean, had lasted more than 33 hours. He had stayed awake the night before his departure; when his head finally hit the pillow early in the morning on the 22nd, he would have to make up for 63 hours of sleeplessness. His feat revealed to the world the great potential of aviation, but it was arguably his plane's primitive technology that kept him alive. Struggling against drowsiness almost from the start, Lindbergh saw ghostly images wander in and out of his cabin twenty hours after takeoff; he was hallucinating and probably would have fallen asleep in the sky were it not for his jerky plane's inability to stabilize.

There must have been times in his remarkable life when Lindbergh wondered whether it was all worth the effort. Upon his arrival in France, a spontaneously gathered crowd of 150,000 revelers mobbed him with giddy enthusiasm. Lindbergh was a global celebrity from that moment until his death in 1974. For years he and his family were hounded by the press—early versions of today's infamous paparazzi. The notoriety that made him a hero led to the kidnapping and death of his first child. The unwanted publicity drove his family into temporary

A. Scott Berg never mythologizes Charles Lindbergh, but he understandably admires him. With honesty and style, he performs the important task of reviving this flawed but essential figure, a true American hero."

exile from the United States, and it also led to a troubled marriage.

In his outstanding biography, A. Scott Berg describes how this shy Midwesterner became "the most famous man on earth" by age 25. Unlike so many of the celebrities who would succeed him, Lindbergh won his fame from an actual accomplishment, one which advanced the common good through a single act of stunning bravery. Upon his return to the United States, Lindbergh participated in parades (roughly 1,285 miles of them) all across the country. An estimated thirty million people one-quarter of the population turned out to see him in scores of public appearances. A new magazine called *Time* launched its "Man of the Year" feature so that it would have an excuse to put Lindbergh on the cover and attract readers. He was the subject of songs and poems; offers came in from Hollywood. "People behaved as though Lindbergh had walked on water, not flown over it," says Berg.

Lindbergh was born of Swedish stock in 1902 in Detroit, but he grew up mainly in Little Falls, Minn., and in Washington, D.C., where his father served as a populist congressman for ten years. He never made good grades, but he showed an aptitude for mechanics. Having enrolled in a Nebraska pilots' academy, he was soon earning a living as a professional barnstormer. Planes were a novelty in the early 1920s, and Lindbergh traveled around the Midwest offering flights to curious customers. He also became a stuntman, occasionally going by the name "The Daredevil Lindbergh," performing as a wingwalker and skydiver, and even participating in an aerial wedding (his plane carried the judge, another one of the bride and groom). According to Berg, "there was one flight—recorded in Lindbergh's papers with the exact location discreetly omitted—

during which a man wanted to fly over his home town and urinate on it . . . a wish Lindbergh granted." He later became one of America's first air-mail carriers.

Fatalities were common during these early days of flight. "Lucky Lindy" had to parachute from faulty planes four times. Despite the risks, aviation technology was steadily advancing to the point where it was becoming possible to contemplate a trip from the United States to Europe. In 1926, Lindbergh began to think seriously about doing it himself. He set about securing the financial backing he would need to custom-build an aircraft; he received most of his help from boosters in St. Louis, a contribution he recognized in christening his plane. A pair of French pilots tries to reach the United States two weeks before Lindbergh's own departure; they disappeared without a trace. Lindbergh would surely have shared their fate were it not for his incredible powers of concentration.

Lindbergh, in fact, was so single-minded about flying that he apparently had never even gone on a date before his historic flight. He just hadn't given much thought to girls. On a trip to Mexico City, however, he met Anne Morrow, the daughter of the American ambassador. They soon married. Although they experienced many periods of great happiness together, Charles at times seemed totally detached from his wife. He had difficulty showing his emotions—Anne never saw him cry, even when their baby was kidnapped. Long business trips did not help matters, and Anne found only limited comfort in her own extraordinary commercial success as a writer and poet. Still, the Lindberghs remained together and watched five children reach adulthood.

Berg, who is the first biographer to receive complete access to the Lindbergh papers as well as the full cooperation of the family, deftly fits the copious details of the Lindbergh's life into these pages. Many or his readers will have assumed that Lindbergh's accomplishments ended in 1927, or that they were restricted to the field of aviation. Flying over the Yucatan in 1929, Lindbergh took aerial photographs of several Mayan ruins, leading to the discovery of as many as six lost cities. Working at a Princeton lab in 1935, he developed the "Lindbergh pump," which made it possible for the first time for an organ to live outside the body. Lindbergh was instrumental in helping rocketry pioneer Robert H. Goddard secure funding for his important work.

Lindbergh also, and less fortunately, became involved in international politics. He encouraged the United States to stay out of the Second World War, taking a prominent position with the anti-interventionist America First Committee. Because of this, Lindberg was widely suspected of being a Nazi sympathizer—a suspicion that Berg effectively lays to rest. It is clear, however, that Lindbergh was at least mildly anti-Semitic (as were so many Americans in those days) and that he seriously underestimated Hitler's evil. As the United States moved closer to war, Lindbergh's anti-intervention rhetoric heated up and his popularity plummeted. ''Few men in American history had ever been so reviled,'' notes Berg.

Lindbergh did strongly support the war effort following the Japanese attack on Pearl Harbor. He served in the Pacific air corps, eventually becoming an expert bombardier. He was truly horrified to learn of the Holocaust, and he even visited the Bergen-Belsen concentration camp in 1945. He continued to defend his pre-war political views, however, and he was too stubborn ever to admit that he had misjudged Hitler.

A modicum of privacy described on Lindbergh in the 1950s and 1960s, and he turned his energies toward global conservation. He even seemed to have second thoughts about the technologies he had helped develop: ''Where civilization is most advanced, few birds exist. I realized that if I had to choose,'' he wrote in 1964, ''I would rather have birds than airplanes.'' Ten years later, surrounded by his family at their vacation home in Hawaii, he succumbed to lymphoma and was given a traditional Hawaiian burial. A. Scott Berg never mythologizes Charles Lindbergh, but he understandably admires him. With honesty and style, he performs the important task of reviving this flawed but essential figure, a true American hero.

Source: John J. Miller, ''The Daredevil Lindbergh,'' in *National Review,* Vol. L, No. 20, October 26, 1998, pp. 50–52.

Sources

Allen, Jamie, ''A. Scott Berg reveals the spirit of Lindbergh,'' in www.cnn.com (September 25, 1998).

Bryant, Eric, et. al., ''Lindbergh,'' in *Library Journal,* Vol. 124, No. 1, January 1999, p. 154.

''Lindbergh,'' in *Booklist,* Vol. 95, March 15, 1999, p. 1295.

''Lindbergh,'' in *Publishers Weekly,* Vol. 245, No. 34, August 24, 1998, p. 38.

Morrow, Lance, ''Lindbergh,'' in *Time,* Vol. 152, No. 12, September 21, 1998, p. 103.

Morton, Desmond, *A Short History of Canada,* McClelland & Stewart, 1998, p. 214.

Stricherz, Mark, ''Enigmatic Aviator,'' in *America,* May 1, 1999, p. 26.

Tanenhaus, Sam, ''Lindbergh,'' in *Commentary,* Vol. 107, January 1999, p. 61.

Ward, Geoffrey C., ''Fallen Eagle,'' in the *New York Times,* September 27, 1998.

Further Reading

Gill, Brandon, *Lindbergh Alone,* Harcourt, Brace & Co., 1977.
Much less detailed than Berg's biography, Gill's book focuses most of its attention on the transatlantic flight.

Langewiesche, Wolfgang, *Stick and Rudder: An Explanation of the Art of Flying,* Tab Books, 1990.
This book, meant to serve as a primer for beginning pilots, helps readers understand the task that Lindbergh faced in flying the *Spirit of St. Louis.*

Lindbergh, Charles, *The Wartime Journals of Charles A. Lindbergh,* Harcourt, Brace, Jovanovich, 1970.
This book provides Lindbergh's thoughts at a particularly trying time in his life when the country was turning against him and branding him a traitor and a coward.

Newton, James, *Uncommon Friends: Life with Thomas Edison, Henry Ford, Harvey Firestone, Alexis Carrel and Charles Lindbergh,* Harcourt, Brace & Co., 1989.
Uncommon Friends is written by a man who knew all of the persons referred to in its title. The book fits each of these men into the larger scheme of the early twentieth century.

The Making of the Atomic Bomb

Richard Rhodes

1987

The Making of the Atomic Bomb, by Richard Rhodes, was first published in 1987. For this detailed documentation of the development of the most destructive war weapon ever to be created, Rhodes received widespread recognition, winning the 1987 National Book Award, the 1988 Pulitzer Prize for General Nonfiction, and the 1988 National Book Critics Circle Award for General Nonfiction.

Rhodes provides extensive information on the biographical background and scientific accomplishments of the international collaboration of scientists that culminated in the creation of the first atomic bomb. In 1939, several scientists became aware of the theoretical possibility of creating an atomic bomb, a weapon of mass destruction vastly exceeding the potential of existing military arsenals. But it was not until the United States entered World War II, late in 1941, that priority was given to funding and organizing research into the creation of such a weapon in a secret operation referred to as the Manhattan Project.

The first test atomic bomb, called Trinity, was exploded in the New Mexico desert on July 16, 1945. On August 6, an atomic bomb was dropped on the Japanese city of Hiroshima. Three days later, another atomic bomb was dropped on the Japanese city of Nagasaki. On August 14, 1945, Japan agreed to an unconditional surrender to the Allies, thus ending World War II.

Rhodes addresses the difficult moral and ethical dilemmas faced by the scientists of the Manhattan Project, particularly the implications of creating such a weapon of mass destruction. Originally concerned with ''pure'' scientific research, those who worked on the Manhattan Project were forced to consider the ultimate effect of their research efforts on the future of the human race.

Author Biography

Richard Lee Rhodes was born in Kansas City, Kansas, on July 4, 1937, the son of Arthur Rhodes, a railroad mechanic and Georgia (maiden name Collier) Rhodes. When he was only thirteen months old, his mother committed suicide. Richard's eldest brother went to live with relatives while Richard and his brother, Stanley, who was two years older, stayed with their father. When Richard was ten, their father remarried, and their stepmother, Anne Ralena Martin, began a reign of terrifying physical and emotional abuse against the boys while their father passively looked on. After two years of deprivation, torture, and violence, Stanley sneaked out of the house to report this abuse to the police. The boys were removed from their home by state officials and placed in the Drumm Institute, a home for boys near Independence, Missouri. Although the Drumm Institute imposed strict rules upon the boys, who were also required to work at farming, Richard thrived in this environment, becoming an avid reader. In 1955, he graduated from high school with a scholarship to Yale University, in New Haven, Connecticut. He attended Yale from 1955 to 1959, graduating with a bachelor's degree in intellectual history.

Rhodes worked as a writer trainee for *Newsweek* magazine in 1959. In 1960, he married Linda Iredell Hampton and began working as a staff assistant for Radio Free Europe, in New York City. Rhodes joined the Air Force Reserve from 1960 to 1965, during which time he worked as an instructor in English at Westminster College, in Fulton, Missouri, (from 1960 to 1961) and found work as an editor. Rhodes became book editing manager for Hallmark Cards in Kansas City, Missouri, from 1962 to 1970. He was a contributing editor to *Harper's* magazine from 1970 to 1974. He divorced Linda in 1974 and began working as a contributing editor for *Playboy* magazine in Chicago from 1974 to 1980. In 1976, he married Mary Magdalene Evans, whom he later divorced. Rhodes became a

Richard Rhodes

contributing editor for *Rolling Stone* magazine, in New York City, from 1988 to 1993. During this time, he was also a visiting fellow in the Defense and Arms Control Study Program at Massachusetts Institute of Technology (1988–1989), and a visiting scholar in the History of Science Department at Harvard University. Although Rhodes had been a severe alcoholic for thirty years, he was inspired to quit drinking by his love for Ginger Untrif, who became his third wife.

Summary

The Scientists

Rhodes describes extensively, up to World War II, the lives and work of an international community of scientists, mostly physicists and chemists, whose work eventually culminated in the making of the first atomic bomb. Theories of the existence of atomic particles date back to Greek philosophy in the fifth century B.C., and, by the seventeenth century A.D. most scientists assumed the existence of the atom. However, no actual proof of the existence of the atom had been formulated until J. J. Thomson discovered the electron in 1897. In 1884, Thomson was chair of the distinguished Cavendish Laboratory at Cambridge where he exerted tremendous influence on a generation of scientists. Einstein's revolutionary theory of relativity was announced in 1915. Leo Szilard, a Hungarian-born Jewish theoretical physicist, entered the University of Berlin in 1921, where he collaborated with Einstein. Ernest Rutherford was a New Zealand born British physicist credited with inventing nuclear physics (also called atomic physics). Rutherford studied under Thomson at the Cavendish Laboratory, replacing Thomson as head of the lab in 1919. Rutherford's most significant accomplishment was the development of a theory of atomic structure called the Rutherford atomic model.

Niels Bohr, a Danish physicist, made significant advances with his formulation of the Bohr atomic model. In 1921, Bohr became director of the Institute for Theoretical Physics in Copenhagen, which, under his direction, soon gained an international reputation as a leading center for research on quantum theory and atomic physics. Bohr broke new ground in the application of quantum theory to the study of atomic and molecular particles. Robert J. Oppenheimer, an American theoretical physicist, studied atomic physics under Rutherford at the Cavendish Laboratory. In 1927, Oppenheimer took a post in physics at The University of California at Berkeley and the California Institute of Technology. In 1932, James Chadwick, an English physicist who worked with Rutherford at the Cavendish Laboratory, discovered the neutron. Otto Hahn, a German chemist who was working with Fritz Strassmann, discovered nuclear fission. The Italian physicist Enrico Fermi conducted important research on nuclear fission at the University of Rome.

When Hitler came to power in Germany in 1933, many of Europe's greatest physicists emigrated in order to flee Nazi persecution, several of them settling in the United States. Szilard emigrated to London, where he first conceived of the possibility of creating an atomic bomb, and later settled in the United States, taking a post at Columbia University. Einstein, in particular danger of Nazi persecution due to his international prominence, fled to the United States, where he took a post at the Institute for Advanced Study at Princeton University, in New Jersey. In 1938, Fermi, under the pretext of traveling with his family to Sweden to receive his Nobel Prize, fled fascist Italy, eventually settling in the United States. Meitner fled Nazi Germany in 1938 to settle in Sweden, where she continued her research with her nephew Otto Frisch. After Nazi Germany invaded Denmark, at the outbreak of World War II, Bohr and his family fled to England and then the United States.

The Manhattan Project

Upon reaching New York in 1939, Bohr alerted Einstein to the possibility of Germany developing an atomic bomb. Along with several colleagues, Bohr persuaded Einstein to write a letter to President Franklin D. Roosevelt, suggesting that the United States initiate research into the development of an atomic bomb before Germany developed one. However, government officials failed to comprehend the enormity of the implications of these new developments, as explained by several brilliant scientists. It was not until the bombing of Pearl Harbor in December of 1941 that the United States entered World War II, at which point the possibility of creating such a military weapon appeared more relevant to government and military officials. The result was the organization in May of 1942 of the secret Manhattan Project, which included several teams of American and British scientists conducting research at such disparate sites as the University of Chicago and Los Alamos, New Mexico. Other locations where scientists were working on the Manhattan Project were the University of California at Berkeley, Columbia University in New York City, and Oak Ridge in Tennessee. It came to be called the Manhattan Project because of the location of the new government office organizing the project, known as the Manhattan Engineer District Office. (The Los Alamos site, however, is most commonly associated with the Manhattan Project.) On July 16, 1945, the first test atomic bomb, named Trinity, was successfully exploded on an air base in Alamogordo, New Mexico. In the meantime, scientists in Great Britain, Germany, Japan, and Russia were coming to the same conclusions about the possibility of creating an atomic bomb. However, several factors discouraged efforts by these nations to develop such a bomb.

Hiroshima and Nagasaki

On April 12, 1945, President Roosevelt died, and Vice President Harry S. Truman was sworn in as president of the United States. Up to that point, Truman had only a vague idea of the goals of the Manhattan Project; he was quickly informed of the significance of its efforts. In May 1945, Germany surrendered to the Allies. Peace negotiations were initiated at the Potsdam Conference, held in a suburb of Berlin, from July 17 to August 2, 1945. President Truman of the United States, Prime Minister Winston Churchill of Great Britain, and Premier Joseph Stalin of Russia, known collectively as the Big Three, were the leading figures in these negotiations. The War with Germany concluded, the Allies sent a message from Potsdam to the Japanese government, calling for unconditional surrender. When Japan refused to surrender, the United States dropped the first offensive atomic bomb on the city of Hiroshima, Japan, on August 6, 1945. The bomb, nicknamed Little Boy, had been carried in a modified B-29 bomber called Enola Gay, flown by Colonel Paul Tibbets. Although the Japanese Emperor Hirohito was willing to surrender, the Japanese military was unyielding, as a result of which the United States dropped a second bomb, nicknamed Fat Man, on the city of Nagasaki, on August 9. Japan immediately surrendered to the Allies. Both Japanese cities were utterly devastated by the bombs. Hiroshima, with a population of about 350,000, suffered the deaths of 140,000 people as a result of the bombing. Two-thirds of the city was demolished in the explosion. Of Nagasaki's 270,000 residents, some 70,000 died as a result of the bombing, and half of the city was demolished. After the war, the United States began work on developing the more powerful hydrogen bomb.

Key Figures

Niels Bohr

Niels Bohr (1885–1962) was a Danish physicist known as the first to apply quantum theory to the study of atomic and molecular particles. He is also known for proposing the liquid model of the atomic nucleus and for formulating the Bohr theory of the atom. Bohr received a doctoral degree from the University of Copenhagen in 1911. He studied under J. J. Thomson at Cambridge University in England, but, when he learned that Thomson was not interested in his work, Bohr left to work under Ernest Rutherford in Manchester, England. There, Bohr distinguished himself by formulating the Bohr atomic model. He returned to Copenhagen in 1912 and in 1921 was named director of the Institute for Theoretical Physics. Under his direction, the Institute soon gained an international reputation for research in quantum theory and atomic physics. Bohr's principle of complementarity offered a theoretical basis for quantum physics, which became widely accepted among many scientists, although Albert Einstein continued to dispute it. Bohr's ground-breaking "liquid drop" model of the atomic

Media Adaptations

- *The Making of the Atomic Bomb*, by Richard Rhodes, was recorded on audiocassette by Books on Tape in 1992.

nucleus and his "compound nucleus" model of the atom led other scientists to the discovery of nuclear fission. With the outbreak of World War II, Nazi Germany invaded Denmark, as a result of which Bohr and his family fled the country for England and then the United States. He worked on the Manhattan Project in Los Alamos, New Mexico, which developed the first atomic bomb. However, Bohr expressed concern throughout his life about the threat to humanity posed by nuclear warfare.

Sir James Chadwick

James Chadwick (1891–1974) was an English physicist credited with the discovery of the neutron, for which he received a Nobel Prize in 1935. Chadwick worked with Ernest Rutherford at the Cavendish Laboratory in Cambridge, England, in researching properties of the atomic nucleus. In 1945, he received the honor of being knighted for his accomplishments.

Arthur Compton

Arthur Compton (1892–1962) was an American physicist who shared the Nobel Prize for Physics in 1927 for his research on X rays. Compton received his doctorate from Princeton University in 1916. In 1920, he was made head of the department of physics at Washington University in St. Louis, Missouri. Compton's research helped to make legitimate Einstein's quantum theory, which was not yet widely accepted among scientists. In 1923, Compton became professor of physics at the University of Chicago, a post that he retained until 1945. He became the chairman of the committee of the National Academy of Sciences that in 1941 conducted research into the potential development of nuclear weapons, ultimately organizing the Manhattan Project. Compton worked on the Manhattan Project as the director of the University of Chicago Metallurgical Laboratory from 1941 to 1945.

Albert Einstein

Albert Einstein (1879–1955) was a German-Jewish physicist whose theories of relativity forever changed scientific approaches to space, time, and gravity. Einstein was awarded the Nobel Prize for physics in 1921. After Hitler came to power in 1933, Einstein fled Nazi Germany, eventually taking a post at the Institute for Advanced Study at Princeton University in New Jersey, where he remained for the rest of his life. In 1939, Niels Bohr alerted Einstein to the possibility that Germany could develop an atomic bomb. Bohr asked Einstein to write a letter to President Franklin D. Roosevelt, suggesting that the United States initiate research on an atomic bomb. Einstein, however, was not involved in the research carried out by the Manhattan Project and was not even aware of the successful development of the atomic bomb until after it was dropped on Hiroshima. In the wake of this event, Einstein became a vocal advocate for world peace and the prevention of further nuclear warfare.

Enrico Fermi

Enrico Fermi (1901–1954) was an Italian-born physicist who won the Nobel Prize for physics in 1938 for his research on nuclear fission. Fermi earned a doctoral degree at the University of Pisa for his research on X rays. In 1926, he became a professor of theoretical physics at the University of Rome, where he was instrumental in developing a community of brilliant young physicists. On the pretext of traveling to Sweden to receive his Nobel Prize, Fermi fled fascist Italy with his family and settled in the United States. In New York City, Fermi met with other nuclear physicists, eventually becoming a part of the Manhattan Project. Based at the University of Chicago, he developed the first self-sustained nuclear chain reaction, which quickly lead to the making of the first atomic bomb. He became an American citizen in 1944 and, in 1946, was named professor of Nuclear Studies at the University of Chicago.

Richard Feynman

Richard Feynman (1918–1988) was an American theoretical physicist who received the Nobel Prize for physics in 1965 for his work on the theory of quantum electrodynamics. Feynman received his doctorate from Princeton University in 1942. From 1941 to 1942, he worked on the Manhattan Project in Princeton, joining the laboratory at Los Alamos, New Mexico, in 1943. Feynman was among the youngest scientists to hold a leadership position at Los Alamos. From 1945 to 1950, he worked as an associate professor at Cornell University, and from 1950 until his retirement he worked as a professor of theoretical physics at the California Institute of Technology. Feynman is considered one of the most brilliant scientific minds of the twentieth century.

Otto Frisch

Otto Frisch (1904–1979) was an Austrian-born physicist who worked on the Manhattan Project at Los Alamos, New Mexico. Frisch earned his doctorate degree at the University of Vienna in 1926. He worked with his aunt, the physicist Lise Meitner, together discovering and naming uranium fission in 1939. After the War, Frisch became director of the nuclear physics department of the Cavendish Laboratory at Cambridge University in England.

Brigadier General Leslie R. Groves

In September 1942, Brigadier General Leslie R. Groves (1896–1970) was named head of the Manhattan Engineer District, in charge of all army activities concerned with the Manhattan Project. Groves was responsible for contracting independent building industries to construct the facilities at the various research and production sites that made up the Manhattan Project, such as a gaseous diffusion separation plant and a plutonium production facility.

Otto Hahn

Otto Hahn (1879–1968) was a German chemist who won the Nobel Prize for chemistry in 1944 for his discovery (along with Fritz Strassmann) of nuclear fission. Hahn received a doctorate degree from the University of Marburg in 1901. At the University of Berlin, he conducted research on radioactivity and in 1911 joined the Kaiser Wilhelm Institute for Chemistry. During World War I, he was instrumental in developing chemical warfare. Although his research was instrumental to the development of the atomic bomb, throughout the remainder of his life he opposed the further development of nuclear weapons.

Lise Meitner

Lise Meitner (1878–1968) was a Jewish Austrian-born physicist whose collaborative research with

Otto Hahn, Fritz Strassmann, and her nephew Otto Frisch resulted in the discovery and naming of uranium fission. Meitner received her doctorate from the University of Vienna in 1906. In 1907, she began working with Hahn in Berlin on research in radioactivity. In 1938, she fled Nazi Germany for Sweden.

Robert Oppenheimer

Robert J. Oppenheimer (1904–1967) was an American theoretical physicist most widely known as the director of the Los Alamos laboratory of the Manhattan Project, which developed the first atomic bomb. Upon graduating from Harvard, Oppenheimer studied atomic physics under Lord Rutherford at the Cavendish Laboratory at Cambridge. He received his doctoral degree from Göttingen University in 1927, after which he taught physics at the University of California at Berkeley and the California Institute of Technology. His collaboration with a team of scientists on the Manhattan Project lead to the first nuclear explosion test in 1945 at Alamogordo, New Mexico. In 1947, Oppenheimer took a post as head of the Institute for Advanced Study at Princeton University. From 1947 to 1952, he was chairman of the General Advisory Committee of the Atomic Energy Commission. In 1953, during the Red Scare in which many intellectuals were accused of treason, Oppenheimer was put on trial for suspicion of having leaked military secrets, based on his earlier sympathies with communism. He was found not guilty, but his position with the Atomic Energy Commission was terminated. The Federation of American Scientists, however, supported Oppenheimer. In 1963, President Lyndon B. Johnson presented Oppenheimer with the Enrico Fermi Award of the Atomic Energy Commission, thus officially retracting all public denunciation of the scientist.

Sir Rudolf Peierls

Rudolf Peierls (1907–1995) was a German-born physicist whose theoretical work was instrumental in the development of the atomic bomb. Peierls worked with Otto Frisch at the University of Birmingham, in England, where they collaborated on a memo explaining the theories that suggested the possibility of creating an atomic bomb. He became a British citizen in 1940 and in 1943 joined the team of British scientists who moved to Los Alamos, New Mexico, to work on the Manhattan Project. After the war, he returned to his post as a professor at Birmingham. In 1963, he left Birmingham to become a professor at the University of Oxford. Peierls was knighted in 1968.

Max Planck

Max Planck (1858–1947) was a German theoretical physicist who was awarded the 1918 Nobel Prize for physics for his formulation of quantum theory. Planck earned his doctoral degree in 1879 from the University of Munich. In 1892, he became a professor at the University of Berlin, a position that he held throughout his life. Although it was not immediately recognized as such by the scientific community, his quantum theory eventually revolutionized theoretical physics. While Einstein was instrumental in championing Planck's achievement, Planck was instrumental in calling attention to the significance of Einstein's theory of relativity. Although Planck was openly opposed to Hitler's racist policies, he remained in Germany throughout World War II to continue his research.

President Franklin Roosevelt

President Franklin Delano Roosevelt (1882–1945) was in his third term of presidency when the United States entered World War II. In 1939, he received a letter from Einstein alerting him to the potential for developing an atomic bomb, but he failed to see the true significance of this information until the United States entered the war in 1941. Roosevelt died in office on April 12, 1945, several months before the dropping of the first atomic bombs and ending of World War II.

Sir Ernest Rutherford

Ernest Rutherford (1871–1937) was a New Zealand-born British physicist awarded the Nobel Prize for chemistry in 1908 for his research that led to the development of nuclear physics (also referred to as atomic physics). In 1895, Rutherford came to the Cavendish Laboratory at Cambridge, in England, where he studied under J. J. Thomson. In 1898, Rutherford took a post as a professor of physics at McGill University in Montreal, Canada. He moved back to England in 1907 to work at the University of Manchester. Rutherford's most important accomplishment was his nuclear theory of atomic structure, called the Rutherford atomic model. In 1914, he was knighted for his many accomplishments. In 1919, he became head of the Cavendish Laboratory.

Major Charles Sweeney

Major Charles W. Sweeney piloted the B-29 bomber, named the Great Artiste, which dropped the atomic bomb over Nagasaki on August 9, 1945.

Leo Szilard

Leo Szilard (1898–1964) was a Hungarian physicist who was a key figure in the formation of the Manhattan Project. Szilard earned his doctoral degree from the University of Berlin in 1922. He worked as a staff member at the Institute of Theoretical Physics at the University of Berlin until 1933, when Hitler came to power, and he left Germany. Szilard worked for several years at the college of St. Bartholomew's Hospital in England, before moving to the United States to occupy a post at Colombia University. From 1942 to 1945, Szilard worked on the Manhattan Project with Fermi's research team at the University of Chicago. After the war, he accepted a position as professor of biophysics at the University of Chicago. Following the war, Szilard became a strong advocate of the use of atomic energy for peaceful purposes and supported limitations on the nuclear arms race.

Edward Teller

Edward Teller (1908-) was a Hungarian-born Jewish nuclear physicist who worked on the Manhattan Project. Teller worked with Enrico Fermi at the University of Chicago before joining the research team at Los Alamos, New Mexico. However, Teller was more interested in research into the development of a hydrogen bomb, which was considered a lesser priority during World War II. After the war, however, Teller became a leading proponent of United States efforts to create a hydrogen bomb, which was potentially more powerful than the atom bomb. In 1951, Teller collaborated with Stanislaw Ulam in a major breakthrough for research on the hydrogen bomb known as the Teller-Ulam configuration. Teller was thus dubbed the "father of the H-bomb."

Sir J. J. Thomson

J. J. Thomson (1856–1940) was an English physicist who discovered the electron in 1897. Thomson began research at the Cavendish Laboratory of Cambridge University in 1880 and in 1884 was made chair of the physics department there. For his accomplishments, Thomson was granted the Nobel Prize for physics in 1906 and was knighted in 1908. Thomson was an influential teacher at Cavendish, and many of his students, including Ernest Rutherford, were awarded Nobel Prizes.

Colonel Paul Tibbets

Colonel Paul W. Tibbets, Jr. was the pilot who flew the B-29 bomber, named Enola Gay, which dropped the atomic bomb on Hiroshima, in Japan, on August 6, 1945.

President Harry Truman

Harry S. Truman (1884–1972) was the thirty-third president of the United States. He took office on April 12, 1945, the day of President Roosevelt's death. Upon being sworn into office, Truman was apprised of the developments of the Manhattan Project, about which he had known little up to that point. While he attended the Potsdam Conference to discuss peace negotiations between the Allies and a defeated Germany, he received notice that the first atomic bomb had been successfully tested by the Manhattan Project on July 16. From Potsdam, a message was sent to Japan, threatening the use of a devastating new weapon unless they agreed to unconditional surrender. When Japan refused this offer, Truman ordered the dropping of the atomic bomb on Hiroshima on August 6, 1945, and on Nagasaki on August 9, 1945.

H. G. Wells

H. G. Wells (1866–1946) was an English writer known today primarily for his classic science fiction novels such as *The Time Machine* (1895), *The Island of Doctor Moreau* (1896), *The Invisible Man* (1897), and *The War of the Worlds* (1898). Wells' novel *The World Set Free* (1914) was prophetic in essentially predicting atomic warfare.

Eugene Wigner

Eugene Wigner (1902–1995) was a Hungarian-born physicist who shared the 1963 Nobel Prize for physics for his work on nuclear physics. Wigner received his doctoral degree in 1925 from the Institute of Technology in Berlin. In 1938, he became a professor of mathematical physics at Princeton University, a position that he held until 1971, when he retired. In 1939, Wigner, with Leo Szilard, helped to convince Albert Einstein to draft a letter to President Roosevelt, alerting him of the possibility of developing an atomic bomb. Wigner worked with

Enrico Fermi at the University of Chicago Metallurgical Laboratory, part of the Manhattan Project.

Themes

Scientific Community

Rhodes devotes almost the entire first third of *The Making of the Atomic Bomb* to introducing the international community of scientists whose work contributed to the development of the first atomic bomb. Rhodes provides biographical background on scientists from Denmark, Germany, Italy, Austria, Hungary, Great Britain, and the United States. Even before the Manhattan Project formally brought these men and women together, many of them were either familiar with one another's work, had communicated with one another, studied with one another, or collaborated on their research. For instance, several of them worked or studied at the Cavendish Laboratory at Cambridge University in England. Further, the oppressive conditions in Germany under Hitler led many of these scientists who were Jewish to flee Nazi Germany, often settling in the United States or Britain. Rhodes explains in detail the ways in which the research, discoveries, and theoretical developments pioneered by each scientist or team of scientists drew from and added to the work of other scientists. Further, several scientists met informally in New York City and in Chicago, before the formulation of the Manhattan Project, to discuss strategies for alerting the United States government to the importance of developing an atomic bomb before Germany achieved the same end. For instance, several of them worked together at various points to draft letters to United States officials, explaining the urgency of the matter. Finally, the Manhattan Project itself, carried out simultaneously in several locations throughout the United States, represents the collaborative efforts of some of the most brilliant scientists of the twentieth century (many of whom were Nobel Prize winners in physics and chemistry).

Weapons of Mass Destruction

Rhodes is particularly concerned with the implications of nuclear warfare on the fate of the human race. Scientists working on the Manhattan Project were painfully aware of the potentially apocalyptic consequences of developing a weapon of mass destruction. Throughout their research, they debated and discussed the fate of world politics in the wake of atomic warfare. They had no doubt that the knowledge and resources to create nuclear weapons would be within the reach of many nations before long and that this could potentially result in mutual mass destruction by warring nations—the self-immolation of the human race. However, others felt convinced that, because such a universally horrific outcome could result from nuclear warfare, it might in fact be the cause of world peace. Some even believed that the potential for nuclear warfare would inevitably result in a new organization of world politics, whereby all nations would become one, and war would be completely abolished. Others were more cynical, foreseeing the horrors of implementing such a weapon. Rhodes spends considerable time quoting from interviews of victims of the bombing of Hiroshima, making vivid and visceral the effects of the bomb on human lives. He provides extensive descriptions of the aftermath of the bombing in which the charred flesh of the survivors, their skin hanging from their bodies like rags, is perhaps the most prominent image. Rhodes thus attempts to provide the reader with an idea of the deeply felt moral and ethical dilemmas of the scientists responsible for the bomb and the pure horror of the human suffering that resulted from their efforts.

Style

Research and Sources

As a work of nonfiction, Rhodes' success in writing *The Making of the Atomic Bomb* is largely due to the thoroughness and skill with which he conducted his research. Rhodes spent five years researching and writing this history, which combines information from a variety of sources. One of his sources was classified government documents, such as the FBI files that include the record of a secret investigation of Szilard, one of the scientists on the Manhattan Project. Another source was first-person accounts by Japanese survivors of the bombing of Hiroshima, describing in graphic detail the devastation caused by the bomb. Another source was reproductions of important correspondence between scientists and politicians, such as the letter written by Einstein to the United States government, warning of the possibility of Germany building an atomic bomb. Yet another source of material Rhodes incorporates into his narrative are anecdotal

Topics for Further Study

- Learn more about the development of methods for harnessing nuclear power as an energy source for peaceful purposes. What scientific research resulted in the construction of nuclear power plants? When was the first nuclear power plant constructed? What types of opposition arose to the development of nuclear power plants? What is the status of nuclear energy as a peacetime power source in the United States today? What about in other nations?

- The research of many scientists throughout the first half of the twentieth century led up to the realization that an atomic bomb was possible.

Pick one of these scientists from the Key Figures list in this entry, and learn more about his or her research up to 1942 when the Manhattan Project was organized. How did this scientist's research contribute to the creation of the first atomic bomb?

- Learn more about the impact of the atomic bomb on Japan. How did the Japanese government and people respond to the horrors of Hiroshima and Nagasaki in the post-war years?

- What is the status of nuclear weapons in the world today? To what extent does nuclear warfare continue to be a threat to the populations of the world?

---

accounts of private conversations between scientists involved in the Manhattan Project.

Nonfiction Genres

Drawing from a wide variety of source materials, Rhodes' narrative also combines elements of a variety of genres, or categories, of nonfiction. His book is part biography, in the sense that he provides extensive biographical background on many of the scientists whose work lead up to the making of the first atomic bomb. It is partly a political history, as Rhodes describes the political and diplomatic significance of historical events surrounding the development of the bomb. It also falls into the category of history of science, as Rhodes traces the series of scientific developments, beginning in the mid-nineteenth century, which made it possible to create an atomic bomb.

Narrative Voice

Rhodes' success with *The Making of the Atomic Bomb* can also be attributed to his capacity for encompassing a massive accumulation of data and several nonfiction genres into a single, coherent, accessible narrative. Rhodes covers a century of history, and an entire globe of political, sociological, and scientific events with a smoothly flowing, comprehensible, as well as comprehensive, third-person narrative voice.

Epigraphs

Rhodes makes use of epigraphs—short, pithy quotations—at the beginning of each of the three parts of the book and facing the table of contents. The very first of these quotes is by Robert Oppenheimer, director of the Los Alamos, New Mexico, branch of the Manhattan Project; it reads: "Taken as a story of human achievement, and human blindness, the discoveries in the sciences are among the great epics." Such a reference to mythological or biblical tales of human heroism and folly is entirely apt as an opening to Rhodes' arguably "epic" nine-hundred page history of the atomic bomb. This quote captures Rhodes' attitude toward the development of the first nuclear weapon, as both a monument to scientific "achievement," and as a testament to a certain moral "blindness" to the horrors that were to result from this achievement. A second opening quote is from Emilio Segré. In this comment, Segré emphasizes a certain element of luck in the various political and scientific efforts that went into the making of the bomb. In offering this quote, Rhodes indirectly comments upon the

extent to which minute facts of physical reality—
"solid numbers based on measurement"—can potentially determine the fate of human history.

Historical Context

World War II

World War II was waged between the Allied
forces and the Axis forces in the years 1939 to 1945.
The first use of the atomic bomb was instrumental in
determining the outcome of the war.

World War II began on August 31, 1939, when
Germany, under Adolph Hitler, invaded Poland. As
a result, Great Britain and France declared war on
Germany on September 3. Soviet troops invaded
Poland's eastern border on September 17, and Germany and the Soviet Union agreed to divide a
defeated Poland between them. By October 10,
Soviet forces easily established themselves in Estonia,
Latvia, and Lithuania. Meanwhile, skirmishes between British naval forces and German U-boats
(submarines) took place in September and October
of that year.

In February 1940, the Soviet Union attacked
Finland, achieving victory by March 6. In April,
Germany successfully invaded and occupied both
Denmark and Norway. In May, Germany successfully invaded and occupied Belgium. From there,
German troops invaded northern France, beating
back French and British troops. On June 10, Italy,
under Mussolini, aligned itself with Germany by
declaring war on France and Great Britain. The
French government surrendered to both Germany
and Italy, agreeing to a partitioning of France into
an occupied zone and an unoccupied zone. In July,
the occupied French government, known as the
Vichy, consented to the creation of a new French
nation under German rule. Accordingly, France
ended its alliance with Great Britain against Germany.

Having broken the French-British alliance, Germany began attacks on British air and naval forces
in an extended conflict known as the Battle of
Britain. When German bombing attacks moved
further into British territory, Great Britain retaliated
by bombing Berlin. Hitler responded to this offensive with the bombing of London and other British
cities. Germany continued air raids over Great Britain into April 1941; however, the British ultimately

held off a German invasion with Britain's superior
radar technology that allowed them to detect and
shoot down many German planes.

In October 1940, Italy began a war against
Greece. In April and May 1941, Germany successfully invaded and occupied both Yugoslavia and
Greece. As a result, Yugoslavia was broken into
several separate states, and Greece was divided
between German and Italian occupation zones. On
June 22, 1941, German troops invaded Russia.

Up to this point, the United States had remained
officially neutral with regard to the war. However,
on December 7, 1941, Japanese forces bombed the
United States naval base at Pearl Harbor in a sur-
prise attack. As a result, on December 8, the United
States declared war on Japan. Japan had invaded
China in the years previous to World War II, and,
immediately after the United States declared war on
Japan, China declared war on Italy, Germany, and
Japan. On April 18, 1942, the United States bombed
Tokyo in an air raid using conventional explosives.
With the United States at war, preparations for the
secret Manhattan Project to develop the first atomic
bomb were made by United States government and
military officials.

In January 1943, Roosevelt and Churchill met
at the Casablanca Conference, as a result of which
Roosevelt announced a request for the uncondi-
tional surrender of Germany, Italy, and Japan. On
July 25 of that year, Mussolini resigned his rule in
Italy, after which the new Italian government se-
cretly negotiated with the Allies. In August, the
Allies took Sicily. In September, the Allies landed
in Italy, which soon surrendered. On October 13,
Italy, now aligned with the Allies, declared war on
Germany.

The decisive event of the war was the invasion
of German occupied Normandy by American, British, and Canadian troops on June 6, 1944, known as
D day. When, in April 1945, Allied troops made
their way into Germany and surrounded Berlin,
Hitler committed suicide. On May 8, 1945, Germany officially surrendered to the Allies.

Meanwhile, war continued on the Pacific front
between the Allies and Japan. The Potsdam Conference, in which the leaders of the Allied forces met in
a suburb outside Berlin, was held from July 17 to
August 2, 1945. During this time, Truman was
notified of the successful testing of the first atomic
bomb, named Trinity, by members of the Manhattan
Project. At this point, Stalin was informed of the

Compare
&
Contrast

- **1949:** The North Atlantic Treaty Organization is founded to create an alliance between the United States and nations of Western Europe in opposition to the military might of the Soviet Union in much of Eastern Europe.

  1955: The Warsaw Pact forms a military alliance between the Soviet Union and other Eastern European nations.

  1963: The Nuclear Test Ban Treaty, signed by the United States, the Soviet Union, and the United Kingdom, bans the testing of nuclear weapons in the earth's atmosphere, in outer space, and underwater; it limits the testing of atomic weapons to underground sites.

  1967: The Outer Space Treaty is signed by the United States, the Soviet Union, the United Kingdom, and other nations; it declares that space exploration be conducted for peaceful purposes only and that no nation may claim sovereignty over the moon or any other region of outer space.

  1968: The Nuclear Non-Proliferation Treaty, signed by the United States, the Soviet Union, the United Kingdom, and many other nations, claims that no nation shall aid another nation that does not possess a nuclear arsenal in the development or build up of nuclear weapons.

  1987: The Intermediate Range Nuclear Forces (INF) Treaty is signed between the United States and the Soviet Union, resulting in the dismantling of some 2,600 missiles and granting each side the right to verify and inspect compliance with the terms of the treaty. This is the first treaty to completely dismantle a particular category of nuclear weapons system.

- **1945:** Over the next forty-five years, the build-up of nuclear arms in the context of the Cold War between the United States and the Soviet Union results in an arms race with the potential to result in mutual mass-destruction.

  1947: The term Cold War is first used to charac-

terize the chilly status of international relations between the United States and the Soviet Union.

1962: During the Cuban Missile Crisis, the United States learns that the Soviets have installed nuclear missiles in Cuba. In the course of a diplomatic standoff between President John F. Kennedy and Soviet Premier Nikita Khrushchev, both sides are on the brink of initiating global nuclear warfare. However, Khrushchev backs down, agreeing to remove all nuclear weapons from Cuba in exchange for a United States promise never to invade Cuba.

1972: The Strategic Arms Limitations Talks (SALT), held between the United States and the Soviet Union, result in the signing of the Anti-Ballistic Missile Treaty (ABM). The ABM Treaty places limitations on the build up of weapons designed to destroy incoming nuclear weapons.

1979: SALT II negotiations result in the proposal of a treaty to limit nuclear weapons, but neither side signs the treaty. However, both sides subsequently adhere to the limitations set by the treaty.

1983: President Ronald Reagan announces his proposal for the development of a Strategic Defense Initiative (SDI), which would include the build up of nuclear weaponry in outer space. However, the "Star Wars" initiative remains controversial throughout the 1980s and is essentially abandoned with the break up of the Soviet Union from 1989–1991.

1989–1991: The collapse of the Soviet Union into fifteen independent, sovereign nations effectively ends the Cold War.

1991–1992: The Strategic Arms Reduction Talks (START) between the United States and the Soviet Union resume the SALT I and SALT II negotiations. With the collapse of the Soviet Union and effective end of the Cold War, both sides agree to significant reduction (of 10–15 percent) in their nuclear arsenal by the dismantling of many existing weapons.

United States' possession of an atomic bomb. The Allies had made much progress in defeating Japanese forces in the Pacific theater of war, and, on July 26, a declaration was sent from Potsdam to Japan, calling for unconditional surrender and warning of reprisals if this demand was not met.

As Japan refused to surrender, the United States dropped an atomic bomb on the city of Hiroshima on August 6. Japanese government authorities did not entirely comprehend the degree of devastation caused by the new weapon and did not surrender until a second atomic bomb was dropped on the city of Nagasaki on August 9. On August 10, Japan communicated its acceptance of an unconditional surrender, officially surrendering to the Allies on August 14. On September 9, Japan formalized their surrender to China, thus ending World War II.

Critical Overview

Upon publication, *The Making of the Atomic Bomb* enjoyed both critical acclaim and popular success. Rhodes was rewarded for his years of meticulous research when he won the 1987 National Book Award, the 1988 Pulitzer Prize for General Nonfiction, and the 1988 National Book Critics Circle Award for General Nonfiction.

Critics praise Rhodes for his exhaustive research, comprehensive scope, even-handed reportage, and narrative skills in rendering a nearly overwhelming array of historical information into a dramatic story, successfully integrating clear explanation of complex scientific concepts with a humanizing account of the scientists, military officials, and political figures involved in the Manhattan Project.

Solly Zuckerman, in a 1988 review in the *New Republic,* calls it "a monumental study," and, echoing the widespread praise Rhodes received, asserts:

> Rhodes' book richly deserves the acclaim that it has already been accorded. He has taken infinite trouble to understand and to outline in simple language the principles of nuclear physics that are the foundation on which the story of the bomb rests. The personalities who move through his book come to life in a way that they are unlikely to have done had they been depicted by a scientist's pen.

Zuckerman further observes, "I have no doubt that his book will stand for years to come as an authorita-

tive account of the way our nuclear age started," adding, "Above all, lengthy as it is, it will be enjoyed as a magnificent read."

In addition to his narrative skills, Rhodes is praised for his balanced treatment of controversial subject matter. David Bennett, in *Dictionary of Literary Biography,* notes that *The Making of the Atomic Bomb* "draws much of its strength and vigor from Rhodes' reporting prowess." He observes, "Despite his own feelings about the subject, Rhodes largely remains a dispassionate narrator, an objective historian, never taking sides on the nuclear debate, giving equal space to myriad points of view."

Rhodes' sequel to *The Making of the Atomic Bomb,* entitled *Dark Sun: The Making of the Hydrogen Bomb* (1995), was named one of the best books of 1995 by *Publishers Weekly.* Critical response to *Dark Sun* expresses praise for Rhodes on similar grounds to that of the earlier book. Richard Stengel, in a review in *Time* magazine, calls it "epic and fascinating." A review in *The Economist* states, "Readers of Mr. Rhodes's magnificent *The Making of the Atomic Bomb* . . . could not wish for a better chronicler for the subsequent installment. The insight, learning and narrative skill displayed in that first volume are gathered here again." A reviewer in *Publishers Weekly* expresses the response of many critics to both books by stating, "Rhodes makes history work as drama."

In addition to *The Making of the Atomic Bomb* and *Dark Sun,* Rhodes has written a wide variety of fiction and nonfiction books that demonstrate the broad scope of his research and writing abilities. In 1973, he published *The Ungodly,* a well-researched fictionalized narrative of the Donner Party, a group of Pioneers who, stranded in the mountains by a snowstorm, resorted to cannibalism to survive. *Farm: A Year in the Life of an American Farmer* (1989), was the culmination of a year spent researching the daily activities and financial struggles of a family of farmers. *A Hole in the World: An American Boyhood* (1990) is Rhodes' autobiographical account of the abuse he and his brother experienced as boys. *Nuclear Renewal* (1993) argues for the expanded use of nuclear power plants, which has come to be largely discounted as an unviable energy source. In *How to Write: Advice and Reflections* (1995), Rhodes offers advice to aspiring writers, based on his own experience. *Trying to Get Some Dignity: Stories of Childhood Abuse* (1996), written with third wife Ginger Rhodes, is based on interview material with survivors of childhood abuse.

An atomic cloud during the July 25, 1946, Baker Day blast on Bikini Atoll in the Pacific Islands; the United States conducted nuclear weapons testing between 1946 and 1958 in this area southwest of Hawaii

Criticism

Liz Brent

Brent has a Ph.D. in American Culture, specializing in film studies, from the University of Michigan. She is a freelance writer and teaches courses in the history of American cinema. In the following essay, she discusses themes of anti-Semitism and Jewish identity in Rhodes' account of the making of the first atomic bomb.

Rhodes devotes considerable attention to the impact of anti-Semitism and Jewish identity on the careers of many of the scientists who contributed to the Manhattan Project. Because of the rise of fascism and anti-Semitism in Germany and other parts of Europe during the 1930s, many Jewish scientists fled to England and the United States where they generally found posts at prominent universities. Jewish nuclear physicists who fled Nazism included Niels Bohr, Albert Einstein, Enrico Fermi, Lise Meitner, Leo Szilard, Edward Teller, and Eugene Wigner, all of whose efforts were essential to the creation of the first atomic bomb. As prominent Jewish scientists, many of these men and women had been particularly vulnerable as targets for assassination by Hitler.

The rise of Hitler in Germany had a cataclysmic effect on the lives of many prominent German-Jewish scientists in the years preceding World War II. Hitler came to power as chancellor of Germany in 1933, at which time he immediately initiated anti-Semitic policies, both official and unofficial. Soon after coming into power, Hitler organized a national boycott of Jewish businesses, which was accompanied by random acts of public violence committed against Jews. A week later, the Law for the Restoration of the Professional Civil Service determined that all non-Aryan, particularly Jewish, university faculty were to be fired from their posts. This was a devastating blow to both the Jewish and the scientific communities of Germany. According to Rhodes, some 16,000 university faculty members lost their jobs, including eleven current or future Nobel Prize winners. A third of the faculty of both the University of Berlin and the University of Frankfurt were let go. Over one hundred physicists, fully one fourth of the physicists in Germany, were fired.

Jewish and non-Jewish scientists in England and the United States quickly founded organiza-

What Do I Read Next?

- *Farm: A Year in the Life of an American Farmer* (1989), by Richard Rhodes, is based on the year Rhodes spent chronicling the daily activities and financial struggles of a Missouri farm family.

- *A Hole in the World: An American Boyhood* (1990), by Richard Rhodes, is Rhodes' autobiographical account of the years of abuse he and his brother suffered at the hands of their stepmother.

- *Dark Sun: The Making of the Hydrogen Bomb* (1995), by Richard Rhodes, is Rhodes' celebrated sequel to *The Making of the Atomic Bomb*, in which he chronicles the research leading to the development of the first hydrogen bomb.

- *Picturing the Bomb: Photographs from the Secret World of the Manhattan Project* (1995), by Rachel Fermi and Esther Samra, is a photographic account of the research and testing done by the Manhattan Project during the development of the first atomic bomb.

- *Hiroshima: Why America Dropped the Atomic Bomb* (1995), by Ronald Takaki, is an analysis of the social, political, and historical context of the American decision to drop the first atomic bomb on Hiroshima, Japan.

- *Weapons for Victory: The Hiroshima Decision Fifty Years Later* (1995), by Robert James Maddox, provides a discussion of the impact of the dropping of the first atomic bomb, in 1945, on politics and international relations in the late twentieth century. This book also offers a discussion of the moral and ethical issues raised by the United States decision to drop the bomb on Hiroshima.

---

tions for the specific purpose of aiding German-Jewish scientists fleeing Nazi Germany. Szilard and Rutherford organized the Academic Assistance Council in England. John Dewey in the United States organized the Faculty Fellowship Fund at Colombia University. Similarly, the Institute for International Education organized the Emergency Committee in Aid of Displaced German Scholars in the United States. Britain and the United States, therefore, harbored a majority of the displaced scientists. Rhodes notes that some one hundred Jewish physicists settled in the United States between 1933 and 1941.

By the 1920s, Einstein, living in Berlin, was among the most celebrated physicists alive. As a Jew, his international prominence marked him as a thorn in the side of Nazi Germany. Einstein had become an outspoken and highly regarded figure of Jewish pride. In a tour of the United States in 1921, where he was warmly received by American Jews, he raised money for a Hebrew university in Palestine (now Israel). As Rhodes observes, Einstein ''was now not only the most famous scientist in the world but also a known spokesman for Jewish causes.'' Einstein's outspoken pacifism during World War I added to anti-Semitic prejudices against him on the part of German nationalists. As Rhodes comments, ''It rankled German chauvinists, including rightist students and some physicists, that the eyes of the world should turn to a Jew who had declared himself a pacifist during the bloodiest of nationalistic wars and who spoke out for internationalism now.'' An anti-Jewish organization, the Committee of German Scientists for the Preservation of Pure Scholarship, met publicly to criticize Einstein's theory of relativity as, according to Rhodes, ''a Jewish corruption.'' In the spring of 1933, Einstein, under the impending threat of assassination by Nazi forces, fled Germany and renounced his German citizenship. He was offered a position at Princeton University, in New Jersey, where he remained throughout the rest of his life.

Bohr, a Danish-Jewish physicist, fled his native Copenhagen in 1943, after it was invaded by Hitler. While Hitler wished to ''eliminate'' Danish Jews, the Danish population rallied in support of its Jew-

> As refugees from Nazi Germany, now working at such institutions as Columbia and Princeton Universities, they were in a unique position to meet and discuss the political implications of recent breakthroughs in the field of nuclear physics."

ish inhabitants, successfully hiding many of them from Nazi officials. Bohr and his son, himself a promising physicist, were specifically targeted by Hitler as prominent scientists. They escaped to Sweden, however, where Bohr made efforts to convince Swedish authorities to publicly announce their willingness to harbor Jews escaping Nazi-occupied Denmark. Rhodes points out that "Niels Bohr played a decisive part in the rescue of the Danish Jews." However, even in Stockholm, Bohr was in danger of assassination by German agents and was secretly flown out of the country in a flight during which he almost died from lack of oxygen. Bohr arrived in England in time to join the British team of scientists who traveled to Los Alamos to work on the Manhattan Project.

Meitner, an Austrian born Jewish physicist, became vulnerable to Nazi persecution after Hitler took Austria in 1938, making it a province of the Third Reich. Meitner contacted a colleague in Holland, who arranged with government officials for her entry into Holland without a visa or passport. Traveling by train from Berlin to Holland, Meitner was in fear for her safety; Rhodes quotes Meitner's explanation that "'I knew that the Nazis had just declared open season on Jews, that the hunt was on.'" With Bohr's help, Meitner was given a post at the Physical Institute of the Academy of Sciences in Stockholm, Sweden, and provided with a grant from the Nobel Foundation.

Although Fermi himself was not Jewish, his wife Laura was. In 1938, they began to make plans for fleeing fascist Italy, then occupied by German forces. Fermi took advantage of the opportunity to travel to Sweden in order to accept his Nobel Prize,

cleverly convincing Italian authorities to allow him to bring his wife with him. He had already accepted a position at Colombia University.

Rhodes discusses the noteworthy phenomenon that "seven of the twentieth century's most exceptional scientists" were Hungarian Jews. Among such notable figures were Leo Szilard, Eugene Wigner, and Edward Teller, all of whom were instrumental in the Manhattan Project. Rhodes explains that the Hungarian Revolution of 1918, known as the Red Terror, was put down in 1919 and replaced with a fascist regime known as the White Terror. What resulted was, as Rhodes describes it, "a selective but unrelenting anti-Semitism that drove tens of thousands of Jews into exile." Szilard fled to Vienna in 1933, then on to London in 1934, arriving in the United States in 1937, where he taught at Colombia University. Teller arrived in the United States in 1935, where he took a post at George Washington University, in Washington, D.C. In 1941, he became a U.S. citizen and relocated to the University of Chicago, where he worked with Fermi, then to the University of California at Berkeley, where he worked with Oppenheimer. Wigner, also a refugee from anti-Semitic Hungary, was hired by Princeton in 1930.

As refugees from Nazi Germany, now working at such institutions as Colombia and Princeton Universities, they were in a unique position to meet and discuss the political implications of recent breakthroughs in the field of nuclear physics. Their sense of urgency in attempting to alert the United States government was in part motivated by a realistic fear that German scientists were coming to the same conclusions and that Nazi Germany, if it developed an atomic bomb before the United States, could succeed in dominating Europe, if not the world. In 1939, Szilard and Wigner were the first scientists to make serious efforts to contact the United States government in regard to the idea of the atomic bomb. Together, they visited Einstein at his home in Princeton, where they explained recent developments in nuclear physics and their implications for atomic warfare. Although he had not been aware of these developments, Einstein immediately understood them and agreed to draft a letter to President Roosevelt. As foreigners, however, these brilliant scientists encountered obstacles in their attempts to communicate with American officials. Einstein's written English was not perfect, so he drafted the letter in German for translation into English; but even a letter from the celebrated Einstein was not enough to convince authorities in Washington. Fermi later traveled to Washington to present their findings before a group of military and government officials. However, having recently escaped fascist Italy, he was met with American prejudice when someone announced his arrival by referring to him as a ''wop,'' a derogatory term for an Italian.

Distrust of Jewish foreigners on the part of United States officials persisted even throughout the Manhattan Project. Einstein himself, due to his lifelong commitment to world peace, was considered a security risk and not informed of the existence of the Manhattan Project; he in fact was not made aware of work on the atomic bomb until after the bombing of Hiroshima. Absurdly, Szilard, the most ardent and persistent in his repeated attempts to inform the United States of the importance of the atomic bomb, came under suspicion and was followed by secret agents during the course of the Manhattan Project. Rhodes observes that reports derived from ''the surveillance of an innocent but eccentric man'' were essentially comedic; official reports included such information as the fact that Szilard, a Hungarian Jew, occasionally spoke in a foreign language, that most of his friends were ''of Jewish extraction,'' and that he frequently shopped at delicatessens.

Anti-Semitism and the Jewish identity of many of the world's most brilliant physicists played a significant role in the series of events that led up to the creation of the first atomic bomb. The rise of Nazism in Europe resulted in the emigration of many scientists to the United States and England. The status of these scientists as refugees from the persecution of Hitler's Germany increased their sense of urgency in desiring that the United States create an atomic bomb before German scientists achieved the same end. As foreigners, however, their vocal and ardent devotion to an Allied victory in World War II did not place them above suspicion in the eyes of the United States government.

Source: Liz Brent, Critical Essay on *The Making of the Atomic Bomb,* in *Nonfiction Classics for Students,* The Gale Group, 2001.

Stephen Raymond Patnode

Patnode is an instructor of American history and the history of medicine. In this essay, he evaluates Rhodes' book with regard to the history of science and the relationship of science to society.

Rhodes' *The Making of the Atomic Bomb* is a well-crafted book with prose that is clear, understandable, and very engaging. Indeed, the book is hard to put down at times. No wonder it was received with almost universal critical acclaim and won three major book awards: the National Book Award, the National Book Critics Circle Award, and the Pulitzer Prize. Rhodes gathers a fascinating cast of characters from the past and tells their stories in a lively, captivating style.

However, this focus on individuals is also one of the weak points of the book. In focusing on personalities, Rhodes gives short shrift to the role of culture and institutions in the historical drama that unfolds. For example, he underestimates the significance of the blind faith Americans had in science during the 1930s and 1940s. This has led society to an overly optimistic belief in the redemptive powers of experts, both historically and in the present. In short, Rhodes' book puts an overly optimistic spin on the relationship between science and society.

One of the cultural influences on science that Rhodes does briefly explore is science fiction. Leo Szilard, one of the developers of the bomb and a central actor in the book, was heavily influenced by the work of H. G. Wells. In particular, Szilard was inspired by *The Open Conspiracy,* which refers to Wells' vision of a public trust of science-minded businessmen and financiers who establish a type of global republic. Their mission is nothing less than the salvation of the world. Rhodes continues, ''Szilard appropriated Wells' term and used it off and on for the rest of his life.'' Indeed, Szilard was so inspired by the idea of the ''Open Conspiracy'' that he tried to create one several times (a clear example of science fiction influencing science practitioners).

The theme of the ''Open Conspiracy'' is an important one; it recurs throughout the book and provides an excellent illustration of the hubris of scientists during this period. This points toward the weakest element of the book: Rhodes' uncritical acceptance of the point of view that dominated the physical sciences during the 1940s. Physicists like Szilard and Niels Bohr (another prominent physicist who thought that the atomic bomb would make war obsolete) believed that science could create a better world. Or, as Rhodes puts it, ''discoveries Szilard made in literature and utopianism opened his mind to new approaches to world salvation.'' The literature in question is actually H. G. Wells' *The World Set Free.* According to Szilard, the novel envisions ''the liberation of atomic energy on a large scale for

> **However, this is not to say that all scientists were bent on a monolithic conspiracy to take over the world.''**

industrial purposes, the development of atomic bombs, and a world war.'' In turn, this book informed Szilard's vision of what the agenda for physicists should be.

Even prior to this, Szilard attempted to create an ''Open Conspiracy'' of his own in Germany in the form of *Der Bund,* which Rhodes translates as ''the order, the confederacy or, more simply, the band.'' This group was comprised of young physicists that Szilard organized in 1930. One of the fine things Rhodes does throughout the book is use extensive quotes from primary sources (in other words, the original documents written by the historical actors he is studying). Thus, he quotes Szilard's own ideas regarding the *Bund,* which is meant to be ''a closely knit group of people whose inner bond is pervaded by a religious and scientific spirit.'' Szilard believed that this group should be able to influence public affairs even if it had no formal power. Or perhaps the *Bund* might even ''take over a more direct influence on public affairs as part of the political system, next to government and parliament, or in the place of government and parliament.'' This quote is indicative of the kind of presumption found among many scientists during the 1930s and 1940s and serves as a cautionary flag for the critical reader.

However, this is not to say that all scientists were bent on a monolithic conspiracy to take over the world. In fact, many of the scientists involved in weapons work had deep-seated misgivings about the moral implications of their work. For example, scientist Edward Teller (who was involved with the development of both fission and fusion bombs) had deep reservations about the morality of his work with weapons. Rhodes quotes him, ''To deflect my attention from physics, my full-time job which I liked, to work on weapons, was not an easy matter.'' Indeed, Teller agonized over the decision for ''quite a time.'' Here Rhodes has an opportunity to explore the internal workings of a scientist who is debating

the course that his discipline has charted during the 1930s and 1940s.

Even though Rhodes includes some of this scientific soul-searching, he downplays its significance. For example, he quickly glosses over Teller's dilemma with a brief story about a speech delivered by Franklin Delano Roosevelt to an audience that included the physicist. In the course of this speech, Roosevelt flatly declared that scientists were not responsible for the terrible destruction of the war. In fact, he says, ''What has come about has been caused solely by those who would use, and are using, the progress that you have made along lines of peace in an entirely different cause.'' In effect, Roosevelt was absolving scientists of any guilt and, moreover, insisting it was their duty to develop weapons. Stirred to action, Teller resolved immediately to focus on weapons work. Rhodes quickly moves on to another subject, never having explored the broader implications of Teller's internal dialogue.

In fact, Rhodes seems to ignore the fact that several of the individuals he discusses actually laid the foundation for the much larger critiques of science that emerged during the latter half of the twentieth century. For example, regarding James B. Conant (a chemist and president of Harvard who was involved with the development of the atomic bomb as well as chemical weapons in World War I), Rhodes simply remarks, ''[He] was a patriot who believed in the application of advanced technology to war.'' This assertion ignores the fact that Conant was directly linked to some of the biggest critics of twentieth century science.

Specifically, Conant helped found one of the programs at Harvard that gave rise to the suspicion of science that followed World War II. As James G. Hershberg recounts in the biography *James B. Conant: Harvard to Hiroshima and the Making of the Nuclear Age,* Conant began teaching a course at Harvard in the early 1940s that was intended for nonscientists and emphasized the ''cultural, intellectual, and political contexts of major advances in scientific knowledge and theory.'' This course led to ''thoughtful criticism'' and became the training ground for preeminent historians of science like Thomas S. Kuhn.

In turn, Thomas Kuhn gained notoriety for his book *The Structure of Scientific Revolutions,* which suggested that science was not as objective as previously thought. Rather, Kuhn argues that scientific achievements are framed by the cultural circumstances that produce them, suggesting that scientific "truth" is far more relative than previously believed. In other words, science is not merely scientific but always has a cultural and political dimension to it as well. If this is the case, then do people need to accept scientific assertions as absolute truth, or are they open to interpretation as products of the culture that created them? This is a shortcoming in Rhodes' book: he disregards the critics of science who have spent the last fifty years questioning the validity of scientific claims and examining the moral implications of scientific achievements like the atomic bomb.

Rhodes' unquestioning acceptance of the scientific worldview comes across most clearly in the epilogue of his book. He notes, "Science is sometimes blamed for the nuclear dilemma." However, he insists this criticism is misplaced. "[Physicists] Otto Hahn and Fritz Strassmann did not invent nuclear fission; they discovered it." Here and elsewhere, Rhodes completely accepts the scientific worldview—the idea that the universe is a static system governed by universal laws that scientists simply need to discover. For example, he asserts that sometimes even other scientists have a hard time remembering that nuclear bombs were developed "not only as weapons of terrible destruction. They were also, as [Italian physicist Enrico] Fermi once said, 'superb physics.'" In this respect, Rhodes presents a very utilitarian interpretation of history, which holds that the events of the twentieth century were preordained.

Again, this completely discounts the importance of the cultural milieu and historical events that framed the "discovery" of the atomic bomb. The discovery of nuclear fission cannot possibly be removed from the events that surrounded it—namely, World War II. These developments were intrinsically linked to the armed conflict. The war framed nuclear fission as a weapon, a tool for total war. Without the conflict, fission may very well have been conceived as an industrial power source; or conversely, it might never have advanced beyond the planning stages because of a lack of initiative from the government and universities that developed it. However, Rhodes' acceptance of the scientific worldview extends beyond simply repeating what the historical actors in his book said.

Rhodes concludes the book by echoing Leo Szilard's ideas regarding the Open Conspiracy. He posits that the dominant organization of political power in the world today, the nation-state, has become nothing but a "death machine." The only

Neils Bohr, a Danish physicist

thing that can resist this organization is the "republic of science." This refers to the larger scientific community, which is "founded on openness" and is "international in scope." For two hundred years, these two systems, the nation-state and the republic of science, coexisted. But then, Rhodes concludes, "In 1945 science became the first living organic structure strong enough to challenge the nation-state itself." The liberation of nuclear energy brought these two systems into direct opposition—science finally produced a weapon that was so terrible, war was no longer possible. Consequently, the nation-state could no longer use war as a means of settling disputes. In other words, the republic of science was the only thing that could save the world from the "death machine" of the modern nation-state by forming an Open Conspiracy of its own.

Rhodes expands this argument, implying that the scientists who invented the nuclear bomb were the true American patriots. He asserts that the intention of the American Revolution was to create an open society. This vision of utopia was not unlike the one that physicist Niels Bohr proposed with his "open world." Bohr believed that the coming of the atomic bomb meant the existing political order of the 1940s would have to be replaced with one based on diplomacy and mutual security. Bohr's "open

> **This failure to recognize the revolutionary nature of the new weapons, against which there is no protection except massive retaliation, Rhodes concludes, misled the politicians and brought us to today's confrontational world."**

world" can be read as another inflection of the idea Szilard borrowed from Wells: the Open Conspiracy.

Rhodes goes on to suggest that the American Revolution and Bohr's "open world" have much in common, "in part because the framers of that revolution and the founders of the republic of science drew from a common body of Enlightenment ideas." The Enlightenment refers to an eighteenth century philosophical movement, which argued that the methods of natural science could be used to discover the laws of nature and human cultures in the interest of creating better societies. By this reasoning, the scientists who invented the bomb were the true patriots; the politicians who stymied their vision of the open world were, in fact, traitors to America's founding fathers.

The problem with this interpretation of history has to do with the distinction that Rhodes draws between the nation-state and the republic of science. Again, science cannot be analyzed apart from its cultural context. In other words, the distinction between science and politics represents a false dichotomy. They are not mutually opposed to one another. Rather, they both form part of a larger process of power relations in American society. Indeed, Rhodes even hints at this himself, noting at one point that "industrial technology and applied science enormously amplified the nation-state's power." Rhodes tries to draw a distinction between two social institutions that cannot be separated.

In conclusion, Richard Rhodes has written a fine book. He makes excellent use of primary sources, has synthesized a vast amount of material, and writes about his subjects with a lively, engaging style. Unfortunately, the focus on individuals is a weak point of the book. It serves to reinforce the beliefs of the scientists that he studies. Rhodes neither offers a critical reflection on the role of science in society nor explores the moral dilemmas of the atomic bomb with sufficient depth. In other words, Rhodes ends up endorsing the scientific worldview of the 1940s without considering the subsequent decades of scholarship that have called it into question. This is the only substantial shortcoming in an otherwise excellent book.

Source: Stephen Raymond Patnode, Critical Essay on *The Making of the Atomic Bomb,* in *Nonfiction Classics for Students,* The Gale Group, 2001.

Zuoyue Wang

In the following review, Wang calls The Making of the Atomic Bomb *"a most up-to-date and surely most readable version of the exciting story."*

This Pulitzer and National Book Prize-winning work (for 1987) by Richard Rhodes is an exceptionally well-written account of the building and use of the first nuclear weapons. Rhodes presents an extensive historical exploration of the scientific and political background to the bomb that focuses on people—the scientists, engineers, and administrators. He synthesizes a large amount of material, most of it published, and ably weaves various lines of development together to render a most up-to-date and surely most readable version of the exciting story.

Starting with Ernest Rutherford's 1911 discovery of the atomic nucleus, the first third of the book is mostly devoted to the history of nuclear physics before World War II. By narrating the milestone events in the field up to the discovery of nuclear fission in 1938, Rhodes does more than provide the necessary scientific framework within which the bomb was created. Scientists' faith in and practice of openness are well illustrated. Scientists are also shown interacting far beyond their national boundaries. Making full use of biographies, Rhodes introduces prominent scientists such as Niels Bohr, Leo Szilard, Albert Einstein, Werner Heisenberg, James Chadwick, Enrico Fermi, Otto Hahn, J. Robert Oppenheimer, Ernest Lawrence, Edward Teller, and many others, when he describes their discoveries. These men eventually became the central figures in the atomic bomb projects on the two sides of World War II.

The American efforts apparently originated in "the Hungarian Conspiracy" led by Szilard. Always concerned about the fate of the world, Szilard, in the days after fission's discovery, was alarmed by the possibility of an atomic bomb and particularly of its being in Nazi hands first. Together with Eugene Wigner and Teller, two fellow Hungarian refugee scientists, he went to see Einstein to encourage him to write what became the famous letter that brought the matter to President Roosevelt's attention. Although given some support in 1939, for bureaucratic and technical reasons the bomb project did not receive full impetus until 1941. Then, a more optimistic feasibility report on the bomb from Britain reached America, and Pearl Harbor brought the nation into war. Thereafter, under the general administration of Vannevar Bush, James Conant, and, more directly, General Leslie Groves, by 1945 the Manhattan Project succeeded, and Hiroshima and Nagasaki were devastated.

Though few engineers are named in the book, engineering was largely at the center of the project. Oppenheimer headed the Los Alamos Laboratory, where the bombs were designed and tested. The problems his people faced, highlighted well by the author, were at least as much technological as scientific. Ordnance experts, applied mathematicians, and engineers from numerous fields worked alongside physicists to understand and perfect the mechanism of implosion.

Industrialists were also an important part of the story. Production of bomb-quality uranium-235 and plutonium meant much more than merely an enlargement of laboratory-size apparatus. It figuratively demanded no less than "turning the whole country into a factory," as predicted by Bohr. Du Pont, Kellex, Union Carbide, and many other industrial giants built plants in Oak Ridge, Tennessee, and Hanford, Washington, under the Army Corps of Engineers. In fact, the Hanford plutonium project was the largest plant Du Pont had ever constructed and operated.

Although this impressive achievement testified to the effectiveness of the collaboration between science and government, Rhodes hardly ignores any of the clashes between the two. Barbed wire at Los Alamos disgusted Edward Condon, a prominent physicist. For questioning the hierarchical structure and military control of the project, and Groves's "compartmentalization" policy, Szilard was almost interned by the general. He was, in any case, under continuous army surveillance. So was Oppenheimer, because of his prewar connection with left-wing organizations. Bohr came close to the same position. He tried to convince Roosevelt

and Winston Churchill of both the great danger and the opportunity the new bomb would bring to the world and urged them to consider international control of nuclear weapons. Churchill, suspicious of Bohr's activities, warned his advisers that "Bohr ought to be confined" to avoid "leakage of information particularly to the Russians." Rhodes highlights these instances to illustrate one of his themes, that "democratic" science conflicts with the "authoritarian" nation-state.

The military use of the atomic bomb also troubled a good many scientists working on the project. When the bombs were nearly ready, Truman's advisers, the Interim Committee, decided to drop them on Japanese cities. While the scientific consultants to this committee saw no other options, a group of Chicago scientists, including Szilard, disagreed. Led by James Franck, they produced the Franck Report, which surprisingly is not mentioned in the book, and suggested a nonmilitary demonstration of the bomb to better the chance for postwar international agreement on the control of nuclear weapons. But the bombs were dropped, and the nuclear arms race was under way.

There was never any serious questioning of the bomb's use on moral grounds. Atrocities in warfare since World War I, so keenly described by Rhodes, had "the long grave already dug." The use of chemical gases and bombing of civilians terrified people. But the Holocaust in the Nazi concentration camps, the Hamburg, Dresden, and Tokyo firebombings, and the December 1937 massacre of Nanjing where Japanese troops killed 300,000 Chinese, all emphatically proclaimed the darker nature of modern warfare. The apt adoption by all belligerents of new military technologies and the strategy of attrition war prepared the stage for the use of atomic weapons. It was merely a "bigger" bomb, as Churchill and many others saw it.

This failure to recognize the revolutionary nature of the new weapons, against which there is no protection except massive retaliation, Rhodes concludes, misled the politicians and brought us to today's confrontational world. The way out of the problem is to negotiate an open world with nuclear arms under international control. This, Rhodes argues, is a direct consequence of science's challenge to the traditional power of nation-states.

Source: Zuoyue Wang, Review of *The Making of the Atomic Bomb,* in *Technology and Culture,* Vol. 30, No. 4, 1989, pp. 1078–1081.

Sources

Bennett, David, *Dictionary of Literary Biography,* Volume 185: *American Literary Journalists, 1945–1995, First Series,* Gale Research, 1997, pp. 241–252.

Hershberg, James G., and James B. Conant, *Harvard to Hiroshima and the Making of the Nuclear Age,* Stanford University Press, 1993.

Review in *The Economist,* Vol. 337, No. 7935, October 7, 1995, p. 99.

Review in *Publishers Weekly,* Vol. 242, No. 40, October 2, 1995, p. 40.

Rhodes, Richard, *The Making of the Atomic Bomb*, Simon and Schuster, 1986

Stengel, Richard, Review in *Time,* Vol. 146, No. 8, August 21, 1995, p. 66.

Zuckerman, Solly, Review in *The New Republic,* Vol. 199, No. 8, August 22, 1988, p. 38.

Further Reading

Allen, Thomas B., and Norman Polmar, *Code-Name Downfall: The Secret Plan to Invade Japan and Why Truman Dropped the Bomb,* Simon & Schuster, 1995.
    Allen and Polmar discuss United States military strategy in respect to President Truman's decision to drop the atomic bomb on Hiroshima.

Alperovitz, Gar, *The Decision to Use the Atomic Bomb and the Architecture of an American Myth,* Knopf, 1995.
    Alperovitz presents a critical historical perspective on the United States military strategy and international relations with the Allied nations during World War II in respect to the dropping of the atomic bomb on Hiroshima.

Larsen, Rebecca, *Oppenheimer and the Atomic Bomb,* F. Watts, 1988.
    Larsen provides a biography of Robert J. Oppenheimer, a leading scientist in the Manhattan Project, which developed the first atomic bomb.

Lifton, Robert Jay, and Greg Mitchell, *Hiroshima in America: Fifty Years of Denial,* Putnam, 1995.
    Lifton and Mitchell discuss the moral and ethical implications of the ways in which the bombing of Hiroshima has been represented in American history.

Rhodes, Richard, *Deadly Feasts: Tracking the Secrets of a Terrifying New Plague*, Simon & Schuster, 1997.
    Rhodes discusses the potential threat to humans from a category of infectious diseases known as "mad cow disease" in its bovine form.

———, *How to Write: Advice and Reflections*, Morrow, 1995.
    Rhodes offers advice to the aspiring writer, based on his personal experience as a journalist, novelist, and nonfiction writer.

———, ed., *Visions of Technology: A Century of Vital Debate About Machines, Systems, and the Human World,* Simon & Schuster, 1999.
    Visions of Technology provides a collection of articles that address the social, historical, and ethical impact of various technological developments throughout the twentieth century.

Rhodes, Richard, and Ginger Rhodes, *Trying to Get Some Dignity: Stories of Triumph Over Childhood Abuse,* W. Morrow, 1996.
    Rhodes and Rhodes compiled *Trying to Get Some Dignity* using interviews with adult survivors of childhood abuse.

My Brother

Jamaica Kincaid

1997

Many readers and critics had long suspected that Jamaica Kincaid's fiction was highly autobiographical, and the publication of *My Brother*, which was nominated for a National Book Award for nonfiction, confirmed those suspicions. Ostensibly inspired by the death of her younger brother Devon Drew from AIDS in 1996, this memoir is most striking for the way that Kincaid presents her own memories and thoughts about her family in light of this tragedy. While her relationship to Devon, who was just three when Kincaid left Antigua in 1966, is important to the book, it's her corrosive and wounded relationship to her mother that readers will remember.

My Brother has been widely praised, and occasionally criticized, for its striking style. Kincaid's sentences are full of short blunt words, but they're intricately constructed, often circling back on themselves in such a way that they mimic the disorderly way that human beings recall their most unsettling memories. Another hallmark of the book is its disarming honesty. Kincaid doesn't shy away from difficult feelings, anger chief among them. Devon's unhappy life is, Kincaid believes, the one she might have lived had she not left Antigua for The United States. Anna Quindlen, writing in the *New York Times,* observes: "Ultimately that is what that memoir is about, about the chasm between the self we might have been and the one that we have somehow, often inexplicably, become. It is about leaving, and leaving people behind, about being a stranger in your own home, to your own family."

Author Biography

In *My Brother*, Kincaid's memoir of the illness and subsequent death of her youngest brother, Devon Drew, many details of her own history emerge. Kincaid has three younger halfbrothers, and the four siblings have all struggled with their difficult mother. Three years after Devon was born, Kincaid left Antigua to live in the United States. The event that precipitates this memoir is the death of Devon on January 19, 1996, at the age of thirty-three. He died of AIDS.

Because *My Brother* is an unconventional memoir, other biographical facts are not revealed. Kincaid was born on May 25, 1949, in St. Johns, Antigua, and was named Elaine Potter Richardson. In 1966, Kincaid immigrated to the United States to be a live-in babysitter for a family in Scarsdale, New York, a job she's told interviewers should be rightfully called "servant." Later, she worked as an au pair for a family in New York City. During these years, Kincaid took classes at Westchester Community College and studied photography at the New School for Social Research. In 1973, she changed her name to Jamaica Kincaid, choosing the new name because *Jamaica* evoked the Caribbean, and *Kincaid,* a name she says she borrowed from a George Bernard Shaw piece, went well with Jamaica; the new name, she says, gave her the freedom to write without worrying about her family's reaction.

While living in New York, Kincaid befriended George Trow, a *New Yorker* columnist who began to quote her observations in the magazine and later helped her get her own work published in the "Talk of the Town" section in the magazine. In 1983, Kincaid published her first book, a collection of short fiction entitled *At the Bottom of the River*; it was immediately hailed as an important work of literature.

A devotee and close friend of former *New Yorker* editor William Shawn, Kincaid, in 1979, married his son, Allen Shawn, a composer and Bennington College professor. The pair live in North Bennington, Vermont, with their two children, Annie and Harold. Kincaid was a longtime staff writer for the *New Yorker* but quit in 1995 after a much-publicized feud with former editor Tina Brown. Kincaid criticized the magazine for treating celebrities and pop culture too reverently. Although Kincaid is often described as "angry," in 1997 she told *Mother Jones* magazine that "whatever I say in my writing, in my personal life I'm really incredibly lucky. I suppose that's what gives me the freedom to express negatives."

Summary

Part I

Kincaid sets the pace for the nonlinear story she tells in the opening paragraph when she describes first visiting Devon in the Gweneth O'Reilly ward of the Holberton Hospital, where he was said to be dying of AIDS; she then skips immediately to the circumstances of his birth. The ostensible connection between these thoughts is tenuous at best: Devon is the only one of Kincaid's mother's four children who was not born in a hospital. The logic of this leap makes increasing sense as the reader learns to follow Kincaid's idiosyncratic and winding thought processes.

Kincaid describes having distanced herself from her family only to have been drawn back into their orbit by her brother's illness. She reminisces about her family, especially her mother, discussing everything from her mother's dislike of her daughter's faculty for remembering to her mother's skill at gardening. She talks of the sorry state of health care in Antigua, the dirtiness of the Holberton Hospital, and the isolation of AIDS patients. At one point, Kincaid thinks that something good has come of Devon's illness: it's made her realize she loves him. She tells Devon of her love, and he responds in kind.

Kincaid procures the AIDS drug AZT for Devon, and he soon begins to recover and eventually leaves the hospital. But wellness is not a perfectly happy state for him. While Devon was hospitalized, his oldest brother, Joe, moved into his house. Devon returns home to live with his mother, sharing a bed with her. Kincaid also learns that Devon is having unprotected sex with a woman who doesn't know of his disease and that he is drinking beer every night. This section ends as Kincaid learns that her brother is once again ill.

Part II

The opening words of this section summarize what's to come: "My brother died." And yet Devon does not die in the simple terms that Kincaid first suggests with that three-word sentence. Instead, his death is relived many times, from different perspectives. First, Kincaid describes the last time she saw her brother alive. She then recalls the moment that she learns he has died. Having returned home from a trip to Miami, she checks on her sleeping children, Harold and Annie, and they ask her to climb into bed with them and snuggle. She falls asleep, and in the morning, her husband wakes her and tells her that Devon has died. Kincaid's first response is to be relieved that the grieving is hers, not his, because she loves her husband dearly and would prefer to be in pain than to worry about his suffering.

Once again, Kincaid circles back to the last time she saw Devon alive, recalling that she didn't kiss him goodbye. At that moment, she felt anger, and "my anger was everything to me, and in my anger lay many things, mostly made up of feelings I could not understand . . ." This mention of anger leads her to a discussion of her mother and the still fresh anger she feels toward her. She then relates the defining story of her relationship to her mother. At fifteen, Kincaid was asked to baby-sit for Devon. Instead of watching the two year old, she spends the day reading, allowing Devon's dirty diaper to go unchanged. The sight of this neglect so enrages Kincaid's mother that she sets fire to Kincaid's most prized possessions: her books.

As is typical of this book, many of the stories are told aslant. Before hearing of Devon's funeral, the reader learns of the funeral of a four-year-old child whose mother vomits thin liquid at the horror of his death. Later, instead of confronting Devon's homosexuality directly (which can't be done; the fact is learned third hand through an Antiguan woman who approaches Kincaid in the United States after he has died), Kincaid writes about Freeston, an openly gay man who feels it's his duty to speak of having the HIV virus but is reviled for his honesty.

Perhaps because grief is irrational and sometimes incoherent, Kincaid's story becomes even more disjointed after Devon's death. Kincaid learns that as Devon was dying, he called out for all the members of his family but not for his sister. His last word is "Styles," his nickname for his brother Joe, the one he didn't get along with as an adult.

The penultimate scene is Devon's funeral. At the funeral, Kincaid is displeased with the minister's sermon. When the minister suggests that the family will be reunited after death, she thinks that

Jamaica Kincaid

she'd rather not see any of these people again. She then discusses how she is writing about her brother's death in order to understand it, how writing has been her salvation. And she ends this memoir on a very personal note, describing how she wrote for William Shawn, the editor of the *New Yorker,* a man she calls "the perfect reader." Although Mr. Shawn has died, she continues to write for him.

Key Figures

Annie Drew

In this portrait of Kincaid's mother, there's one central and shocking truth that Kincaid revisits many times: "my mother hates her children." In an interview in the *Boston Globe*, Kincaid said, "Mother loves us best when we are dying. We need her. It's when we're walking around that she's critical of us. When we're thriving." In an interview in *Salon* Kincaid says that the core of her novel *The Autobiography of My Mother* is "drawn from an observation I've about my own mother: That all her children are quite happy to have been born, but all of us are quite sure she should never have been a mother."

Media Adaptations

- *My Brother* was adapted into an audio book performed by Jamaica Kincaid. The audio book runs for 360 minutes and was published by Penguin Audiobooks.

Capable of deep maternal devotion, Annie Drew cares for Devon tirelessly and with great tenderness when he is ill. Likewise, Kincaid recalls that when she was a child with a clogged nose, her mother would suck the mucus from her nostrils, and, when eating felt too tiring, her mother would chew her daughter's food and then return it to her mouth. Drew possesses the traits of a maternal woman; she is a gardener with a knack for growing all sorts of vegetables and herbs.

Although occasionally kind, Annie Drew's cruelty is what strikes the reader most forcefully. When Kincaid is struggling to become a writer in New York City, her mother's words are typically harsh: "It serves you right, you are always trying to do things you know you can't do." Not only is she capable of blistering cruelty, but Annie Drew is a woman who refuses to apologize for her actions, nor will she ever subordinate herself to anyone. Kincaid's brothers live with their mother, not vice versa, because she would never allow herself to be in the position of living with anyone. Drew has so enraged her grown children that neither Jamaica nor Dalma, who lives with his mother, will eat any food she's prepared. Dalma and Devon until he becomes ill refuse to call Annie Drew "mother," instead calling her "Mrs. Drew." Dalma believes his mother is evil and will not speak to her. Once when Joseph, the oldest of the three brothers, dated a woman against his mother's wishes, Annie Drew was so furious that she threw stones at him.

When Kincaid returns to Antigua after having spent twenty years distancing herself from her family, she looks at a soursop tree that is now nothing more than a charred trunk. Kincaid's mother says that the tree became the home of a colony of parasitic insects and to rid herself of the insects, she burned down the tree. Kincaid attributes this easy way with destruction to her mother's powerful sense of herself. She sees her mother as a tyrant. "It's possible that in another kind of circumstance the shape of the world might have been altered by her presence. But this woman, my mother, had only four people to make into human beings."

Dalma Drew

Dalma is the middle brother, and he is eleven years younger than Kincaid. In contrast to Devon, who was careless with his life and health, Dalma is industrious. At the time of Devon's death, Dalma held down three jobs: accountant, peddler of imported foods, and bass steel-drum player in the most prominent steel band in Antigua. Yet for all his hard work, Dalma must live with his mother, a woman whom he describes as evil and to whom he no longer speaks. He refuses to eat anything his mother has cooked, and he refers to her as "Mrs. Drew," not "mother."

Devon Drew

Born at home on May 5, 1962, Devon Drew was intelligent, well-read, athletic, and deeply troubled. Kincaid is frank about his shortcomings. At age fourteen, Devon was involved in a gas station robbery in which the attendant was murdered; Devon testified against his friends, and his mother used her political connections to reduce his sentence, but he still spent time in jail. As an adult, he lived as a Rastafarian, a religious group whose members view Africa, and especially Ethiopia, as the promised land. Devon also used marijuana and cocaine, had many sexual partners, both men and women, and stole from his mother and brother Joe.

Despite his many failings, Devon was deeply charming. Kincaid sees him as a brilliant man who would have spoken to the world in an important way. Although Devon appreciates what Kincaid says about him, he can neither act on nor even fully imagine her vision of him:

> But he was not even remotely aware of such a person inside him. It is I who told him this and he agreed with me at the moment I told him this, and he said yes, and I saw that he wished what I said were really true, would just become true, wished he could, wished he knew how to make the effort and make it true. He could not. In his daydreams he became a famous singer, and women removed their clothes when they heard him sing.

Above all, Kincaid sees her brother Devon as a dreamer, an observer, and a man who never fully knew himself. For the reader, Devon is a disturbing figure. When his AIDS virus goes into remission, Devon becomes convinced he's been cured, and he resumes sexual relations without using adequate protection. After Devon dies, Kincaid learns that her brother was probably a homosexual, a man who couldn't admit his own sexual inclinations to his family and friends in Antigua.

Joseph Drew

The oldest of the three brothers, Joe, is an electrician. Devon nicknamed him "Styles" because he is meticulous about how he dresses. Once, after his mother became irrationally angry at him and began to stone him, he threw her to the ground and broke her neck.

Jamaica Kincaid

Jamaica Kincaid, the narrator of *My Brother*, is an Antiguan who left home as a teenager and is compelled to return only when she learns her much younger brother is dying of AIDS. Because of her geographical distance, Kincaid can understand and comment upon the Antiguans and the family members she left behind. She is now a successful writer in the United States, happily married with a husband, two children, and a garden, and she's put so much distance between herself and her past that she can barely understand the Antiguan patois that her family speaks. Equally, they find her diction either funny or incomprehensible.

Because Kincaid is the narrator of this story, her character traits tend to emerge by inference. Readers know that she has an exceptional memory, a faculty that she feels her family, especially her mother, resents. "This is what my family, the people I grew up with, hate about me. I always say, Do you remember?" As a child, Kincaid's memory was a source of pride to her mother, but as she grew up, it became an irritant. Kincaid speculates that her mother hates her daughter's ability to remember because Kincaid recalls unpleasant things that her mother wants forgotten.

Kincaid is an enormously honest narrator, one who doesn't shy away from confronting contradictions and even perversities in her own personality. For instance, she both enjoys her role as healer, the successful family member who can now afford the AIDS drug, AZT, while feeling weighed down by the responsibilities she's assumed. Nor is Kincaid afraid to articulate the negative feelings she harbors. Kincaid tells us that she wishes her brother would die and be done with it. When she returns to the United States, she feels relief, but she also admits, "I missed him. I missed seeing him suffer." One way that Kincaid and Devon are alike is that both are dreamers; she describes Devon as an observer, a man who likes events best when they ask nothing of him, and this description fits Kincaid as well. That the illness of her brother forces her to become an active participant in her brother's tragedy is apparently the source of some of her anger.

Finally, Kincaid is deeply curious about people and their motives, eagerly delving into her brother's life and death, so that she can better understand herself. Kincaid wonders what her own life would have been like, "if I had not been so cold and ruthless in regard to my own family, acting only in favor of myself when I was a young woman." In that way, there's yet another source of kinship with Devon, who acts on his own sexual urges despite his highly contagious disease.

Dr. Prince Ramsey

Dr. Ramsey is a figure of Antiguan possibility, and his goodness stands in contrast to most of the other islanders. He is, for instance, punctual, something Kincaid says that most Antiguans are not. "He was something I had long ago thought impossible to find in an Antiguan with authority: he was kind, he was loving toward people who needed him, people who were less powerful than he; he was respectful."

Allen Shawn

Kincaid tells us that she loves her husband deeply and that he's a man who "takes suffering too seriously, too hard."

Mr. William Shawn

The fabled editor of the *New Yorker* was Kincaid's mentor. She says she was driven to write because she loved his praise. Knowing Mr. Shawn would read her work made writing worthwhile. Kincaid describes Mr. Shawn, as she calls him, as having been curious about things that he would not have wanted to know about. She envisions him as the person she writes for: the perfect reader.

Topics for Further Study

- Research how Antigua became independent from British rule and discuss the implications of that event for the modern-day Antigua of Kincaid's memoir.

- Kincaid never discusses psychology explicitly, but she is clearly interested in the mother-daughter dynamic. Research what psychologists say about children separating from their mothers and apply it to the feelings Kincaid harbors toward her mother.

- Up until very recently, people suffering from AIDS in the United States didn't want to discuss their disease publicly. Research how attitudes toward people with AIDS have changed, concentrating on how legal protection against discrimination of people suffering from this disease has helped change attitudes.

- Consider how *My Brother* differs from more conventionally structured family memoirs. Ask yourself why Kincaid chose to arrange her story the way she did.

- Kincaid describes at length how encountering the Antiguan woman from her AIDS support group and learning that Devon was a practicing homosexual was not like the falling and breaking of a miniature water-filled glass dome that is associated with childhood. Why does Kincaid use the metaphor of the glass dome in such a contradictory fashion?

Themes

Anger

Anger is a recurring theme in both Kincaid's feelings toward her family and toward Antigua, the country of her birth. Kincaid reflects on her own anger, admitting that anger often manifests itself in small transactions. When Devon asks Kincaid to go for a walk alone with him, she suspects that he'll ask her for something of hers and that she'll resent the request. She remembers how Devon had once asked her for the khaki shorts she was wearing and can articulate why the request annoyed her: "I did not like giving them to him at all. I did not want them back, I wanted not to have had to give them in the first place."

In Kincaid's family, quarreling is a way of life. One family member often stops talking to another, and these angry silences take on a life of their own. At one point, Kincaid identifies her own mother as "his mother," meaning Devon's mother, noting that "she is my mother, too, but I wasn't talking to her then, and when I am not talking to her, she is someone else's mother, not mine." After Devon temporarily recovers, she remembers, "He and my mother had huge quarrels and unforgivable things were said, but after the quarrels were over, they would both feel that everything said had not really been meant." Anger has its own rules in Kincaid's family, and people who have done and said terrible things can also be unexpectedly loving.

Mothers and Motherhood

Closely linked to the theme of anger are issues of mothering and its aftereffects. Kincaid says that the extraordinary thing about her mother's love for her children is its ability "to turn into a weapon for their destruction." Critics have observed that Kincaid's fascination with mother-daughter relationships stems from her preoccupation with colonialism, which is essentially the coercive and quasi-parental relationship of one nation toward another. In *A Small Place*, Kincaid spoke of the English people who colonized Antigua in terms that would also have described her mother's parenting style: "no natural disaster imaginable could equal the harm they did."

Although Kincaid is unequivocal in her harsh portrayal of her mother, she understands that the role of mother must almost, by definition, inspire negative feelings from time to time. Kincaid talks about how her son loves her and hates her, and how this is necessary and right: "This state of profound contradiction, loving me and hating me, is what will be for the rest of his life, if I am a good mother to him. This is the best that it can be. If I should fail him—and I very well might, the prime example I have is not a good one—he will experience something everlastingly bitter and awful: I know this, the taste of this awfulness, this bitterness, is in my mouth every day."

Gardening

Gardening is one link connecting Kincaid with her mother. Kincaid recognizes that her own love of gardening, as does Devon's, springs from her mother. "What would my brother say were he to be asked how he became interested in growing things? He saw our mother doing it. What else?"

Throughout, gardening is Kincaid's metaphor for nurturing. When she talks of Freeston, the Antiguan who openly acknowledges that he has AIDS, the harmony of his family is apparent in the flourishing houseplants: "he lived with [his mother] in a house with a beautiful garden full of zinnias and cosmos and some impatiens and all sorts of shrubs with glossy and variegated leaves." Yet the gardening metaphor is most effective and poignant when Kincaid uses it to describe Devon: "in his life there had been no flowering, his life was the opposite of that, a flowering, his life was like the bud that sets but, instead of opening into a flower, turns brown and falls off at your feet."

Sex and sexuality

Gardening can be equated with nurturing, but it also is a link to Kincaid's themes of birth, death, and sexuality. Sexuality is central to this memoir because Devon has contracted a fatal disease through his own undisclosed sexual activities. One of the discoveries Kincaid finds most disturbing about her brother Devon is that even though he has a fatal disease that's transmitted through sexual contact, he continues to have sex with women, without first informing them he has AIDS. Devon is not particularly concerned about the danger to which he exposes his sexual partners; his rationale for his irresponsible behavior is "that he could not live without sex, that if he went without sex for too long he began to feel funny." His attitude seems consistent with prevailing views in Antigua. There, men who attend Dr. Ramsey's lectures on AIDS leave and go imme-

diately to the section of town where the prostitutes are found. It's well known that a majority of these women ("butter women" they're called because they're from Santo Domingo and have light skin) are HIV positive. The men cavalierly tell Dr. Ramsey that "they would rather die than leave the butter women alone."

Like other subjects, sexuality is not simple to Kincaid. She is frank about her own interest in sex: "on the whole I like to know whom people have sex with, and a description of it I find especially interesting. My own life, from a sexual standpoint, can be described as a monument to boring conventionality. And so perhaps because of this I have a great interest in other people's personal lives." Yet for all her desire to glean facts about her brother's sexual past, she doesn't learn the truth until after Devon's death, when she's told that he sometimes had sex with other men.

Style

Diction

The diction of each family member is revealing. Kincaid's writing is formal, almost distant, and her carefully constructed sentences stand in direct contrast to the casual island diction of her mother and brothers. Devon speaks in an island dialect by which AIDS is always referred to as "de chupidness." Kincaid can no longer readily understand her brother—she's always asking him to repeat himself—and he finds her way of speaking comical.

Metaphor

Diction is one metaphor for what separates Kincaid from the family in which she was raised. There's also a sense in which the cruelty of Kincaid's childhood has now manifested itself as adult sickness, a physical metaphor for the psychological pain she and her brothers experience. Not only has Devon become fatally ill, but after Kincaid's mother visits her in the United States, she recalls, "I was sick for three months. I had something near to a nervous breakdown, I suffered from anxiety and had to take medicine to treat it; I got the chicken pox, which is a disease of childhood and a disease I had already had when I was a child."

In Kincaid's memoir, metaphor sometimes leads in unexpected directions. When Kincaid learns that her brother was probably a closet homosexual, she sees his life as a flower that failed to bloom, the bud becoming brown and dropping off at her feet. And here, the failure of metaphor to carry her readers to its logical end haunts her. ''But the feeling that his life with its metaphor of the bud of a flower firmly set, blooming, and then the blossom fading, the flower setting a seed which bore inside another set of buds, leading to flowers, and so on and so on into eternity—this feeling that his life actually should have provided such a metaphor, so ordinary an image, so common and so welcoming had it been just so, could not leave me . . .''

Although Kincaid uses metaphor throughout this memoir, she's also distrustful of the potential for using the device to reach overwrought or incorrect conclusions. When Kincaid hears the opening of the zipper on the bag that contains her dead brother Devon, she compares it to a dangerous reptile announcing its presence.

Style

Here's how Anna Quindlen describes Kincaid's writing style in a 1997 *New York Times* review of *My Brother*: ''The stylistic ground she covers in this book is also recognizable from her past work, the endless incantatory sentences a contrast to the simple words and images—a tower built of small bricks.''

Kincaid's style is consistent both with a rigorous search for truth and an acknowledgement that the truth can never be known. As Kincaid repeatedly tells the reader things they take for granted—that Kincaid's husband is the father of her children, that Kincaid's mother is the mother of her brothers—she makes the point that there are no givens, everything must be examined and either confirmed or refuted.

Repetition is a style consistent with not knowing where one's thoughts are leading or should lead. At her most ambivalent, Kincaid is also her most repetitive. ''My talk was full of pain, it was full of misery, it was full of anger, there was no peace to it, there was much sorrow, but there was no peace to it.'' Twice in a single sentence, Kincaid reminds us that she derives no peace from talking about her brother and his illness.

Historical Context

Antigua is a small West Indian island, twelve miles long and nine miles wide. Christopher Columbus arrived in Antigua in 1493, and he named the tiny island after the Church of Santa Maria de la Antigua in Sevilla, Spain. Soon after, Antigua was settled by the Spanish, French, and British, and in 1667 it became a British colony under the Treaty of Breda.

Although Antigua was still governed by the British, when Kincaid was growing up there, it became self-governing on February 27, 1967, and was known for the next fourteen years as an Associated State of Britain. In 1981, Antigua became an independent nation within the Commonwealth. Because Antigua was an outpost of British rule for so long, the educational system was British, which accounts for the fact that Kincaid and Devon both love John Milton, and Devon's favorite sport is cricket. In a *New York Times* interview, Kincaid said, ''In my generation, the height of being a civilized person was to be English and to love English things and eat like English people. We couldn't really look like them, but we could approximate being an English person.''

In *A Small Place*, Kincaid recalls that May 24th, Queen Victoria's birthday, was a holiday in Antigua. Instead of being incensed because the birthday of this unappealing person was meaningless to Antiguans, the Antiguans were grateful for a holiday from work. When Kincaid grows up and finds herself sitting across from an Englishman at a dinner party, he laments that he too celebrated the meaningless event. Her response is that at least he understood that Queen Victoria was dead. In that angry book, Kincaid writes that she has no tongue other than that of the criminal and that her language is built to express Englishmen's points of view. English cannot, she believes, adequately contain or express the horror, injustice, and agony of the criminal's deeds.

One of Kincaid's trademarks is writing about the curiously ambivalent feelings the colonized harbor toward the colonizers. This is evident in her fiction as well as in *My Brother*. She recalls that Devon was obsessed with ''the great hero–thieves of English maritime history: Horatio Nelson, John Hawkins, Francis Drake . . . he thought (as do I) that this history of ours was primarily an account of theft and murder (''Dem tief, dem a dam tief''), but presented in such a way as to make the account seem inevitable and even fun . . . he liked the people who won, even though he was among the things that had been won.''

Kincaid writes about the odd ways of Antigua in *A Small Place*. She describes her birth place as hopelessly disorganized; for instance, a sign saying the library was damaged in the earthquake of 1974 and is pending repairs, hung there for more than a decade without the repairs being made. And yet she doesn't feel that it's right to criticize today's Antigua without noting that the country is the way it is because Antiguans lived under the dysfunctional and infantilizing relationship of colonialism for so long.

Critical Overview

Fittingly enough, one of Kincaid's fortes—writing about anger—has earned her extreme critical reactions. One review of *My Brother* opens this way: "Jamaica Kincaid is great at describing rage." Sarah Kerr, the author of that review, believes that Kincaid's memoir of her brother succeeds because it ultimately moves beyond rage. "Still, rage is only one shade on the spectrum of human experience. Kincaid's new memoir is more expansive than her fiction—and at times more moving—because in it, she begins to explore some of the others."

In one of the more glowing reviews of *My Brother*, Anna Quindlen praises Kincaid in the *New York Times* for her ability to recreate the disorderly way human beings remember their lives. "Memory feels exactly like *My Brother*," Quindlen writes. And later she observes, "Kincaid moves with strange naturalness from the dying of her brother to his birth to his place in their family to her own place, providing, among other things, the deep satisfaction of recognition. This is what the mind does when it remembers. This is not real life, but real life recollected."

Not all critics are so enthusiastic. Some take Kincaid to task for writing an ostensible memoir of her brother that isn't really all that concerned with his life. Diane Hartman, writing for the *Denver Post,* comments that it's "hard to figure why Kincaid wrote this book." She also complains, "the book isn't a tribute or memorial and has no moral or discernible point." Writing in *Time,* John Skow calls *My Brother* "an irritating navel contemplation," in which Kincaid "repeats the pattern of familiar, well-written complaint." His central criticism revolves around the fact that the memoir is only glancingly a portrait of Kincaid's half-brother and its "real subject is Kincaid's scalded psyche."

Perhaps the most controversial aspect of *My Brother* is its style. Some critics applaud the circularity of the sentences, while others are put off by the repetitiousness. Hartman calls the style "infuriating," noting that Kincaid "repeats facts over and over, not adding a different perspective or subtle shade of meaning, just providing the same facts. This may remind someone of Gertrude Stein; I found it condescending." And while Quindlen is mainly enthusiastic about Kincaid's style, she thinks the experimentation sometimes goes too far. "There are pitfalls to this," she writes. "Some of the sentences are snarled string, some of the repetitions a tiresome tic."

Criticism

Elizabeth Judd

Judd is a freelance writer and book reviewer for Salon *and the* New York Times Book Review. *In the following essay, she discusses the ways in which Kincaid uses various stylistic devices to explore and illustrate the dynamics of familial distance within her memoir* My Brother.

"Desire," wrote Longinus, a philosopher in ancient Greece, "is full of endless distances." In *My Brother*, Kincaid makes a related but highly personal point: "I am so vulnerable to my family's needs and influence that from time to time I remove myself from them. I do not write to them. I do not pay visits to them. I do not lie, I do not deny, I only remove myself." *My Brother* is Kincaid's account of both the strong desire she feels for her family when separated from them and of the time she spends back in their orbit. From the safe distance of her new life as a successful American writer, she can plumb the depths of who her brother Devon is and what she herself might have become had she not left Antigua at the age of sixteen. In an interview in *People Weekly,* Kincaid says she wanted to write *My Brother* because "I just knew instinctively that my brother's life was parallel to mine. We were both dreamers, both lived in our heads. I thought, 'This could be me.'"

One reason why Kincaid's writing has been described as economical is that she takes a single idea—distance is just one example—and lets it gather meaning until it comes to represent many

A street in Antigua, where Kincaid was raised

important and complex truths. The distance Kincaid has personally travelled is evident in many ways, and Kincaid explores all of them, including geographical and cultural distance. Seeing the hospital where Devon is being treated, she is appalled. At Holberton Hospital, the furniture is dirty, the dusty ceiling fans present a danger to patients who have trouble breathing, and even something as ordinary as aspirin is sometimes impossible to come by. As an American, Kincaid is easily able to procure the AIDS medicine AZT for her brother, and the hospital staff is amazed when Devon begins to gain weight and recover his strength.

Physical distance is the most concrete type of distance in this memoir, but emotional distance is what's central to Kincaid's project. The gravity of Devon's illness collapses some of the longstanding emotional barriers in Kincaid's family. Kincaid once again returns to Antigua, allowing herself to be affected by the tragedy of one of her family members. Kincaid's mother excels at caring for her adult son, going so far as to sleep in the same bed with him. Yet most members of this family have also taken drastic steps to distance themselves. When Devon was a drug addict, he stole valuable tools from his oldest brother, Joe, and then sold them; to protect his property, Joe ran a live wire around his

bedroom with enough current that it electrocuted a puppy. This dangerously charged wire represents the power of Joe's desire to keep Devon out of his life.

Yet the children reserve their most ingenious distancing maneuvers for their mother. One form of rebuke is refusing to eat the food she's prepared. When Devon rejects her cooking, Kincaid considers his action ''part of a separation he wished to make between himself and his family.'' For Kincaid even distancing herself from her mother represents a sort of twisted intimacy, because the habit of refusing her mother's food began when she was a young child: ''not eating food my mother cooked for me as a sign of distancing myself from her was a form of behavior I had used a long time ago, when I felt most close to and dependent on her.''

In this family, quarrelling is perfectly natural. At any given time, one family member is generally not speaking to another. Like communication, silence has its own code of conduct: ''(and this not speaking to each other has a life of its own, it is like a strange organism, the rules by which it survives no one can yet decipher; my mother and I never know when we will stop speaking to each other and we never know when we will begin again).'' By downplaying these silences, placing the explanation of them within parentheses as if such silences are so

What Do I Read Next?

- National Book Critics Circle Award winner *The Spirit Catches You and You Fall Down* (1997) is Anne Fadiman's nonfiction story of a Hmong child diagnosed with severe epilepsy. The girl's parents, now living in Merced, California, are refugees from Laos, and their notions of what will cure their daughter are desperately at odds with the American medical establishment.

- Kincaid's *Annie John* (1985) is a coming-of-age story told in eight separate chapter vignettes, stories that span the Antiguan girl's childhood from the age of ten to seventeen. Like much of Kincaid's work, the stories are preoccupied with Annie's love for (and subsequent anger with) her mother. At the end of the book, Annie leaves home, headed for England.

- The slim but emotionally intense *A Small Place* (1998) has been described as an "anti-travel narrative." It's Kincaid's imagined visit by a North American or European tourist to a Carib-

bean island that his or her people have colonized. Although Kincaid is critical of the corruption of present-day Antigua, she repeatedly reminds the reader that the island's problems stem from its long history of colonialism.

- Like all of Kincaid's work, *Lucy* (1990) borrows heavily from the details of the author's life. Having moved from her Caribbean home to New York City, Lucy works as an au pair in the home of an upper-middle-class couple, and there she witnesses the disintegration of the couple's marriage.

- In her novel *Breath, Eyes, Memory* (1998), Edwidge Danticat covers much of the same emotional terrain as Kincaid does. The novel begins when Sophie leaves her happy existence with her aunt and grandmother in rural Haiti to live with the mother she's never known in New York.

---

commonplace they need no elaboration, Kincaid paradoxically heightens their significance. Only a member of a deeply troubled family would deem withholding speech unremarkable.

For the members of Kincaid's family, emotional distancing is a form of self-protection. On the morning when Kincaid learns of Devon's death, she chats with the other mothers at the bus stop, and she discovers she can enjoy herself by not acknowledging her brother has died. At another key moment, when Kincaid is visiting Devon two months before his death, she writes,

> "I was thinking of my past and how it frightened me to think that I might have continued to live in a certain way, though, I am convinced, not for very long. I would have died at about his age, thirty-three years, or I would have gone insane. And when I was looking at him through the louvered windows, I began to distance myself from him, I began to feel angry at him, I began to feel I didn't like being so tied up with his life, the waning of it, the suffering in it. I began to feel it

> would be so nice if he would just decide to die right away."

When truth becomes too uncomfortable, Kincaid finds refuge in anger and emotional distance.

Distance, Kincaid believes, was necessary for her to fulfill herself. She writes, "I could not have become a writer while living among the people I knew best, I could not have become myself while living among the people I knew best." Similarly, Kincaid views Devon's decision to become a Rastafarian as a distancing maneuver, one she applauds. "The impulse was a good one, if only he could have seen his way to simply moving away from [our mother] to another planet, though perhaps even that might not have been far enough away." Kincaid's outlook on death is naturally shaped by her own longing for separation, since death is the ultimate distance between individuals. Although she mourns her brother, she's displeased by the minister's suggestion in his funeral sermon that the

> Kincaid's repetitions are another stylistic decision that reinforces the emotional distancing underway. By repeating herself, Kincaid both emphasizes her various messages and then desensitizes the reader to the painful meaning of her words."

family will be reunited at some later date: "I did not want to be with any of these people again in another world."

One of Kincaid's most intriguing strategies for creating and enforcing distances is her writing style. Diction is the most noticeable sign of the chasm that now separates Kincaid from her brother.

> I had lived away from my home for so long that I no longer understood readily the kind of English he spoke and always had to have him repeat himself to me; and I no longer spoke the kind of English he spoke, and when I said anything to him, he would look at me and sometimes just laugh at me outright. You talk funny, he said."

How each sibling speaks is a sign of who he or she has become, but Kincaid consciously magnifies the gulf in the way she chooses to describe the problem. The semicolon in that long first sentence indicates the barrier between two linguistic worlds. In the first half of the sentence, Kincaid is a famous writer speaking as Americans do; in the second half, she's a person whose speech is outlandish to her own brother. Each separate truth exists on its own side of a grammatical divide.

Kincaid's repetitions are another stylistic decision that reinforces the emotional distancing underway. By repeating herself, Kincaid both emphasizes her various messages and then desensitizes the reader to the painful meaning of her words. Hearing that someone's brother has died carries an emotional charge. But when the fact of that death is repeated several times in close succession, the reader becomes deadened to the impact of that sorrow, and the emotions become more remote. Thus, when Kincaid writes, "And my brother died, for he kept

dying; each time I remembered that he had died it was as if he had just at that moment died, and the whole experience of it would begin again; my brother had died and I didn't love him," the death itself ceases to shock, but the emotional distance of the speaker and her lack of love for her brother are now what capture the reader's attention.

Distance may be a necessity, but throughout, Kincaid wishes her life could have been otherwise, that she had loved her brother and that her mother wasn't someone she needed to escape. In *Interview* magazine, Kincaid says that she would have preferred a less remarkable mother than the force of nature who, in fact, raised her: "An ordinary mother would have served me better, one that didn't require great distance to escape from." Distance has saved Kincaid from Devon's fate, but she also realizes that emotional distance comes at a high price because it is the pain of closeness that makes life meaningful. On the morning Kincaid learns that Devon has died, she begins to wish "that this, my brother dying, had not happened, that I had never become involved with the people I am from again, and that I only wanted to be happy and happy and happy again, with all the emptiness and meaninglessness that such a state would entail." Her three repetitions of "happy" make the state seem vapid, frivolous, undesirable.

Perhaps the most wrenching sign of familial distance is conveyed by the way these individuals address one another. Kincaid explains that Devon and Dalma call their mother "Mrs. Drew," and at many times in the memoir, Kincaid is equally unwilling to claim kinship with her. She writes, "He stole from his mother (our mother, she was my own mother, too, but I was only in the process of placing another distance between us, I was not in the process of saying I know nothing of her, as I am doing now)." The language is convoluted because the emotions are snarled, impossible to make simple and smooth again. For a writer who never lets any judgment pass unquestioned, one who always denotes relationships with hairsplitting accuracy (her mother is Mrs. Drew or the mother of her brothers), Kincaid has chosen the most poignant of all possible titles for her memoir. In the intimacy of writing this book, Kincaid has claimed Devon as her own again. By naming Devon's relationship to her with the utmost directness, the two words "my brother" become the sweetest of all possible endearments.

Source: Elizabeth Judd, Critical Essay on *My Brother,* in *Nonfiction Classics for Students,* The Gale Group, 2001.

Adrian Blevins

Adrian Blevins is a poet and essayist who has taught at Hollins University, Sweet Briar College, and in the Virginia Community College System. In this essay, she explores how the digressions and contractions in Jamaica Kincaid's My Brother *ultimately help the author explore her reactions to a family tragedy reveal the way the self is often split between love and hate, obligation and self-preservation, and action and inaction.*

Toward the end of *My Brother*, Jamaica Kincaid says that she "became a writer out of desperation." She elaborates in this way: "when I first heard my brother was dying I was familiar with the act of saving myself: I would write about him. I would write about his dying." Like much of Kincaid's memoir, this statement is ironic because *My Brother* is not really, and certainly not only, about Kincaid's brother's sickness and death. As many critics have observed, it does not move in a straight line through Devon's illness and eventual death in order to give us an honest and straightforward account of the horrors of acquired immunodeficiency syndrome (AIDS) in a developing country or anywhere else. Instead, Kincaid *uses* her brother Devon's illness with AIDS and his eventual death as the axis for meditations on a whole series of complex themes about the self in relation to itself, others, and the world. This method—which produces a "sustained meditation on the grinding wheel of family," as American writer Anna Quindlen says—has been underappreciated by too many critics. Diane Hartman, in a review of *My Brother* for *The Denver Post,* says that Kincaid

> has a way of writing—described by one critic as "the circularity of her thought patterns"—that can be infuriating. She repeats facts over and over, not adding a different perspective or subtle shade of meaning, but just the same facts. This may remind someone of Gertrude Stein; I found it condescending.

Yet it is this very "way of writing"—the way Kincaid allows "the circularity of her thought patterns" to dictate structure and theme—that makes *My Brother* an interesting and memorable book. As Quindlen says, "this is what the mind does when it remembers. This is not real life, but real life recollected." *My Brother* ultimately explores one person's reactions to a family tragedy in order to reveal the way the self is often split between love and hate, obligation and self-preservation, and action and inaction. Kincaid manages to weave these paradoxes into the story of her brother's illness and death by being true to the nature of memory. That is, *My*

> One of the oddest repetitions in *My Brother* is the idea that Devon's father (Mr. Drew) is not Kincaid's own father. . . . This repetition works as a kind of refrain in the book, revealing how important it is for Kincaid to separate herself from the family she was born into."

Brother mimics the way memory actually works, moving in time and place in an effort to uncover the astonishing self at work within the most unpleasant of circumstances.

The basic narrative of the memoir does follow a straight and even predictable line: the author finds out her brother has AIDS, goes to visit him in Antigua, and sends AZT from the United States, which she buys with her own money. Although the AZT helps for a while, allowing Devon to convince himself he isn't sick at all and to have unprotected sex with women on the island, eventually Devon does die, and the author returns to Antigua for his funeral. Kincaid narrates the details of these main events masterfully, giving us specific images to authenticate the experience and reveal how her brother's life "was like the bud that sets but, instead of opening into a flower, turns brown and falls off at your feet." She says:

> His lips were scarlet red, as if layers and layers of skin had been removed and only one last layer remained, holding in place the dangerous fluid that was his blood. His face was sharp like a carving, like an image embossed on an emblem, a face full of deep suffering, beyond regrets or pleadings for a second chance.

These details of Devon's illness as well as images of Devon after he has died (when his "eyes had been sewn shut," and he looked "like an advertisement for the dead") work as the book's main plot device, tying the memoir into one coherent piece. Because they are so graphic and horrible, however, they are difficult images to sustain for a long period of time. Thus Kincaid's digressions, or her sometimes-startling leaps in time, place, and theme, work to relieve us of the graphic nature of the situation she's describing: they move us from the dying or dead body, from images of ''penises that looked like lady fingers left in the oven too long and with a bite taken out ... and.... labias covered with thick blue crusts'' to images of the *living,* of living people struggling to understand and know the self and the world. Toward the end of the book, Kincaid says:

> I am remembering the life of my brother, I am remembering my own life, or at least a part of my own life, for my own life is still ongoing, I hope, and each moment of its present shapes its past and each moment of its present will shape its future and even so influence the way I see its future; and the knowledge of all this leaves me with the feeling: And what now, and so, yes, what now. *What now!*

The sense of wonder expressed in this passage works to counter the images of death and dying in Kincaid's memoir. Kincaid's digressions—made up of memories and observations written in her famously meandering sentences, repetitions, and interruptions—help her produce a tone that is oddly evasive and hesitant, revealing that the crisis (and interest) of a tragedy is not often the tragedy itself, but the make-up of selves that live before and after and within it—the mix of personalities that witness (and may even cause) the self-destruction of some people.

The first sentence in the book sets us up for the story of sickness and dying, but that expectation is frustrated very quickly. ''When I saw my little brother again after a very long time, he was lying in a bed in the Holberton Hospital, in the Gweneth O'Reilly ward, and he was said to be dying of AIDS,'' Kincaid begins. But she digresses in the very next sentence, moving backwards in time to tell us about how ''the routine of [the family's] life was upset'' by Devon's birth. We learn that Devon, unlike Kincaid and her other brothers, was born at home, and that an army of red ants attacked him while he lay beside his mother in bed on his second day of life. This one incident reveals that Hartman is mistaken to suggest that Kincaid ''repeats facts over and over, not adding a different perspective or subtle shade of meaning,'' since Kincaid does return to the story of the ants later in the book, telling us how her mother burned the tree that gave the ants a path through the window to the bed. Kincaid then ties this story to the memory of her mother burning her books, creating a motif of fire that works, to make the book a coherent whole.

After she narrates the day Devon is born, Kincaid moves backward in time to narrate events and meditate on them: the reader finds out that she and her mother ''were in a period of not speaking to each other'' when the telephone call from her mother's friend comes, and the reader witnesses Kincaid's meditation on a series of questions about how Devon got AIDS in the first place. These details and questions deepen the tension already established by the book's main narrative premise, suspending specific information about Devon and his sickness while we learn about the speaker and her family, specifically their long struggle to separate themselves from their mother's ''spectacular'' and ''unequaled'' love.

These details are interesting because they are oddly universal. They reveal the contradictions at work in the self and in the family, and, since they produce a conversational and informal tone appropriate to a meditation that can ultimately ask more questions than it can answer, they do serve the book's ultimate aim. Kincaid suggests toward the beginning of the book that she realized when she first came to see Devon that she loved him. She says: ''it surprised me that I loved him; I could see that what I was feeling, love for him, and it surprised me because I did not know him.'' Then, still in the book's first section, she says:

> when I was no longer in his presence, I did not think I loved him. Whatever made me talk about him, whatever made me think of him, was not love, just something else, but not love; love being the thing I felt for my family, the one I have now, but not for him, or the people I am from, not love, but a powerful feeling all the same, only not love.

The apparent contradiction between these statements reveals that it is possible to love and ''notlove'' at the same time; it reveals that it is not only possible, but perfectly human, to be a ''combustion of feelings.'' Other similar paradoxes infuse *My Brother*, deepening its complexity and appeal. Kincaid tells us that her mother ''loves her children. . . . in her way'' and, later in the book, she says: ''I felt I hated my mother, and even worse, I felt she hated me, too.'' During the passage in which she remembers the day she was supposed to take care of Devon and failed to change his diaper because she was too busy reading, she even says that ''when my mother saw [Devon's] unchanged diaper ... she wanted me dead.''

Kincaid also tells us that sometimes she is ''so vulnerable to [her] family's needs and influence that she. . . . removes [herself] from them.'' Still, she visits Antigua many times, buys AZT and a coffin, and becomes so obsessed with the idea of Devon dying that she ''felt she was falling into a deep hole.'' The contradiction expressed between

Kincaid's actions and her words shows us how easy it is to act against our own feelings, especially when we're faced with another's suffering. Kincaid reveals the reasons she feels she must remove herself from her family (in an alternative act of self-preservation) when she tells us what happened after her mother came for a visit to Vermont:

> . . . after my mother left, I was sick for three months. I had something near to a nervous breakdown, I suffered from anxiety and had to take medicine to treat it; I got the chicken pox, which is a disease of childhood and a disease I had already when I was a child. Not long after she left, I had to see a psychiatrist.

Kincaid's repetitions also serve an important purpose. One of the oddest repetitions in *My Brother* is the idea that Devon's father (Mr. Drew) is not Kincaid's own father. She tells us, often parenthetically, that this is the case, sometimes rephrasing, sometimes using the exact same phrase. This repetition works as a kind of refrain in the book, revealing how important it is for Kincaid to separate herself from the family she was born into. Toward the end of the book, she says that she won't forget Devon "because his life is the one I did not have, the life that, for reasons I hope shall never be too clear to me, I avoided or escaped." Kincaid's repetition about Mr. Drew not being her father has prepared us for this statement, which might otherwise seem to lack compassion. This statement also underscores the fact that the central theme of Kincaid's memoir is not Kincaid's brother or his sickness and death, but Kincaid herself—her realizations about herself and her family that Devon's sickness and death have brought forth.

In his introduction to *The Art of the Personal Essay*, Phillip Lopate reminds us that "the personal essayist looks back at the choices that were made, the roads not taken, the limiting familial and historic circumstances, and what might be called the catastrophe of personality" in order to arrive at realizations that are, amazingly enough, "appetizing and even amusing to the reader." By "catastrophe," Lopate doesn't mean that the essayist must necessarily meditate on the way a self might fail and falter in the world, though this might be (and has been) a fertile topic for our most notable practitioners. Lopate means rather that personal essayists must investigate their own reactions to the world and to themselves as honestly as possible in order to arrive at a full picture of what it means to be human. Kincaid's digressions, interruptions, and repetitions serve the book's purpose because they combine to produce an apt vehicle for the expression of the "catastrophe of personality" that led Devon Drew to his death and,

conversely, his sister to an articulation of the complex feelings at work in people who struggle to understand who they have become.

Source: Adrian Blevins, Critical Essay on *My Brother*, in *Nonfiction Classics for Students,* The Gale Group, 2001.

Gay Wachman

In the following review, Wachman finds that My Brother *exhibits less anger than Kincaid's previous works and focuses on "the authenticity of the voice—her brother's or her own."*

To read Jamaica Kincaid's memoir, *My Brother*, is to re-experience her unforgettable narrative voice, revisiting Antigua over the three years that Devon is dying of AIDS, and re-characterizing the island, her mother and the child/adolescent self chronicled in her earlier books. The lucid, assertive, deceptively simple voice takes its time in fleshing out the figures of the memoir, both in their present and in the past, circling around Devon and the multiple meanings of his life, illness and death. The narrative loops between the United States and Antigua, contrasting Kincaid's "now privileged North American way" with the lives of her brothers and mother. It recalls both the double setting of *Lucy* and the triple denunciation in *A Small Place* of tourist complacency, imperialist oppression and government corruption.

But Kincaid's voice is less angry here, and more reflective. Indeed, she explicitly distances herself from *A Small Place,* "a . . . book in which I did nothing but cast blame and make denunciations." There is still rage, however, against conditions in Antigua, where she finds her youngest brother in hospital, dying of opportunistic infections because there is no AZT. But this is a reality that can be altered by individual, middle-class agency: Kincaid buys Devon three more years of life with AZT from the States. And although she is unable to change his living conditions either in the hospital, which isolates AIDS patients in a small, dirty room, or at home when he returns to live with their mother, she finds cause for hope as soon as she meets Dr. Prince Ramsey, the leader of the fight against AIDS on the island. Kincaid is astonished to find such a doctor in Antigua: "He was kind, he was loving toward people who needed him, people who were less powerful than he; he was respectful. . . . He is a very loving man and the other reason I have for saying this is I saw that wherever he went, people, ordinary people, would go out of their way to greet him and ask him how he was, but not because they

Devon was a Rastafarian, like the man seen here

really wanted to know: it was just to hear his voice.'' Kincaid knows how people respond to love. It is the gap between this knowledge and her feelings about her mother that makes much of her writing so poignant.

From the beginning of this book it is clear that this relationship remains at least as troubled as that represented in *Lucy*; Kincaid's life has been punctuated by long periods of not speaking to her mother. But her mother cares untiringly for Devon while he is sick:

> My mother loves her children, I want to say, in her way! . . . It has never occurred to her that her way of loving us might have served her better than it served us. And why should it? Perhaps all love is self-serving. I do not know, I do not know . . . All the same, her love, if we are dying, or if we are in jail, is so wonderful, a great fortune, and we are lucky to have it. My brother was dying; he needed her just then.

The pain in the repeated ''I do not know'' reflects Kincaid's continuous state of conflict about her mother; for a moment she doubts her judgment of her mother's love and also of her own love for others. She acknowledges, too, that her mother's bitter cruelty dates only from the family's descent into poverty when Kincaid was about 13 years old, but she cannot forgive her for burning her books in a rage, taking her out of school to look after her

brothers and sending her away alone to earn money for the family. The depth of her distrust is shown by her refusal, along with two of her three brothers, to eat any food her mother cooks. Kincaid knows that ''the powerful sense my mother has of herself'' is a danger for any thing or person who gets in her path; she is finally convinced that ''my mother hates her children.''

When *Lucy* was published in 1990 I was struck by the number of reviewers who were puzzled or offended by Lucy's unremitting anger, directed at both her mother and her privileged but well-meaning white employer. I have never been able to withstand the relentless analytical clarity of Kincaid's narrative voice. Whatever her narrators tell me about their feelings, however unpleasant or extreme they may be, I accept, as long as I'm reading, as ''true.'' (It doesn't matter whether Kincaid's mother really hates her children; what matters is Kincaid's experience.) So, because the narrative persuaded me to focus on her response to her brother rather than on my own experience and knowledge of AIDS, I believed as I read three-quarters of *My Brother* that Devon was a heterosexual drug user who did not inject drugs. After he is dead, Kincaid learns that he was in fact bisexual, but Antiguan homophobia is such that Devon has encouraged his sister's supposition that "he got the virus through . . . heterosexual sex." He boasts that he is sexually irresistible to women and constantly speaks of his desire for them.

Devon is a man who talks a lot when he is well enough to do so; he seems to be compulsively sociable. Kincaid, back in Vermont, imagines him "sitting on my mother's little front porch":

> Whenever anyone passed by, he would have to call out to them a greeting regardless of whether they were familiar to him or not. He would not be able to bear the emptiness of silence . . . He was not meant to be silent. He was a brilliant boy, he was a brilliant man. Locked up inside him was someone who would have spoken to the world in an important way. I believe this . . . But he was not even remotely aware of such a person inside him.

Kincaid also sees him as a man who stole and lied and "did unspeakable things . . . he was unable to speak openly about. He could never say that anything in front of him was his own, or that anything in front of him came to him in a way that he did not find humiliating." But, her heterosexual privilege blinds her to what is really unspeakable—to her, at any rate—in his life.

When Devon dies, Kincaid is in the middle of her book tour for *The Autobiography of My Mother*; she takes it up again after the funeral. At a reading in a Chicago bookstore she sees a woman she recognizes; they had met once in Antigua three years earlier at an AIDS support group organized by Dr. Ramsey. This white "lesbian woman"—the redundancy of "woman" concisely conveys how strange lesbianism is to Kincaid—knows that Devon is dead. She tells Kincaid how, saddened by "the scorn and derision heaped on the homosexual man," she had opened up her home on Sundays and "made it known that . . . men who loved other men could come to her house in the afternoon and enjoy each other's company." The reader is left wondering about this gay Antiguan subculture, wanting to know more about these meetings and what they meant to Devon. The gaps in Kincaid's knowledge of her brother are finally exposed. Reading as a "lesbian woman," I am momentarily estranged from this unreliable narrator.

But this estrangement may be the crux of the memoir, emphasizing the unknowability of those whom we love as of those whom we have made Other. After the lesbian's revelation, Kincaid feels a new empathy with her brother:

> Who he really was—not a single sense of identity but all the complexities of who he was—he could not

> The narrative loops between the United States and Antigua, contrasting Kincaid's 'now privileged North American way' with the lives of her brothers and mother. It recalls both the double setting of *Lucy* and the triple denunciation in *A Small Place* of tourist complacency, imperialist oppression and government corruption."

express fully: his fear of being laughed at, his fear of meeting with the scorn of the people he knew best were overwhelming and he could not live with all of it openly. His homosexuality is one thing, and my becoming a writer is another altogether, but this truth is not lost to me: I could not have become a writer while living among the people I knew best, I could not have become myself while living among the people I knew best . . . in his life there had been no flowering.

This identification with Devon escapes being an appropriation because Kincaid's resolute sense of self is vital to the authenticity of the voice—her brother's or her own—that she is right to value so highly. At Devon's funeral, distanced by the unreality of his body after the ministrations of the undertakers, she mourns what she knows to be loss: "his farawayness so complete, so final, he shall never speak again; he shall never speak again in the everyday way that I speak of speech." *My Brother* is a memoir of a voice.

Source: Gay Wachman, "Dying in Antigua," in *The Nation*, Vol. 265, No. 14, November 3, 1997, pp. 43–44.

Sources

"Don't Mess with Gardener and Author Jamaica Kincaid," in *Boston Globe,* June 20, 1996.

Garis, Leslie, "Through West Indian Eyes," in *New York Times,* October 7, 1990, p. 42.

Garner, Dwight, "Jamaica Kincaid," in *Salon,* November 8, 1995.

Goldfarb, Brad, ''*My Brother,*'' in *Interview,* Vol. 27, No. 10, October 1997, p. 94.

Hartman, Diane, Review, in *Denver Post,* December 7, 1997.

Kerr, Sarah, ''The Dying of the Light,'' in *Slate,* October 21, 1997.

Lopate, Phillip, Introduction to *The Art of the Personal Essay,* Doubleday, 1994.

Quindlen, Anna, ''The Past is Another Country,'' in *New York Times,* October 19, 1997.

Skow, John, Review, in *Time,* Vol. 150, No. 20, November 10, 1997, p. 108.

Snell, Marilyn, ''Jamaica Kincaid Hates Happy Endings,'' in *Mother Jones,* September–October 1997.

Further Reading

Bloom, Harold, ed., ''Jamaica Kincaid,'' in *Caribbean Women Writers,* Chelsea House, 1997, pp. 104–116.
    This overview of Kincaid's work was written prior to the publication of *My Brother.*

Graham, Renee, ''A Death in the Family: Jamaica Kincaid's Wrenching, Incantatory Story of her Brother Devon,'' in *Boston Globe,* November 2, 1997, p. N1.
    Graham describes Kincaid's memoir as one of ''unsparing honesty'' in this detailed review of her book.

Hainley, Bruce, ''*My Brother,*'' in *Artforum,* Vol. 36, No. 3, November 1997, p. S27.
    In this book review of *My Brother,* Hainley compares Kincaid to writers Michel Leiris and Elizabeth Bishop.

Kaufman, Joanne, ''Jamaica Kincaid: An Author's Unsparing Judgments Earn Her an Unwanted Reputation for Anger,'' in *People Weekly,* Vol. 48, No. 24, December 15, 1997, p. 109.
    This interview with Kincaid following the nomination of *My Brother* for a National Book Award touches on topics ranging from Tina Brown, editor of *The New Yorker,* to Kincaid's family history, her conversion to Judaism, and her passion for gardening.

Kurth, Peter, ''*My Brother:* A Memoir,'' in *Salon,* October 9, 1997.
    Kurth's book review focuses on Kincaid's relationship with her mother, comparing *My Brother* to *The Autobiography of My Mother.*

Paula

Isabel Allende

1994

Paula, published in Spanish in 1994 and English in 1995, is the first nonfiction book by Isabel Allende, one of today's most influential Latin-American authors. An autobiography framed by the author's experience of watching her only daughter's slow death, the book is "equal parts heartbreak, humor and wisdom," as described by Cynthia Dockrell in her review for the *Boston Globe*. Allende wrote the book while her daughter Paula was in a coma from 1991 to 1992 and uses her writing to preserve memories as she teaches herself to let her daughter go. Like with her first, landmark novel, *The House of the Spirits*, Allende followed a personal tradition of letter-writing to begin *Paula* and did not think of the audience: "It was meant to become a journal that I would give to my children and my grandchildren," she said to Dockrell. The book that was never meant to be published became an instant bestseller in several countries.

Many reviewers have pointed out that Allende's first work of nonfiction reads like a novel—in fact, German and Dutch translations of *Paula* were subtitled "A Novel"—but the author differentiates between genres even in the book itself. When describing the evening she met her second husband, on a night of the full moon with Sinatra singing from the restaurant's speakers, Allende adds: "This is the kind of detail that is forbidden in literature . . . The problem with fiction is that it must seem credible, while reality seldom is." This time around, the

reality behind the inspirations for many eccentric, mystical, larger-than-life characters and adventures in Allende's earlier works are revealed in her descriptions of actual people and events—proving that her fictional work often stems from the author's life itself.

I finished the book has been like a catharsis in many ways. So, when I started writing [*Paula*], my only goal was to survive.''

Recent novels include *Aphrodite: A Memoir of the Senses* (1998) and *Daughter of Fortune* (1999).

Author Biography

Allende was born on August 2, 1942, in Lima, Peru, the first child of affluent Chilean parents: her parents were Tomas, a diplomat and the nephew of future Chilean President Salvador Allende, and Francisca (Llona Barros) Allende. Following the couple's divorce three years later, the author's mother returned to her parents' home in Santiago where Allende grew up. In 1953, her mother married Ramon Huidobro, a Chilean diplomat who took his new family to his posts in Bolivia, Europe, and Lebanon over the next five years. Allende graduated from a private high school in Santiago, Chile, and shortly after married Miguel (Michael) Frias.

After working as a secretary for a couple of years, Allende began successful careers in the theatre and print and broadcast journalism. She also had two children. In 1970, Salvador Allende won the popular election and became president of Chile, only to die three years later in a right-wing military coup. Allende lost her job on political grounds and the family began receiving threats from supporters of the new regime; they fled Chile and sought asylum in Venezuela in 1975. During Allende's life in exile, her marriage fell apart; eventually, she remarried and now lives in California with her second husband.

While in exile, Allende began a letter to her grandfather that turned into her first novel, *The House of the Spirits*; published in 1982, it quickly became a bestseller in several countries. *Paula*, published in 1995, is Allende's autobiography, contextualized by her daughter's death in 1992, a year after Paula fell into a coma due to a rare blood disease. As Allende states in an interview with Farhat Iftekharuddin for *Speaking of the Short Story: Interviews with Contemporary Writers:* ''I think that I am still in [the] tunnel of pain, but the fact that

Summary

Part One: December 1991 to May 1992

Sitting by Paula's hospital bed in Madrid and waiting for any sign of improvement as her daughter lies in a coma caused by a rare blood disease, Allende begins to tell the story of her life with the purpose of offering her own past to her ill daughter. ''Listen, Paula. I'm going to tell you a story, so that when you wake up you will not feel so lost.''

Allende begins with her Chilean heritage and national history, her family tree, the controversial circumstances of her parents' marriage, and Allende's birth. Often switching between the vivid memories of the past and the silent waiting of the present by Paula's hospital bed, the narrator introduces a complex web of relatives that surrounded her during her childhood, after the scandalous divorce of her parents: her father abandoned the family after a political scandal at the Peruvian embassy, in which he might have been involved. Back in her maternal grandparents' home in Chile, little Allende forms strong and lasting bonds with family members and begins to develop a sense of liberal politics as she observes the lives of her family's servants. She also learns the art of storytelling from her spirit-summoning grandmother Meme and her grandfather Tata. After her mother's marriage to Chilean diplomat Tio Ramon, the family moves again, and Allende spends her teenage years in Lebanon. Because of the political unrest in the region during the 1950s, she is sent back to Santiago to finish school; there she meets her first husband Michael. They have two children, Paula and Nicolas.

Allende proceeds to write about her professional adventures, from her work for the United Nations to her work as a journalist. During the 1960s, Allende relates how she developed into a feminist liberal while traveling and greatly expanding her social life. When she attempts to interview poet Pablo Neruda, he advises her to use her creative talents to write fiction; advice she will eventually take. Further, the author recalls the victory of Salvador Allende in 1970, only to contrast it with the events three years later when the military coup under Augusto Pinochet fully disrupts the life she had in Chile. The first part of the book ends with the heavy atmosphere of a Chilean police state and terror that is yet to be fully comprehended.

Part Two: May to December 1992

In the second part of the book, as she learns of Paula's brain damage and the impossibility of her recovery, Allende abandons the letter format of her writing and proceeds to tell a story as an autobiography. While moving Paula to California, where she can take care of her in her home, the author begins to recall the years of her life after 1973, when her homeland changed forever.

Many people around Allende suffer under the Pinochet regime, and she and her family organize ways of helping those in need, always afraid of possible consequences. The author loses her job as a journalist for political reasons, and the family begins to feel the pressure of anonymous threats. In 1975, they flee Chile and seek asylum in Venezuela, where Allende experiences one of the worst periods of her life. With great difficulty, she finds a job as a school administrator, but the rest of her life seems to be falling apart. As her relationship with Michael begins to disintegrate, Allende looks for comfort in an affair that ultimately ends her marriage. Exasperated and depressed, the author begins to write to her dying grandfather (Tata) in Chile; the letter becomes a novel, *The House of the Spirits*. At this point, Allende explains the somewhat superstitious process she goes through in her work, the purpose of her writing, and the techniques she employs; she also recalls the connections between the real people and events in her life and the characters and adventures described in her fiction.

Allende's marriage seems beyond salvation, so she divorces her first husband in 1987; about a year later, she meets Willie and remarries, moving to California with him. Settling into her new life and new professional identity as a writer in America, Allende criticizes the role of the United States in Latin America. At the house she shares with Willie, she takes care of Paula and slowly accepts the inevitable. She lets her go with a final goodbye, and

Isabel Allende

the book ends with Paula's departure into the world of spirits, exactly one year after she fell into a coma.

Key Figures

Isabel Allende

Isabel Allende, narrator and protagonist, emerges as strong, imaginative, passionate, and loving but also impulsive, prone to mistakes, and, at times, guilt ridden. In the year of silence and sadness at her daughter's bedside, she struggles against Paula's death the best way a storyteller can—by capturing memories. Allende survives exile in Venezuela for the sake of her children; she survives her marriage by finding a creative outlet in a letter to her grandfather—which turns into her first novel. She uses writing again to cope with her daughter's coma and death. Allende comes through as a survivor in spirit and finds love with her second husband. Throughout the book, she demonstrates an energetic spirit as the main caregiver for her daughter during her illness and finds strength in her love for her daughter in the moment of Paula's death.

Media Adaptations

- Channel BBC1 in the United Kingdom did a production of *Listen Paula* in September of 1995. The special, focusing on Allende, Paula, and the family's history, received much public attention.

Juan Allende

Plagued with illness from the moment of his birth, Juan is the narrator's weak, but likeable, youngest brother. As an adolescent, he joins the National Air Academy only to learn that he detests military life. Always considered the intellectual genius of the family, Juan becomes a professor of political science but turns to divinity studies when he experiences a spiritual crisis.

Pancho Allende

Pancho is the narrator's brother, their parents' second child, and a troublemaker from his teenage years on. Allende recalls his tendency to vanish for months and years at a time to go on daring spiritual quests. As an adult, he is estranged from his family.

Salvador Allende

Salvador Allende, the founder of Chile's Socialist Party and the world's first freely elected Marxist president, is the uncle of the narrator's father, Tomas. Although the narrator's familial relation to Salvador Allende ends with the divorce of her parents, the influential "uncle" continues a cordial relationship with the family. He is described as a loyal friend, sharp and energetic, arrogant and charming, and with a witty sense of humor. Allende writes that in her view, his main traits were "integrity, intuition, courage, and charisma." During the three years of his presidency (1970–1973), Chile is divided by fear and harsh, unchanging economic conditions. In 1973, the president's political enemies, headed by General Augusto Pinochet, take over the country in a violent military coup during which Salvador Allende allegedly commits suicide.

Tomas Allende

Tomas, the narrator's estranged father, disappears from her life too early for personal memories. Allende describes him as a "clever man with a quick mind and merciless tongue . . . [and] a murky past," whose lineage (he is the cousin of Salvador Allende) granted him certain political standing. After the wedding, Tomas takes his bride to Peru where he is appointed secretary of the Chilean embassy. Their three children, the narrator being the oldest, are born in Lima. Tomas' career and marriage come to an abrupt end with the scandalous news of sexual perversions involving an important politician. Allende never encounters him again until, ironically, she is called in to identify his body.

Ernesto

Ernesto, Paula's husband, is an electronics engineer in Madrid. Allende writes that, the day after Paula met him, she called to tell her mother she'd found the man she was going to marry. Allende describes her son-in-law as a sensitive, tender, emotional, yet strong and exuberant young man, very supportive of his wife. The couple lives in Madrid until Paula's illness; she falls into a coma before their first wedding anniversary. Allende describes the details of the young husband's suffering, noticing that even the nurses at the hospital feel envious—"[they] wish they could be loved like that."

Fisherman

The fisherman in Allende's story is a part of her memory of her first secret sexual experience at the age of eight and of the moral crisis that ensued.

Celia Frias

Celia is Allende's daughter-in-law, another example of the many radical conversions in the family: strictly religious and highly prejudiced at the time of her marriage to Allende's son Nicolas, Celia becomes a free spirit in time, eventually giving birth at the home of her mother-in-law.

Michael Frias

Michael is the narrator's first husband and the father of her three children; they meet in Santiago and marry young, after three years of chaste courtship. Michael is a member of an English family, which has lived in Chile for generations but maintains British mannerisms: he grows up treated like a "young lord," taught to control and conceal his emotions. Although a patient and supportive husband, he becomes distant and emotionally estranged from the narrator, especially during the second half of their marriage, which is spent in exile. During that time, he works on a dam deep in the Venezuelan jungle and visits his family every six weeks. Allende has an affair with an Argentinian musician with whom she spends three months in Spain, but she cannot stay away from her children and comes back. Despite many attempts to remedy their marriage, the two eventually divorce.

Nicolas Frias

Allende's son Nicolas is described as an imaginative albeit morbid teenager who tortures his mother with pretend suicides; eventually, he becomes an explorer-turned-computer expert. Nicolas is also very close to his sister and a great pillar of support for the narrator during Paula's illness.

Paula Frias

The author's daughter gives her name to this autobiography, as her tragic illness inspires Allende to write the book while taking care of her. Paula is the narrator's first child and only daughter; born in 1963, she grows up during her mother's professional rise in Chilean television. While her parents are at work and engaged in a lively social scene of 1960s Chile, Paula becomes "a complete lady in miniature" by the age of two in the hands of her paternal grandparents. Paula is spoiled yet mature, stubborn yet a quiet accomplice in acts of kindness—like hiding her grandmother's drinking habit by burying the empty bottles in the yard. Paula's idyllic childhood comes to an abrupt end when the family flees to Venezuela. There, Paula does volunteer work in the slums of Caracas, just as she helped classmates in post-coup Chile whose parents were persecuted by the new government.

After graduation, Paula marries Ernesto and moves to Spain with him; in a moment of clairvoyance, she writes a letter to be opened after her death, in which she bids everybody farewell. At the beginning of the book, she has just been confined to a hospital in Madrid, Spain, diagnosed with porphyria, a rare metabolic disease of the blood. Paula falls into a coma from which she never wakes up, and she dies exactly a year later.

Granny

Allende's first mother-in-law and Paula's paternal grandmother, Granny is a sensitive and loving English lady, who adores her grandchildren and spends the last years of her life taking care of them. With the social deterioration in Chile, she becomes depressed and turns to alcohol; after her grandchildren leave to seek exile in Venezuela, she loses touch with reality, repeatedly asks for them, and gradually dies—of alcoholism and loneliness.

Meme

The author has few memories of Meme, her maternal grandmother and Tata's wife who passes away early in the narrator's childhood, but her spirit seems to follow Allende throughout her life. Ethereal and mystical, the grandmother is a comforting presence and an essential part of the narrator's inspiration. Meme was training her granddaughter to become a seer but died before Allende developed her mystical gifts; with her death, the household became quiet and cheerless.

Mother

Brought up in a sheltering world of wealth and privilege, Allende's mother faces a life of disgrace after her divorce and suffers a long illness. Her health improves but her social status worsens when she falls in love with a married Chilean diplomat, Tio Ramon, whom she eventually marries. In the beginning of her second marriage, while the family lives in Lebanon, Allende's mother becomes an "expert in the supreme art of keeping up appearances" due to the family's modest income. Although often weakened by illness and stress, the narrator's mother remains a pillar of strength and encouragement in her life. When Allende returns to Chile, the two maintain a rich daily correspondence and visit each other at times of crisis.

Pablo Neruda

Probably Chile's most famous poet, the winner of the Nobel Prize for literature, Pablo Neruda is a great influence in the narrator's writing career. During her job as a reporter, Allende visits him for lunch, hoping to get an interview; however, the poet laughs at the idea, calling her the country's worst journalist—lacking in objectivity, placing herself in the middle of all her stories, inventing and falsifying news. He finally gives her advice that will ultimately change her life: "Why don't you write novels instead? In literature, those defects are virtues."

General Prats

One of Salvador Allende's most loyal supporters, Prats dies with the defeat of his government in the military coup; however, the narrator salutes his ghost, which allegedly haunts the presidential palace during Pinochet's reign to remind its occupants of the terror they have imposed on the country.

Tio Ramon

Tio Ramon is Allende's stepfather, who enters her life shortly after her parents' separation. Entirely smitten by the beauty and vulnerability of the narrator's mother, he divorces his wife (with whom he has four children) and begins a life filled with financial struggles but entirely fulfilling. A diplomat assigned to various Chilean embassies, Tio Ramon takes his new family along and successfully weathers the many trials of raising another man's children. When Salvador Allende becomes president, Ramon gets a high and well-paid post in Argentina, only to leave after the coup; in his old age and in exile, he looks for work in Venezuela. Intelligent and charming, never uttering a word of complaint, he sets an example of courage and optimism that follows the narrator through her life's struggles.

Even though at their first meeting Allende declares she has "never seen such an ugly man" and becomes jealous of her mother's attention given to this stranger, she eventually develops a deep respect and love for her new father, whose vivacity and fairy-tale imagination make the years of modest living feel like they are filled with splendor. Although tough and persistent in making the narrator face her insecurities, Tio Ramon is also disarmingly supportive of her: when his fourteen-year-old stepdaughter doesn't want to go to a dance at her school in Lebanon out of fear of being the wallflower, he "closed the consulate and dedicated the afternoon to teach [her] to dance."

Tata

Tata is Allende's grandfather. As a young man, he is described as exhibiting "the concentration and integrity that were his characteristics; he was made of the same hard stone as his ancestors and, like many of them, had his feet firmly on the ground." Nevertheless, he marries his absolute opposite, a beautiful clairvoyant with telekinetic powers. In his old age, Tata remains a stubborn and proud man "who [believes] discomfort was healthful and that central heating sapped the strength." When he develops a heavy cough and high fever, he drives himself into a stroke with self-imposed remedies: "He buckled a saddle cinch around his waist and when he had a coughing fit gave himself a brutal tug to 'subdue his lungs'" and "tried to cure [the fever] with ice cold showers and large glasses of gin."

Allende acknowledges Tata's influence in her development as a writer as she recalls the long conversations she had with him, stating: "My daily visits with Tata provided me with enough material for all the books I have written, possibly for all I will ever write." She describes him as a "virtuoso storyteller, gifted with perfidious humor, able to recount the most hair-raising stories while bellowing with laughter." While in exile, Allende hears that Tata is dying and begins to write him a letter—which becomes a best-selling novel.

Willie

Willie is the narrator's second husband, a California lawyer with an aristocratic appearance and a frustratingly messy household life. The two meet after both of their lives have suffered a shipwreck of sorts, and they marry shortly thereafter. Allende falls in love with his life story and uses it in one of her novels.

Themes

Humor

Although *Paula* arises from an emotionally difficult time in the author's life and is permeated with her pain at losing her child to a long and excruciating illness, the writing is more often than not colored with Allende's wry sense of humor. For example, in describing the painful separation and social disgrace of losing her father after Tomas abandons his family, Allende recalls that her mother gladly returned to him his coat of arms, which featured three starving dogs—an ironic reference to the blue blood that Tomas brought to the family, then took away. As she writes of the sad days of her exile, the narrator also infuses her recollections with humorous remarks: she points out the loudness and vivacity of the Venezuelans, stating that, compared to them, "discreet Chileans with their high-pitched voices and delicate Spanish seemed like dolls on the wedding cake."

A crucial element of much of Allende's fiction, humor serves a double role in *Paula*. It emphasizes the magnitude of the narrator's pain through contrast: after entertaining anecdotes, Allende switches back into the reality of waiting, silence, and suffering in her daughter's inanimate presence. It also testifies to Allende's ability to find beauty, life, and strength in the face of tragedy, thus becoming a document of survival. Even while she writes about

Topics for Further Study

- The hereditary blood disease, porphyria, has its own rich mythological background. Investigate both the fiction and the facts about this rare illness. Discuss the reality and mythology of the disease in terms of the depiction of Paula as a character in the book.

- Select a few culturally specific narratives that negotiate a period of historical trauma. Such narratives might arise out of wars, like the Vietnam War or the Korean Conflict, or genocide, such as the Holocaust or the Indian Wars in the American West. How do narratives reveal variations in the representation of trauma based on their purpose (e.g. historical works, sociological studies, and fictional accounts)?

- The interest amongst Americans in their genealogy exploded during the 1990s. Investigate this recent interest in terms of best-selling works, like Allende's, that emphasize family trees.

- Although *Paula* reflects the author's Chilean heritage, in what ways does her work also take part in the creation of an international literature? How does Allende continue the spirit of ''El Boom''?

- What is Marxism and why has it receded as a viable alternative to capitalism? What was so unique about the experience of Marxism in Chile compared to other attempts to create a socialist state?

Paula's days in the hospital, the narrator notices the humor in the patients around her—like in the woman awaiting brain surgery who blames her condition on her husband's impotence. Allende's use of humor speaks of her personal ways of coping with pain and serves to balance out the emotional impact of the book, offering hope amid times of sadness.

Memory

In works that fall within the genre of autobiography, such as *Paula*, the author's memories are the essential component of the text. However, Allende arranges hers within the framework of the present, always reverting to her time with her daughter—the intended audience and the reason for telling the story of her life. The narrator's memories involve the recollections of others, as when she writes about the events that took place before her birth or in her early childhood; also, Allende acknowledges the changing nature of memory with aging and time, saying that people often make up in imagination for what they lack in memory of important participants in their lives. In describing her grandmother Meme, Allende says: ''I heard people talk about her, and I hoard her few remaining relics in a tin box. All the rest I have invented, because we all need a grand-

mother.'' However, because she is telling the story to her daughter, Allende writes that she is trying to be as faithful as possible to what really happened.

The author further explains the personal significance of memory in her life as she recalls that her family members who passed away were preserved as alive in survivors' memories of them. Allende's grandfather, Tata, maintains his relationship with his wife through memories: '''She lives on,' he said, 'because I have never forgotten her, not for a single minute.''' Faced with Paula's slow death, the narrator examines the importance of memory for the connection with one's loved ones when they pass on to spiritual existence; she writes that, once gone from the material world, they remain present only as spirits and memories, living intangible lives within those left behind.

Family

Amidst the narrator's recollections of personal growth, historical events, and cultural changes witnessed in her past are the detailed descriptions of the members of her family tree, with special emphasis on those who shaped her life and personality. Allende emphasizes the importance of family in her life over and over again, examining her own genetic and social heritage through the portraits of those that preceded her. When she describes the way her mother and grandmother "kidnapped" her from the hospital after she was born, Allende writes: "It is possible that in their haste they traded me for another baby, and that somewhere there is a woman with spinach-colored eyes and a gift for clairvoyance who is taking my place." However, the family relations created after her birth prove to be more important to Allende; based on the relationships she forms with various family members, she develops not only a large part of her personality but also her identity as a storyteller. Family also forms a basis for her sense of cultural identity, as she recalls the views and actions of those who have influenced her in determining her world views.

The situation of Paula's illness is also crucial for the author's sense of family, as she loses a part of her own. Allende writes: "Since the day [my children] were born, I have never thought of myself as an individual but as part of an inseparable trio." Given the sad occasion of Paula's dying, the family becomes closer and more significant for everybody involved, as is illustrated in the book's final pages when the family members gather to bid Paula goodbye.

Style

Autobiography

The genre of *Paula* is apparent in several elements of the book's construction. First of all, it is written in first person narrative, which the author specifies is her own voice; she names herself clearly in the text as Isabel Allende, not a character with the same name. Then, the foreword situates the work in relation to actual events in the author's life: Allende opens the book by stating, "These pages were written during the interminable hours spent in the corridors of a Madrid hospital. . . as well as beside [Paula's] bed in our home in California." Throughout the rest of the book, specific references are made within this time frame: the first part is written during the stay in the Madrid hospital; the second part continues in the author's house and ends with Paula's death. Allende further specifies the nature of her writing in *Paula* when she states that she will try to tell the truth about her life without embellishing the facts.

Style

Many critics have noted that *Paula* resembles Allende's fictional works because the real characters, situations, and events from her life are described in the same style as her fictional ones. Style, defined as a specific way of using elements of writing composition to convey ideas and to give the text a stamp of the author's personality, is an indication of Allende's presence in all of her works. In *Paula*, when the narrator speaks of her identity as a writer, she admits to creating her novels and short stories on the basis of real-life encounters. For example, Allende focuses on family and culture as important topics covered in *Paula*, and there are detailed descriptions of individual characters as well as historical events. Also, the realistic presentation of facts is diluted by the author's references to ethereal, mystical visions and events; this is a technique that classifies Allende as a writer in the tradition of magic realism—a genre of modern Latin American novels that addresses social issues but keeps them veiled in "magical" symbolism.

Flashback

Allende creates a parallel plot in *Paula* by switching between two story lines: one in the present, in which she takes care of her daughter in her illness, and the other in the past, presented more or less in a linear fashion, in which the narrator tells the story of her life. The second story line is a flashback, a device used in literature to showcase events that took place before the story's beginning. Allende goes back and forth in her memory although she mostly maintains chronological order in the flashback, starting with a broad and unspecified description of her ancestry and going through the various stages of her life until the present time.

The benefit of using a flashback to tell a story is that the narrator knows what eventually happens; therefore, and especially since *Paula* is an autobiographical work, the author often comments on the future events in her story line while contextualizing a character or discussing an event. This way, Allende reorganizes the book to accommodate the development of certain themes: she groups them together by shifting the chronological order of her memories somewhat. For example, when talking about her estranged father at the book's beginning, Allende points out the irony of being called in to identify his body years later because she never knew what he looked like; she tells Paula all of his photographs were burned decades ago. This reference makes a link between the narrator's present, in which she tells Paula about a family photo from her childhood, and her past, in which the flashback continues with a description of the problematic marriage of Allende's parents.

Historical Context

NAFTA

The North American Free Trade Agreement (NAFTA) went into effect on January 1, 1994. This trilateral agreement between Canada, the United States, and Mexico created an economic zone free from tariff barriers. During the period of negotiations, the countries of the American Hemisphere left out of the agreement began to create their own trading blocks or to improve existing ones. In December 1994, the Summit of the Americas was held in Miami, Florida. All the nations of the hemisphere were present, and trade was high on the agenda. The dream of a hemisphere trading block was resuscitated, but nothing was immediately agreed upon due to the myriad of existing blocks that would need to be aligned.

For example, Argentina, Brazil, Chile, and Uruguay had, in 1990, formed Mercosur (a Spanish acronym that, in English, translates as the Common Market but is sometimes referred to as the Andean Group). However, the economies involved in this trading block did not begin to boom until 1992 when nearly every regional tariff between the member nations was removed. The 1992 agreement was in response to the NAFTA negotiations as well as the desire by individual countries, especially Chile, to eventually win inclusion into NAFTA. By 1997, Chile was approaching fast-track inclusion in NAFTA.

Chile

Chile's return to democracy began in 1987 when Pope John Paul II visited Chile and accused General Augusto Pinochet Ugarte's regime of human rights violations. In the political fracas that ensued, Pinochet agreed to a confidence plebiscite, a vote in which the people would decide whether to allow Pinochet to reign as president for another eight years. Sixteen of the opposition parties banded together to form a "No" coalition, and in the fall of 1988 Pinochet lost the plebiscite. Consequently, new elections were held the following year. In 1990, the Christian Democrat Patricio Aylwin, who represented the seventeen-party coalition Concert of

Parties for Democracy, became president. Pinochet became "Senator for Life."

Aylwin succeeded in maintaining civilian rule by continuing to decrease the power of the military. His ability to avoid an overthrow of the government was successful. During the Aylwin administration, the Rettig Commission began to collect information on the human rights violations committed by the Pinochet regime. In the 1993 elections, democracy was assured with the election of Christian Democrat Eduardo Frei Ruiz-Tagle.

America's Republican Revolution

Responding to a potential ideological vacuum, left by the Cold War's end, to President Clinton, and to the demographic shift in America, which had made the suburbs an electoral power in their own right, the Republicans took a commanding control of Congress in 1994 under the leadership of Newt Gingrich. This takeover has been called the Suburban Congress, the Republican Revolution, or the Newtonian Revolution. The extreme rhetoric of the revolutionary Gingrich eventually led to his political demise but not before seriously heightening the drama of the culture wars by reducing the National Endowment for the Arts and changing the structure of the welfare system.

Assisted Suicide

The "right to die" became a serious debate in the United States in response to a Michigan pathologist who became known as Dr. Death. By 1996, Jack Kevorkian had enabled thirty people to use his "suicide machines" to end their lives. Several states pursued murder charges against Kevorkian but three such cases failed. Several states put the issue to referendum votes.

Critical Overview

The critical reception of *Paula* was divided: although most reviewers praise the book as a passionate and candid voyage through memory and grief, some find it disappointing after Allende's previous work. Negative reviews range from criticism of the author's use of her daughter's tragedy as a peg on which to hang the story of her own life to seeing the book as an overly romanticized autobiography relying on questionable facts, to pointing out that the author's kitschy rhetoric camouflages the book's introspective parts. However, the majority of critics applauded Allende's effort in her first nonfiction work and admitted to feeling drawn into the story's powerful emotional pull.

In a review for the *San Francisco Chronicle,* Patricia Holt praises the book and writes: "In her feverish determination to bring it all to life, and Paula along with it, Allende produces some of her best writing." Her writing, Holt says, is "voluptuous" and universally moving, as she seeks "answers to life's largest questions" in wondering about loss, death, revival, and acceptance. Liz Warwick writes in a Montreal *Gazette* review that *Paula* is "a haunting memoir of [Allende's] life and a poignant meditation on her daughter's year-long descent into death." Warwick also recognizes the honesty with which Allende reveals the many layers of her personal and public personae, including the one of writer, while remaining humble throughout. As Allende states in the interview with Warwick:

> Mothers across the world for millennia have experienced the loss of their children. Why should I, in my terrible arrogance, imagine that I don't deserve this or that my daughter didn't deserve to die young? This is what life is about—coming into the world to lose everything we have . . . And from each loss, we learn and grow.

In the introduction to *Conversations with Isabel Allende,* John Rodden recognizes the stages in Allende's work as indivisible from her personal life and notes that *Paula* is a testimony to the author's individual development, saying: "Allende's courage and openness have also extended to a greater capacity for self-disclosure about her private demons." Rodden also points out the author's personal investment in the book, made remarkable by her willingness to share the experience with an audience of her readers. He further observes, in "After Paula," another chapter of the same book, that the magic in *Paula*, criticized for its presence in an autobiography, is in fact strangely existent in her life: a psychic once told Allende that her daughter would become known all over the world, which "was to come ironically true in another way: by the end of April 1995, *Paula* was number eight on the *New York Times* best-seller list, after having already become a best-seller throughout Europe."

Criticism

Jeremy W. Hubbell

Hubbell is a Ph.D. candidate in history at the State University of New York at Stony Brook. In this essay, *he examines the literary expression of traumatic symptoms and the author's coping strategies in Allende's* Paula, *evident in the content as well as in the textual elements of the book.*

During the 1990s, the concept of trauma entered the American cultural spotlight and found its place in the spheres of "psychoanalysis, psychiatry, sociology, and even literature," as Cathy Caruth writes in the book *Trauma and Experience: Explorations in Memory.* The public interest in the literature of this issue became apparent when autobiographical works focusing on a traumatic experience, such as *Angela's Ashes, My Sergei: A Love Story,* and *Tuesdays with Morrie,* reached and stayed on national bestseller charts throughout the decade.

The symptoms of trauma, as outlined by Caruth, are the following: intense personal suffering, avoidance or delay in emotional response that is too overwhelming to be experienced all at once, repetition and reliving of the experience in an attempt to recapture it, and the sufferer's becoming possessed by the overwhelming event. Underlying these symptoms is the sufferer's sense of fragmentation, disorientation in space and time, an apparently irrational desire to hang onto the trauma as a definition of self, and, if it is a trauma of loss, to retain a kind of memorial to the deceased within oneself. In her autobiography dedicated to her daughter, Allende finds an outlet for at least some of her traumatic symptoms by recording them in her writing and in the process creates a document that testifies to her pain and survival.

Allende exhibits several traumatic symptoms as she writes *Paula*; the two story line threads (of the narrator's past and of her daughter's present) reflect the return of old traumas from her life. The most obvious traumatic event—the one that propels her into writing the book in the first place—is Paula's sudden tragic illness and the deterioration of her condition while she is in a coma. Allende's response of beginning a letter to her daughter can be seen as a form of avoidance of pain; in the beginning of the book, as she introduces the agonizing circumstances of her writing, she states: "I plunge into these pages in an irrational attempt to overcome my terror."

Allende's choice of the book's content also speaks of her need to escape the painful present as she reverts to memory and returns to the past—far from Paula's imminent tragedy. By writing of her own past, not exclusively Paula's, Allende signifies

Isabel Allende's uncle, Chilean President Salvadore Allende

her desire to find self-affirmation outside her suffering as well as to remove herself from the source of unbearable pain. This attempt repeatedly fails because the author cannot help but return to the inanimate figure in the hospital bed. Allende speaks of her fear that Paula will not wake up intact from her coma, of guilt at placing her in a hospital where she was misdiagnosed and mistreated, of struggling not to lose hope in face of the doctors' grim predictions, of not being able to survive the loss; she speaks of these emotions in temporally distributed intervals, placing enough textual distance between them to make them manageable. Thus, the structure of the book demonstrates the author's way of coping with the trauma of Paula's illness. Further, the author documents a typical defense mechanism of trauma victims who are too overwhelmed by the event to face its horror in reality: she describes several dreams in which her worst fears are expressed, thus finding an outlet for her feelings in nightmares. The most disturbing dream is one in which she sees her daughter's death and cannot prevent it:

> I dreamed that you were twelve years old, Paula . . . You were standing in the center of a hollow tower, something like a grain silo filled with hundreds of fluttering doves. Meme's voice was saying, 'Paula is dead.' You began to rise off the ground . . . I tried to hold you back by your clothing; I called to you, but no sound came.

An important way in which the text reflects Allende's traumatization is the juxtaposition of past and present events: when she accepts the news of Paula's brain damage and loses hope for her full recovery, the author also reaches the peak of pain in the story of her life—her unwanted exile in Venezuela after the assassination of her uncle, Chilean president Salvador Allende. This mirroring of an old trauma with a new one shows a repeating pain in the author's life, in both cases caused by unwanted abandonment, first of her country (which at the time did not have a chance of ''recovery''), then of her hope for Paula's physical and mental recovery from her illness. Other losses come into the story as well: that of Meme and Tata (grandparents who die years apart, leaving both emptiness and fulfillment in the author's heart), of her own father who deserts the family before she can ever remember him, of her favorite uncle, of her brothers who become estranged, of her first marriage, which disintegrates while in exile, and so forth. These painful experiences range from personal to national, showing that trauma as a phenomenon exists and shapes not only individual lives but the lives of cultures, histories, and societies as well. When the doctors test Paula's peripheral nerves by administering electric shocks

What Do I Read Next?

- Allende's *Daughter of Fortune*, published in 1999, is the author's sixth novel. Set in the 1800s, it tells the story of a young woman who takes the road less traveled in pursuit of her own identity and happiness. Like Allende's former fictional works, this one also presents characters that span many generations, plots that converge, and questions issues of class and ethnicity.

- *Angela's Ashes: A Memoir* is Frank McCourt's 1996 book, which quickly became a bestseller; it was eventually followed by *'Tis,* a sequel to his autobiography. McCourt recalls his childhood and life in Ireland and New York City, painting a poignant yet often humorous picture of a life of poverty, spent among many siblings and with an alcoholic father.

- Richard Wright's semi-fictional autobiography *Black Boy,* originally published in 1945, came out in a new edition in the 1990s. A moving story of a young boy's coming of age, this book is a seminal text in American history about the experience of black men in the American South during the Jim Crow years.

- *Tuesdays with Morrie: An Old Man, a Young Man and Life's Greatest Lesson,* published in 1997, is journalist Mitch Albom's recollection of the relationship he had with his mentor, Morrie Schwartz, before his mentor's death from a terminal illness.

- Ekaterina Gordeeva's 1996 book *My Sergei: A Love Story* is an autobiographical account by the young widow after her husband's untimely death. The book details the professional and intimate relationship between the author and her husband/skating partner Sergei Grinkov, the famous Russian two-time Olympic gold medalists in pairs skating.

---

to her arms and legs, Allende is "thinking of all the men and women and children in Chile who were tortured in a very similar way with electric prods."

Allende's recollections of these various traumatic events serve a twofold purpose in the text. First, they reveal what the author has already survived and how she and those around her dealt with these losses; and second, they document her attempt to survive the tragedy at hand, perhaps by remembering the coping strategies she used in the past. Admittedly, the most powerful strategy for Allende is writing; at the beginning of the book, she says to Paula that her first novel (*The House of the Spirits*) began as a letter to her dying grandfather in an effort to deal with the pain she felt about his death and her own life in exile. Writing can be an effective way to relive the traumatic experience without being overwhelmed by it. In fact, Allende relates the accumulation of her life's traumas to her need to organize her memories so that she can deal with Paula's situation. Trying to fight off the sufferer's

disorientation in time, she writes: "I am trampled by memories, all happening in one instant, as if my entire life were a single, unfathomable image." The text further reveals the traumatic nature of Allende's memory in its uncontrollability: "My past has little meaning; I can see no order in it, no clarity, purpose, or path, only a blind journey guided by instincts and detours caused by events beyond my control." Yet, writing has the benefit of giving trauma shape and some unity and of taking it from the abstract realm of one's mind into the concrete realm of text:

> Looking back, I view the totality of my fate and, with a little luck, I shall find meaning for the person I am . . . My grandmother wrote in her notebooks to safeguard the fleeting fragments of the days and outwit loss of memory. I am trying to distract death."

Another symptom of trauma apparent in Allende's writing of *Paula* is a sense of fragmentation she repeatedly describes. For example, when her husband Willie visits her in Madrid, the author experiences her physical existence once again and reaffirms herself: she touches parts of her body and rediscovers life in it. Putting these parts together is a process that Allende employs in writing the book itself—taking pieces of her past, segments of memory, and putting them together into an autobiography. That way, she can once again find stability in a life ruptured by sadness. After months of feeling overwhelmed by Paula's tragedy, the author attempts to reestablish a sense of self outside the trauma that has come to define her everyday existence: "This is me, I'm a woman, I'm Isabel, I'm not turning into smoke, I have not disappeared."

The fact that Allende wrote an autobiography at this point in her life can be seen as an effort to negotiate the importance of the traumatic event as well as to let go of it. In preserving her feelings of loss and desperation in text, Allende manages to retain the event—in a way, "saving" the trauma on paper—and thus acknowledges the significance of losing Paula from her life. However, because the author writes about her life's experiences in the book, she also recognizes and reestablishes herself through the cycle of life that keeps her going. The fact that the book about the mother's life is dedicated to her dying daughter is a recovery that works in two ways: although she has created a tangible memorial to Paula, Allende has also contextualized the event as a part of her existence instead of the other way around. By the book's end, it becomes obvious that the author has learned to negotiate with her feelings and that she is ready to let Paula go into the spiritual realm that encompasses all existence: "I am the void, I am everything that exists, I am in every leaf of the forest, in every drop of the dew, in every particle of ash carried by the stream, I am Paula and I am also Isabel, I am nothing and all other things in this life and other lives, immortal. Godspeed, Paula, woman. Welcome, Paula, spirit."

Overall, Allende's autobiography is an ultimate testimony to survival after a tragic loss. The style and structure of *Paula* ultimately reveal the writer's state of mind although many other textual elements counter her record of her suffering. The book's humorous and buoyant tone, picturesque descriptions, magical depictions of everyday reality, and a cast of life-affirming personae are nevertheless delicately balanced against the author's painful attempts to deal with trauma in her life as well as in her literary work. An exemplary document of private as well as public trauma, *Paula* is a case study of the presence of an author's emotion in literature.

Source: Jeremy W. Hubbell, Critical Essay on *Paula*, in *Nonfiction Classics for Students,* The Gale Group, 2001.

> In her autobiography dedicated to her daughter, Allende finds an outlet for at least some of her traumatic symptoms by recording them in her writing and in the process creates a document that testifies to her pain and survival."

Barbara Mujica

In the following interview-essay, Allende discusses with Mujica her writing technique, criticism of her works, and the uniqueness of Paula.

The night before this interview I attended a talk by Isabel Allende at Georgetown University—a stop on a long publicity tour for her memoir, *Paula* (HarperCollins). Allende spoke about her book, which she began in 1991 in a hospital in Madrid, where her daughter was being treated for porphyria. A beautiful, intelligent, active young woman in her late twenties, Paula had just married a young Spaniard. She was working as a volunteer with poor children at a Catholic school in Madrid when she became ill. Although porphyria is rarely fatal, due to an error in procedure, an accident, or some other unknown circumstance, Paula never came out of her coma and died on December 6, 1992. In spite of the fact that *Paula* was engendered by a tragedy, this is not a sad book, for Allende emphasizes the beautiful moments she spent with her daughter as much as the physical destruction caused by the disease.

In her presentation, Allende spoke of the most difficult moments of her long, hard ordeal, but she also read humorous passages about her own life, including one in which she recounts her experiences as a chorus girl at the follies, when she was researching an article for a feminist magazine. I was impressed with the ease with which she passed from terribly painful to amusing segments of the book, laughing and provoking laughter, telling embarrassing anecdotes, answering difficult questions. Small, pretty, and very sharp, in front of an audience Allende is a professional in complete control of her

> Allende believes that *Paula* is different from everything else she has written. 'I can't judge it from a literary perspective,' she says, 'and I can't compare it with other books because it would be unfair both to this book and the others; they're two different genres.'"

medium—perhaps due to the long years she worked on Chilean television. It was obvious that this presentation had been carefully orchestrated and rehearsed, one of many that she was giving to promote her new book in countless cities. And yet, one sensed terrible sadness behind the protective shield. After the talk, several listeners remained in their seats sobbing disconsolately.

I asked Allende where she found the strength and vitality to do these presentations night after night, week after week—how she could go on talking about Paula and laughing, how she managed to get on with her life—because her energy was indeed amazing. "When the idea to do this book tour came up, I was terrified," she admits. "I thought I wouldn't be able to do it. Obviously because the topic is very hard for me to deal with, and also because it's all still very fresh in my mind. Two things have helped me a lot. One is people's reaction. There's a marvelous energy that the public transmits. You can feel people's affection, their openness, their tolerance, their understanding. So many people come up to me with a letter they've written on the back of a ticket, a little note, or a gift to tell me that they've lost someone close . . . Or often very young girls who identify with Paula . . . The second thing is that I read these texts in English, and the language constitutes a filter. These aren't the words that I wrote; they're the words of my translator, and that creates a little space between the text and me, which helps. But those few times I'll have to do it in Spanish I think will be very hard."

In her talk at Georgetown Allende spoke of the mask of language she hides behind. Nevertheless, people penetrate that mask and feel her pain. "It's

that the pain is always there," she explains. "It's part of my nature. It's like wrinkles and grey hair. Those things are part of me now. I welcome a feeling that I know will be with me the rest of my life. Each time I see a long-haired girl in blue jeans walking down the street, I think it's Paula. And often I find myself with my hand on the phone ready to call her—because I called her all the time, almost every day—and then I realize that there's no place to call her. What I'm saying is, that's going to be with me always . . . and I have to live with it."

Four years ago Allende was at a party celebrating the publication of *The Infinite Plan* (HarperCollins), feeling elated, triumphant, thinking that she had reached the high point of her career, when she received the call that Paula was in the hospital. When she arrived at the intensive care unit and was informed of her daughter's state, she was convinced that Paula would get better. She began to write during the long hours of waiting at the hospital; it was a way of killing time. Besides, she thought that Paula might not remember certain things when she awakened, and the book—a long memoir of the author's life with family anecdotes and descriptions of the political situation—would serve to orient her.

"My mother told me: 'Write or you'll die,'" says Allende, "and I started to think that as long as I wrote, Paula would stay alive. It was a way of defying death. My mother saw the end way before I did. Life is full of signs and premonitions, if only we knew how to read them. I had a lot of trouble coming to terms with the truth."

Allende began jotting down her thoughts and recollections on a yellow pad. She didn't intend to write a book, so the procedure never became a literary project. "At least not while I was writing," she says. "Now it is, because it's out of my hands. But writing was so tied to everything that happened . . . From the moment when Paula got sick I began to write, and I wrote during the entire year she was ill and during the fist year of mourning. It was like part of the process, I never separated it completely. There are no variations in an illness like this one, nothing ever happens. There are no reactions. I wrote a lot of letters to my mother . . . when I went back over them I saw that none of them revealed any kind of change . . . Everything is the same from the first day to the last. Writing was a means of separating the days, of allowing time to pass and fixing it in my memory. It was like, by writing the day, the day happened. Without that, everything was the same. Writing was so tied to the process of grieving and also trying to help Paula that the book never developed an independent life. It's just that it wasn't a book. It started to be a book a lot later. So it never had its own life. When I wrote the last draft of the book, we still hadn't decided whether or not to publish it because I wasn't really writing it for anyone but myself, first of all, and then for my son, Nicolás, and my grandchildren. Porphyria is a genetic problem. Nicolás may have it. It might possibly show up in the children. It's a dominant gene, so it's very possible that the children have it. I thought it was important to leave them a testimony of what happened. Who knows when it might happen again?''

Nevertheless, today book publishing has become a commercial enterprise. Under the circumstances, marketing *Paula* must have been tremendously difficult for Allende. ''I never had to do this before *The Infinite Plan,*'' she explains. ''When I changed publishers, HarperCollins stipulated in the contract that I had to do book tours. And I did the one for *The Infinite Plan* under terrible conditions because my daughter had died some six months before. I had to go all over the country, to eighteen cities, talking about *The Infinite Plan,* which didn't have anything to do with Paula's story, with a truly broken heart. So that was a really traumatic experience. This time, as well, I approached it with certain terror, but it hasn't been so bad. Of course, I don't think of it as selling the book. Instead, I think of it as talking about Paula. And somehow a sort of spiritual clearing forms in which I can take refuge, even on this trip, because the topic is a spiritual one.''

There has been a lot of talk about the influence of other writers, especially Gabriel García Márquez, on Allende's work. However, in *Paula* there can be no question of imitation. The tone is intimate and the voice, absolutely authentic. The author insists that the question was raised years ago with respect to *The House of Spirits* (Knopf, 1985) but hasn't come up since. ''I believe that every story has its own way of being told, every story has its own tone,'' she says. ''I had never written nonfiction before . . . well, of course, when I was a journalist, but I'd never written a whole book that wasn't fiction. But the tone of this book is very different from that of the others. This one is written the way I speak.''

Allende believes that *Paula* is different from everything else she has written. ''I can't judge it from a literary perspective,'' she says, ''and I can't compare it with other books because it would be unfair both to this book and the others; they're two

different genres . . . I don't know what I'm going to write in the future. I don't even know if I'm going to write. I feel that during my whole life I was preparing to write this book. And what comes after, I don't know. I have the impression that nothing. All I feel is a great emptiness.''

As for her evolution as a writer, she says: ''I've learned very little. I've learned to cut a lot, to be more and more critical of my own work. But I have the impression that for each book you have to start from scratch. I know certain things that I'll never do again. For example, I can't try to force the story or the characters in a particular direction because I have a preconceived notion of how things should be, because that doesn't work for me. When I try to do that, everything falls apart. I have to follow the natural course the story takes all by itself. As if I could just interpret something that's in the air, but not create something new. That's something I've learned. And I've learned to be disciplined. I don't believe in inspiration. I believe in work. In my case, inspiration doesn't cut it; what cuts it is sitting all day, six or eight hours, and working. And that's something I know now, so I don't even wait for the story to fall out of the blue because I know that won't happen. And to edit, to do a lot of editing. But I always have the impression when I start on a new project that I don't know anything. Nothing.

''It seems to me that all my books are written differently. *The House of the Spirits* has an oneiric, magical tone. *Of Love and Shadows* (Knopf, 1987) is a police story that could have been written by a journalist. *Eva Luna* (Knopf, 1988) has a very different tone because there's a strong element of irony; it's a book that can be read on a lot of different levels. On the first, it could just be the story of *Eva Luna;* on another, the story that she invents about herself; on another, the soap opera that she's writing about the story that she's inventing about herself. There are a lot of steps to reading it. And that sensation of peeling an onion, I had it while I was writing. It's very different from my other books. *The Infinite Plan* is a story that was already there. My job was to re-create it, but all the characters already existed, and the entire story existed. Even the title existed because my husband's father was the one who invented the religion called the Infinite Plan, and that's where the story came from. So I even stole the title from him. Everything!''

Allende also has a popular collection of short fiction, *The Stories of Eva Luna* (MacMillan, 1991). ''People are always asking me for stories, but they're difficult to write,'' she says. ''Stories are like apples. They come to you whole, round. Any little thing that's off, the story is ruined. There's one advantage, though: it's that you can work in segments, in segments of time. In two or three weeks, you can write a story. On the other hand, a novel is a commitment that can last two, three years. It's like falling in love. On the other hand, a short story is like a one-night stand!''

When she's working on a book, Allende follows a rigid schedule. She has one day—January 8—when she begins all her projects, ''because it's too easy to put off writing,'' she says. ''There's always something better to do, like play with the grandchildren, for example, so I need the discipline of always beginning on the same day. And once I begin, I don't start any other project until I finish the first one. I write just one book at a time, I never have several projects going at the same time. I write in the morning rather than in the afternoon because I'm more creative and energetic in the morning than in the afternoon. I get up very early, at six, and I go to another town, where I have a study, a garage that my husband fixed up like a study, and that's where I work. In the afternoon, at about two more or less, I have to take care of my correspondence. There's always more and more mail; we're forever waiting for it to crest and die down, but it doesn't, it just . . . it's like bureaucracy, it can only grow. Unless it's contracts, invitations . . . my assistant—who fortunately is also my daughter-in-law, Celia in the book—she takes care of all that. She deals with it . . . she's really my boss. The letters, the fan letters, I answer them all personally. Because, if a person is kind enough to write me a letter, to look up my address and send it to me, at least I can answer it. That takes quite a bit of time.

''Generally, I type right into the computer a draft into which I pour everything. That's the part I like best, telling the story, without worrying about how it will come out. And after I've written the whole story, which takes about three or four months, I print it and read it for the first time. Then I know what it's all about. After that, I begin to clean it up, to leave the main story and get rid of all the extraneous material. That's for a novel, not for a memoir or stories, which are different. And then, there's a second draft in which the story is there, defined, and another in which I only worry about tension, language . . . I polish it, I polish it carefully . . . I don't know how long that takes because with the computer you correct and overcorrect and correct again right on the screen . . . I don't print it each time. And when I have the feeling that it's pretty much ready, I print it out and send it to my mother in Chile.

''My mom reads it with a red pencil. Then she gets on the first plane she can find and comes to California. We lock ourselves up in the dining room to fight, and we fight for about a month. There's no better editor than my mother. She's heartless, absolutely cruel. She says things that would destroy any writer . . . If she weren't my mother, I'd have killed her already! But I know she does it because she loves me. She demands a lot from me because she loves me so much. She's not jealous of me, and she doesn't have a preconceived notion of what will sell, the way an editor from a publishing house might. A professional editor might be thinking . . . well, if we put a sex scene on page 40, we'll sell more copies. Such an idea would never occur to my mother. She just goes by the quality. She insists and insists. We polish it between the two of us, and then she leaves and I continue polishing the draft by myself, incorporating a large number of my mother's suggestions, but not all of them, because my mom, for example, is shocked by the fact that I include sex scenes in my books. Sometimes I don't even show them to her. Now, with the computer, I censor them before she sees them.'' Allende bursts out laughing, proof that she hasn't lost her sense of humor. ''If there's some reference to the pope, I censor that too,'' she says, still laughing.

Although Allende's books have been translated into many languages and are praised all over the Western world, she has not been immune to negative criticism. I asked her how adverse commentaries affect her, whether they hurt her or simply roll off her back. ''It depends,'' she answers. ''There are criticisms that are just negative and others that are malicious. And there's quite a difference. I can accept that someone doesn't like what I write for some reason. But at times I perceive meanness in the criticism. Meanness that comes from the fact that I wrote something that someone doesn't understand for any particular reason. Or because there was antagonism there to start with. Sometimes it's happened to me that another writer, often a man, criticizes my work, and you can tell from his comments that he is envious. His tone is nasty. That bothers me. But it doesn't bother me that much, because in reality, public response is what really matters in the long run. There are criticisms that are very destructive. The worst review in the history of literature appeared in the *New York Review of Books* on *Eva Luna*. This is an important piece because it goes to all the bookstores, all the libraries, so any students or other people who are studying my work or want to know anything about me, the first thing they'll do is go to the library and look for criticism, and the first thing they'll find is that one, which is horrible. A man who is an expert on baseball and took a trip to Latin America wrote it. Someone thought that because he had traveled in Latin America, he was the person to write about *Eva Luna*. He didn't understand the book at all, and he tore it apart in the most vicious way possible. And that bothered me because, who is this guy? What moral or literary authority does he have to take a book he didn't even understand and tear it apart?''

In spite of being the subject of many studies and theses, Allende admits that she doesn't keep up with the latest literary criticism. ''I never studied literature,'' she explains. ''And I haven't taught it, either. I've taught creative writing, which isn't the same thing. So fortunately, I'm not up on all the theories, which terrify me! But I get a lot of studies done by students, books written by professors on my work . . . Generally, I don't understand them. I think it's the same with most writers. One writes as one can, the best one can, and it's the job of other people to vivisect what one produces, to explain it, but it's difficult for a writer to explain her own work. I have maybe four papers on Barrabás, the dog in *The House of the Spirits* . . . what the dog symbolizes . . . It was just a dog who lived in my house and his name was Barrabás, that's all! But how can I explain to a student who has been working on a thesis on Barrabás for a year that he's just a dog? I'd feel awful!'' The author laughs as she remembers the strange explanations that some critics have given to different characters or episodes in her books. ''I think it can also be very paralyzing if you have that kind of explanation in your head . . . if you're always thinking about those theories, about what the critics are going to say,'' she says. ''You wind up writing for professors and critics, which is very dangerous.''

Some feminist critics have insisted that there is such a thing as ''women's writing,'' which, according to the French theorist Hélène Cixous, is more spontaneous, natural, and fluid than men's writing. Allende approaches these theories rather cautiously because, in her opinion, ''women have been segregated from everything in life, including writing. So, when we talk about literature, we just suppose it's masculine and it's not qualified by an adjective. When women write, they call it 'women's literature' as if it were a minor genre. I think we women

have to be careful not to fall into that trap ourselves. Nevertheless, on the one hand, literature is always the same and language, the instrument that we use, is always the same. But, of course, it's also true that there's such a thing as point of view, perspective, which is determined by one's sex, one's age, one's place of birth, the social class one is born into, the race one is born into. All these things determine a biography, a world view and, therefore, a form of writing. Why do women chose subjects different from the ones men choose? Why do women read certain books that just don't interest men, and vice versa? Because certain things are common to our sex.''

The House of the Spirits, the book that launched Allende's career, continues to be her most highly praised work. In spite of this, however, it seems that certain aspects of the novel have been understood only superficially by readers outside of Chile. For example, *The House of the Spirits* is one of the few books that really show the diversity of opinion among conservatives during the socialist regime in Chile. Many of the conservatives of the generation of Esteban Trueba, the protagonist's grandfather, were afraid of change and unable to support socialism on ideological grounds, but felt that when Salvador Allende fell, Chile would return to its democratic roots. When they saw what Pinochet's dictatorship brought, they were horrified. Outside Chile, there is a tendency to classify the opponents of socialism automatically as supporters of the dictatorship. Nevertheless, Allende shows that this was not the case.

I asked her if she feels that readers grasp this aspect of the novel. ''Some, yes,'' she says. ''But others get angry. For example, when *The House of the Spirits* was published, it was during the worst part of the repression in Chile. And the message at the end is reconciliation. Not forgetting, but yes, reconciliation, with the idea that a new country could be built—or the country could be restored—only on a foundation of national reconciliation. It just wasn't possible to go on proliferating hatred systematically forever and ever, on and on, because that way we would never end the violence. That set very badly among the people who had suffered repression firsthand in Chile, because it was practically asking them to forgive in a period when no one was entertaining that idea yet. So I had a very negative reaction from the people on the left, and of course, a horrible one from the people on the right, because I tried to explain the circumstances under which the coup occurred; I spoke clearly of torture and the horror that took place under the military regime, which, back then, it was still possible to deny because we were living with censorship and self-censorship, so nothing was being published about it and people could say no, those are just Communist rumors and not accept what was really happening in Chile. Nowadays it's almost impossible for people to keep on denying it. It's very difficult. There are still people who do, but those are just dinosaurs who really don't matter. So I had bad reactions from both sides. But there was a huge number of people in the middle who did understand the subtleties of how things were, because in every family there were people on both sides. The country was divided, families were divided, couples were divided. So a lot of people did understand, and the book was very well received by those people in the middle. Now, how the public understands it in the United States or in, say, Denmark, I don't know. I just don't know.''

In 1994 a film based on *The House of the Spirits* was released, with Jeremy Irons, Meryl Streep, Glenn Close, Winona Ryder, and Antonio Banderas. It received mixed reviews, but the author liked it a lot. However, she says, ''I felt a few things were missing. The lack of humor, that's what bothered me the most. I don't know if you know Jeremy Irons . . . he's the funniest person imaginable. I think that in the book, in *The House of the Spirits,* except in the very most tragic moments, there's a current of irony and humor that just isn't in the movie. I found that lacking, and also a more Latin touch . . . I would have liked more . . . more of that Latin tone. But I did like the film very much.''

It is hard to believe, in spite of what she says, that Allende has no plans for the future. She is too dynamic to remain inactive, and she loves writing too much to give it up. She admits that she has already begun another project: ''Well, January 8 always prompts me to begin another book,'' she says. ''And I did begin something. Let's see when I finish with all this, if I can spend time on it and create another book. But I don't feel the passion to write it that I've felt before, with other books. I think it's because *Paula* is still too fresh. I just finished the memoir last October. It was published immediately in Spain in December. Everything has gone so fast that I haven't had time to breathe. It's been too fast.''

In spite of how hard it has been, at least she is fortunate enough to be able to count on the support of her family: ''I have a husband, a son, and a daughter-in-law, who want only for me to write, because that way I don't bother them. They want me to be locked up writing all the time. My husband met me because he fell in love with one of my books . . . *Of Love and Shadows* . . . He read it in English, he fell in love with it, and so he went to San José [California] when I was on a book tour, and that's where he met me. So, he came to me because he admired my work. And his admiration for my work hasn't diminished at all. It's a nice feeling because, as a Latin woman, I've had to struggle my whole life against the lack of respect of the male establishment . . . in every aspect of my life. For example, it took many years before my stepfather, whom I adore, was able to respect me professionally, in my career. He automatically respected the male children. Women, we have to earn respect from one day to the next. It's hard. To have to fight like that during your whole life leaves you scarred.''

But Allende hasn't lost faith in people. She sees her book *Paula* as a celebration of existence, of all the things in the world that are beautiful and worthwhile. She concludes a conversation with these words: ''The only thing I want to say is that this book, in spite of the tragic subject matter and the tragic circumstances under which I wrote it, is not a book about death. It's not a sad book. I think it's a book about life . . . about family . . . about relationships . . . about love . . . about all the things that are important and should be celebrated in my life and in Paula's.''

Source: Isabel Allende and Barbara Mujica, ''The Life Force of Language,'' in *Americas,* Vol. 47, No. 6, November/December 1995, pp. 36–43.

Ruth Behar

In the following review, Behar calls Paula *a "memoir of devastating passion," citing its "charged poetry."*

''Listen, Paula, I am going to tell you a story, so that when you wake up you will not feel so lost.'' With those simple, enchanted words, the Chilean novelist Isabel Allende begins *Paula,* a memoir of devastating passion dedicated to her daughter. Sadly, unlike Sleeping Beauty, Paula Frias Allende will never awaken to hear her mother's tale. She has fallen, at the age of 28, into a sudden coma caused by the rare illness of porphyria, which has left her speechless, motionless, lost in an angelic stupor that is broken only rarely by tears and trembling. As her mother unfolds her tale, patiently seeking to awaken Paula and bring her back to the world of the living, Paula

La Moneda, *the Government Palace, the site of Salvadore Allende's regime in Santiago, Chile*

edges closer to death. By the end, she becomes a gentle spirit who appears to her mother in the night, asking to be released from the suffering and weight of her body. Allende must finally confront a harsh truth: not only that her tale won't save her daughter, but that she must cease her storytelling altogether, that it is keeping Paula strapped to a reality she no longer inhabits.

Paula, despite the title, is not a biography or even an account of the life of Isabel Allende's daughter. It is Allende's own autobiography, told to a daughter who has entered a limbo between life and death. Paula's entrance into that border zone becomes the occasion for Isabel Allende to tell her own life story. The dying daughter becomes a mirror in which the mother reaffirms her reality and comes to terms with the decisions she has made as a woman and a writer. In the cruelest possible twisting of the order of things, Paula must die before her mother, must become a daughter who gives birth to her mother. This unflinchingly honest self-portrait becomes Allende's parting gift to her daughter.

How inspiring it is for any woman who feels she has yet to do the work that really matters to read Isabel Allende's story of how she found her calling

as a novelist. Allende recalls, "New Year's, 1981. That day brought home the fact that soon I would be forty and had not until then done anything truly significant. Forty! that was the beginning of the end, and I did not have to stretch too much to imagine myself sitting in a rocking chair knitting socks." Unable to imagine what she might do that would seem significant in her own eyes, she makes a number of sensible New Year's resolutions. She resolves to stay indefinitely in Venezuela, where she'd gone into exile with her husband, her two children, her mother and her stepfather in 1975 after General Pinochet toppled the democratic government of her uncle, Salvador Allende, and instituted a regime of repression, torture and terror. She resolves to continue working steadily at a school in Caracas for children with emotional problems, which will provide security and stability. And she resolves to "sacrifice love" for the "noble companionship" of a good husband, for whom she no longer feels any passion.

"The plan was entirely rational—and it lasted not quite a week," Allende tells us. On January 8, in a phone call from Santiago de Chile, she learns that Tata, her beloved grandfather, soon to turn one hundred years old, is dying. She begins to write a

" ** *Paula* **is a heartbreaking lament, written with the charged poetry that emerges at those times when there is an urgent need to speak, though one knows that words, no matter how ravishingly spoken, will change nothing."

letter "to tell him he could go in peace because I would never forget him and planned to bequeath his memory to my children and my children's children." That letter, like a wild weed, quickly and unexpectedly grows into the five hundred pages of her novel, *The House of the Spirits,* and it is Paula who, in another strange gesture of premonition, tosses the coin that helps Allende choose the title of the book that will completely change her life.

Not long after, Allende writes a second novel, *Of Love and Shadows,* to prove to her literary agent in Spain that she is a serious writer and not just the accidental lucky author of a bestseller. All her sensible plans for a quiet and predictable life joyfully unravel. She quits her job at the school, gracefully undoes her marriage in a single afternoon and lets passion sweep over her in California, where she meets Willie, a cowboy-booted lawyer who'd given up on women, and overnight convinces herself and him that they have found in each other the passion of a lifetime. Sound romantic? Well, it is, and Allende, a magical writer, makes you believe that "happily ever after" is still possible, and in the very prime of a woman's life.

Now, Allende desperately wishes she could trade her life for her daughter's life. She is a privileged woman, in that she can afford to be present constantly at Paula's bedside and can hire others to help with all the complicated details of her daughter's daily care. But like Job she struggles with God, asking why her daughter had to be anointed early, so early, as a spirit? For a writer whose first best-selling novel was entitled *The House of the Spirits,* it is ironic to see that fictional house of spirits transformed into her real-life daughter's home.

Indeed, the Premonitions of her fiction haunt Allende throughout the writing of *Paula.* Especially eerie to her is the foresight embedded in her short story, "And Of Clay Are We Created," which was inspired by the 1985 avalanche in Colombia that buried a village in mud. Among those trapped was Omaira Sánchez, a thirteen-year-old girl who became the focus of attention of news-hungry photographers, journalists and television cameras that fixed their curious and helpless eyes on the girl who kept her faith in life as she bravely met her death. In that horrid audience of onlookers, there was one man, a reporter, who made the decision to stop observing Omaira from the lens of his camera and lay down in the mud to offer her what comfort he could as her heart and lungs collapsed. Allende, who was obsessed by "the torment of that poor child buried alive," wrote her story from the perspective of a woman—and she was that woman—"who watches the televised struggle of the man holding the girl."

Allende assumed that once the story was published (in *The Stories of Eva Luna*), Omaira would disappear from her life. But Omaira, she discovers, is

> a dogged angel who will not let me forget her. When Paula fell into a coma and became a prisoner in her bed, inert, dying slowly before the helpless gaze of all around her, I remembered the face of Omaira Sánchez. My daughter was trapped in her body, as the girl had been trapped in mud. Only then did I understand why I had thought about her all those years, and finally could decipher the message in those intense black eyes: patience, courage, resignation, dignity in the face of death.

She reaches a paradoxical conclusion: "If I write something, I fear it will happen, and if I love too much, I fear I will lose that person; nevertheless, I cannot stop writing or loving . . ."

Like the reporter who joins the girl in the mud, Allende, too, relinquishes the detached observer position. For her, this means exiling herself from the territory of fiction, which in the past has allowed her to invent the destinies of her characters and so removed reality to a safe and controllable distance. Until her daughter fell ill, she remarks, she much preferred to write fiction. But with Paula's descent into death, Allende comes to feel she can only write about the world that lies insistently before her as if

> a dark curtain has separated me from the fantasy world in which I used to moves so freely, reality has become intractable . . . Everything is suspended, I have nothing to tell, the present has the brutal certainty of tragedy. I close my eyes and before me rises the painful image of my daughter in her wheelchair, her eyes staring toward the sea, her gaze focused beyond the horizon where death begins.

The pages of the memoir that Allende writes at her daughter's bedside in a Madrid hospital and later in her home in California are

> an irreversible voyage through a long tunnel; I can't see an exit but I know there must be one. I can't go back, only continue to go forward, step by step, to the end. As I write, I look for a sign, hoping that Paula will break her implacable silence and answer somehow in these yellow pages . . .

Paula is a heartbreaking lament, written with the charged poetry that emerges at those times when there is an urgent need to speak, though one knows that words, no matter how ravishingly spoken, will change nothing. Isabel Allende couldn't save her daughter by writing *Paula,* nor even by enlisting every kind of therapy and remedy, from the most advanced biomedical techniques to acupuncture and astrology. And yet it is a tribute to Allende's skill as a writer and the depth of her soul-searching that *Paula,* written on the eve of death, is immensely life-affirming. This is one of those unusual books about suffering that has no use for pity, that manages, somehow, in a situation of utter depletion, to give much more to the reader than would have seemed possible. One reads *Paula* with gratitude for the way it poignantly marks the loss of a daughter while restoring faith in the power of language to free those of us women who are still in this world and still caught in the labyrinths of our own lives. And Margaret Sayers Peden's translation into English is so exquisite that the unpretentious lyricism of Allende's Spanish seems to glow on the page.

In the face of her daughter's dying, Allende may have felt unable to write fiction, but like Eva Luna, the protagonist of her third book, she has clearly set out to live her life "like a novel." Or at least, to her daughter, Paula, to try to awaken her, she *tells* her life as if it were a novel. In that novel of her life, Isabel Allende emerges as a woman who isn't afraid of her own desire, or her own happiness. She is able to admit, at one of the worst moments of her grief, "I have lived nearly half a century, my daughter is dying, and still I want to make love. I think of Willie's reassuring presence and feel goosebumps rise on my skin, and can only smile at the amazing power of desire that makes me shiver despite my sorrow, even push death from my mind." Embracing life and love with all her might, Allende honors the memory of Paula and lets her go, gently, back out into the universe.

Source: Ruth Behar, "In the House of Spirits," in *Women's Review of Books,* Vol. XIII, No. 2, November 1995, p. 8.

Sources

Caruth, Cathy, ed., *Trauma: Explorations in Memory,* Johns Hopkins University Press, 1995.

Dockrell, Cynthia, "The Spirits of Isabel Allende," in *Boston Globe,* city edition, May 24, 1995, p. 75.

Holt, Patricia, "Love Letter to a Dying Daughter," in *San Francisco Chronicle,* Sunday edition, April 9, 1995, p. 1.

Iftekharuddin, Farhat, "Writing to Exorcise the Demons," in *Conversations with Isabel Allende,* edited by John Rodden, University of Texas Press, 1999, pp. 351–363.

Rodden, John, "After Paula" in *Conversations with Isabel Allende,* edited by John Rodden, University of Texas Press, 1999, pp. 409–420.

———, "Introduction" in *Conversations with Isabel Allende,* edited by John Rodden, University of Texas Press, 1999, pp. 1–31.

Warwick, Liz, "A Daughter's Death: 'The fact that Paula was born is more important than the fact that she died,' writes Isabel Allende," in *Gazette* (Montreal), final edition, June 5, 1995, p. C3.

Further Reading

Allende, Isabel, *Aphrodite: A Memoir of the Senses,* HarperFlamingo, 1998.
    Continuing in the vein of (at least somewhat) autobiographical writing, Allende composes a playful examination of the history of aphrodisiacs—including an appropriate cookbook.

———, *The House of the Spirits*, Bantam Books, 1982.
    Allende's first book and an international bestseller, *The House of the Spirits* is a vaguely autobiographical story of several generations of one family as it weathers the changes in Latin America during the twentieth century. Often compared to Gabriel Garcia Marquez' *One Hundred Years of Solitude*, Allende's debut novel offers a magical depiction of her society through the female point of view.

———, *Of Love and Shadows*, Bantam Books, 1988.
    Allende's novel describes a military dictatorship in a Latin American country and the protagonists' pursuit of truth which puts their lives at risk. Although veiled in the author's imagination and her characteristically mystical style, the novel is a documentary of Allende's experience in post-1973 Chile.

Pilgrim at Tinker Creek

Annie Dillard

1974

Pilgrim at Tinker Creek, published in 1974, is a nonfiction work that defies categorization. The winner of the Pulitzer Prize for general nonfiction, it is often read as an example of American nature writing or as a meditation. Annie Dillard, the author, resists these labels, preferring to think of the book as a theological treatise. The book is frequently described as a collection of essays, but Dillard insists that the work is an integrated whole. Perhaps it is because the book succeeds on so many levels that it has been so widely read and admired.

The book is a series of internal monologues and reflections spoken by an unnamed narrator. Over the course of a year, she walks alone through the land surrounding Tinker Creek, located in the Blue Ridge Mountains near Roanoke, Virginia. As she observes the changing of the seasons and the corresponding behaviors of the plants and animals around her, she reflects on the nature of the world and of the God who set it in motion. The narrator is determined to present the natural world as it truly is, not sentimentally or selectively. Therefore, she is as likely to reflect on a frog being sucked dry by an insect as on the slant of light that strikes a certain springtime tree. Whether the images are cruel or lovely, the language is beautiful and poetic, and insistently celebratory.

Author Biography

Meta Ann Doak was born into an upper-middle-class family on April 30, 1945, in Pittsburgh, Pennsylvania. She and her two younger sisters were raised under the influences of their free-thinking parents, their wealthy paternal grandparents who lived nearby, and an African-American domestic servant. "Annie" was encouraged from the beginning to think and act independently, to tell stories, and to read books. She took piano and dance lessons, socialized at the country club, and attended the Ellis School, a private school for girls where she studied Latin, French, and German. But she had a keen interest in the natural world even as a girl, and assembled collections of rocks, bugs, and other elements of nature, as well as a collection of favorite poems. Dillard has recounted her early years in an autobiography, *An American Childhood* (1987).

Dillard's high school years were turbulent. Like many teenagers, she took up smoking and driving fast, and wrote angry poetry about the hypocrisy and emotional impoverishment of the adults around her. For a time, she even stopped attending the Presbyterian Church she had belonged to since childhood, but she soon felt the loss and returned. Dillard's struggle to understand God and religion and her fascination with poetic language—even her smoking—surface throughout her writing, including *Pilgrim at Tinker Creek*.

After high school, Dillard attended Hollins College, a women's college near Roanoke, Virginia, and studied creative writing and religion. At the end of her sophomore year, she married one of her creative writing professors, Richard Dillard. Richard was a strong influence on her writing, encouraging her to develop her skills as a poet and a natural historian. During the marriage, Dillard finished her undergraduate degree in English literature and completed a master's. The topic of her master's thesis was Henry David Thoreau's *Walden; or, Life in the Woods* (1854). Later, she would use *Walden* as the model for *Pilgrim at Tinker Creek*.

For the next few years, Dillard painted, wrote poetry, read widely, volunteered at local community agencies, and kept extensive journals of her observations and thoughts. In 1973, she turned those journals into *Pilgrim at Tinker Creek*, working as many as fifteen hours a day to complete the manuscript. She described the process of writing the book in *The Writing Life* (1989). Individual chapters of *Pilgrim* were published as essays in influen-

Annie Dillard

tial magazines, and when the full book was published in 1974, it was an immediate success. The book won the 1975 Pulitzer Prize for general nonfiction. At the time, Annie Dillard was just thirty years old. She eventually divorced Dillard and, in 1980, married writer Gary Clevidence.

Over the past quarter century, Dillard has published eight more books, including a novel, two collections of poetry, and several nonfiction volumes. These books have been well received, but Dillard is still known primarily as the author of *Pilgrim at Tinker Creek*. She married another professor and writer, Robert D. Richardson Jr. in 1988.

Summary

Chapter One: "Heaven and Earth in Jest"

The opening of *Pilgrim at Tinker Creek* is one of the most famous passages from the book. "I used to have a cat," the book begins. The narrator reports that she was in the habit of sleeping naked in front of an open window, and the cat would use that window to return to the house at night after hunting. In the morning, the narrator would awaken to find her body ''covered with paw prints in blood; I looked as though I'd been painted with roses.''

This opening passage introduces several important ideas and approaches that will operate through the entire book. Dillard insistently presents the natural world as both beautiful and cruel, like the image of roses painted in blood. She demonstrates throughout the book that to discover nature, one must actively put oneself in its way. The narrator sleeps naked, with the windows open, to put no barriers between herself and the natural world. But the natural world is a manifestation of God, and it is God she is really seeking to understand through the book. Dillard introduces the theme of religion as the narrator washes the bloodstains off her body, wondering whether they are ''the keys to the kingdom or the mark of Cain.'' Finally, the anecdote structure itself is typical; throughout the book, Dillard weaves together passages of reflection, description, and narration.

The book's structure is loosely chronological, moving from January to December. ''Heaven and Earth in Jest'' is set in January, and several passages in present tense read like a naturalist's journal. But Dillard freely uses memories from other seasons and other years. ''I am no scientist. I explore the neighborhood,'' the narrator says, explaining both her method and her purpose.

Chapter Two: ''Seeing''

The ten sections of chapter two all explore the question of what it means to really see. The narrator explains how she has trained herself to see insects in flight, hidden birds in trees, and other common occurrences in nature that most people miss because the events are too small or happen too quickly. She spends hours on a log watching for muskrats and brings home pond water to study under a microscope. In a long passage, she tells about patients who benefitted from the first cataract operations, and their difficulties in trying to see with their eyes after a lifetime of blindness. As the narrator contemplates different ways of seeing, she realizes, ''I cannot cause light; the most I can do is try to put myself in the path of its beam.''

Chapter Three: ''Winter''

''Winter'' begins on the first of February with the movements of large flocks of starlings that live in the area. Down by the creek, the narrator watches a coot and thinks about the frogs and turtles asleep under the mud. Her forays outside are shorter, and she spends evenings in front of the fireplace reading books about travel and about nature. Her only companions are a goldfish named Ellery Channing (after a friend of Henry David Thoreau) and the spiders that are allowed ''the run of the house.''

Chapter Four: ''The Fixed''

In this chapter, the narrator discusses insects and stars. She has learned to recognize praying mantis egg cases in the wild, and she has brought one home and tied it to a branch near her window so she can observe the hatching. In the cold of February, she thinks about June and the steadiness of insects and the seeming fixedness of the stars.

Chapter Five: ''Untying the Knot''

This short chapter takes its title from a snake skin the narrator finds in the woods. The skin appears to be tied in a knot, continuous, as the seasons are ''continuous loops.'' The narrator contemplates the changing of the seasons and hopes to be alert and notice the exact moment when winter becomes spring.

Chapter Six: ''The Present''

It is March. Surprisingly, as the chapter opens, the narrator is at a gas station on an interstate highway, talking with the station attendant. But it is not the conversation that is important; rather, the narrator focuses on a beagle puppy, whose fur she rubs as she sips her coffee. For a moment, she feels entirely alive: ''This is it, I think, this is it, right now, the present, this empty gas station here, this western wind, this tang of coffee on the tongue, and I am patting the puppy, I am watching the mountain.''

The narrator reflects on human consciousness and self-consciousness, which act against being in the present and against being in the presence of God. She affirms her intention to push away connections with cities, with people. The flowing creek is new every second, and it is in the creek that grace can be found.

Chapter Seven: ''Spring''

Spring unfolds through April and May, and the narrator has missed spring's beginning. Plants are greening and flowering, and hibernating animals are reappearing. The narrator feels an urgency to examine every creature quickly before summer comes and they begin to decay and devour each other.

Chapter Eight: "Intricacy"

This chapter contains more meditation than anecdote. In June, the narrator ponders the smallest things—red blood cells in a goldfish's tail, blooming plankton, the horsehair worm, molecules, and atoms. In the intricacy of the universe, she finds confirmation of God's presence and plan: "Beauty itself is the fruit of the creator's exuberance that grew such a tangle."

Chapter Nine: "Flood"

Like many of Dillard's chapter titles, "The Flood" is meant to be taken both literally and figuratively. This chapter, which opens with the first day of summer, describes an actual flooding of Tinker Creek and its effects on the landscape, the animals, and the narrator's human neighbors. It is among the most consistently narrative chapters of the book. The rising water brings with it a flood of emotions and thoughts, leaving the narrator feeling "dizzy, drawn, mauled."

Chapter Ten: "Fecundity"

Fecundity means "fruitfulness," and this chapter explores plants and animals, including fish, poppies, field mice, and bamboo, that grow quickly or produce large numbers of offspring. Of course, these creatures are so prolific because they must be: of a million fish eggs laid, only a few will survive to hatch. "What kind of a world is this, anyway," the narrator asks. "Are we dealing in life, or in death?"

Chapter Eleven: "Stalking"

As summer progresses, the narrator practices her skills at stalking animals, especially animals that do not wish to be seen, including fish, herons, and muskrats. As she watches fish, she thinks about fish as an ancient symbol for Christ and for the spirit. In a long passage, she describes how she has spent years learning to stalk muskrats. But stalking animals is not the end in itself: "You have to stalk the spirit, too."

Chapter Twelve: "Nightwatch"

In late summer, the narrator watches grasshoppers and locusts. She takes a sleeping bag and a sandwich to spend a night outside. As she watches the sunset and listens to the night sounds, she thinks, "this is my city, my culture, and all the world I need."

Chapter Thirteen: "The Horns of the Altar"

At mid-September, the narrator ponders poisons, parasites, and pests. In the natural world, creatures eat one another or die of other causes. The chapter title refers to altars used for sacrifices in the Old Testament of the Judeo-Christian Bible. Animals to be sacrificed would be tied to "horns," or rising side pieces, so that they would be suspended above burning coals. The narrator is aware of herself as a potential sacrifice, as eventual food for maggots and parasites. "I am aging and eaten and have done my share of eating too."

Chapter Fourteen: "Northing"

As October and November pass, the narrator thinks about heading north, facing directly into the coming winter. Watching butterflies and geese migrating south, she wishes to go north, to find a place where the wind and the view will be unimpeded, where she can find an austere simplicity. She believes that stillness will open her up to the presence of God.

Chapter Fifteen: "The Waters of Separation"

At the winter solstice, the weather is unusually warm. The narrator wanders through the brown landscape following a bee and reflecting on the year that has passed. The chapter title refers to ceremonial water used in the Old Testament for purifying the unclean. For Dillard, Tinker Creek flows with "the waters of beauty and mystery" and also with the waters of separation. In contemplating the natural world, she approaches God but separates herself from other people and from the things of this world. She drinks of this water willingly and with thanks.

Key Figures

The Narrator

Pilgrim at Tinker Creek is written in the first person; that is, the narrator continually refers to herself as "I." But the book is not an autobiography, and the author is not the narrator. In fact, an early draft of the manuscript was set in New England and was narrated by a young man. For Dillard, the identity of the speaker was not central to her explorations. The narrator of *Pilgrim at Tinker Creek*, then, may more properly be thought of as a persona than as Dillard herself.

Media Adaptations

- *Pilgrim at Tinker Creek* was published as an unabridged audio book by the American Library Association in 1995. The reading is by Barbara Rosenblat.

- Another unabridged edition on audiocassette, read by Grace Conlin, was produced by Blackstone Audio Books in 1993. This version is no longer available on cassettes, but http://www.audible.com offers it for sale as a downloadable file.

Few biographical details can be discerned about the narrator. She lives near Tinker Creek in the Blue Ridge Mountains of Virginia. She is well-educated and has read widely, and she spends most of her time alone, closely observing the natural world. She seems to have no daily responsibilities or occupations, but has the time and the patience to spend hours alone in one place watching the light changing or a duck eating. She once had a cat, but she does not mention any family, and she does not seek the company of other humans except for an occasional evening game of pinochle with unnamed friends. No other person plays a significant role in the book.

Themes

Faith and Spirituality

As the first word of the title suggests, *Pilgrim at Tinker Creek* is primarily a book about seeking God. A ''pilgrim'' may be merely a person who travels, but more commonly the word is used to describe someone who travels to a holy place. For the narrator, the creek itself is as sacred as a church; it is here that she encounters God's grace in its purest form: ''So many things have been shown me on these banks, so much light has illumined me by reflection here where the water comes down, that I can hardly believe that this grace never flags.'' In using water as a symbol of God's presence and grace, Dillard is drawing on centuries of religious tradition.

Throughout the book, Dillard balances the seemingly opposing forces of heaven and Earth, of God as the creator of beauty and of horror. Much of the imagery in the book is of the beauty and complexity of nature, reflecting God's grace. In every sunset, every egg case, every snake skin, the narrator sees God's generosity. But at times, reading about a praying mantis that has devoured her mate or contemplating hoards of parasites, she rails against the cruelties of nature, asking, ''What kind of a world is this, anyway?'' She wonders whether the mystery of cruelty is not part of God's plan. ''It could be,'' she muses, that God has spread ''a fabric of spirit and sense so grand and subtle, so powerful in a new way, that we can only feel blindly of its hem.'' She seems to conclude that, ultimately, humans must accept the contradictions of this world—must embrace death and darkness as part of the cycle of life and light.

Dillard has carefully studied the Bible, as demonstrated by the many biblical quotations and allusions throughout the book. But essential to Dillard's vision is the belief that the natural world is also a vehicle for spiritual insight. Just as the narrator has had to train herself to stalk wild animals to be in their presence, so she must also stalk God, seeking Him out where He is and as He is.

Individual and Society

A recurring idea in *Pilgrim at Tinker Creek* is the narrator's belief that she must choose between embracing nature and embracing human society. In fact, she does not seem to have close ties with any living humans. She alludes occasionally to playing baseball or pinochle—games that cannot be played in solitude—but she never names her companions. She is aware of neighborhood boys, and she knows the names of the people who own the property along Tinker Creek and of those who are endangered by the flood. But there is no strong feeling, positive or negative, expressed in any of her human contacts. While a puppy or a sunrise can leave her breathless, people do not.

Her isolation is both inevitable and intentional. On the one hand, she feels unlike other people. She does not know others who rhapsodize as she does

Topics for Further Study

- Find out more about the Roman Catholic monk Thomas Merton, who was also a poet and a political activist. What causes did he speak out about? How did he understand the ideal balance between a life of contemplation and a life of activism?

- Read some excerpts from Henry David Thoreau's *Walden; or, Life in the Woods,* especially one or two passages in which he gives detailed accounts of his observations of nature. In terms of the amount of precise detail, how do his accounts compare with Dillard's? How would you compare the conclusions Thoreau and Dillard draw from their observations?

- For a short time, Dillard considered submitting her manuscript to publishers under the name "A. Dillard" so the publishers would assume the author was a man. Do you think this would have fooled them? If you did not know the name of the author of *Pilgrim at Tinker Creek*, what clues in the text would suggest a female author? Consider language, imagery, and attitude.

- Using balls to represent the Earth and the Sun, demonstrate the meanings of the terms "winter solstice" and "summer solstice." Explain how the position of the Earth relative to the Sun at each solstice affects the weather where you live.

- Spend an hour or more alone, replicating one of Dillard's activities: Stalk a muskrat or other animal to see how close you can get; sit still outside at sunrise or sunset and watch the light change; or pat a puppy and try to think of nothing else except what you are doing. Write a brief essay in which you describe the experience.

---

over slugs and spiders, and at times she feels like "a freak." More importantly, she has willed herself to be alone, to live in the world of nature instead of the world of the city. She has experienced both, and remembers in "The Present" the "human companionship, major-league baseball, and a clatter of quickening stimulus like a rush from strong drugs that leaves you drained." But human connection is a distraction, making it difficult to live in the present. In the same chapter, she almost drifts away into a memory of dancing and music years before, and she forcefully wills herself to abandon the memory: "I stir. The heave of my shoulders returns me to the present . . . and I yank myself away, shove off, seeking live water."

Although the persona who explores Tinker Creek from January to December 1972 lives alone with only goldfish and spiders for company, Annie Dillard was married and living with her husband at the time she wrote the book. She spent a great deal of time volunteering in her community, meeting with a writing group, and socializing with friends. The solitude of the narrator is, therefore, an intentional creation of the writer. As the narrator explains in "Fecundity," "I must go down to the creek again. It is where I belong, although as I become closer to it, my fellows appear more and more freakish, and my home in the library more and more limited. Imperceptibly at first, and now consciously, I shy away from the arts, from the human emotional stew."

Nature

Although it does not seem to be what Dillard intended, *Pilgrim at Tinker Creek* is perhaps most frequently read as a piece of nature writing. The book is filled with narratives, descriptions, and unusual facts about a catalog of plants and animals. Some of the most famous passages in the book come from the writer's own observations; for example the description of the tomcat with bloody paws, the frog being sucked dry by a giant water bug, or the young muskrat floating on its back. Dillard is just as vivid when her narrator is retelling an observation she has read somewhere else: J. Henri Fabre's caterpillars walking a never-ending circular trail around the mouth of a vase, or his female praying mantis mating with a male whose head she has already eaten. For many readers, these glimpses of the world outside are valuable in themselves, without symbolizing anything beyond the literal.

On a practical level, the reader of *Pilgrim at Tinker Creek* learns a great deal about the natural world, primarily about the flora and fauna in the area around Tinker Creek. Readers who care to learn may gather enough information to begin their own explorations—to identify a monarch butterfly pupa or a sycamore tree. They may also put together an impressive reading list of some of the books from which Dillard has taught herself. Dillard combines her own observations with those of other writers to produce a record of the changing natural world through the calendar year, from January to December. In doing so, and in making it seem so beautiful and fascinating, she encourages the reader to do the same. Dillard has learned much of her natural history from reading books, and her own book similarly instructs her readers.

Science and Technology

As she pieces together an understanding of God and the natural world, the narrator also considers what science can and cannot tell her. Repeatedly, she looks through microscopes or telescopes, using technology to see things that the naked eye cannot reveal. Several of her stories, including the account of the caterpillars following each other around the rim of a vase, demonstrate knowledge gained through scientific experimentation. In her acceptance of animal behavior in all its seeming cruelty, the narrator exhibits a scientist's objectivity. But she is fully aware of the limits of science. In ''Stalking,'' for example, she discusses the principle of indeterminacy, which governs the study of atomic particles. The more scientists learn, she says, the more they become aware that they can never truly know: ''we know now for sure that there is no knowing. . . . The use of instruments and the very fact of an observer seem to bollix [bungle] the observations; as a consequence, physicists are saying that they cannot study nature per se, but only their own investigation of nature.''

Dillard comes back to the limits of science several times throughout *Pilgrim at Tinker Creek*. Ultimately, the impossibility of knowing everything both frustrates and comforts the narrator. She would like to find things out, and she keeps return-ing to books and to observation, but she will never know it all. On the other hand, the very fact of the world being beyond human comprehension is, for her, confirmation of the existence of God.

Style

Structure

The fifteen essays or chapters of *Pilgrim at Tinker Creek* are organized into two parallel structures. The more obvious structure follows the calendar year from January, in the chapters ''Heaven and Earth in Jest'' and ''Seeing,'' through spring, summer, and autumn to December 21 in the last chapter, ''The Waters of Separation.'' The book is meant to resemble a polished journal that the narrator kept of her observations through one year, but in fact, the material was pulled together from twenty volumes of journals that Dillard kept over several years. The calendar year structure, describing the changes in the seasons, is a convention of American nature writing that has been used by Henry David Thoreau, Edwin Way Teale, Henry Beston, Aldo Leopold, and others.

A less obvious structure has been pointed out by Dillard herself and supports her insistence that the book be read as a whole, not as a collection of essays. As quoted in Sandra Humble Johnson's *The Space Between: Literary Epiphany in the Work of Annie Dillard,* Dillard explains that the structure of the book follows the path of the medieval mystic toward God. The first seven chapters represent the *via positiva,* or ''the journey to God through action & will & materials.'' In these chapters, Dillard focuses on the beauty and intricacy of nature. After a meditative eighth chapter, ''Intricacy,'' the last seven chapters represent the *via negativa,* or ''the spirit's revulsion at time and death.'' In this half of the book, beginning with the destruction of ''Flood,'' Dillard's anecdotes are more negative, focusing more on parasites, poisons, and death.

Setting

Pilgrim at Tinker Creek is set, as the title suggests, ''by a creek, Tinker Creek, in a valley in Virginia's Blue Ridge'' in the year 1972. The creek is outside the small town of Hollins, home of Hollins College. Dillard completed her bachelor's and master's degrees at Hollins College and lived near Tinker Creek for nine years in the late 1960s and early 1970s. Although the book appears to be a factual representation of place and time, the real Tinker Creek is not so isolated and wild as readers may assume. Through careful selection of detail, Dillard makes the area seem quiet, undeveloped, and largely uninhabited. Compare the impression of wilderness Dillard creates for this book to the way she describes the same locations in a later essay, "Living Like Weasels": "This is, mind you, suburbia. It is a five-minute walk in three directions to rows of houses, though none is visible here. There's a 55 m.p.h. highway at one end of the pond, and a nesting pair of wood ducks at the other. . . . The far end is an alternating series of fields and woods, fields and woods, threaded everywhere with motorcycle tracks." For *Pilgrim*, she has narrowed her focus to specific moments and specific images, leaving out the details that work against her purpose. The setting of *Pilgrim at Tinker Creek* is, therefore, a slightly fictionalized version of a real place.

Similarly, the book appears to record the events of one calendar year, 1972. Obviously, the chapters also include information from the narrator's reading and from her past. The stories from her own past are clearly tagged with phrases like "several years ago" or "once." These narratives are written in the past tense. Narratives that are meant to be immediate ("I am sitting") or very recent ("yesterday") are presented as though they occurred in the order told and within one year. These observations actually occurred over a period of several years.

Although *Pilgrim at Tinker Creek* is classified as nonfiction, it has elements of fiction in its setting. It has the appearance of a journal or an autobiography, but it is not one. Rather, it is a series of reflections set into a journal form.

Figurative Language

One of the most admired qualities of *Pilgrim at Tinker Creek* is the beauty and power of its language. Dillard studied creative writing at Hollins College and has published two volumes of poetry. Her concern with figurative or "poetic" language is apparent on every page. Because nature is so evocative for Dillard, she uses grand language to describe it, particularly when she is awed. Describing her reaction to "the tree with the lights in it," she writes, "The vision comes and goes, mostly goes, but I live for it, for the moment when the mountains open and a new light roars in spate through the crack, and the mountains slam." In this line, she is speaking metaphorically, especially with the verbs "open," "roars" and "slam." The line is made more powerful by the repetition of "comes and goes, mostly goes" and "I live for it, for the moment," and the unusual word "spate" elevates the line further. This line and countless others like it strike many readers as more like poetry than like prose.

Historical Context

The 1960s and 1970s

The years during which Dillard lived in the Blue Ridge Mountains, keeping her journals and writing *Pilgrim at Tinker Creek*, were among the most turbulent in recent United States history. In the five years before she began writing in 1973, civil rights leader Martin Luther King, Jr., and presidential candidate Robert F. Kennedy were assassinated; the United States withdrew from Vietnam after a long and unsuccessful military action in which tens of thousands of Americans died; the presidency of Richard Nixon had started to unravel because of the scandal known as "Watergate"; the nation was feeling the first effects of an energy crisis; an Equal Rights Amendment to the U.S. Constitution, addressing gender equality issues, was passed by Congress but never ratified by the states.

It is striking, then—and for some critics at the time it was disturbing—that Dillard mentions none of these things in her book. Dillard's focus is both inward and outward, but her concerns are spiritual, not social or political. She is aware of what is going on in the world; she pores over the newspapers and spends time in the library. She reads and admires the monk Thomas Merton, who balanced a contemplative life with activism against nuclear weapons. But Dillard chooses in this work to direct her gaze away from social concerns, as she explains in "Intricacy": "I would like to see it all, to understand it, but I must start somewhere, so I try to deal with the giant water bug in Tinker Creek and the flight of three hundred redwings from an Osage orange, with the goldfish bowl and the snakeskin, and let those who dare worry about the birthrate and population explosion among solar systems."

Compare & Contrast

- **1970:** On April 22, the first Earth Day is observed, marking a strong interest in environmental issues across the United States.

  Today: Although a small group of environmental advocates tries to create a sensation, the thirtieth anniversary of Earth Day receives scant attention in the nation's newspapers.

- **1974:** Dillard considers submitting her manuscript of *Pilgrim at Tinker Creek* under the name "A. Dillard," because she does not believe that a book with theological themes written by a woman will sell many copies.

Today: Although publications by men still outnumber those by women in the fields of religion and philosophy, women are accepted as making important contributions in these disciplines.

- **1975:** Environmental literature is popular with general readers and with critics. Annie Dillard wins the Pulitzer Prize for general nonfiction for *Pilgrim at Tinker Creek* and Gary Snyder wins the Pulitzer Prize for poetry for *Turtle Island,* a collection of nature poems.

Today: Nature writers including Terry Tempest Williams, Rick Bass, and Ann Zwinger reach a small but dedicated readership.

Nature Writing

Although *Pilgrim at Tinker Creek* has proven difficult for readers to categorize, it is most often located in the genre of nature writing. Nature writing is not so strictly defined as the sonnet or the novel, but there are several criteria that critics agree upon. Generally, nature writing is nonfiction prose set in the wilderness or in a rural area. Its primary focus is on accurate but beautifully rendered descriptions of the natural phenomena that occur in one limited place, not on political or social commentary. The speaker or narrator of a piece of nature writing reports her own observations; she does not interfere with nature, but carefully and patiently records every detail. Most importantly, she is well-educated and checks her facts. It is not enough to write gushing prose about the beauty of a heron at sunset; the nature writer must have enough scientific knowledge to place the scene in its biological, climatological, and even cosmological context.

Early English writers, who lacked what we would consider today to be basic scientific knowledge of the world, must have found nature to be as unpredictable and frightening as it was beautiful and awe-inspiring. They did not know much about the natural world except how it affected them, and in accordance with Judeo-Christian thought of the time, they believed that humans were set apart from nature by God—apart from it and above it. Images of nature in literature tended to be used as a backdrop for more important human activity, or as a symbol of human emotions and spirit. In these works, nature exists to serve and to represent humans. Details about flowers or birds or mountains tend to be vague and impressive, rather than detailed and accurate. Writers and readers alike had little knowledge about the behavior of muskrats, and little interest in obtaining more. What was more important was what a muskrat could represent—mystery, or industry, or beauty, or danger.

In the nineteenth century, however, two important books changed the way writers and others looked at the natural world, and became the origins of what is today called nature writing or environmental literature. The first book, published in 1845, by Henry David Thoreau, was *Walden, or, Life in the Woods. Walden,* considered one of the classic works of American literature, is an account of two years Thoreau spent living in a small cabin on the shore of Walden Pond near Concord, Massachusetts. Thoreau combines passages of reflection on daily life, government, and society with passages of close examination of worms and beans and rain. Others had looked at nature objectively, and for its own sake, without attributing human characteristics to it, but Thoreau's work was so beautifully written and clearly argued that it reached a large audience and endured.

The second important book was Charles Darwin's 1859 *On the Origin of Species by Means of Natural Selection, or the Preservation of Favoured Races in the Struggle for Life.* Darwin's book proposed for the first time that humans, and all living creatures, have evolved over time from previous species. It is difficult for us today to understand how shocking this idea was for Darwin's first readers. Darwin was saying that humans are not above nature, but a part of it; he claimed that life has evolved in a continuing pattern, rather than being set down on earth for the pleasure and use of humans. With this new sense of nature and human-kind's role in it, there came a new interest in studying and classifying the natural world, in under-standing it on its own terms.

The tradition of nature writing in the United States can be traced to the journals and essays of the earliest explorers in the New World. The most important works include Henry David Thoreau's *Walden; or, Life in the Woods* (1845); John Muir's *The Mountains of California* (1894); Mary Austin's *The Land of Little Rain* (1903); and Aldo Leopold's *A Sand County Almanac* (1949). The last third of the twentieth century saw a new wave of nature writing, and it is this movement in which *Pilgrim at Tinker Creek* is frequently placed. Some critics have taken issue with Dillard's identification as a nature writer because of what Linda Smith, author of *Annie Dillard* in Twayne's United States Authors Series, calls her "consistent—even stubborn—devotion to traditional Christianity" and her "concern with aesthetics." But many critics have gone so far as to rank *Pilgrim at Tinker Creek*, as John Tallmadge did in his essay "Beyond the Excursion: Initiatory Themes in Annie Dillard and Terry Tempest Williams," as one of "the most powerful works to appear in the current renaissance of American nature writing."

Critical Overview

Pilgrim at Tinker Creek is widely recognized as an important personal essay, uniquely and powerfully combining theology and nature writing. Nancy Parrish reports in *Lee Smith, Annie Dillard, and the Hollins Group: A Genesis of Writers* that the book's success was immediate: "thirty-seven thousand copies of *Pilgrim* were sold within two months of first publication; the book went through eight printings in the first two years; paperback rights and Book-of-the-Month Club selection brought her $250,000 within three months." The book was awarded the Pulitzer Prize for general nonfiction.

Most early reviewers responded favorably to the book, including Eva Hoffman, writing for *Commentary,* who termed Dillard a "connoisseur of the spirit" and praised her for her "rare ability to create emotional tone." Others, including the fiction and essay writer Eudora Welty (herself a Pulitzer Prize winner), found Dillard's language and structure needlessly opaque. In a review for the *New York Times Book Review,* Welty quoted Dillard's passage about the "great dog Death" at the end of the "Fecundity" chapter and commented, "I honestly do not know what she is talking about at such times. The only thing I could swear to is that the writing here leaves something to be desired."

Aside from reviews, there was no criticism of the book for several years. In 1983, Margaret Loewen Reimer's *Critique* article, "The Dialectical Vision of Annie Dillard's *Pilgrim at Tinker Creek*," initi-ated a small body of criticism dealing with Dillard's religious themes. This body of criticism, which frequently debates whether Dillard is more an exis-tentialist or a transcendentalist, tends to be written in academic language that makes it difficult for beginning students.

More accessible, and more common, are the critics who address Dillard as a nature writer. Vera Norwood's "Heroines of Nature: Four Women Respond to the American Landscape," in *The Ecocriticism Reader,* examines Dillard as playing an important role in the development of female nature writers and finds that she is among those who "freely choose to seek out wild nature and defend it, thus defying the traditions limiting women access to and appreciation of the natural environment, but who also conclude their explorations in a state of ambivalence." Linda Smith, author of the Twayne's United States Authors series volume *Annie Dillard,* argues that, because of its concern with religion, the book is not primarily nature writing. But James McClintock, in "'Pray Without Ceasing': Annie Dillard among the Nature Writers," disagrees, stat-

Dillard's hermit-like existence upon the banks of Tinker Creek was influenced by the poet-theologian Thomas Merton, who lived a life of contemplation as a Trappist monk

ing, ''Nature writing in America has always been religious or quasi-religious.'' He concludes that Dillard does belong ''among the nature writers'' because, ''In Dillard's essays, the same persona speaks to us as from the works of other nature writers—the solitary figure in nature, moved to philosophical speculation and, finally, to awe and wonder.''

While most critics have admired Dillard's acute powers of observation and her powerful connection with the natural world, more than a few have found her seeming lack of connection with human society unsettling. The poet Hayden Carruth, in his early review in *Virginia Quarterly Review,* found that the book made ''little reference to life on this planet at this moment, its hazards and misdirections, and to this extent it is a dangerous book, literally a subversive book.'' Gary McIlroy acknowledges in his essay ''*Pilgrim at Tinker Creek* and the Social Legacy of *Walden*'' that this book has less human interaction than the work Dillard patterned it after, *Walden,* but argues that solitude is appropriate for her spiritual quest: ''Annie Dillard goes into the woods to claim her spiritual heritage. Like a prophet, she travels alone.'' In the field of literary criticism about nature writing, Dillard is a major figure. Nearly every significant collection of essays about nature writing, or ecocriticism (the belief that women share a special bond with nature and that both women and nature have been exploited by men) or ecofeminism (the study of literature and the environment) includes an essay about *Pilgrim at Tinker Creek*.

Criticism

Cynthia Bily

Bily is an instructor of writing and literature at Adrian College in Adrian, Michigan. In this essay, she explores the role of reading in Dillard's vision of the student of nature.

The term *nature writing* refers to the work of those writers since the time of Thoreau and Darwin who have consciously tried to go out into nature, look at it closely, and report what they see, without sentimentalizing or anthropomorphizing, without getting in the way of the natural events they observe, and without using nature as a backdrop for a political or social commentary. It is into this genre of writing that Annie Dillard's *Pilgrim at Tinker Creek* is usually classified. Dillard wrote her master's thesis on *Walden,* and used Thoreau's book as a model for her own.

Dillard's reliance on Thoreau is interesting in many ways. Looking at both books together, readers can learn a great deal about how the world changed in the hundred or so years between publications. What information was available to Dillard that Thoreau did not have? What were the new advancements in science? What had naturalists observed and recorded about the behaviors of living creatures? To what extent *can* a person step out of the technological world and encounter nature purely, on its own terms? All of these are interesting questions, worthy of consideration. But this essay is more interested in something that binds Thoreau and Dillard together across the span of a hundred years: their lives as readers and writers. Although they believe that people must clear their minds and open their hearts to nature, without interjecting their intellect and their expectations, they turn again and again to books for confirmation or clarification of what they have seen.

What Do I Read Next?

- Henry David Thoreau's *Walden; or, Life in the Woods,* published in 1854, was Dillard's most important model for *Pilgrim at Tinker Creek.* In *Walden,* Thoreau describes the two years he spent living alone in a cabin on Walden Pond near Concord, Massachusetts, recording his thoughts and his observations of the natural world through the changing seasons.

- *Teaching a Stone to Talk: Expeditions and Encounters* (1982) is a collection of essays by Dillard. These pieces are similar to *Pilgrim at Tinker Creek* in observing and reflecting on the natural world, but they move beyond Virginia as far away as Ecuador.

- *The Writing Life*, published in 1989, is Dillard's exploration of her own creative process and search for an understanding of inspiration. She incorporates literal and metaphorical narratives, including the story of how she composed *Pilgrim at Tinker Creek.*

- Terry Tempest Williams' *An Unspoken Hunger: Stories from the Field* (1995) is a collection of essays about connections between the natural world and our spiritual selves. Most of Williams's essay are set in the American West, and unlike Dillard, she is ever mindful of her place in a human community.

- Another classic work of American nature writing is Henry Beston's 1928 book *The Outermost House: A Year of Life on the Great Beach of Cape Cod.* The book is an account of one year—from autumn to autumn—that Beston spent living alone in a one-room house on the shore of the Atlantic Ocean.

Thoreau devotes an entire chapter to "Reading," and mentions the subject throughout his book. He brings little with him to his cabin in the woods, but he does bring books, as he explains: "My residence was more favorable, not only to thought, but to serious reading, than a university; and though I was beyond the range of the ordinary circulating library, I had more than ever come within the influence of those books which circulate round the world." He keeps a copy of the *Iliad* on his table, and like most of his contemporaries he knows much of the Bible by heart. In Thoreau's mind, studying books and studying nature are paired, and "We might as well omit to study Nature because she is old" as give up studying the classics. The written word, he says, "is the work of art nearest to life itself."

Yet a lover of the written word must be careful not to let books replace actual experience. Thoreau writes, "No method nor discipline can supersede the necessity of being forever on the alert. What is a course of history, or philosophy, or poetry, no matter how well selected . . . compared with the discipline of looking always at what is to be seen?" For his first summer in the cabin, Thoreau put his books away.

Dillard faces the same struggle to balance her essential trust in the written word and the need to get out and *see.* Unlike Thoreau, Dillard has a great variety of books to tempt her indoors. As she admits early on, she is not a scientist; much of what she knows about plants and animals she has learned through reading. The references to reading are endless: "I had read about the giant water bug, but never seen one"; "a book I read when I was young recommended an easy way to find caterpillars to rear"; "I saw color-patches for weeks after I read this wonderful book." Dillard is clearly an insatiable reader, but the reading is not an end in itself. She uses what she reads to direct her gaze, and help her process what she sees.

Reading about travel is a guilty pleasure for both writers. Thoreau tells readers that he turned to this kind of reading while he was building his cabin:

> **This essay is interested in something that binds Thoreau and Dillard together across the span of a hundred years: their lives as readers and writers. Although they believe that people must clear their minds and open their hearts to nature, without interjecting their intellect and their expectations, they turn again and again to books for confirmation or clarification of what they have seen."**

"I read one or two shallow books of travel in the intervals of my work, till that employment made me ashamed of myself, and I asked where it was then that I lived." Dillard, too, reads stories of travel and exploration by "Knud Rasmussen, Sir John Franklin, Peter Freuchen, Scott, Peary, and Byrd; Jedediah Smith, Peter Skene Ogden, and Milton Sublette; or Daniel Boone singing on his blanket in the Green River Country." (It seems notable that there are no women on Dillard's list.) But she reads these books in the winter, when there is not much happening outside. Balance is important. It is pleasant to read about going places, but how much better to actually go.

Dillard is nagged by the need to strike this balance. On the one hand, the written word aids in understanding: "At night I read and write, and things I have never understood become clear; I reap the harvest of the rest of the year's planting." On the other hand, the very act of committing a sensation to words strips it. Dillard describes the moment of patting the puppy and being in the present, and then realizes, "the second I verbalize this awareness in my brain, I cease to see the mountain or feel the puppy." She finds any kind of writing irresistible, and even shares a passage from an article about building a snowman, but then wonders, "Why, why in the blue-green world write this sort of thing? Funny written culture, I guess; we pass things on."

Why write things down? An essential question for a writer. One reason is to share information, to pool knowledge. Dillard remarks that "the world is full of creatures that for some reason seem stranger to us than others, and libraries are full of books describing them." But reading is not enough. She continues, "What I aim to do is not so much learn the names of the shreds of creation that flourish in this valley, but to keep myself open to their meanings." To learn the names, Dillard consults her books, but to find the meanings she must put them aside.

Dillard never resolves the issue. In "Fecundity," she is as ambivalent as ever about her books. Emotions, she writes, do more harm than good because they cause people to question and challenge and mourn. She proposes a solution, then takes it back: "let us all go have lobotomies to restore us to a natural state. We can leave the library then, go back to the creek. . . . You first." A paragraph later, she repeats the idea of abandoning books: "I must go down to the creek again. It is where I belong, although as I become closer to it, my fellows appear more and more freakish, and my home in the library more and more limited. Imperceptibly at first, and now consciously, I shy away from the arts, from the human emotional stew." Her will is to empty herself of thought and knowledge, to stand empty and ready. But she is a writer; ironically, readers know about her wish to turn away from the written word because she wrote it down.

Historians of nature writing state that this reliance on books is common, and desirable. Richard G. Lillard, in an essay titled "The Nature Book in Action," defines nature writing and the nature writer. He explains that "The nature book is a personal statement, often charmingly literary, told at firsthand by a well-rounded observer who is as much at home in the humanities as in the natural sciences, especially the biological studies. . . . The nature writer studies both books and nature." Those who come after these writers, who are enriched by reading their works, benefit from the writers' deft balancing act of books and nature. But Thoreau and Dillard help readers see that reading a work of nature writing is an empty exercise, unless it prompts them to get up and go outside.

Source: Cynthia Bily, Critical Essay on *Pilgrim at Tinker Creek,* in *Nonfiction Classics for Students,* The Gale Group, 2001.

Jim Cheney

In the following essay, Cheney analyzes Pilgrim at Tinker Creek *as a feminist postmodern work, asserting that Dillard's approach ''effects a transformation of the dominant Western theological tradition.''*

Postmodernism and the Sacred

I used to have a cat, an old fighting tom, who would jump through the open window by my bed in the middle of the night and land on my chest. I'd half-awakened. He'd stick his skull under my nose and purr, stinking of urine and blood. Some nights he kneaded my bare chest with his front paws, powerfully, arching his back, as if sharpening his claws, or pummeling a mother for milk. And some mornings I'd wake in daylight to find my body covered with paw prints in blood; I looked as though I'd been painted with roses.

It was hot, so hot the mirror felt warm. I washed before the mirror in a daze, my twisted summer sleep still hung about me like sea kelp. What blood was this, and what roses? It could have been the rose of union, the blood of murder, or the rose of beauty bare and the blood of some unspeakable sacrifice or birth. The sign on my body could have been an emblem or a stain, the keys to the kingdom or the mark of Cain. I never knew. I never knew as I washed, and the blood streaked, faded, and finally disappeared, whether I'd purified myself or ruined the blood sign of the passover. We wake, if we ever wake at all, to mystery, rumors of death, beauty, violence . . .

So begins Annie Dillard's *Pilgrim at Tinker Creek*. One sentence later we read:

These are morning matters, pictures you dream as the final wave heaves you up on the sand to the bright light and drying air. You remember pressure, and a curved sleep you rested against, soft, like a scallop in its shell. But the air hardens your skin; you stand; you leave the lighted shore to explore some dim headland, and soon you're lost in the leafy interior, intent, remembering nothing.

Pilgrim at Tinker Creek is concerned with morning matters, the articulation of a sacred dimension of existence while walking lost ''in the leafy interior,'' by Tinker Creek. ''What blood [is] this, and what roses?'' What is this life, this creek, this ''faint tracing on the surface of mystery, like the idle, curved tunnels of leaf miners on the face of a leaf?'' Annie Dillard's reflections on these morning matters are given voice within a postmodernist ambience in which, as Heisenberg says, ''method and object can no longer be separated.'' We are caught up, and all routes back to (and through) that ''curved sleep'' are mythical tracings on and in the

> **Annie Dillard's exploration at Tinker Creek is the weaving of a world—not so much a search for Truth as a matter of description, an account which answers to her (and our) needs. Mythical narrative. Truth as response, embeddedness, ethical or religious vernacular.''**

''looped soil'' of our lives and land. We wake, not to truth, but to myth, ''to mystery, rumors of death, beauty, violence.''

Annie Dillard's exploration at Tinker Creek is the weaving of a world—not so much a search for Truth as a matter of description, an account which answers to her (and our) needs. Mythical narrative. Truth as response, embeddedness, ethical or religious vernacular. It is not just method and object that cannot be separated in these mythical tracings; neither can the thread of valuation be teased from the cloth of description. They are ineluctably interwoven, nurturing one another, calling one another forth.

The questions and accounts elicited by Tinker Creek are of the sacred—the sacred not as a world apart, but a dimension of the here-and-now, ''the mystery of the continuous creation and all that providence implies: the uncertainty of vision, the horror of the fixed, the dissolution of the present, the intricacy of beauty, the pressure of fecundity, the elusiveness of the free, and the flawed nature of perfection.'' The questions posed, the experiences undergone, and the need to speak these forth in a narrative intertwined with ceremony and ritual are properly termed 'sacred', not because of the nature of the subject matter, but because of the shape, the contour, the texture of the cloth required to weave them into coherence. The cloth, moreover, is woven in a sacred manner. It is not possible, finally, to tease apart question, experience, need, account, ceremony, ritual, fact and value.

Pilgrim at Tinker Creek does not give credence to Enlightenment (modernist) conceptions of epistemology and metaphysics as these are reflected in the correspondence theory of truth and the metaphysical distinction between fact and value. But neither is language on a holiday in this work, freed from the requirements of fidelity to this world. Rejection of traditional epistemology does not release language from the pull of the world, but frees it into a deeper commitment, a deeper faithfulness— or the promise of one—to the complex interplay of question, experience, narrative, ceremony, and world. It returns language to the world, recognizing it as an expression of the world, emergent from it. In this, *Pilgrim at Tinker Creek* is an exemplary text of *feminist* postmodernism.

Postmodernist rereadings of the notion of truth all too often reflect merely the negative dimension of our distance from the Enlightenment—constituting a masculinist reaction to the sundering of language from world. The Enlightenment subjective self remains intact in these versions of the postmodernist world: It is the place of language's exile. With the dissolution of the modernist subjective self in many feminist postmodernist accounts, however, language returns to the world, not as its mirror, but as emergent from it and therefore embedded in it.

But what guarantees do emergence and embeddedness provide? Emergent, therefore true? With the dissolution of Enlightenment epistemology and metaphysics the notion of truth becomes less useful, plays less of a role than it once did. But the notion that words give expression to the world does not mean that issues cousin to those of truth and falsity no longer arise. In the spirit of a contextualist or coherentist and naturalized epistemology which seems most appropriate to feminist postmodernism, Annie Dillard's text suggests that the central concern is fidelity to the complex interplay of question, experience, narrative, ceremony and world. The epistemological issues are those of fitness, appropriate care, and health, to name but three of a large network of terms which suggest that epistemology itself is a matter of social negotiation. These do not stand outside the interplay of question, experience, and narrative, policing these concepts. They are additional components of the weave. They are, or ought to be, central and pivotal notions, analogues of modernist criteria of truth embedded in foundationalist epistemologies. But their centrality does not place them outside the tapestry. Rather, their function is to orient particular inquiries at the same time as they are influenced and shaped by them.

Naturalized Theology

> King David leaped and danced naked before the ark of the Lord in a barren desert. Here [at Tinker Creek] the very looped soil is an intricate throng of praise.

> Hasidism has a tradition that one of man's purposes is to assist God in the work of redemption by "hallowing" the things of creation. By a tremendous heave of his spirit, the devout man frees the divine sparks trapped in the mute things of time; he uplifts the forms and moments of creation, bearing them aloft into that rare air and hallowing fire in which all clays must shatter and burst. Keeping the subsoil world under trees in mind, in intelligence, is the *least* I can do.

> The mountains . . . are a passive mystery, the oldest of all. Theirs is the one simple mystery of creation from nothing, of matter itself, anything at all, the given. Mountains are giant, restful, absorbent. You can heave your spirit into a mountain and the mountain will keep it, folded, and not throw it back as some creeks will. The creeks are the world with all its stimulus and beauty; I live there. But the mountains are home.

There is a tension *Pilgrim at Tinker Creek* between, on the one hand, a thoroughly naturalized and contextualized inquiry into the sacred and, on the other hand, the Western theological tradition of a transcendent creator-god which provides much of the explicitly theological vocabulary at work in the text. One of the joys of reading this book is savoring the interplay of these two aspects of the text. Annie Dillard uses, appreciates, and accepts the Western tradition within the ambience of her own orientation to the sacred. The dominant Western theological tradition is not part of her approach, or complementary to it—it is transformed by it.

The problem Annie Dillard sets herself is seemingly posed for her by the Western theological tradition in the form of the problem of evil:

> Cruelty is a mystery, and the waste of pain. But if we describe a world to compass these things, . . . then we bump against another mystery: the inrush of power and light, the canary that sings on the skull.

But even here the traditional problem of reconciling the existence of pain and suffering with belief in an all-powerful, all-knowing, perfectly benevolent God is transformed into the problem of providing a description that will "compass" both "the waste of pain" and "the inrush of power and light." An a priori description of God is not the fixed point of Annie Dillard's exploration. An account of the sacred does not precede and shape her description of the world; rather, such an account emerges from the description. The vocabulary of the theological tradition is pulled into the description as experience requires—pulled in and transformed. She takes seriously the rhetorical question from the Koran: "The heaven and the earth and all in between, thinkest thou I made them *in jest?*.'' The tradition is not saved, in the face of ''the waste of pain,'' by the neo-Gnostic notion of a *Deus Absconditus.* If there is a focus, a fixed—or relatively fixed—point, it is her faithfulness to Tinker Creek (''I live there,'' although ''the mountains are home''). And so the tradition is transmuted by the creek: ''It could be that God has not absconded but spread . . . to a fabric of spirit and sense so grand and subtle, so powerful in a new way, that we can only feel blindly of its hem.'' There is an older, more venerable, less masculine conception of the problem of evil at work here: ''the waste of pain,'' not as challenge to theology, but as stimulus to it; not escape into theology, but presence to the world:

> Now also in the valley night a skunk emerged from his underground burrow to hunt pale beetle grubs in the dark. A great horned owl folded his wings and dropped from the sky, and the two met on the bloodied surface of earth. Spreading over a distance, the air from that spot thinned to a frail sweetness, a tinctured wind that bespoke real creatures and real encounters at the edge.

''God has not absconded but spread.'' And so, Annie Dillard says,

> I propose to keep here what Thoreau called a ''meteorological journal of the mind,'' telling some tales and describing some of the sights of this rather tamed valley, and exploring, in fear and trembling, some of the unmapped dim reaches and unholy fastnesses to which those tales and sights so dizzyingly lead.

She ''would like to know the grasses and sedges—and care,'' not just because (as she says here) her exploration would be ''a series of happy recognitions,'' but because, as she says elsewhere, these matters have moral and religious significance. ''I suspect,'' she says, ''that the real moral thinkers end up, wherever they may start, in botany.'' Botany itself (or zoology or geology—the geology of the *mindscape/landscape* of Tinker Creek—or . . .) is a moral (or religious) exercise:

> What I aim to do is not so much learn the names of the shreds of creation that flourish in this valley, but to keep myself open to their meanings, which is to try to impress myself at all times with the fullest possible force of their very reality. I want to have things as multiply and intricately as possible present and visible in my mind.

Meaning is not an overlay on experience in this text; it is inextricably bound up with having things as ''multiply and intricately'' present as possible. Meaning, valuation, religious significance and description emerge as dimensions of her textured and narrative embeddedness in the valley through which flows the ''active mystery'' of Tinker Creek.

These meanings emerge, not from the world-as-object, but from the world-with-her-in-it, ''lost in the leafy interior,'' remembering ''pressure, and a curved sleep.''

> A little blood from the wrists and throat is the price I would willingly pay for that pressure of clacking weights on my shoulders, for the scent of deserts, groundfire in my ears—for being so in the clustering thick of things, rapt and enwrapped in the rising and falling real world.

The chapter titled ''Winter''—a time for reading and preparation, a time when the world *is* object to the inquiring mind—ends, not simply with the winter thought that ''things are well in their place'', but with a sense of the uncanny, a premonition of the breaking in upon her of a new order of meaning:

> If I go downstairs now will I see a possum just rounding a corner, trailing its scaled pink tail? I know that one night, in just this sort of rattling wind, I will go to the kitchen for milk and find on the back of the stove a sudden stew I never fixed, bubbling, with a deer leg sticking out.

And the ''Nightwatch'' chapter, which is the structural parallel of the ''Winter'' chapter (and prepares her and the reader for the final meditations of the book), ends with a sense of being ''rapt and enwrapped in the rising and falling real world.''

Annie Dillard's approach, as I have said, effects a transformation of the dominant Western theological tradition. The mountains may be home, but the creeks are the world and where she lives; and her theology flows from (in) the creeks, not from the mountains. The hallowing of creation consists, not in the (Hasidic/Gnostic) freeing of ''divine sparks trapped in the mute things of time,'' ''bearing them aloft into that rare air . . . in which all clays must shatter,'' but in ''keeping the subsoil world under trees in mind.'' The ''very looped soil,'' not a dance ''before the ark of the Lord in a barren desert,'' is, for her, ''an intricate throng of praise.''

These contrasts exemplify a consistent thread running through *Pilgrim at Tinker Creek.* Annie Dillard's naturalized theology isn't a move from the particularities of this world to religious hypotheses concerning its origin or significance. Rather, the very act of keeping the world ''in mind, in intelligence'' is conceived of as a religious act. This is an important aspect of what I have in mind when I call her naturalized theology a *contextualized* theology. There is a parallel here with ethical contextualism. To contextualize ethical deliberation is, in some sense, to provide a narrative, or story, from which the solution to the ethical dilemma emerges as the fitting conclusion. The particular problems posed by the attempt to articulate a satisfactory environmental ethic, for example, press for a naturalization and contextualization of ethics. The complex understanding that comes from the day-to-day observations of the field naturalist is usually sufficient to generate a sense of care and responsiveness to the biotic community. It is a matter of ''compelling representation.'' The style of arriving at moral insight exemplified by Aldo Leopold's *A Sand County Almanac,* for example, is interestingly similar to the style of moral deliberation we see in Carol Gilligan's subjects in *In a Different Voice.*

Annie Dillard's explorations at Tinker Creek do not provide the *data* for religious deliberation; they are themselves *religious observances.* This is faith in a larger sense. Such a faith does not involve *belief* in specific doctrines; rather, it consists in living this life, and walking on this earth, in a sacred manner. ''The question from agnosticism is, Who turned on the lights? The question from faith is, Whatever for?'' Faith in this larger sense does not *start* with the assumption that God is good—or that there *is* a God; it acknowledges the possibility that we may be ''dealing with a maniac.'' ''[F]aithlessness is a . . . massive failure of imagination.''

The imagination which is faith reveals, perhaps, that ''the creek is the mediator, benevolent, impartial, subsuming my shabbiest evils and dissolving them, transforming them into live moles, and shiners, and sycamore leaves.'' Think of a faith and imagination large and expansive enough to say this, not as conceit, but as truth—that is, as *true* symbol, that which, emerging from genuine encounter, carries, sustains, and shapes thought. Tinker Creek transforms, subsumes, the concepts of grace and forgiveness—and God. The *creek* forgives—by dissolving evils, transforming them into sycamore leaves. If this sounds odd, Annie Dillard suggests, we might wash ourselves in the waters of Tinker Creek, any creek, and muse on the traditional concept of God on some true dawn, some true morning in our lives.

It is a measure of the naturalism and contextualism of Annie Dillard's thought that, given the concerns that provide the focus for her book, Gnosticism is not a temptation. She notes the evidence that points the Gnostic way:

I have to acknowledge that the sea is a cup of death and the land is a stained altar stone. We the living are survivors huddled on flotsam, living on jetsam. We are escapees. We wake in terror, eat in hunger, sleep with a mouthful of blood.

And I can I think call the vision of the cedar and the knowledge of these wormy quarryings twin fjords cutting into the granite cliffs of mystery . . .

But she doesn't take the bait:

The thistle is part of Adam's curse. . . . But does the goldfinch eat thorny sorrow with the thistle, or do I? If this furling air is fallen, then the fall was happy indeed. . . . Creation itself was the fall, a burst into the thorny beauty of the real.

She agrees with Pascal that ''Every religion that does not affirm that God is hidden is not true,'' but she prefers not to take this in a Gnostic direction: ''It could be that God has not absconded but spread.'' Transcendental theology figures into her argument only as ''a relatively narrow column of God as air.''

There is nothing of the masculine drama of alienation from God in Annie Dillard, and nothing of the related masculine penchant for taking the transcendent, the spiritual, the abstract as the real, the true, what is of value—and the opposite of these as less real, the source of error, of less value. A nice example is her notion of the *gratuitousness* of the things of this world—not contingency, but gratuitousness. For the most part (as in Aquinas's third proof for the existence of God) the dominant Western theological tradition has acknowledged and even insisted upon the contingency of this world in contrast to the presumed necessity of God's existence. But its gratuitousness is as often, if implicitly, denied. Western theology is marked by its urgent need to understand the world as *required,* as necessitated by God. It is as though the world is something of an embarrassment to the masculine theological mind, an anomaly, a surd which must be assigned a derivative necessity and intelligibility in virtue of its relationship to the necessary existence and goodness of God—as though to say that only the transcendent is real and that this world should be here, could be here, only if it *must* be here, only if God's existence or goodness requires it.

For Annie Dillard, on the other hand, the starting point is the gratuitousness and extravagance of the world's ''spotted and speckled detail.''

I would like to see it all, to understand it, but I must start somewhere, so I try to deal with the giant water bug in Tinker Creek and the flight of three hundred redwings from an Osage orange. . . . And it occurs to me more and more that everything I have seen is wholly gratuitous. The giant water bug's predations, the frog's croak, the tree with the lights in it are not in any real sense necessary per se to the world or to its creator. Nor am I. . . . [I]t accumulates in my mind as an extravagance of minutiae. The sheer fringe and network of detail assumes primary importance. That there are so many details seems to be the most important and visible fact about the creation. . . . The first question—the one crucial one—of the creation of the universe and the existence of something as a sign and an affront to nothing, is a blank one. I can't think about it. So it is to the fringe of that question that I affix my attention, . . . the intricacy of the world's spotted and speckled detail.

For her, theology in the dominant tradition of the West is not a deposit of faith with which she proposes to reconcile the giant water bug's predations, but a source of understandings provided by mythical tracings. All routes back to—and through—that "curved sleep" are mythical tracings on and in the "looped soil" of our lives and land. "What I have been after all along is not an explanation but a picture."

Annie Dillard is not after a *reductive* account, an understanding of this world as a manifestation of God's goodness, for example. Nor is she after a *consistent* account:

> The creator goes off on one wild, specific tangent after another . . . with an exuberance that would seem to be unwarranted, and with an abandoned energy sprung from an unfathomable font. What is going on here? The point of the dragonfly's terrible lip, the giant water bug, birdsong, or the beautiful dazzle and flash of sunlighted minnows, is not that it all fits together like clockwork—for it doesn't, particularly, not even inside the goldfish bowl—but that it all flows so freely wild, like the creek, that it all surges in such a free, fringed tangle.

With the Principle of Plenitude and the Great Chain of Being it *is* the fit that counts, the a priori dictates of unity and a transcendental theology; with Annie Dillard it is the fact or experience of the "free, fringed tangle" that matters. Her method is not that of generalization; nor is her aim to find unity in diversity, a coherent and consistent account. Rather she wishes to paint a satisfying picture—where satisfaction consists in *fidelity*—a picture intricate enough, detailed enough, to answer to her desire to be so tuned to Tinker Creek that her questions are answered, her needs met, by narrative or ceremonial continuances of her mythical tracings on and in the "looped soil" of her life and land.

Terror and a Beauty Insoluble: Twin Fjords in the Granite Cliffs of Mystery

The problem—emblematically—is with insects:

> Fish gotta swim and bird gotta fly; insects, it seems, gotta do one horrible thing after another. I never ask why of a vulture or shark, but I ask why of almost every insect I see. More than one insect—the possibil-

ity of fertile reproduction—is an assault on all human value, all hope of a reasonable god.

Several things are notable about this passage. First, that Annie Dillard's concern—or one of them—*is* about insects. Second, that her concern has little or nothing to do with the effect of insects on humans but with the sheer manner of their existence: "not only did the creator create everything, but . . . he is apt to create *anything*. He'll stop at nothing." Third, that her concern is not with the creator's goodness but with the creator's reasonableness. Fourth, looking beyond the quoted passage, we are not shown either the reasonableness or the goodness of God. *Pilgrim at Tinker Creek* is not a theodicy. While theodicies begin with a fixed point, the goodness (or reasonableness) of God, in this text God is anything but a fixed point, a theological given. The term 'God' functions, in part, as a stand-in for whatever account emerges from her exploration. It organizes the inquiry; it influences not only perception but also the kind of reflectiveness woven into her experience.

Is the use of the dominant tradition in this way fruitful, revelatory? To answer this question we must answer another: What ultimately gives shape to Dillard's text, determines its texture? Is the text—though it makes use of the tradition—faithful to its empirical grounding (or watering) in Tinker Creek? Does Annie Dillard's use of the tradition help to articulate her experience, bring it to narrative or ceremonial coherence and intelligibility? Or does it function (as does totalizing discourse) to block perception? What shapes the discourse, what is it *faithful* to? To an a priori theological metaphysics or to the texture of experience? My sense is that the texture of experience shapes the discourse and that the use of the tradition serves to mark and shape that discourse as *sacred*.

So, emblematically, the problem is with insects, the intelligibility within a religious ambience of the world with its "uncertainty of vision, the horror of the fixed, the dissolution of the present, the intricacy of beauty, the pressure of fecundity, the elusiveness of the free, and the flawed nature of perfection." The question concerns what it might mean to walk in a sacred manner, in the fecund world of insects in which "every glistening egg is a memento mori." The first step is to gather the data, and to note clearly one's responses to that world.

> I don't know what it is about fecundity that so appalls. I suppose it is the teeming evidence that birth and growth, which we value, are ubiquitous and blind, that life itself is so astonishingly cheap, that nature is as

careless as it is bountiful, and that with extravagance goes a crushing waste that will one day include our own cheap lives. . . . Every glistening egg is a memento mori . . . [T]he notion of the infinite variety of detail and the multiplicity of forms is a pleasing one; in complexity are the fringes of beauty, and in variety are generosity and exuberance. But all this leaves something vital out of the picture. It is not one pine I see, but a thousand. I myself am not one, but legion. And we are all going to die.

In this repetition of individuals is a mindless stutter, an imbecilic fixedness that must be taken into account. The driving force behind all this fecundity is a terrible pressure I must also consider, the pressure of birth and growth, the pressure that splits the bark of trees and shoots out seeds, that squeezes out the egg and bursts the pupa, that hungers and lusts and drives the creature relentlessly toward its own death. Fecundity, then, is what I have been thinking about, fecundity and the pressure of growth. Fecundity is an ugly word for an ugly subject. It is ugly, at least, in the eggy animal world. I don't think it is for plants.

This gathering of data is infused with valuation and with elements of the cultural tradition that connects her to human history. What emerge are patterns, smaller and larger coherences. There is no attempt to *force* these recognitions into a larger unity. She does not pull God's reasonableness or goodness out of the hat; nor does she go in the other, equally popular, direction of offering a value-neutral scientific account (''This is the way the world is . . .''), eliding value, treating it as a subjective overlay on world-description.

The patterns that concern Annie Dillard are of two kinds. The articulation of these and the refusal to join them in some higher synthesis are refrains throughout the text, as though both the recognition and the refusal are at the heart of the matter. ''Terror and a beauty insoluble,'' she says, ''are a ribband of blue woven into the fringes of garments of things. . . . No culture explains, no bivouac offers real haven or rest.'' Variations on this theme:

> What geomancy reads what the windblown sand writes on the desert rock? I read there that all things live by a generous power and dance to a mighty tune; or I read there that all things are scattered and hurled, that our every arabesque and grand jeté is a frantic variation on our one free fall.

> Beauty itself is the fruit of the creator's exuberance that grew such a tangle, and the grotesques and horrors bloom from that same free growth, that intricate scramble and twine up and down the conditions of time.

> Beauty is real. I would never deny it; the appalling thing is that I forget it. Waste and extravagance go together up and down the banks, all along the intricate fringe of spirit's free incursions into time.

Related to the ontological/valuational categories of ''beauties'' and ''horrors'' are the terms 'mystery' and 'knowledge,' respectively. ''Knowledge,'' she says, ''does not vanquish mystery, or obscure its distant lights.'' Likewise, ''it would be too facile to pull everything out of the hat and say that mystery vanquishes knowledge.'' She considers and rejects the standard modes of reconciliation. She says, for example, that

> Although my vision of the world of the spirit would not be altered a jot if the cedar [the tree with the lights in it] had been purulent with galls, those galls actually do matter to my understanding of this world. Can I say then that corruption is one of beauty's deep-blue speckles, that the frayed and nibbled fringe of the world is a tallith, a prayer shawl, the intricate garment of beauty? It is very tempting, but I honestly cannot.

> I am not washed and beautiful, in control of a shining world in which everything fits, but instead am wandering awed about on a splintered wreck I've come to care for, whose gnawed trees breathe delicate air, whose bloodied and scarred creatures are my dearest companions, and whose beauty beats and shines not *in* its imperfections but overwhelmingly in spite of them, under the wind-rent clouds, upstream and down.

Annie Dillard's argument does not move toward an ontologically or epistemologically unified account: ''*Sub specie aeternitatis* this may all look different. . . . Here may not be the cleanest, newest place, but that clean timeless place that vaults on either side of this one is noplace at all.'' Such an account is born of alienation and arrogant perception. Rather, her words are addressed to the specific circumstances of her ''fellow survivors''; they emerge from, and give rise to, loving perception and respect. ''Let us love the country of here below,'' she says with Simone Weil, ''It is real; it offers resistance to love.''

Dillard considers the splitting apart of nature and culture and the devaluation of the former:

> It looks for the moment as though I might have to reject this creek life unless I want to be utterly brutalized. Is human culture with its values my only real home after all? . . . This direction of thought brings me abruptly to a fork in the road where I stand paralyzed, unwilling to go on, for both ways lead to madness.

> Either this world, my mother, is a monster, or I myself am a freak.

The first fork, the Pascalian/Gnostic/Existentialist fork, is rejected outright; its masculinist transcendentalism and dualism haven't enough purchase on her soul, with its particular sense of the spiritual geography of Tinker Creek.

The second fork—"that creation itself is blamelessly, benevolently askew by its very free nature, and that it is only human feeling that is freakishly amiss"—although she prefers it to the first, is nonetheless problematic, the best of "two ridiculous alternatives." What is ridiculous, it seems, is understanding this fork as an *explanation,* a theodicy. As a *picture,* however, which is what she says she has been after all along, it works; it establishes the context in which she can explore what I take to be the central concern of this work: the (or *a*) proper human response to the situation in which we find ourselves, namely, as survivors wandering awed on a wreck we have (or might) come to care for. The thought that our "emotions are the curse, not death," "that it is only human feeling that is freakishly amiss," is mentioned not as theodicy—she is quite aware that there would still be a theological problem ("What creator would be so cruel, not to kill otters [or humans], but to let them care?—but as datum, an answer to which we must *respond.* And what that answer seems to require is something between lobotomy and Gnostic rejection of this world. And what *that* leaves us with, she says, is the unanswerability of the "old, old mystery," the problem of evil. What she has done is precisely *not* solve or dissolve that problem but place it center stage as definitive of what it is to be a pilgrim at Tinker Creek. The tension this creates takes shape as a (perhaps *the*) central existential fact of her spiritual landscape. This tension is poignantly expressed in the words of an Eskimo shaman, whom she quotes: "ife's greatest danger lies in the fact that men's food consists entirely of souls." As far as theodicy goes—or redemption, or saving knowledge—what the world offers is this:

> There is not a guarantee in the world. Oh your *needs* are guaranteed, your needs are absolutely guaranteed by the most stringent of warranties, in the plainest, truest words: knock; seek; ask. But you must read the fine print. "Not as the world giveth, give I unto you." That's the catch. If you can catch it it will catch you up, aloft, up to any gap at all, and you'll come back, for you will come back, transformed in a way you may not have bargained for—dribbling and crazed. The waters of separation, however lightly sprinkled, leave indelible stains. Did you think, before you were caught, that you needed, say, life? Do you think you will keep your life, or anything else you love? But no. Your needs are all met. But not as the world giveth. You see the needs of your own spirit met whenever you have asked, and you have learned that the outrageous guarantee holds. You see the creatures die, and you know you will die. And one day it occurs to you that you must not need life. Obviously. And then you're gone. You have finally understood that you're dealing with a maniac.

Walking in a Sacred Manner

A central concern of *Pilgrim at Tinker Creek* is the articulation of a ceremonial response to "terror and a beauty insoluble." One of my concerns in the preceding sections has been to provide a context for the articulation of that response, to place it as a naturalized postmodernist theology, the point of which is to preserve openness to contradiction and difference, a place in which the Other can be recognized, truly seen, and in which one can, in the presence of this world, this creek, *awaken.* "We wake, if we ever wake at all, to mystery, rumors of death, beauty, violence." It is in this context that we can understand the radicalness of Annie Dillard's use of ceremony and ritual.

As a touchstone for this understanding I look at another contemporary account of ceremony, that which emerges in an interview with the West Coast poet, Gary Snyder:

> [INTERVIEWER]: Whether you're eating vegetables, meat, or sand, you're involved in the ripoff [the exploitation of nature].
>
> SNYDER: I don't think eating is ripping off. We can't look at it that way . . . because we're edible too.
>
> [INTERVIEWER]: But I'm not offering myself up to somebody as food.
>
> SNYDER: You'd better. Sooner or later. . . . If you look at life itself as a ripping off process, then your metaphysics are hopeless. Your only choice then is to reject the world and opt entirely for spirit. Which has meant historically to neglect the biological and to really rip off nature consequently. . . . But you hit on a very sensitive thing, which is that relationship with food. If you think of eating and killing plants or animals to eat as an unfortunate quirk in the nature of the universe, then you cut yourself from connecting with the sacramental energy-exchange, evolutionary mutual-sharing aspect of life . . . that sharing of energies, passing it back and forth, which is done by literally eating each other. And that's what communion is. . . . That's one of the healthiest things about the primitive worldview is that it's solved one of the critical problems of life and death. It understands how you relate to your food. You sing to it. You pray to it, and then you enjoy it.

Snyder invokes a gift economy, typical of tribal communities, in which goods and services flow through the community (and between the human community and the rest of nature) as gifts rather than as commodities for which we barter or contract in the marketplace. In gift communities the gift (from other people or nonhuman nature) must be consumed, it cannot pile up like capital in the hands of the recipient; and it must be passed on—it increases and confers its benefits on the community and its individuals *only* by being passed on. In the case of food, literally, and in the case of much else metaphorically, we die into one another's lives and live one another's deaths.

The view invoked by Snyder's interviewer in his claim that eating is a ripping-off process is, by contrast, a market economy notion. The "right to life" which we violate when we eat plants and animals, as with individual rights in general, is a means of stockpiling capital in the form of potentially satisfiable interests or desires, possible satisfactions which might accrue to the individual. On one level, then, we can understand Snyder as recommending a return to the notion of a gift economy as the organizing principle of community.

What, however, of the fact that in Snyder's view the passing of the gift is conceived of ritualistically, as communion; and what of his endorsement of the "primitive worldview" which understands our relationship to food as involving singing to it, praying to it, and then enjoying it? Much of this can be readily understood as part of the acknowledgment involved in the giving and receiving of gifts. But there is a note that isn't captured in saying this, a slight air of tragedy, some acknowledgment of the fact that though we may die into one another's lives, we nonetheless *die*. There is some suggestion that it isn't simply and straightforwardly all right to kill and consume other creatures. There is also the suggestion that this can be *made* all right, but only by permission given from the animal. Or, perhaps, the thought is that there are certain dangers inherent in living the death of another, dangers which can be avoided only by the performance of certain rituals. Is the thought that other creatures possibly have an *equal* claim, or right, to life which can be overridden only by permission?

We might speculate that in a tribal situation in which there is as yet no conception of moral hierarchy, ritual expresses the beginnings of a tradition of individual rights. In such a society the sense that there are claims or rights which others might press upon us must be dealt with by supplication or the asking of permission. Perhaps ritual atonement, appeasement, and supplication are the precursors within an egalitarian society—where, also, the nonhuman has equal status with the human—of the moral hierarchy established by a theory of rights and its associated rank-ordering of values.

On this speculative account ritual straddles two worlds and is ambiguous for that reason. It has one foot in the contemporary world of moral hierarchy and human domination. It has another foot in the tribal world of usufruct—the use of the fruit. The bridge between these two worlds is, oddly enough, the concept of equality, the idea that other creatures and I are morally on a par. This is a highly abstract concept and poses a problem for usufruct which is resolved by the notion of ritual supplication, permission, courtesy, and the idea of reciprocity in the web of relationships between people and nonhuman nature. There is a sense in which these rituals are also highly abstract; that is, both the problem and the solution presuppose a certain conceptual and emotional distancing from the ongoing activities of eating, birthing, and dying. Such ritual points to a deeper understanding and appreciation of the world, but it also points to dilemmas not *revealed* by this deeper understanding but, rather, *created* by it, and to solutions which accentuate the distance and alienate us from the Eskimo shaman's observation that "Life's greatest danger lies in the fact that men's food consists entirely of souls."

Ritual, on this speculative account, is a crossroads. Moving from ancient to modern times it represents a movement away from embeddedness in the flow of life toward an abstract and managerial relation toward it. Ritual, as a way of establishing relationships to nature, at the present time, however, represents, at its best, a movement back toward a more caring response to the world, an attempt to acknowledge the presence of a world for which it is possible, and good, to care.

In my account of ritual and ceremony—seeing in their early manifestations the seeds of moral hierarchy and in their contemporary manifestations the hope of a return to a more egalitarian, nondomineering relationship with one another and with nonhuman nature—I have bypassed an empirical investigation of their actual function in traditional cultures. The account does allow us, however, to discern a particular danger inherent in contemporary uses of ritual and ceremony.

One of our inheritances from modernism (though it is not unique to modernism) is the totalizing and colonizing use of discourse for the advancement of cultural imperialism on all levels of society. Myth, ritual, and ceremony are, as this century has shown, enlisted into the cause of cultural imperialism. Cultural imperialism is currently quite pervasive in the dominant culture, even among those who take themselves to be combatting it. This has become clear, for example, in recent criticism of white, middle-class feminist theory by women of color, criticism that has revealed pervasive totalizing, colonizing, and, therefore, racist tendencies within that body of theory. In another place I have discussed similar tendencies within male-authored radical environmentalism. The fact that such proclivities are found at the very heart of liberatory movements has been one of the motives for the development of feminist "standpoint epistemologies" and a "politics of difference." It is in this context that I read Annie Dillard's use of ceremony and ritual as a means for both acknowledging and living with contradiction and difference.

It is in her mystical passages and in her use of ritual and ceremony that Annie Dillard seems most susceptible to a traditional theological reading. And yet it is just here, when read in the light of her naturalized and contextualized theology, that she often seems to depart most radically from the tradition out of which she speaks.

Judith Plaskow has given us a detailed account of the ways in which the theologies of Reinhold Niebuhr and Paul Tillich provide us, not with an account of the *human* condition and redemption from that condition, but, rather, an account of a typically male form of alienation. This is not the place to argue for the view, but it can be plausibly maintained that most (if not all) of the salvific techniques of the major world religions were designed to redeem the alienated masculine ego, to undo the excessive focus on the self which leads to, or constitutes, that alienation. I emphasize in my portrait the *alienation* resulting from that self-centeredness, rather than the self-centeredness itself, because it points to the fact that most redemptive strategies envision the overcoming of alienation as the overcoming of *difference.* The overcoming of difference takes many forms, but basically, alienating difference is seen as ultimately illusory. One might say that in the interests of redemption, the world is colonized. A colonizing understanding of the world—the interior counterpart of the imperialism which has come to be characteristic of the "civilized" world—is internalized as part of the redemptive process.

Of course, such "redemptive" processes are not truly redemptive. Only a politics of difference will make possible the genuine redemption of members of the dominant culture (and the correlative liberation of oppressed cultures).

Annie Dillard's use of mysticism, ritual, and ceremony can plausibly be read, not as a way of overcoming difference, but of preserving it, of resisting the temptations of colonizing consciousness. Much of *Pilgrim at Tinker Creek* is a meditation on difference—not on *dualism*—and a refusal to resolve the threat of difference through the colonization of that difference. Yet the question remains: How does one live with the consciousness of difference revealed in Annie Dillard's encounters at Tinker Creek? This is the role of ceremony and ritual in *Pilgrim at Tinker Creek*. Ceremony and ritual (the "waters of separation") provide means of living with the understanding that we are "dealing with a maniac."

Seen in this light the mystical images scattered throughout the text take on new significance:

> I am an explorer, then, and I am also a stalker, or the instrument of the hunt itself. . . . I am the arrow shaft, carved along my length by unexpected lights and gashes from the very sky, and this book is the straying trail of blood.

The image of the hunt is not used to identify with the hunted animal as a condition of overcoming alienation from it. Its sense, rather, is brought out in the image that follows, that of being played on like a pipe, being pummeled by barely sheathed power. It is further clarified in the next sentence by the reference to Eskimo breath-singing, in which the singers sit "cross-legged on the ground, mouth on mouth, blowing by turns each other's throat cords, making a low, unearthly music." The image is not one of incorporation, assimilation, or of destruction and domination, but one of openness to the Other, what Jessica Benjamin has called "genuine self-other recognition"—that discovery and understanding of the self which occurs within the space provided by clear perception of, and acceptance by, the Other. This reading also makes sense of the following passage:

> I have never understood why so many mystics of all creeds experience the presence of God on mountaintops. Aren't they afraid of being blown away? . . . It often feels best to lay low, inconspicuous, instead of waving your spirit around from high places like a lightning rod. For if God is in one sense the igniter, . . . God is also in another sense the destroyer. . . . You get a comforting sense, in a curved, hollow place, of being vulnerable to only a relatively narrow column of God as air.

This states precisely the distance that separates Annie Dillard from those traditions in which redemption *does* consist in being "blown away," destroyed by God. Unlike the mountaintop, which is the place of self-obliteration, the place of passing over into *unity* with God, or the place of reception of the mind of Christ, the "curved, hollow place" is the space of genuine self-other recognition.

But Annie Dillard *does* talk of selflessness in rather traditional ways, such as when she speaks of finding a balance and repose by retreating "not inside myself, but outside myself, so that I am a tissue of senses. . . . I am the skin of water the wind plays over; I am petal, feather, stone"; or when she says that "experiencing the present purely is being emptied and hollow"; or in the following passage:

> The death of the self . . . is no violent act. It is merely the joining of the great rock heart of the earth in its roll. It is merely the slow cessation of the will's sprints and the intellect's chatter . . .

These passages, however, are not joined to a metaphysical system in which selflessness is understood as, for example, union with God or *Brahman,* or identification with the divine *logos.* In these systems the "cessation of the will's sprints and the intellect's chatter" and the overcoming of alienation are achieved by the internalization of a metaphysics of unity—an internalization that blocks genuine recognition and acceptance of difference by colonizing that difference. (Notice the image of the *joining* of the "great rock heart of the earth.")

Themes of longing and denial are also pervasive, particularly in the last part of the work, in which mystical and ritual aspects come to the fore But the objective of the mystical and ritual honing of the spirit is not to overcome longing, not to achieve some desired rest in unity, but to *clarify* longing, to make of it an instrument of perception and recognition:

> It is possible, in deep space, to sail on solar wind. Light, be it particle or wave, has force: you rig a giant sail and go. The secret of seeing is to sail on solar wind. Hone and spread your spirit till you yourself are a sail, whetted, translucent, broadside to the merest puff.

> I am buoyed by a calm and effortless longing, an angled pitch of the will, like the set of the wings of the monarch which climbed a hill by falling still.

In the two central mystical experiences of *Pilgrim at Tinker Creek*—the experience of the cedar tree on which shone "the steady, inward flames of eternity" and the pure experience of the present when patting the puppy—pride of place, for Annie Dillard, goes to the experience of the tree with lights ("The vision comes and goes, mostly goes, but I live for it.") Nonetheless, "on both occasions I thought, with rising exultation, this is it, this is it" and "although the door to the tree with the lights in it was opened *from* eternity, as it were, and shone on

that tree eternal lights, it nevertheless opened on the real and present cedar. It opened on time."

> I am a sacrifice bound with cords to the horns of the world's rock altar, waiting for worms. I take a deep breath, I open my eyes. Looking, I see there are worms in the horns of the altar like live maggots in amber. . . . A wind from noplace rises. A sense of the real exults me; the cords loose; I walk on my way.

The honing of the spirit *is* a preparation for the gift of the tree with the lights in it; but, more importantly, it is the austerity necessary for living with difference, the "twin fjords in the granite cliffs of mystery," the "horns of the world's rock altar."

Chapters on clarity of perception ("Seeing," "The Present," and "Stalking"; chapters 2, 6, and 11) immediately precede chapters ("Winter," "Spring," and "Nightwatch"; 3, 7, and 12) which can be read as preparations of the soul for its meditations on terror and beauty in the chapters which follow ("The Fixed," "Intricacy"/"Fecundity," and "The Horns of the Altar"; 4, 8/10, and 13). The first sequence brings the problem—emblematically, that of insects—into focus; the second refuses totalizing answers, leaving in place the "twin fjords in the granite cliffs of mystery"; the third gathers up the themes of the first two in a reprise in which the theoretical conclusion of the second sequence is affirmed in this world: "Let us love the country of here below. It is real; it offers resistance to love" (quotation from Simone Weil).

It is in this context that we should listen to the last two chapters of *Pilgrim at Tinker Creek.* These two ("Northing" and "The Waters of Separation") constitute a fourth sequence, similar to the other three but in which the seeing, the preparation, and the understanding are deepened, embedded in a ritualized or ceremonial relationship to the world necessary for their acceptance and maintenance in good faith, necessary in order that the perception that "You have finally understood that you're dealing with a maniac" not slide into banality or be subsumed (totalized, colonized) by a "higher" understanding in which difference disappears, in which the Otherness of this world is colonized and we need no longer fear that one night "I will go to the kitchen for milk and find on the back of the stove a sudden stew I never fixed, bubbling, with a deer leg sticking out." In "Northing" we read:

> I have glutted on richness and welcome hyssop [used in purification rites]. . . . I stand under wiped skies directly, naked, without intercessors.

In this way true seeing, true preparation of the soul for life along Tinker Creek is accomplished.

And meditation on the twin fjords in the granite cliffs of mystery (in "The Waters of Separation") is itself a ceremony:

> This Tinker Creek! It was low today, and clear. On the still side of the island the water held pellucid as a pane, a gloss on runes of sandstone, shale, and snail-inscribed clay silt; on the faster side it hosted a blinding profusion of curved and pitched surfaces, flecks of shadow and tatters of sky. These are the waters of beauty and mystery, issuing from a gap in the granite world; they fill the lodes in my cells with a light like petaled water.... And these are also the waters of separation: they purify, acrid and laving, and they cut me off.

> And so

> ... I go my way, and my left foot says "Glory," and my right foot says "Amen": in and out of Shadow Creek, upstream and down, exultant, in a daze, dancing, to the twin silver trumpets of praise.

Source: Jim Cheney, "'The Waters of Separation': Myth and Ritual in Annie Dillard's *Pilgrim at Tinker Creek,*" in *Journal of Feminist Studies in Religion,* Vol. 6, No. 1, Spring 1990, pp. 41–63.

Elaine Tietjen

In the following essay, Tietjen recounts her early impressions of Pilgrim at Tinker Creek *along with her experience as a student of Dillard's, then offers a later analysis of Dillard's work.*

She stared as if she were about to tell me that she dreamed last night of hanging in space above our blue planet. With her leather jacket, loose wool pants, serious hiking boots, and a collecting pouch slung over her neck, she looked the perfect image of the woodswoman I desperately wanted to become. Her cornsilk hair was lit up like a lamp. Annie Dillard sat on a ledge in a clearing, beckoning the reader to come into her woods. I held her Pulitzer Prize-winning book on my lap in the back of an old bus, headed for Canyonlands.

Pilgrim at Tinker Creek was one of three books I took into the wilderness for a semester of expeditions in the Rockies. Edward Abbey's *Desert Solitaire* and Aldo Leopold's *Sand County Almanac* both waited in my pack. Up until two weeks before, I had never heard of Dillard, but the sheer force of her image on the cover convinced me to buy her book. The cover said *Pilgrim* was "a mystical excursion into the natural world." So I read it first. I was glad the trip to Utah was a long one; I had to savor each paragraph three or four times and stare out the window at the rolling world, dumbfounded.

Dillard liked to exaggerate, I discovered, but she convinced me to believe her buoyant claims. Here was a power in language I had never heard before from a woman, or from anyone really—a freedom to be wild, deep, outrageous, exposed. Her voice was confident, striding, and then unashamedly silly. Dillard had me to herself for days.

I had enrolled in this outdoor education program to experience the "essence" of wilderness. I wanted an ultimate physical and spiritual baptism, to see if I, like Thoreau, could live deliberately. As I opened Dillard's book I was looking for a like mind and an affirmation that life meant something serious. Surrounded by sixteen fellow students who spent the bus ride comparing beer brands and former girlfriends, I wanted to talk about evolution, plant dispersal, buzzards, sunsets. We were living in alpine meadows, at the base of desert cliffs, in silent caves, on the ridgelines of Wind River peaks—and I needed to exclaim wonder with someone. Annie Dillard hit that deepest chord.

"I wish I could get hold of this country. I wish I could breathe it into my bones," I wrote with pained longing from a cramped position in a wind-whipped tent. It was the late seventies. I had grown up reading *Audubon* magazine, hiking in the Adirondacks, and attending school assemblies on Earth Day. At college I had just lived for a year in Ecology House—where I finally learned what multi-national corporations did. Wilderness was being destroyed at an alarming rate, I discovered, and few people seemed to care. Hardly anyone had even *heard* of the Congressional debate over the future of Alaska when I knocked on their doors with a petition in hand. How could human culture survive if we eliminated the very foundation of what made us human? I wanted to experience wilderness before it was too late. I was ready to devote myself to saving it.

It's no wonder that Dillard's apparent "visionary naturalism" (to quote one critic) became a kind of intellectual template for me. Dillard went into the natural world to SEE, the way children and adults blind from birth with cataracts, and given sight through a special operation, suddenly could see the world for the first time. They found it either horrifying or beautiful. Dillard wanted to see the world freshly, as if for the first time—a flat plane of "color patches" raw and real—the world unfiltered by human senses, untrammeled by human meaning.

> Peeping through my keyhole I see within the range of only about thirty percent of the light that comes from

Near Tinker Creek is the 2031-mile long Appalachian Trail linking New England to the South. Here three white-tailed does eat from shrubs along a portion of the Appalachian Trail in Shenandoah National Park in Virginia

the sun; the rest is infrared and some little ultraviolet, perfectly apparent to many animals, but invisible to me. A nightmare network of ganglia, charged and firing without my knowledge, cuts and splices what I do see, editing it for my brain. Donald E. Carr points out that the sense impressions of one-celled animals are *not* edited for the brain: ''This is philosophically interesting in a rather mournful way, since it means that only the simplest animals perceive the universe as it is.''

Undaunted by this information, Dillard set out to observe the universe as it really is. Both scientist and poet, she wrestled with the spiritual underpinnings of each field, gathering information by the armload to sort into colorful patterns. She was an explorer and stalker, she tells us, determined to discover the meaning of life—or rather, of suffering, pain, and death, for these are the phenomena that do not make coherent sense. Dillard wanted to get below and around human perceptual limitations. She would have liked to see God in the face if she could do so without dying.

On a first reading of *Pilgrim*, I identified with Dillard's brave explorations. Life is rough, she seemed to say, and the world unfair and insane; all creatures suffer; we're all in this together. She was

willing to grant that the rest of life besides us humans mattered. She quoted John Cowper Powys, who said, ''We have no reason for denying to the world of plants a certain slow, dim, vague, large, leisurely semiconsciousness.'' Dillard added, ''The patch of bluets in the grass may not be long on brains, but it might be, at least in a very small way, awake.''

This writer was a keen observer, and a collector of incredible facts. Through her eyes natural history came alive for me. I was a biology student who wrote poetry; Dillard seemed to be a poet who conducted experiments on life. She waited on the bridge for hours to catch a glimpse of a muskrat. She stuffed praying mantis egg-cases in her pockets and attached them to a bush outside her window where she would be sure to see them hatch. She tried to untie a snakeskin; chased grasshoppers; shouted into the cliffs to see if the echo would disturb a bee foraging at her elbow.

All of life was worth noticing to Dillard because any piece of it could lead to revelation. The natural world, if we could only perceive it as it really is, would provide us with a door into mystery.

Then one day I was walking along Tinker Creek thinking of nothing at all and I saw the tree with the lights in it. I saw the backyard cedar where the mourning doves roost charged and transfigured, each cell buzzing with flame. I stood on the grass with the lights in it, grass that was wholly fire, utterly focused and utterly dreamed. It was less like seeing than like being for the first time seen, knocked breathless by a powerful glance. The flood of fire abated, but I'm still spending the power. Gradually the lights went out in the cedar, the colors died, the cells unflamed and disappeared. I was still ringing. I had been my whole life a bell, and never knew it until at that moment I was lifted and struck.

This was the way I had been struck, too, I exclaimed to myself, one night in the mountains when I had perched on a rock mid-stream and stared at the stars until I could actually see the distances between them, and could feel the earth turn under me, a round speck I rode through a vast reality usually ignored. Dillard, "the arrowshaft," went purposefully in life, seeking and readying herself for such moments of revelation. It was up to us, she exhorted by example or directive, to be seekers and look for the world's meaning. She looked on faith and expected meaning to be real—on faith and on the non-rational knowledge of having seen the tree with the lights in it. Her seeking led her to eventually hold horror in one hand, beauty in the other, and to give thanks for all of it; she exits the book with her left foot saying "Glory" and her right foot "Amen": "in and out of Shadow Creek, upstream and down, exultant, in a daze, dancing, to the twin silver trumpets of praise."

I remember closing the book with reverence, breathless myself, convinced that I was parting from a soul-mate. Surely, I thought, if we were to meet, oh surely we would become the closest of friends. I could not have guessed then how wrong I was, and how young.

The following fall I returned to college for my senior year. Standing outside the English office, inspecting the schedule of new courses taped to the door, I nearly exploded with adrenaline when I read "A. Dillard." Rushing to my house, I called Dillard immediately to ask her to be my advisor for an honors project I had just that minute created. We had a long talk, at the end of which she flatly refused, having inquired why in the world I would want to write about environmental problems when "it's been done before." The encounter deflated me for weeks.

The next semester I was on the class list for Dillard's "Writing Poetry" course. It proved to be

> **Looking so closely at eternity, Dillard was torn between beauty and horror throughout her 'mystical excursion' in *Pilgrim*. The *logos* force compelled her to explore, analyze, and question the meaning of existence, and eventually to write a reasoning book."**

one of the most hypnotizing and frustrating I had as an undergraduate. At one point Dillard admitted that she would have called the course "Writing and Living Poetry"—"this class is really about writing as a way of life," she said. "You must turn away from the pleasure of being one of the people of the world. The mission of endeavor is more important than the pleasure of life." If we had a choice, she asked us, of going to Afghanistan or reading in the library, which should we do? I thought of her forays onto the island in Tinker Creek. I thought of her standing on the bridge over the creek one summer in a hurricane while the flood waters swirled a few inches below her feet. I thought of her longing to go "northing"—to see the caribou for herself perhaps, hear their hoof joints clicking. Of course, I thought, GO, I would go. "The library," she said.

When Dillard first walked into that classroom I had been struck by how young she looked—too young to have absorbed so much wisdom. Her hair was long and loose like many of the young women in the class. She was soft-skinned but put a hard set in her jaw when she wanted to. She liked to wear hats. She talked about softball. She liked to smoke at the head of the wide rectangular conference table around which we thirty students sat, and willingly, I forgave her. She remained distant and private about her own life, and devoted herself to the class. She was tough, demanding: every poem came back with comments all over it. In the margins of mine she admonished me to "eschew sentimentality." By the middle of the semester I finally got the hang of her all-encompassing definition for that oft-repeated word—anything that had been done before: anything that came too easily; anything that borrowed its power from the world, instead of creating its own; anything that was too comfortable, that did not dare and plunge.

One day she asked how many of us would be writing poems ten years from now. The week before we had heard, ''The people who are accomplishing things are the people sitting in their rooms missing life.'' Most of the hands in the room went up. She was surprised; her eyes softened a bit. ''Good for you,'' I think she said. The look on her face was pained, pleased, worried—writing mattered too much. I think we made her day. I think we made her anxious.

Confronted each week by such declarations, I soon wondered what had happened to the woodswoman I had first met. Hadn't she stalked a coot all of one afternoon, listened to insects, attained a glorious moment while patting a puppy? Her classroom directives for a strict intellectualism did not fit the sense-based ''experiential'' image I had of her from the book. In an interview with Mike Major for *America* in 1978, Dillard set the record straight: ''. . . people want to make you into a cult figure because of what they fancy to be your life style, when the truth is your life is literature! You're writing consciously, off of hundreds of index cards, often distorting the literal truth to achieve an artistic one . . . [People] think it happens in a dream, that you just sit on a tree stump and take dictation from some little chipmunk!''

My new role model appeared progressively more disciplined, more severe, and more driven than I would have guessed from reading *Pilgrim,* but she was no environmentalist. One day she commented that she didn't see how any of us would want to be vegetarians; it took too much time away from writing to cook that stuff. She showed no allegiance to any political causes that I could detect. Her sole cause was Meaning and Art.

We budding poets learned that our purpose was to take the whole world as material and bend it to make Art. Art objects had to cohere, with every part utterly clear and the meanings interconnected. Even if the intent was to portray the meaninglessness of the world, the artist did it ''the usual way, the old way, by creating a self-relevant artistic whole,'' by imposing ''a strict order upon chaos,'' wrote Dillard in *Living by Fiction,* a book she was working on while teaching our class. ''In this structural unity lies integrity, and it is integrity which separates art from nonart.''

Pilgrim is a non-fiction work with fiction in it. Its author sought the integrity of the very world, and so blurred her own distinction between art and nonart. One expectation behind many of her questions in this book is that life should behave coherently. Conscious observant seeking should reveal the world to be an art object itself—unified, ordered, and resplendent. But the chaotic world resists the attempt to impose order on it, presenting instead raw pain, illogical death, and suffering. Thus, the world she sees engenders Dillard's ever more determined struggle to find Reason at the foundation of life.

Artistic energy in a work is derived from the material, instructed this teacher. You need real objects in the real world to write successfully, but writing, ultimately, is *about* something abstract. For Dillard, the relationship between time and eternity stimulated her work. ''I've devoted my life to trying to figure this out,'' she said, implying that each of us in the class should find an equally worthy goal and stick to it fiercely as a life project.

Looking so closely at eternity, Dillard was torn between beauty and horror throughout her ''mystical excursion'' in *Pilgrim.* The *logos* force compelled her to explore, analyze, and question the meaning of existence, and eventually to write a reasoning book. *Logos* also, necessarily, divided her from the very world she sought, while the force of *eros* compelled her toward integration. *Pilgrim* is Dillard's effort to find a balance point between reason and intuition, classification and unification. As an art work, the book rings and reverberates with its own energy—but can the inner light of mystical knowledge manifest into words on a page? *Pilgrim* records the attempt, but cannot validly represent Nature itself, for the author tips the balance in favor of *logos.* One could say, as did Kabir, a fifteenth-century poet (quoted by Lewis Hyde in *The Gift*) that ''. . . all our diseases/are in the asking of these questions.'' Dillard remains too focused on her own idiosyncratic life projects to achieve a convincing epiphany by the end of her book. Although many readers admire her as both a naturalist and a mystic, she is primarily, fundamentally, an artist, and the core of her book is not about the whole of Nature, but only one small part—*Pilgrim* is about human beings.

Dillard immediately interprets every one of her observations in spiritual terms, in relation to human life. The ''tree with the lights in it'' represents spiritual revelation at its finest. The collapsed body of the frog eaten by a giant water bug becomes

Dillard's refrain for suffering and insane death. The Polyphemous moth reappears again and again—it hatched in a jar in young Dillard's classroom and could not spread its beautiful wings to dry. Released an hour later, the crippled insect crawled down the school driveway at Dillard's feet. She never forgot its crumpled useless wings, and the moth crawls into her narrative in *Pilgrim* repeatedly to symbolize the part we humans play in the fabric of nature's horror. The creek—to whose side Dillard's house is clamped like an "anchor-hold"—is "continuous creation"—pure energy, flux, the rush of the future and the promise of rebirth, while the mountains hold up eternity: "Theirs is the one simple mystery of creation from nothing, of matter itself, anything at all, the given". Dillard uses all the elements of her landscapes to search for God, just as she uses the library. The natural world is itself a text. This pilgrim uses Nature as a bridge to a direct relationship with God, following a long tradition of American nature writers, it is true, but failing to free herself from her own personality in her search. Dillard did not escape her perceptual filtering systems, and in some ways, she did not try to escape them. Some danger lies in taking this work as a model for natural history or metaphysical explorations, since it offers a specifically human-centered view of reality.

Dillard actually went out into the natural world to learn about her own unwilling role in the cycles of horror. This is the darker side of Thoreau and Melville that Dillard bravely explores, but she does not go quite far enough. This road can only lead to the embrace of paradox. On a first reading, under the huge skies of the Rockies, I was convinced that Dillard had found Meaning by the end of the book, as she sways with confidence, clasping beauty and horror together in thanksgiving. Reading *Pilgrim* again, I have to wonder whether her quest had actually ended—or did the book simply need finishing? Her exultations seem forced—an intellectually conscious construction, a loud shouting to drown out the tremendous fear that still tips the balance.

Other critics have noted Dillard's unusual focus on the particular as a path toward the universal. In fact, this focus also limited her. She insisted on seeing creatures and plants as individuals with identities that are bounded by their skins or shells or coats. But this way of seeing overlooks some basic lessons of ecology. Individuals often do not matter in the network of energy exchanges as much as do whole systems. Is this necessarily a horrifying idea? Perhaps it is, if it threatens the human ego's sense of

identity and autonomy. Horror here is an artifact of the drive to differentiate the world into parts. The patterns that might really be operating in the world do not carry as much weight as the chaos Dillard chose to perceive. Life ought to make sense, she asserted, the way it makes sense to *us*.

Even though revelatory experiences succeed in dissolving the ego completely, if only for a brief moment, Dillard could not maintain the vision of the tree with the lights in it. Near the end of the book, she hoists herself out of despondency by focusing on a particular maple key seed, a symbol of renewal.

> Hullo. I threw it into the wind and it flew off again, bristling with animate purpose, not like a thing dropped or windblown, pushed by the witless winds of convection currents . . . , but like a creature muscled and vigorous, or a creature spread thin to that other wind, the wind of the spirit which bloweth where it listeth, lighting, and raising up, and easing down. O maple key, I thought, I must confess I thought, o welcome, cheers.

But a little later she is gone again into the dark:

> The waters of separation, however lightly sprinkled, leave indelible stains. Did you think, before you were caught, that you needed, say, life? Do you think you will keep your life, or anything else you love? But no. Your needs are all met. But not as the world giveth. You see the needs of your own spirit met whenever you have asked, and you have learned that the outrageous guarantee holds. You see the creatures die, and you know you will die. And one day it occurs to you that you must not need life. Obviously. And then you're gone. You have finally understood that you're dealing with a maniac.

At times, Dillard's outward seeking attention led her to moments of truth. She saw the tree with the lights in it, or a monarch butterfly climbing a hill by coasting, or some other miracle of affirmation. But she never fully considered that the horrors she perceived might reflect her Self. *Logos* keeps us within the confines of our own minds, while *eros* breaks us out. Italo Calvino wrote, in *The Uses of Literature,* that "The power of modern literature lies in its willingness to give a voice to what has remained unexpressed in the social or individual unconscious: this is the gauntlet it throws down time and again. The more enlightened our houses are, the more their walls ooze ghosts. Dreams of progress and reason are haunted by nightmares."

Could it be that many of Dillard's awestruck fears in confronting the alien world of insects come from her own unresolved experiences in her unconscious? Dillard's own sorts of ghosts rise up in nearly every chapter, most frequently in the bodies of insects who do "one horrible thing after another." In her recently published memoir, *An American Childhood,* Dillard described several incidents that had enormous emotional and psychological power over her. One day a dead, dried butterfly fell out from between the pages of a book she was reading. The wings and body crumbled to bits that slipped under her shirt and stuck to her chest. One day she returned home from summer vacation to discover a carrion beetle still alive in her insect collection box. Stuck through with a pin, it had been swimming in the air for days. The contribution she made to the crippling of the Polyphemous moth had haunted her ever since. Dillard's unusual obsession with the horrors of the alien lives of insects could be, in part, an effort to accommodate the dark side of her own psyche. Is the terror that she faces the terror of nightmares rather than a directly perceived external reality? Perhaps the darker side of God, the face he will not show us, hides a uniquely human image.

> I used to kill insects with carbon tetrachloride—cleaning fluid vapor—and pin them in cigar boxes, labeled, in neat rows. That was many years ago: I quit when one day I opened a cigar box lid and saw a carrion beetle, staked down high between its wing covers, trying to crawl, swimming on its pin. It was dancing with its own shadow, untouching, and had been for days. If I go downstairs now will I see a possum just rounding a corner, trailing its scaled pink tail? I know that one night, in just this sort of rattling wind, I will go to the kitchen for milk and find on the back of the stove a sudden stew I never fixed, bubbling, with a deer leg sticking out.

As much as Dillard insists that she focuses on the world, her witty, jerking, twisting, or joking language frequently draws attention to herself. Dillard's portrait on the cover of *Pilgrim* was not entirely out of place, since she so often serves as subject as well as author of her book. Dillard the artist brings these "horror-show" images together; Dillard the poet makes the point.

Spiritual seeking and mystical experiences have been recorded and discussed for centuries. Dillard does not have much that is new to say about revelation, although her path, that focuses on the particular and the alien, is somewhat new. Her overriding concern with structured meaning and coherent integrity leads her more easily to her ego Self than to the gate of the raw universe.

In *Living by Fiction* Dillard wonders, "Do artists discover order, or invent it? Do they discern it, or make it up?" In *Pilgrim,* the question of whether Meaning is absolute seems urgent, for our very sanity might depend on the answer. We can

explain the horrors of the world either because the God that made the world is a monster and our own ordered minds are freaks, or because the horrors are themselves projections or reflections of a Mind that is a monster in an ordered universe.

Although this woods explorer poses both sides of the question in *Pilgrim,* she addresses them unequally. More ready and willing to call God a maniac and the world insane, she resists abandoning her own ego to consider that life may not Mean in the way we human beings assume it to mean. Afraid to redefine her understanding of beauty, she asks, as might each of us, "Or is beauty itself an intricately fashioned lure, the cruelest hoax of all?". She recounts an Eskimo tale in which an ugly old woman kills her beautiful daughter and skins the daughter's face to wear as a mask, so as to fool her daughter's husband into sleeping with her. "Could it be that if I climbed the dome of heaven and scrabbled and clutched at the beautiful cloth till I loaded my fists with a wrinkle to pull, that the mask would rip away to reveal a toothless old ugly, eyes glazed with delight?" To revive herself from this tug of horror Dillard again focuses on the outer "real" world:

> A wind rose, quickening; it seemed at the same instant to invade my nostrils and vibrate my gut. I stirred and lifted my head. No, I've gone through this a million times, beauty is not a hoax—how many days have I learned not to stare at the back of my hand when I could look out at the creek? Come on, I say to the creek, surprise me; and it does, with each new drop. Beauty is real. I would never deny it; the appalling thing is that I forget it. Waste and extravagance go together up and down the banks, all along the intricate fringe of spirit's free incursions into time. On either side of me the creek snared and kept the sky's distant lights, shaped them into shifting substance and bore them speckled down.

To see beauty as pure energy flung alongside time, one has to escape one's sense of self; one has to swim in the wild, free, crazy, shifting creek. Dillard cannot stay there—perhaps none of us can. But we might come closer to seeing Meaning consistently if we were to step outside of the anthropomorphic framework Dillard assumes. Her insistence that the parts of the world *fit* misleads the reader, intentionally or not, into regarding the natural world as a forum for human Idea. The world can be taken and used in our art works, but the world remains mysterious, completely autonomous from that art.

Reading *Pilgrim* again, I am still swept by Dillard's nimble language, by her wit and curiosity, by her sheer boldness to expose her fears, and by her intense driven vision. But I am also unsatisfied. Dillard's god is too profoundly human. She expects a Him of some kind, related to her in some way, operating out of rationality. I do not feel the horror she does when considering how a female dragonfly consumes its mate, for instance—I am fascinated. This precise behavior may have made the species better able to adapt. Dillard's horror is misplaced, for if life, like all matter, is simply made of light energy, then the particular forms life takes are not as significant as the flow of energy life participates in. Creatures consume other creatures; energy changes and transforms. Quite likely, the dragonfly does not experience death in the way that we would. The dragonfly's death may not make sense on the level of the individual, but on the level of the community or the biosphere such a death may be quite beautiful. So, too, might a human death be beautiful, if it can be perceived as a transformation to another form. This idea, of course, is the ultimate challenge of faith, and the foundation of knowledge for mystics. We are all part of a pattern larger than we can ever see, more complex than we can rationally comprehend. What if the Meaning of it all—the ultimate pattern of the universe—is not discernible in human terms? What if the Meaning requires that we abandon our "human-ness" to understand it, or accept that it can never be expressed in rational words? For all her bravery, Dillard seems to resist this question, perceiving Nature as a collection of discrete parts that ought to illuminate her own life. In a world rapidly becoming dominated and destroyed by human needs and rational human meaning, it may be time to consider the human mind as the monster.

To allow for the possibility of an ultimate or absolute pattern in the universe, we should make an effort to leap outside of the limitations of rational perception. It is not simply a matter of seeing "color patches" in a flat plane. It may require us to abandon the notion of the sanctity of the "individual" above all else. Simplifying the reality of the natural world by disconnecting its interlocking parts will not lead to Truth. At her revelatory moments in *Pilgrim*, Dillard understands this, but a good deal of the book reveals her ego's attempt to come to terms with its own destruction. The ultimate pattern of the universe—whatever it may be—seems to insist on such a dissolution.

People who come to this book, as I did originally, looking for an ecology of perception, will misread *Pilgrim*. Dillard sometimes too consciously exploits the natural world for her own artistic pur-

poses. Today, in the late eighties, we need to consider more than humanly defined identity in our efforts to seek wisdom.

Interestingly, the authors of the other two books I carried to Canyonlands offer quite different ethical views of Nature. In *Dessert Solitaire,* Edward Abbey tells us he is not writing *about* the desert: "The desert is a vast world, an oceanic world, as deep in its way and complex and various as the sea. Language makes a mighty loose net with which to go fishing for simple facts, when facts are infinite. If a man knew enough he could write a whole book about the juniper tree. . . . Since you cannot get the desert into a book any more than a fisherman can haul up the sea with his nets, I have tried to create a world of words in which the desert figures more as medium than as material." Dillard uses Tinker Creek as medium also, but doesn't admit to this as clearly.

Abbey foresees that he will be criticized for dealing "too much with mere appearances, with the surface of things," and for failing "to engage and reveal the patterns of unifying relationships which form the true underlying reality of existence." To this idea he responds: "Here I must confess I know nothing whatever about true underlying reality, having never met any." Abbey shies away from calling himself a mystic. He regards the world from a biocentric point-of-view—the natural world has intrinsic value wholly apart from its relationship to us. If this desert lover had to make a choice between killing a rare wildflower or killing a man, he probably would choose the man—or so he says.

In contrast, Aldo Leopold embodies another sort of vision, one that in my mind provides a more ethically coherent framework for a perception of the true "reality" of the natural world. In *Sand County Almanac,* the former forester proposes a Land Ethic based on the value of a whole system, including human beings. "A thing is right when it tends to preserve the integrity, stability, and beauty of the biotic community. It is wrong when it tends otherwise." This is an ecocentric perspective, and it is also holistic because it does not perceive the world as composed of discrete parts. Isn't this view, in so many words, the essence of mystical wisdom also? Leopold is considered by many the founder of environmental ethics, having successfully combined the romantic tradition of nineteenth-century naturalists with the rational knowledge of twentieth-century ecological sciences.

Life cannot be divided into parts at any level really, whether cell, organism, species, population, or community. Dillard persists in seeing horror because she insists on focusing on the particular *too closely*. She divides and separates and catalogues, and seems to forget that she has reduced her field of vision, and so perceives the horror as the real, the raw stuff of the universe.

Leopold may have had a better footing in addressing the question of whether artists perceive meaning, or make it up. Dillard tried to perceive meaning based on the existence of individual, discrete egocentric lives. Leopold said: "The ordinary citizen today assumes that science knows what makes the community clock tick; the scientist is equally sure that he does not. He knows that the biotic mechanism is so complex that its workings may never be fully understood." Leopold proposed a shift in consciousness. When considering the human use of wilderness areas, he suggested that "Recreational development is a job not of building roads into lovely country, but of building receptivity into the still unlovely human mind."

At moments, Dillard succeeds in dissolving her Mind's autonomy to perceive the patterns of which she is a part. At these moments, *Pilgrims* remains a gripping book, nearly accomplishing the impossible task of transmitting in words an experience that is outside logical processes, independent of time, and impenetrable by reason. For this effort on her part, I still close the book with reverence. *Pilgrim* is not a dangerous book—*if* the reader understands that the natural world portrayed in it is more a vision of a human mind, limited, self-focused, and filtering, than of the universe. We may yet find that it is human meaning that does not make sense. We may discover that the natural world is not here as a bridge for us, that our personal journeys are part of a pattern we will never fully comprehend.

Source: Elaine Tietjen, "Perceptions of Nature: Annie Dillard's *Pilgrim at Tinker Creek*," in *North Dakota Quarterly,* Vol. 56, No. 3, Summer 1988, pp. 101–13.

Sources

Carruth, Hayden, "Attractions and Dangers of Nostalgia," in *Virginia Quarterly Review,* Vol. 50, Autumn 1974, p. 640.

Hoffman, Eva, "Solitude," in *Commentary,* Vol. 58, October 1974, p. 87.

Lillard, Richard G., "The Nature Book in Action," in *Teaching Environmental Literature: Materials, Methods, Resources,* edited by Frederick O. Waage, Modern Language Association of America, 1985, p. 36.

McClintock, James I., "'Pray Without Ceasing': Annie Dillard among the Nature Writers," in *Earthly Words: Essays on Contemporary American Nature and Environmental Writers,* edited by John Cooley, University of Michigan Press, 1994, pp. 69, 85.

McIlroy, Gary, "*Pilgrim at Tinker Creek* and the Social Legacy of *Walden*," in *Earthly Words: Essays on Contemporary American Nature and Environmental Writers,* edited by John Cooley, University of Michigan Press, 1994, p. 100.

Norwood, Vera L., "Heroines of Nature: Four Women Respond to the American Landscape," in *The Ecocriticism Reader: Landmarks in Literary Ecology,* edited by Cheryll Glotfelty and Harold Fromm, University of Georgia Press, 1996, pp. 325–26.

Parrish, Nancy C., *Lee Smith, Annie Dillard, and the Hollins Group: A Genesis of Writers,* Louisiana State University Press, 1998, p. 124.

Reimer, Margaret Loewen, "The Dialectical Vision of Annie Dillard's *Pilgrim at Tinker Creek,*" in *Critique,* Vol. 24, No. 3, Spring 1983, pp. 182–91.

Smith, Linda L., *Annie Dillard,* Twayne, 1991, p. 42.

Tallmadge, John, "Beyond the Excursion: Initiatory Themes in Annie Dillard and Terry Tempest Williams," in *Reading the Earth: New Directions in the Study of Literature and Environment,* edited by Michael P. Branch, Rochelle Johnson, Daniel Patterson, and Scott Slovic, University of Idaho Press, 1998, p. 197.

Thoreau, Henry David, *Walden; or, Life in the Woods,* Dover Thrift, 1995, pp. 65–67, 72.

Welty, Eudora, Review in *New York Times Book Review,* March 24, 1974, p. 4.

Further Reading

McClintock, James I., "'Pray Without Ceasing': Annie Dillard among the Nature Writers," in *Earthly Words: Essays on Contemporary American Nature and Environmental Writers,* edited by John Cooley, University of Michigan Press, 1994, pp. 69–86.

In this brief essay, McClintock locates two of Dillard's books, *Pilgrim at Tinker Creek* and *Holy the Firm,* within the tradition of American nature writing, focusing on the religious elements of her writing.

Norwood, Vera L., "Heroines of Nature: Four Women Respond to the American Landscape," in *Environmental Review: An International Journal of History and the Humanities,* Vol. 8, Spring 1984, pp. 23–31.

Norwood traces the differences between men's and women's nature writing in the United States, claiming that while men seek to dominate and conquer the landscape, women tend to embrace and defend it. This article examines writings by Dillard, Rachel Carson, Isabella Bird, and Mary Austin.

Parrish, Nancy L., *Lee Smith, Annie Dillard, and the Hollins Group: A Genesis of Writers,* Louisiana State University Press, 1998.

Parrish explores the work and lives of a remarkable group of women writers who attended Hollins College in Virginia in the early 1970s. In a chapter entitled ''Annie Dillard: *Pilgrim at Tinker Creek,*'' she tells some of the stories behind the writing and reveals more intimate personal information than Dillard gives in her own autobiographical works.

Radford, Dawn Evans, ''Annie Dillard: A Bibliographical Survey,'' in *Bulletin of Bibliography,* Vol. 51, No. 2, June 1994, pp. 181–94.

Radford provides an overview of Dillard's career and of the central issues addressed by critics of her work, followed by an annotated bibliography of nearly two hundred of the most important primary and secondary works. Radford's annotations are succinct and sub-stantive, making this bibliography invaluable for research.

Smith, Linda L., *Annie Dillard,* Twayne's United States Authors Series, 1987.

Smith's overview is an excellent starting place for students who wish to learn more about Dillard's life and work. In jargon-free and engaging prose, it presents a brief biography, a chapter about each of Dillard's major books, a chronology of important dates, and an annotated bibliography.

Tietjen, Elaine, ''Perceptions of Nature: Annie Dillard's *Pilgrim at Tinker Creek*'' in the *North Dakota Quarterly,* Vol. 56, No. 3, Summer 1988, pp. 101–13.

Tietjen gives a personal response to her reading of *Pilgrim at Tinker Creek*, comparing Dillard's reactions to the natural world with her own. Tietjen also had the opportunity to take a class taught by Dillard. She attempts in this essay to make sense of the differences between her idealized conception of Dillard and the real woman and to move beyond her first awe-struck reading of the work.

A Preface to Morals

Walter Lippmann

1929

Walter Lippmann was an influential journalist and political theorist of the twentieth century. *A Preface to Morals*, his most well-known and influential book, was first published in 1929.

In *A Preface to Morals*, Lippmann argues that in modern society traditional religious faith has lost its power to function as a source of moral authority. He asserts that ancient religious doctrine is no longer relevant to the conditions of modern life: governments have become increasingly democratized, populations have moved from rural to urban environments, and tradition in general is not suited to the dictates of modernity. Further, the democratic policy of the separation of church and state has created an atmosphere of religious tolerance, which suggests that religious faith is a matter of preference. In addition, the development of scientific method has created an atmosphere of doubt as to the claims made by religious doctrine.

Lippmann offers humanism as the philosophy best suited to replace the role of religion in modern life. He notes that the teachers of humanism are the wise men or sages, such as Aristotle, Buddha, Confucius, Plato, Socrates, and Spinoza, and that it is up to the individual to determine the value of their wisdom. He goes on to observe that one of the primary functions of religion is to teach the value of asceticism, or voluntary self-denial, as essential to human happiness. Lippmann describes an attitude of ''disinterestedness'' as essential to the develop-

ment of a humanistic morality. Disinterestedness, for Lippmann, is an approach to reality that puts objective thought before personal desire. He claims that the role of the moralist in modern society is not, as in traditional religions, to chastise and punish but to teach others a humanistic morality that can fulfill the human needs traditionally filled by religion.

Lippmann's central themes in *A Preface to Morals* concern religion, modern society, moral authority, and humanism.

Author Biography

Walter Lippmann was born on September 23, 1889, into a German-Jewish family in New York City. He was the son of Jacob Lippmann, a clothing manufacturer, and Daisy (maiden name Baum) Lippmann. From 1896 to 1906, he was enrolled in Sachs school for boys. In 1906, he entered Harvard University, completing his degree in only three years. At Harvard, he found that he was excluded from the popular social clubs because he was Jewish. While still in college, he organized the Harvard Socialist Club. In 1909, Lippmann began graduate study at Harvard, working as a teaching assistant for George Santayana in the philosophy department. During this time, he worked as a reporter for *Boston Common* as well as for *Everybody's Magazine*. In 1912, Lippmann had a short-lived stint in political life when he served as executive secretary to George R. Lunn, the socialist mayor of Schenectady, New York. Disillusioned with politics, he resigned his post after several months. His political concerns, however, were not abated, and soon afterward he joined the Socialist party of New York County. His first book, *A Preface to Politics*, was published in 1913. In 1914, he was invited to join the founding editors of the *New Republic* magazine. In 1917, he married Faye Albertson.

When the United States entered World War I in 1917, Lippmann was recruited to serve in various capacities, formulating war and peace policy. That year he left the *New Republic* to serve an appointment as assistant to Newton D. Baker, United States Secretary of War. He was then appointed to serve as secretary of the Inquiry, a think tank secretly organized by the United States government to conduct research in preparation for the Paris Peace Conference. In 1918, he was commissioned as a captain in Army Military Intelligence and appointed a member of the American Commission to Negotiate Peace.

Walter Lippmann

He was a key figure in the development and writing of President Wilson's Fourteen Points policy in regard to postwar Europe. In 1919, he was included in a delegation that accompanied President Wilson to the Paris Peace Conference. However, Lippmann quickly became disillusioned with the terms of the peace negotiations and resigned with an honorable discharge from military service.

Lippmann returned to his position as editor of the *New Republic* in 1919. In 1920, he started a regular column in *Vanity Fair*. In 1922, he started working as an editorial writer for the *New York World* and in 1924 became the editor of the *New York World*. *A Preface to Morals*, Lippmann's tenth book of political philosophy, was published in 1929. In 1931, the *New York World* published its last issue, and Lippmann began a regular column, ''Today and Tomorrow,'' for the *New York Herald-Tribune,* which remained a regular feature until 1962. In 1937, after he was caught having an affair with Helen Byrne, a married woman, he divorced Faye, and Helen divorced her husband. In 1938, Lippmann and Byrne were married and moved to Washington, D.C. In 1944, during World War II, he worked as a war correspondent in Europe. He was awarded a Pulitzer Prize for editorial comment in 1958 and a Pulitzer Prize for reporting of international affairs in 1962. In the early 1960s, he began to appear in television interviews. In 1963, Lippmann's "Today and Tomorrow" column was moved to the *Washington Post,* and he began a regular column for *Newsweek.* He was honored by Lyndon B. Johnson with the Presidential Medal of Freedom in 1964. In 1967, Lippmann published his last "Today and Tomorrow" column, and he and Helen moved from Washington, D.C., to New York City. Helen died in February of 1974, and Lippmann died on December 14 of that year.

Summary

Religion in the Modern World

Lippmann addresses what he sees as a crisis facing modern society due to the increasing number of people whose lives are no longer ordered by religious conviction. He asserts that modern humanity in increasingly democratic secular societies needs to look to some form of "new orthodoxy" by which to live. He notes that it is certainly true that many in the modern world still believe in God. However, he argues, the nature of this belief, even among the clergy, is of a different nature from what it once was so that now people make a distinction between the factual world and the spiritual world. Lippmann observes that fundamentalism in religion is the exception that proves this rule: fundamentalist movements arise in reaction to the overwhelming trend in modern society toward religious doubt. He notes that this "loss of certainty" regarding religion had led to a change in how the Bible is understood. Whereas it was once understood by most as literal (yet also symbolic), it has come to be interpreted as literary analogy. Further, it is only in modern history that the concept of a conflict between religion and reason evolved. He argues that, even among the faithful, there is a seed of doubt, based upon the conception of faith as less certain than rational, scientific knowledge. He goes on to argue that a society's concept of God is always a reflection of that society's governmental system—so that, in a monarchical society God is conceived as a kingly ruler; in a feudal society, as a landholding lord, and so forth. Lippmann thus notes that in a modern democratic society, conceptions of God have lost the image of all-powerful, patriarchal authority. Further, he asserts that the modern crisis in faith is due to the fact that, over the past four hundred years, daily life has resembled less and less the conception of the universe put forth by religion.

Faith and Tradition in Modern America

Lippmann focuses on the particular character of America by pointing out a variety of reasons for the loss of religious faith that characterizes modernity. The rapid pace of change in modern society has left people without permanent landmarks by which to make sense of a religion that is based on an ancient society. Further, because America is a nation of immigrants, socially and geographically mobile, the old religions no longer resemble anything in modern life. In addition, he argues, whereas agrarian life, dependent on tradition and subject to the forces of nature, is in keeping with religious tradition and conviction, urban life dispenses with tradition and is beholden to technology rather than the natural world. Finally, Lippmann puts forth, figures of authority in American society are merely a class of wealthy socialites who possess no moral high ground in the eyes of the masses.

Separation of Church and State

Lippmann goes on to observe that the crisis of faith in modern society is partly due to changes in the relationship between church and state. The separation of church and state results in a society in which the church is no longer the overarching societal authority. Particularly, the policy of "tolerance" among religions implies that no one religion can assert supreme authority over all citizens. As a result, the individual citizen, even while faithful to his or her own religion, does not consider it to be the dominant authority in civil life. Lippmann suggests that patriotism, particularly in time of war, has to some extent supplanted the all-encompassing religious faith once exerted by the church. Further, in a capitalist society, that which represents authority in the realm of business is considered separate from religious authority. Modern society thus lacks the sense of an all-encompassing meaning and direction to human life, which was once provided by religious doctrines of destiny. Lippmann further claims that the separation of church and state has led to a separation within the individual self, in which daily human activities have no sense of one great overarching meaning. In this context, there is no "moral certitude," and no all-encompassing system of values has emerged to take its place.

Science and Religion

Lippmann observes that the role of miracles in traditional religion has been used as a source of concrete physical evidence of the existence of God.

However, the development of modern science has outmoded religion in its capacity to provide concrete evidence in support of claims to truth. He asserts that the ascendance of science as a claim to truth has always posed a threat to people's capacity for religious faith. He notes that attempts to develop religious beliefs based on scientific discovery have failed on two counts: first, because scientific theory is always subject to change as a result of further scientific discovery; and second, because the assertions of science, no matter how true, can never serve the human needs traditionally satisfied by religious faith.

Humanism

Lippmann explains that, in traditional religious practice, morality was based on "divine authority," and the believer strove to act in accordance with the will of God. Since "divine authority" no longer holds the power it once did in the human mind, he asserts, modern society must find some alternative basis for morality. He puts forth that humanism is the ideal basis for moral authority in the modern world. Lippmann offers the wisdom of such figures as Aristotle, Buddha, Confucius, Plato, Socrates, and Spinoza, whose teachings form the basis of humanism. However, he points out that those who espouse humanism "have no credentials" on the order of the moral authority of God. Rather, the sages of humanism derive their authority from the self-government of the individual, who is required to take full responsibility for adhering to humanist teachings.

Desire and Asceticism

Lippmann discusses the persistent concern, among the "popular" religions (as he calls them), as well as the sages, with the need to place restrictions upon human desire. He asserts that asceticism (the self-imposed denial of basic human desires) is central to human happiness and "the good life." Modern capitalist society, by contrast, promotes the idea that humans should seek to freely satisfy all possible desires. Based on the theories of Sandor Ferenczi, Lippmann traces human psychological development from childhood to maturity as a process of slowly but surely learning that the world can never satisfy all of one's desires. Maturity, thus, is defined as the state of bringing one's desires into line with reality. He explains that religion has always played the part in society of imposing external standards of asceticism and self-denial on the

general public. The sages, however, have confined their advice regarding asceticism to a small circle of pupils. Because, according to Lippmann, religion has ceased to serve the function of disciplining desire in modern society, there is no generalized societal code designed to enforce the curbing of individual human desires.

Evil, Disinterestedness, and the Moralist in the Modern Age

Lippmann observes that the concept of evil has been altered in the age of modernity. He explains that, traditionally, evil is seen as a matter of the judgment of God, whereas in modern society, evil is seen as a phenomenon that is created by humanity and can thus be eradicated by human action.

He asserts that in the modern world it is necessary to cultivate an attitude of "disinterestedness" in matters of moral concern. By "disinterest," Lippmann means an ability to judge matters from an objective perspective not necessarily in keeping with the personal interests of the individual. He cites scientific method as the epitome of "disinterested" endeavor. For Lippmann, "disinterestedness" is the key to formulating standards of morality in the modern world. Particularly in business, government, and sexual relations, the "three great phases of human interest," an attitude of "disinterest" is all-important.

Lippmann observes that the role of the moralist in modern society has been misconstrued. It is no longer the place of the moralist to control and punish the populace to elicit moral behavior. Rather, the role of the moralist in modern society is to teach others how to place limits on their own desires for the sake of "the good life." Lippmann describes the ideal replacement for traditional religion as a "religion of the spirit," which does not conform to a strictly defined set of beliefs but to whatever values are in the interest of "the quality of human desire."

Key Figures

Aristotle

Aristotle (384–322 B.C.) was the third of the three great Greek philosophers whose ideas immeasurably influenced Western thought. Aristotle is one of the sages Lippmann regards as a source of "well-tested truths," the wisdom of which may serve the function once filled by religious doctrine. He mentions Aristotle as one among many sages who have advocated asceticism as essential to happiness. Lippmann later quotes from Aristotle's *Ethics* in relating the idea of virtue as a golden mean between extremes of any quality or characteristic in a person. He explains that, in contrast to the commandments of traditional religion, the ideals of human behavior espoused by Aristotle are a matter of the education and discipline of the "human will."

Buddha

The Indian-born teacher Lippmann refers to as Buddha, or Gautama Buddha, lived in the fifth or sixth century B.C. and was the founder of Buddhism, the predominant religion throughout much of Asia. Buddha is one of the sages Lippmann regards as a source of "well-tested truths," the wisdom of which may serve the function once filled by religious doctrine. Buddha is among the wise men who taught the value of asceticism for the achievement of "the good life." Further, Lippmann points out that Buddha, among other sages, was concerned with teaching and self-discipline rather than with imposing commandments for human behavior. Lippmann cites Buddha as an example of a sage who did not expect more than a small number of men to live according to the ideals that he taught.

Confucius

Confucius (551–479 B.C.), born in China, became the most revered and influential teacher and philosopher in Eastern Asia. Confucius is one of the sages Lippmann regards as a source of "well-tested truths," the wisdom of which may serve the function once filled by religious doctrine. Lippmann mentions the wisdom Confucius, which is that, to be happy, one must bring one's desires in line with reality. He refers to Confucius as among the sages whose wisdom was directed toward the self-discipline of the individual rather than toward the issuing of commandments for human behavior.

Havlock Ellis

Havlock Ellis (1859–1939) was an English essayist and physician known for his open-minded and controversial writings on human sexuality. Lippmann refers to the ideas of Havlock Ellis in his discussion of the effect of readily available contraception on sexual mores in the modern age.

Dr. S. Ferenczi

Sándor Ferenczi (1873–1933) was a Hungarian psychoanalyst closely associated with Sigmund Freud. Lippmann explains the psychological theory of human development from infancy to maturity, according to Dr. S. Ferenczi, as a matter of the child's process of learning to accept the submission of his own desires to the dictates of reality.

Jesus

Jesus is one of the sages Lippmann regards as a source of "well-tested truths," the wisdom of which may serve the function once filled by religious doctrine. He mentions Jesus among many sages who have advocated asceticism as essential to happiness. Lippmann, however, distinguishes between Jesus as a teacher of a relatively small following during his lifetime, and Christianity as an organized "popular religion" that arose centuries after the death of Jesus.

Plato

Plato (428–348 B.C.) was the second of the three great Greek philosophers whose ideas immeasurably influenced Western thought. Plato is one of the sages Lippmann regards as a source of "well-tested truths," the wisdom of which may serve the function once filled by religious doctrine. He mentions Plato among many sages who have advocated asceticism as essential to happiness.

Socrates

Socrates (470–399 B.C.) was the first of the three great Greek philosophers whose ideas immeasurably influenced Western thought. Socrates is one of the sages Lippmann regards as a source of "well-tested truths," the wisdom of which may serve the function once filled by religious doctrine. He mentions Socrates among the sages who advocate some form of asceticism as essential to "the good life." He cites Socrates' *Phaedo,* which claims that the human body is an impediment to "a philosopher in search of truth." Lippmann further mentions Socrates as one who advocated self-conscious examination of one's personal motives.

Spinoza

Spinoza (1632–1677) was a Dutch-Jewish philosopher known for his development of the ideas of seventeenth century rationalism. Spinoza is one of the sages Lippmann regards as a source of "well-tested truths," the wisdom of which may serve the function once filled by religious doctrine. He mentions Spinoza among the sages who advocate some form of asceticism as essential to "the good life." He refers to Spinoza as among the sages whose wisdom was directed toward the self-discipline of the individual rather than toward the issuing of commandments for human behavior.

Themes

Religion

The premise of Lippmann's argument in *A Preface to Morals* is that, in modern society, traditional religious beliefs have broken down. He makes clear that this is not to say that no one believes in God any more. Rather, he explains, the nature of religious belief has altered radically. Religion is no longer regarded as an undisputed fact but is placed in a context of doubt, even among true believers. Further, the traditional religious hierarchy, according to which God the father is all-powerful, is no longer in keeping with the power structures of a democratic society. In sum, religion no longer holds the all-encompassing authority it once held in society. Because of this, Lippmann asserts, modern society is in need of some system of values that can serve the function once served by religion.

Modern Society

Lippmann's argument is based upon the assertion that, historically, unprecedented changes have been wrought in modern society. He states that the "acids of modernity" have eaten away at traditional belief systems. Central to his thesis is the argument that traditional religion is no longer in keeping with the realities of everyday life in modern society. Because of these discrepancies, he argues, it is impossible for people in modern society to accept religious doctrine with the same unquestioning faith that was common earlier in eras of human history. He asserts that the democratization of modern societies renders many traditional beliefs meaningless. Thus, the modern citizen in a democratic society sees evidence all around that leads to doubt. For instance, the habit of religious tolerance that accompanies the democratic separation of church and state implies that no one religion can claim

legitimacy over all others. Lippmann also points out that modern society has become increasingly urban, rather than rural, and that urban life is not compatible with tradition or traditional beliefs. Further, the social and geographic mobility that characterizes modern living standards encourages a habit of leaving tradition behind. For all of these reasons, Lippmann argues, modern society is not compatible with traditional religious belief and doctrine.

Moral Authority

Lippmann is particularly concerned with what he perceives to be a modern crisis of moral authority. He argues that, in modern society, the moral authority, which was once under the jurisdiction of religious belief, has lost its power. It is Lippmann's opinion that this breakdown in traditional faith is an inevitable result of the realities of modern life. He asserts that, to the extent that there is a need for moral authority, it is not because citizens in modern society are depraved but because they have lost faith in traditional religious authority. Lippmann suggests that the wisdom of the sages, both modern and ancient, is the best source from which to derive a moral authority appropriate to the modern age. Wise men such as Aristotle, Buddha, Confucius, Jesus, Plato, Socrates, Spinoza, and others may fill this role. However, he argues that the basis for moral authority in modern society must come from the judgment of the individual, based on her or his own assessment of the wisdom of others.

Humanism

Lippmann offers humanism as a standard for moral authority, which could appropriately replace religion in modern society. Lippmann explains that the values of humanism are derived on the basis of "human experience" rather than in accordance with divine will. Humanism, according to Lippmann, "is centered not in superhuman but in human nature." Humanism is based in the ideal of acting in accordance with that which best facilitates "human happiness," rather than an ideal dictated by some higher authority. Further, humanism does not subscribe to rigid doctrine but must adapt and respond to an ever-changing and increasingly complex society. Humanism is thus based in human experience and can be tested only by means of trial and error, and its value is determined only by the scrutiny of the individual. Lippmann explains that he subscribes to humanism because, to his mind, it is the

Topics for Further Study

- Lippmann's basic premise in *A Preface to Morals* is that religious authority has been essentially eroded in the modern world. To what extent do you agree with this assessment? As a replacement for traditional religion, Lippmann suggests a philosophy of humanism, drawing from the timeless wisdom of sages throughout history. To what extent do you agree or disagree with this solution? What might you propose instead as a system of moral authority suitable to the modern age?

- Lippmann refers repeatedly to sages throughout history, such as Aristotle, Buddha, Confucius, Jesus, Plato, and Spinoza. Learn more about one of these figures. What are his basic teachings? To what extent do you find his ideas useful as a guide to human thought and behavior in modern society?

- Lippmann is often seen as a product of the Progressive Era in American history, lasting from the 1890s through 1920. Learn more about the Progressive Era. Who were some of the key figures in the Progressive movement? What changes were made in America at the economic, legal, political, and social levels? To what extent have the changes made during the Progressive Era survived today?

- Two of the primary influences on Lippmann's political philosophy were his teachers George Santayana and William James. Learn more about one of these men. What were his central tenets? What are his major works? To what extent does Lippmann's argument in *A Preface to Morals* reflect this influence? To what extent does Lippmann deviate from the ideas of his teachers?

- In 1914, Lippmann was one of the founding members of the *New Republic,* a weekly magazine focused on discussion of political concerns. Find a recent issue of the *New Republic.* What general political standpoint do the articles seem to support? Pick one article on a topic of interest to you. To what extent do you agree or disagree with this article?

---

only system of values appropriate to modern society that can fulfill the needs hitherto fulfilled by religion.

Style

Writing Style

Lippmann has been critically acclaimed for his lucid writing style, by which he translates complex ideas, as well as historical and political analysis, into thoughtful, easily readable prose. Critics agree that this stylistic virtuosity largely accounts for Lippmann's popularity and vast readership, of both his journalistic columns and his books of political philosophy. Ronald Steel, in *Walter Lippmann and the American Century,* praises Lippmann for his "superbly lucid literary style." Barry D. Riccio, in *Walter Lippmann,* mentions that Lippmann "wrote in the vernacular rather than in the argot of the specialist." D. Steven Blum, in *Walter Lippmann,* observes that Lippmann "tackled enduring political and moral controversies in an unaffected idiom, accessible to the general educated reader." Hari N. Dam, in *The Intellectual Odyssey of Walter Lippmann,* makes note of "the superb craftsmanship" of Lippmann's writing style, commenting, "Lippmann's writing has all the classical virtues—balance, precision, purity and clarity." David Elliot Weingast, in *Walter Lippmann,* characterizes the essence of Lippmann's impressive style as "clear, logical, and inevitably persuasive." John Patrick Diggins, in a 1982 introduction to *A Preface to Morals*, likewise describes Lippmann's literary style as "at once relaxed, lucid, crisp, and unencumbered by heavy philosophical jargon." Diggins adds, "As a journalist as well as an author, Lippmann displayed a felicity of expression that often rose to epigrammatic brilliance.''

Epigraph

Lippmann begins each of the three parts of *A Preface to Morals* with an epigraph or brief quote. Each epigraph sums up in a few words the essence of Lippmann's message within the proceeding section of the book. Part I, "The Dissolution of the Ancestral Order," opens with "Whirl is King, having driven out Zeus," a quote from the ancient Greek playwright Aristophanes. Zeus thus represents the God of an ancient belief system, or "ancestral order," which has been "driven out" of or dissolved by modern culture, leaving only "Whirl," or chaos, in its place. This idea mirrors Lippmann's central argument that the "acids of modernity" have dissolved faith in traditional religion, leaving a moral vacuum in its place. Part II, "The Foundations of Humanism," opens with "The stone which the builders rejected / That same is become the head of the corner," from Luke XX:17. Through this quote, Lippmann implies that humanism ought to become the cornerstone of a new structure of moral authority in the modern age. Part III, "The Genius of Modernity," opens with "Where is the way the light dwelleth?" from Job 38:19. Whereas the first two epigraphs are statements, the third is a question. It poses to the reader the question of where the "light" of moral authority can be found if not in traditional religion. It is interesting to note that, while Lippmann's central argument poses that traditional religions are no longer viable in the modern age, he begins two of the three main sections of *A Preface to Morals* with epigraphs drawn from Biblical sources. Lippmann thus appeals to the role of religion in addressing certain timeless human concerns although he argues that religion is no longer able to satisfy these concerns adequately.

Historical Context

The Industrial Revolution

Lippmann's central argument in *A Preface to Morals* concerns the status of religion in the "modern age," or the "age of modernity." Lippmann does not define precisely when he considers modernity to have begun but makes broad generalizations regarding historical trends in the West over the past several centuries. However, he frequently makes reference to the changes wrought by the Industrial Revolution, by which many date the coming of the modern age. The Industrial Revolution broadly defines developments that gained momentum in the early nineteenth century, first and foremost in England, which encouraged rural, agrarian economies to become urban, industrial economies.

The Progressive Era

Lippmann's early writing and political thought is frequently associated with the outlook of the Progressive Era in American history. The Progressive movement names a trend in American political activism that began in the 1890s as a response to economic depression in both rural and urban areas. Progressivism, which achieved many successes over a twenty- to thirty-year period, was characterized by a push for social reform and the placement of legal limitations on the power of industrialists. Social services were organized to aid the poor and underprivileged, while legal measures were instituted to curb industrial monopolies. In 1894, the National Municipal League was organized to clean up corruption at the level of local government. Other Progressive movement concerns included workers' rights and benefits, such as child labor laws. The presidential terms of Theodore Roosevelt (from the assassination of President McKinley in 1901 through the 1904 election to 1908) was characterized by great strides in Progressive movement issues. The two terms of President Woodrow Wilson (1912–1920) were also characterized by a strong showing of Progressive movement concerns.

World War I

World War I was a major concern early in Lippmann's career as a journalist and public policy maker. When the war broke out in Europe in 1914, the American policy was firmly one of neutrality, but as the war wore on the United States became increasingly (unofficially) sympathetic to the Allies and increasingly defensive toward Germany. A series of incidents functioned to turn the tide of American popular opinion, as well as government policy, toward military intervention in Europe. In May 1915, a German submarine sank the British *Lusitania*, an unarmed liner, without warning, killing 128 Americans (as well as others). Early in 1917, Germany opted for extensive submarine warfare against nonmilitary as well as military vessels, as a result of which the United States broke diplomatic relations with Germany. After the Germans began sinking American ships, the United States was drawn into the war in April of 1917. The entry

Compare & Contrast

- **1890s:** Economic depression in the United States helps to spark a mass movement toward economic and social reform known as the Progressive movement.

  1930s: Just months after the publication of Lippmann's *A Preface to Morals,* the stock market crash of 1929 begins the Depression era in the United States. Increased production as a result of Europe's entry into World War II lifts the United States out of the Depression.

  1990s: The United States enjoys a period of economic prosperity characterized by low unemployment as well as many average Americans profiting from stock market investments.

- **1914–1918:** World War I breaks out in Europe. The United States enters the war in 1917, helping to turn the tide in favor of the Allied forces. The postwar peace negotiations are made in 1919 at the Paris Peace Conference. Lippmann attends the Paris Peace Conference as a member of President Wilson's special delegation but is disillusioned by the terms of the peace treaty and resigns his post.

  1939–1945: World War II breaks out in Europe. The United States enters the war in 1941 after the Japanese bombing of Pearl Harbor. Lippmann serves as a war correspondent in Europe.

  1990–1991: In August 1990, Iraq, under President Saddam Hussein, invades the neighboring oil-rich nation of Kuwait. The Persian Gulf War begins on January 16, 1991 when the United States, along with forces from British, French, Egyptian, and other nations, leads an air offensive against Iraq in a military operation known as Desert Storm. The armed conflict ends on February 28, 1991 with the liberation of Kuwait from Iraq.

- **1914:** Lippmann is one of the founding editors of the *New Republic,* a weekly magazine promoting the values of the Progressive movement.

  1917–1919: Lippmann engages in war-related government service, taking an unofficial hiatus from his editorial position at the *New Republic*.

  1946: Former Vice President Henry A. Wallace becomes editor of the *New Republic* but is asked to resign due to his leftist political stance.

  1980s: The *New Republic* becomes less liberal in political orientation, reflecting a range of political stances.

  1990s: The *New Republic* continues to be a highly influential journal of political commentary.

- **1919:** The League of Nations is established as part of the Treaty of Versailles. The League of Nations is an organization designed to promote ''collective security'' among the nations of the world. The world headquarters are established in Geneva, Switzerland. The United States, however, never joins the League of Nations.

  1940s: During World War II, the League of Nations has no power or influence over international conflicts and is dissolved. In 1946, the United Nations is established to replace the League of Nations. The United Nations includes the United States, and the world headquarters are located in New York City.

  1990s: The dissolution of the Soviet Union and end of the Cold War brings new challenges to the United Nations in mediating international conflicts as well as violent conflicts between ethnic groups within single nations.

of the United States on the side of the Allies led to victory against the Central Powers late in 1918.

President Wilson and the Paris Peace Conference

Early in 1918, President Wilson presented to Congress the Fourteen Points that became the signature of his presidency. Lippmann had been recruited as one of the members of the Inquiry, a think-tank organized by Wilson to research, formulate, and write the Fourteen Points, which spelled out Wilson's recommendations for postwar world peace. Among these points was a call for self-determination among nations currently struggling for national independence and for the organization of a League of Nations to protect world peace. In January 1919, the Paris Peace Conference met to determine the outcome of World War I, based on Wilson's recommendations in the Fourteen Points. Lippmann was invited to join Wilson's delegation to Paris but soon resigned his post due to his disillusionment with the peace negotiations. The Versailles Treaty was the document that resulted from international negotiations over the Fourteen Points, many of which were retained, though others were compromised or dispensed with. However, the United States Congress voted twice against signing the Treaty of Versailles, and America never became a member of the League of Nations.

Critical Overview

Lippmann's Influence

Walter Lippmann is generally considered to be the most important, most popular, and most widely influential political journalist of the twentieth century.

Clinton Rossiter and James Lare, in *The Essential Lippmann,* consider him ''perhaps the most important American political thinker of the twentieth century'' and ''a major contributor to the American way of life and thought.'' D. Steven Blum, in *Walter Lippmann*, asserts that Lippmann is ''the century's foremost political journalist'' and ''the preeminent chronicler of the political events of the age.'' Ronald Steel, in *Walter Lippmann and the American Century*, asserts that Lippmann ''was without a doubt the nation's greatest journalist.''

In addition to his critical acclaim, Lippmann's books of political philosophy and regular newspaper and magazine columns were extraordinarily popular. Marquis Childs, in *Walter Lippmann and His Times*, describes Lippmann as ''a critic who, more than any other American today, has achieved through his pen a worldwide audience.'' Lare and Rossiter concur, ''his audience has been the largest and most insatiable ever to pay the homage of thoughtful attention to a serious-minded American writer.'' Larry L. Adams, in *Walter Lippmann*, states that Lippmann was ''beyond question the most widely read American social thinker of the twentieth century and one of the most respected.'' David Elliott Weingast, in *Walter Lippmann*, likewise declares that Lippmann's influence ''has helped to determine the opinions of the American people on many urgent issues.''

While popular among a worldwide audience of readers, Lippmann remained, throughout his career, extremely influential among major political figures in the United States and abroad. As quoted in *Walter Lippmann and the American Century,* when Lippmann was only twenty-five, Theodore Roosevelt dubbed him the '''most brilliant young man of his age in all the United States.''' Steel goes on to describe the scope of Lippmann's political influence, noting, ''Influence was Lippmann's stock-in-trade . . . what made him a powerful public figure.''

> He commanded no divisions, but he did have enormous power over public opinion. This in turn gave him a power over Presidents, politicians and policymakers. They did not, by any means, always do what Lippmann advised. But they listened to him and sought his support—and they learned not to take his opposition lightly. Lippmann commanded a loyal and powerful constituency, some ten million of the most politically active and articulate people in America. Many of these people literally did not know what they ought to think about the issues of the day until they read what Walter Lippmann had said about them. A politician could ignore that kind of power only at his own risk.

Lare and Rossiter further describe Lippmann's high-ranking political influence:

> in most of the great political and moral dialogues of modern America, Walter Lippmann has been a leading participant. In his own style, at his own pace, and largely on his own terms, he has spoken out on the issues of the age—and spoken with an authority that persuades presidents, premiers, foreign ministers, and perhaps even cardinals and commissars to pause and listen.

Praise for A Preface to Morals

A Preface to Morals, first published in 1929, was an immediate success and remained Lippmann's most popular book. Within the first year of publica-

Lippmann's editorials on the trial of John T. Scopes, seen here, nurtured the moral sensitivity evident in A Preface to Morals. *Scopes was charged with violating Tennessee state law by teaching the theory of evolution.*

tion, six editions were sold out, and the book was translated into a dozen different languages. *A Preface to Morals* was soon selected for the extremely popular Book-of-the-Month Club. Several critics have tried to account for the book's success. Michael Kirkhorn in *Dictionary of Literary Biography* referring to it as "one of the most, if not the most, profoundly knowing" of Lippmann's books, observes, "The book struck a chord for a generation seeking recovery from the disillusionment of the late 1920s." Steel notes that *A Preface to Morals* was none less than "a popular sensation" and was "perfectly attuned to its times, codifying anxieties of a generation." Steel goes on to explain,

> Lippmann had put his finger on the problem of the moment, laid it out in terms simple to grasp, phrased it in a vocabulary that flattered the reader's intelligence, and proposed a self-sacrificing but noble way out of the maze.

In addition to its timeliness upon initial publication, *A Preface to Morals* remains an important commentary on current societal concerns. John Patrick Diggins in a 1982 introduction to *A Preface to Morals* asserts that Lippmann's "heroic book speaks forcefully to us today." Diggins continues, "every generation interested in the relationship of politics

to morals must come to terms with Lippmann's seminal work." Further, Diggins observes,

> it is a measure of a great book that, in addition to reflecting the immediate context in which it was written, it illuminates issues that transcend the context, issues not less universal than alienation, authority, knowledge, and morality.

Diggins concludes, "It is precisely because the problems he raised remain unresolved today that we need to consider them."

Criticism of A Preface to Morals

A Preface to Morals, however, received its fair share of criticism. Reviewers in religious periodicals criticized Lippmann for being too disdainful of religion while atheistic reviewers criticized him for espousing religiosity. His own teacher and mentor, George Santayana, even offered harsh criticism of Lippmann's work. While praising the work on many counts, Blum concurs that *A Preface to Morals* "*was* gravely flawed." Common criticisms of Lippmann's broader body of work were also applied to *A Preface to Morals*. Steel notes that Lippmann "was not always right and he was not universally popular." The most common criticism of Lippmann's work is that it is inconsistent, even characterized by self-contradiction. Adams observes, "Most students of Lippmann's work have been troubled by what they find to be a lack of consistency in his work, contradictions which reach his fundamental assumptions." Weingast comments, "Although Lippmann has clarified countless individual issues for his readers, he has offered a number of interpretations of dubious merit" and cautions readers to read Lippmann with a degree of skepticism:

> Any tendency to rely on him as a source of final authority is unmerited. He is to be read with skepticism, with the feeling that his views are the serious reflections of a highly literate, well-informed mind, but also with the feeling that he has been wrong before and will very likely err again.

However, Adams asserts, "The inconsistencies in Lippmann's lifework are interesting and important; but of more enduring interest is their underlying unity, which mirrors his own search for meaning and coherence in a chaotic century." Weingast concludes that, although Lippmann's body of journalism and political philosophy is of singular merit, "his views, nevertheless, are to be taken as suggestive rather than definitive."

Lippmann's Legacy

Hari N. Dam in *The Intellectual Odyssey of Walter Lippmann* sums up Lippmann's legacy as a political philosopher of the modern age:

> Whatever the verdict of posterity, Lippmann, with his hatred of tyranny and oppression, with his passion for freedom and justice, with his mellowed sapience and charity, with his abundant optimism and earnestness, with his serene temper and calm dignity, is today and will always be a source of comfort, hope and inspiration for free men in this troubled world of ours.

Criticism

Liz Brent

Brent has a Ph.D. in American culture, specializing in film studies, from the University of Michigan. She is a freelance writer and teaches courses in the history of American cinema. In the following essay, she discusses the relationship between art and religion in Lippmann's work.

In a chapter of Walter Lippmann's *A Preface to Morals* entitled "Lost Provinces," Lippmann discusses three areas of human society that are "lost provinces" of religious authority: business, the family, and art. Of the three, Lippmann reserves his most extensive discussion for the history of artistic creation in relation to the history of religion. He argues that while art was for centuries almost entirely dictated by religious doctrine, in the modern age art has lost its moorings to religion and now drifts in the realm of philosophical uncertainty and chaos. Although Lippmann's discussion of art represents a small section of *A Preface to Morals*, it serves as a concrete example of the far-reaching impact that the status of religion in the modern age has upon all aspects of human society. In the course of his discussion, Lippmann makes reference to several centuries of the history of the relationship between art and religion. A closer look at Lippmann's brief discussion of art will help to illuminate his broader argument about the place of religion in the modern world.

In a section entitled "The Disappearance of Religious Painting," Lippmann describes the traditional relationship between art and religion, and the dissolution of this relationship by the "acids of modernity." Lippmann argues that religion is no longer the predominant theme in modern art because "the great themes of popular religion have ceased to inspire the imagination of modern men." He traces the course of this disillusionment from the fifteenth to the twentieth centuries. Lippmann explains that, by the end of the fifteenth century, art began to reflect the fact that religious faith was no longer "naively believed" as it had once been. In the sixteenth century, he continues, with the Reformation and Counter Reformation, as well as with the rise of industrial capitalism, artists became increasingly less concerned with religious themes. He concludes that, in the nineteenth and twentieth centuries, artists have engaged in "feverish experimentation" in the context of "our present bewilderment" over the loss of religion as an organizing principal for artistic creation. Lippmann argues *against* the theory that artists have ceased to paint religious themes because those with the power and money to buy art are no longer interested in religion. Rather, he asserts, religion is no longer the central thematic concern of artists in the modern age because "the will to produce" such works has been dissolved by "the acids of modernity."

In a section entitled "The Loss of Heritage," Lippmann further points out that the Protestant Reformation and the Catholic Counter Reformation have functioned to his dissolve the traditional rela-

What Do I Read Next?

- In *Public Opinion* (1922), one of Lippmann's most influential works, he argues that the mass public is not capable of forming rational opinions on matters of national and international concern.

- *Essays in the Public Philosophy* (1955) represents a culmination of Lippmann's political philosophy, in which he again asserts the need for authority based on rational thought as a moral compass in the modern world.

- *Aristotle for Everybody: Difficult Thought Made Easy* (1978), by Mortimer J. Adler, provides a basic explanation of the central ideas of Aristotle, one of the sages whom Lippmann regards as a teacher of timeless wisdom.

- *George Santayana* (1987), by John McCormick, is a biography of the modern philosopher who was one of Lippmann's teachers and primary influences.

- *Plato for Beginners* (1990), by Robert J. Cavalier, presents an introduction to the central ideas of Plato, one of the sages whom Lippmann regards as a teacher of timeless wisdom.

- *The Original Analects: Sayings of Confucius and His Successors* (1997) provides an updated translation, by E. Bruce Brooks and A. Taeko Brooks, of the basic teachings of Confucius, one of the sages whom Lippmann regards as a teacher of timeless wisdom.

- *Spinoza: A Life* (1999), by Steven M. Nadler, is a biography of the seventeenth century philosopher Benedictus de Spinoza, one of the sages whom Lippmann regards as a teacher of timeless wisdom.

- *A Simple Path: Basic Buddhist Teachings* (2000), by the Dalai Lama, provides an introduction to the central ideas of Buddha, one of the sages whom Lippmann regards as a teacher of timeless wisdom.

---

tionship between religion and art. He observes that, in a world without religious doubt, the artist was free to represent religious themes in concrete images, such as depicting God as ''a benign old man.'' However, during the Reformation and Counter Reformation, religious doctrine became more complex and abstract in response to new expressions of religious doubt. Artistic representations of religious themes could no longer be represented through concrete and simple images. Lippmann asserts that the growth of religious ''skepticism'' thus ''dissolves the concreteness'' of religious imagery with the expression of abstractions. He notes that although this separation between art and religion has developed over some four hundred years, it is only in recent generations that its effect has been manifested. Thus, only in the last hundred years has the artist been faced with the task of representing ''a world without any accepted understanding of human life,'' once supplied by religious doctrine.

In a section entitled ''The Artist Formerly,'' Lippmann explains the historical circumstances that dictated artistic representation of religious themes up to the modern age. He notes that while originally the work of the artist was to be kept within certain guidelines of religious doctrine, in the beginnings of the modern age religious authorities felt the need to determine more strictly the exact specifications of the artist's representation of religious themes. In particular, he observes the religious doubt initiated by the Protestant Reformation in the sixteenth century completely changed the relationship of art to religion. The Catholic Counter Reformation, coming on the heels of the Reformation, attempted to counteract this trend by further codifying the role of the artist in depicting specific religious images.

In a section entitled ''The Artist as Prophet,'' Lippmann observes that in the modern age artists have been left to their own devices to define their relationship to society. He notes that two possible solutions to this dilemma have been offered: either that artists are themselves "prophets" of spiritual insight or that artists have no connection to the expression of greater meaning and create art only for "art's sake." Addressing the first solution, Lippmann argues that artists are indeed *not* prophets. He asserts that, in general, artists are not "thinkers," and they have no particular claim to "wisdom" but are merely craftsmen with a talent for representing objects in a visual medium. He goes on to note that in the absence of religious themes by which artistic creations derive greater meaning, "the modern painter has ceased not only to depict any theory of destiny but has ceased to express any important human mood in the presence of destiny."

In a section entitled "Art for Art's Sake," Lippmann explores the second solution to the question of the role of art in modern society: "art has nothing to do with prophecy, wisdom, and the meaning of life, but has to do only with art." This conception of art, born of the age of modernity, is known as "art for art's sake." Lippmann contends that most modern artists subscribe to the concept of "art for art's sake," which implies that it is not the role of the artist to imbue life with any greater meaning. He goes on to observe, however, that no art is without philosophical implications, as "some sort of philosophy is implied in all human activity." He thus concludes that modern "art for art's sake" expresses an essentially atheistic philosophy, whereby "Experience has no underlying significance, man himself has no station in the universe, and the universe has no plan which is more than a drift of circumstances, illuminated here and there by flashes of self-consciousness."

In a section entitled "The Burden of Originality," Lippmann argues that the very notion of the artist's claim to "originality" is a symptom of the modern age. Throughout most of history, artists have been required to depict images derived from traditional religious doctrine. Therefore, "originality" was never considered to be the domain of the artist. However, in the modern age, artists are required to be "original" because they have no tradition from which to draw their subjects and themes. He observes that the very notion of the artist as a tortured "soul" undergoing "storm and stress" is a symptom of the modern artist's unprecedented task of creating "order out of the chaos of experience" to create a work of art. He goes on to say that, as religion no longer functions to provide an overarching sense of meaning upon which artists

> **Lippmann argues that the very notion of the artist's claim to 'originality' is a symptom of the modern age. . . . Artists are required to be 'original' because they have no tradition from which to draw their subjects and themes."**

can base their work, artists are left to flounder in a chaotic world of disconnected ideas and philosophies out of which the significance of their art must be gleaned. Because these ideas are no longer universal or generally understood, Lippmann claims, modern art is often "uninteresting" and "confusing" to most people.

Lippmann's discussion of the changing relationship between art and religion that developed in the age of modernity serves as an extended example of his larger thesis regarding the effects of the "acids of modernity" on the role of religion in modern life. He asserts that "What was happening to painting is precisely what has happened to all the other separated activities of men." In art, as well as in other realms of modern life, the dissolution of religious faith has meant the loss of a sense of "cosmic order" unifying all of human activity and experience.

Source: Liz Brent, Critical Essay on *A Preface to Morals,* in *Nonfiction Classics for Students,* The Gale Group, 2001.

Kelly Winters

Winters is a freelance writer and editor. In the following essay, she discusses themes in, and critical responses to, Walter Lippmann's A Preface to Morals.

When Walter Lippmann's book, *A Preface to Morals,* was published in 1929, many people in American society were perplexed by a growing sense of alienation and disillusionment. Old religious values, faith in the forward progress of science, and optimism no longer seemed appropriate in a world that had seen the unprecedented horrors of World War I—horrors that were unrelieved by religion accompanied by carnage that was assisted, not prevented, by modern science. Many people, like Lippmann, felt that the old sources of authority in society—the church, the government, and other traditional authorities such as the family and class structure—were no longer relevant and that faith in them had been irretrievably corrupted by the changes of modern life. Some of these people advocated that people return to more orthodox, traditional religions as an antidote to the despair so prevalent in modern life, but Lippmann believed it was too late for that.

As Lippmann points out, many people in earlier ages who believed wholeheartedly in traditional religion had a sense of order and destiny. They may have argued about the details and even had wars over them, but, he writes, "They had no doubt that there was an order in the universe which justified their lives because they were a part of it. The acids of modernity have dissolved that order for many of us." As critic Edmund Wilson remarks, Lippmann believed that the churches, and belief in them, have become "impossible" for most modern people.

Some people are unperturbed by their loss of faith, but for many others this loss of authority and meaning is a problem. "Among those who no longer believe in the religion of their fathers, some are proudly defiant, and many are indifferent. But there are also a few, perhaps an increasing number, who feel that there is a vacancy in their lives," Lippmann writes. He also notes that, when questioned, most of these people would say that without a religious faith they have no certainty that there is any significance or value to their lives or that anything they do really matters in the larger scheme of things—since there apparently is no larger scheme of things. In other words, without the compelling moral codes handed down by tradition and religion, how do people determine what is right or wrong? How do people decide what to do with their lives? How do people find meaning in the way they spend their time?

Lippmann was not interested in attacking the faith of those who were religious; he notes at the beginning of the book that if some people still have a traditional faith, then he is happy for them, but his book is addressed specifically to unbelievers who are trying to answer these questions.

In addition to traditional religion, Lippmann also questions traditional political views and obedience to them. He asks readers to consider words such as "the state, sovereignty, independence, democracy, representative government, national honor,

liberty and loyalty," and he comments that very few people could define these terms but that despite this lack of understanding, most would fight to the death to defend them. These terms, like religious ideas, have become mere "push buttons" that set off "emotional reflexes," and blind patriotism, like blind faith, is no longer an option for most people.

In *A Preface to Morals*, Lippmann tries to create a philosophy of morality and authority that is not based in any religion and is also not based on the traditional sources of authority in Western civilization: the state, class differences, family, law, or custom. All these old structures of authority demand obedience to particular codes of behavior but can not provide logical reasons *why* their codes should be obeyed; they are much like a parent who says, "Because I said so," to a questioning child. Lippmann believes that this is not a good enough reason for obedience and indeed that the very notion of obedience to some petty, man-made authority should be tossed out.

Lippmann advocates "disinterest" as the cornerstone of the new, enlightened person; "disinterest" implies detachment from one's own self-interest. To achieve this state of calm disinterest, he believes that people need to become more self-aware, with the help of modern psychology, which can aid them in becoming aware of their previously unexamined thoughts and feelings and ultimately in becoming detached from them. He writes, "To become detached from one's passions and to understand them consciously is to render them disinterested. . . . This is the principle by which a humanistic culture becomes bearable." He also notes that throughout human history, and in all known religions, the qualities that are most highly valued are based on disinterest: "courage, honor, faithfulness, veracity, justice, temperance, magnanimity, and love."

He also writes that if the reader is able to observe their feelings, they should take note of them, consider them objectively, and determine why they have them, so they can be liberated from them. "To detach ourselves from our own fears, hates, and lusts, to examine them, name them, identify their origin, and finally to judge them, is somehow to rob them of their imperiousness." Once this conscious awareness and freedom is achieved, the energy formerly wasted on them can be used in more productive pursuits.

He also writes that human suffering is often caused not by an actual event but by our response to that event and the meaning we give to the event. For example, a marathoner approaching the last mile of a 26.2-mile race may be in a great deal of pain but won't experience the pain as such if she is winning the race. On the other hand, someone forced to run 26.2 miles as a punishment would experience the same physical sensations but would suffer greatly because a very different meaning is attached to all those miles.

Lippmann believes that things and events are not necessarily inherently evil; what is perceived as evil is not an innate quality but comes from an attitude toward the thing or event and a reaction to it. "For things are neutral and evil is a certain way of experiencing them," he writes. "To realize this is to destroy the awfulness of evil."

Lippmann gives various examples in the book, but he doesn't say how to respond to events that most people would perceive as truly evil—regardless of the attitude of the participants—such as the Holocaust of World War II, when millions of innocent people were tortured and killed. Could those people simply change the way they responded to their fate and thereby lessen the evil of what happened to them? This is doubtful, and it would seem that, no matter what attitude one took, it would be difficult to "destroy the awfulness" of such events by changing one's mental attitude or cultivating disinterestedness. Of course, Lippmann wrote his book before the immense atrocities of World War II. On a smaller scale, however, consider the case of a child who is starving to death; it doesn't seem likely that the child's suffering could be lessened by a change in attitude.

However, Lippmann's analysis is true for many events in modern life: attitude is everything. His description of the enlightened modern person seems almost Buddhist at times; in fact, he does mention the Buddha repeatedly, along with other spiritual and philosophical teachers. "Buddha did, to be sure, teach that craving was the source of all misery, and that it must be wholly extinguished." Lippmann illustrates how a man free from desire is able to live more easily:

> The mature man would take the world as it comes, and within himself remain quite unperturbed. . . . Would he be hopeful? Not if to be hopeful was to expect the world to submit rather soon to his vanity. Would he be hopeless? Hope is an expectation of favors to come, and he would take his delights here and now. Since nothing gnawed at his vitals, neither doubt, nor ambition, nor frustration, nor fear, he would move easily through life.

> " Without the compelling moral codes handed down by tradition and religion, how do people determine what is right or wrong? How do people decide what to do with their lives? How do people find meaning in how they spend their time?"

A Preface to Morals became an immediate bestseller, despite its philosophical subject matter, and was praised by a wide variety of writers and thinkers, as well as by the public, who were captivated by Lippmann's application of philosophy to ordinary modern life. Arthur M. Schlesinger Jr. writes in *Walter Lippmann and His Times,* "At the depths of the Depression (if my memory is correct), the *New Yorker*'s 'Talk of the Town,' commenting on the reported formation of the Monarchist party in the United States, said that many Americans would be glad to settle for Walter Lippmann as king."

Lippmann's style is remarkably clear, considering his subject matter; he writes in an elegant but almost conversational manner and provides examples from ancient philosophers, modern psychologists and writers, the Bible, and other religious works, as well as from history and modern life, to give readers a clearer understanding of his ideas.

In *From the Uncollected Edmund Wilson,* in an essay on *A Preface to Morals,* critic Edmund Wilson describes the book as "beautifully organized, beautifully clear . . . both outspoken and persuasive in bringing news which has been uneasily awaited," and he writes, "No one else that I have read has performed this task of discrediting traditional religion at once so tactfully and so uncompromisingly as Lippmann." However, he also praises the fact that Lippmann doesn't simply discredit faith in traditional religion and then leave the reader in despair. He writes, "I recommend this book as an antidote to. . . [the work of] critics who tend to despair of modern civilization."

Wilson also writes that Lippmann's criticism of popular religion is unsurprising, given that many other critics have noted the same gap between belief and modern religious attitudes, but that Lippmann's criticism of government and traditional politics is refreshing and surprising. However, Wilson notes, Lippmann's belief that everyone in society, and society as a whole, could become enlightened and run on the basis of benign disinterest seems somewhat naïve. Nevertheless, he writes, "these considerations do not, in any case, damage Lippmann's principal arguments."

In *Walter Lippmann,* Larry L. Adams writes that *A Preface to Morals* is one of Lippmann's "best received and most widely read books" but notes that Lippmann's former professor and philosophical hero, George Santayana, whose influence Lippmann acknowledges in the book, wrote an ambiguous but "generally skeptical" review of it, in which he implies that Lippmann's view is naïve. Santayana also remarks, with irony, that it would be interesting to see what will be "the ruling passions, favorite pleasures, and dominant beliefs of mankind when the hitherto adventurous selfish human animal has become thoroughly socialized, mechanized, hygienic, and irreligious." Adams also comments that one weakness in the book is the fact that Lippmann's emphasis on disinterest is directly counter to the prevailing values of American culture, which emphasizes individualism and hearty self-interest as the basis of economic and social freedom. However, Adams writes, Lippmann is correct in pointing out that no society could survive and thrive without some form of moral structure, and he finds Lippmann ahead of his time because he draws wisdom not only from the Western religious and philosophical traditions but also from the sages of other cultures, such as Buddha and Confucius.

In his introduction to the Transaction Publishers' edition of the book, John Patrick Diggins notes that the great praise lavished on Lippmann's book is not universal: liberals criticize Lippmann because his vision of a new society doesn't provide for any restraints on individuals' desires; other, more radical critics note that this kind of enlightened society, based on benign disinterest, could not succeed until all vestiges of injustice and strife are eliminated. Diggins, like Adams, also comments that although these critics don't mention it, an inherent conflict exists between Lippmann's ideal—disinterest and freedom from desire—and the demands of a free, capitalistic society, which of course is based on "maximiz[ing] desire through the pleasures of consumption."

However, Diggins praises Lippmann's ability to "turn the mundane issues of life into philosophical riddles" as well as his style, which is "at once relaxed, lucid, crisp, and unencumbered by heavy philosophical jargon." He also praises Lippmann's "daring enterprise" of attempting to create a framework of moral authority not grounded in old institutions that would not withstand a true intellectual challenge to their orders. Diggins writes, "That is why his book speaks forcefully to us today, when our emotions feel the need for authority but our mind demands that authority be rational and just."

Source: Kelly Winters, Critical Essay on *A Preface to Morals,* in *Nonfiction Classics for Students,* The Gale Group, 2001.

Joyce Hart

Hart has degrees in English literature and creative writing, and she is a copyeditor and published writer. In this essay, she examines Lippmann's definitions of asceticism and humanism, as well as the purposes he proposes for turning to them.

Walter Lippmann wrote *A Preface to Morals* in 1929, so it might be necessary for some readers to practice some forgiveness in reference to Lippmann's sometimes elitist and sexist attitude. That being said, there is no denying that Lippmann was an intelligent man with a wide scope of interests that spanned topics in philosophy, theology, psychology, sociology, and science. Although some of his information may be outdated by the discoveries in quantum physics and psychology that have taken place in the seventy plus years that have passed since his book was published, his insights and his understanding of human nature far exceed his time. His inquiry into the history of theology and its implications for modern society still hold a valid position today. His discussion of the demise of popular religion based on old orthodoxy offers an explanation for a continued uneasiness felt in contemporary society; and his theories of humanism based on a self-regulated asceticism, provide an interesting and stimulating discussion of human nature.

Lippmann claims, in his opening remarks, that there is an increasing number of people in modern society, "who feel that there is a vacancy in their lives." And it is to these people, the so-called unbelievers, that Lippmann directs his thoughts. For those who are "perplexed by the consequences" of their lack of religion or disturbed by the hole that the lack of religion has placed in their lives, Lippmann digs into his own repertoire of collected knowledge in an attempt to extract some new insights. His attempts are aimed at putting a sense of significance and morality back into the soul of the unbeliever, qualities that are lost when a religion no longer makes sense to people who find that the teachings of the old orthodox churches no longer apply to their modern concepts of life.

By the old orthodoxy, Lippmann refers to religions that are based on a somewhat literal interpretation of the Bible, a book they believe was created with "wisdom backed by the power of God himself." These religions teach that the Bible contains the truths of life that cannot be wrong. They also teach that there is a Supreme Being, "who is more powerful than all the kings of earth together." He is also the "ultimate judge of the universe." For these believers, God is a "magical King" who rules the universe and issues all commands for living a good life. If followed, the commandments will lead the believers to salvation. For these believers, life has meaning, and that life is built on a solid foundation of morality that is defined through the church by the word of God. These people "felt themselves to be living within the framework of a universe which they called divine because it corresponded with their deepest desires." For this "common man," as Lippmann puts it, life is more satisfying because rules are laid out, and the dictates of life are sanctified. A person knows what they have to do to make it through this life and eventually reap the benefits of a "concrete world hereafter." Believing in a god who not only knows a person's "deeds but their motives" means that there is "no hole deep enough into which a man could crawl to hide himself from the sight of God." Morality, then, in this kind of belief is easily defined. All a person has to do is bend his or her own will to the will of God. People who believe in this type of religion have no choice but to obey this divine and omniscient ruler. Their codes of morality include all distinctions between what is considered good and what is evil, as well as how they should conduct themselves in private life and in their society.

A way of life driven by the laws of God survives without much interpretation or questioning as long as people lived close to the soil, states Lippmann. Their "ways of living changed little in the course of generations," and because their ways rarely changed, there were always at hand typical solutions to every problem, based on practical experiences from the past. But it is not so easy for the modern population who live, more than likely, in an

> " Humanists believe in a morality in which virtue is not commanded by an outside divine force, but rather virtue 'must be willed out of the personal conviction and desire' of the individual."

urban society that is far removed from family and their stories of generational experience. Added to this is the fact that in the last four hundred years, and more significantly since the nineteenth century, there have been many influences that have "conspired to make incredible the idea that the universe is governed by a kingly person."

Lippmann does not mean to say that most people living in modern cities do not believe in God. What he does mean is that many people now "no longer believe in him simply and literally." They "can no longer honestly say that he exists." At best, the modern person is left with what Lippmann refers to as an indefinite God. In addition to this, science, with its strong influence on modern society, has made people believe that before something can be stated as a fact, it has to be proven. This concept has eroded the possibility of modern society accepting anything without first questioning it. This weakens religious beliefs and once the basic beliefs of religion are weakened, "the disintegration of the popular religion begins." In the place of all people living under the dictates of one, true religion, modern society is made up of many "detached individuals."

As a result of this disintegration, old religious orthodoxy becomes at best a "somewhat archaic . . . quaint medley of poetry, rhetoric, [and] fable." The lessons of the Bible might still ring true, but the authority behind the words is missing, and there exists no basis for a functioning morality because there is no longer certainty in a god to fear, a god who knows all thoughts and will pronounce the last judgment. Although people can themselves conceive ethical codes, there no longer exists a belief in a power strong enough to demand compliance with those codes. Humans are fallible; therefore, their ethical codes would be fallible. If God is an uncertainty, then the punishment for disobeying the codes as well as the rewards for obeying them are uncertain. With this cloud of uncertainty prevailing over modern society, with no definite God looking over and watching their every move and thought, people feel they no longer have a sense of self-importance. It is from this lack of importance that the hole, or vacant feeling, is created.

This questioning, uncertainty, and feeling of insignificance intensifies the "separated activities" of modern people. There is nothing remaining that pulls people together. From the disintegration of the church follows the disintegration of state and family. In earlier times, the laws of a single god governed everything from government to family, art, science, and morality. In modern times, everyone works toward his or her own separate interest. Therein lies another problem for the moralist. Not only is there no remaining authority to demand obedience to a code of ethics; no longer is there infallible belief in the old code; but also there no longer is anything strong enough to pull people together to even think about creating a new, unified code. In modern society, there are only individuals left to their own devices to define their own private codes. These individuals are also left with only a vague sense of punishment or reward as consequences to either breaking or following those codes.

It is from this state of confusion and individualism that Lippmann suggests humanism, a philosophy that puts a positive spin on this situation, recognizing not the weaknesses of individuals but rather the potential ability of an individual to define a viable code of morals for him- or herself. Humanists believe in a morality in which virtue is not commanded by an outside divine force, but rather virtue "must be willed out of the personal conviction and desire" of the individual. In other words, a person must will him- or herself to know and to act upon the difference between what they believe is right and wrong. But how do individuals come to these conclusions? How do they come to understand themselves well enough to make rational definitions about something as abstract as morals? To these questions, Lippmann offers the remaining chapters of his book.

"In a world where no man desired what he could not have, there would be no need to regulate human conduct and therefore no need for morality," states Lippmann. But modern society is in no way close to that utopia. People have needs. People have desires. And not all needs and desires can be fulfilled. There is a belief, however, that modern society appears to have assumed, and it is a belief that "the human passions, if thoroughly liberated from all tyrannies and distortions, would by their fulfillment achieve happiness." This is a false belief, according to Lippmann, because he believes that there are not enough resources in this world to satisfy the needs of every person. "Desires are . . . unlimited and insatiable, and therefore any ethics which does not recognize the necessity of putting restraint upon naive desire is inherently absurd." And it is at this point in his discussion that Lippmann turns to his definition of asceticism and shows how it can be used in conjunction with the philosophy of humanism to help individuals define a code of morality.

Asceticism is a practice or discipline that helps to curb desires. It is not a total dismissal or denouncement of desires, as is popularly held, but rather a "discipline of the mind and body to fit men for the service of an ideal." No one can make a list of what is good and what is bad because this would be "an attempt to understand something which is always in process of change." The task of disciplining, defining, weighing, and interpreting, according to humanism, relies totally on the individual; and the individual must rely on "his own intuitions, commonsense, and sense of life." The goal of asceticism is maturity. Toward this goal, Lippmann suggests, the education of the individual should be set up. The educators should base their lessons on the teachings of the sages of "high religion," who include great thinkers such as Spinoza, Confucius, Jesus Christ, and the Buddha. Through the teachings of these sages, one would learn the art of living, which would show every individual how "to pass gracefully from youth to old age," and eventually, "to learn to die."

The principle underlying this educational process is that individuals need to recognize the meaning of their desires. In doing this, they will learn that their emotions are often irrational. Many desires are remnants from childhood that are carried over into adult life. Once these desires are made rational, the individual would realize that many of the immediately desirable objects are not quite as desirable as once thought. Also, with a rational understanding, the undesirable would become more tolerable. When the emotions and desires of a child are carried over into the adult world, the consequences are that the individual begins to assume, when things go wrong, that the world is out to get him or her and that life owes him or her something. The immature individual also grabs at everything that passes by and covets it in fear that someone might someday take it away.

In contrast, the mature person, having disciplined his or her emotions, will learn to want ''what he can posses . . . learn to hold on to things which do not slip away . . . to hold on to them . . . not by grasping . . . but by understanding them and by remembering them.'' Through the alteration of immature emotions, people learn that being good is not good just because God demands it, but because through experience they will come to find that being good ''yields happiness, serenity, wholeheartedness.'' Salvation, according to the teachings of the high religion, is not achieved by appeasing an almighty judge but rather ''a condition of the soul which is reached only by some kind of self-discipline.''

So if asceticism is a discipline that makes people fit for the service of an ideal, the final question to be answered would necessarily be, what is the ideal? Lippmann defines his concept of the ideal in his last chapter. First he describes the role of the moralist, who cannot, in a time of unsettled customs such as in modern times, ''teach what is revealed,'' for there are no revelations that fit contemporary models, but rather, ''he must reveal what can be taught. He has to seek insight rather than to preach.'' Lippmann then refers to Aristotle, who lived in an age that also was unsettled, somewhat similar to contemporary society. The function of the moralist, states Aristotle, is to ''promote good conduct by discerning and explaining the mark at which things aim.'' An individual as well as a whole nation, must know what its ideals are to understand why the discipline is needed in the first place. It is through the moralist that people need to be reminded what they are moving toward. In general, by quoting Confucius, Lippmann states the goal of human effort as following ''what the heart desires without transgressing what is right.'' Lippmann calls this the ''religion of the spirit.'' It is a religion that does not depend on commandments, does not profess to know the truth, and is only concerned with ''the quality of human desire.''

Lippmann does not direct his comments to everyone. He realizes that many people are very comfortable in their beliefs. But to those who are searching for answers, his book provides stimulating insights into questions that may have begun with Aristotle, but continue to haunt contemporary society. By looking back into history, as well as ahead to possible consequences if answers are not found, Lippmann opens the mind of the reader and in essence says, here, if you are confused or feeling empty about life, why not try this one.

Source: Joyce Hart, Critical Essay on *A Preface to Morals,* in *Nonfiction Classics for Students,* The Gale Group, 2001.

Sources

Adams, Larry L., *Walter Lippmann,* Twayne Publishers, 1977, pp. 9–10.

Blum, D. Steven, *Walter Lippmann: Cosmopolitanism in the Century of Total War,* Cornell University Press, 1984, pp. 9–11, 97.

Childs, Marquis, Introduction to *Walter Lippmann and His Times,* edited by Marquis Childs and James Reston, Harcourt, Brace and Company, 1959, p. 2.

Dam, Hari N., *The Intellectual Odyssey of Walter Lippmann,* Gordon Press, 1973, pp. 161–162.

Diggins, John Patrick, Introduction to *A Preface to Morals,* by Walter Lippmann, Transaction Publishers, 1982, pp. x–xi, xiv, xiv, xxxv–xxxvi, xli.

Kirkhorn, Michael, *Dictionary of Literary Biography,* Volume 29: *American Newspaper Journalists, 1926–1950,* edited by Perry J. Ashley, Gale Research, 1984, pp. 174–189.

Riccio, Barry D., *Walter Lippmann: Odyssey of a Liberal,* Transaction Publishers, 1994, p. xii.

Rossiter, Clinton, and James Lare, eds., *The Essential Lippmann: A Political Philosophy for Liberal Democracy,* Random House, 1963, pp. xi, xiii.

Steel, Ronald, *Walter Lippmann and the American Century,* Atlantic Monthly Press, 1980, pp. xiii–xvi, 263.

Weingast, David Elliott, *Walter Lippmann: A Study in Personal Journalism,* Rutgers University Press, 1949, pp. xiii, 125, 127, 130.

Further Reading

Adams, Larry L., ''The New Morality,'' in *Walter Lippmann,* Twayne Publishers, 1977, pp. 123–147.
  Adams discusses the philosophical, religious, and social underpinnings of Lippmann's work.

Auchincloss, Louis, *Woodrow Wilson,* Viking Penguin, 2000.
  Woodrow Wilson is a biography of the progressive President Woodrow Wilson by whom Lippmann was recruited to develop international policy for peace in postwar Europe.

Cooper, John Milton Jr., *Pivotal Decades: The United States, 1900–1920,* W. W. Norton, 1990.

Pivotal Decades is a history of the United States during the first decades of the twentieth century, the period during which Lippmann's fundamental political philosophy was developed.

Diggins, John Patrick, "Introduction to the Transaction Edition: Walter Lippmann's Quest for Authority," in *A Preface to Morals*, by Walter Lippmann, Transaction Publishers, 1999, pp. ix–liii.

Diggins describes Lippmann's career as a writer and thinker, as well as factors that make his book an important contribution to American moral philosophy.

Diner, Steven J., *A Very Different Age: Americans of the Progressive Era,* Hill & Wang, 1998.

A Very Different Age is a history of the United States during the Progressive era of the 1890s to 1920s.

Knock, Thomas J., *To End All Wars: Woodrow Wilson and the Quest for New World Order,* Oxford University Press, 1992.

To End All Wars provides a historical discussion of the efforts of President Wilson to formulate a program for international peace in the wake of World War I.

Lamont, Corliss, *The Philosophy of Humanism,* Continuum Press, 1990.

Philosophy of Humanism is an introduction to humanism, a moral philosophy that Lippmann advocates as the most appropriate replacement for religion in the age of modernity.

Reston, James, "Conclusion: The Mockingbird and Taxicab," in *Walter Lippmann and His Times,* edited by Marquis Childs and James Reston, Harcourt Brace & Co., 1959, pp. 226–238.

The book describes Lippmann's daily life and work habits, in part derived from the conclusions he drew in *A Preface to Morals.*

Riccio, Barry Daniel, *Walter Lippmann: Odyssey of a Liberal,* Transaction Press, 1994.

In *Walter Lippmann,* Riccio traces the development of Lippmann's liberal, humanist political philosophy over half a century of publication.

Wilson, Edmund, "Walter Lippmann's *A Preface to Morals,*" in *From the Uncollected Edmund Wilson,* edited by Janet Groth and David Castronovo, Ohio University Press, 1995, pp. 108–114.

This early review of Lippmann's book originally appeared in the *New Republic* in July of 1929.

Wolfe, Gregory, ed., *The New Religious Humanists: A Reader,* Free Press, 1997.

The New Religious Humanists is an overview of philosophies of religious humanism in the late twentieth century.

Zieger, Robert H., *America's Great War: World War I and the American Experience,* Rowman and Littlefield, 2000.

America's Great War provides a history of United States participation in World War I.

Silent Spring

Rachel Carson

1962

First published in the United States in 1962, *Silent Spring* surveys mounting evidence that widespread pesticide use endangers both wildlife and humans. Along the way, Rachel Carson criticizes an irresponsible chemical industry, which continues to claim that pesticides are safe, and imprudent public officials, who accept without question this disinformation. As an alternative to the "scorched earth" logic underlying accepted pest-control practices, the author outlines the "biotic" approach—cheaper, safer, longer acting, natural solutions to pest problems (for example, controlling the Japanese beetle by introducing a fungus that causes a fatal disease in this insect).

The primary inspiration for the book was a friend of Carson's who was concerned about dying birds in her hometown where the authorities had sprayed DDT to control mosquitoes. At about the same time, a disastrous pesticide campaign against the fire ant of the Southeast was receiving national attention. Formerly a science writer for the United States Fish and Wildlife Service, Carson already had some acquaintance with research on pesticides, and she was ready to speak out. Originally planned as an article, *Silent Spring* became a book of more than two hundred pages when the only outlet she could find was the book publisher Houghton Mifflin.

Though *Silent Spring* is without question her best-known book today, Carson was already a national literary celebrity when it came out. As work

of social criticism, *Silent Spring* represented a considerable departure from the natural history with which she had made a name for herself. Whether this would have been a turning point in her career or merely a detour is impossible to know because Carson succumbed to breast cancer only a year and a half after *Silent Spring* appeared. What is clear, however, is that her public image was irrevocably transformed. Average Americans came to see her as a noble crusader while the chemical industry would quickly spend more than a quarter of a million dollars to discredit her.

Few books have had as much impact on late twentieth-century life as Carson's *Silent Spring*. Though an environmental consciousness can be discerned in American culture as far back as the nineteenth century, environmentalism as it is known today has only been around for about forty years, and Carson's book is one of its primary sources. Her tirade against humankind's attempt to use technology to dominate nature wrenched environmentalism from its relatively narrow, conservationist groove and helped transform it into a sweeping social movement that has since impacted almost every area of everyday life.

Author Biography

Rachel Louise Carson was born on May 27, 1907, in Springdale, Pennsylvania, the daughter of Robert Warden Carson and Maria Frazier McLean. The family had very little money—Robert Carson made only a slim living as a salesman and utility employee—but thanks to their talented and well-educated mother, Rachel and her older brother and sister enjoyed a comparatively stimulating childhood. A great reader and passionate naturalist, Maria Carson left an especially deep imprint on her youngest child. While still quite young, Rachel began writing stories about animals, and by age ten, she had published a prize-winning magazine piece.

In 1925, Carson earned a scholarship for Pennsylvania Women's College where she hoped to prepare herself for a literary career by majoring in English. As had always been her habit in school, the bright but reserved student focused on academics rather than socializing and was soon one of the college's top scholars. Less expected was Carson's changing her major to biology after taking a class taught by a captivating young zoology professor named Mary Scott Skinner. In 1929, after graduating with high honors, the writer who would someday earn fame for her work on marine life got her first look at the sea as a summer intern at Woods Hole Laboratory on Cape Cod. Later that year, Carson began graduate work in zoology at Johns Hopkins University, but in 1935, when her father suddenly died, family responsibilities put an end to her formal studies. By 1937, she was the sole provider for both her mother and the children of her now deceased sister.

It was at this point that she embarked on her long career as a civil servant, an endeavor that would occupy her for the next decade and a half and the crucible out of which would come the influential nature writing of her later life. Producing publications for the Bureau of Fisheries and the United States Fish and Wildlife Service, Carson increased her already considerable expertise in biology and honed her skills as a writer. The bureaucratic elements of such work do not seem to have been at all stifling; in *Notable American Women,* Paul Brooks credits Carson for setting ''a new standard for government publication.'' It was inevitable that such work would someday come to the notice of a wider circle of readers, as it did in 1941, when she published *Under the Sea Wind,* a work of natural history that originated in an article she had written for a Bureau of Fisheries publication in the late 1930s. Though it was well received by reviewers, the book was something of a false start: the entrance of the United States into World War II led to poor sales, and Carson herself soon had to put other such projects aside to deal with growing responsibilities at Fish and Wildlife. (By 1949, she was editor of all agency publications.)

It wasn't until 1951 that her next and most popular book, *The Sea Around Us,* appeared. It was among the first examples of what was to become an important late twentieth-century genre, science as literature. On the *New York Times* bestseller list for eighty-six weeks, this volume earned Carson enough royalties to enable her to retire from government work and focus on the projects that most interested her.

After completing the third and final volume of her ''biography of the sea,'' *The Edge of the Sea,* and a handful of smaller projects, Carson was prompted by a series of events to write the book that would make her one of the most important women of the twentieth century. Carson was recruited to help a friend from Duxbury, Massachusetts, challenge a state mosquito control program that seemed to be wiping out birds. This and another widely publicized controversy over a similar development in the Southeast led Carson to write on the mounting scientific evidence about the risks of pesticides. Doubting that she could find a magazine that would publish an article on so gloomy a topic, Carson produced an entire book for an interested editor at Houghton Mifflin. Serialized by the *New Yorker* in advance of its 1962 publication, *Silent Spring* became the focus of intense attention, not least because the chemical industry responded with a quarter-million-dollar campaign to discredit the author. Before the controversy cooled, a presidential commission began looking into the problem, and Congress began considering tougher restrictions on dangerous chemicals. (Carson herself testified before Congress.) Already a prize-winning writer, Carson was now elevated to the ranks of the nation's most important public figures. The true magnitude of her accomplishment would only become clear some months later, when Carson died on April 14, 1964, in Silver Springs, Maryland. During the four years that she worked on *Silent Spring*, Carson also had been battling cancer.

Rachel Louise Carson

Summary

Chapter One

Carson's survey of the research on pesticides opens in a most unscientific fashion with a tale about an American town that has suffered a series of plagues. At chapter's end, Carson acknowledges that the town is an imaginary one, but lest the tale be dismissed as mere fantasy, she hastens to add that each of the catastrophes it catalogs ''has actually happened somewhere, and many real communities have already suffered a substantial number of them.''

Chapters Two and Three

Not until chapter two does Carson identify the source of the ills described in chapter one: potent synthetic poisons of relatively recent design, proliferating at the rate of about five hundred a year, applied in massive quantities virtually everywhere, with disastrous short- and long-term consequences for both wildlife and humans. To convey the grave danger that these substances represent, she introduces an analogy that will resurface over and over in *Silent Spring*: pesticides are like atomic radiation— invisible, with deadly effects that often manifest

themselves only after a long delay. Chapter three identifies a small handful of qualities that make the new pesticides so much more dangerous than their predecessors: 1) greater potency 2) slower decomposition and 3) a tendency to concentrate in fatty tissue. Carson clarifies the significance of the last two characteristics by pointing out that a toxin that might not constitute a danger in small doses will ultimately do so if it accumulates in the body, and also that substances with this propensity concentrate as one moves up the food chain.

Chapters Four, Five, and Six

Chapters four, five and six form a triptych that stresses the highly interconnectedness of life in three biological systems—plant systems and those centered in water or soil. Given its fluidity and interconnectedness, water is an extremely difficult place to contain a problem, Carson points out. As an unintended result of runoff from agricultural spraying and of poisons sometimes directly introduced in the water supply, groundwater nearly everywhere is tainted with one or more potent toxins. The full extent of the problem, she worries, cannot even be precisely measured because methods for screening the new chemicals have yet to be routinized. In some instances, the danger lies in substances formed by unexpected reactions that take place between individual contaminants; in such cases, toxins might escape detection even where tests are available. Chapter five explains the life cycle within soil-based ecosystems: rich soil gives rise to hearty plant life; then the natural process of death and decay breaks down the plants, and the soil's vitality is restored. Pesticides threaten this fundamental dynamic—fundamental not just for plants but also for the higher organisms that live on plants. An insecticide applied to control a particular crop–damaging insect depletes the microbial life within the soil that facilitates the essential enrichment cycle, hence the millions of pounds of chemical fertilizer required each year by factory–farms. In chapter six, Carson's focus shifts from insecticides to herbicides. The general picture that emerges is of a deceptive chemical industry and ill–informed public authorities spending large sums of taxpayers' money undermining whole ecosystems to eradicate one or two nuisance species.

Chapter Seven

In "Needless Havoc," Carson's attention turns to the people behind pesticides, the public officials who are responsible for the widespread use of these dangerous chemicals. What has typified their behavior in her view is almost unbelievable recklessness followed by an irrational unwillingness to reckon with the catastrophes they have wrought. Exhibit A is the infamous campaign against the Japanese beetle, a frenzy that swept the Midwest in the late fifties. In the first place, Carson argues, there was no real evidence that the beetle constituted a serious threat. Secondly, officials failed to warn the public of potential risks involved in combating the insect with pesticides.

Chapter Eight

Not surprisingly, at the very heart of *Silent Spring* lies a chapter called "And No Birds Sing," where the author recounts the true stories from whence the book's most unforgettable image comes. The chemical villain in these tragedies is the notorious DDT; the principal victims are the robin, beloved herald of spring, and the eagle, revered symbol of national spirit. That the shrewd writer chose species with so much emotional resonance is hardly an accident. Both birds' fates bring the discussion back to the problem of bio–magnification, the concentration of toxins as they pass from one organism to the next along the food chain: the robin receive fatal doses from consuming poisoned worms and other insects, the eagle from pesticide–carrying fish.

Chapter Nine

Chapter nine explains how blanket pesticide spraying—of forests, crop fields, and suburban lawns—is wreaking havoc on aquatic life in the streams, estuaries, and coastal waters that receive runoff from treated areas. The chapter's most frightening observation is that runoff concentrates in marshes and estuaries where freshwater meets the seas, extraordinarily fragile ecosystems and the primary feeding and spawning grounds for many species—the foundation of much aquatic life.

Chapter Ten

Reviewing two more disastrous eradication efforts, chapter ten sounds many of the same notes as chapter eight. What chapter ten adds to this now fairly well-developed picture is a clearer sense of the colossal blunder that was aerial spraying. Carson reports that pilots were paid according to how much pesticide they sprayed, and so they drenched the countryside with toxic chemicals, contaminating orchards and gardens, killing birds, bees and other wildlife, poisoning milk cows and even soaking humans who happened to get in the way.

Chapter Eleven

Chapter eleven concerns the minute but repeated exposures to pesticides that every man, woman, and child suffers in all but the most isolated regions of the planet. Carson lays the blame for the breathtaking diffusion of dangerous chemicals in everyday life on the deceptive marketing campaigns of pesticide makers, which insist these products are safe, and government agencies like the Department of Agriculture and the FDA, which not only countenance such disinformation but actively promoted the use of synthetic poisons.

Chapters Twelve, Thirteen, and Fourteen

Chapters twelve, thirteen and fourteen focus on the effects of pesticides on people. Chapter twelve stresses two key issues: first, that pesticides are absorbed by fat, a widely dispersed tissue, and so they insinuate themselves in virtually every part of the system, including the ever so crucial organs and fundamental cell structures; and second, because most people accumulate these toxins by way of repeated minute exposure of which they are rarely aware, it difficult to trace the resulting pathologies to their true cause. Chapter thirteen explains one of the book's main refrains—that pesticides are so very dangerous because they disrupt basic biological processes like oxidation (cell metabolism) and mitosis (cell reproduction). The central claim here is that pesticides are probably responsible for cancer, birth defects, and a wide array of chromosomal abnormalities. Scientific research in this area was still in an early stage when Carson wrote *Silent Spring*, but plant and animal studies were already suggesting what had long been known about radiation, namely that pesticides had powerful mutagenic properties. Chapter fourteen chronicles the history of the carcinogen, a term that has become only more familiar since 1962. It was first surmised that cancer related to environmental conditions in the eighteenth century, when a London physician noted an extremely high incidence of scrotal tumors among the city's chimney sweeps, who were all day covered in soot. During the nineteenth century, with the rise of industry, several other suspicious relationships had been observed. But with World War II and the rise of widespread pesticide use, the risk of cancer confronted not just members of certain occupational groups but virtually everyone.

Chapters Fifteen and Sixteen

Chapters fifteen and sixteen discuss in a comprehensive way one of Carson's most damning criticism of pesticides, but one she has thus far only voiced in passing: not only are pesticides expensive and extremely dangerous, but they are also terribly ineffective. The trouble is twofold. Chapter fifteen focuses on the first part of the problem; current pesticide practice, Carson argues, is like trying to repair a delicate watch with a sledgehammer. Massive applications of highly toxic substances reverberate through whole ecosystems, upsetting delicate balances and often compounding the original problem. Chapter sixteen highlights the tendency of pesticides to lose effectiveness quickly as insects and other nuisance organisms develop resistance. The problem arises from the indefatigable reality of natural selection. Within any given pest species, some number of organisms will be less susceptible to pesticides as a function of ordinary genetic variety within the species. Pesticide kills off the weak, leaving the pesticide–resilient to thrive and establish a new generation of super bugs. Of particular concern is the loss of effective tools in the fight against disease carrying insects like the mosquito.

Chapter Seventeen

Since so many of the book's chapters conclude with some mention of safer alternatives to current pesticide practices, it is hardly surprising that the book itself concludes with an extended discussion of what Carson calls "biotic controls." One of the main arguments of the chemical industry in the face of mounting evidence about the dangers of pesticides is that the risks are justified by benefits to agriculture and other areas. By laying out in fine detail cheaper, safer, and more effective alternatives, Carson pulls the rug out from under the industry with its self–interested talk of pesticide benefits. Broken into three sections, each of which focuses on a slightly different basic strategy, chapter seventeen offers a cogent overview of the elegant science of natural pest control. Part one explains how chemicals derived from the insects themselves can be used as repellants or lures for traps that pose no risk to humans. Part two shows how repeatedly introducing sterilized males into target populations can bring about a gradual decline of pests. And part three reports on the use of natural enemies—bacterial insecticides and predator species—to combat pests.

Key Figures

The Chemical Industry

Because Carson refrains from naming particular corporations, the pesticide makers assume the monolithic shape of an evil empire in *Silent Spring*. Yet Carson does not preach at the industry. Yes, it develops hundreds of new deadly toxins a year, and, through disinformation and pressure on government agencies, it promotes their widest possible use—the book is very clear about these things. But Carson seems to view such activity as natural to the commercial enterprise and wastes no time calling on pesticide producers to reform themselves.

The Government

The government is the other great villain in Carson's story, and though one might think it is the chemical industry that bears primary responsibility for what has occurred, she is much more critical of public servants. Her thinking seems to be that more is to be expected of government. In succumbing to political pressure and helping pesticide makers promote their products, she argues, government has lost sight of its *raison d'etre* (reason for being), protecting the public interest. Carson holds that instead of echoing industry disinformation and spend-

Media Adaptations

- The documentary *The ''Silent Spring'' of Rachel Carson,* produced by CBS Reports in 1963, captures the mood of the times when the book first appeared.

- In 1993, PBS produced and presented *Rachel Carson's ''Silent Spring''* as part of its ''American Experience'' series. The film features interviews with several of the writer's colleagues and critics.

- Durkin Hayes published an abridged version of *Silent Spring* on audiocassette in 1993. The text is read by actress Ellen Burstyn.

ing taxpayers' money on reckless pest eradication programs, agencies like the Department of Agriculture and the Food and Drug Administration ought to impose stricter controls on the development, sale, and use of dangerous chemicals and to fund more research.

Nature

An overview of key figures in *Silent Spring* that did not mention nature would be quite incomplete. In terms of the amount of attention that is devoted to them, plant and animals are the most important ''characters'' in the book, surpassing humans by a wide margin, who are the focus of just a few chapters. Still, despite the almost infinite variety of life forms that Carson mentions, there emerges a single image of nature that has a crucial function in Carson's case against pesticides: nature as a fabric of life in which all things are connected, from the smallest of soil microbes to human beings and other large mammals. If readers accept such a view, they must also agree with Carson that the sledgehammer-like approach of current pest control—introducing large amounts of extremely toxic chemicals into the environment to eradicate a few species of insects—is indefensible.What poisons one part of the fabric of life poisons the whole.

The Public

Along with wildlife, the public is a major concern in *Silent Spring*. The image the book projects of this collective entity is that of a victim of the chemical industry, betrayed by irresponsible public officials and exposed to toxic pesticides at every turn. As the terrible side effects of pesticides become clearer, the public begins to ask questions, demand answers, and insist on greater responsiveness from government agencies.

The Visionaries

The heroes of *Silent Spring* come from several walks of life: scientists laboring patiently in an often tedious and seriously underfunded area of research to determine the precise scope of the pesticide threat; birders and other amateur naturalists, whose careful observation of wildlife in the field yields essential information about the problem; activists driven by a deep concern for their communities and the natural environment to challenge industry and government to behave more responsibly; and philosophers, writers, and other thinkers who help citizens understand the cultural sources not just of the pesticide problem but of the whole range of trouble that modern civilization has stirred up with technology.What all of these individuals share is an uncommon power discernment. Simply recognizing the broad impact of pesticides on the environment and health is a significant achievement. What makes Carson's visionaries even more remarkable is their having probed this tricky problem with great precision in the face of widespread disinformation and obstruction.

Themes

The Science of Pesticides

One of the great insights of *Silent Spring* is its grasp of the pesticide problem as a compound one. On one hand, there are the intrinsic dangers of these chemicals: their capacity to disrupt basic biological processes, their persistence in the environment, and so forth. But Carson knew that the manner in which a dangerous substance is also crucial. To understand how compounds like DDT and malathion have come to threaten life on a global scale, one has to examine what has been done with them. Each of the major themes of *Silent Spring* belongs then to one of two lines of argument; the first concerns the raw toxicity of pesticides, the second the recklessness with which they have been employed.

Along with atomic fallout, the synthetic pesticides that came into wide use after World War II are the most dangerous substances man has ever created. The heart of the problem, science has shown, is the pesticides' unique capacity for disrupting critical biological processes like metabolism and cell division. Acute exposure can cause catastrophic systemic problems—paralysis, immune deficiency, sterility, etc.—and small doses repeated over time can lead to grave illnesses like cancer.

Carson attributes this radically disruptive potential to the distinctive molecular structure of synthetic pesticides. Part carbon, they mimic the substances that are crucial to life (enzymes, hormones, etc.) and so gain entrance to sensitive physiological systems. Once inside these vital systems, the elements to which the carbon is bound (chlorine and other deadly materials) wreak havoc on the organism.

Two other properties that increase the hazard of pesticides are, first, the slow rate at which they break down and become less toxic, and, second, their tendency to accumulate in fat tissue. It is these characteristics that make even low-level exposure to pesticides so dangerous. A dose that is too small to cause immediate harm is stored in the body and remains active for a considerable period; with each subsequent exposure the cumulative "body burden" increases, and along with it the chance of serious illness. These properties also put species at the top of the food chain at special risk because they absorb large amounts of pesticide from the lower organisms they consume, a process called "biomagnification."

The Culture of Pesticides

Carson takes great pains to show that it is the imprudent use of pesticides, as much as their intrinsic properties, which makes them one of the worst health threats of the twentieth century. Dosing blankets with DDT, spraying densely populated neighborhoods from the air, and pouring pesticide into ponds to kill mosquitoes might have poisoned the planet if not for *Silent Spring*. From the vantage point of a more environmentally conscious age, it is difficult to understand how such practices could have been so popular. Years ahead of her time, Carson was dumbfounded.

As nearly as Carson could figure, mid-twentieth-century attitudes toward synthetic pesticides were warped by a trio of interacting forces: the chemical industry, government, and what she calls "Neanderthal science." In calling science "Nean-

Topics for Further Study

- Look carefully at the material on pesticides at the web site of the Environmental Protection Agency (http://www.epa.gov/ebtpages/pesticides.html). Does the government's attitude toward these products seem different today than it was in 1962, as described in *Silent Spring*? Report your findings in a one-page summary.

- Imagine that it is 1962. Write a one- or two-page letter using what you learned from the book to persuade your state representative or senator to do something about the problem Carson describes. Be sure to tell your representative specifically what you would like him or her to do.

- Identify three passages in *Silent Spring* that seem particularly compelling. Does Carson's language (word choice, tone, images, etc.) contribute something to the force of these excerpts. How? Summarize your observations in a brief essay.

- Examine the labels of some pesticide products around the house, taking note of their active ingredients. At http://www.epa.gov/pesticides/info.htm, see what you can find out about the health hazards of these products. Report your findings in a one-page summary.

derthal," she has two characteristics of contemporary methodology in mind. The first is the extraordinarily high degree of specialization. Knowledge might appear to advance at a faster pace along the narrow paths of modern research, but it has also become more fragmented; the entomologist developing a pesticide to control the hungry gypsy moth, for example, is unlikely to know much about the chemical's harmful effects on non-targeted organisms such as birds and fish. The second defect of science, especially in the applied areas, is its habit of conceiving problems in military terms, an outlook it shared to some degree with culture as a whole in the aftermath of World War II. Solutions are always seen to depend on exerting the greatest possible force over an "enemy." This logic expresses itself in pest management strategies that advocate applying the most lethal substances available in saturating quantities to eradicate entire species. As an alternative to the "total war" approach to solving problems, Carson proposes an approach that exploits the natural tendency of systems to seek balance; with a little help, it has been proven time and time again, the natural environment can solve its own problems cheaply, safely, and effectively. *Silent Spring* recounts some elegant, low-intensity, "biotic" interventions, such as cultivating certain plants to encourage species that compete with pests or introducing a pest-specific disease into a blighted area.

The second major culprit behind the overuse of pesticides is the chemical industry itself. The corporate giants use their enormous political leverage to co-opt government agencies and engage in large scale disinformation campaigns to defuse growing public concern about synthetic poisons. To a certain degree, the short-sightedness of science described above is itself a product of industry influence: because pesticide makers are the largest funders of research in the field, most investigation tends to harmonize with corporate interests; hence the paucity of knowledge about the risks of synthetic chemicals and the limited effort to develop safer, "biotic" alternatives. It is worth noting that, as outrageous as the posture of the industry might appear to some, Carson eschews moralistic argument to make a case that is all the more compelling for its sheer pragmatism. Pesticide makers, she concedes, will always have as their sole concern the profitable sale of pesticides. But if it is absurd to expect them to take a broader view, she concludes, it is just as unreasonable to allow them any role in the process by which public policy on pesticides is determined, a process in which the primary concern must always be saftey.

Style

Clarity

A writer's style is always at some level shaped by her purposes, and these can usually be identified without too much difficulty in a work of nonfiction. Indeed, in the case of *Silent Spring*, Carson really only has one aim: to raise public awareness about the dangers of pesticides with the ultimate goal of bringing about more prudent pest-management practices. What stylistic necessities does this task impose on the writer? The first is accessibility. If her message is aimed at the public, then she must write in a manner that is suitable for the widest possible circle of readers.

The second imperative arises from her determination not merely to inform readers but to motivate them to activism. Carson must put the case in such a way that individuals feel obliged to get involved.

Finding a style that is suitable for a general audience is tricky in writing a book like *Silent Spring* where so much technical information must be presented. The writer must make the complex comprehensible but avoid doing so in a manner that oversimplifies and therefore undermines the authority of scientific information. Carson had been doing just that for over two decades, first as a science writer for the federal government, then as a bestselling interpreter of marine biology. Not surprisingly, her technique is easiest to examine in those sections of *Silent Spring* that focus on the most complicated matters—chapters like "Elixirs of Death" (on pesticide chemistry) and "Through a Narrow Window" (on cell biology).

In these two chapters readers find chemical nomenclature ("dichlor-diphenyl-trichloroethane"!), passages on neurophysiology, debate about toxicity reckoned in "parts per million," and exotic terminology drawn from cell biology. Though one might think it counterproductive to include such language in a book aimed at a general audience, Carson is careful not to go too far, and the ultimate effect is quite positive. Not only does the scientific nitty-gritty lend the argument an irresistible objectivity and authority, but the author's own ease with this complicated material builds trust in the reader. What keeps readers afloat in this tide of esoterica (knowledge or information known only to a small group) are Carson's clear explanations. Never does she touch on a technical subject without a clarifying digression, even if it requires a paragraph or two. The unfailing success of these passages lies mainly in her ability to make the abstract concrete. For example, organic chemistry is elucidated through metaphor; the component substances are described as "building blocks" that chemists assemble into more elaborate "Lego"-like compounds. The effects of pesticides on cellular metabolism are likened to the overheating of an engine.

Persuasiveness

Carson hopes to incite her readers to action, and the scientific data, no matter how well explained, lacks the requisite emotional appeal. To get readers to care about problems like the estrogenic properties of organic chemicals and the depletion of adenine triphosphate, Carson must make them not only understandable but also meaningful.

Carson's solution is to use highly charged language to keep the human implications of the pesticide problem in the foreground. For every use of the word "herbicide," for example, there is one of "weed-killer." The following fragments are culled from just the first few pages of *Silent Spring*: "Lethal," "battery of poisons," "endless stream" of new chemicals, "violent crossfire" of pesticide use, "fanatic zeal" of pest-control agencies, "tranquilizing pills" of chemical industry disinformation, "agents of death," "havoc," "indiscriminate" spraying.

Still more striking are those passages in which Carson uses such language to paint unsettling images of acute poisoning in animals and humans: birds losing balance, suffering tremors and convulsions, and then abruptly dying; a baby vomiting, experiencing a seizure and unconsciousness, and ending up a "vegetable"; a housewife wracked by fever and never-ending joint pain. Few things affect readers as powerfully as the specter of death, and Carson conjures it again and again in *Silent Spring*. Pesticides are associated with some of people's worst fears, and she does not hesitate to exploit the connection, evoking among other things the long agony of cancer and the heartbreaking spectacle of children plagued by birth defects.

In such a fashion, the writer virtually assures that readers will become anxious about the problem. Many commentators have noted that Carson very cannily draws an analogy between pesticides and radioactive fallout, a comparison that could not have failed to unnerve readers at the height of the Cold War. But there is quite enough haunting imagery in *Silent Spring* for it to have stirred up the public even without that powerful association.

Historical Context

The Rise of Synthetic Pesticides

So influential a role did Carson's *Silent Spring* play in the quickening of concern about pesticides that it is often assumed that she was the first to call attention to the problem. But pesticides had been in wide use since the nineteenth century, and debates about their effects on health had been going on for decades. But the nature of the chemical threat changed dramatically after World War II, and Carson was the first popular writer to explain this development to Americans.

During the early twentieth century, the most commonly used chemical pesticides were arsenic compounds. They were deadly enough to cause a few health scares, but a far cry from the poisons that wartime chemical weapons research bequeathed to the world—an entirely new and ever expanding family of man-made toxins called organochlorines, the most notorious of which was DDT. The new pesticides were more lethal than their predecessors, more numerous, and more widely used. They also stayed toxic over a long period, accumulated in the body, and concentrated in the food chain. By the late 1950s, a handful of scientists, naturalists, and attentive citizens could hear the "rumblings of an avalanche"; ecological and public health problems of unprecedented proportion were beginning to come into view. Rachel Carson was the first to bring this emerging crisis to the attention of the general public in a compelling way.

Science, Technology, and Nature

Since the very first days of the industrial revolution, technology has always been a mixed blessing. It has helped humans to create and to destroy; it has both enriched life and impoverished it. Until perhaps the present moment, which has seen such extraordinary breakthroughs in information science, genetics, and astrophysics, the mid-twentieth century was the most dizzying era of all time on the technological front. The pace of progress, the breadth of innovation, and the size of the strides were quite unprecedented. It was the age in which humanity got its first taste of ultimate power in areas such as organic chemistry where scientists created substances that never occurred in nature, and physics, which spawned the atomic bomb.

Rapid progress has always been intoxicating, and the mid-century boom was no different in this respect. In the heady early years, it seemed that the new know-how would allow civilization to solve all of its problems. But soon this optimism disintegrated in the usual way: the physical universe turned out to be more complicated than it had appeared, and once-powerful tools rapidly exhausted their usefulness. What set this particular phase of disillusionment apart from earlier ones was civilization's recognition that, for the first time in history, technology could threaten life on a global scale. The

Compare & Contrast

- **1962:** Thalidomide, often prescribed for morning sickness, is suspected of causing birth defects, adding to already widespread concern about the dangers of synthetic chemicals.

  Today: The Environmental Protection Agency requires pesticide makers to submit data that will allow the agency to determine the special risks of their products for children.

- **1962:** Watson, Crick, and Wilkins win a Nobel Prize for describing the molecular structure of DNA.

  Today: Scientists complete a provisional map of the entire human genome.

- **1963:** President Lyndon Johnson signs the Clean Air Act, legislation designed to protect air quality in the United States.

  Today: The United Nations agree to the Kyoto Protocol, a plan for reducing emission of greenhouse gases.

---

end result was not just more modest expectations about what science could achieve at that moment, but a series of major social movements (environmentalism, the anti-nuclear movement, etc.) that saw humanity's only hope for survival in a radical reconception of its relationship to the natural world. *Silent Spring* sprang from this loss of faith in science and technology and also intensified it.

Critical Overview

Critics writing about *Silent Spring* when it first appeared disagreed very little about the author's literary gifts. An anonymous reviewer for *Life* magazine called the book vivid, a work of great "grace" by a "deliberate researcher and superb writer." *Time*'s reviewer echoed much of this praise; once again, Carson was said to be a "graceful writer" who demonstrated considerable "skill in building her frightening case." In assessing the book's claims, however, the early reviews were sharply divided. Periodicals aimed at birders and other nature-oriented readers, who likely already knew something about dangers of pesticides, found Carson's argument unassailable. The mainstream press, on the other hand, was skeptical on the whole. Some of the resistance stemmed from a natural reluctance to accept what was, after all, a shocking proposition—

the technological "miracle" of pesticides, long claimed to be safe by the chemical industry and trusted government officials, was a Trojan horse that threatened life on a global scale. For example, the reviewer for *Life* found much that was compelling in Carson's "amply buttressed" argument, anxiously hoped that she had "overstated her case" in predicting widespread destruction.

> The scenes she describes so vividly—the neighborhood where all the robins perished after eating DDT-engorged earthworms, the woman who died of leukemia after repeatedly spraying spiders in her cellar, the salmon streams emptied by seeping poisons—are all true enough. But they are isolated examples.

One can only conclude that the critic was groping for reassurance here in turning away from the obvious point of Carson's catalog of pesticide disasters, which was that the incidents alluded to were harbingers of worse, more widespread trouble. That he largely shared the author's concerns is clear enough in the review's conclusion where he called for the very same remedies that *Silent Spring* urges: tougher restrictions on pesticide use and more government funding for research.

Not all of the skeptical reviews were as friendly as *Life* magazine's; *Silent Spring* was the target of a well-funded smear campaign by the chemical industry, and a startling number of the early critics align themselves with that effort in one way or another. Indeed, in a magazine as influential in the

A worker in a protective suit sprays pesticide on ferns inside a greenhouse

shaping of public opinion as *Time,* there appeared a review that so harmonized with the position of pesticide makers that its author, if he was not in fact an industry hatchet man, might as well have been. Calling Carson a "hysterical" woman, the reviewer employed the industry's favorite attack on her and then presented fragments of some of the harshest passages of *Silent Spring* in an attempt to make its author seem unbalanced. For example, he cited her "emotion fanning" claim that DDT is found in mother's milk and her claim that people "can't add pesticide to water anywhere without threatening the purity of water everywhere." Elsewhere the distortions are even more pronounced, as where he called the writer's advocacy of biologic pest management "reckless primitivism." So egregious are the misreadings and lapses that it is hard not to conclude that the review's object was damage control, not rational debate about the issue.

Since the publication of *Silent Spring,* critical opinion of the book has changed in three important ways. First, no one questions the soundness of Carson's argument anymore; forty years of scientific research has confirmed virtually all of the book's major claims. The second change is related to the historical importance of *Silent Spring,* often called the *Uncle Tom's Cabin* of modern environ-

mentalism. In "The Reception of *Silent Spring,*" Craig Waddell offered one of the most concise assessments of the book's significance.

> Ernest Hemingway once wrote that "[a]ll modern American literature comes from one book by Mark Twain called *Huckleberry Finn.*" It would not be too much of an exaggeration to make a similar claim for *Silent Spring*'s relationship to the modern environmental movement. Although the American environmental movement traces its roots to such nineteenth-century visionaries as Henry David Thoreau, George Perkins Marsh, and John Muir—all of whom were concerned with the preservation of the wilderness— the modern environmental movement, with its emphasis on pollution and the degradation of the quality of life on the planet, may fairly be said to have begun with one book by Rachel Carson called *Silent Spring.*

Today, more and more critics are turning their attention to historical considerations. Several examples of such work appear in a recently published anthology of essays called *And No Birds Sing;* for instance, Ralph Lutts argues that the book's initial popularity was in some large measure attributable to the panic over atomic fallout, and Cheryll Glotfelty shows how Carson's critique of "man's [pesticide] war against nature" exploits the tropes of Cold War discourse.

The third major change in the criticism of *Silent Spring* might be guessed from comparisons of Carson's book to *Uncle Tom's Cabin* and *Huckleberry Finn.* Having earned a place among the American classics for its historical significance, it is now the object of the close textual scrutiny always given to such works. *Silent Spring* is treated as a literary text across the usual range of interests: in "An Inventional Archaeology," Christine Oravec looks at Carson's manuscript to learn about the book's composition; Edward Corbett's "A Topical Analysis" examines the argument through the lens of classical rhetoric; and "*Silent Spring* and Science Fiction" by Carol Gartner points to its generic kinship with science fiction. Given Carson's considerable talents as a writer, this recent interest in literary dimensions of *Silent Spring* seems on the whole a promising development.

Criticism

Joyce Hart

Hart has degrees in English literature and creative writing, and she is a copyeditor and published writer. In this essay, she examines Carson's references to potential human suffering as a result of the overuse of chemicals as presented in her book Silent Spring.

Given time, states Carson in her book *Silent Spring,* nature will heal itself. "Life adjusts." At least this was true through the previous millennia. But in the modern world, humans are quickly running out of time. Carson even says that "there is no time" left, because modern-day humans are creating havoc at a pace too fast for nature to heal. Modern civilizations are not only quick in creating devastation, they are also broad-ranged, as they are creating synthetic substances that have "no counterparts in nature." Nature will need generations of time to cleanse herself from the toxic pollutants. Carson wrote her book in 1962 as a warning, and since then, things have only gotten worse.

It is through no fault of Carson's that people have not heeded her warnings. Actually, many people have heeded them, but still the chemical companies prevail. Carson died in 1964 of cancer. Who knows if the source of her illness was the chemical carcinogens in her environment. Maybe she sensed her own fate, and tried with her writing to save the generations that were to come after her. How she did this can be found in her book in which she carefully lists all the chemicals that were being

produced in her lifetime, as humanity made every attempt to control nature. But her book is not just a catalog of deadly poisons; it is a book about suffering, potential as well as actual. It is about nature suffering in all levels of her myriad forms. It is also a book of what people are doing to one another and to themselves.

Humans are subjected to "dangerous chemicals, from the moment of conception until death," Carson states. Chemicals are everywhere. They are in the soil, water, and air. They are found in almost every household: under the bathroom sink in the form of cleaners, on shelves in the garage in forms of paint thinners and glues, in the kitchen in form of insecticides, in the bedroom in the forms of hair sprays and other cosmetics. They are present in food and drink, even in the milk that mothers produce from their own bodies; they are even present "in the tissues of the unborn child."

The chemicals that Carson focuses on are those whose prevalence began during World War Two, "in the course of developing agents of chemical warfare," and were first promoted on a commercial level when it was discovered that these chemicals were useful in killing insects. But what Carson believed was the worst element of these chemicals was not that they were capable of poisoning but that these new chemical discoveries were capable of making potent and irreversible changes on a deep, biological level in every living thing on earth. These new synthetic chemicals could enter the plants as well as animals and "change them in sinister . . . ways. . . . They prevent the normal functioning of various organs, and they may initiate in certain cells the slow and irreversible change that leads to malignancy." Carson was ahead of her time. She sensed scientific truths that would not be proven until after her death. She sensed the cancers that would become more and more commonplace.

Carson warns mankind in part by listing details of the incredible number of new chemicals that are being produced each year. She lists their names and their effects, explaining that "if we are going to live so intimately with these chemicals—eating and drinking them, taking them into the very marrow of our bones—we had better know something about their nature and their power." But it is not until she gets very up close and personal in her discussions that the full power of her book takes effect. The lists of chemicals and their potential power are daunting, nightmarish material, but names don't make the same impact as the fear of suffering and pain. And

What Do I Read Next?

- Before she published *Silent Spring*, Rachel Carson wrote three popular works of natural history on the ocean, the best known of which is *The Sea Around Us* (1951).

- Jonathan Harr's *A Civil Action* (1995) tells a powerful story about one community that looked to the law to protect it from dangerous chemicals.

- Another classic work of environmental literature is John McPhee's *Encounters With the Archdruid* (1971), an engaging meditation on the then-current conflict over land use.

- In *Losing Ground: American Environmentalism at the Close of the Twentieth Century* (1996), Mark Dowie chronicles the history of the movement with an eye to the errors that have kept it from realizing its full potential.

---

the source of some of that potential suffering might be as close as the nearest water fountain. For example, it is alarming to know that chemists are creating excessive quantities of chemical compounds in their laboratories, but it is even more frightening to find out that even more deadly compounds are being created in the water that people drink. Runoffs from various chemical sources meet one another in the water resources of this earth, such as when fertilizers mix with insecticides in ground water and create "mingled chemicals that no responsible chemist would think of combining in his laboratory." Even if chemists know the effects that their chemical compounds might have on the living things of nature, they do not, Carson warns, know the effects of the compounds being created on their own in the rivers, the lakes, and the sewers.

Another interesting but scary fact that Carson presents is that chemicals from insecticides and fertilizers can remain in the soil more than twelve years after they have been applied. What does this imply for the farmer who wants to grow foods organically? Just how organic can food be if there is no virgin soil left in which to plant crops? Even if the ideal of organic produce is discarded, oftentimes a chemical used to control insects on one plant kill the rotating crop that is planted the following season, and the season following that one, too. For instance, in the state of Washington, farmers successfully used a chemical to kill a bug that was harming a grain called hops. Later, when grapes were planted in these same fields, the roots of the grape vines died. When planted again the next year, the result was the same. Carson was very concerned that applying these chemicals without fully realizing their potential for destruction was courting ecological disaster.

Carson talks about all kinds of potential disasters, some more severe than others. On the lighter side, she mentions a more aesthetic kind of disaster, one that wipes out the beauty of nature. Using the excuse of traffic control and safety, there was, in Carson's time, and largely remains today, the practice of spraying weeds with an herbicide along all the country's roadsides and highways. In a poetic voice, Carson declares that in those rare places where herbicides had not been sprayed, she would drive along the country roads and her spirit would be lifted by "the sight of the drifts of white clover or the clouds of purple vetch with here and there the flaming cup of a wood lily." These are not weeds that need to be controlled, she says. They are places of great, wild beauty. There is seldom a need to kill back the wildflowers, especially in the dimensions that are employed. In some states, the height at which the spraying occurs is from road level to eight feet above the road. This is needless overuse, Carson contends. She also cites other abuses like the contractor who was caught discharging the herbicides from his trunk into a protected wood side area, a place where no spraying had been authorized. Another contractor's negligence was a little more severe. He purchased chemicals from a "zealous chemical salesman." The herbicide contained arse-

" Another interesting but scary fact that Carson presents is that chemicals from insecticides and fertilizers can remain in the soil more than twelve years after they have been applied. What does this imply for the farmer who wants to grow foods organically?"

nic, which eventually ended up killing twelve cows. This was all done in the name of killing weeds. Herbicides, states Carson, "give a giddy sense of power over nature to those who wield them." In the process of using them, herbicides destroy natural beauty. They leave behind a "sterile and hideous world."

More important and much more painful for humans, is the effect of chemicals on their own bodies. In particular, Carson expresses her views on some very serious, life-threatening diseases that have been linked to the use of man-made chemicals. She begins by explaining that cancer-causing agents are as old as the earth. Radiation from the sun and certain rocks in earth's crust has always been capable of producing malignancies. Over time, human biology adapted to these radiations in varying degrees. But with the rapid development of man-made carcinogens, a medical term for cancer-producing substances, human biology has not been able to keep pace. "As a result these powerful substances could easily penetrate the inadequate defenses of the body." Added to this problem is the inadequate research done on the causes of cancer. Chemical use is approved without fully understanding the potential complications. Often it takes years of use before the slow but steady buildup of chemicals in a human body results in a malignancy. Admonishing the government as well as the chemical companies who produce the insecticides and pesticides, Carson writes, "Our recognition of the agents that produce it [the cancerous malignancies] has been slow to mature."

All humans are susceptible to cancers. No age is immune. As a matter of fact, Carson reports that in the beginning of the nineteenth century, it was a rarity to find cancer in children. But by the time her book was published, not only was it not considered rare for children to have cancer, children were being born with cancer already growing inside their bodies. Apparently the developing fetus is the most susceptible to cancer-producing agents. Whereas the pregnant mother may not be affected, the agents may penetrate her body and the placenta and "act on the rapidly developing fetal tissues." As newer and more powerful chemicals are used in the production of food, pregnant women, who eat this food, pass on the carcinogens to their children unaware. Chemicals are used on food without full knowledge of their effects as well as without full disclosure of their potential danger. The result is that cancer rates climb.

There has also been a rise in cases of leukemia, a malignant blood disorder. Whereas malignant cancerous growths may take years to develop, leukemia can occur soon after exposure to radiation and toxic chemicals. In 1960, the Mayo Clinic, a world-famous medical institution, published an opinion that stated that the increase in leukemia could almost definitely be linked to an over-exposure to pesticides. Some of the case studies involved people doing simple tasks around their homes, such as the woman who tried to rid her house of spiders or the man who tried to kill the cockroaches in his office. Both used commercial bug sprays. Both were afflicted with sudden painful symptoms that were eventually diagnosed as leukemia. Both died. Another case involved two farm workers whose job it was to unload bags of insecticide. In all these cases, death was swift.

The world is quickly becoming a sea of carcinogens, says Carson. And carcinogens are linked to death. But unlike the last century, where mankind's biggest health concern was contagious disease, carcinogens could be easily removed from the earth's environment. At least a majority of the man-made carcinogens could. She suggests that in addition to looking for a cure for cancer, people should be re-evaluating chemical use. How much is really necessary? Chemicals, she writes, "have become entrenched in our world in two ways: first, and ironically, through man's search for a better and easier way of life; second, because the manufacture and sale of such chemicals has become an accepted part of our economy and our way of life." In other words, if mankind put them here, mankind surely could get rid of them. And along with ridding this earth of chemicals, civilization would rid their own bodies of cancer.

Carson ends her book with a bit of irony and finally with a hint of hope. The irony is that in mankind's efforts to control nature, people are poisoning not only themselves, their food, their water, but their future generations. Added to this is the most ironic fact of all. In an effort to rid the world of pests, to make this world a better place to live, mankind has tried to kill every insect that gets in the way. As a result, insecticides have killed the weak. Stronger insects have not only survived, they have created insecticide-resistant offspring. Added to this is the fact that in killing the insects that were detrimental, mankind has also killed the beneficial insects that helped to maintain a balance in the sheer numbers of insects. So now the earth is suffering through stronger and more powerful plagues.

But there is hope. Carson discusses in her last chapter some of the research that was going on in the 1960s, research that is continuing today. There is the research in the relationships between different kinds of insects in the hopes that by encouraging one type of benevolent insect, a farmer might curb the propagation of destructive types without the use of chemicals. Some researchers were looking into the possibility of sterilizing male insects as a way of controlling their numbers. Others were working on the creation of natural lures or introducing natural predators.

Carson encourages her readers at the end of her book to take a holistic approach to life. She reminds people, who are trying to create favorable environments for themselves, that they are not the only ones living in that environment. Humans are not the only creatures on earth. "Only by taking account of such life forces and by cautiously seeking to guide them into channels favorable to ourselves can we hope to achieve a reasonable accommodation between the insect hordes and ourselves," she writes. A lot of suffering has been caused by the rush to use man-made chemicals, a rush to find a quick fix to stop mosquitoes from biting, stop cockroaches from raiding trash cans, stop grubs from consuming the roots of that all-perfect lawn. The suffering is everywhere, in the fish in the water, the birds in the air, the people who live in the cities, the people who live on farms. Carson's book is a portrayal of that suffering. It is also a portrayal of the causes of that suffering, and its very simplistic cure. Curb the use of chemicals.

Source: Joyce Hart, Critical Essay on *Silent Spring,* in *Nonfiction Classics for Students,* The Gale Group, 2001.

Yaakov Garb

In the following essay, Garb explores how Silent Spring*'s emphasis on "natural balance and the web of life" rather than politics led to its wide acceptance, and impacted the book's logic.*

Scattered reports of problems with pesticides had appeared in the technical literature from the fifties onwards, but it was only in 1962 that a wide-ranging critique of pesticides was published for a popular audience. Brought out by a major trade press, this book charted the tremendous increase in the production and use of these chemicals since World War II, and documented their failings. Focusing on chlorinated hydrocarbons and DDT in particular, it described their physiological effects, their impact on human health and wildlife, and the inadequacy of existing pesticide regulation. The book demonstrated how pesticides were not only harmful, but ultimately self-defeating, since pests soon developed resistance while beneficial insects and animals that helped keep them in check were killed. Further pesticide applications to counter a resurgence of the targeted species and infestations of new insects that weren't a problem before began an escalating cycle. The book proposed replacing this hubristic attempt to master nature, which was destroying the earth's capacity to support human life, with a philosophy of wise management of ecosystems and the development of ecologically sound biological control of pests. These changes, the author stressed, should not jeopardize nutrition and the American economy, and pesticides should not be banned, only used very selectively.

The book flopped, it received short negative reviews in the literary supplements of the *New York Times* and the *Times* of London, and not much else, and soon disappeared. I doubt many of you have heard of its author, Lewis Herber, or remember its title, *Our Synthetic Environment.* A few months later, however, in three June issues of the *New Yorker* magazine and then in the fall as a book, Rachel Carson's critique of pesticides was published. Her *Silent Spring* contained in amplified form every one of the charges against pesticides I have just listed for Herber's work, but no substantially new ones. Yet Carson's critique created an immediate storm of media and governmental attention. There was much praise, as well as angry rebuttal and attacks, including a fierce and well-funded campaign by the chemical industry to counter Carson's message. Within a year of its publication, *Silent Spring* had prompted programs for sci-

> ❝ But although it provided Carson with a versatile conceptual framework and familiar stirring images, there are difficulties in founding a treatment of environmental destruction on a depoliticized notion of 'nature.'❞

entific research into the hazards of pesticides, brought significant changes in their regulation, spurred public debate on environmental practices more generally, inspired a younger generation of environmental activists, and made ecology a household word. Carson's initially embattled viewpoint on pesticide problems rapidly became absorbed into public sentiment. It is standard in the historiography of environmentalism to speak of the book as a—perhaps the—watershed of the modern environmental movement.

Why did these two works have such a different fate? What enabled *Silent Spring*'s critique of pesticides to become so broadly accepted in middle-class America? Part of the answer lies, no doubt, in luck and in the *New Yorker* forum. Also contributing to the book's success were Carson's standing and skills as a gifted writer and her biological training, which Herber lacked. She was able to offer a terrifyingly eloquent portrait of what it would mean to inhabit an increasingly toxic landscape. Building on postwar anxieties about technological excess and radioactivity, Carson's novel descriptions of our vulnerability to new chemicals that acted in eerie and unexpected ways were shocking and galvanizing.

In this essay, however, I want to consider how *Silent Spring*'s success depended on its politics and, relatedly, its conception of nature. By not grappling head on with the political and economic factors that led to the entrenchment of pesticides in postwar America, and by centering its arguments instead on conceptions of natural balance and the web of life, the book was made palatable to a wide audience. I want to explore the mixed results of this success. The book's broad acceptance gave it considerable if circuitous political-economic impact. At the same time, its avoidance of politics troubled the logic of Carson's argument.

Herber's unnoticed book can scarcely serve as a model for a more politically desirable intervention, but it does highlight another conception of politics and nature that was possible, if not broadly acceptable, in that moment. Written pseudonymously by the journalist and anarchist theorist Murray Bookchin, who later became well known as the founder of social ecology, *Our Synthetic Environment* briskly covered almost all of the substance of Carson's critique of pesticides in less than twenty pages. The rest of the book documented the many other ways in which human health was compromised by the industrialized, urbanized way of life that increasingly characterized postwar America. Chemical hazards to human food supplies other than pesticides (synthetic hormones, antibiotics, and additives) were described in detail, as was the degradation and erosion of soil by large-scale agriculture, and the deterioration of the nutritional quality of crops raised on synthetic fertilizers. And beyond these problems of the food system, Bookchin described how health was endangered by a polluted, stressful, and dehumanizing urban environment; by the radioactive byproducts of nuclear testing and energy production; and by the rise in heart disease and cancer associated with lifestyle and environmental causes.

This range of assaults to human well-being and nature, claimed Bookchin, were of a piece, and originated in unviable social arrangements. They demanded a return to rural and agricultural communities of human scale through deindustrialization, decentralization, and a reining in of the profit motive, so that the "most pernicious laws of the market place" were not "given precedence over the most compelling laws of biology." Individual action or even remedial legislation were not, in his mind, sufficient to get at the heart of these problems; a sound ecological practice was synonymous, for Bookchin, with shaping a satisfying social life. Bookchin's pill was clearly too big, bitter, and unfamiliar for most Americans to swallow at that time. His book was dismissed as "nice sentiments, only impossible," as "numbing" or "unmanageable" in its scope, and as offering only "incoherent," "intangible," or hopelessly utopian proposals.

Carson's Nature

Whereas the focus of Bookchin's analysis was "the relationship between human and human," *Silent Spring*'s center of gravity lay in Carson's reworking of deeply conventional conceptions of the balance of nature and the web of life. When the president of the chemical manufacturing company Monsanto characterized her as "a fanatic defender of the cult of the balance of nature," he was reacting to what is indeed the book's central metaphor. Carson's nature—a "complex, precise, and highly integrated system" characterized by relations of "interdependence and mutual benefit," and regulating checks and balances—was the new science of ecology's rendition of a conception that goes back to antiquity. In its explicitly theological eighteenth-century form, for example, the harmony and order underlying nature's economy had a divine source: God's providence ensured a system of perpetual balance among all living things, in which each creature had its allotted place. The "balance of nature" provided Carson with a norm against which human interference could be assessed and challenged. The existing "system of relationships between living things," she claimed, "cannot be safely ignored any more than the law of gravity can be defied with impunity." A second guiding metaphor in the book is the related notion of an "ecological web of life" whose "threads" "bind" together organisms and their environment so that even minute changes in one area reverberate over space and time.

These notions—the balance of nature, the ecological web, "the natural"—do a tremendous amount of persuasive work. Nature whole is the basis for *Silent Spring*'s unsettling tidings of balance lost. It allowed Carson to invert a tradition of nature writing that celebrated harmony and connectedness to cast pesticides as unnatural and sinister. Thus the book is dense with images of dislocation: a living world "shattered," landscapes "bludgeoned," threads "broken," fabric "ripped apart," delicate processes "uncoupled." Carson brought a tone of elegy into conventions of wonder by introducing her reader to the unseen dynamics and relations of the natural world (a hidden sea of groundwater, invisible bird flyways and fish migration paths, teeming microscopic soil life) through portraying their disruption by pesticides. And by including the delicate internal realms of human and animal physiology within nature's balanced and interconnected system, she seamlessly and chillingly joined inner and outer landscapes, ecology and human health, launching a new phase of environmental concern.

But although it provided Carson with a versatile conceptual framework and familiar stirring images, there are difficulties in founding a treatment of

environmental destruction on a depoliticized notion of "nature." Terms like the "natural," or the "balance of nature" can obscure the social relations and priorities that go into evaluating environmental practices. Take, for example, Carson's preference for biological rather than chemical methods of pest control as less disturbing of "nature's balance." This term reifies judgments about the respective benefits and costs—to humans—of these methods, creating internal contradictions in Carson's account. Why, for instance, is the importation of an exotic pathogen (a bacteria) to kill the Japanese beetle a "natural" means of control? Is this intervention—which Carson notes in passing kills not only the target species but at least forty other species in the scarabaeid family—more respectful of the balance of nature than certain pesticides?

Similar questions could be asked about each of the biological control technologies Carson celebrates: juvenile hormones, chemical attractants, repellent sounds, microbial and viral infection of insects, introduced predators and parasites. For example, she enthusiastically endorses the dispersal of X-ray-sterilized male screw-worms and heralds the "complete extinction of the screw-worm in the Southeast" as a "brilliant success" and "a triumphant demonstration of the worth of scientific creativity." Slipping into the militaristic imagery she objects to in the proponents of pesticide spraying, she talks approvingly of research that turns "insect sterilization into a weapon that would wipe out a major insect enemy." But surely the difference between this celebrated method and the chemical practices Carson castigates lies not in their inherent degrees of "naturalness" but in (human) judgments about their respective impacts. Had Carson chosen to cast the X-ray sterilization of males as unnatural, the rhetorical resources she uses to disparage pesticides could easily have been redirected, as in the following imagined rendition of the same facts Carson gives in her celebratory account.

> Rather than seeking to understand the intricate life cycle and ecology of this tiny insect, scientists invented a scheme that would allow them, by infiltrating the very heart of their natural reproductive cycle, to sever the link between generations. Day after day, in huge "fly factories," technicians bombarded male insects with mutagenic radiation and then, using 20 light planes working 5 to 6 hours daily, these insidious carriers of genetically altered material were dispersed over huge areas. Unsuspecting females mated with these seemingly normal products of the laboratory. While these unions produced eggs, these were, without exception, sterile. In less than two years, the species had vanished.

The ease with which a creative triumph becomes a tragedy of technological hubris highlights the instability of the categories of natural and unnatural.

Bookchin's analysis in *Our Synthetic Environment,* which didn't rest on notions of "the balance of nature," is spared these particular paradoxes. As part of nature, humans are justified, claims Bookchin, in making the world's fate up as they go—if they do so with an eye first and foremost toward "promoting human health and fitness." There is, he argues, no preordained state that must be preserved forever, and the "quasi-mystical" and unreserved valorization of "nature" and the "natural" is misguided, "an impediment to a rational outlook." For him human emotions in the presence of nature are not an indication of nature's special metaphysical status (as they were for the Transcendentalists with whom Carson sympathized), and reticence in using technology to remake nature in service of our needs should not be sentimentalized. "Our nostalgia," he claims, "springs from a growing need to restore the normal, balanced, and manageable rhythms of *human* life—that is, an environment that meets *our* requirements as individuals and biological beings" (emphasis mine). (Note that having forgone biological nature as a guide for human action, Bookchin immediately recovers another nature: the "normal" and "balanced" rhythms of human life.)

Politics, and Its Avoidance

The massive adoption of synthetic pesticides in the postwar decades in America was facilitated by a densely interrelated network of factors. The dynamics of the competitive free market pressured farmers, suppliers of farm technology, and food processors toward pesticide use. In addition, pesticides were first tested and mass produced during a period when priorities were skewed by wartime agendas; they were institutionally and culturally entrenched at the war's end. Existing standards and legal procedures were not fitted to enforce the regulation and testing of this new technology, nor to establish liability for damages it caused. And a pest-control method that was chemical-based, fast-acting, broad-spectrum, and seemed to offer total eradication accorded well with certain American cultural values. In the face of these forces, the underfunded and mismanaged biological control methods that had shown great promise in the decades prior to the war did not stand a chance, and were soon eclipsed.

Silent Spring, however, made visible only a tiny part of this network of factors. This is because

Carson cast the entrenchment of pesticides and the call for their replacement as primarily an epistemic and moral problem, rather than a political-economic one. This, I believe, is a large part of what allowed her work to be so broadly accepted.

The book's muted political stance was in part a consequence of its author's background. Carson came to her book as a biologist, as an author immersed in the nature writing tradition since adolescence, and as a former writer and editor of public information publications for the Fish and Wildlife Service. (Bookchin was steeped in the writings of the Frankfurt School, in anarchist theory, and Marxism.) But an avoidance of overt politics was also a strategic choice, one of several Carson made in carefully shaping a defensible challenge of pesticide practices. Linda Lear in her forthcoming biography of Carson shows, for example, how Carson chose to include only a small amount of the extensive evidence she had for the environmental origins of cancer, and declined to mention organic gardening for fear of being associated with food faddists. Nor did Carson invoke the biocentric convictions about the inherent worth of other forms of life that she expressed in other writing. Similarly, while it is clear from her remarks in interviews and from her collaboration with the politically outspoken director of the U.S. Department of Agriculture Biological Survey, Clarence Cottam, that Carson was keenly aware of the financial incentives that skewed the development, use, and evaluation of pesticides, she kept this out of the book.

Carson had been warned of the hostility her pesticide work would invoke. She wrote in a period that some have called the "McCarthy era of the environmental movement," in which those who questioned the use of pesticides were specifically branded as being against the spirit of free enterprise. After the appearance of the *New Yorker* articles, for example, Louis A. McLean, secretary and general counsel of Velsicol, the sole manufacturer of chlordane and heptachlor, sent a five-page registered letter to Houghton Mifflin suggesting that it might want to reconsider publishing *Silent Spring.* His letter built up to the following statement:

> In such a climate even some members of theUnfortunately, in addition to the sincere opinions by natural food faddists, Audubon groups and others, members of the chemical industry in this country and in Western Europe must deal with sinister influences whose attacks on the chemical industry have a dual purpose: (1) to create the false impression that all business is grasping and immoral, and (2) to reduce the use of agricultural chemicals in this country and in

the countries of Western Europe, so that our supply of food will be reduced to east-curtain parity. Many innocent groups are financed and led into attacks on the chemical industry by these sinister parties.

In such a climate even some members of the Sierra Club's board of directors opposed the appearance of a positive review of *Silent Spring* in the Club Bulletin. A more forthrightly "political" analysis would probably not have survived to have *Silent Spring*'s political impact. At the same time, however, Carson's avoidance of politics left unchallenged the structural underpinnings of pesticide use that are with us still.

One concrete way in which politics was avoided in her text was through the circumlocutions she substituted for the names of chemicals, their manufacturers, or other delinquent parties in order to avoid lawsuits. With the exception of the Army Chemical Corps, Carson did not name a single manufacturer of chemicals or pesticide brand name. For example, her extended description of the biological havoc caused by pesticide wastes dumped over the course of ten years by "a chemical plant" doesn't say which. Her discussion of a new carcinogenic chemical used against mites and ticks requires a stream of nonspecific designations: "a chemical;" "this chemical," "the chemical," "the product," "the suspected carcinogen," and so on, rather than Aramite, the product's name. Even when protesting the fact that certain innocuously named weed killers sold for suburban lawns didn't list their ingredients, including chlordane and dieldrin, nor mention their dangers, she withheld the names of these products at this tantalizingly apt point, when mentioning them would have worked directly to end their facade of benignity. But even in the absence of potential legal action, claims Linda Lear, Carson might not have mentioned specific names; contention about specific culprits, Carson felt, would have distracted from her central message.

On a larger scale, Carson downplayed the political implications of her account through a consistently elliptical capping of its descriptions of irrational pesticide use. Repeatedly she argued that the instances of spraying she describes were not only harmful to humans and wildlife, but unjustified even in terms of biological effectiveness or economic payoff to farmers. Why did spraying take place nonetheless? Carson's scenarios demand an answer, but hers is vague or often lacking altogether. Readers are left to make their own inferences or, more likely, to ignore the troubling questions these narrative lapses signal. This kind of

hanging question is most comfortably accommodated at the end of sections. "The science of range-management," she says in the last sentence of chapter six, "has largely ignored [the] possibility [of biological control of weeds by plant-eating insects] although these insects . . . could easily be turned to man's advantage." She concludes another section with the observation that "there is no dearth of men who understand these things . . . but they are not the men who order the wholesale drenching of the landscape with chemicals." Elsewhere she describes how "funds for chemical control came in never-ending streams, while the biologists . . . who attempted to measure the damage to wildlife had to operate on a financial shoestring." Why the marginalization of effective biological control? the distance between those who know and those who order? the discrepancy between budgets for inventing chemicals and for studying their damage? Carson's silence on these questions buries the problem of the democratic control of science, technology, and production.

To the extent that Carson does trace the origins of the destruction whose "irrationality" she has exposed, her account of agency is feeble and diffuse, her blame mild. Destruction of the environment stems from people's failure to "read" the "open book" of the landscape; facts about pesticides' destructiveness are denied out of "short-sightedness;" spraying continues because of "entrenched custom," or "surely, only because the facts are not known." "We are walking in nature like an elephant in the china cabinet," she quotes a scientist whose "rare understanding" she respects, implying "our" problem to be one of clumsiness.

Even at the level of single sentences Carson frequently masks agency and blame through passive or negative sentence constructions. She tells, for example, of farmers who chose to spray crows rather than switch to a variety of corn that didn't attract birds because they "*had been persuaded* of the merits of killing by poison" (emphasis mine). Her excision of the subject here closes down a crucial line of inquiry. A similar negative formulation lessens blame even as it assigns it. "Because the spray planes were paid by the gallon rather than by the acre," Carson says, "there was no effort to be conservative." How much more powerful would this sentence have been had its latter part been directly and positively phrased: "there was incentive to use as much as possible"? (It would also have helped had she unreified "spray planes" to make more visible which *people* were paid.)

This photo of a woman spraying DDT over her child was printed in 1945 to illustrate the idea that the spray is only harmful to insects

Carson's reticence about the political and economic forces encouraging heedless pesticide use made it hard for her to talk about fundamental social interventions as part of a solution. Her proposals, therefore, gravitate toward the only resource left to her: a respect for the balance of nature and ecological interconnectedness, to be achieved through attitudinal reform and the technologies of biological control. Her call for new attitudes is a reasonable, even inspiring, repudiation of human arrogance in favor of an attitude of cautious ''guidance'' reasonable ''accommodation,'' sensitive ''management,'' and an ethic of ''sharing'' rather than ''brute force.'' These are valuable orientations in themselves, but their mildness and abstraction bespeak the book's missing politics.

Carson offers the biological control of pests as the technical manifestation of this more humble attitude. One could not hope for a more symbolically-appealing solution: Yankee ingenuity in service of a pastoral ideal. By pastoral here I am referring to what Leo Marx points to as the most long-lived Western model for an appropriate relation to nature, which proposes a middle ground between the wild

and the overcivilized. *Silent Spring* opens with such a middle ground in its rustic idyll of ''a town in the heart of America where all life seemed to live in harmony with its surroundings.'' This prosperous town is far from the trouble of cities, but also safely removed from wild nature, signified by the barking of foxes in the distant hills. Pesticides are an evil blight disrupting this harmony, killing the town's birds and animals and bringing a strange stillness, a silent spring. At the end of the book, in the last chapter, entitled ''The Other Road,'' Carson offers her proposal for regaining this lost balance through various forms of biological pest control. It too is structured as a middle ground, a way of navigating between the technological hubris of pesticides on the one hand, and a vulnerability to nature's wildness in the form of pests on the other. It embodies the pastoral vision of enjoying the best of human artifice and inventiveness while preserving a closeness to natural cycles and creatures.

Yet Carson had evidence suggesting that humility and artifice alone often did not determine the choice of pest control methods. She herself describes the repeated bypassing of forms of biological control *known* to be cheap, effective, and harmless in favor of harmful chemicals. And she knew that for decades prior to World War Two, before they were eclipsed by faster acting and profit-producing insecticides, biological methods had been investigated and adopted not because they offered a more ''natural'' or ethically superior solution but because they were cheap and effective. Nor were the many problems that plagued chemical pesticides (resistance, resurgence, toxicity, bioaccumulation) a surprise that surfaced with their widespread agricultural use in the postwar years; most were recognized decades before *Silent Spring* was published.

Carson mentions some of these early successes as well as several contemporary ''shining models'' of nonchemical methods of pest control in her chapter on biological control. And in her next chapter, on the problems of chemical control, she describes prominent early disasters and the intensification of pesticide side effects in the late fifties. Once again, she has juxtaposed facts that pose a pointed question: why has a problematic form of pest control replaced an effective one? Here she offers the book's sole explicitly structural analysis, consisting of the two paragraphs about chemical industry funding for university research mentioned earlier, whose impact is soon diluted with more idealist explanations. The chapter continues to talk of people being ''slow to recognize'' problems with pesticides, and of chemical research drawing the best people because it seems "more exciting," and Carson concludes it with a quotation that exemplifies the book's dominant message.

> We need a more high-minded orientation and a deeper insight, which I miss in many researchers. Life is a miracle beyond our comprehensions, and we should reverence it. . . . The resort to weapons such as insecticides to control it is a proof of insufficient knowledge . . . . Humbleness is in order; there is no excuse for scientific conceit here.

Bookchin makes a different use of the past in his somewhat broader and more forthright account of how vested interests have shaped the directions taken by modern agriculture. He discusses, for example, how the food industry undermined enlightened standards for food purity in place at the beginning of the century, and nibbled away at the Delany clause protecting consumers from carcinogens. For Bookchin, these early achievements are not simply models for what could be achieved again in the future; his description of the eclipse of sane ways of doing things points his readers to the political struggle necessary to establish and upbold these.

Pushing the Limits

Silent Spring presented facts that brought its readers to the threshold of difficult questions about how pest control might be guided by biological knowledge and democratically determined priorities, rather than the logic of capital accumulation. But Carson's avoidance of politics, abetted by her conceptions of nature, helped lead them away again. Through these she taught her readers to see pesticide problems as resulting from oversight and carelessness, or at the most arrogance, rather than from greed or systemic structural factors. By casting the problem of pest control as primarily an issue of achieving a harmonious relationship to "nature," with little reference to the social criteria embedded in the term, nor the changes in social institutions necessary to achieve this harmony, Carson stripped her book of overtly political analysis or claims. She seemed to believe that it was enough to present the facts and let public opinion take over.

My goal, however, is not to judge the book politically ineffective or undesirable, only to highlight the limits of what could be said and widely heard in that particular moment. The disappearance of Bookchin's work and the furor over even the politically restrained *Silent Spring* suggest that Carson stood close to these limits. A broadly understandable and persuasive challenge to the pesticide

> **Tragically, the USDA/ARS bureaucracy simply never grasped the fundamental challenge of *Silent Spring*. Dismissing Carson and the growing ecology movement as an inconsequential minority of 'bird and bunny lover,' animal and food faddists, and religious cultists with no political or economic clout, they never imagined that the accepted course of technological progress could be seriously challenged."**

paradigm had both to criticize and placate, to extend and maintain existing worldviews. Carson's book did not call for nor achieve a fundamental democratization of research, technology, and production. But it did frighten people, link health to nature for the first time as a topic of heated public debate, and draw on familiar conceptions of nature to undermine the postwar aura of pesticides as a marvelous technical achievement and cast them as sinister and stupid instead.

The book's political consequences are complex, and still unfolding. It prompted a debate that led to legislation banning some pesticides and tightening the procedures for testing, registering, and using others. But with political-economic ground rules remaining intact, agriculture and the chemical industry could respond to these developments relatively easily. Restrictions placed several years later on organochlorines, the earliest generation of synthetic pesticides such as DDT, for example, didn't halt their continued manufacture for export, nor the development and profitable production of other pesticides, nor recent attempts to genetically engineer profitable and hazardous pest and pesticide resistant crops. More generally, these reforms did nothing to stop the trend toward increasingly mechanized and large-scale agriculture that made pesticides unavoidable. On the thirtieth anniversary of *Silent Spring*'s publication the executive director of the National Coalition Against the Misuse of Pesticides could still describe America as standing at the crossroads between ''promoting safer alternative pest management techniques or simply substituting less toxic inputs into conventional pesticide-intensive practices.''

At the same time, however, other longer term and more subtle effects of the sea-change Carson helped initiate are only now beginning to surface. For example, the cost of approving a new pesticide and the demand for ''organic'' produce have both grown to a point where alternative forms of pest management are now becoming economically feasible. Curiously, it may have required an ''apolitical'' challenge to pesticides to initiate this process.

Source: Yaakov Garb, ''Rachel Carson's *Silent Spring*,'' in *Dissent,* Fall 1995, pp. 539–46.

Sources

Brooks, Paul, ''Rachel Louise Carson,'' in *Notable American Women: The Modern Period,* Harvard University Press, 1980, pp. 138–41.

Corbett, Edward P. J., ''A Topical Analysis of 'The Obligation to Endure,''' in *And No Birds Sing: Rhetorical Analyses of Rachel Carson's ''Silent Spring,''* Southern Illinois University Press, 2000, pp. 60–72.

''The Gentle Storm Center,'' in *Life,* Vol. 53, October 1962, pp. 105–106.

Glotfelty, Cheryll, ''Cold War, *Silent Spring:* The Trope of War in Modern Environmentalism,'' in *And No Birds Sing: Rhetorical Analyses of Rachel Carson's ''Silent Spring,''* Southern Illinois University Press, 2000, pp. 157–73.

Killingsworth, M. Jimmie, and Jacqueline S. Palmer, ''*Silent Spring* and Science Fiction: An Essay in History and Rhetoric of Narrative,'' in *And No Birds Sing: Rhetorical Analyses of Rachel Carson's ''Silent Spring,''* Southern Illinois University Press, 2000, pp. 174–204.

Lear, Linda J., ''Rachel Louise Carson,'' in *American National Biography,* Oxford University Press, 1999, pp. 474–76.

Lutts, Ralph, ''Chemical Fallout: *Silent Spring,* Radioactive Fallout, and the Environmental Movement,'' in *And No Birds Sing: Rhetorical Analyses of Rachel Carson's ''Silent Spring,''* Southern Illinois University Press, 2000, pp. 17–41.

Oravec, Christine, ''An Inventional Archaeology of 'A Fable for Tomorrow,''' in *And No Birds Sing: Rhetorical Analyses of Rachel Carson's ''Silent Spring,''* Southern Illinois University Press, 2000, pp. 42–59.

''Pesticides: The Price for Progress,'' in *Time,* Vol. 80, September 1962, pp. 45–48.

Sale, Kirkpatrick, *The Green Revolution: The American Revolution, 1962–1992,* Hill and Wang, 1993, pp. 25 and 94.

Steingraber, Sandra, *Living Downstream: An Ecologist Looks at Cancer and the Environment,* Addison-Wesley, 1997, pp. 31–117.

Waddell, Craig, ''The Reception of *Silent Spring:* An Introduction,'' in *And No Birds Sing: Rhetorical Analyses of Rachel Carson's ''Silent Spring,''* Southern Illinois University Press, 2000, pp. 1–16.

Further Reading

Graham, Frank, *Since ''Silent Spring,''* Houghton Mifflin, 1970.
   Graham's book offers a detailed account of the pesticide controversy that followed the publication of *Silent Spring.*

Lear, Linda, *Rachel Carson: Witness for Nature,* Henry Holt & Co., 1997.
   Rachel Carson: Witness for Nature is widely regarded as the definitive biography of Carson.

Waddell, Craig, ed., *And No Birds Sing: Rhetorical Analyses of Rachel Carson's ''Silent Spring,''* Southern Illinois University Press, 2000.
   The essays in this volume all focus on the language of *Silent Spring,* not always from the standpoint of the rhetorician, as the title suggests, but in the manner of literary critics more generally—one examining Carson's manuscripts for clues about the her intentions, another attempting to classify the book in terms of genre, etc.

Wargo, John, *Our Children's Toxic Legacy: How Science and Law Fail to Protect Us from Pesticides,* Yale University Press, 1996.
   As the book's title indicates, Wargo asks whether current pesticide regulations adequately safeguard children, but *Our Children's Toxic Legacy* also provides an excellent overview of the pesticide problem, including a detailed description of the contemporary regulatory process. Along with Steingraber's *Living Downstream,* Wargo's book is essential reading in this area.

The Souls of Black Folk

W. E. B. Du Bois

1903

W. E. B. Du Bois introduces *The Souls of Black Folk* with the forethought:

> herein lie buried many things which if read with patience may show the strange meaning of being black here in the dawning of the twentieth century. This meaning is not without interest to you, gentle reader; for the problem of the twentieth century is the problem of the color-line.

These succinct lines summarize the aim of the collection, which is to impress upon the world the particular experience of being an African American some forty years after the Civil War. The work consists of fourteen essays on various topics, from a history of the U.S. government's efforts at Reconstruction to a discussion of the role of religion in he black community. First published in 1903, it was reprinted twenty-four times between then and 1940 alone; it is easily Du Bois' most widely read book and is considered a masterpiece. Coined the Father of social science, Du Bois brings together a blend of history, sociological data, poetry, song, and the benefit of his personal experience to propose his vision of how and why color poses such a dilemma at the turn of the twentieth century. His assertion is fortuitous, and the collection continues to provide insight into the ways that the African-American culture is intrinsic to the larger American culture, and how history has made that relationship inherently problematic.

Author Biography

William Edward Burghardt Du Bois was born on February 23, 1868, into a large white community in Great Barrington, Massachusetts. The racism he experienced as a child in New England formed the basis of his lifelong struggle for equal rights. Endowed with outstanding intellect, Du Bois traveled to Nashville, Tennessee to attend Fisk College on scholarship in 1885. His contact with the post-Civil War South in the capacity of student and teacher solidified his commitment to education and mobilization of African Americans. Following three years in the South, Du Bois completed his undergraduate and graduate degrees at Harvard, focusing on history and philosophy. He completed the bulk of his doctoral work during two years in Berlin, where he came to the understanding of racism as a worldwide issue, opposed to a national issue.

Following the completion of his doctoral thesis entitled *The Suppression of the African Slave Trade in America*, Du Bois began his lifelong career as educator, researcher and social advocate. His studies embodied the first scientific approach to examining social issues, and as a result he is considered to be the father of social science. Du Bois worked for social reform through his study of all aspects of African-American life, in an effort to educate blacks and promote understanding between the relationship of blacks to white America. Du Bois was diametrically opposed to the philosophy of Booker T. Washington, the most popular black man in America, who espoused the idea that African Americans should accept their low social status and work for modest goals through technical training only (foregoing civil rights, higher education and political power). In 1906, Du Bois founded the Niagra Movement, an organization of black men aimed at aggressive advocacy for civil rights. The organization was joined by a group of white liberals to form the National Association for the Advancement of Colored People (NAACP). For twenty-five years Du Bois edited the NAACP magazine *The Crisis,* strongly advocating that blacks lead themselves out of oppression, with whites serving only as support.

Trips to Africa and Russia in the 1920s resulted in a revision of Du Bois' ideology; he became convinced that integration in America was unrealistic, and that white capitalism was geared toward keeping minorities down. By 1933 he had left the NAACP and resumed teaching, writing and organizing the Pan-African conference. During World War II and the beginning of the Cold War he became a peace advocate and spoke out strongly against the use of atomic weapons, resulting in his indictment as a foreign agent by the Department of Justice. Although he was acquitted, the incident served to further alienate him from the nation of his birth. In 1959, he moved to Ghana and became a Ghanaian citizen and a member of the Communist party. He died in Accra, Ghana, on August 27, 1963, the day before the "March On Washington."

Summary

Du Bois begins his work by stating his objective in no uncertain terms; his goal is to represent what it is like to be black in America at the beginning of the twentieth century because he is convinced that race is the central problem of the century to come. He states this in his forethought and follows with a loose thematic grouping of the essays to follow.

The first three chapters in *The Souls of Black Folk* address historical and political issues. He begins "Of Our Spiritual Strivings" with a provocative question underlying all other questions posed to him: "how does it feel to be a problem?" The essay addresses this fundamental question in a discussion of the contradictions inherent in the process of "striving." Here Du Bois discusses efforts made toward winning the ballot and literacy and outlines the topics to follow in what amounts to an extended prologue. "Of the Dawn of Freedom" is a straightforward history of the ways the U.S. government attempted to deal with the "problem" of African Americans just before, during, and after the Civil War, over the years 1861 through 1872. The essay amounts to an even-handed analysis of the policies of the Freedmen's Bureau, including both strengths and shortcomings, and the ways that its unfinished work laid an outline for the social and race problems to follow. "Of Mr. Booker T. Washington and Others" is an attack on the policies of the famous educator and speaker who at the time of the essay was Du Bois' philosophical opponent and rival. In the course of his essay, Du Bois suggests that Washington's work reflects his indoctrination in the most superficial of American value-systems, commercialism and materialism, and that his work is self-motivated. He goes on to analyze the historical precedents of Washington's policies of submission and technical education, and addresses in detail the shortcomings and inevitable results of those policies.

In the next six chapters, Du Bois moves from the general to the specific, in his own words taking the reader "within the veil." In these chapters, he offers stories from his life experience in the South, presents portraits of actual people, and infuses them with his sociological understanding of them. He offers anecdotes about teaching school during his time as a student at Fisk College, details the conditions of workers in cotton mills, and describes the transformation of Atlanta and her outskirts from pastoral idyll to industrial wasteland. He narrates a drive through the black belt of Georgia and scrutinizes the legacy of slavery in the relationship between the races in the South in "Of the Sons of Master and Man." These stories expose the hardships of poor, uneducated black people and solicit compassion on the part of the reader. Du Bois' testimonial tales and picturesque depictions of the Southern countryside are balanced by his analyses of the development of black education, and his argument that intellectual training can only benefit the entire culture of the South.

The last five chapters entail African-American spirituality, both in analytic discussion and personal anecdote. In "The Faith of Our Fathers," Du Bois discusses the history and influence, power, and self-contradiction of religion for black Americans. He describes his own grief process over the death of his son in "Of the Passing of the First Born." In "Of Alexander Crummel," he gives a biographical sketch of one man's efforts to uplift his people. "Of the Coming of John" is a short parable detailing the terrible potential outcome of the "veil." Finally, "Of the Sorrow Songs" discusses the history, power, and purpose of the music preceding each of the chapters.

Key Figures

Alexander Crummel

Alexander Crummel is the first African-American man ordained an Episcopalian priest. Over the course of his long life, he established his own parish, seeks counsel and inspiration in England, and ministers in Africa out of the ardent desire to uplift his people. As a man who strives to aid his people with very little support or recognition, his life is a great inspiration to Du Bois.

W. E. B. Du Bois

W. E. B. Du Bois

W. E. B. Du Bois is the author of *The Souls of Black Folk* and, because the essays reflect his own experience, the hero, he narrates the collection, moving from the third to the first person and back, in an effort to represent the fullness of the African-American experience by representing his own.

John Jones

John Jones is the protagonist in the fiction story "Of the Coming of John." He is a young black man from southeastern Georgia who is sent north to school in hopes that he will return home a teacher. Although at first he is a lax student, once he sets his mind to study he becomes committed to education and self-improvement. As he learns and gains exposure to the Northern culture, he feels more and more acutely the stigma of racism, and after being slighted at a New York concert on account of his color, he determines to return home to teach. Once home, he inadvertently offends the white community with what appears to be provocative ideas. Given his exposure to a better, more informed lifestyle in the North, John's resentment over the disparity between blacks and whites overtakes him. When he comes upon his former playmate (a white bigot also named John) trying to kiss his sister, he flies into a

Media Adaptations

- *The Souls of Black Folk* is available in the form of an e-book, available from Microsoft Reader.

- *The Souls of Black Folk* is also available on four audiocassettes from Walter Covell.

rage and kills the friend of his youth. When the authorities come to arrest him, he throws himself into the sea, seeing no option for freedom aside from death.

Josie

Josie is a farm girl whom Du Bois befriends while teaching in Tennessee. She is a tireless worker and aspires to an education, but dies as a result of her difficult circumstances. As a victim of the hardships placed on African Americans, Josie's life is tragic in Du Bois' eyes.

Booker T. Washington

At the end of the nineteenth century, Booker T. Washington was considered to be the most popular black man in America, at least as far as whites were concerned. Longtime principal of the Tuskegee Institute, Washington is known for his 1895 compromise speech. In the speech, he urges African Americans to accept their position as socially inferior and strives for personal improvement through vocational training, foregoing political power and higher education. Du Bois was diametrically opposed to the politics and philosophy of Booker T. Washington, and he details the reasons for his opposition in "Of Booker T. Washington and Others."

Themes

Dualism

In "Of Our Spiritual Strivings," Du Bois makes reference to the experience of "double-conscious-ness, this sense of always looking at one's self through the eyes of others." This concept of dual identity appears throughout the text in nearly every essay and is central to the author's goal in making the African-American condition understood. Du Bois contends that African Americans experience a split in self-concept because they are regarded with "contempt and pity" by the majority of their fellow Americans. As both "Negro" and American, black people are organized into public and private identities, neither regarded as whole by mainstream, white America. This theme extends into the contradictory nature of American policies toward black people during the time the work was written. For example, although as an African American in New England, Du Bois was able to attend Harvard University and was afforded many of the privileges of any citizen, whereas when he lived in the South he was subject to Jim Crow laws. The United States is comprised of both the North and South, but race policy for the nation is split.

The "Veil"

Du Bois first mentions the "veil" in his forethought, and extends the metaphor throughout the text. The "veil" is a metaphoric film between black people and white America that obscures the true identity of black people. Du Bois attributes the confused dual identity of his people to the "veil," which makes it impossible for blacks to see themselves in entirety as well. According to Arnold Rampersad, author of *The Art and Imagination of W. E. B. Du Bois,* however, the "veil" also "unites Black men. They are drawn together for reasons sprung 'above all, from the sight of the "veil" that hung between us and Opportunity.'" Du Bois extrapolates on his metaphor with extensive use of visual imagery, or the impairment thereof. Darkness, light, brightness, shadow, and haze appear throughout the text. In effect, according to Du Bois, difficulty in perception is fundamental to being African American.

Style

Form

The collection consists of fourteen chapters, an introduction, and an afterward. With one exception, each of the chapters (an essay or story) opens with a quotation of verse from a famous source in the

Western literary canon followed by lines of music from African-American oral tradition. The result is a frame for each essay, both from the recognized cultural establishment and from the unrecognized, yet widely known tradition of slave songs and spirituals. The effect is an impression of support, both from within the black community and from without, and puts the two formats on par with one another. The first essay, "Of Our Spiritual Strivings," begins with verse depicting ceaseless yearning, and the final piece, "The Song of Sorrows," ends in song cheering the weary traveler with hope, effectively enclosing all of the essays in brackets of song describing the poles of black experience. These in turn are bracketed by the introduction, which makes an appeal to the reader to read with charity and patience for the author's cause, and ends with the After-Thought, a similar appeal in stylized, poetic form.

Point of View

Most of the work in *The Souls of Black Folk* takes the form of essay, written in third person prose. The tone is didactic, marked by formality and the long, classical sentence structure characteristic of nineteenth century prose. The lyricism of the prose and flexibility of form throughout the text suggest the influence of Romanticism, a period ending loosely around the end of the nineteenth century, blended with the rationalism of Du Bois' data, experience, and analysis. Arnold Rampersad, in *The Art and Imagination of W. E. B. Du Bois,* notes that "devices of the traditional pastoral elegy are present in modified but distinct form," such as the depiction of withering roses in his essay about the death of his infant son. Occasionally, Du Bois uses the second person, particularly in the introduction when he states his objectives, urging the reader in how and why he should read the text. His tone in these instances is an appeal and is emphatic about the truth and importance of his work. "Of the Coming of John" is distinct from the other essays in that it is a parable; also poetry, both by Du Bois and by other authors, appears in the text.

Symbolism

Du Bois' primary use of symbolism revolves around vision. The "veil" is his main metaphor for the distance and misconception between black and white Americans, and is responsible for the way African Americans see themselves as dualistic and distorted. Darkness generally symbolizes ignorance

Topics for Further Study

- Consider Du Bois' and Washington's assertions about educational opportunities for African Americans. Given recent controversy over affirmative action policies, where do you think the two would locate themselves in this debate, and why.

- Consider the role of song in the text. Given Du Bois' discussion of what he terms "Negro music" in *"The Sorrow Songs,"* how might he interpret the evolution of African-American music in the last century?

- In *The Souls of Black Folk* Du Bois makes use of a blend of shifting tones and forms. Discuss how this versatility reflects and impacts the thematic material, and what the author's intent may have been.

and despair, such as in the opening to "The Sorrow Songs"; enslaved black people in the past are termed "they that walked in darkness." Similar use of imagery concerning impaired vision includes haze, dimness, dusk, shadow, and mist.

Historical Context

All of the essays in *The Souls of Black Folk* were written around the turn of the century, a pivotal time in United States history in regard to race relations. In response to the end of the war, the fourteenth and fifteenth amendments had been passed in 1868 and 1870 to recognize black Americans as U.S. citizens and to provide them with equal protection under the law. Despite these amendments, by the turn of the century, segregation was still intact, particularly in the South. Although the Southern states had received assistance during the Reconstruction period, the region was still feeling the effects of the Civil War by the end of the nineteenth century and race

Compare & Contrast

- **1900:** At least two thousand blacks are lynched or burned to death in the fifteen years prior to the turn of the century. White murderers go unpunished.

  Today: Racially motivated hate crimes are a rarity, but still exist, as in the case of James Byrd Jr. In 1998, three white men drag Byrd behind their car, resulting in Byrd's death. The men who committed the crime are convicted and sentenced to death.

- **1896:** In the case of *Plessy v. Ferguson,* the Supreme Court upholds the constitutionality of racially segregated railroad cars.

  1955: In the case of *Brown v. Board of Education,* the Supreme Court rules that racial segregation of schools is unconstitutional. Despite the ruling, education remains largely segregated in the South.

  Today: Despite disparities in some schools based on socioeconomic factors, no schools in the United States are segregated.

- **1903:** In *The Souls of Black Folk,* Du Bois advocates equal opportunity and treatment for whites and blacks, including equal standards for competency.

  1972: The Equal Opportunity Act of 1972 expands Title VII protections to schools, extending affirmative action policies to colleges and universities in the interest of aiding minorities.

  1995: Governor Pete Wilson and the University of California vote to end affirmative action in both hiring and admissions statewide.

---

relations reflected hostility on the part of whites for blacks. Limitations were placed on black employment opportunities and property ownership, interracial marriage was illegal in every state, and all public facilities, including schools, restaurants, hospitals, and public transportation were divided by race. At its most terrifying extreme, violation of the unspoken code of segregation resulted in murder; between the years of 1884 and 1900, two thousand blacks were killed by lynch mobs in the United States.

During this time, there were some organized attempts at legal challenge to segregation. For example, in 1896, a group of African-American and white citizens challenged the constitutionality of separate railroad cars for blacks and whites in the Supreme Court case *Plessy v. Ferguson.* The constitutionality of segregated cars was upheld, but the case marked the beginning of organized response to Jim Crow conditions. National trends tended toward policies limiting the rights of black people; in 1898, the Supreme Court, in the case of *Williams v. Mississippi,* approved a system of poll taxes and literacy testing as requirements for voters in an

effort to keep African Americans away from the polls. At the turn of the century Booker T. Washington, the principal of the Tuskegee Institute for black education in Tuskegee, Alabama, was the most popular and powerful African-American man in the United States, at least among whites. In 1895, he delivered his famous compromise speech in which he advocated that black people accept low social status, forego political power, and pursue vocational education rather than higher education. Around the same time, Du Bois was coming into the public eye as a sociologist, activist, and spokesperson advocating equal rights and higher education for African Americans. The Industrial Revolution was underway in America, drawing more blacks to urban centers and exploiting them, resulting in poverty and ghettos; Du Bois was at work to prove that such conditions for blacks were symptomatic of the system rather than inherent to the group. He and other more militant African Americans publicly opposed Washington, and as individuals, they represented the philosophical division over race relations. In the next several years, Du Bois' work would result in the organization of the NAACP, an organization that would change the face of race relations in the United States forever.

Critical Overview

In his introduction to the 1989 edition of *The Souls of Black Folk*, Henry Louis Gates, Jr. asserts that the book "has served as a veritable touchstone of African-American culture for every successive generation of black scholars since 1903." He goes on to say that "Du Bois' contemporaries, and subsequent scholars, generally have agreed that two of the uncanny effects of *The Souls* are that it is poetic in its attention to detail, and that it succeeds, somehow, in 'narrating' the nation of Negro Americans at the turn of the century, articulating for the inarticulate insider and for the curious outsider ... the cultural particularity of African Americans." Although at the time of publication some white critics were skeptical about the work, black critics were overwhelmingly enthusiastic for what Wendell Phillips Dabney, in the Ohio Enterprise, calls "a masterpiece."

The *New York Times* review from 1903 calls *The Souls of Black Folk* "sentimental, poetical, picturesque," and asserts "the acquired logic and the evident attempt to be critically fair-minded is strangely tangled with these racial characteristics and racial rhetoric." The reviewer concedes that the book "throws much light upon the complexities of the Negro problem." He is convinced that as a Northerner, Du Bois "probably does not understand his own people in their natural state" in the South. Not all of Du Bois' opponents were as even-handed in their criticism; Gates quotes the Louisville Courier-Journal, which took the book to be "crudely written" and "characterized by incoherent statements and disconnected arguments." Ten years later, however, in *The African Abroad,* William H. Ferris calls Du Bois' work "the most brilliant and suggestive book ever written by a Negro" and the "political bible of the Negro race." Gates echoes Ferris when he ventures to say "no other text, save possibly the King James Bible, has had a more fundamental impact on the shaping of the Afro-American literary tradition." These assessments reflect the consensus by African-American writers in the years since the book's publication; as Gates illustrates, from Langston Hughes to Ralph Ellison, *The Souls of Black Folk* has been a timeless influence and inspiration.

Criticism

Jennifer Lynch

Lynch is a writer and teacher in Northern New Mexico. In the following essay, she examines ways that the text of The Souls of Black Folk *embodies Du Bois' experience of duality as well as his "people's."*

In Du Bois' "Forethought" to his essay collection, *The Souls of Black Folk*, he entreats the reader to receive his book in an attempt to understand the world of African Americans—in effect the "souls of black folk." Implicit in this appeal is the assumption that the author is capable of representing an entire "people." This presumption comes out of Du Bois' own dual nature as a black man who has lived in the South for a time, yet who is Harvard-educated and cultured in Europe. Du Bois illustrates the duality or "two-ness," which is the function of his central metaphor, the "veil" that hangs between white America and black; as an African American, he is by definition a participant in two worlds. The form of the text makes evident the author's duality: Du Bois shuttles between voices and media to express this quality of being divided, both for himself as an individual, and for his "people" as a whole. In relaying the story of African-American people, he relies on his own experience and voice and in so doing creates the narrative. Hence the work is as much the story of *his* soul as it is about the souls of all black folk. Du Bois epitomizes the inseparability of the personal and the political; through the text of *The Souls of Black Folk*, Du Bois straddles two worlds and narrates his own experience.

Du Bois expands on his reference to duality and the "veil" in "Of Our Spiritual Strivings" with the explanation, "It is a peculiar sensation, this double-consciousness, this sense of always looking at one's self through the eyes of others, of measuring one's soul by the tape of a world that looks on in amused contempt and pity." He goes on to describe "two-ness" as being "an American, a Negro; two souls, two thoughts, two unreconciled strivings; two warring ideals in one dark body." The world of the African American, he asserts, is one split by perception from the exterior of mainstream America and in conflict with the experience of oneself. These conflicting selves result in an obscured sense of identity. Du Bois' use of the "veil" describes an obstacle that prevents white America from true perception of African Americans. The veil is mentioned at least once in each of the essays; Du Bois sees it as

A white waiting-room sign at a Greyhound bus depot in Mississippi in 1961

inseparable from African-American identity in that blacks live within it, yet also live in America, and thus lead double lives. Arnold Rampersad, in *The Art and Imagination of W. E. B. Du Bois,* suggests that the word "'souls' in the title is a play on words, referring to the 'two-ness' of the black American." His assertion supports a reading of Du Bois' work as aimed not only at addressing the African American as a whole but at addressing his experience as an individual who is inherently divided.

As an active participant in two worlds, Du Bois embodies his assessment of life within the "veil"— and to the extreme. Raised in New England and possessed of superior intellect, he completed his undergraduate, master's, and Ph.D. degrees at Harvard University and spent several years working on his dissertation in Europe. His extensive education makes him a renowned scholar and a man exceptional for his time; he was the first African American admitted to Harvard. As a student of history and philosophy at the end of the nineteenth century, Du Bois was versed in the classics according to the traditional curriculum of the time. Hence, although the focus of his work is the liberation of African-American people, his academic life was necessarily steeped in Western, and largely white, culture. Because of financial limitations, Du Bois com-

pleted the first three years of his undergraduate education at Fisk College in Tennessee and spent his summers teaching deprived southern blacks each of those years, a period that comprises his main experience of the South. Because most of his life was spent in the North, critics of his work at the time called into question his ability to understand the lives of southern African Americans. For example, the 1903 *New York Times* review of *The Souls of Black Folk* asserts, "probably he does not understand his own people in their natural state." Such statements not only support Du Bois' interpretation of the way African Americans are viewed by white America but also reflect the way he himself was viewed as not a "natural" black man, and, in fact, divided from his people.

Several of the essays in *The Souls of Black Folk* are delivered in a third-person, rhetorical tone that calls to mind Du Bois' superior education and attention to the classics. "Of the Dawn of Freedom" and "Of Mr. Booker T. Washington and Others" in particular reflect Du Bois' intellect and ability as on par with white intellectuals, in the forum of white intellectuals. Other first-person narratives, such as "Of the Meaning of Progress," retain the previous essays' formality of tone and, in Rampersad's words, mark their "literary antecedents as clearly classi-

What Do I Read Next?

- *Black Reconstruction* is Du Bois' refutation of the traditional historical view of the contributions of African Americans during the Reconstruction period.

- *Dusk of Dawn* is Du Bois' 1940 book concerning his views on both the African's and African American's quest for freedom in the twentieth century.

- Du Bois' doctoral thesis, *The Suppression of the African Slave Trade* (1894) is a definitive work about the social, economic, and historical reasons for the end of the slave trade.

- Jean Toomer's 1923 collection of stories and poetry, *Cane*, is an eloquent and aesthetically beautiful representation of the many versions of African-American life. His layered use of form reflects the direct influence of *The Souls of Black Folk*.

- James Weldon Johnson's novel *Autobiography of an Ex-Colored Man* (1912) concerns one man's struggle with racial identity, and includes mention of Du Bois' influence over the protagonist.

- *The Souls of Black Folk* is paired with Booker T. Washington's autobiography and James Weldon Johnson's novel in *Three Negro Classics: Up From Slavery, The Souls of Black Folk*, and *Autobiography of an Ex-Colored Man*, Mass Market Paperback, 1976.

---

cal.'' Since the goal of the work is to convince mainstream America of the wholeness and humanity of a disenfranchised people, Du Bois clearly seeks to make his work viable in terms of the mainstream and thus uses the language of the mainstream. According to Rampersad,

> In its variety and range *The Souls of Black Folk* indicates Du Bois' appreciation and mastery of the essay form as practiced in the nineteenth century . . . Sensitive to the many purposes to which the form could be put, he used the essay to capture the nuances of his amorphous subject, the multiple disciplines involved in his explication, and the different and sometimes conflicting expressions of his temperament.

His writing is by turns romantic, didactic, passionate, qualitative, poetic and rational; he uses the popular styles of the times to his advantage. These styles do not so much represent the fullness of Du Bois' experience as an African American as his experience as a nineteenth-century scholar from a white institution. His more personal accounts, however, bridge the gap between his largely white audience and his experience as a black man. For example, in ''Of the Meaning of Progress'' Du Bois describes the harsh conditions of his students and ultimately the death of a prized pupil. Du Bois generates compassion on the part of the reader by narrating the story as a personal experience, rather than by listing statistics. Similarly, when he describes the impact of the birth and death of his son in ''Of the Passing of the First-Born,'' he uses language that is stylistically grandiose and formal, atypical of African-American speech and writing at the time. However, he conveys a story that is both extremely intimate and illustrative of his highly developed human emotions. Thus Du Bois uses the personal narrative to bridge the gap between the white world he knows and wishes to inform and the black world of which he is also a part.

Du Bois' most explicit literary device for demonstrating the dual nature of his world, however, is his use of double epigraphs to begin each essay. With the exception of the last piece, which directly addresses the meaning of sorrow songs in the context of African-American culture, each essay begins with a line of verse from the Western literary canon, followed by a line from African-American song. The effect is double. On one hand, the placement of the contrasting lines puts the sorrow songs on par with the literary canon. On the other hand, the accepted verse appears in English and is easily

> In relaying the story of African-American people, Du Bois relies on his own experience and voice and in so doing creates the narrative."

understandable, while the lesser known songs appear as music scores without lyrics, thus their meaning is less accessible than the lines that precede them. The meaning of the sorrow songs bears explanation, which is provided by Du Bois in the chapter devoted to them: it serves as a metaphor for black culture in general, which also requires an explanation to be understood by the mainstream audience. Of the songs Du Bois writes, "I know that these songs are the articulate message of the slave to the world." He attests to their artistic worth when he writes that the music "remains the singular spiritual heritage of the nation and the greatest gift of the Negro people." The contrasting lines of verse and song, although distinct and from separate traditions, are inextricably intertwined, as are the lives of black and white Americans.

Toward the close of "The Sorrow Songs" Du Bois wonders, "Would America have been America without her Negro people?" Apparently he concludes it would not. In his aim to represent the African-American people to mainstream America, Du Bois offers his own narrative, in a variety of voices, to represent the whole. His various means of expression represent his particular experience, which is in many ways exceptional and outside of the norm for his time. This sets him apart from the mainstream of black America, yet also highlights his experience of dualism as an African American. Despite the fact that as a cultured Northerner he has access to the resources of white America, his testimony shows that he is "bone of the bone and flesh of the flesh of them that live within the Veil."

Source: Jennifer Lynch, Critical Essay on *The Souls of Black Folk,* in *Nonfiction Classics for Students,* The Gale Group, 2001.

Scott Herring

In the following essay, Herring examines The Souls of Black Folk *within a historical and cultural context, specifically focusing on the book's reaction to minstrelsy.*

W.E.B. Du Bois's *The Souls of Black Folk* is not a book that can be read in ignorance of its historic milieu; to focus exclusively on the text would be to cripple it. First published in 1903, it was written in an America in which the white majority only grudgingly accepted the idea that black folk even had souls. The images most white Americans had of blacks were stereotypical; blacks were a demonized group which had to be controlled by terror or an idealized group of self-sacrificing Uncle Toms and Mammys; they were seen as embodying a sexual potency and promiscuity secretly envied by whites, or they were represented as primitive, laughable clowns. All these stereotypes were given form and (for many Northerners) largely brought into being by the century-old tradition of minstrelsy, in which white comics blackened their faces with burnt cork and performed an imitation of black life for a (usually delighted) white audience. It is this tradition and its effects that Du Bois seeks to subvert in *The Souls of Black Folk;* he removes what Houston Baker calls the "minstrel mask" from his entire race, taking back from the blackface theater the characteristic art form of his race, its music, which the minstrels had appropriated for their own purposes.

I read *The Souls of Black Folk* as a political text, embedded in its historical environment and at odds with the dominant culture—a reading shaped by some of the insights of new historicism. New historicists, such as Stephen Greenblatt, have posited "transactions" or "negotiations" between components of a society (Greenblatt's term is "exchanges" in his essay on Shakespeare and the exorcists, to which my title pays an oblique homage). This essay will use the term "appropriation" for the process of cultural exchange, because the exchange that motivates *The Souls of Black Folk* is less a transaction than a theft. The blackface theater appropriated black music and transformed it to suit its own ends, the fairly straightforward ones of getting laughs and making money. Not all but a significant number of whites adopted the images of the minstrel fiction and applied them to the African American reality, seeing in the streets characters from the stage; blacks very quickly learned, in their dealings with whites, to put on the mask. For Du Bois, the mask is a Veil to be rent. In *Souls,* he addresses two audiences: for white readers, he wishes to demonstrate the worth—even the humanity—of the race many have imagined the minstrel comedian to adequately represent; and to blacks, especially young black artists, he communicates the richness of their heritage. The latter project is accomplished largely by the re-appropriation and rehabilitation of the music that minstrelsy had deformed, music being a vital form of expression for a people only recently literate (and, in 1903, still only partly so). After considering some of the implications of minstrelsy's variegated appropriation and distortion of black culture, and popular response to it, this essay will examine Du Bois's project of retaking black American music.

The long, long run enjoyed by minstrel acts on the stages of America (comics blacking their faces with burnt cork to perform ''darky'' roles has been traced back at least as far as 1975) is a phenomenon familiar to anyone reasonably conversant with the history of the nineteenth century, as is the great love of so many Americans for this curious distraction. What is not as well known is that this love affair is not a simple or straightforward matter; neither was the form itself consistent. Minstrelsy changed frequently throughout its evolution, starting as a forum for a single performer, most famously Thomas Dartmouth Rice, originator of the Jim Crow routine. It changed in the 1840s, after the advent of the Virginia Minstrels, to a highly ritualized two- or three-part show by four musicians/comedians/acrobats, shifting again in the 1850s with the popularity of ''Tom shows'' (minstrel versions of Uncle Tom's Cabin), and again after the war, with blacks entering the business and white troupes swelling to form massive traveling spectacles. It finally faded only after first penetrating the motion picture industry (Amos and Andy, played on radio by white actors, represent a strong late survival of the tradition). And while this evolution is clear in retrospect, it was surely less clear at the time; the various forms overlapped, co-existed, borrowed from each other, and were subject to great variability within individual acts, matched by a high variability in the reaction of the audience.

For instance, when one thinks of the minstrel stage, one may picture its characters as happy and carefree. However, the minstrel character was not always happy; from the 1840s on, tearjerkers were common on the blackface stage. ''By focusing on farcical elements it is easy to overlook the fact that minstrelsy was a very sentimental art form,'' Gary Engle writes in his introduction to a reprint of the 1871 blackface lachrymatory Uncle Eph's Dream. He continues: ''The minstrel show's first part invariably included mother songs or pathetic ballads which helped balance the comic songs and ex-

> **Du Bois reveals that he is very much aware that an appropriation has taken place, and he specifically identifies the minstrel theater as a culprit.''**

changes between interlocuter and end men. Numerous performers were renowned for their ability to leave audiences weeping.'' This sounds like a sympathetic broadcasting of the slave's (or, in 1871, freedman's) plight, of which Du Bois might conceivably have approved. Uncle Eph's Dream shows that this is not the case. Eph mourns his lost wife and children, but he also mourns the loss of Mr. Slocum: ''He used to be my massa and a mighty good massa he was too-but we got no more massas now; de poor old slaves will hab to look out for demselves.'' Happy or sad, here is one aspect of minstrel characters which appears often: whatever their age, they have a tendency to be not fully adult. Despite the mutability of the form the minstrel show took during its century of ascendency, certain themes do emerge.

The variability of audience response is perhaps the most complex aspect of the minstrel phenomenon. A major attempt to sort out this complexity of both performance and response is Eric Lott's recent Love and Theft: Blackface Minstrelsy and the American Working Class. In minstrelsy, he sees a dialectic play of opposites, not merely a putdown of blacks:

What I have called the social unconscious of blackface suggests that the whites involved in minstrelsy were far from unenthusiastic about black cultural practices or, conversely, untroubled by them, continuous though the economic logic of blackface was with slavery. As often as not, this involvement depended on an intersection of racial and class languages that occasionally became confused with one another, reinforcing the general air of political jeopardy in minstrel acts. . . At every turn blackface minstrelsy has seemed a form in which transgression and containment coexisted, in which improbably threatening or startlingly sympathetic racial meanings were simultaneously produced and dissolved. Neither the social relations on which blackface delineations depended, the de-

In perhaps the most famous essay in the collection, "Of Mr. Booker T. Washington and Others," Du Bois addresses the attitudes of the influential black educator, which Du Bois feels promote the subservience and inferiority of blacks

lineations themselves, their commercial setting, nor their ideological effects were monolithic or simply hegemonic.

Instances of this co-existence of transgression and containment abound; one example is the Tom show, which enjoyed such an extraordinary run from the 1850s until well into this century. Because "no laws existed copyrighting fictional material for stage use", Harriet Beecher Stowe had no control over the form her novel would take when dramatized; her only profit was a free seat when one of the many productions came to Hartford, during the performance of which she had to ask her companion to explain the plot. The 1850s saw a plethora of wildly variable versions of Uncle Tom's Cabin, some broadly abolitionist, some anti-abolitionist, with a few that contrived to be a little of both, the theatrical situation reflecting the broader political disintegration of the country. But despite the complexity of Lott's reading of minstrelsy, he does recognize certain broad features shared by many of

its productions, from which he begins his "complication" of the phenomenon:

> While it was organized around the quite explicit "borrowing" of black cultural materials for white dissemination, a borrowing that ultimately depended on the material relations of slavery, the minstrel show obscured these relations by pretending that slavery was amusing, right, and natural. Although it arose from a white obsession with black (male) bodies which underlies white racial dread to our own day, it ruthlessly disavowed its fleshly investments through ridicule and racist lampoon. For the present purpose—examining Du Bois's attitude toward minstrelsy-this essay will focus on these two tendencies in blackface: minstrelsy was an appropriation of black culture, and it deformed what it appropriated.

Its very beginning was an act of theft; Thomas Dartmouth Rice's famous Jim Crow routine was "borrowed" from a crippled stablehand of that name. That Rice had been the one who discovered and appropriated Jim Crow's song, dance, and name was established by the 1880 autobiography of Rice's employer, thus settling an old controversy. "The foggy folklore and apocrypha regarding the origins of 'Jim Crow' vary with the interpreter and with the time of retelling. Jim Crow has been authoritatively and geographically discovered in Louisville, Pittsburgh, Cincinnati, New Orleans, and obscure outposts of the Great Southwest. Progenitors of 'Jim Crow' surfaced all over the land." Although scholars have traced the origins of the Jim Crow stage routine, separating Rice's valid claim from those resulting from faulty memory or worse, few have considered the deeper meaning of its vague etiology and multiple discoverers. In one sense, this "foggy folklore and apocrypha" is not constructed merely of falsehoods; rather, it represents accurately the relationship which developed between the minstrel theater and the innumerable, nameless black informants who gave the theater its material. Thomas Rice's appropriation of Jim Crow's song was a prototype from which thousands of copies sprang. Rice's stellar success led other performers to take up his technique of appropriation, mingling among the slaves and free blacks of antebellum America in search of ready-made routines. Robert Toll, who describes this process as "primitive fieldwork," quotes a number of the early minstrel stars on the topic, like Billy Whitlock, who while touring the South would "steal off to some negro hut to hear the darkies sing and see them dance, taking a jug of whisky to make things merrier."

Such direct testimony is uncommon; "black-face performers rarely credited specific material to blacks because they wanted to be known as creative artists as well as entertainers." Creative they were; it would be a grave mistake to imagine that productions of minstrelsy adequately represented nineteenth century black culture. Indeed, after the Civil War, minstrel troupes began to include stereotyped German, Jewish, Italian, Irish, and Chinese characters, portrayed in blackface, in their shows, a move which Gary Engle credits to competition from the ethnic comedies of variety theater. Any connection with African American reality, in these shows at least, was stretched beyond the breaking point. The content of many blackface performances, however, reveals that minstrels did borrow heavily from black culture; they "used Afro-American dances and dance-steps, reproduced individual Negro's songs and 'routines' intact, absorbed Afro-American syncopated rhythms into their music, and employed characteristically Afro-American folk elements and forms." Plainly, a very one-sided exchange-an appropriation-took place. Black informants (there must have been an enormous number of them, during the long history of minstrelsy) surrendered bits and pieces of their culture to the minstrels, who proceeded to put them to use. Many of the latter grew wealthy, while the former got nothing (before Abolition, at least) and rarely survive even as names. But it is not merely the act of appropriation which is of interest here. Just as important is the use to which this appropriated culture was put, a use which had the final effect of hanging the minstrel mask on black America; it is this use which motivates Du Bois's work of re-appropriation in *The Souls of Black Folk.*

In the absence of any real communication between the races-an absence Du Bois seeks to fill-the minstrel show defined what blacks were for most of its audience. What was the black "reality" created by the average minstrel show? Its characteristics are still well known, perhaps because traces of the minstrel form survived so long in the motion picture industry and showed a remarkable resiliency in live theater. Ralph Ellison, in a recent introduction to a new edition of Invisible Man, reports witnessing a Tom show in Vermont during World War II, and Harry Birdoff writes that there were still a few Tom troupes scattered around the country as late as 1947. Again, this reality was a complex one, but often the black, as portrayed by the blackface theater, was a buffoon: "With their ludicrous dialects, grotesque make-up, bizarre behavior, and simplistic carica-tures, minstrels portrayed blacks as totally inferior." For pre-war Northern audiences, minstrels frequently created fantasy plantations populated by fantasy slaves who-like Uncle Eph—were happy in their bondage, devoted to their masters, content to frolic like children all day. Beginning in 1853, Christy Minstrels produced one of the more popular inverted versions of Uncle Tom's Cabin. The following lyric, from the piece entitled Happy Uncle Tom, captures its spirit:

Oh, white folks, we'll have you to know Dis am not de version of Mrs. Stowe; Wid her de Darks am all unlucky But we am de boys from Old Kentucky, Den hand de Banjo down to play We'll make it ring both night and day And we care not what de white folks say Dey can't get us to run away.

When the (mistakenly) desired gift of freedom was granted the minstrel slave, it might be voluntarily surrendered, as in Stephen Foster's 1851 "Ring, Ring de Banjo!": Once I was so lucky, My massa set me free, I went to old Kentucky To see what I could see: I could not go no farder, I turn to massa's door, I lub him all de harder, I'll go away no more.

Lott sees in this a contradictory message, as one might expect, given that his project is-rightly-to complicate our perception of minstrelsy. He considers it as one of many minstrel songs that "briefly or obliquely kick against plantation authority"; later in the song, massa dies, a "death that may be a murder," but, he continues, "is just as surely an unfortunate orphaning." For all its complexity, it was very often the case that the "minstrel show's message was that black people belonged only on Southern plantations and had no place at all in the North. 'Dis being free,' complained one minstrel character who had run away from the plantation, 'is worser dem being a slave.'" Before it became the anthem of the white Confederacy, that characteristic example of Southern homesickness expressed in music, "Dixie," had been a minstrel song. Minstrelsy often created for its audience a black America which wanted only security and endless play-which could exist only in a state of arrested childhood.

The entry of freedmen into the theater did little to change this situation. Blacks were largely excluded from both the audience and stage of the pre-Civil War white theater. With Abolition, this situation changed rapidly, with many freedmen taking to the stage and adopting the minstrel forms unaltered. It is not surprising that this first black venture into theater was a venture into minstrelsy; the audiences of these new troupes were mostly white, and pre-war minstrelsy had led them to expect nothing else. During the waning decades of the nineteenth century, a number of black minstrel performers became quite successful. Perhaps the most famous was Billy Kersands. Houston Baker, in Modernism and the Harlem Renaissance, likens Booker T. Washington's "mastery of minstrel form" (Washington's ability, when needed, to selectively play the minstrel clown for the edification of white philanthropists) to that of Kersands; both took up "types and tones of nonsense to earn a national reputation and its corollary benefits for the Afro-American masses." It is a pragmatic attitude, and a very sane one. What else could Washington, or Kersands, or any other ambitious black person do in the hostile environment of late nineteenth century America? Besides, as Nathan Huggins notes, "some black performers attempted to achieve the distance between the stage character and themselves by the very extremities of the exaggeration." Kersands, for example, became famous for his ability to deliver a speech with a mouth full of billiard balls. "Grotesques, themselves, could allow black men, as they did white men, the assurance that the foolishness on stage was not them." Nevertheless, the common delusion that minstrelsy and African American reality were one could only have been strengthened by the presence of "the real thing" on stage.

After the war, partly in response to the competition of the new black troupes, white minstrel shows began to swell. By 1880, the United Mastadon Minstrels, to give only one example, "featured a 'magnificent scene representing a Turkish Barbaric Palace in Silver and Gold' that included Turkish soldiers marching, a Sultan's palace, and 'Baseball.' And that was just one feature of the first part of the show." It is a long way from crippled Jim Crow to Turkish Barbaric Palaces in Silver and Gold, but by 1880, any minstrel show which relied on the old stereotypes-especially in the North, where the black population grew daily-was becoming an exercise in schizophrenia. The black minstrels who put on the old make-up and performed the old routines were, as one scholar has put it, "an imitation of an imitation of plantation life of Southern blacks." White minstrels had appropriated such elements of black culture as they thought would sell theater seats, ignoring some elements, highlighting others. When audiences exercised their economic power over the performers-their power, that is, to choose the most pleasing performance-the minstrel spectacle took another step away from the black reality. Between the black minstrel and his white audience there hung a veil of misunderstanding and make-believe: the black partially-selectively-silenced, the whites paying to see a cherished fantasy made briefly real. When members of the white audience left the theater, they hoped, often expected, sometimes demanded, that the minstrel play continue among the blacks they met in the street. Such was the environment in which *The Souls of Black Folk* was produced. In Du Bois's America, the color line had been partly drawn by the forward edge of the minstrel stage.

In their break with formalist criticism, the new historicists have perhaps been most radical in their insistence that, since all texts are embedded in the ideological discourse of their time, none are uninfluenced by ideology; all texts are political. While he is, of course, not a new historicist critic, Du Bois could hardly agree more with this insistence. "All art is propaganda and ever must be, despite the wailing of purists," he writes in "Criteria of Negro Art":

I stand in utter shamelessness and say that whatever art I have for writing has been used always for propaganda for gaining the right of black folk to love and enjoy. I do not care a damn for any art that is not used for propaganda. But I do care when propaganda is confined to one side while the other is stripped and silent. Much of Du Bois's career was devoted to breaking this silence. The main work of Souls is anticipated by his 1901 New York Times articles, in which he invites white readers to place themselves within the negro group and by studying that inner life look with him out upon the surrounding world. When a white person comes once vividly to realize the disabilities under which a negro labors, the public contempt and thinly veiled private dislike, "the spurns that patient merit of the unworthy takes"—when once one sees this, and then from personal knowledge knows that sensitive human hearts are enduring this, the question comes, How can they stand it?

When the question is finally asked by enough whites, he believes, social change for the better, for "the right of black folk to love and enjoy," will finally happen. This project is continued two years later in *The Souls of Black Folk,* which is thus first and foremost a political text; Du Bois speaks for the folk who, except for the unreal language of minstrelsy, had long been stripped and silent. Du Bois's fundamental design-his political agenda-is to subvert the color line which minstrelsy has helped to construct.

Du Bois aims to accomplish this end by offering convincing detail that black folk are just as human as any other folk. By focusing each chapter on a different aspect of black life, he demonstrates that "the longing of black men must have respect: the rich and bitter depth of their experience, the unknown treasures of their inner life, the strange rendings of nature they have seen, may give the world new points of view and make their loving, living, and doing precious to all human hearts." Du Bois argues that, although they do not yet know it, whites have much to gain from black culture. Du Bois's enemy is ignorance, both the ignorance of poor, unlettered blacks and that of whites still enamored of the minstrel fantasy. His audience lies within both races, but his terms of address are pointed mostly toward whites. Thus, in his "Forethought," he explains that he has "stepped within the Veil, raising it that you may view faintly its deeper recesses,—the meaning of its religion, the passion of its human sorrow, and the struggle of its greater souls." His ultimate goal is to arouse not pity, but acknowledgment of a shared humanity. In "Of Alexander Crummel," he writes of the nineteenth century as

> the first century of human sympathy,—the age when half wonderingly we began to descry in others that transfigured spark of divinity which we call Myself; when clodhoppers and peasants, and tramps and thieves, and millionaires and-sometimes—Negroes, became throbbing souls whose warm pulsing life touched us so nearly that we half gasped with surprise, crying, "Thou too!"

Having entered the twentieth century, his goal is to extend this sympathy to African Americans until it is no longer occasional, a deviation from the norm.

Du Bois's dominant metaphor for the communicative impasse which exists between the races is the Veil. It is an image that has received considerable critical attention. For such African American critics as Houston Baker, the metaphor is comprehensive: it "signifies a barrier of American racial segregation that keeps Afro-Americans always behind a color line—disoriented—prey to divided aims, dire economic circumstances, haphazard educational opportunities, and frustrated intellectual ambitions." Keith Byerman sees the persona narrating "Of the Passing of the First Born"—who is consoled by the thought that his dead son will not grow up "choked and deformed within the Veil" as "a man robbed of his vitality and jealous of his son for dying. What he has been made to feel as a result of his skin color has left him only with a death-wish.

He has suffocated beneath the Veil." Jerold Savory identifies a possible Biblical source of the Veil image; the "most frequent Biblical use of the term," he writes," is in reference to the Temple in which a large curtain (sometimes a double curtain) was hung to separate the 'holy of holies' from the public." Only high priests could pass within the veil; it is thus associated with power and oppression, and is "rent in twain" when Christ dies on the cross. Savory sees a connection with Du Bois's "conviction that the rending of the Veil must begin 'at the top' through the enlightened efforts of the 'Talented Tenth' of liberally educated Blacks qualified to assume positions of educational, economical, and political leadership." Arnold Rampersad sees an even more powerful connection between metaphor and actual oppression. According to Rampersad, Du Bois "links his image of the veil to the symbol of an ongoing slavery; at one and the same time, he records 'the wail of prisoned souls within the veil, and the mounting fury of shackled men.'" Into this single image, then, the color line and all the evils that flow from it are compressed.

Like the color line, the veil is insubstantial; it is much more a construct of perception and attitude than of any tangible difference. It is a creation of, among other influences, the minstrel fantasy. The fantasy itself is destructive (for instance, what banker would risk a loan to a black when he believes this person to be a happy, childlike clown?), and by showing black folk to be as human as white folk, Du Bois seeks to deconstruct both the fantasy and the color line. Although he does not often mention minstrelsy by name, he challenges the minstrel tradition quite clearly in his commitment to re-appropriating the Sorrow Songs.

Du Bois reveals that he is very much aware that an appropriation has taken place, and he specifically identifies the minstrel theater as a culprit. "Away back in the thirties the melody of these slave songs stirred the nation, but the songs were soon half forgotten. Some, like 'Near the lake where drooped the willow,' passed into current airs and their source was forgotten; others were caricatured on the 'minstrel' stage and their memory died away." He understates the popularity and staying power of the many hit songs minstrelsy produced, all based ultimate on slave music: "Turkey in the Straw," "Dixie," "Camptown Races," "Old Folks at Home," "My Old Kentucky Home," "Old Black Joe," "Beautiful Dreamer," all were minstrel songs. They also all exhibit key elements of the minstrel fantasy; when sung by the blackface performer, they expressed the sentiments of a simple, playful people, homesick for massa and the plantation. Along with other "debasements and imitations," Du Bois in *The Souls of Black Folk* refers to the minstrel tradition as "a mass of music in which the novice may easily lose himself and never find the real Negro music. . . ." In subverting the minstrel renditions by returning to the forgotten roots from which these songs sprang, his work of re-appropriation is partly a means to an end; showing black folk to possess a creative art form uniquely their own further rends the Veil. "They tell us in these eager days that life was joyous to the black slave, careless and happy. I can easily believe this of some, of many. But not all the past South, though it rose from the dead, can gainsay the heart-touching witness of these songs."

But Du Bois's re-appropriation is also an end in itself; his recovery of the Sorrow Songs is a project which underlies the entire book. We see this in those odd, enigmatic bars of music which stand as silent epigraphs at the head of each chapter. To the reader who cannot decipher music notation—which is to say, most readers today-they are as meaningful as the lines of poetry which accompany them would be to an illiterate slave. It is not until the final chapter that we learn the names of the songs to which these bars of music belong, and their lyrics. It is so by design. By the end of the book, the white reader has been introduced to life behind the Veil. If Du Bois's aim has been fulfilled, he or she will know that black folk possess souls as intricate as his or her own. If not thus prepared, the white reader might dismiss these slave songs as minstrel foolishness. *The Souls of Black Folk* is at least partly structured to enable such a reader to accept these songs as works of art.

It would be difficult to overemphasize the marginal status of the Sorrow Songs, from the time of their composition until Du Bois came to their aid. Most are religious in nature, but they were rarely permitted to be sung in church, especially before Emancipation. In the North, even black ministers disapproved of them as vulgar. Daniel Alexander Payne, for instance, at different times a minister, historian, and bishop of the African Methodist Episcopal Church, condemned the Sorrow Songs, calling them "cornfield ditties." In the South, religious gatherings of slaves, like all gatherings, were suppressed; but even in their secret gatherings, or in those permitted by lenient masters, "the slaves generally adhered to conventional forms of worship," singing only psalms and hymns approved by

the Methodist or Baptist churches. "Judging from the evidence, the singing of religious folksongs was not encouraged in formal services. [Plantation owner and memoirist R. Q. J. Mallard seemed to be proud of the fact that sometimes, when in a generous mood, he would let the slaves sing 'their own improvised spiritual' at church services." And while the success of the Fisk Jubilee Singers, among other touring black college groups, certainly lifted the status of the Sorrow Songs, such performances were no longer what they had been, by Du Bois's day.

When the spirituals were removed from the original setting of the plantation or the Negro Church and sung by persons who had not directly experienced slavery, these songs no longer served their primary function. Concert singers could present to the public only an approximation of how the spirituals had been sung by the slaves.

Independent of the liberties minstrelsy had taken with slave music, it enjoyed no great prestige when Du Bois took up its cause.

Du Bois communicates his sense of the cultural importance the Sorrow Songs possess in the first chapter: "there is no true American music but the wild sweet melodies of the Negro slave." This statement is reinforced by, again, Du Bois's dual chapter epigraphs. In this case, he plays a subtle and little noticed joke on the white reader. All fourteen of the slave song epigraphs are examples of "true American music," works of art belonging to a genre which is distinctly ours. But what of the poets whose works stand above those of the anonymous slaves? Byron, Elizabeth Barrett Browning (twice), Swinburne, Tennyson, Arthur Symons—the list is rather British. "The music of Negro religion . . . [,]despite caricature and defilement, still remains the most original and beautiful expression of human life and longing yet born on American soil."

But the importance of the Sorrow Songs does not lie merely in their ability to satisfy the literary nationalist; its potential role is too vital for that. As noted, Du Bois is confident that black folk have much to offer whites, and one of their latent gifts is their music. "Will America be poorer if she replace . . . her vulgar music with the soul of the Sorrow Songs?" Robert Stepto refers to this as Du Bois's "call for a truly plural American culture", involving "nothing less than his envisioning fresh spaces in which black and white Americans discover bonds beyond those generated by social-structured race rituals." The Veil is not merely to be lifted; positive cultural bonds are to replace it.

Du Bois's re-appropriation of the Sorrow Songs is not, however, a project aimed at rehabilitating them in the eyes of white Americans alone. Even more important is their rehabilitation in the eyes of the Talented Tenth of his fellow blacks.

The innate love of harmony and beauty that set the ruder souls of his people a-dancing and a-singing raised but confusion and doubt in the soul of the black artist; for the beauty revealed to him was the soulbeauty of a race which his larger audience despised, and he could not articulate the message of another people.

According to James Weldon Johnson, Du Bois succeeded. In *Along This Way,* Johnson refers to *The Souls of Black Folk* as ''a work which, I think, has had a greater effect upon and within the Negro race in America than any other single book published in this country since Uncle Tom's Cabin.'' Du Bois was not the first to treat the slave songs as something more than the raw material for minstrel buffoonery. As noted, the Fisk Jubilee Singers had already brought the Sorrow Songs before the white public, and with considerable success, earning the astonishing sum of $150,000 toward the support of Fisk University. Du Bois, however, may be the first to argue that the Sorrow Songs are works of art as important-and really no different than the high poetry with which they share his chapter headings. In this way, Du Bois's project of re-appropriation anticipates in a surprising way—and by about eight decades—one of the central arguments of new historicism—that the border between the literary and non-literary, between high art and low pastime, is an artificial construct of the ideology that prevails at any given time, and that such borders are permeable. His violation of the boundaries between high and low art is a radical one; beneath each of his chapter titles, the very highest and very lowest mix as equals. It is not so surprising when one reflects that all cultures possess a literature. In an analphabetic culture, the literature will be an oral one. The legendary Homer, the anonymous Beowulf poet, the ''Turoldus'' who recites the Song of Roland (and who is to us, like Jim Crow, no more than a name)—all three, whoever they were, produced works regarded as great literature by Du Bois's America, and our own. Though the forms are different (''primary'' epic versus folk song), they were engaged in the same cultural pursuit as the slaves who created the Sorrow Songs. Still, for Du Bois to equate the Sorrow Songs with the work of Byron, Tennyson, Shiller, and all the others is a subversive act indeed.

In so doing, he lays the foundations of the Harlem Renaissance, during which Alain Locke would declare black spirituals to be

> thematically rich, in idiom of rhythm and harmony richer still, in potentialities of new musical forms and new technical traditions so deep as to be accessible only to genius, they have the respect of the connoisseur even while still under the sentimental and condescending patronage of the amateur.

The Renaissance would have happened without Du Bois, of course. However, his confident assertion of equality between native black forms of aesthetic expression and those of the white majority—remarkably confident, at that early date—is an important precursor to Locke's very similar assertion. By re-appropriating the music which minstrelsy had debased, Du Bois provides the Harlem Renaissance with an example of an art form which is distinctively African American. His was the pioneering voice. As Johnson's Ex-Colored Man puts it, the future black novelist or poet will have an opportunity ''to give the country something new and unknown, in depicting the life, the ambitions, the struggles, and the passions of those of their race who are striving to break the narrow limits of traditions. A beginning has already been made in that remarkable book by Dr. Du Bois, *The Souls of Black Folk.''*

Source: Scott Herring, ''Du Bois and the Minstrels,'' in *MELUS,* Vol. 22, No. 2, Summer 1997, pp. 3–16.

Sources

Du Bois, W. E. B., *The Souls of Black Folk,* Library of America, 1986, pp. 3–191.

Ferris, William H., ''*The Souls of Black Folk:* The Book in Its Era,'' in *Critical Essays on W. E. B. Du Bois,* edited by William L. Andrews, G. K. Hall & Co., 1985, pp. 125–27.

Gates, Henry Louis, Jr., Introduction to *The Souls of Black Folk,* by W. E. B. Du Bois, Bantam, 1989, pp. xiv–xvii.

Rampersad, Arnold, *The Art and Imagination of W. E. B. Du Bois,* Harvard University Press, 1976, pp. 72–88.

Review in *New York Times,* April 25, 1903.

Further Reading

Broderick, Francis L., *W. E. B. Du Bois: Negro Leader in a Time of Crisis,* Stanford University Press, 1959.

Broderick, writing during Du Bois' lifetime, discusses Du Bois' life and achievements.

Gutman, Herbert G., *The Black Family in Slavery and Freedom 1750–1925,* Random House, 1976.
Gutman provides the definitive sociological and historical work on African-American life during and immediately after slavery.

Rampersad, Arnold, *The Art and Imagination of W. E. B. Du Bois,* Harvard University Press, 1976.
Rampersand provides a thorough discussion of Du Bois' stylistic approach to writing.

Tuttle, William M., *Great Lives Observed: W. E. B. Du Bois,* Prentice-Hall, 1973.
This is a collection of articles and essays concerning Du Bois' work in the context of his life.

A Study of History

Arnold J. Toynbee

1934–1961

Arnold Toynbee's multi-volume *A Study of History* is one of the major works of historical scholarship published in the twentieth century. The first volume was published in London in 1934, and subsequent volumes appeared periodically until the twelfth and final volume was published in London in 1961. A two-volume abridgement of volumes 1–10 was prepared by D. C. Somervell with Toynbee's cooperation and published in 1947 (volume one) and 1957 (volume two) in London.

A Study of History in its original form is a huge work. The first ten volumes contain over six thousand pages and more than three million words. Somervell's abridgement, containing only about one-sixth of the original, runs to over nine hundred pages. The size of the work is in proportion to the grandeur of Toynbee's purpose, which is to analyze the genesis, growth, and fall of every human civilization ever known. In Toynbee's analysis, this amounts to five living civilizations and sixteen extinct ones, as well as several that Toynbee defines as arrested civilizations.

Toynbee detects in the rise and fall of civilizations a recurring pattern, and it is the laws of history behind this pattern that he analyzes in *A Study of History*.

From the outset, *A Study of History* was a controversial work. It won wide readership amongst the general public, especially in the United States, and after World War II Toynbee was hailed as a

prophet of his times. On the other hand, his work was viewed with skepticism by academic historians, many of whom argued that his methods were unscientific and his conclusions unreliable or simply untrue. Despite these criticisms, however, *A Study of History* endures as a provocative vision of where humanity has been, and why, and where it may be headed.

Author Biography

Arnold J. Toynbee was born in London on April 14, 1889, the son of Harry V. Toynbee, a social worker, and Sarah Edith Marshall Toynbee, a historian. Showing academic promise at a young age, Toynbee won scholarships to attend Winchester School from 1902 to 1907, and then Balliol College, Oxford, where he studied Classics and graduated in 1911. In the same year, Toynbee pursued his interest in ancient Greek history by studying at the British Archeological School in Athens. In 1912, he became a fellow and tutor at Balliol College, a position he held for three years. Unable to perform military service because of his health, during World War I he worked in the Political Intelligence Department of the War Office and was a member of the British delegation at the Paris Peace Conference in 1919. He also held the Koraes Chair of Byzantine and Modern Greek Studies at London University in 1919.

In 1925, Toynbee began a thirty-year tenure as director of studies at the Royal Institute of International Affairs and professor of international history at London University. He was a prolific author, writing more than 140 articles and books between 1921 and 1934, including *The Western Question in Greece and Turkey* (1922), *Greek Historical Thought* (1924), *Greek Civilisation and Character* (1924), the annual *Survey of International Affairs* (1923–1927), and *A Journey to China* (1931). He was also at work on *A Study of History*, for which he is best known. The first three volumes of this investigation into the rise and fall of civilizations were published in 1934; volumes 4–6 followed in 1939.

From 1943 until 1946, Toynbee directed the Research Department at the Foreign Office. He also attended the second Paris Peace Conference as a British delegate. In 1954, volumes 7–10 of *A Study of History* were published. An abridged version,

prepared by D. C. Somervell with Toynbee's cooperation, appeared in two volumes (1947 and 1957).

Toynbee's massive work made him one of the best-known historians of his time although it also proved controversial. The final, twelfth volume, *Reconsiderations* (1961), was an attempt to answer his many critics.

After finishing *A Study of History*, Toynbee continued to publish at a prolific rate. Between 1956 and 1973, he wrote sixteen books. These included *An Historian's Approach to Religion* (1956), in which he advocated a return to spiritual values, *Change and Habit: The Challenge of Our Time* (1966), in which he suggested that China might emerge as a unifying influence in world affairs, and the autobiographical *Experiences* (1969).

Toynbee married Rosalind Murray in 1912, and they had two children. The marriage ended in divorce in 1945. In 1946, Toynbee married Veronica Marjorie Boulter, a research associate and writer. They collaborated in writing the *Survey of International Affairs*.

Toynbee died in York, England, on October 22, 1975.

Summary

Chapter 1: The Unit of Historical Study
In *A Study of History*, Toynbee first identifies the unit that should be the object of the historian's study. This unit is not an individual nation but an entire civilization. Toynbee identifies five living civilizations: Western Christian, Orthodox Christian, Islamic, Hindu, and Far Eastern. In addition there are sixteen extinct civilizations from which living civilizations developed. Toynbee then makes a distinction between primitive societies, of which there are many, and civilizations, which are comparatively few. He dismisses the idea that there is now only one civilization, the West, and also the notion that all civilization originated in Egypt.

Chapter 2: Geneses of Civilizations
How do civilizations emerge from primitive societies? For Toynbee, the answer does not lie in race; nor does an easy environment provide a key to the origins of civilization. On the contrary, civilizations arise out of creative responses to difficult situations. It is difficulty, rather than ease, that proves the stimulus. Toynbee identifies five chal-

lenges that aid the process: a hard environment; a new environment; one or more "blows," such as a military defeat; pressures, such as a frontier society subjected to frequent attack; and penalizations, such as slavery or other measures in which one class or race is oppressed by another. Some challenges, however, prove to be too severe and do not result in a civilization's growth.

Chapter 3: Growths of Civilizations

After examining why some civilizations (Polynesian, Eskimo) cease to develop, Toynbee discusses how the growth of a society is to be measured. He concludes that neither military nor political expansion, nor advances in agricultural or industrial techniques, are reliable criteria. These are external indicators, whereas what is important is "etherialization." In this process, the energies of a society are directed away from external material obstacles, which have been overcome, towards challenges that arise from within and require an inner or spiritual response. Growth happens because of creative individuals who exhibit a pattern of withdrawal from and return to society.

Arnold J. Toynbee

Chapter 4: Breakdowns of Civilizations

The breakdown of a civilization, Toynbee holds, is not due to some inevitable cosmic law. Nor is it caused by loss of control over the physical or human environment, a decline in technology, or military aggression. A breakdown happens when the creative minority loses its creative power and the majority no longer follows it, or follows it only because it is compelled to do so. This results in a loss of social unity and the emergence of a disaffected "proletariat." Creative minorities lose their power because they have a habit of "resting on their oars" following their success and becoming infatuated with the past. Therefore they fail to meet the next challenge successfully.

Chapter 5: Disintegration of Civilizations

When a civilization disintegrates, it splits into three factions: a "dominant minority," which is a degenerate stage of a formerly creative minority; an "internal proletariat," which is a mass of people within the civilization who no longer have any allegiance to the dominant minority and may rebel against it; and an "external proletariat" that exists beyond the frontiers of the civilization and resists being incorporated into it. An internal proletariat may react violently against the dominant minority,

but later there may be a more peaceful reaction, culminating in the discovery of a "higher religion."

Social changes in a disintegrating civilization are accompanied by changes in behavior, beliefs, and ways of life. There is either a sense of "drift," in which people believe the world is ruled by chance, or a sense of sin, both of which are substitutes for the creative energy that has been lost. There may also be "archaism," a desire to return to the past, or "futurism," a revolutionary mode in which old institutions are scrapped. Disintegration of a civilization proceeds in a rhythm of "routs" followed by "rallies." During this process, creative personalities will emerge as different kinds of "saviours."

Chapter 6: Universal States

A universal state appears as part of the "rally" stage in the disintegration of a civilization; it follows a "Time of Troubles" and brings political unity. However, it is still part of the process of disintegration. Although universal states fail to save themselves, they do offer unintended advantages to other institutions, such as the higher religions of their internal proletariats. Universal states provide high "conductivity" between different geographic areas and between social classes. They are often ruled with tolerance, which helps to facilitate the spread of higher religions. Many of the institutions established by a universal state, such as communications, legal systems, weights and measures, money, and civil services, are made use of by communities other than those for which they were designed.

Chapter 7: Universal Churches

Toynbee analyzes the relationship between churches and civilizations. He repudiates the idea that a church is like a social cancer that leads to the decline of the universal state. But the idea that churches act as chrysalises, keeping civilization alive as it evolves from one manifestation into the next, is not the entire truth either, he writes. Toynbee argues that, rather than religion being a by-product of civilization, the whole purpose of a civilization is to provide an opportunity for one of the higher religions (Christianity, Hinduism, Buddhism, Islam) to emerge.

Chapter 8: Heroic Ages

When a disintegrating civilization is destroyed by barbarians who have previously co-existed alongside it, the result is a Heroic Age. The barbarians are not sufficiently advanced to benefit from the legacy of the civilization they have destroyed although they may commemorate their victories in epic poetry. A Heroic Age is an interlude between the death of one civilization and the birth of another. It leads to a Dark Age, out of which civilization reemerges.

Chapter 9: Contacts between Civilizations in Space

When diverse civilizations come into contact with each other, there is usually conflict, with disastrous results. A civilization under assault may fight back by military means; with ideological propaganda (as the Soviet Union did against the West); by intensely cultivating its own religion; or by creating a higher religion. A victorious civilization will sometimes become militarized, to its own ultimate cost. It also pays the price of having the culture of the alien civilization seep into its own social life, which may have adverse consequences. A civilization that subjugates another may make the mistake of regarding the conquered people as ''heathens,'' ''barbarians,'' or ''natives.''

Chapter 10: Contacts between Civilizations in Time

Toynbee surveys the many renaissances in history in which one civilization has drawn new inspiration from a civilization of the past. The best-known example is the influence of the dead Hellenic civilization on Western Christendom in the late medieval period (the Italian Renaissance).

Chapter 11: Law and Freedom in History

Does history unfold according to laws of nature or is the process random? Toynbee argues for the former. He cites examples from human affairs such as business and economics that show the operation of predictable laws. Then he points to a cyclic pattern of war and peace in modern Western history and notes that disintegrating civilizations follow a similar pattern of rout-and-rally. Humankind can harness these laws of nature to its benefit although the extent to which it is able to do so depends on its own psychology and on its relationship with God, who represents a higher law than the law of nature.

Chapter 12: Prospects of Western Civilization

Worship of the nation-state and militarism are negative aspects of modern Western civilization, Toynbee holds, but it has also achieved positive results in promoting democracy and education. Toynbee discusses prospects for world peace, world government, and issues arising from modern technology. The price a society pays for freedom from want is increasing regimentation, which encroaches on personal freedom. Toynbee holds out the hope that in a mechanized society in which there is more leisure, people will have more energy to devote to spiritual matters.

Key Figures

Andean

The Andean civilization in Peru emerged on the Andean coast and plateau around the beginning of the Christian era. The challenge it had to overcome was a bleak climate on an almost soil-less plateau. It is not known when its Time of Troubles began, but it lasted until 1430 A.D. and was followed by the universal state of the Inca Empire. A time of peace followed until 1533, when the empire was destroyed by the arrival of the Spanish.

Arabic

The Arabic civilization developed out of the Syriac civilization and flourished mainly in Syria and Egypt. It was similar to the Iranic civilization; the main difference was that in the Iranic civilization, the predominant faith was Islamic Shi'ism, whereas in the Arabic civilization, Sunnism predominated.

Arrested Civilizations

Arrested civilizations are those that have stayed alive but have failed to grow. They arose in response to a physical or human challenge of unusual severity, on the borderline between the degree that gives stimulus to greater development and that which brings about defeat. They attempted and achieved a *tour de force* but could not grow any further. Examples include, in response to physical challenges, the Polynesians, Eskimos, and Nomads; and in response to human challenges, the Spartans in the Hellenic world and the Osmanlis in the Orthodox Christian world

Babylonic

Babylonic civilization emerged in Iraq before 1500 B.C. out of the disintegrating Sumeric civilization with which it continued to have much in common. It endured a Time of Troubles during the seventh century B.C. in which it was at war with the Assyrians. Following this, a Neo-Babylonic Empire (a universal state) was established from 610 to 539 B.C. under the reign of Nebuchadnezzar. After conquest by Cyrus the Persian, the Babylonic universal state was swallowed up by the universal state of the Achaemenian Empire of Cyrus; Babylonian civilization was absorbed into the Syriac civilization.

Egyptaic

The Egyptaic civilization emerged in the Nile River Valley before 4000 B.C. The challenge it faced was environmental: to clean, drain, and cultivate what was formerly a jungle-swamp uninhabited by man. It reached a peak of growth and creativity in the fourth dynasty with major achievements in engineering (including the pyramids), political administration, art, and religion. Decline set in with the Time of Troubles from circa 2424 to 2070/60 B.C., and this resulted in a universal state, which lasted from c. 2000 to 1788 B.C. The universal state was overthrown by invasion of the Hykos but was later reestablished as the New Empire. Each universal state produced a "universal peace," the second of which lasted until 1175 B.C. The Egyptaic civilization became extinct in the fifth century A.D. It had no forebears and no successors.

Far Eastern Christian

The Far Eastern Christian civilization arose in Central Asia and perished in 737–741 A.D. when it was annexed to the Arab Empire. It had been separate from the rest of the Syriac world for nearly nine hundred years.

Far Eastern—Japanese Offshoot

The Japanese offshoot of the main body of Far Eastern civilization arose in the Japanese Archipelago after 500 A.D. It endured a Time of Troubles from 1185 to 1597 in which there was political disunity and civil war. This period was followed by a universal state until 1863. Japanese civilization produced the religion of Zen Buddhism. It is now in a state of disintegration because of the impact of Western civilization.

Far Eastern—Main Body

The Far Eastern civilization emerged in China before 500 A.D. out of the disintegrating Sinic civilization. It began to break down in the late ninth century A.D. Its Time of Troubles lasted from about 878 to 1280, followed by successive universal states founded by barbarians. The first was the Mongol Empire (1280–1351); another was the Manchu Empire (1644–1853). The Far Eastern remains a living civilization.

Far Western Christian

The Far Western Christian civilization arose mainly in Ireland after c. 375 A.D. The Celts molded Christianity to fit their own social heritage, and their originality can be seen in their church organization, literature, and art. This civilization was destroyed by a combination of the Vikings from the ninth to eleventh centuries, the ecclesiastical authority of Rome, and the political authority of England in the twelfth century.

Hellenic

The Hellenic civilization was loosely affiliated with the Minoan; its offspring were the Western and Orthodox Christian civilizations. It first emerged in the coasts and islands of the Aegean before 1100 B.C.; the challenge it faced was to overcome barren land, the sea, and the disintegrating Minoan society. The Hellenic civilization's Time of Troubles began in 431 B.C. with the outbreak of the Peloponnesian war, which ended in victory for Sparta in 404 B.C. The Time of Troubles continued until 32 B.C. when a universal state, the Roman Empire, was established. A time of peace endured to 378 A.D. The Hellenic civilization collapsed with the downfall of the Roman Empire in the fifth century A.D. It produced great achievements in politics, art, literature, architecture, science, and philosophy. Notable individuals included Plato, Aristotle, Pythagoras, Socrates, Aeschylus, Sophocles, and Zeno.

Hindu

The Hindu civilization arose in North India before 800 A.D. out of the disintegrating Indic civilization. Its Time of Troubles was 1175–1572 A.D., followed by a universal state, the Mughal Empire, 1572–1707. When this collapsed it was replaced within a century by the British Raj, from 1818 to 1947. The Hindu civilization developed the religions of Sikhism and Hinduism. The latter is associated with the name of Sankara, who lived about 800 A.D. The Hindu civilization remains a living one.

Hittite

The Hittite civilization emerged from Cappadocia, just beyond the borders of the Sumeric civilization, before 1500 B.C. Its main challenge was to deal with the disintegrating Sumeric civilization. The Hittites were constantly at war with Egypt from 1352 to 1278 B.C. Hittite civilization was overwhelmed by a wave of migration from 1200 to 1190 B.C.

Indic

The Indic civilization emerged circa 1500 B.C. in the Indus and Ganges river valleys from where it spread to cover the entire Indian subcontinent. The environmental challenge to which it had to respond was the luxuriant tropical forests in the Ganges valley. Indic civilization went through a Time of Troubles up to 322 B.C. after which a universal state, the Mauryan Empire, came into being, 322–185 B.C. Another universal state, the Guptan Empire, arose c. 375–475 A.D.; it was followed by three hundred years of invasion by Huns and Gurjaras. Indic civilization produced the religion of the Vedas, the Buddha (567–487 B.C.), and Jainism.

Iranic

The Iranic civilization was affiliated with the Syriac. It arose in Iran, Iraq, Syria, and North Africa before 1300 A.D. out of the disintegrating Syriac civilization. The chrysalis that enabled it to emerge was the Islamic Church. Its ''twin'' civilization was the Arabic with which it fused in 1516 to form the Islamic civilization. In modern times, the Pan-Islamic movement has suggested the coming of a universal state, but this state has not so far occurred.

Mayan

The Mayan civilization emerged in the Central American tropical forests before c. 500 B.C. Its challenge was to overcome the luxuriance of the forest. A Time of Troubles occurred from an unknown date until 300 A.D. after which the First Empire of the Mayas was formed. Although not technologically advanced, the Mayas achieved a high level of civilization, excelling in astronomy. The Mayan civilization came to a rapid and mysterious end in the seventh century A.D. Its ruined cities still remain in the midst of tropical forests.

Mexic

The Mexic civilization arose from the disintegration of the Mayan civilization and it fused with the Yucatec to form a Central American civilization. A Time of Troubles occurred up to 1521 A.D.; the Aztecs were on the verge of establishing a universal state when the Spanish arrived. With the coming of Western civilization, the Mexic civilization lost its distinctive identity.

Minoan

The Minoan civilization emerged in the Aegean islands before 3000 B.C. Its main challenge was the sea. It underwent a Time of Troubles from an unknown date to 1750 B.C. before being unified in a universal state known as the Thalassocracy of Minos. It enjoyed 350 years of peace. The Heroic Age that followed the invasion by barbarians and the disintegration of the Minoan universal state can be glimpsed in the epic poetry of Homer's *Iliad* and *Odyssey*.

Orthodox Christian—Main Body

The Orthodox Christian civilization is, with Western civilization, a twin offshoot of Hellenic civilization. It emerged as a result of a schism in the Catholic Church into two bodies, the Roman Catholic Church and the Orthodox Church. This split began with the Iconoclastic controversy in the eighth century and became final in 1054. Orthodox Christian civilization went through a Time of Troubles between 977 and 1372; this period ended with the establishment of a universal state, the Ottoman Empire, which lasted from 1372 to 1768. Orthodox Christianity is found mainly in southern and eastern Europe.

Orthodox Christian—Russian Offshoot

The Russian offshoot of the Orthodox Christian civilization emerged in Russia in the tenth century. Its Time of Troubles began in the twelfth century with the break-up of the Russian Principality of Kiev into warring states; it was aggravated by the invasion of the Mongols in 1238. The Time of Troubles did not end until 1478, when a universal state was established through the union of Muscovy and Novgorod, a state that lasted until 1881. Like all living civilizations, the Russian branch of the Orthodox civilization has been heavily influenced, to the point of breakdown, by Western civilization.

Scandinavian

The Scandinavian civilization emerged after the break-up of the Roman Empire. The Scandinavians had been isolated from Roman Christendom, and their pagan civilization grew as a result of Viking conquests from the eighth to the eleventh century. The civilization was doomed, however, after the Icelanders were converted to Christianity in the year 1000.

Sinic

The Sinic civilization developed in the lower valley of the Yellow River in northern China around 1500 B.C. It had to overcome the challenge of marshes, floods, and extremes of temperature. Its Time of Troubles was from 634 to 221 B.C., after which a universal state, the Ts'in Empire (and later the Han Empire) was formed. The Sinic civilization produced the philosopher Confucius and the great works of Taoism and is also associated with Mahayana Buddhism, which reached it from the Indic civilization.

Sumeric

The Sumeric civilization began in the lower Tigris-Euphrates valley c. 4300–3100. B.C., where it had to overcome the difficult jungle-swamp environment. It faced a Time of Troubles from c. 2677–2298 B.C., in which Sumerian city-states were at war. After this the Empire of Sumer and Akkad established unity and peace in a universal state that lasted until 2230 B.C. It was restored by Hammurabi c. 1947 B.C. and broke up after his death.

Syriac

The Syriac civilization emerged in Syria before 1100 B.C. out of the disintegrating Minoan civilization. From c. 937 to 525 B.C. it went through a Time of Troubles before becoming a universal state in the form of the Achaemenian Empire, c. 525–332 B.C. In the last century B.C., it absorbed the Babylonic civilization. A second universal state occurred during the Arab Caliphate, 640–969 A.D. Three great achievements of Syriac society were the invention of the alphabet, the discovery of the Atlantic Ocean, and a monotheistic conception of God that is common to Judaism, Zoroastrianism, Christianity, and Islam. Through its universal church, Islam, Syriac civilization contributed to the rise of the Iranic and Arabic civilizations.

Western

Western civilization arose in Western Europe before 700 A.D. Affiliated with the Hellenic civilization, it arose out of the chaos that followed the break-up of the Roman Empire. In the eighth century, it covered only Britain and the dominions of Charlemagne in Western Europe, but it has shown a tendency to expand its boundaries. This expansion began in earnest in the last quarter of the fifteenth century. Since then, Western civilization has spread across the globe, encroaching on or absorbing all other living civilizations. This is particularly apparent in the economic and political spheres; this ascendency has not yet obliterated the distinctive cultures of the other civilizations. Western Civilization can be divided into four periods or chapters: the Dark Ages (675–1075); Middle Ages (1075–1475); Modern (1475–1875); and from 1875 on, which Toynbee tentatively describes as Postmodern.

Yucatec

The Yucatec civilization was the offspring of the Mayan civilization. It arose after 629 A.D. on a desolate limestone shelf of the Yucatan peninsula and had to overcome the dry, treeless terrain. It also had the challenge of forming an identity distinct from the disintegrating Mayan civilization. Although its people were skilled in metallurgy, the Yucatec civilization never achieved the heights that the Mayan had; it was absorbed by the Mexic civilization in the twelfth century.

Themes

Laws of History

The basic premise of *A Study of History* is that civilizations emerge, grow, break down, and disintegrate according to a consistent, recurrent pattern. Since Toynbee believed that the universe was not

Topics for Further Study

- Why has the West assumed such a dominant role in the world today? Is the West a force for good? If it is, why do many other countries, particularly in Asia and the Arab world, resent Western influence in their affairs?

- Are Western democracy and capitalism always the best ways to organize human society, or might other ways be equally valid? If so, what might those ways be, and in what situations might they work? (You might want to consider tribalism, socialism, communism, monarchy, and/or dictatorship.)

- Is Toynbee's law of challenge-and-response an adequate explanation of the genesis of civilizations? According to Toynbee's law, a difficult environment is more conducive to growth than an easy one. Might such a law apply in the lives of individuals, too? Can you list any examples from your own life when hardship produced more success than ease might have done?

- Explore Toynbee's law of withdrawal and return in the lives of creative people. He gives examples from the lives of seven great men: St. Paul, St. Benedict, St. Gregory the Great, the Buddha, Muhammad, Machiavelli, and Dante. Research two more historical figures and show how the same law operated to produce some of their significant achievements. Also, think of achievements in your own life. Was a rhythm of withdrawal and return operating there, too?

---

chaotic but subject to laws, he argued that those laws must also be observable in human history.

Although *A Study of History* is a voluminous work, the basic outline of this pattern of laws operating in history is quite simple. A primitive society evolves into a civilization because it successfully responds to a challenge in either the physical or the human environment. This pattern of challenge and response continually recurs because each successfully met challenge generates another challenge, which demands another creative response, and so on. Employing terms taken from Chinese philosophy, Toynbee identifies this as a movement from the state of Yin (rest) to that of Yang (action) and declares it to be one of the fundamental rhythms of the universe.

The engines of societal growth are creative individuals and groups. They also obey a law, which Toynbee defines as withdrawal-and-return. They withdraw from society, whether literally or figuratively, and develop knowledge, wisdom, or power, and then return to society and bring the benefits of their labors to everyone. The majority then follows this creative minority in a process of mimesis, or imitation, and so the civilization advances. Toynbee points out that the law of withdrawal-and-return can be found not only in the human sphere but also in the annual withdrawal and return of agricultural crops. He also notes that the same law applies to human spiritual growth, especially in the Christian doctrine of resurrection. This is typical of the way Toynbee uses analogies from the natural world and from spheres of human activity other than the political to emphasize his point about recurring patterns and laws.

The breakdown of a civilization also follows predictable laws. It occurs when the creative minority is no longer able to meet a challenge successfully. The "internal proletariat" no longer sees any reason to follow it, and the "external proletariat" (those groups outside the civilization's formal borders who are influenced by developments within it) becomes hostile. Social disruption and wars follow, a stage that Toynbee calls a Time of Troubles. Out of the Time of Troubles emerges a conqueror, who imposes peace through a universal state, which is an attempt to reverse the decline. An example of a universal state, and one of the many models that Toynbee discusses, is the Roman Empire, which was born out of the disintegration phase of Hellenic civilization. But the universal state cannot permanently reverse the decline or avoid the eventual collapse of the civilization.

Everywhere Toynbee looks, he sees patterns, laws, rhythms, and cycles, not only in the broad rise and fall of civilizations, but in smaller details, too. For example, when analyzing modern Western history over the previous four hundred years, he discerns a recurring pattern of four cycles, which he even puts in tabular form in chapter 11: first there is an ''overture'' in which minor wars serve as a prelude to what is to come; this is followed first by a ''general war,'' then by a ''breathing space'' of relative peace, then by a ''supplementary war'' (which he calls the Epilogue), and finally by a ''general peace.'' Toynbee states that similar patterns can be found in the Hellenic and Sinic civilizations.

Toynbee was aware that in developing the concept of laws of history he was going against the grain as far as the modern trend of historical study was concerned. He noted that many modern historians rejected the idea that history could be understood in terms of an orderly pattern based on the operation of discernible laws. He quoted an unidentified English novelist who, wishing to express the idea that history was merely a succession of meaningless events, coined the word ''Odtaa,'' standing for ''one damn thing after another.'' But Toynbee begged to differ.

One consequence of Toynbee's system is that, if accepted, it would make the entirety of human history intelligible. It would also mean that given the presence of recurring patterns, the historian would be in a position to offer predictions about the future course of human history, a task that Toynbee did indeed undertake, if somewhat reluctantly, in chapter 12 of *A Study of History*.

Religion

Writing in 1955, Toynbee stated, ''Religion has come, once again, to take the central place in my picture of the Universe.'' This is made clear in chapter 7 of *A Study of History*. In earlier chapters, Toynbee takes the view that civilizations are the dominant element in history, and that the higher religions (Christianity, Buddhism, Islam, and Hinduism) are only by-products, coming into existence as the civilizations disintegrate. In chapter 7, he describes a new view. Rather than seeing religions in terms of civilizations, he now sees civilizations in terms of religions. According to this view, the whole purpose of civilization is to provide an opportunity for a higher religion to come into being. (By ''higher religions'' Toynbee means those religions that are universal, as opposed to the lower religions that are merely local and restricted to one tribe or parochial state.) A consequence of Toynbee's new perspective is that the breakdown and disintegration of a civilization does not mean that it has failed; on the contrary, it may have succeeded in its main task. Rather than being a by-product of a civilization that may have some other main purpose, religion is civilization's most valuable fruit.

Toynbee uses an analogy of the wheel to explicate his view further. He sees the rising and falling of civilizations like revolutions of a wheel, which ''carry forward the vehicle which the wheel conveys.'' The vehicle conveyed by Toynbee's wheel is religion.

The same image helps Toynbee explain why the higher religions are born during the downward turns of the wheel, in periods of decline. He argues that this is necessary because there is a spiritual law according to which progress comes only through suffering. Low points in secular life may be high points in spiritual history.

Although he is steeped in the Christianity of his own civilization, Toynbee does not regard Christianity as the only route to spiritual enlightenment. He sees all the higher religions as having a role to play, particularly in the modern age in which global communications have facilitated an unprecedented level of contact between different faiths. He considers the possibility that in a forthcoming universal state that includes the whole world

> the respective adherents of the four living higher religions might come to recognize that their once rival systems were so many alternate approaches to the One True God along avenues offering diverse partial glimpses of the Beatific Vision.

Toynbee even envisions the possibility that in the future, the diverse religions might come together and form a single church.

Style

Simile and Analogy

Toynbee frequently makes use of similes and analogies in which two apparently dissimilar things are compared. The purpose of these similes is to enable the reader to visualize the concept that is being presented and make it easier to grasp. One extended simile recurs at several points in the book, and that is Toynbee's comparison of civilizations to humans climbing a mountain. Primitive civilizations are like people lying asleep on a ledge with a precipice below and a precipice above. No further progress is possible for them. Arrested civilizations are like climbers who have reached a certain height but now find themselves blocked; they can go neither forward nor backward. Civilizations that are ready to grow, however, are like climbers who have just risen to their feet and are beginning to climb the face of the cliff. They cannot stop until they either fall back to the ledge or reach another, higher ledge.

In another extended simile, Toynbee compares the influence of a creative minority in a civilization to a physical beam of light that radiates outward. He calls this a "culture ray," in which the economic, political, and cultural aspects of a civilization radiate to those living outside its formal borders. His description of the process is an example of the poetic quality of much of Toynbee's prose:

> The light shines as far as, in the nature of things, it can carry until it reaches its vanishing-point. The gradations are infinitesimal, and it is impossible to demarcate the line at which the last glimmer of twilight flickers out and leaves the heart of darkness in undivided possession.

Toynbee believes the culture ray to be a very powerful force because although civilizations are a comparatively recent development in human history, they have succeeded during that period in permeating, to a greater or lesser extent, virtually every primitive society.

A third extended simile is that of a dam. Toynbee uses this to illustrate the way a disintegrating civilization creates a military barrier to insulate itself from the alienated people outside its borders. The barrier acts like a physical dam. However, in the long run it is always breached. In chapter 8, Toynbee elaborates at great length and sophistication, in terms of his simile of the dam, on how this happens. The water that is piled up above the dam (the equivalent of the civilization's hostile external proletariat) seeks to find the same level as the water below it (the civilization), and it continually exerts pressure to that effect. Just as engineers construct safety valves in the form of sluices, so does the defending civilization attempt techniques that will keep its own "dam" from collapsing. One technique is to enlist some of their barbarian adversaries on their own side. But the safety valves fail because the forces outside the military barrier (the equivalent of the water above the dam) are forever on the rise. When the barbarians finally break through, the result, as with the bursting of a physical dam, is calamity all round.

Style

A Study of History has been compared to a mighty river, meandering along its course and gathering strength from many tributary streams. It might also be thought of as a great cathedral, in which every stone, every stained-glass window, and every historical monument in the interior help to create the final edifice that reveals the grandeur of humanity's spiritual aspiration. In constructing this imposing edifice, not only does Toynbee seem to know almost everything about so many different civilizations, his style of exposition is equally eclectic. In addition to the facts and historical research that are the tools of the historian's profession, he makes frequent use of mythology and world literature. He has an eye for the apt quotation that perfectly captures his idea, as when a passage from a poem by American poet Walt Whitman illustrates the Toynbee theory of a recurring rhythm of challenge and response through which a civilization grows: "It is provided in the essence of things that from any fruition of success, no matter what, shall come forth something to make a greater struggle necessary." Shakespeare is employed to illustrate the idea that civilizations are destroyed not by outside forces but from within; Shakespeare is brought in again to illustrate the Toynbee law of "etherialization," in which the vital sphere of a growing civilization shifts from the external to the internal world. Goethe's poem *Faust* is used to illustrate the challenge and response pattern, and references to the Bible and classical myths are too numerous to detail. Toynbee uses this eclectic approach to his subject to capture a vital dimension of human history that may be unobtainable by a method that deals only with strict empirical facts.

Historical Context

Nationalism

The growth of nationalism was one of the most important developments in nineteenth- and twentieth-century Western history. Toynbee disliked nationalism, regarding it as one of the besetting evils of the modern world. He believed it was the cause of war. He also believed that emphasis on the nation-state led to distorted versions of history. This was why he took civilizations rather than nations as the

Compare & Contrast

- **1950s:** The Cold War between the United States and the Soviet Union dominates the political landscape of the world.

  Today: The world is no longer divided into two competing superpowers. The United States is generally considered to be the sole superpower, but there are other regional centers of power, such as the countries that comprise the European Union, as well as Japan, Russia, and China.

- **1950s:** There is a wide expectation in the industrialized world that machines and robots will soon take over many of the tasks now performed by humans. This is expected to result in greater leisure. Toynbee believes this may mean that people will spend more of their time participating in religious practices.

  Today: The average American works more hours than his or her counterpart did a generation ago.

Mechanization has not resulted in more leisure although technology has produced a greater variety of choices as to how leisure time is spent.

- **1950s:** Global population nears three billion, and efforts to curb it begin. The Population Council is formed by John D. Rockefeller III; the International Planned Parenthood Federation is also formed.

  Today: The United Nations estimates that world population passed six billion in late 1999 and is growing at the rate of seventy-seven million a year. Efforts at population control emphasize not only contraception and family planning but also the improvement of every aspect of women's lives, including health, education, political rights, and economic independence. High levels of education, coupled with economic prosperity, are known to correlate with lower birth rates.

---

units of historical study. Toynbee also wanted to combat another dangerous modern tendency, that of Eurocentric or Western bias, which he called an "egocentric illusion." He did not view Western civilization as the apex of human development since this left no room for objective evaluation of civilizations originating in China and India, let alone South and Central American civilizations.

World Wars I and II

A Study of History was influenced by the times in which Toynbee lived. In 1920, Western civilization was facing the challenge of recovering after the devastation of World War I. It was in that year that Toynbee first conceived the idea that there might be uniform laws governing the rise and fall of civilizations. He noted striking parallels between the situation facing the West and the challenge faced by the Hellenic civilization following the Pelopponesian war in the fifth century B.C. This parallel between the two civilizations was the seed idea that led to the structure elaborated in *A Study of History*.

World War II also affected Toynbee's work. Volumes 4–6 of *A Study of History* were published the year the war broke out. Since they dealt for the most part with the breakdown and disintegration of civilizations, they were very timely.

Toynbee was unable to resume his work until 1947 because of the war. His views had been modified by the intervening events. Because of the destructive power of the newly created atomic bomb, he now possessed a more pessimistic view of the future prospects for Western and other civilizations. He also allocated a far more important place to the higher religions of the world than before.

The Cold War

When Toynbee was writing his final volumes, the Cold War between the United States and Russia, the two superpowers that had emerged after World War II, dominated the world. Toynbee gave considerable attention to this situation in chapter 12 of *A Study of History*. He noted that if a third world war should break out, the result might be the annihilation of human life on Earth. He concluded that the only alternative was to move toward political unification of the world with control of nuclear weapons in the hands of one power. He did not see the United Nations as capable of fulfilling such a role. Instead, it would have to be carried out by one of the two superpowers. Of these two powers, Toynbee held a more favorable view of the United States. Toynbee found the United States, with its history of federalism, more suited to assuming the principal position in a world government.

Population Growth

In the second half of the twentieth century, one of the major problems facing the world, Toynbee believed, was unchecked population growth. He pointed out that the population of China had doubled in the hundred years from the middle of the nineteenth century to the middle of the twentieth. India and Indonesia, two of the most populous countries in the world, showed a similar rate of population growth. Much of the growth was due to reduced infant and child mortality rates. Toynbee believed that if the trend continued, world population would outstrip the earth's capacity to feed everyone. Even the most sophisticated technology would not be able to prevent this. After all, Toynbee argued, the Earth's surface is finite; only so much food can be produced from it. The result of over-population would be famine unless a world government was formed to restrict the rights of humans to procreate. Toynbee acknowledged the many difficulties and tensions this loss of personal liberty would create.

Critical Overview

There were two markedly different reactions to *A Study of History*. The general public gave the book an enthusiastic reception, but academic historians were in general severely critical of Toynbee's work.

In 1947, when Somervell's abridgement of volumes 1–6 appeared, Toynbee won wide popular acclaim in the United States. E. D. Myers' review in the *Nation* was typical of the praise heaped on the book by nonspecialists. Myers commented that Toynbee's concepts and analysis were ''of sufficient importance and excellence to merit serious study; his presentation is as 'entrancing' as Mr. Somervell suggests it is.'' Myers suggested that if

readers had time to read only one book that year, they should select *A Study of History*.

Much of the American book-buying public felt the same way. The abridged version became a Book-of-the-Month club selection and a bestseller. In 1947 alone, over 129,000 copies were sold, and total sales in the next few years reached almost 250,000. Toynbee himself became a minor celebrity. He was invited to give a lecture series at Bryn Mawr College, and in March 1947, his photograph appeared on the cover of *Time* magazine, which contained a lengthy and laudatory review of *A Study of History*. There were numerous discussions of the book in the press and on radio and television, and Toynbee was hailed as a prophet for the post-World War II era. In *Toynbee and History: Critical Essays and Reviews,* published in 1956, M. F. Ashley Montagu commented that the book ''constitutes one of the most famous and most widely discussed books of its time.''

However, most professional historians did not share this exalted opinion of their colleague's work. In 1954, following the publication of volumes 7–10 of *A Study of History* (abridged by Somervell in 1957), there was a barrage of harsh criticism by historians. Prominent British historian Hugh Trevor-Roper wrote in the *Sunday Times* (reprinted in *Toynbee and History*):

> Not only are Professor Toynbee's basic assumptions often questionable, and his application of them often arbitrary, but his technical method turns out to be not 'empirical' at all. The theories are not deduced from the facts, not tested by them: the facts are selected, sometimes adjusted, to illustrate the theories, which themselves rest effortlessly on air.

Another distinguished British historian, A. J. P. Taylor, was equally dismissive of Toynbee's work. Declaring in London's *New Statesman* (reprinted in *Toynbee and History*) that the work was not what he understood history to be, Taylor commented:

> Professor Toynbee's method is not that of scholarship, but of the lucky dip, with emphasis on the luck. . . . The events of the past can be made to prove anything if they are arranged in a suitable pattern; and Professor Toynbee has succeeded in forcing them into a scheme that was in his head from the beginning.

Other academic critics weighed in with similar criticisms, attacking Toynbee's methods and his conclusions. Some said the work was a failure, that Toynbee got his facts wrong and also mixed up his history with too much theology and metaphysics, trying to take on the mantle of prophet and religious moralist. Specialists in different fields of history

The Egyptian Sculpture Room at the British Museum in London. Toynbee acquired an interest in Egyptian civilization by gazing at their exhibits in the British Museum

attempted to refute what Toynbee had written about their particular area of expertise.

There was similar criticism of Toynbee's work from academic historians in America, although Pitirim Sorotkin, an eminent sociologist wrote a more positive article that was published in *The Journal of Modern History* (and reprinted in *Toynbee and History*). Although he disputed Toynbee's fundamental idea that a civilization is a unified whole and argued that Toynbee's fitting of all civilizations into a pattern of genesis, growth, and decline was far too rigid, he still expressed the view that Toynbee's

work was ''one of the most significant works of our time in the field of historical synthesis.''

It is customary for major works, of history or any other discipline, to undergo periodic reevaluation, and *A Study of History* has been no exception. In 1989, two books were published to celebrate the centenary of Toynbee's birth. In the essays collected in *Toynbee: Reappraisals,* it is clear that professional historians were now prepared to look more favorably on Toynbee's achievement. And in his biography *Toynbee: A Life,* William H. McNeill, himself a noted historian, made a persuasive case for the positive reevaluation of Toynbee's work. It seems likely that, criticisms notwithstanding, *A Study of History* will endure, along with Oswald Spengler's *The Decline of the West* (1918–1923), as one of the most learned and provocative works of historical analysis written in the twentieth century.

Criticism

Bryan Aubrey

Aubrey holds a Ph.D. in English. In this essay, he explores the eclectic methods that Toynbee employed in writing A Study of History, *including the use of mythology, Jungian psychology, and unusual personal experiences.*

The twentieth century was an age of increasing specialization in all fields of knowledge, a trend that remains with us today. Knowledge grows at a rapid pace, but what is lacking is a connecting link among different fields of knowledge. The physical scientist has little to say to the humanist scholar; the social scientist and the mathematician speak different languages; and so on. Even within disciplines, knowledge has become compartmentalized. A professor of, say, literature may spend his or her entire career developing expertise in one small area and may know little not only of other fields of knowledge but also of what his or her colleagues in the same department are teaching and researching.

These issues were central to Toynbee's purpose in writing *A Study of History*. He pointed out that a historian must do two things: study history in detail but also as a whole. There had to be a balance between general views and the accumulation of facts. Toynbee believed that during the twentieth century the balance had swung too far in the direction of specialized studies that gave no sense of the whole picture. His fellow historians could no longer see the forest for the trees. Toynbee's gigantic attempt to view the whole of history from a universal perspective therefore stood at odds with the trend of the time toward specialization. This accounts in part for the disdain with which professional historians have often viewed his work.

A consequence of Toynbee's approach to history was that he was far more eclectic in his methods than the contemporary rationalistic approach would permit. He decided that if he was going to survey the whole of civilization, he would also employ in his task the whole of the human mind—its imaginative, nonrational, artistic, and spiritual capabilities as well as its rational and scientific powers. This approach can be seen, first, in Toynbee's reliance, at crucial moments in his argument, on mythology; second, in his use of the psychological theories of Carl Jung; third, in his inclusion of personal experiences, some of which can only be described as mystical; and fourth, in his insistence that the purpose of history must ultimately be sought in a religious view of the universe.

Central to Toynbee's account of the genesis of civilizations is his law of challenge and response: a civilization is born when a society successfully overcomes a major challenge. Toynbee derived this law not from any scientific method but from mythology. He pointed to various stories of encounters between two superhuman personalities in which the actions of one are in response to a challenge posed by the other. The story he relied on most was Goethe's dramatic poem, *Faust,* in which God, knowing that man is always too eager to fall back into a state of slumber and inertia, uses the Devil, in the form of Mephistopheles, to goad Faust into action. Mephistopheles wagers that he can give Faust delightful experiences that will satisfy him more than any man has ever been satisfied. Faust takes on the bet, saying that he will never rest content, whatever the Devil offers him. If he should ever cease from striving for greater fulfillment, then the Devil will win the wager and can have his soul.

In the simile that Toynbee uses several times, Faust is like a climber on a cliff who is awakening from sleep and is about to seek the next ledge above. For Toynbee, this was the essential step in moving from the inactive state of Yin to the active state of Yang. He found the same message in another mythological work, Homer's *Odyssey,* in which many of the temptations that Odysseus faces are in situations where he is promised that he can rest eternally in a delightful paradise. But Odysseus knows that he must remain active and press on with his mission to return home.

Toynbee's belief that mythology could embody a truth that was beyond the reach of the rational mind was stimulated by his reading of Plato, who often used imaginative myths to explore the nature of reality. This ability to use both reason and imagination in a search for the truth was, to Toynbee, a sign of the ''humility and the audacity of a great mind.''

Toynbee's interest in mythology was shared by Jung, and it is not surprising that Toynbee incorpo-

What Do I Read Next?

- Journalist Robert D. Kaplan, in *The Coming Anarchy: Shattering the Dreams of the Post Cold War* (2000), argues that the post-Cold War world, far from being the prelude to an era of peace, is likely to be a bleak place for all but a few.

- J. M. Roberts' *History of the World* (1993) is a well-illustrated one-volume survey of human history that describes the nature and main lines of development of many of the civilizations that Toynbee discusses although Roberts also includes African civilizations, which Toynbee ignores.

- *A World History,* by William H. McNeill (1998),

is a popular one-volume history that emphasizes the civilizations that have arisen in the Middle East, India, China, and Europe. McNeill makes excellent use of recent archaeological discoveries and explains how they have impacted historical scholarship. This edition also includes a discussion of the most important events in world history since 1976.

- Toynbee's *Christianity among the Religions of the World* (1957) consists of lectures given by Toynbee in the United States in 1955. He discusses the attitude of Christians toward followers of the other great living religions—both what that attitude is and what it should be.

---

rated a number of Jungian ideas in his work. In his search for knowledge of the totality of the psyche, Jung developed the concept of the collective unconscious, a universal pool of psychic energy that manifests in archetypal images and dreams. The existence of a collective unconscious also explains the phenomenon Jung described as synchronicity in which individuals or groups seem able to communicate with others with whom they are not in direct contact. Toynbee may have drawn on this concept when he explained how the culture of a civilization, in its disintegration phase, is transmitted to its external proletariat, the groups that live outside its boundaries: "A rain of psychic energy, generated by the civilization . . . is wafted across a barrier." This concept of a society receiving and absorbing the influx of "alien psychic energy" seems to depend on what Jung, drawing on ancient philosophy, referred to in *Memories, Dreams, Reflections* as "the sympathy of all things." It operates on a level much deeper than the explicit intermixing of ideas.

Jung also believed that the subconscious contained repressed psychic energies that exerted great, if hidden, power over human desires and actions. Toynbee noticed a social parallel to this repression

of elements of the conscious mind into the subconscious. This is when the creative minority in a society loses touch with its creative impulse and deteriorates into a mere dominant minority, resulting in the creation of a proletariat. The effect is that a society that was formerly unified is now split into two parts, each of which is hostile to the other, just as conscious and subconscious elements of the mind are frequently at odds with each other.

As Kenneth Winetrout points out in *Arnold Toynbee,* Toynbee also developed a schematic interpretation of religion that drew on Jung's classification of four psychological types—thinking, feeling, sensation, and intuition—and two psychological "attitudes," introversion and extraversion. The introverted thinking type corresponds to Hinduism; introverted feeling, to Buddhism; extraverted thinking, to Islam; and extraverted feeling (love), to Christianity.

Some may find this too much of a broad generalization. However, the attempt to discover a consistent pattern in diverse phenomena, both inner and outer, is characteristic of Toynbee's habit of thought.

The third aspect of Toynbee's unconventional method of studying history is the influence of a

> " Toynbee's belief that mythology could embody a truth that was beyond the reach of the rational mind was stimulated by his reading of Plato, who often used imaginative myths to explore the nature of reality."

number of unusual personal experiences. He records in volume 10 of the unabridged *A Study of History* that on no fewer than six occasions he had found himself in direct personal communion with certain events in history as if those events that had happened hundreds or thousands of years ago were literally unfolding in front of his eyes. The experiences were triggered by viewing the scenes where those events took place. Toynbee then records yet another experience, even "stranger" (his word) than the others. It occurred not long after World War I. Toynbee was walking down a London street when he

> found himself in communion, not just with this or that episode in History, but with all that had been, and was, and was to come. In that instant he was directly aware of the passage of History gently flowing through him in a mighty current, and of his own life welling like a wave in the flow of this vast tide.

One can only guess what this remarkable experience must have been like and what effect it had on Toynbee's later work. But mystical or not, it seems entirely in line with the thrust of *A Study of History*, in which Toynbee seeks to grasp the whole of history in a meaningful pattern and by doing so acquire insight into what the future might hold.

It is clear from this that Toynbee was no ordinary historian. Perhaps the essential nature of his work can be better grasped if he is viewed as an artist and *A Study of History* as a kind of prose epic. One reads Toynbee not so much for the facts, although there are plenty of those, but for the vision, the informing pattern, the unity in diversity that he discerns in the sweep of human history. In this respect, Toynbee's work resembles the work of another scholar in another field, Joseph Campbell. Campbell's *A Hero With a Thousand Faces,* pub-

lished in 1949 as Toynbee was working on his final volumes, did for mythology what Toynbee did for history, identifying a single recurring pattern in all the diverse mythology of the world.

The fourth and final aspect of Toynbee's distinctive method as a historian was that he strived to see the unfolding of civilizations in terms not merely of humanity. He thought that to view history merely from a human perspective led to a dangerous worship of the creations of man. As a historian, he could not ignore the importance of the spiritual dimension. He believed that this was by far the most important angle of vision from which to study history. In fact, he declared that the whole purpose of the turning wheel of history was to bring forth spiritual truth. History gives "a vision of God's creation on the move"; creation travels from God, by way of history, back to God. The contribution of the historian is to point this out for others to contemplate.

Such a vision also formed part of Toynbee's own spiritual quest. Although later in his life he would describe himself as an agnostic, in volume 10 of *A Study of History*, in a passage that was not included in Somervell's abridgement, he looked forward to a fellowship with others through the grace of God, whose "presence and participation transfigure a precarious Brotherhood of Man into a Communion of Saints in which God's creatures are united with one another through their union with their Creator."

Toynbee expressed the same idea, in less highflown language, when he wrote of his practical purpose as a historian. In his pamphlet, "How The Book Took Shape" (reprinted in *Toynbee and History*), he remarks that in a world in which nuclear annihilation is a possibility, there is one thing a historian can do:

> He can help his fellow man of different civilizations to become more familiar with one another, and, in consequence, less afraid of one another and less hostile to one another, by helping them to understand and appreciate one another's histories and to see in these local and partial stories a common achievement and common possession of the whole human family. . . . And it *is* one family; it always *has* been one family in the making.

To a fractious world that has still not learned what it needs to know, Toynbee's gentle words, all the more eloquent for their simplicity, bear repeating.

Source: Bryan Aubrey, Critical Essay on *A Study of History,* in *Nonfiction Classics for Students,* The Gale Group, 2001.

Kenneth W. Thompson

In the following essay, Thompson analyzes Toynbee's theories and formulas and their application to Western society.

Most critics would agree that Toynbee's *Study of History* is a work of epic proportions. Several commentators have noted that Toynbee, as a historian who zealously recorded the many contrasting beats of history, himself injected a marked counterbeat into historical writing. Since 1910 few works have exceeded one volume; in literature the short story has been threatening the novel. In contrast, both the length and the temper of *A Study of History* are exceptions to the prevailing ethos. Toynbee consciously struck a blow against the fashionable specialized and "scientific" studies which isolate tiny fragments of experience for the most intensive study. His chief foe, however, was not the discrete use of scientific techniques but rather the idolatry of that method and the ready acceptance of the superficial philosophy of "scientism" with its easy optimism and materialism. His method, in its turn, must be critically assessed, for the boldness of his approach makes it inevitable that certain questions and criticisms should be raised. The first person to anticipate this would have been Toynbee himself, who observed at the time he was launching his major work: "In the world of scholarship, to give and take criticism is all in the day's work and, each in our day, we may criticize our predecessors without becoming guilty of presumption so long as we are able to look forward without rancour to being criticized in our turn by our successors when our day is past."

All historians, including those who construct theories of universal history, have their special competence. Toynbee's was Graeco-Roman history. Its lands and people were so familiar to him as to make them his second "homeland." However, it is exactly his attachment to Hellenic history which causes readers some uneasiness about the pattern of world history he discovered. His conceptual scheme was suspiciously well tailored to the decline and fall of one civilization but it hung rather awkwardly on the twenty-odd others. It is apparent from even a cursory reading that Hellenic civilization had its "Time of Troubles," "Universal State," and "Universal Church" in relentless and seemingly preordained succession. This pattern was more difficult to maintain when Toynbee discussed other civilizations. He was obliged to confess that Egyptiac history comprised one kind of exception (for its

> **❝** When a reader attempts to apply the conceptual scheme derived principally from Hellenic civilization to, for example, Western civilization, Toynbee's problem at once becomes clear."

universal state was revived after it had run its normal course), Arabic civilization was another exception, and other civilizations were in other ways exceptions too.

When a reader attempts to apply the conceptual scheme derived principally from Hellenic civilization to, for example, Western civilization, Toynbee's problem at once becomes clear. In a table designed to portray the stages in history of the various civilizations, the "Time of Troubles" for Western civilization was charted as having occurred between 1378 and 1797. Elsewhere in the *Study,* Toynbee was more cautious, leaving the impression that although many symptoms of decay may be present, one must wait and see before conceding this decline. If growth and disintegration are as clear-cut as was elsewhere implied, it is curious that the stage in history at which the West finds itself should remain so beclouded for Toynbee.

Furthermore, critics point to flaws in Toynbee's pattern of history which are distinct from the problem of its concrete application to contemporary civilizations. The basic concept in his schema is *civilization,* and yet he never defined by more than a few illustrations precisely what he meant by this term or how it could be distinguished from *society.* As the analysis proceeded he nevertheless talked about these units as if he were using them with all the precision of a zoologist. Yet the species *civilization* appears to be used interchangeably with the generic category society. Most of his definitions are literary rather than scientific, and much of his terminology has that breadth and vagueness which generally characterizes spiritual interpretations of history. For example, in his treatment of the withdrawal and return of creative leaders who inspired growth in civilization, the reader must somehow divine the precise common denominator for the experiences of some thirty individuals. If Toynbee had used Buddha, Caesar, Peter the Great, Kant, and Lenin to point up an interesting parallel, this flaw would not be particularly significant. When he used their experiences to establish scientific formulas and laws, the practice may legitimately be questioned. Indeed, his discussion is curiously marred by the unequal attention given the various personalities and minorities responsible for civilizational growth. In some cases, Toynbee presented shortened life histories of the creative leaders, and the data while interesting often have little to do with the point at issue. At other times, he allowed a paragraph or two to suffice. This difference in treatment can hardly be based upon any systematic principle. Moreover, it is difficult to appreciate the similarity he detected between the quiet habits of Kant, whose thoughts, to be sure, made an impact throughout the world, and the withdrawal and return of Peter the Great, who returned to Russia from Europe with new ideas which he personally put into practice.

This concept is also obscure in Toynbee's discussion of particular creative nations. The notion that England withdrew from the Continent between the sixteenth and eighteenth centuries, only to return as the center of world trade and world power in the nineteenth century, has more meaning as a description of the general foundations of British foreign policy than as an exact statement of historical fact. That is, British policy was based upon England's relative insularity, but this hardly constituted withdrawal. If it is farfetched to assume that a nation even in the sixteenth century could withdraw from relations with others, it is no less extravagant to imagine that other nations in the thick of European power politics would be incapable of making a creative contribution. Any theory which excluded seventeenth- and eighteenth-century France as a creative force would hardly receive support. Yet it would also be erroneous to ignore the fact that the concept of Withdrawal and Return, whether because or in spite of its utter intangibility, illuminates some of the shadowy corners of history which scientific studies have left untouched. However, Toynbee's overly ambitious claims invite critical responses by some honest observers.

Another principle or law which is so indefinite that almost any historical episode can be molded to fit its broad outlines is Challenge and Response. Spiritual and scientific interpretations of history have consistently asked, What is the true mechanism of history? For some, such as Hegel and Marx, it is a particular dialectic or process. Others have found the mechanism in economic conditions or geographical factors. Toynbee's formula is more difficult to verify objectively and more likely to encompass a wider range of events. Between an environment that is too severe and one that is too easy, there is a "golden mean" where civilization can flourish. In general, the basis for this optimum condition is a favorable climate and adequate land and natural resources.

Scientific historians would object that this concept is too simple. New nations and societies have achieved their positions in history because of such rudimentary factors and because the whole context of their historical experience was favorable. The American colonies were blessed with a broad continent with resources of unparalleled variety and richness. This privileged position, however, was only one fragment of the larger historical development in which factors such as outside assistance and unexpected freedom from colonial domination were also involved. There is some question whether Toynbee's formula of challenge and response is sufficiently broad to encompass these various factors and concrete enough to permit their separate consideration. In the eyes of most modern scientific historians, every historic event is a separate entity and therefore so infinitely complex that an observer can evaluate it only in terms of its concreteness. Only by patient research and painstaking scrutiny can such an event be clearly illuminated.

There is a final assumption to which modern historians would probably take exception. Toynbee postulated that civilizations break down and decay because elements within them are inherently self-destructive. Yet the early American civilizations, particularly those of the Incas and Aztecs, were destroyed by external forces. But a spiritual interpretation of history could hardly concede such a point. So *A Study of History* maintained that these civilizations had already succumbed to the most profound internal malaise before they were invaded and conquered by Spanish adventurers. It is of course likely that societies have been weakened by internal dissension and decay before falling prey to a more powerful foe. It seems naïve to imagine, however, that history does not offer numerous cases of brute force triumphing over weakness and virtue. This has surely been the fate of small nations throughout history. It would be surprising indeed if the same were not true of civilizations such as the early American ones. Toynbee's assumption of transcendent spiritual factors in history makes it difficult if not impossible for him to accept the primacy of force and power as the cause of death for a civilization. His "Time of Troubles" explanation indirectly assumes that the successful conqueror has not himself suffered the same self-inflicted blow and is therefore morally and politically superior. If pursued to its logical conclusion, this principle would mean that in all important respects a conquering invader would surpass his victim. Any list of victorious conquerors shows how fantastic this assumption is. It symbolizes the great weakness in those spiritual versions of history which too complacently identify virtue and power. It reflects the tragic paradox of our times that in Western civilization with the breakdown of common moral standards even the spiritual historian becomes a utopian of power. He finds ways of justifying the proposition that might makes right.

Furthermore, the dilemma which confounds students of human affairs is reflected in the dual problem with which Toynbee grappled. In seeking to establish general principles and laws of history, he chose as his subject great civilizations and found over twenty separate examples. Thus a student of history has the same kind of individual facts with which the physical sciences have traditionally dealt. Civilizations are "affiliated" and "apparented," but this very concept may have served to obscure the empirical unity of history. Particular cultures are interrelated in complex ways, and only in the last volumes of the *Study* did Toynbee demonstrate the degree to which he plumbed the profound and mysterious relations between various societies in history.

Although Toynbee called upon this physical-sciences analogy, he at the same time abandoned a practice central to all scientific pursuits. The criticism leveled most frequently against him has been that his "well-beloved empiricism" is in fact no empiricism at all. He selected his data and imperturbably used them to build a system. But each datum can be used in a variety of ways, and Toynbee may not always have cited those facts which would not support his principal theses. However valid this criticism may be for Toynbee's empiricism in particular, it is unerringly true with respect to empiricism in general. The cauldron of history is so immense that the individual historian can serve up but a spoonful, and whether this can represent the whole is always doubtful. The limits of Toynbee's history are those of his subject matter. The infinite variety of history is the chief factor which creates the eternal boundaries within which any student must formulate his principles.

There is a further standard by which *A Study of History* can be judged. In sheer erudition and learning, the work is breathtaking and matchless. It is more wide-ranging than Spengler's masterpiece, and its pages literally teem with brilliant passages and flashes of insight. One section includes an extensive account of the history of warfare; another describes the colonization of North America. His accounts of the history of the Jewish people in Eastern Europe and Spain, of the Spartan form of society, and of the Ottoman slave-court illustrate the amplitude of historical experience to which the reader is introduced. Even if one finds that some of Toynbee's main theses are untenable, only the most uninspired of readers would be unable to gain new perspectives on the world. The value of Toynbee's work does not depend on the acceptance of each of its parts as if it were a Euclidean demonstration. It is so rich in historical allusions that the study of its pages has a value independent of full agreement with its assumptions and conclusions.

As a philosopher of history, Toynbee himself held up a warning to all historians and political scientists. He steadfastly maintained the proposition that history in general is unpredictable. The soundest estimates will be confounded by elements of chance and contingency. No one can say in advance how leading participants in the historical drama will act and few have prophesied accurately the more far-reaching events in history. Some think the gradual elimination of this uncertainty will occur when the specialized social sciences delve more carefully into the wellsprings of human behavior. Toynbee affirmed his confidence in the use of some of these techniques, particularly social psychology and statistics. It would be stretching a point, however, to imply that he shared the cheerful and extravagant expectations of some social scientists about the elimination of chance in discoveries that are possible through the use of rigorous social surveys.

In talking about the growth and decay of civilizations, Toynbee necessarily wrote social history. This is particularly the case in *A Study of History,* for the fundamental criterion by which growth is measured is not geographical expansion but, more unusual, self-determination. It is obvious that a society which turns inward in this way must face up to its social problems. Therefore one finds in the

Study a large number of rich insights into social ills and social institutions.

Sociologists as a group have laid great stress on case studies, maintaining that a student must first get inside a particular society and appraise it on its own terms. A prominent American social theorist has held that the only clear "case study" in Toynbee's writing is his analysis of Hellenic civilization. Even the staunchest admirer of Toynbee must confess that sometimes the social data hardly provide a clear picture of the uniqueness of a particular community. It is probably fair to say that Toynbee made little or no contribution to the cultural "case study" method as interpreted by modern sociology.

He has, however, provided empirical sociologists with a series of fertile hypotheses which remain to be tested and verified. His theory of challenge and response is of this order. Some of his formulas, however, have already been analyzed more fully, among them his theory of cultural diffusion or radiation wherein a society that has accepted a certain aspect of an alien culture must subsequently acquire all others. Moreover, as early as the turn of the century, modern sociology considered the social phenomenon of imitation, for which Toynbee has constructed his theory of mimesis. One of the social classics anticipated *A Study of History* on this point by nearly half a century: "A society is a group of people who display many resemblances produced either by imitation or by *counter-imitation.* For men often counter-imitate one another, particularly when they have neither the modesty to imitate directly nor the power to invent." There are fewer allusions to the findings of modern sociology in Toynbee's great work than there are to comparable studies in political science and history. Yet it is significant that great social theorists such as Merton have found a community of interest with Toynbee.

The major difference between Toynbee and contemporary sociologists is his individualistic interpretation of social change. Toynbee ascribed to great personalities and leaders what sociologists would insist, through more extensive analysis and study, could be attributed to underlying social forces. Research and new theoretical tools may yield the causes of fundamental change in man's social relations and institutions. The neophyte in sociology may be tempted to dissent vigorously from its obsessions with classification, from its sometimes pedantic distinctions between *society* and *community* or between subtypes of sacred and secular

societies; he may likewise disagree with Toynbee's extreme individualism. On this point, nonetheless, the paths of the historian and his contemporaries in sociology and anthropology sharply and probably irrevocably diverge.

Students of contemporary religion have been at least as critical of some of Toynbee's views as have scholars in the social sciences. It is most unlikely that philosophers and specialists in comparative religion would accept the strong currents of Christian determinism which emerge in his general conclusion that Christianity is the culmination of religious history. Indeed, by abandoning the neutrality about religions which he maintained throughout earlier accounts, Toynbee invited the unanimous criticism of all relativists in philosophy and religion.

Within religious circles, moreover, particularly among traditionalists, one would expect further differences of opinion on many of the points Toynbee raised. He stated, for example, that religious progress occurred during the breakdown and decay of civilizations. It is historically accurate to say that periods of decay have frequently been marked by profound religious insight. In times of crisis, the idolatrous worship of governments and social institutions has frequently been supplanted by new faiths or old religions. It is far less certain that in all of history, the progress of religion has been an inevitable concomitant of cultural disintegration. One exception is the growth of religious indifference in the past four centuries, during what may prove to be our own "Time of Troubles." Further, it might well be argued that there has been a tendency for religions to identify so closely with historic civilizations that the destruction of one has meant that the other would likewise perish. Toynbee is right if in ideal terms religions prove able to stand apart from their native societies and in times of catastrophe display the courage of interpreting these tragedies as judgments by God. One looks in vain in the New Testament, however, for a concept of religion mounting to higher dimensions of insight through impending societal breakdowns and destruction. On the stage of human experience, there is always a chance that evil will triumph over the good and an eternal peril that religion itself will be destroyed. From this standpoint, the latter-day revisions of Toynbee's morphology of history may be subject to criticism and possible emendation.

Toynbee also tended to identify religion too completely with a particular ecclesiastical institution. It is not everywhere clear what he meant by his frequent references to the ''Church''—sometimes it was the Roman Catholic, elsewhere the Greek Orthodox, and occasionally the Church of England. In general, his hopes for the future were related to the revival of a universal Roman Catholic church under a modern Hildebrand. Thus, the greatest of all questions to be answered in the twentieth century is, ''Can Hildebrand arise again in his might to heal the wounds inflicted upon the souls of his flock by the sins of a Rodrigo Borgia and a Sinibaldo Fieschi?'' There is a curious naïveté to his statement that although ''the Church may actually never yet have expressed Christianity to perfection, there is at least no inherent impediment here to the attainment of a perfect harmony.'' Elsewhere he seemed acutely aware that all institutions are likely, through domination by hierarchies of leaders, to become closed corporations in which there can be little progress. In general, Toynbee tended to overvalue the virtues of ecclesiasticism and to treat cavalierly the whole tradition of Protestantism. It is one thing to deal realistically with the implications of religious universalism for international affairs. It is something else again to draw further conclusions about the intrinsic merits of religions on that basis. In his emphasis on the primacy of institutional religion, Toynbee surely parted company with Bergson and Augustine.

For the analysis and study of religion, however, Toynbee's contribution is of greatest significance. He identified the particular religions which have been important in various civilizations. He discussed their influence and shortcomings with great insight and unquestioned familiarity. That a secular historian should pay such heed to the religious theme in history has been one of the momentous factors influencing the role of religion in the mid-twentieth century.

More than the majority of historians, Toynbee wrote about political events and trends from the viewpoint of political science. In numerous ways, this approach was apparent in estimates of political developments in England and the United States, in analysis of the influence of forms of government upon international politics, and in discussions of political power. But the issues Toynbee spoke of most frequently and on which he propounded formal theories are the nature of political leadership and the nature of the modern state. Each theory carries important implications for democratic theory and practice in the West.

In one view, the leader is merely an expression of prevailing customs or ideas in any society. He is thus an agent for that commonalty and can act only upon its mandate. Toynbee assumed, however, that it is primarily through the energy of the successful creative leader that a society moves forward. Moreover, the bonds of community between him and his followers are so fragile that only through imitation and ''social drill'' can they respond to his program.

The question one must ask is whether Toynbee's conception leads directly to antidemocratic politics. It is important to observe here that the fundamental assumption upon which a theory of creative leadership is based is not inconsistent with some of the findings of contemporary scholarship in political science and sociology. There is an inherent tendency, we have discovered, for ''elitist groups'' to ascend to power in both autocratic and democratic governments. The role of the ''charismatic'' leader is central in this process. The great personality or hero in Toynbee's scheme must first convince the people of his intrinsic worth as a leader before his creative program will be given a try. This would hardly be true for governments which were tyrannies or depotisms, although modern totalitarianism may present a somewhat different case.

On this count, Toynbee's thesis is unqualifiedly democratic, for the great mass of uncreative followers retain the right to accept or reject the leader who is appealing to them. On other grounds, however, there are reasons for some uncertainty. Once a leader who has risen to power has lost his creativity, machinery must be in place to make possible his removal and to assure succession. On this crucial point, Toynbee's references to revolution are inconclusive. Moreover, the system of popular elections, the principal means for disposing of unsatisfactory leaders, is not referred to at any point. If we conceive of Toynbee's theory of political leadership as a detailed account of the political process, then this omission becomes so serious that we may classify his views as antidemocratic. If, on the other hand, we appraise it as a fragment of a broad theory of history, then some qualifications are necessary. In general, spiritual interpretations have tended to accent the importance of struggle, which has often obscured their insight into the indirect channels by which these contests are resolved. If one assumes that the most profound human experiences are a monopoly of the few, it is difficult to build on this foundation a steadfastly democratic philosophy. Yet political leadership, for most moderns, remains little less than an ''enigma wrapped in a riddle.'' It is symbolic of this dilemma that Toynbee should join an intensely individualistic social philosophy with a theory of political leadership which has aristocratic overtones.

Toynbee's view of the state is that of a contemporary English Liberal. In his view, political units in both socialist and free enterprise states have been moving, through trial and error, toward a common set of functions. The major problem in interpreting the role of the state is to bring the discussion to the level of practical experience. If it were possible to find some palliative for the enormity of recurrent wars, then states everywhere could act in many more ways to promote the general welfare. It may be said that Toynbee's conception of political problems is hardly that of a systematic political theorist. To a surprising number of perplexing issues, however, he brings the fresh and creative outlook of a thinker whose intuition has exceeded his ability to formulate general principles and theories.

We have been primarily concerned with Toynbee's theory of international politics. If the scheme he devised for interpreting and evaluating all history moved through successive stages, it is even more true that his concept of international politics was evolutionary. Indeed, his whole outlook on the forces and principles of international affairs was painfully and slowly harmonized with reality.

Toynbee was, in both religion and politics, originally a staunch idealist. His thinking about foreign policy and diplomacy was imprisoned within a crusading nationalism. Sometime during the 1930s, the decade of unparalleled catastrophe, however, he began to employ the tools and principles that four hundred years of modern diplomacy have taught. For an absolutist in religious matters, this shift to relativism in politics could not have been easy. He sometimes seized upon new instruments for peace and order as enthusiastically as he had taken to simple formulas.

Thus in the early stages of the experiment with collective security, Toynbee was convinced that this "new dispensation" had taken the place of the old balance of power. The particular problems of collective security with which he was forced to deal concretely were probably what carried him toward political realism. The pathos of these experiences liberated his theory from its earlier utopian fetters. This tendency in his thinking reached its culmination in the counsel he offered for the mitigation of the perilous struggle between East and West since

World War II. In time of greatest crisis, no rational student of international politics could afford to ignore the lessons of diplomatic history. Toynbee turned to traditional diplomacy and its well-tested procedures and techniques because he properly identified that struggle as a worldwide political contest.

Moreover, in practice, Toynbee's viewpoint was eclectic. He was able to distinguish between immediate and ultimate objectives. The former can be pursued as practical alternatives; the latter must be conceived as long-range aims which can be achieved only by prudent choices among competing principles. What is striking about Toynbee's theory is that on most fundamental issues he succeeded in maintaining one set of interests without sacrificing the other. Since 1947 he steered the perilous course between a cynical realism and the fatuous assumptions of utopianism. In the 1930s, he was not always able to find this channel but at the height of the cold war when the highest political wisdom is called for, he adjusted his theory to current problems.

Whether the most prudent political insight can carry Western civilization beyond the reach of ultimate destruction is something about which Toynbee was none too sanguine. All he would say was that in the task which confronts Western society and against the catastrophes of internecine warfare, our best hope was in bargaining for time. Toynbee's theory of international politics was transformed because modern society must try to avert its doom. In this common enterprise, the historian of great civilizations and the student of unrelenting struggles for political power offered the same counsel.

Source: Kenneth W. Thompson, "A Critical Evaluation," in *Toynbee's Philosophy of World History and Politics,* Louisiana State University Press, 1985, pp. 215–26.

William H. McNeill

In the following essay, McNeill discusses how the great range and eclectic nature of A Study of History *make uncovering consistent and unified themes in the work difficult.*

There are at least three points of view from which the worth of a book of history may be assessed. One may ask whether the book is accurate, that is, whether it deals fairly and skillfully with the data upon which it is based. Secondly, one may turn the historian's characteristic tools back upon himself and ask: How did this book come to be written? What is its relation to the individual life of the author, and more particularly, what is its relation to the age in which he lived? And, thirdly, one may ask what basic ideas, assumptions, or intellectual methods may underlie the text, governing its scope and proportion, shaping its emphasis, and giving a sort of artistic or intellectual unity to the whole.

When, however, we attempt to focus upon a book so vast and various as Toynbee's *A Study of History* from any of these viewpoints, difficulties at once arise. His basic ideas seem to have shifted radically during the thirty-odd years he spent producing the ten volumes, so that many discrepancies between the earliest and latest volumes may be found. Moreover, our times are too much with us to make it possible to see his book clearly in relation to the currents of thought and feeling that still run among us. We cannot say which of the many contradictory strands will predominate or seem most significant to later generations. Finally, the scope of his inquiries is so wide, and his erudition so various that the job of checking up on his accuracy must be resigned to experts in one or another of the fields of history with which he deals. Yet this is in some degree unjust, for errors of fact or judgment, which may seem monstrous to the narrow expert, need not necessarily invalidate the book as a whole. If we listen only to indignant specialists, the real greatness of the *Study* (which must surely lie in the effort to reduce all the multifariousness of human history to a comprehensible order) may quite escape us.

Indeed, on this point I venture the opinion, absurd though it may seem, that even if all but a few fragments of Toynbee's text should prove vulnerable to attack on the ground of factual inaccuracy, still the book will stand in the public eye, and also I believe in the judgment of posterity, as a notable monument of our century's intellectual history. Quite apart from the impression his ideas have made upon the general lay public—and this in itself becomes an incident in the intellectual history of our times—Toynbee has presented the community of academic and professional historians with an important challenge. It may or may not be taken up seriously by future generations; and the long-term influence of his book will in part depend upon the reaction we and our successors make to the challenge he has set before us.

The nature of Toynbee's challenge is twofold. First, he has boldly overridden the conventional boundaries between specialisms in the field of history. Taking all the knowable human past as his province, he has found rhythms and patterns which

Toynbee was inspired by the fifth-century Greek historian Thucydides

any less panoramic view could scarcely have detected. I am, for myself, profoundly convinced that there are insights attainable by taking large views of the past which cannot be had from close inspection of the separated segments of history. I once had an experience in New York City which for me has come to stand as a symbol of the advantage which may accrue to a man taking such an intellectual position. Once on a hot summer's evening when I was walking on Morningside Heights looking down upon the Hudson, the traffic on the Parkway beneath caught my attention. It was heavy, and to my surprise I saw that the cars were grouped along that ribbon of concrete in the alternating nodes and antinodes of a longitudinal wave, precisely like the diagram I remembered from my physics textbook illustrating the propagation of a sound wave. Moreover, the waves of traffic moved along the Parkway at a rate considerably faster than the progress of any car and were regular in length as well as in their speed. Here was a truth about stop-and-go driving on a crowded road which I had never known before, even though I had more than once been a particle in such a jam. Only the long perspective of Morningside Heights permitted me to apprehend this aspect of the phenomenon. Observers closer to the roadside might see individual cars going by; might calculate

> "The development of Toynbee's mind, in response to the public and private experiences of his mature lifetime, obviously involved discrepancies and changes of emphasis, if not outright contradictions, between the earliest and latest volumes of his *A Study of History*."

their speed or tabulate their makes, study the varieties of hubcaps or measure the pollution of the air from the exhausts; but from the very proximity of their vantage points our imaginary observers could have understood the wave-character of the traffic only through exact and painstaking statistical analysis of a sort usually impossible in historical study from lack of sufficient data. Yet a Toynbee-like vision of universal history, I believe, opens the possibility of short-circuiting statistical methods, as my glance from Morningside Heights could do. New insights may arise with breadth of view; fallible and never completely provable perhaps, yet enormously stimulating to exact and careful study which may find new questions to ask of familiar data in the light of general ideas generated by men like Toynbee. No multiplication of specialisms or narrowing down of fields of history in the interest of more perfect accuracy can by itself hope to achieve such an enrichment of our understanding of man's past. Interaction between large views, bold hypotheses, fallible intuitions, and exact, detailed scholarship is what we need. If we concentrate upon the latter alone, by drawing ever closer to the facts and seeing details ever more completely, we may blind ourselves to other aspects of reality. We may, in the terms of my parable, see only the hubcaps and radiator grilles in the parade of traffic and miss the waves entirely.

This, then, is the first great challenge which Toynbee's *A Study of History* has put before us. It is a real challenge; for most academic historians, because they have made accuracy their major concern, have shrunk from universal history. After all,

no man, not even a man as gifted as Toynbee, can hope to have more than a superficial acquaintance with all the fields of history; and until Toynbee came along, the English-speaking world had, for at least two generations, left universal history to brilliant amateurs like H. G. Wells, or, in this country, to the writers of undergraduate textbooks, whose efforts were directed not so much to new synthesis as to the cataloguing of more or less well-assorted information culled from the work of specialists.

The second great challenge Toynbee has put before us is similar in that it constitutes a breakthrough of the traditional limits of our discipline, not horizontally, so to speak, but vertically. What I mean is this: Toynbee has felt himself free to connect his studies of history with ultimate philosophical and theological questions. His study of the human past has confronted him with such questions as: What is the destiny of mankind? What laws are human societies subject to? What part does God play in human affairs? Perhaps because we wished to be scientific, and were temperamentally cautious, professional historians have tended to skirt these major riddles of the human condition; but Toynbee has boldly rushed in where we have feared to tread and come up with his own individual answers. Quite apart from the question whether they are good answers or not, answers are there in his book; and I believe that much of his popularity arises from the explicitness with which he has confronted these ultimate questions which haunt, and have always haunted, the minds of reflective men.

We all know the enrichment which came to the traditions of political history when men began to delve into economic aspects of the past; and Toynbee, it seems to me, offers a similar enrichment by challenging us to bring our historical truths into relation with sociological, philosophical, and theological theories and beliefs.

Yet in attempting so grandiose a synthesis, accuracy of fact and accuracy of detailed interpretation inevitably suffer. Omniscience is beyond mankind, and in proportion as one ideal of history is emphasized another must be crowded into the shadows. This is, no doubt, the case with Toynbee, who, in undertaking to say something about everything, has laid himself open to expert criticism over and over again. Yet criticism directed merely toward correctness will miss the heart of his book, disguise its importance, and can do little to explain (or to destroy) its significance for our age in general and for professional historians in particular.

Let me leave the matter of Toynbee's accuracy at that. However mistaken or wrong-headed he may be on particular points, the *Study* still stands before us, grand and imposing.

Perhaps we can hope to come nearer to an understanding of his significance by taking up the second critical standpoint, asking ourselves: How did this book come to be written? What is its relation to Toynbee's and our own time?

Two preliminary observations are perhaps worth making in this connection. First, the scope and content of *A Study of History* is dependent on the work done by archaeologists, much of it within the present century. If the goodly company of the archaeologists had not discovered and studied Sumerian, Babylonian, Assyrian, Minoan, Mycenaean, Hittite, Indus, Shang, and Mayan civilizations, Toynbee could not have conceived history as he did. In this most elementary sense, his book is a product of our age. Secondly, the great popular reception his ideas have met in this country—a reception far warmer than they have had in England, or in any other country so far as I know—is undoubtedly connected with an easy inference to be made from his pattern of the development of civilizations. If the Western world is now becoming ripe for the emergence of a universal state, as his pages seem to suggest, the United States is clearly a contender for the role once played by Rome. Such a role flatters the national ego. If this is to become the American century, it is, to say the least, comforting to know the historical inevitability thereof in advance. In some influential quarters Toynbee's ideas were, I believe, so interpreted, and the publicity his books received depended in some measure upon this fact.

But these observations merely skirt the question of the relation between *A Study of History* and our times. Fortunately, Toynbee has himself given a reasonably clear account of how he first conceived the germ of the *Study*. In 1914, soon after the First World War broke upon an unsuspecting Europe, Toynbee, in the course of his academic duties as a young Oxford don, found the pages of Thucydides pregnant with new meanings, and applicable, with surprising precision, to the contemporary struggle in Europe. In Toynbee's own words:

> . . . suddenly my understanding was illuminated. The experience that we were having in our world now had been experienced by Thucydides in his world already . . . Thucydides, it now appeared, had been over this ground before. He and his generation had been ahead of me and mine in the stage of historical experience

we had respectively reached; . . . Whatever chronology might say, Thucydides' world and my world had now proved to be philosophically contemporary. And, if this were the true relation between the Graeco-Roman and the Western civilizations, might not the relation between all the civilizations known to us turn out to be the same?

A sudden flash of insight, then, communicated from the pages of Thucydides in a time when the familiar landmarks of European civilization seemed about to collapse, raised a tantalizing question in Toynbee's mind; and as soon as the pressure of war duties in the British Foreign Office was removed, he set out to try to find an answer. If it were true that European historical development in the twentieth century A.D. was in some sense running parallel to the historical development of the Greek city-states of the fifth century B.C., was this mere accident, or part of a larger parallelism between the whole life course of the two civilizations? And could similar parallels be discovered in the histories of other peoples? Was there, in short, a sort of plot or rhythm common to human civilizations?

As we all know, Toynbee's investigations gave affirmative answers to these questions. As early as 1921 he was able to jot down a draft outline of the work we know as *A Study of History*, and during the next eight years he worked out details and prepared notes to flesh out that preliminary outline.

During these germinative years, and down until 1933 when work on the first three volumes was completed, Toynbee remained strongly under the spell of the classical education he had received in school and at Oxford. This shows through quite clearly in the first three volumes, where he regularly used the history of the Greco-Roman world as the archetype and measuring rod against which to plot the careers of other civilizations. Indeed, the method he used to identify his separate civilizations was to search for analogues of the three leading phenomena which accompanied the decay of the ancient classical world—a universal state, a universal church, and barbarian invasions; and when some parallels to these phenomena were discovered, he was prepared to recognize the death of an older and the birth of a new civilization.

There is, here a certain ambiguity in Toynbee's thought—or so it seems to me. He never gives a systematic, careful definition of what the term "civilization" means, but in later passages refers to it as a "state of the soul." Yet his criteria for recognizing separate civilizations are political, and as his book unfolds one discovers that the breakdowns of civilizations occur on the political plane also. I do not think Toynbee contradicts himself by such a procedure, for he could plausibly enough assert that the gross political manifestations which he used to discover the major outlines of the careers of civilizations were no more than outward and easily discovered manifestations of the state of the souls of the millions of men concerned with each civilization. Yet he has not spelled out what he means by his central concept of a civilization, and in his first three volumes he sometimes gives the impression that the political framework is at least for practical purposes identical with the civilization itself.

Such an emphasis upon politics is thoroughly in the tradition of classical thought; and there is still another sense in which his early inspiration derived from the ancients. From at least the time of Plato it had been a commonplace of Greek and Roman literature to hold that history moved in cycles. In its extreme form, as in the fourth of Vergil's *Eclogues,* this theory asserted that identical acts would recur time and again as the Great Year rolled round anew; in less fantastic form, men like Plato and Polybius held that constitutions underwent a regular cycle of change, rising toward an apex and then inevitably undergoing decay and eventual dissolution until the cycle began once more. Toynbee's view of the life pattern of civilizations, as advanced in his early volumes, was nothing but a translation of this classical commonplace onto a larger scene, substituting civilizations for the constitutions of city-states, and the globe, as known to contemporary Western historians, for the Mediterranean world of Plato and Polybius.

Yet however deeply Toynbee's mind in his early manhood was imbued with Greek and Roman literature, it remained true that, like Western civilization itself, his precocious childhood had been even more profoundly affected by exposure to an intense, evangelical Christianity, which gave him an abiding familiarity with the King James Bible. In the later 1930's when the progress of public events cast the long shadow of the Second World War upon the scene, and when personal problems also distressed him deeply, Toynbee's classicism began to wear thin. By degrees Toynbee the Hellenist gave way to Toynbee the man of religion, not quite Christian perhaps, since the creeds and formalism of organized Christianity repelled his mind. But still his new frame of mind may, I think, fairly be described as an enriched and sophisticated version of the Christianity of his childhood. One can see the beginning of this transformation in the middle group

of his volumes, published on the eve of World War II, and the change in outlook became explicit and complete in the four concluding volumes published in 1954.

This gradual conversion was Toynbee's personal response o the challenge of personal sorrow and public disaster. The phrase from Aeschylus's *Agamemnon, "pathei mathos"* (learning through suffering), which had echoed in his mind even in his most Hellenized years, came to have an ever growing significance for his view of the history and destiny of mankind. For through suffering, he came to believe, specially gifted men might attain a sensitivity, otherwise beyond their powers, to the divine reality behind mundane appearances; and, as teachers and prophets, could share their enhanced vision of the nature and purposes of God with their fellow men, whose minds had been readied for the reception of their message by the same suffering.

From this point of view, the cyclical rise and fall of civilizations came to have a new meaning. In his earlier, Hellenizing years, the recurrent breakdown and dissolution of civilizations had stood as a self-contained tragedy, attesting the limitations of human powers and the blindness of human passions. The consolation of history, as he then apprehended it, was a sort of Stoic heroism in the face of foreknown disaster. The three quotations which he prefixed to his first volumes: "Work . . . while it is day . . ."; "Nox ruit, Aenea . . ."; and "Thought shall be the harder, Heart the keener, Mood shall be the more, As our might lessens," accurately catch the tone of his mind, deeply affected as it then was by the war of 1914–1918.

But from his new standpoint of the later 1930's and after, this resigned pagan heroism began to seem mere blindness to the most basic reality of the world. Instead of being mere disaster, the long drawn-out human suffering involved in the dissolution of a civilization now appeared as the greatest of all challenges offered to men, creating for them the indispensable social matrix for reception of divine self-revelation. Thus the entire historic process changed its character in Toynbee's eyes. History was no longer simply cyclical; one civilization was no longer strictly equivalent to another. Instead, through the establishment of religions during the declining phases of a civilization's existence, a permanent addition to human knowledge of God was painfully attained. Universal history thus appeared as a gradual, stage-by-stage revelation of God to man. Religions replaced civilizations as the supremely valuable and significant forms of human association. God displaced man as the protagonist of history.

In this revised picture it is not difficult to recognize the lineaments of the traditional Judaic-Christian interpretation of history. Faith in progress, which Toynbee had rather scornfully rejected during his Hellenized years, was now restored, though not in its secularized eighteenth- and nineteenth-century form. To be sure the cycles of civilization remained; but they served, like the wheels of some great chariot, to carry humanity onward, ever onward toward some divinely appointed and unforeknowable but plainly desirable end.

The development of Toynbee's mind, in response to the public and private experiences of his mature lifetime, obviously involved discrepancies and changes of emphasis, if not outright contradictions, between the earliest and latest volumes of his *A Study of History*. These discrepancies may, perhaps, illustrate a changing temper of our times; I do not know. Certainly his growing religiosity is not unique; other sensitive spirits, too, have turned toward God as he has done; but whether he and they comprise only a minority in the intellectual community of our time, or whether they will appear in later times as pioneers of a new age remains to be seen. However that may be, Toynbee's volumes may be better understood and their discrepancies appreciated only if the reader sets them, as I have tried to do, against the background of the years in which they were written.

It remains, now, to take up our third vantage point and examine Toynbee's work in itself, asking what basic assumptions and intellectual methods underlie his book. It is here, I believe, that we can discover a measure of consistency and unity in his whole thought, despite the disparate conclusions which have at different stages of his life dominated his mind. For Toynbee the Hellenist and Toynbee the man of religion both used much the same methods of inquiry, and at least one common assumption underlies both the earlier and later versions of his vision of history.

Let me say something about Toynbee's methods of inquiry first, and turn to his assumptions at the end of this paper.

Toynbee likes to call himself an empiricist, and repeatedly describes his procedure in seeking illustrations for some general proposition about human history as an "empirical survey." Yet it seems to me that his use of this word is distinctly misleading. For his "empiricism" is an empiricism which already is keenly aware of what it is seeking; and in such a difficult and multifarious study as history, it is all too easy to find evidence to "prove" almost any proposition. The reason is simple. The potential data of history are limitless, and by selecting for attention only those bits and pieces that fit in with one's notions, a convincing "empirical" validation of the preconception with which one started out may often, if not always, be achieved. Yet this is the procedure by which Toynbee again and again seeks to prove or justify his generalizations. It follows, I think, that whatever value they may have—and in my opinion many of them have a great value—does not rest upon the empirical surveys of which he seems so fond.

Indeed, Toynbee's self-proclaimed empiricism seems to me largely a pose, adopted originally, perhaps, partly in an effort to distinguish his thought from Spengler's; and one which has been largely abandoned in his later volumes. Rather, the heart of Toynbee's intellectual procedure has always been the sudden flash of insight such as that which, on his own account, launched him originally on *A Study of History*. The experience of suddenly seeing some new relationship or pattern emerging from a confusion of elements previously unrelated is one which I presume all thinking men experience from time to time; and such experiences often carry with them a considerable emotional force which almost compels assent even before the details and implications of the new insight have been tidily arranged and worked out. Such I conceive to have been the method by which Toynbee worked his way through history; and being endowed by nature with an unusually powerful memory and an even more powerful imagination, his flashes of original insight have been numerous and far ranging. Many of them are, at least for me, profoundly illuminating. Let me just mention two examples from European history where my information is adequate to make it possible for me to control, in some measure, the data Toynbee worked upon. I find, for example, his concept of an abortive Far Western civilization on the Celtic fringe of Europe in the early Middle Ages, and his account of the competition between what he calls the "city-state cosmos" and the national state organization of late medieval and early modern Europe eminently enlightening. His analysis of the successive phases through which Greek and Roman society passed, and especially of the early phases of the growth of Greek civilization, seem to me masterful and entirely persuasive; and to go somewhat further afield, in his anatomy of the Ottoman Empire in particular and of nomad empires in general, he seems to me to be barking up the right tree, though his analysis may be a bit too schematic to fit each case exactly. It is passages such as these, where the free exercise of a synthetic imagination has succeeded in suggesting novel relationships or discerning new points of view, which, in my opinion, make Toynbee a truly great historian.

But I must also confess that there are other passages in his book where his imagination seems to run amuck. In the interest of fitting his data into a pattern he sometimes seems to cut and slice reality in an arbitrary and even fantastic fashion. I will mention only one instance of this: His description of the Arab caliphate as the resumption of a Syriac universal state after a millennium of Hellenic intrusion does not convince me in the least. Yet once the equation is made, throughout the rest of the book it is baldly taken for granted, and the sense in which the caliphate was also heir to Greek and Roman culture is nowhere seriously taken into account.

Such contrasts as these point up the difficulties of Toynbee's intellectual method. The sort of insights upon which the book is founded come in a flash or not at all, arising, in large, part, from the hidden and unconscious levels of the mind. Their nature is closer akin to the vision of the artist than to strictly rational or merely inductive mental processes. But rational and inductive processes contain their own controls, being bound by logic and sense perception; whereas the constructive imagination lacks such controls, and may go sadly astray by virtue of the very freedom which in lucky instances permits it to strike home to the truth.

My first point, then, about Toynbee's intellectual procedure is his reliance upon insight and imagination rather than upon arguments or induction. In this he is true to the Platonic intellectual tradition of which he is a latter-day representative; for Plato, too, and all good Platonists after him, have experienced and, having experienced, have valued above all else the flash of intellectual insight—the vision of the Idea—which Plato set as the apex of intellectual endeavor.

This suggests another important characteristic of Toynbee's procedure: for just as Plato in the *Republic* falls back upon a myth when he wishes to describe the Idea of the Good, so also Toynbee at critical points in his book resorts to myth and metaphor, and finds in these an otherwise unattainable path to the solution of problems he has set himself.

I need scarcely remind you of the freedom with which he resorts to these devices. Images such as the elaborate metaphor of the climbers on the rock face or the pollarded willow of the first volume give a picturesque sharpness to his concepts; and, more than this, seem sometimes for their author to take on an independent life and reality of their own. Toynbee's mind tends to move freely among visual images, metaphors, and figures of speech, finding baldly abstract and severely verbal formulae a pallid substitute for fully embodied imagination.

One may, indeed, say that his habit of mind is poetic, and it would be a mistake not to recognize his book as a prose epic, whatever else it may be besides. If his literary style were more austere and polished, his book could, I think, stand comparison with Dante, or better, with Milton. Indeed, in Toynbee's own spirit one might make up a table of literary parallels: As Herodotus is to Homer, and as Thucydides is to Aeschylus, so Toynbee is to Milton. Like Milton, he combines classical humanism with evangelical religion; but Toynbee lacks the doctrinal certainty of his predecessor. In much the same way the two great Greek historians accepted the fundamental intellectual frame-work of their poetic forerunners, but could not accept the pantheon of Olympus.

Toynbee's use of myth as a guide and suggestion to argument occurs at critical turning points in his book rather than throughout. But in falling back on Goethe's *Faust* for hints as to the manner in which a civilization comes into being, in summoning Aeschylus's Prometheus to assist him in comprehending the processes of civilization's growth; or in resorting to the language of Christian theology when discussing the relations of law and freedom in history, Toynbee is reproducing for his readers the processes of mind through which he himself passed in order to arrive at his conclusion.

Toynbee has confessed that this procedure at first filled him with misgiving, flying, as it did, in the face of accepted, scientific, sober-minded, intellectual method. But whether by birth or training, he found peculiar stimulus in the world of poetry and myth, and decided to plunge ahead and follow the suggestions that came to him from these sources in plotting out the drama of human history. In later years, he found a theoretical justification for what he had done. "I have now lived to see," he writes, "the subconscious well-spring of Poetry and Prophecy restored to honour in the Western World by the genius of C. G. Jung; but, before Jung's star at last rose above my horizon, Plato's example . . . had given me courage to part company with an early-twentieth-century Western Zeitgeist whose . . . only realities were those that could be weighed and measured.''

As I understand Toynbee's mature conviction (and I am not sure that I do understand his rather oblique and fleeting references to this arcanum of his thought), mythology represents an attempt to express in figurative and narrative language an intuitive grasp of the deepest reality of the human condition: a reality which can tamely but only inadequately be expressed in sober, severely intellectual discourse. And since the intellect is only part of man, and not necessarily the most far-ranging or reliable part at that, he now feels that he was right in relying upon the inspiration of myths to guide his thoughts, for they represent free intuitions of the soul, whose universal value has been tested by their survival through many ages and countless retellings.

For my present purposes, however, there is no need to explore or to criticize Toynbee's *ex post facto* justification for his procedure. The important point is the procedure itself—a movement of mind and method of thought very deeply implanted in him, and as characteristic of his early Hellenized as of his more recent Christianized outlook.

I think he would agree that Plato is his intellectual master of masters; and this is true not only in his reliance upon flashes of insight, and in his use of metaphor and of myth to convey or suggest meanings which sober matter-of-fact language leaves lifeless, but also in the habit of mind which strives in the face of all the diversity of experience and of history to arrive at the interconnectedness of things— to see multiplicity and discrepancy reduced to unity and order, to see the whole in the parts, the One in the Many. This is, indeed, the most basic and fundamental quality of Toynbee's mind, a quality perhaps unusual in an historian, who is normally liable to be arrested and intrigued by the variety and multiplicity of things and to take the data of history more or less for what they are—infinitely various, changeable, shifting, and interesting.

The impulse to find a unity in history implies, of course, that there is such a unity to be discovered; and this seems to me to be the bedrock of Toynbee's entire intellectual enterprise. Here is the basic assumption of his *A Study of History:* that there is intelligible unity behind all the diversity of human historical experience. Moreover, it is possible to characterize the unity Toynbee believes he has discovered; for alike in his earlier as in his later phases of thought, he has seen history as essentially a drama in which the human spirit is confronted with an Other, suffers frustration, and is provoked to respond by changing itself, thus growing, or, when the response falls short of success, suffering decay; but in either case making history. The nature of the Other which confronts the human spirit may vary: it may be physical nature, it may be other men, it may be God; and the later phases of his thought are distinguished from the earlier by the greater emphasis he now puts on the third of these alternatives. Yet in the fundamental picture of the historic process, and in the assumption that there is a Form or Idea (in the Platonic sense) to that process, he has remained entirely consistent, so far as I can see, from beginning to end.

I must confess that I am myself sufficiently close-wedded to the Zeitgeist of the twentieth century to be disturbed by some of Toynbee's mythological and theological language. Yet I find it possible to abstract sound sense from his pages. History, I agree, is change, and change in human society is, I believe, provoked by challenges (of whatever sort) from outside the closed circle of custom and institutional precedent which binds the normal day-by-day life of men together. And the reality of rhythms and patterns in history I am not disposed to deny. No doubt such crude paraphrase would, for Toynbee himself, lose all the barely expressible overtones and utterly distort the truth he has sought to convey. Such imperfect communication is, however, normal in intellectual discourse and should surprise no one. My point is merely this: I find much scintillating suggestion and stimulation to thought in Toynbee's pages; he has opened vistas of history and put questions before me as no other single author has done. For this I am grateful, and insofar as he does the like for others of the historical profession, we should all be grateful. He has certainly not spared himself in pursuing a high goal. I hope that future historians may find inspiration in his example, and will test, criticize, correct, and not entirely forget to emulate his efforts. If we do, the study of history cannot fail to be enriched, and we will worthily uphold Clio's oft-disputed claim to reign a queen among the sciences.

Source: William H. McNeill, ''Some Basic Assumptions of Toynbee's *A Study of History*,'' in *The Intent of Toynbee's History,* edited by Edward T. Gargan, Loyola University Press, 1961, pp. 29–46.

Sources

Gargen, Edward T., ed., *The Intent of Toynbee's History,* Loyola University Press, 1961, pp. 1–46.

Jung, C. G., *Memories, Dreams, Reflections,* Collins, 1967, pp. 159–60.

McIntire, C. T., and Marvin Perry, *Toynbee: Reappraisals,* University of Toronto Press, 1989.

McNeill, William H., *Toynbee: A Life,* Oxford University Press, 1989.

Montagu, M. F. Ashley, ed., *Toynbee and History: Critical Essays and Reviews,* Porter Sargent, 1956, pp. 3–11, 115–17, 122–24, 172–90.

Myers, E. D., Review in *Nation,* Vol. 164, April 19, 1947, p. 455.

Spengler, Oswald, *The Decline of the West,* Oxford, 1991.

Winetrout, Kenneth, *Arnold Toynbee: The Ecumenical Vision,* Twayne, 1975, pp. 17–38, 120.

Further Reading

Geyl, Peter, *Debates with Historians,* Meridian Books, 1958. Geyl's text includes four chapters that deal with *A Study of History*. Geyl criticizes Toynbee's method as not being genuinely empirical, and he also disputes Toynbee's pessimistic assessment of the state of Western civilization.

Ortega y Gasset, Jose, *An Interpretation of Universal History,* translated by Mildred Adams, W. W. Norton, 1973. This work is compiled from a lecture course that Ortega gave on Toynbee. Largely hostile to Toynbee, Ortega accuses him of having a mystical approach to history and of relying too much on Greco-Roman history as the key to all other civilizations. Ortega also claims that Toynbee makes major factual errors.

Samuel, Maurice, *The Professor and the Fossil,* Knopf, 1956. Samuel disputes Toynbee's description of the Jews as fossils of the extinct Syrian civilization with its implication that Jewish culture is lifeless and unproductive.

Stromberg, Roland N., *Arnold J. Toynbee: Historian for an Age in Crisis,* Southern Illinois University Press, 1972. This is a concise introduction and a balanced and fair-minded evaluation of Toynbee's thought, excellent for those who are studying him for the first time.

Glossary of Literary Terms

A

Abstract: Used as a noun, the term refers to a short summary or outline of a longer work. As an adjective applied to writing or literary works, abstract refers to words or phrases that name things not knowable through the five senses. Examples of abstracts include the *Cliffs Notes* summaries of major literary works. Examples of abstract terms or concepts include ''idea,'' ''guilt'' ''honesty,'' and ''loyalty.''

Absurd, Theater of the: See *Theater of the Absurd*

Absurdism: See *Theater of the Absurd*

Act: A major section of a play. Acts are divided into varying numbers of shorter scenes. From ancient times to the nineteenth century plays were generally constructed of five acts, but modern works typically consist of one, two, or three acts. Examples of five-act plays include the works of Sophocles and Shakespeare, while the plays of Arthur Miller commonly have a three-act structure.

Acto: A one-act Chicano theater piece developed out of collective improvisation. *Actos* were performed by members of Luis Valdez's Teatro Campesino in California during the mid-1960s.

Aestheticism: A literary and artistic movement of the nineteenth century. Followers of the movement believed that art should not be mixed with social, political, or moral teaching. The statement ''art for art's sake'' is a good summary of aestheticism. The movement had its roots in France, but it gained widespread importance in England in the last half of the nineteenth century, where it helped change the Victorian practice of including moral lessons in literature. Oscar Wilde is one of the best-known ''aesthetes'' of the late nineteenth century.

Age of Johnson: The period in English literature between 1750 and 1798, named after the most prominent literary figure of the age, Samuel Johnson. Works written during this time are noted for their emphasis on ''sensibility,'' or emotional quality. These works formed a transition between the rational works of the Age of Reason, or Neoclassical period, and the emphasis on individual feelings and responses of the Romantic period. Significant writers during the Age of Johnson included the novelists Ann Radcliffe and Henry Mackenzie, dramatists Richard Sheridan and Oliver Goldsmith, and poets William Collins and Thomas Gray. Also known as Age of Sensibility

Age of Reason: See *Neoclassicism*

Age of Sensibility: See *Age of Johnson*

Alexandrine Meter: See *Meter*

Allegory: A narrative technique in which characters representing things or abstract ideas are used to convey a message or teach a lesson. Allegory is typically used to teach moral, ethical, or religious lessons but is sometimes used for satiric or political purposes. Examples of allegorical works include Edmund Spenser's *The Faerie Queene* and John Bunyan's *The Pilgrim's Progress.*

Allusion: A reference to a familiar literary or historical person or event, used to make an idea more easily understood. For example, describing someone as a ''Romeo'' makes an allusion to William Shakespeare's famous young lover in *Romeo and Juliet.*

Amerind Literature: The writing and oral traditions of Native Americans. Native American literature was originally passed on by word of mouth, so it consisted largely of stories and events that were easily memorized. Amerind prose is often rhythmic like poetry because it was recited to the beat of a ceremonial drum. Examples of Amerind literature include the autobiographical *Black Elk Speaks,* the works of N. Scott Momaday, James Welch, and Craig Lee Strete, and the poetry of Luci Tapahonso.

Analogy: A comparison of two things made to explain something unfamiliar through its similarities to something familiar, or to prove one point based on the acceptedness of another. Similes and metaphors are types of analogies. Analogies often take the form of an extended simile, as in William Blake's aphorism: ''As the caterpillar chooses the fairest leaves to lay her eggs on, so the priest lays his curse on the fairest joys.''

Angry Young Men: A group of British writers of the 1950s whose work expressed bitterness and disillusionment with society. Common to their work is an anti-hero who rebels against a corrupt social order and strives for personal integrity. The term has been used to describe Kingsley Amis, John Osborne, Colin Wilson, John Wain, and others.

Antagonist: The major character in a narrative or drama who works against the hero or protagonist. An example of an evil antagonist is Richard Lovelace in Samuel Richardson's *Clarissa,* while a virtuous antagonist is Macduff in William Shakespeare's *Macbeth.*

Anthropomorphism: The presentation of animals or objects in human shape or with human characteristics. The term is derived from the Greek word for ''human form.'' The fables of Aesop, the animated films of Walt Disney, and Richard Adams's *Watership Down* feature anthropomorphic characters.

Anti-hero: A central character in a work of literature who lacks traditional heroic qualities such as courage, physical prowess, and fortitude. Anti-heros typically distrust conventional values and are unable to commit themselves to any ideals. They generally feel helpless in a world over which they have no control. Anti-heroes usually accept, and often celebrate, their positions as social outcasts. A well-known anti-hero is Yossarian in Joseph Heller's novel *Catch-22.*

Antimasque: See *Masque*

Antithesis: The antithesis of something is its direct opposite. In literature, the use of antithesis as a figure of speech results in two statements that show a contrast through the balancing of two opposite ideas. Technically, it is the second portion of the statement that is defined as the ''antithesis''; the first portion is the ''thesis.'' An example of antithesis is found in the following portion of Abraham Lincoln's ''Gettysburg Address''; notice the opposition between the verbs ''remember'' and ''forget'' and the phrases ''what we say'' and ''what they did'': ''The world will little note nor long remember what we say here, but it can never forget what they did here.''

Apocrypha: Writings tentatively attributed to an author but not proven or universally accepted to be their works. The term was originally applied to certain books of the Bible that were not considered inspired and so were not included in the ''sacred canon.'' Geoffrey Chaucer, William Shakespeare, Thomas Kyd, Thomas Middleton, and John Marston all have apocrypha. Apocryphal books of the Bible include the Old Testament's Book of Enoch and New Testament's Gospel of Peter.

Apollonian and Dionysian: The two impulses believed to guide authors of dramatic tragedy. The Apollonian impulse is named after Apollo, the Greek god of light and beauty and the symbol of intellectual order. The Dionysian impulse is named after Dionysus, the Greek god of wine and the symbol of the unrestrained forces of nature. The Apollonian impulse is to create a rational, harmonious world, while the Dionysian is to express the irrational forces of personality. Friedrich Nietzche uses these terms in *The Birth of Tragedy* to designate contrasting elements in Greek tragedy.

Apostrophe: A statement, question, or request addressed to an inanimate object or concept or to a nonexistent or absent person. Requests for inspiration from the muses in poetry are examples of apostrophe, as is Marc Antony's address to Caesar's corpse in William Shakespeare's *Julius Caesar:* ''O, pardon me, thou bleeding piece of earth, That I am meek and gentle with these butchers!... Woe to the hand that shed this costly blood!... ''

Archetype: The word archetype is commonly used to describe an original pattern or model from which all other things of the same kind are made. This term was introduced to literary criticism from the psychology of Carl Jung. It expresses Jung's theory that behind every person's ''unconscious,'' or repressed memories of the past, lies the ''collective unconscious'' of the human race: memories of the countless typical experiences of our ancestors. These memories are said to prompt illogical associations that trigger powerful emotions in the reader. Often, the emotional process is primitive, even primordial. Archetypes are the literary images that grow out of the ''collective unconscious.'' They appear in literature as incidents and plots that repeat basic patterns of life. They may also appear as stereotyped characters. Examples of literary archetypes include themes such as birth and death and characters such as the Earth Mother.

Argument: The argument of a work is the author's subject matter or principal idea. Examples of defined ''argument'' portions of works include John Milton's *Arguments* to each of the books of *Paradise Lost* and the ''Argument'' to Robert Herrick's *Hesperides.*

Aristotelian Criticism: Specifically, the method of evaluating and analyzing tragedy formulated by the Greek philosopher Aristotle in his *Poetics.* More generally, the term indicates any form of criticism that follows Aristotle's views. Aristotelian criticism focuses on the form and logical structure of a work, apart from its historical or social context, in contrast to ''Platonic Criticism,'' which stresses the usefulness of art. Adherents of New Criticism including John Crowe Ransom and Cleanth Brooks utilize and value the basic ideas of Aristotelian criticism for textual analysis.

Art for Art's Sake: See *Aestheticism*

Aside: A comment made by a stage performer that is intended to be heard by the audience but supposedly not by other characters. Eugene O'Neill's *Strange Interlude* is an extended use of the aside in modern theater.

Audience: The people for whom a piece of literature is written. Authors usually write with a certain audience in mind, for example, children, members of a religious or ethnic group, or colleagues in a professional field. The term ''audience'' also applies to the people who gather to see or hear any performance, including plays, poetry readings, speeches, and concerts. Jane Austen's parody of the gothic novel, *Northanger Abbey,* was originally intended for (and also pokes fun at) an audience of young and avid female gothic novel readers.

Avant-garde: A French term meaning ''vanguard.'' It is used in literary criticism to describe new writing that rejects traditional approaches to literature in favor of innovations in style or content. Twentieth-century examples of the literary *avant-garde* include the Black Mountain School of poets, the Bloomsbury Group, and the Beat Movement.

B

Ballad: A short poem that tells a simple story and has a repeated refrain. Ballads were originally intended to be sung. Early ballads, known as folk ballads, were passed down through generations, so their authors are often unknown. Later ballads composed by known authors are called literary ballads. An example of an anonymous folk ballad is ''Edward,'' which dates from the Middle Ages. Samuel Taylor Coleridge's ''The Rime of the Ancient Mariner'' and John Keats's ''La Belle Dame sans Merci'' are examples of literary ballads.

Baroque: A term used in literary criticism to describe literature that is complex or ornate in style or diction. Baroque works typically express tension, anxiety, and violent emotion. The term ''Baroque Age'' designates a period in Western European literature beginning in the late sixteenth century and ending about one hundred years later. Works of this period often mirror the qualities of works more generally associated with the label ''baroque'' and sometimes feature elaborate conceits. Examples of Baroque works include John Lyly's *Euphues: The Anatomy of Wit,* Luis de Gongora's *Soledads,* and William Shakespeare's *As You Like It.*

Baroque Age: See *Baroque*

Baroque Period: See *Baroque*

Beat Generation: See *Beat Movement*

Beat Movement: A period featuring a group of American poets and novelists of the 1950s and 1960s—including Jack Kerouac, Allen Ginsberg, Gregory Corso, William S. Burroughs, and Lawrence Ferlinghetti—who rejected established social and literary values. Using such techniques as stream of consciousness writing and jazz-influenced free verse and focusing on unusual or abnormal states of mind—generated by religious ecstasy or the use of drugs—the Beat writers aimed to create works that were unconventional in both form and subject matter. Kerouac's *On the Road* is perhaps the best-known example of a Beat Generation novel, and Ginsberg's *Howl* is a famous collection of Beat poetry.

Black Aesthetic Movement: A period of artistic and literary development among African Americans in the 1960s and early 1970s. This was the first major African-American artistic movement since the Harlem Renaissance and was closely paralleled by the civil rights and black power movements. The black aesthetic writers attempted to produce works of art that would be meaningful to the black masses. Key figures in black aesthetics included one of its founders, poet and playwright Amiri Baraka, formerly known as LeRoi Jones; poet and essayist Haki R. Madhubuti, formerly Don L. Lee; poet and playwright Sonia Sanchez; and dramatist Ed Bullins. Works representative of the Black Aesthetic Movement include Amiri Baraka's play *Dutchman,* a 1964 Obie award-winner; *Black Fire: An Anthology of Afro-American Writing,* edited by Baraka and playwright Larry Neal and published in 1968; and Sonia Sanchez's poetry collection *We a BaddDDD People,* published in 1970. Also known as Black Arts Movement.

Black Arts Movement: See *Black Aesthetic Movement*

Black Comedy: See *Black Humor*

Black Humor: Writing that places grotesque elements side by side with humorous ones in an attempt to shock the reader, forcing him or her to laugh at the horrifying reality of a disordered world. Joseph Heller's novel *Catch-22* is considered a superb example of the use of black humor. Other well-known authors who use black humor include Kurt Vonnegut, Edward Albee, Eugene Ionesco, and Harold Pinter. Also known as Black Comedy.

Blank Verse: Loosely, any unrhymed poetry, but more generally, unrhymed iambic pentameter verse (composed of lines of five two-syllable feet with the first syllable accented, the second unaccented). Blank verse has been used by poets since the Renaissance for its flexibility and its graceful, dignified tone. John Milton's *Paradise Lost* is in blank verse, as are most of William Shakespeare's plays.

Bloomsbury Group: A group of English writers, artists, and intellectuals who held informal artistic and philosophical discussions in Bloomsbury, a district of London, from around 1907 to the early 1930s. The Bloomsbury Group held no uniform philosophical beliefs but did commonly express an aversion to moral prudery and a desire for greater social tolerance. At various times the circle included Virginia Woolf, E. M. Forster, Clive Bell, Lytton Strachey, and John Maynard Keynes.

Bon Mot: A French term meaning "good word." A *bon mot* is a witty remark or clever observation. Charles Lamb and Oscar Wilde are celebrated for their witty *bon mots.* Two examples by Oscar Wilde stand out: (1) "All women become their mothers. That is their tragedy. No man does. That's his." (2) "A man cannot be too careful in the choice of his enemies."

Breath Verse: See *Projective Verse*

Burlesque: Any literary work that uses exaggeration to make its subject appear ridiculous, either by treating a trivial subject with profound seriousness or by treating a dignified subject frivolously. The word "burlesque" may also be used as an adjective, as in "burlesque show," to mean "striptease act." Examples of literary burlesque include the comedies of Aristophanes, Miguel de Cervantes's *Don Quixote,*, Samuel Butler's poem "Hudibras," and John Gay's play *The Beggar's Opera.*

C

Cadence: The natural rhythm of language caused by the alternation of accented and unaccented syllables. Much modern poetry—notably free verse—deliberately manipulates cadence to create complex rhythmic effects. James Macpherson's "Ossian poems" are richly cadenced, as is the poetry of the Symbolists, Walt Whitman, and Amy Lowell.

Caesura: A pause in a line of poetry, usually occurring near the middle. It typically corresponds to a break in the natural rhythm or sense of the line but is sometimes shifted to create special meanings or rhythmic effects. The opening line of Edgar Allan Poe's "The Raven" contains a caesura following "dreary": "Once upon a midnight dreary, while I pondered weak and weary. . . ."

Canzone: A short Italian or Provencal lyric poem, commonly about love and often set to music. The *canzone* has no set form but typically contains five or six stanzas made up of seven to twenty lines of eleven syllables each. A shorter, five- to ten-line "envoy," or concluding stanza, completes the poem. Masters of the *canzone* form include

Petrarch, Dante Alighieri, Torquato Tasso, and Guido Cavalcanti.

Carpe Diem: A Latin term meaning "seize the day." This is a traditional theme of poetry, especially lyrics. A *carpe diem* poem advises the reader or the person it addresses to live for today and enjoy the pleasures of the moment. Two celebrated *carpe diem* poems are Andrew Marvell's "To His Coy Mistress" and Robert Herrick's poem beginning "Gather ye rosebuds while ye may. . . ."

Catharsis: The release or purging of unwanted emotions— specifically fear and pity—brought about by exposure to art. The term was first used by the Greek philosopher Aristotle in his *Poetics* to refer to the desired effect of tragedy on spectators. A famous example of catharsis is realized in Sophocles' *Oedipus Rex,* when Oedipus discovers that his wife, Jacosta, is his own mother and that the stranger he killed on the road was his own father.

Celtic Renaissance: A period of Irish literary and cultural history at the end of the nineteenth century. Followers of the movement aimed to create a romantic vision of Celtic myth and legend. The most significant works of the Celtic Renaissance typically present a dreamy, unreal world, usually in reaction against the reality of contemporary problems. William Butler Yeats's *The Wanderings of Oisin* is among the most significant works of the Celtic Renaissance. Also known as Celtic Twilight.

Celtic Twilight: See *Celtic Renaissance*

Character: Broadly speaking, a person in a literary work. The actions of characters are what constitute the plot of a story, novel, or poem. There are numerous types of characters, ranging from simple, stereotypical figures to intricate, multifaceted ones. In the techniques of anthropomorphism and personification, animals—and even places or things—can assume aspects of character. "Characterization" is the process by which an author creates vivid, believable characters in a work of art. This may be done in a variety of ways, including (1) direct description of the character by the narrator; (2) the direct presentation of the speech, thoughts, or actions of the character; and (3) the responses of other characters to the character. The term "character" also refers to a form originated by the ancient Greek writer Theophrastus that later became popular in the seventeenth and eighteenth centuries. It is a short essay or sketch of a person who prominently displays a specific attribute or quality, such as miserliness or ambition. Notable characters in literature include Oedipus Rex, Don Quixote de la Mancha, Macbeth, Candide, Hester Prynne, Ebenezer Scrooge, Huckleberry Finn, Jay Gatsby, Scarlett O'Hara, James Bond, and Kunta Kinte.

Characterization: See *Character*

Chorus: In ancient Greek drama, a group of actors who commented on and interpreted the unfolding action on the stage. Initially the chorus was a major component of the presentation, but over time it became less significant, with its numbers reduced and its role eventually limited to commentary between acts. By the sixteenth century the chorus—if employed at all—was typically a single person who provided a prologue and an epilogue and occasionally appeared between acts to introduce or underscore an important event. The chorus in William Shakespeare's *Henry V* functions in this way. Modern dramas rarely feature a chorus, but T. S. Eliot's *Murder in the Cathedral* and Arthur Miller's *A View from the Bridge* are notable exceptions. The Stage Manager in Thornton Wilder's *Our Town* performs a role similar to that of the chorus.

Chronicle: A record of events presented in chronological order. Although the scope and level of detail provided varies greatly among the chronicles surviving from ancient times, some, such as the *Anglo-Saxon Chronicle,* feature vivid descriptions and a lively recounting of events. During the Elizabethan Age, many dramas— appropriately called "chronicle plays"—were based on material from chronicles. Many of William Shakespeare's dramas of English history as well as Christopher Marlowe's *Edward II* are based in part on Raphael Holinshead's *Chronicles of England, Scotland, and Ireland.*

Classical: In its strictest definition in literary criticism, classicism refers to works of ancient Greek or Roman literature. The term may also be used to describe a literary work of recognized importance (a "classic") from any time period or literature that exhibits the traits of classicism. Classical authors from ancient Greek and Roman times include Juvenal and Homer. Examples of later works and authors now described as classical include French literature of the seventeenth century, Western novels of the nineteenth century, and American fiction of the mid-nineteenth century such as that written by James Fenimore Cooper and Mark Twain.

Classicism: A term used in literary criticism to describe critical doctrines that have their roots in ancient Greek and Roman literature, philosophy, and art. Works associated with classicism typically exhibit restraint on the part of the author, unity of design and purpose, clarity, simplicity, logical organization, and respect for tradition. Examples of literary classicism include Cicero's prose, the dramas of Pierre Corneille and Jean Racine, the poetry of John Dryden and Alexander Pope, and the writings of J. W. von Goethe, G. E. Lessing, and T. S. Eliot.

Climax: The turning point in a narrative, the moment when the conflict is at its most intense. Typically, the structure of stories, novels, and plays is one of rising action, in which tension builds to the climax, followed by falling action, in which tension lessens as the story moves to its conclusion. The climax in James Fenimore Cooper's *The Last of the Mohicans* occurs when Magua and his captive Cora are pursued to the edge of a cliff by Uncas. Magua kills Uncas but is subsequently killed by Hawkeye.

Colloquialism: A word, phrase, or form of pronunciation that is acceptable in casual conversation but not in formal, written communication. It is considered more acceptable than slang. An example of colloquialism can be found in Rudyard Kipling's *Barrack-room Ballads:* When 'Omer smote 'is bloomin' lyre He'd 'eard men sing by land and sea; An' what he thought 'e might require 'E went an' took—the same as me!

Comedy: One of two major types of drama, the other being tragedy. Its aim is to amuse, and it typically ends happily. Comedy assumes many forms, such as farce and burlesque, and uses a variety of techniques, from parody to satire. In a restricted sense the term comedy refers only to dramatic presentations, but in general usage it is commonly applied to nondramatic works as well. Examples of comedies range from the plays of Aristophanes, Terrence, and Plautus, Dante Alighieri's *The Divine Comedy,* Francois Rabelais's *Pantagruel* and *Gargantua,* and some of Geoffrey Chaucer's tales and William Shakespeare's plays to Noel Coward's play *Private Lives* and James Thurber's short story "The Secret Life of Walter Mitty."

Comedy of Manners: A play about the manners and conventions of an aristocratic, highly sophisticated society. The characters are usually types rather than individualized personalities, and plot is less important than atmosphere. Such plays were an important aspect of late seventeenth-century English comedy. The comedy of manners was revived in the eighteenth century by Oliver Goldsmith and Richard Brinsley Sheridan, enjoyed a second revival in the late nineteenth century, and has endured into the twentieth century. Examples of comedies of manners include William Congreve's *The Way of the World* in the late seventeenth century, Oliver Goldsmith's *She Stoops to Conquer* and Richard Brinsley Sheridan's *The School for Scandal* in the eighteenth century, Oscar Wilde's *The Importance of Being Earnest* in the nineteenth century, and W. Somerset Maugham's *The Circle* in the twentieth century.

Comic Relief: The use of humor to lighten the mood of a serious or tragic story, especially in plays. The technique is very common in Elizabethan works, and can be an integral part of the plot or simply a brief event designed to break the tension of the scene. The Gravediggers' scene in William Shakespeare's *Hamlet* is a frequently cited example of comic relief.

Commedia dell'arte: An Italian term meaning "the comedy of guilds" or "the comedy of professional actors." This form of dramatic comedy was popular in Italy during the sixteenth century. Actors were assigned stock roles (such as Pulcinella, the stupid servant, or Pantalone, the old merchant) and given a basic plot to follow, but all dialogue was improvised. The roles were rigidly typed and the plots were formulaic, usually revolving around young lovers who thwarted their elders and attained wealth and happiness. A rigid convention of the *commedia dell'arte* is the periodic intrusion of Harlequin, who interrupts the play with low buffoonery. Peppino de Filippo's *Metamorphoses of a Wandering Minstrel* gave modern audiences an idea of what *commedia dell'arte* may have been like. Various scenarios for *commedia dell'arte* were compiled in Petraccone's *La commedia dell'arte, storia, technica, scenari,* published in 1927.

Complaint: A lyric poem, popular in the Renaissance, in which the speaker expresses sorrow about his or her condition. Typically, the speaker's sadness is caused by an unresponsive lover, but some complaints cite other sources of unhappiness, such as poverty or fate. A commonly cited example is "A Complaint by Night of the Lover Not Beloved" by Henry Howard, Earl of Surrey. Thomas Sackville's "Complaint of Henry, Duke of Buckingham" traces the duke's unhappiness to his ruthless ambition.

Conceit: A clever and fanciful metaphor, usually expressed through elaborate and extended comparison, that presents a striking parallel between two seemingly dissimilar things—for example, elaborately comparing a beautiful woman to an object like a garden or the sun. The conceit was a popular device throughout the Elizabethan Age and Baroque Age and was the principal technique of the seventeenth-century English metaphysical poets. This usage of the word conceit is unrelated to the best-known definition of conceit as an arrogant attitude or behavior. The conceit figures prominently in the works of John Donne, Emily Dickinson, and T. S. Eliot.

Concrete: Concrete is the opposite of abstract, and refers to a thing that actually exists or a description that allows the reader to experience an object or concept with the senses. Henry David Thoreau's *Walden* contains much concrete description of nature and wildlife.

Concrete Poetry: Poetry in which visual elements play a large part in the poetic effect. Punctuation marks, letters, or words are arranged on a page to form a visual design: a cross, for example, or a bumblebee. Max Bill and Eugene Gomringer were among the early practitioners of concrete poetry; Haroldo de Campos and Augusto de Campos are among contemporary authors of concrete poetry.

Confessional Poetry: A form of poetry in which the poet reveals very personal, intimate, sometimes shocking information about himself or herself. Anne Sexton, Sylvia Plath, Robert Lowell, and John Berryman wrote poetry in the confessional vein.

Conflict: The conflict in a work of fiction is the issue to be resolved in the story. It usually occurs between two characters, the protagonist and the antagonist, or between the protagonist and society or the protagonist and himself or herself. Conflict in Theodore Dreiser's novel *Sister Carrie* comes as a result of urban society, while Jack London's short story "To Build a Fire" concerns the protagonist's battle against the cold and himself.

Connotation: The impression that a word gives beyond its defined meaning. Connotations may be universally understood or may be significant only to a certain group. Both "horse" and "steed" denote the same animal, but "steed" has a different connotation, deriving from the chivalrous or romantic narratives in which the word was once often used.

Consonance: Consonance occurs in poetry when words appearing at the ends of two or more verses have similar final consonant sounds but have final vowel sounds that differ, as with "stuff" and "off." Consonance is found in "The curfew tolls the knells of parting day" from Thomas Grey's "An Elegy Written in a Country Church Yard." Also known as Half Rhyme or Slant Rhyme.

Convention: Any widely accepted literary device, style, or form. A soliloquy, in which a character reveals to the audience his or her private thoughts, is an example of a dramatic convention.

Corrido: A Mexican ballad. Examples of *corridos* include "Muerte del afamado Bilito," "La voz de mi conciencia," "Lucio Perez," "La juida," and "Los presos."

Couplet: Two lines of poetry with the same rhyme and meter, often expressing a complete and self-contained thought. The following couplet is from Alexander Pope's "Elegy to the Memory of an Unfortunate Lady": 'Tis Use alone that sanctifies Expense, And Splendour borrows all her rays from Sense.

Criticism: The systematic study and evaluation of literary works, usually based on a specific method or set of principles. An important part of literary studies since ancient times, the practice of criticism has given rise to numerous theories, methods, and "schools," sometimes producing conflicting, even contradictory, interpretations of literature in general as well as of individual works. Even such basic issues as what constitutes a poem or a novel have been the subject of much criticism over the centuries. Seminal texts of literary criticism include Plato's *Republic,* Aristotle's *Poetics,* Sir Philip Sidney's *The Defence of Poesie,* John Dryden's *Of Dramatic Poesie,* and William Wordsworth's "Preface" to the second edition of his *Lyrical Ballads.* Contemporary schools of criticism include deconstruction, feminist, psychoanalytic, poststructuralist, new historicist, postcolonialist, and reader-response.

D

Dactyl: See *Foot*

Dadaism: A protest movement in art and literature founded by Tristan Tzara in 1916. Followers of the movement expressed their outrage at the destruction brought about by World War I by revolting against numerous forms of social convention. The Dadaists presented works marked by calculated madness and flamboyant nonsense. They stressed total freedom of expression, commonly through primitive displays of emotion and illogical, often senseless, poetry. The movement ended shortly after the war, when it was replaced by surrealism. Proponents of Dadaism include Andre Breton, Louis Aragon, Philippe Soupault, and Paul Eluard.

Decadent: See *Decadents*

Decadents: The followers of a nineteenth-century literary movement that had its beginnings in French aestheticism. Decadent literature displays a fascination with perverse and morbid states; a search for novelty and sensation—the "new thrill"; a preoccupation with mysticism; and a belief in the senselessness of human existence. The movement is closely associated with the doctrine Art for Art's Sake. The term "decadence" is sometimes used to denote a decline in the quality of art or literature following a period of greatness. Major French decadents are Charles Baudelaire and Arthur Rimbaud. English decadents include Oscar Wilde, Ernest Dowson, and Frank Harris.

Deconstruction: A method of literary criticism developed by Jacques Derrida and characterized by multiple conflicting interpretations of a given work. Deconstructionists consider the impact of the language of a work and suggest that the true meaning of the work is not necessarily the meaning that the author intended. Jacques Derrida's *De la grammatologie* is the seminal text on deconstructive strategies; among American practitioners of this method of criticism are Paul de Man and J. Hillis Miller.

Deduction: The process of reaching a conclusion through reasoning from general premises to a specific premise. An example of deduction is present in the following syllogism: Premise: All mammals are animals. Premise: All whales are mammals. Conclusion: Therefore, all whales are animals.

Denotation: The definition of a word, apart from the impressions or feelings it creates in the reader. The word "apartheid" denotes a political and economic policy of segregation by race, but its connotations— oppression, slavery, inequality—are numerous.

Denouement: A French word meaning "the unknotting." In literary criticism, it denotes the resolution of conflict in fiction or drama. The *denouement* follows the climax and provides an outcome to the primary plot situation as well as an explanation of secondary plot complications. The *denouement* often involves a character's recognition of his or her state of mind or moral condition. A well-known example of *denouement* is the last scene of the play *As You Like It* by William Shakespeare, in which couples are married, an evildoer repents, the identities of two disguised characters are revealed, and a ruler is restored to power. Also known as Falling Action.

Description: Descriptive writing is intended to allow a reader to picture the scene or setting in which the action of a story takes place. The form this description takes often evokes an intended emotional response—a dark, spooky graveyard will evoke fear, and a peaceful, sunny meadow will evoke calmness. An example of a descriptive story is Edgar Allan Poe's *Landor's Cottage,* which offers a detailed depiction of a New York country estate.

Detective Story: A narrative about the solution of a mystery or the identification of a criminal. The conventions of the detective story include the detective's scrupulous use of logic in solving the mystery; incompetent or ineffectual police; a suspect who appears guilty at first but is later proved innocent; and the detective's friend or confidant— often the narrator—whose slowness in interpreting clues emphasizes by contrast the detective's brilliance. Edgar Allan Poe's "Murders in the Rue Morgue" is commonly regarded as the earliest example of this type of story. With this work, Poe established many of the conventions of the detective story genre, which are still in practice. Other practitioners of this vast and extremely popular genre include Arthur Conan Doyle, Dashiell Hammett, and Agatha Christie.

Deus ex machina: A Latin term meaning "god out of a machine." In Greek drama, a god was often lowered onto the stage by a mechanism of some kind to rescue the hero or untangle the plot. By extension, the term refers to any artificial device or coincidence used to bring about a convenient and simple solution to a plot. This is a common device in melodramas and includes such fortunate circumstances as the sudden receipt of a legacy to save the family farm or a last-minute stay of execution. The *deus ex machina* invariably rewards the virtuous and punishes evildoers. Examples of *deus ex machina* include King Louis XIV in Jean-Baptiste Moliere's *Tartuffe* and Queen Victoria in *The Pirates of Penzance* by William Gilbert and Arthur Sullivan. Bertolt Brecht parodies the abuse of such devices in the conclusion of his *Threepenny Opera.*

Dialogue: In its widest sense, dialogue is simply conversation between people in a literary work; in its most restricted sense, it refers specifically to the speech of characters in a drama. As a specific literary genre, a "dialogue" is a composition in which characters debate an issue or idea. The Greek philosopher Plato frequently expounded his theories in the form of dialogues.

Diction: The selection and arrangement of words in a literary work. Either or both may vary depending on the desired effect. There are four general types of diction: "formal," used in scholarly or lofty writing; "informal," used in relaxed but educated conversation; "colloquial," used in everyday speech; and "slang," containing newly coined words and other terms not accepted in formal usage.

Didactic: A term used to describe works of literature that aim to teach some moral, religious, political, or practical lesson. Although didactic elements are often found in artistically pleasing works, the term "didactic" usually refers to literature in which the message is more important than the form. The term may also be used to criticize a work that the critic finds "overly didactic," that is, heavy-handed in its delivery of a lesson. Examples of didactic literature include John Bunyan's *Pilgrim's Progress,* Alexander Pope's *Essay on Criticism,* Jean-Jacques Rousseau's *Emile,* and Elizabeth Inchbald's *Simple Story.*

Dimeter: See *Meter*

Dionysian: See *Apollonian and Dionysian*

Discordia concours: A Latin phrase meaning "discord in harmony." The term was coined by the eighteenth-century English writer Samuel Johnson to describe "a combination of dissimilar images or discovery of occult resemblances in things apparently unlike." Johnson created the expression by reversing a phrase by the Latin poet Horace. The metaphysical poetry of John Donne, Richard Crashaw, Abraham Cowley, George Herbert, and Edward Taylor among others, contains many examples of *discordia concours.* In Donne's "A Valediction: Forbidding Mourning," the poet compares the union of himself with his lover to a draftsman's compass: If they be two, they are two so, As stiff twin compasses are two: Thy soul, the fixed foot, makes no show To move, but doth, if the other do; And though it in the center sit, Yet when the other far doth roam, It leans, and hearkens after it, And grows erect, as that comes home.

Dissonance: A combination of harsh or jarring sounds, especially in poetry. Although such combinations may be accidental, poets sometimes intentionally make them to achieve particular effects. Dissonance is also sometimes used to refer to close but not identical rhymes. When this is the case, the word functions as a synonym for consonance. Robert Browning, Gerard Manley Hopkins, and many other poets have made deliberate use of dissonance.

Doppelganger: A literary technique by which a character is duplicated (usually in the form of an alter ego, though sometimes as a ghostly counterpart) or divided into two distinct, usually opposite personalities. The use of this character device is widespread in nineteenth- and twentieth- century literature, and indicates a growing awareness among authors that the "self" is really a composite of many "selves." A well-known story containing a *doppelganger* character is Robert Louis Stevenson's *Dr. Jekyll and Mr. Hyde,* which dramatizes an internal struggle between good and evil. Also known as The Double.

Double Entendre: A corruption of a French phrase meaning "double meaning." The term is used to indicate a word or phrase that is deliberately ambiguous, especially when one of the meanings is risque or improper. An example of a *double entendre* is the Elizabethan usage of the verb "die," which refers both to death and to orgasm.

Double, The: See *Doppelganger*

Draft: Any preliminary version of a written work. An author may write dozens of drafts which are revised to form the final work, or he or she may write only one, with few or no revisions. Dorothy Parker's observation that "I can't write five words but that I change seven" humorously indicates the purpose of the draft.

Drama: In its widest sense, a drama is any work designed to be presented by actors on a stage. Similarly, "drama" denotes a broad literary genre that includes a variety of forms, from pageant and spectacle to tragedy and comedy, as well as countless types and subtypes. More commonly in modern usage, however, a drama is a work that treats serious subjects and themes but does not aim at the grandeur of tragedy. This use of the term originated with the eighteenth-century French writer Denis Diderot, who used the word *drame* to designate his plays about middle- class life; thus "drama" typically features characters of a less exalted stature than those of tragedy. Examples of classical dramas include Menander's comedy *Dyscolus* and Sophocles' tragedy *Oedipus Rex.* Contemporary dramas include Eugene O'Neill's *The Iceman Cometh,* Lillian Hellman's *Little Foxes,* and August Wilson's *Ma Rainey's Black Bottom.*

Dramatic Irony: Occurs when the audience of a play or the reader of a work of literature knows something that a character in the work itself does not know. The irony is in the contrast between the intended meaning of the statements or actions of a character and the additional information understood by the audience. A celebrated example of dramatic irony is in Act V of William Shakespeare's *Romeo and Juliet,* where two young lovers meet their end as a result of a tragic misunderstanding. Here, the audience has full knowledge that Juliet's apparent ''death'' is merely temporary; she will regain her senses when the mysterious ''sleeping potion'' she has taken wears off. But Romeo, mistaking Juliet's drug-induced trance for true death, kills himself in grief. Upon awakening, Juliet discovers Romeo's corpse and, in despair, slays herself.

Dramatic Monologue: See *Monologue*

Dramatic Poetry: Any lyric work that employs elements of drama such as dialogue, conflict, or characterization, but excluding works that are intended for stage presentation. A monologue is a form of dramatic poetry.

Dramatis Personae: The characters in a work of literature, particularly a drama. The list of characters printed before the main text of a play or in the program is the *dramatis personae.*

Dream Allegory: See *Dream Vision*

Dream Vision: A literary convention, chiefly of the Middle Ages. In a dream vision a story is presented as a literal dream of the narrator. This device was commonly used to teach moral and religious lessons. Important works of this type are *The Divine Comedy* by Dante Alighieri, *Piers Plowman* by William Langland, and *The Pilgrim's Progress* by John Bunyan. Also known as Dream Allegory.

Dystopia: An imaginary place in a work of fiction where the characters lead dehumanized, fearful lives. Jack London's *The Iron Heel,* Yevgeny Zamyatin's *My,* Aldous Huxley's *Brave New World,* George Orwell's *Nineteen Eighty-four,* and Margaret Atwood's *Handmaid's Tale* portray versions of dystopia.

E

Eclogue: In classical literature, a poem featuring rural themes and structured as a dialogue among shepherds. Eclogues often took specific poetic forms, such as elegies or love poems. Some were written as the soliloquy of a shepherd. In later centuries, ''eclogue'' came to refer to any poem that was in the pastoral tradition or that had a dialogue or mono-logue structure. A classical example of an eclogue is Virgil's *Eclogues,* also known as *Bucolics.* Giovanni Boccaccio, Edmund Spenser, Andrew Marvell, Jonathan Swift, and Louis MacNeice also wrote eclogues.

Edwardian: Describes cultural conventions identified with the period of the reign of Edward VII of England (1901-1910). Writers of the Edwardian Age typically displayed a strong reaction against the propriety and conservatism of the Victorian Age. Their work often exhibits distrust of authority in religion, politics, and art and expresses strong doubts about the soundness of conventional values. Writers of this era include George Bernard Shaw, H. G. Wells, and Joseph Conrad.

Edwardian Age: See *Edwardian*

Electra Complex: A daughter's amorous obsession with her father. The term Electra complex comes from the plays of Euripides and Sophocles entitled *Electra,* in which the character Electra drives her brother Orestes to kill their mother and her lover in revenge for the murder of their father.

Elegy: A lyric poem that laments the death of a person or the eventual death of all people. In a conventional elegy, set in a classical world, the poet and subject are spoken of as shepherds. In modern criticism, the word elegy is often used to refer to a poem that is melancholy or mournfully contemplative. John Milton's ''Lycidas'' and Percy Bysshe Shelley's ''Adonais'' are two examples of this form.

Elizabethan Age: A period of great economic growth, religious controversy, and nationalism closely associated with the reign of Elizabeth I of England (1558-1603). The Elizabethan Age is considered a part of the general renaissance—that is, the flowering of arts and literature—that took place in Europe during the fourteenth through sixteenth centuries. The era is considered the golden age of English literature. The most important dramas in English and a great deal of lyric poetry were produced during this period, and modern English criticism began around this time. The notable authors of the period—Philip Sidney, Edmund Spenser, Christopher Marlowe, William Shakespeare, Ben Jonson, Francis Bacon, and John Donne—are among the best in all of English literature.

Elizabethan Drama: English comic and tragic plays produced during the Renaissance, or more narrowly, those plays written during the last years of and few years after Queen Elizabeth's reign. William Shakespeare is considered an Elizabethan dramatist in the broader sense, although most of his work was produced during the reign of James I. Examples of Elizabethan comedies include John Lyly's *The Woman in the Moone,* Thomas Dekker's *The Roaring Girl, or, Moll Cut Purse,* and William Shakespeare's *Twelfth Night.* Examples of Elizabethan tragedies include William Shakespeare's *Antony and Cleopatra,* Thomas Kyd's *The Spanish Tragedy,* and John Webster's *The Tragedy of the Duchess of Malfi.*

Empathy: A sense of shared experience, including emotional and physical feelings, with someone or something other than oneself. Empathy is often used to describe the response of a reader to a literary character. An example of an empathic passage is William Shakespeare's description in his narrative poem *Venus and Adonis* of: the snail, whose tender horns being hit, Shrinks backward in his shelly cave with pain. Readers of Gerard Manley Hopkins's *The Windhover* may experience some of the physical sensations evoked in the description of the movement of the falcon.

English Sonnet: See *Sonnet*

Enjambment: The running over of the sense and structure of a line of verse or a couplet into the following verse or couplet. Andrew Marvell's "To His Coy Mistress" is structured as a series of enjambments, as in lines 11-12: "My vegetable love should grow/Vaster than empires and more slow."

Enlightenment, The: An eighteenth-century philosophical movement. It began in France but had a wide impact throughout Europe and America. Thinkers of the Enlightenment valued reason and believed that both the individual and society could achieve a state of perfection. Corresponding to this essentially humanist vision was a resistance to religious authority. Important figures of the Enlightenment were Denis Diderot and Voltaire in France, Edward Gibbon and David Hume in England, and Thomas Paine and Thomas Jefferson in the United States.

Epic: A long narrative poem about the adventures of a hero of great historic or legendary importance. The setting is vast and the action is often given cosmic significance through the intervention of supernatural forces such as gods, angels, or demons. Epics are typically written in a classical style of grand simplicity with elaborate metaphors and allusions that enhance the symbolic importance of a hero's adventures. Some well-known epics are Homer's *Iliad* and *Odyssey,* Virgil's *Aeneid,* and John Milton's *Paradise Lost.*

Epic Simile: See *Homeric Simile*

Epic Theater: A theory of theatrical presentation developed by twentieth-century German playwright Bertolt Brecht. Brecht created a type of drama that the audience could view with complete detachment. He used what he termed "alienation effects" to create an emotional distance between the audience and the action on stage. Among these effects are: short, self-contained scenes that keep the play from building to a cathartic climax; songs that comment on the action; and techniques of acting that prevent the actor from developing an emotional identity with his role. Besides the plays of Bertolt Brecht, other plays that utilize epic theater conventions include those of Georg Buchner, Frank Wedekind, Erwin Piscator, and Leopold Jessner.

Epigram: A saying that makes the speaker's point quickly and concisely. Samuel Taylor Coleridge wrote an epigram that neatly sums up the form: What is an Epigram? A Dwarfish whole, Its body brevity, and wit its soul.

Epilogue: A concluding statement or section of a literary work. In dramas, particularly those of the seventeenth and eighteenth centuries, the epilogue is a closing speech, often in verse, delivered by an actor at the end of a play and spoken directly to the audience. A famous epilogue is Puck's speech at the end of William Shakespeare's *A Midsummer Night's Dream.*

Epiphany: A sudden revelation of truth inspired by a seemingly trivial incident. The term was widely used by James Joyce in his critical writings, and the stories in Joyce's *Dubliners* are commonly called "epiphanies."

Episode: An incident that forms part of a story and is significantly related to it. Episodes may be either self-contained narratives or events that depend on a larger context for their sense and importance. Examples of episodes include the founding of Wilmington, Delaware in Charles Reade's *The Disinherited Heir* and the individual events comprising the picaresque novels and medieval romances.

Episodic Plot: See *Plot*

Epitaph: An inscription on a tomb or tombstone, or a verse written on the occasion of a person's death. Epitaphs may be serious or humorous. Dorothy Parker's epitaph reads, "I told you I was sick."

Epithalamion: A song or poem written to honor and commemorate a marriage ceremony. Famous examples include Edmund Spenser's

"Epithalamion" and e. e. cummings's "Epithalamion." Also spelled Epithalamium.

Epithalamium: See *Epithalamion*

Epithet: A word or phrase, often disparaging or abusive, that expresses a character trait of someone or something. "The Napoleon of crime" is an epithet applied to Professor Moriarty, arch-rival of Sherlock Holmes in Arthur Conan Doyle's series of detective stories.

Exempla: See *Exemplum*

Exemplum: A tale with a moral message. This form of literary sermonizing flourished during the Middle Ages, when *exempla* appeared in collections known as "example-books." The works of Geoffrey Chaucer are full of *exempla*.

Existentialism: A predominantly twentieth-century philosophy concerned with the nature and perception of human existence. There are two major strains of existentialist thought: atheistic and Christian. Followers of atheistic existentialism believe that the individual is alone in a godless universe and that the basic human condition is one of suffering and loneliness. Nevertheless, because there are no fixed values, individuals can create their own characters—indeed, they can shape themselves—through the exercise of free will. The atheistic strain culminates in and is popularly associated with the works of Jean-Paul Sartre. The Christian existentialists, on the other hand, believe that only in God may people find freedom from life's anguish. The two strains hold certain beliefs in common: that existence cannot be fully understood or described through empirical effort; that anguish is a universal element of life; that individuals must bear responsibility for their actions; and that there is no common standard of behavior or perception for religious and ethical matters. Existentialist thought figures prominently in the works of such authors as Eugene Ionesco, Franz Kafka, Fyodor Dostoyevsky, Simone de Beauvoir, Samuel Beckett, and Albert Camus.

Expatriates: See *Expatriatism*

Expatriatism: The practice of leaving one's country to live for an extended period in another country. Literary expatriates include English poets Percy Bysshe Shelley and John Keats in Italy, Polish novelist Joseph Conrad in England, American writers Richard Wright, James Baldwin, Gertrude Stein, and Ernest Hemingway in France, and Trinidadian author Neil Bissondath in Canada.

Exposition: Writing intended to explain the nature of an idea, thing, or theme. Expository writing is often combined with description, narration, or argument. In dramatic writing, the exposition is the introductory material which presents the characters, setting, and tone of the play. An example of dramatic exposition occurs in many nineteenth-century drawing-room comedies in which the butler and the maid open the play with relevant talk about their master and mistress; in composition, exposition relays factual information, as in encyclopedia entries.

Expressionism: An indistinct literary term, originally used to describe an early twentieth-century school of German painting. The term applies to almost any mode of unconventional, highly subjective writing that distorts reality in some way. Advocates of Expressionism include dramatists George Kaiser, Ernst Toller, Luigi Pirandello, Federico Garcia Lorca, Eugene O'Neill, and Elmer Rice; poets George Heym, Ernst Stadler, August Stramm, Gottfried Benn, and Georg Trakl; and novelists Franz Kafka and James Joyce.

Extended Monologue: See *Monologue*

F

Fable: A prose or verse narrative intended to convey a moral. Animals or inanimate objects with human characteristics often serve as characters in fables. A famous fable is Aesop's "The Tortoise and the Hare."

Fairy Tales: Short narratives featuring mythical beings such as fairies, elves, and sprites. These tales originally belonged to the folklore of a particular nation or region, such as those collected in Germany by Jacob and Wilhelm Grimm. Two other celebrated writers of fairy tales are Hans Christian Andersen and Rudyard Kipling.

Falling Action: See *Denouement*

Fantasy: A literary form related to mythology and folklore. Fantasy literature is typically set in non-existent realms and features supernatural beings. Notable examples of fantasy literature are *The Lord of the Rings* by J. R. R. Tolkien and the Gormenghast trilogy by Mervyn Peake.

Farce: A type of comedy characterized by broad humor, outlandish incidents, and often vulgar subject matter. Much of the "comedy" in film and television could more accurately be described as farce.

Feet: See *Foot*

Feminine Rhyme: See *Rhyme*

Femme fatale: A French phrase with the literal translation "fatal woman." A *femme fatale* is a sensuous, alluring woman who often leads men into danger or trouble. A classic example of the *femme fatale* is the nameless character in Billy Wilder's *The Seven Year Itch,* portrayed by Marilyn Monroe in the film adaptation.

Fiction: Any story that is the product of imagination rather than a documentation of fact. characters and events in such narratives may be based in real life but their ultimate form and configuration is a creation of the author. Geoffrey Chaucer's *The Canterbury Tales,* Laurence Sterne's *Tristram Shandy,* and Margaret Mitchell's *Gone with the Wind* are examples of fiction.

Figurative Language: A technique in writing in which the author temporarily interrupts the order, construction, or meaning of the writing for a particular effect. This interruption takes the form of one or more figures of speech such as hyperbole, irony, or simile. Figurative language is the opposite of literal language, in which every word is truthful, accurate, and free of exaggeration or embellishment. Examples of figurative language are tropes such as metaphor and rhetorical figures such as apostrophe.

Figures of Speech: Writing that differs from customary conventions for construction, meaning, order, or significance for the purpose of a special meaning or effect. There are two major types of figures of speech: rhetorical figures, which do not make changes in the meaning of the words, and tropes, which do. Types of figures of speech include simile, hyperbole, alliteration, and pun, among many others.

Fin de siecle: A French term meaning "end of the century." The term is used to denote the last decade of the nineteenth century, a transition period when writers and other artists abandoned old conventions and looked for new techniques and objectives. Two writers commonly associated with the *fin de siecle* mindset are Oscar Wilde and George Bernard Shaw.

First Person: See *Point of View*

Flashback: A device used in literature to present action that occurred before the beginning of the story. Flashbacks are often introduced as the dreams or recollections of one or more characters. Flashback techniques are often used in films, where they are typically set off by a gradual changing of one picture to another.

Foil: A character in a work of literature whose physical or psychological qualities contrast strongly with, and therefore highlight, the corresponding qualities of another character. In his Sherlock Holmes stories, Arthur Conan Doyle portrayed Dr. Watson as a man of normal habits and intelligence, making him a foil for the eccentric and wonderfully perceptive Sherlock Holmes.

Folk Ballad: See *Ballad*

Folklore: Traditions and myths preserved in a culture or group of people. Typically, these are passed on by word of mouth in various forms—such as legends, songs, and proverbs— or preserved in customs and ceremonies. This term was first used by W. J. Thoms in 1846. Sir James Frazer's *The Golden Bough* is the record of English folklore; myths about the frontier and the Old South exemplify American folklore.

Folktale: A story originating in oral tradition. Folktales fall into a variety of categories, including legends, ghost stories, fairy tales, fables, and anecdotes based on historical figures and events. Examples of folktales include Giambattista Basile's *The Pentamerone,* which contains the tales of Puss in Boots, Rapunzel, Cinderella, and Beauty and the Beast, and Joel Chandler Harris's Uncle Remus stories, which represent transplanted African folktales and American tales about the characters Mike Fink, Johnny Appleseed, Paul Bunyan, and Pecos Bill.

Foot: The smallest unit of rhythm in a line of poetry. In English-language poetry, a foot is typically one accented syllable combined with one or two unaccented syllables. There are many different types of feet. When the accent is on the second syllable of a two syllable word (con- *tort*), the foot is an "iamb"; the reverse accentual pattern (*tor* -ture) is a "trochee." Other feet that commonly occur in poetry in English are "anapest", two unaccented syllables followed by an accented syllable as in inter-*cept*, and "dactyl", an accented syllable followed by two unaccented syllables as in *su*-i- cide.

Foreshadowing: A device used in literature to create expectation or to set up an explanation of later developments. In Charles Dickens's *Great Expectations,* the graveyard encounter at the beginning of the novel between Pip and the escaped convict Magwitch foreshadows the baleful atmosphere and events that comprise much of the narrative.

Form: The pattern or construction of a work which identifies its genre and distinguishes it from other genres. Examples of forms include the different genres, such as the lyric form or the short story form, and various patterns for poetry, such as the verse form or the stanza form.

Formalism: In literary criticism, the belief that literature should follow prescribed rules of construction, such as those that govern the sonnet form. Examples of formalism are found in the work of the New Critics and structuralists.

Fourteener Meter: See *Meter*

Free Verse: Poetry that lacks regular metrical and rhyme patterns but that tries to capture the cadences of everyday speech. The form allows a poet to exploit a variety of rhythmical effects within a single poem. Free-verse techniques have been widely used in the twentieth century by such writers as Ezra Pound, T. S. Eliot, Carl Sandburg, and William Carlos Williams. Also known as *Vers libre.*

Futurism: A flamboyant literary and artistic movement that developed in France, Italy, and Russia from 1908 through the 1920s. Futurist theater and poetry abandoned traditional literary forms. In their place, followers of the movement attempted to achieve total freedom of expression through bizarre imagery and deformed or newly invented words. The Futurists were self-consciously modern artists who attempted to incorporate the appearances and sounds of modern life into their work. Futurist writers include Filippo Tommaso Marinetti, Wyndham Lewis, Guillaume Apollinaire, Velimir Khlebnikov, and Vladimir Mayakovsky.

G

Genre: A category of literary work. In critical theory, genre may refer to both the content of a given work—tragedy, comedy, pastoral—and to its form, such as poetry, novel, or drama. This term also refers to types of popular literature, as in the genres of science fiction or the detective story.

Genteel Tradition: A term coined by critic George Santayana to describe the literary practice of certain late nineteenth- century American writers, especially New Englanders. Followers of the Genteel Tradition emphasized conventionality in social, religious, moral, and literary standards. Some of the best-known writers of the Genteel Tradition are R. H. Stoddard and Bayard Taylor.

Gilded Age: A period in American history during the 1870s characterized by political corruption and materialism. A number of important novels of social and political criticism were written during this time. Examples of Gilded Age literature include Henry Adams's *Democracy* and F. Marion Crawford's *An American Politician.*

Gothic: See *Gothicism*

Gothicism: In literary criticism, works characterized by a taste for the medieval or morbidly attractive. A gothic novel prominently features elements of horror, the supernatural, gloom, and violence: clanking chains, terror, charnel houses, ghosts, medieval castles, and mysteriously slamming doors. The term "gothic novel" is also applied to novels that lack elements of the traditional Gothic setting but that create a similar atmosphere of terror or dread. Mary Shelley's *Frankenstein* is perhaps the best-known English work of this kind.

Gothic Novel: See *Gothicism*

Great Chain of Being: The belief that all things and creatures in nature are organized in a hierarchy from inanimate objects at the bottom to God at the top. This system of belief was popular in the seventeenth and eighteenth centuries. A summary of the concept of the great chain of being can be found in the first epistle of Alexander Pope's *An Essay on Man,* and more recently in Arthur O. Lovejoy's *The Great Chain of Being: A Study of the History of an Idea.*

Grotesque: In literary criticism, the subject matter of a work or a style of expression characterized by exaggeration, deformity, freakishness, and disorder. The grotesque often includes an element of comic absurdity. Early examples of literary grotesque include Francois Rabelais's *Pantagruel* and *Gargantua* and Thomas Nashe's *The Unfortunate Traveller,* while more recent examples can be found in the works of Edgar Allan Poe, Evelyn Waugh, Eudora Welty, Flannery O'Connor, Eugene Ionesco, Gunter Grass, Thomas Mann, Mervyn Peake, and Joseph Heller, among many others.

H

Haiku: The shortest form of Japanese poetry, constructed in three lines of five, seven, and five syllables respectively. The message of a *haiku* poem usually centers on some aspect of spirituality and provokes an emotional response in the reader. Early masters of *haiku* include Basho, Buson,

Kobayashi Issa, and Masaoka Shiki. English writers of *haiku* include the Imagists, notably Ezra Pound, H. D., Amy Lowell, Carl Sandburg, and William Carlos Williams. Also known as *Hokku.*

Half Rhyme: See *Consonance*

Hamartia: In tragedy, the event or act that leads to the hero's or heroine's downfall. This term is often incorrectly used as a synonym for tragic flaw. In Richard Wright's *Native Son,* the act that seals Bigger Thomas's fate is his first impulsive murder.

Harlem Renaissance: The Harlem Renaissance of the 1920s is generally considered the first significant movement of black writers and artists in the United States. During this period, new and established black writers published more fiction and poetry than ever before, the first influential black literary journals were established, and black authors and artists received their first widespread recognition and serious critical appraisal. Among the major writers associated with this period are Claude McKay, Jean Toomer, Countee Cullen, Langston Hughes, Arna Bontemps, Nella Larsen, and Zora Neale Hurston. Works representative of the Harlem Renaissance include Arna Bontemps's poems ''The Return'' and ''Golgotha Is a Mountain,'' Claude McKay's novel *Home to Harlem,* Nella Larsen's novel *Passing,* Langston Hughes's poem ''The Negro Speaks of Rivers,'' and the journals *Crisis* and *Opportunity,* both founded during this period. Also known as Negro Renaissance and New Negro Movement.

Harlequin: A stock character of the *commedia dell'arte* who occasionally interrupted the action with silly antics. Harlequin first appeared on the English stage in John Day's *The Travailes of the Three English Brothers.* The San Francisco Mime Troupe is one of the few modern groups to adapt Harlequin to the needs of contemporary satire.

Hellenism: Imitation of ancient Greek thought or styles. Also, an approach to life that focuses on the growth and development of the intellect. ''Hellenism'' is sometimes used to refer to the belief that reason can be applied to examine all human experience. A cogent discussion of Hellenism can be found in Matthew Arnold's *Culture and Anarchy.*

Heptameter: See *Meter*

Hero/Heroine: The principal sympathetic character (male or female) in a literary work. Heroes and heroines typically exhibit admirable traits: ideal-ism, courage, and integrity, for example. Famous heroes and heroines include Pip in Charles Dickens's *Great Expectations,* the anonymous narrator in Ralph Ellison's *Invisible Man,* and Sethe in Toni Morrison's *Beloved.*

Heroic Couplet: A rhyming couplet written in iambic pentameter (a verse with five iambic feet). The following lines by Alexander Pope are an example: ''Truth guards the Poet, sanctifies the line,/ And makes Immortal, Verse as mean as mine.''

Heroic Line: The meter and length of a line of verse in epic or heroic poetry. This varies by language and time period. For example, in English poetry, the heroic line is iambic pentameter (a verse with five iambic feet); in French, the alexandrine (a verse with six iambic feet); in classical literature, dactylic hexameter (a verse with six dactylic feet).

Heroine: See *Hero/Heroine*

Hexameter: See *Meter*

Historical Criticism: The study of a work based on its impact on the world of the time period in which it was written. Examples of postmodern historical criticism can be found in the work of Michel Foucault, Hayden White, Stephen Greenblatt, and Jonathan Goldberg.

Hokku: See *Haiku*

Holocaust: See *Holocaust Literature*

Holocaust Literature: Literature influenced by or written about the Holocaust of World War II. Such literature includes true stories of survival in concentration camps, escape, and life after the war, as well as fictional works and poetry. Representative works of Holocaust literature include Saul Bellow's *Mr. Sammler's Planet,* Anne Frank's *The Diary of a Young Girl,* Jerzy Kosinski's *The Painted Bird,* Arthur Miller's *Incident at Vichy,* Czeslaw Milosz's *Collected Poems,* William Styron's *Sophie's Choice,* and Art Spiegelman's *Maus.*

Homeric Simile: An elaborate, detailed comparison written as a simile many lines in length. An example of an epic simile from John Milton's *Paradise Lost* follows: Angel Forms, who lay entranced Thick as autumnal leaves that strow the brooks In Vallombrosa, where the Etrurian shades High over-arched embower; or scattered sedge Afloat, when with fierce winds Orion armed Hath vexed the Red-Sea coast, whose waves o'erthrew Busiris and his Memphian chivalry, While with perfidious hatred they pursued The sojourners of

Goshen, who beheld From the safe shore their floating carcasses And broken chariot-wheels. Also known as Epic Simile.

Horatian Satire: See *Satire*

Humanism: A philosophy that places faith in the dignity of humankind and rejects the medieval perception of the individual as a weak, fallen creature. "Humanists" typically believe in the perfectibility of human nature and view reason and education as the means to that end. Humanist thought is represented in the works of Marsilio Ficino, Ludovico Castelvetro, Edmund Spenser, John Milton, Dean John Colet, Desiderius Erasmus, John Dryden, Alexander Pope, Matthew Arnold, and Irving Babbitt.

Humors: Mentions of the humors refer to the ancient Greek theory that a person's health and personality were determined by the balance of four basic fluids in the body: blood, phlegm, yellow bile, and black bile. A dominance of any fluid would cause extremes in behavior. An excess of blood created a sanguine person who was joyful, aggressive, and passionate; a phlegmatic person was shy, fearful, and sluggish; too much yellow bile led to a choleric temperament characterized by impatience, anger, bitterness, and stubbornness; and excessive black bile created melancholy, a state of laziness, gluttony, and lack of motivation. Literary treatment of the humors is exemplified by several characters in Ben Jonson's plays *Every Man in His Humour* and *Every Man out of His Humour.* Also spelled Humours.

Humours: See *Humors*

Hyperbole: In literary criticism, deliberate exaggeration used to achieve an effect. In William Shakespeare's *Macbeth,* Lady Macbeth hyperbolizes when she says, "All the perfumes of Arabia could not sweeten this little hand."

I

Iamb: See *Foot*

Idiom: A word construction or verbal expression closely associated with a given language. For example, in colloquial English the construction "how come" can be used instead of "why" to introduce a question. Similarly, "a piece of cake" is sometimes used to describe a task that is easily done.

Image: A concrete representation of an object or sensory experience. Typically, such a representation helps evoke the feelings associated with the object or experience itself. Images are either "literal" or "figurative." Literal images are especially concrete and involve little or no extension of the obvious meaning of the words used to express them. Figurative images do not follow the literal meaning of the words exactly. Images in literature are usually visual, but the term "image" can also refer to the representation of any sensory experience. In his poem "The Shepherd's Hour," Paul Verlaine presents the following image: "The Moon is red through horizon's fog;/ In a dancing mist the hazy meadow sleeps." The first line is broadly literal, while the second line involves turns of meaning associated with dancing and sleeping.

Imagery: The array of images in a literary work. Also, figurative language. William Butler Yeats's "The Second Coming" offers a powerful image of encroaching anarchy: Turning and turning in the widening gyre The falcon cannot hear the falconer; Things fall apart. . . .

Imagism: An English and American poetry movement that flourished between 1908 and 1917. The Imagists used precise, clearly presented images in their works. They also used common, everyday speech and aimed for conciseness, concrete imagery, and the creation of new rhythms. Participants in the Imagist movement included Ezra Pound, H. D. (Hilda Doolittle), and Amy Lowell, among others.

In medias res: A Latin term meaning "in the middle of things." It refers to the technique of beginning a story at its midpoint and then using various flashback devices to reveal previous action. This technique originated in such epics as Virgil's *Aeneid.*

Induction: The process of reaching a conclusion by reasoning from specific premises to form a general premise. Also, an introductory portion of a work of literature, especially a play. Geoffrey Chaucer's "Prologue" to the *Canterbury Tales,* Thomas Sackville's "Induction" to *The Mirror of Magistrates,* and the opening scene in William Shakespeare's *The Taming of the Shrew* are examples of inductions to literary works.

Intentional Fallacy: The belief that judgments of a literary work based solely on an author's stated or implied intentions are false and misleading. Critics who believe in the concept of the intentional fallacy typically argue that the work itself is sufficient matter for interpretation, even though they may concede that an author's statement of purpose can be useful. Analysis of William Wordsworth's *Lyri-*

cal Ballads based on the observations about poetry he makes in his ''Preface'' to the second edition of that work is an example of the intentional fallacy.

Interior Monologue: A narrative technique in which characters' thoughts are revealed in a way that appears to be uncontrolled by the author. The interior monologue typically aims to reveal the inner self of a character. It portrays emotional experiences as they occur at both a conscious and unconscious level. images are often used to represent sensations or emotions. One of the best-known interior monologues in English is the Molly Bloom section at the close of James Joyce's *Ulysses.* The interior monologue is also common in the works of Virginia Woolf.

Internal Rhyme: Rhyme that occurs within a single line of verse. An example is in the opening line of Edgar Allan Poe's ''The Raven'': ''Once upon a midnight dreary, while I pondered weak and weary.'' Here, ''dreary'' and ''weary'' make an internal rhyme.

Irish Literary Renaissance: A late nineteenth- and early twentieth-century movement in Irish literature. Members of the movement aimed to reduce the influence of British culture in Ireland and create an Irish national literature. William Butler Yeats, George Moore, and Sean O'Casey are three of the best-known figures of the movement.

Irony: In literary criticism, the effect of language in which the intended meaning is the opposite of what is stated. The title of Jonathan Swift's ''A Modest Proposal'' is ironic because what Swift proposes in this essay is cannibalism—hardly ''modest.''

Italian Sonnet: See *Sonnet*

J

Jacobean Age: The period of the reign of James I of England (1603-1625). The early literature of this period reflected the worldview of the Elizabethan Age, but a darker, more cynical attitude steadily grew in the art and literature of the Jacobean Age. This was an important time for English drama and poetry. Milestones include William Shakespeare's tragedies, tragi-comedies, and sonnets; Ben Jonson's various dramas; and John Donne's metaphysical poetry.

Jargon: Language that is used or understood only by a select group of people. Jargon may refer to terminology used in a certain profession, such as computer jargon, or it may refer to any nonsensical language that is not understood by most people. Literary examples of jargon are Francois Villon's *Ballades en jargon,* which is composed in the secret language of the *coquillards,* and Anthony Burgess's *A Clockwork Orange,* narrated in the fictional characters' language of ''Nadsat.''

Juvenalian Satire: See *Satire*

K

Knickerbocker Group: A somewhat indistinct group of New York writers of the first half of the nineteenth century. Members of the group were linked only by location and a common theme: New York life. Two famous members of the Knickerbocker Group were Washington Irving and William Cullen Bryant. The group's name derives from Irving's *Knickerbocker's History of New York.*

L

Lais: See *Lay*

Lay: A song or simple narrative poem. The form originated in medieval France. Early French *lais* were often based on the Celtic legends and other tales sung by Breton minstrels—thus the name of the ''Breton lay.'' In fourteenth-century England, the term ''lay'' was used to describe short narratives written in imitation of the Breton lays. The most notable of these is Geoffrey Chaucer's ''The Minstrel's Tale.''

Leitmotiv: See *Motif*

Literal Language: An author uses literal language when he or she writes without exaggerating or embellishing the subject matter and without any tools of figurative language. To say ''He ran very quickly down the street'' is to use literal language, whereas to say ''He ran like a hare down the street'' would be using figurative language.

Literary Ballad: See *Ballad*

Literature: Literature is broadly defined as any written or spoken material, but the term most often refers to creative works. Literature includes poetry, drama, fiction, and many kinds of nonfiction writing, as well as oral, dramatic, and broadcast compositions not necessarily preserved in a written format, such as films and television programs.

Lost Generation: A term first used by Gertrude Stein to describe the post-World War I generation of American writers: men and women haunted by a sense of betrayal and emptiness brought about by the destructiveness of the war. The term is commonly applied to Hart Crane, Ernest Hemingway, F. Scott Fitzgerald, and others.

Lyric Poetry: A poem expressing the subjective feelings and personal emotions of the poet. Such poetry is melodic, since it was originally accompanied by a lyre in recitals. Most Western poetry in the twentieth century may be classified as lyrical. Examples of lyric poetry include A. E. Housman's elegy "To an Athlete Dying Young," the odes of Pindar and Horace, Thomas Gray and William Collins, the sonnets of Sir Thomas Wyatt and Sir Philip Sidney, Elizabeth Barrett Browning and Rainer Maria Rilke, and a host of other forms in the poetry of William Blake and Christina Rossetti, among many others.

M

Mannerism: Exaggerated, artificial adherence to a literary manner or style. Also, a popular style of the visual arts of late sixteenth-century Europe that was marked by elongation of the human form and by intentional spatial distortion. Literary works that are self-consciously high-toned and artistic are often said to be "mannered." Authors of such works include Henry James and Gertrude Stein.

Masculine Rhyme: See *Rhyme*

Masque: A lavish and elaborate form of entertainment, often performed in royal courts, that emphasizes song, dance, and costumery. The Renaissance form of the masque grew out of the spectacles of masked figures common in medieval England and Europe. The masque reached its peak of popularity and development in seventeenth-century England, during the reigns of James I and, especially, of Charles I. Ben Jonson, the most significant masque writer, also created the "antimasque," which incorporates elements of humor and the grotesque into the traditional masque and achieved greater dramatic quality. Masque-like interludes appear in Edmund Spenser's *The Faerie Queene* and in William Shakespeare's *The Tempest.* One of the best-known English masques is John Milton's *Comus.*

Measure: The foot, verse, or time sequence used in a literary work, especially a poem. Measure is often used somewhat incorrectly as a synonym for meter.

Melodrama: A play in which the typical plot is a conflict between characters who personify extreme good and evil. Melodramas usually end happily and emphasize sensationalism. Other literary forms that use the same techniques are often labeled "melodramatic." The term was formerly used to describe a combination of drama and music; as such, it was synonymous with "opera." Augustin Daly's *Under the Gaslight* and Dion Boucicault's *The Octoroon, The Colleen Bawn,* and *The Poor of New York* are examples of melodramas. The most popular media for twentieth-century melodramas are motion pictures and television.

Metaphor: A figure of speech that expresses an idea through the image of another object. Metaphors suggest the essence of the first object by identifying it with certain qualities of the second object. An example is "But soft, what light through yonder window breaks?/ It is the east, and Juliet is the sun" in William Shakespeare's *Romeo and Juliet.* Here, Juliet, the first object, is identified with qualities of the second object, the sun.

Metaphysical Conceit: See *Conceit*

Metaphysical Poetry: The body of poetry produced by a group of seventeenth-century English writers called the "Metaphysical Poets." The group includes John Donne and Andrew Marvell. The Metaphysical Poets made use of everyday speech, intellectual analysis, and unique imagery. They aimed to portray the ordinary conflicts and contradictions of life. Their poems often took the form of an argument, and many of them emphasize physical and religious love as well as the fleeting nature of life. Elaborate conceits are typical in metaphysical poetry. Marvell's "To His Coy Mistress" is a well-known example of a metaphysical poem.

Metaphysical Poets: See *Metaphysical Poetry*

Meter: In literary criticism, the repetition of sound patterns that creates a rhythm in poetry. The patterns are based on the number of syllables and the presence and absence of accents. The unit of rhythm in a line is called a foot. Types of meter are classified according to the number of feet in a line. These are the standard English lines: Monometer, one foot; Dimeter, two feet; Trimeter, three feet; Tetrameter, four feet; Pentameter, five feet; Hexameter, six feet (also called the Alexandrine); Heptameter, seven feet (also called the "Fourteener" when the feet are iambic). The most common English meter is the iambic pentameter, in which each line contains ten syllables, or five iambic feet, which individually are composed of an unstressed syllable followed by an accented syllable. Both of the following lines from Alfred, Lord Tennyson's

''Ulysses'' are written in iambic pentameter: Made weak by time and fate, but strong in will To strive, to seek, to find, and not to yield.

Mise en scene: The costumes, scenery, and other properties of a drama. Herbert Beerbohm Tree was renowned for the elaborate *mises en scene* of his lavish Shakespearean productions at His Majesty's Theatre between 1897 and 1915.

Modernism: Modern literary practices. Also, the principles of a literary school that lasted from roughly the beginning of the twentieth century until the end of World War II. Modernism is defined by its rejection of the literary conventions of the nineteenth century and by its opposition to conventional morality, taste, traditions, and economic values. Many writers are associated with the concepts of Modernism, including Albert Camus, Marcel Proust, D. H. Lawrence, W. H. Auden, Ernest Hemingway, William Faulkner, William Butler Yeats, Thomas Mann, Tennessee Williams, Eugene O'Neill, and James Joyce.

Monologue: A composition, written or oral, by a single individual. More specifically, a speech given by a single individual in a drama or other public entertainment. It has no set length, although it is usually several or more lines long. An example of an ''extended monologue''—that is, a monologue of great length and seriousness—occurs in the one-act, one-character play *The Stronger* by August Strindberg.

Monometer: See *Meter*

Mood: The prevailing emotions of a work or of the author in his or her creation of the work. The mood of a work is not always what might be expected based on its subject matter. The poem ''Dover Beach'' by Matthew Arnold offers examples of two different moods originating from the same experience: watching the ocean at night. The mood of the first three lines— The sea is calm tonight The tide is full, the moon lies fair Upon the straights. . . . is in sharp contrast to the mood of the last three lines— And we are here as on a darkling plain Swept with confused alarms of struggle and flight, Where ignorant armies clash by night.

Motif: A theme, character type, image, metaphor, or other verbal element that recurs throughout a single work of literature or occurs in a number of different works over a period of time. For example, the various manifestations of the color white in Herman

Melville's *Moby Dick* is a ''specific'' *motif,* while the trials of star-crossed lovers is a ''conventional'' *motif* from the literature of all periods. Also known as *Motiv* or *Leitmotiv.*

Motiv: See *Motif*

Muckrakers: An early twentieth-century group of American writers. Typically, their works exposed the wrongdoings of big business and government in the United States. Upton Sinclair's *The Jungle* exemplifies the muckraking novel.

Muses: Nine Greek mythological goddesses, the daughters of Zeus and Mnemosyne (Memory). Each muse patronized a specific area of the liberal arts and sciences. Calliope presided over epic poetry, Clio over history, Erato over love poetry, Euterpe over music or lyric poetry, Melpomene over tragedy, Polyhymnia over hymns to the gods, Terpsichore over dance, Thalia over comedy, and Urania over astronomy. Poets and writers traditionally made appeals to the Muses for inspiration in their work. John Milton invokes the aid of a muse at the beginning of the first book of his *Paradise Lost:* Of Man's First disobedience, and the Fruit of the Forbidden Tree, whose mortal taste Brought Death into the World, and all our woe, With loss of Eden, till one greater Man Restore us, and regain the blissful Seat, Sing Heav'nly Muse, that on the secret top of Oreb, or of Sinai, didst inspire That Shepherd, who first taught the chosen Seed, In the Beginning how the Heav'ns and Earth Rose out of Chaos. . . .

Mystery: See *Suspense*

Myth: An anonymous tale emerging from the traditional beliefs of a culture or social unit. Myths use supernatural explanations for natural phenomena. They may also explain cosmic issues like creation and death. Collections of myths, known as mythologies, are common to all cultures and nations, but the best-known myths belong to the Norse, Roman, and Greek mythologies. A famous myth is the story of Arachne, an arrogant young girl who challenged a goddess, Athena, to a weaving contest; when the girl won, Athena was enraged and turned Arachne into a spider, thus explaining the existence of spiders.

N

Narration: The telling of a series of events, real or invented. A narration may be either a simple narrative, in which the events are recounted chronologically, or a narrative with a plot, in which the account is given in a style reflecting the author's artistic concept of the story. Narration is sometimes used as a synonym for "storyline." The recounting of scary stories around a campfire is a form of narration.

Narrative: A verse or prose accounting of an event or sequence of events, real or invented. The term is also used as an adjective in the sense "method of narration." For example, in literary criticism, the expression "narrative technique" usually refers to the way the author structures and presents his or her story. Narratives range from the shortest accounts of events, as in Julius Caesar's remark, "I came, I saw, I conquered," to the longest historical or biographical works, as in Edward Gibbon's *The Decline and Fall of the Roman Empire,* as well as diaries, travelogues, novels, ballads, epics, short stories, and other fictional forms.

Narrative Poetry: A nondramatic poem in which the author tells a story. Such poems may be of any length or level of complexity. Epics such as *Beowulf* and ballads are forms of narrative poetry.

Narrator: The teller of a story. The narrator may be the author or a character in the story through whom the author speaks. Huckleberry Finn is the narrator of Mark Twain's *The Adventures of Huckleberry Finn.*

Naturalism: A literary movement of the late nineteenth and early twentieth centuries. The movement's major theorist, French novelist Emile Zola, envisioned a type of fiction that would examine human life with the objectivity of scientific inquiry. The Naturalists typically viewed human beings as either the products of "biological determinism," ruled by hereditary instincts and engaged in an endless struggle for survival, or as the products of "socioeconomic determinism," ruled by social and economic forces beyond their control. In their works, the Naturalists generally ignored the highest levels of society and focused on degradation: poverty, alcoholism, prostitution, insanity, and disease. Naturalism influenced authors throughout the world, including Henrik Ibsen and Thomas Hardy. In the United States, in particular, Naturalism had a profound impact. Among the authors who embraced its principles are Theodore Dreiser, Eugene O'Neill, Stephen Crane, Jack London, and Frank Norris.

Negritude: A literary movement based on the concept of a shared cultural bond on the part of black Africans, wherever they may be in the world. It traces its origins to the former French colonies of Africa and the Caribbean. Negritude poets, novelists, and essayists generally stress four points in their writings: One, black alienation from traditional African culture can lead to feelings of inferiority. Two, European colonialism and Western education should be resisted. Three, black Africans should seek to affirm and define their own identity. Four, African culture can and should be reclaimed. Many Negritude writers also claim that blacks can make unique contributions to the world, based on a heightened appreciation of nature, rhythm, and human emotions—aspects of life they say are not so highly valued in the materialistic and rationalistic West. Examples of Negritude literature include the poetry of both Senegalese Leopold Senghor in *Hosties noires* and Martiniquais Aime-Fernand Cesaire in *Return to My Native Land.*

Negro Renaissance: See *Harlem Renaissance*

Neoclassical Period: See *Neoclassicism*

Neoclassicism: In literary criticism, this term refers to the revival of the attitudes and styles of expression of classical literature. It is generally used to describe a period in European history beginning in the late seventeenth century and lasting until about 1800. In its purest form, Neoclassicism marked a return to order, proportion, restraint, logic, accuracy, and decorum. In England, where Neoclassicism perhaps was most popular, it reflected the influence of seventeenth- century French writers, especially dramatists. Neoclassical writers typically reacted against the intensity and enthusiasm of the Renaissance period. They wrote works that appealed to the intellect, using elevated language and classical literary forms such as satire and the ode. Neoclassical works were often governed by the classical goal of instruction. English neoclassicists included Alexander Pope, Jonathan Swift, Joseph Addison, Sir Richard Steele, John Gay, and Matthew Prior; French neoclassicists included Pierre Corneille and Jean-Baptiste Moliere. Also known as Age of Reason.

Neoclassicists: See *Neoclassicism*

New Criticism: A movement in literary criticism, dating from the late 1920s, that stressed close textual analysis in the interpretation of works of literature. The New Critics saw little merit in historical and biographical analysis. Rather, they aimed to examine the text alone, free from the question of how external events—biographical or otherwise—may have helped shape it. This predominantly American school was named "New Criticism" by one of its practitioners, John Crowe Ransom. Other important New Critics included Allen Tate, R. P. Blackmur, Robert Penn Warren, and Cleanth Brooks.

New Negro Movement: See *Harlem Renaissance*

Noble Savage: The idea that primitive man is noble and good but becomes evil and corrupted as he becomes civilized. The concept of the noble savage originated in the Renaissance period but is more closely identified with such later writers as Jean-Jacques Rousseau and Aphra Behn. First described in John Dryden's play *The Conquest of Granada,* the noble savage is portrayed by the various Native Americans in James Fenimore Cooper's "Leatherstocking Tales," by Queequeg, Daggoo, and Tashtego in Herman Melville's *Moby Dick,* and by John the Savage in Aldous Huxley's *Brave New World.*

O

Objective Correlative: An outward set of objects, a situation, or a chain of events corresponding to an inward experience and evoking this experience in the reader. The term frequently appears in modern criticism in discussions of authors' intended effects on the emotional responses of readers. This term was originally used by T. S. Eliot in his 1919 essay "Hamlet."

Objectivity: A quality in writing characterized by the absence of the author's opinion or feeling about the subject matter. Objectivity is an important factor in criticism. The novels of Henry James and, to a certain extent, the poems of John Larkin demonstrate objectivity, and it is central to John Keats's concept of "negative capability." Critical and journalistic writing usually are or attempt to be objective.

Occasional Verse: poetry written on the occasion of a significant historical or personal event. *Vers de societe* is sometimes called occasional verse although it is of a less serious nature. Famous examples of occasional verse include Andrew Marvell's "Horatian Ode upon Cromwell's Return from England," Walt Whitman's "When Lilacs Last in the Dooryard Bloom'd"— written upon the death of Abraham Lincoln—and Edmund Spenser's commemoration of his wedding, "Epithalamion."

Octave: A poem or stanza composed of eight lines. The term octave most often represents the first eight lines of a Petrarchan sonnet. An example of an octave is taken from a translation of a Petrarchan sonnet by Sir Thomas Wyatt: The pillar perisht is whereto I leant, The strongest stay of mine unquiet mind; The like of it no man again can find, From East to West Still seeking though he went. To mind unhap! for hap away hath rent Of all my joy the very

bark and rind; And I, alas, by chance am thus assigned Daily to mourn till death do it relent.

Ode: Name given to an extended lyric poem characterized by exalted emotion and dignified style. An ode usually concerns a single, serious theme. Most odes, but not all, are addressed to an object or individual. Odes are distinguished from other lyric poetic forms by their complex rhythmic and stanzaic patterns. An example of this form is John Keats's "Ode to a Nightingale."

Oedipus Complex: A son's amorous obsession with his mother. The phrase is derived from the story of the ancient Theban hero Oedipus, who unknowingly killed his father and married his mother. Literary occurrences of the Oedipus complex include Andre Gide's *Oedipe* and Jean Cocteau's *La Machine infernale,* as well as the most famous, Sophocles' *Oedipus Rex.*

Omniscience: See *Point of View*

Onomatopoeia: The use of words whose sounds express or suggest their meaning. In its simplest sense, onomatopoeia may be represented by words that mimic the sounds they denote such as "hiss" or "meow." At a more subtle level, the pattern and rhythm of sounds and rhymes of a line or poem may be onomatopoeic. A celebrated example of onomatopoeia is the repetition of the word "bells" in Edgar Allan Poe's poem "The Bells."

Opera: A type of stage performance, usually a drama, in which the dialogue is sung. Classic examples of opera include Giuseppi Verdi's *La traviata,* Giacomo Puccini's *La Boheme,* and Richard Wagner's *Tristan und Isolde.* Major twentieth- century contributors to the form include Richard Strauss and Alban Berg.

Operetta: A usually romantic comic opera. John Gay's *The Beggar's Opera,* Richard Sheridan's *The Duenna,* and numerous works by William Gilbert and Arthur Sullivan are examples of operettas.

Oral Tradition: See *Oral Transmission*

Oral Transmission: A process by which songs, ballads, folklore, and other material are transmitted by word of mouth. The tradition of oral transmission predates the written record systems of literate society. Oral transmission preserves material sometimes over generations, although often with variations. Memory plays a large part in the recitation and preservation of orally transmitted material. Breton lays, French *fabliaux,* national epics (including the Anglo- Saxon *Beowulf,* the Spanish *El Cid,* and the Finnish *Kalevala*), Native American myths and legends, and African folktales told by plantation slaves are examples of orally transmitted literature.

Oration: Formal speaking intended to motivate the listeners to some action or feeling. Such public speaking was much more common before the development of timely printed communication such as newspapers. Famous examples of oration include Abraham Lincoln's "Gettysburg Address" and Dr. Martin Luther King Jr.'s "I Have a Dream" speech.

Ottava Rima: An eight-line stanza of poetry composed in iambic pentameter (a five-foot line in which each foot consists of an unaccented syllable followed by an accented syllable), following the ababbcc rhyme scheme. This form has been prominently used by such important English writers as Lord Byron, Henry Wadsworth Longfellow, and W. B. Yeats.

Oxymoron: A phrase combining two contradictory terms. Oxymorons may be intentional or unintentional. The following speech from William Shakespeare's *Romeo and Juliet* uses several oxymorons: Why, then, O brawling love! O loving hate! O anything, of nothing first create! O heavy lightness! serious vanity! Mis-shapen chaos of well-seeming forms! Feather of lead, bright smoke, cold fire, sick health! This love feel I, that feel no love in this.

P

Pantheism: The idea that all things are both a manifestation or revelation of God and a part of God at the same time. Pantheism was a common attitude in the early societies of Egypt, India, and Greece— the term derives from the Greek *pan* meaning "all" and *theos* meaning "deity." It later became a significant part of the Christian faith. William Wordsworth and Ralph Waldo Emerson are among the many writers who have expressed the pantheistic attitude in their works.

Parable: A story intended to teach a moral lesson or answer an ethical question. In the West, the best examples of parables are those of Jesus Christ in the New Testament, notably "The Prodigal Son," but parables also are used in Sufism, rabbinic literature, Hasidism, and Zen Buddhism.

Paradox: A statement that appears illogical or contradictory at first, but may actually point to an underlying truth. "Less is more" is an example of a paradox. Literary examples include Francis Ba-

con's statement, "The most corrected copies are commonly the least correct," and "All animals are equal, but some animals are more equal than others" from George Orwell's *Animal Farm*.

Parallelism: A method of comparison of two ideas in which each is developed in the same grammatical structure. Ralph Waldo Emerson's "Civilization" contains this example of parallelism: Raphael paints wisdom; Handel sings it, Phidias carves it, Shakespeare writes it, Wren builds it, Columbus sails it, Luther preaches it, Washington arms it, Watt mechanizes it.

Parnassianism: A mid nineteenth-century movement in French literature. Followers of the movement stressed adherence to well-defined artistic forms as a reaction against the often chaotic expression of the artist's ego that dominated the work of the Romantics. The Parnassians also rejected the moral, ethical, and social themes exhibited in the works of French Romantics such as Victor Hugo. The aesthetic doctrines of the Parnassians strongly influenced the later symbolist and decadent movements. Members of the Parnassian school include Leconte de Lisle, Sully Prudhomme, Albert Glatigny, Francois Coppee, and Theodore de Banville.

Parody: In literary criticism, this term refers to an imitation of a serious literary work or the signature style of a particular author in a ridiculous manner. A typical parody adopts the style of the original and applies it to an inappropriate subject for humorous effect. Parody is a form of satire and could be considered the literary equivalent of a caricature or cartoon. Henry Fielding's *Shamela* is a parody of Samuel Richardson's *Pamela*.

Pastoral: A term derived from the Latin word "pastor," meaning shepherd. A pastoral is a literary composition on a rural theme. The conventions of the pastoral were originated by the third-century Greek poet Theocritus, who wrote about the experiences, love affairs, and pastimes of Sicilian shepherds. In a pastoral, characters and language of a courtly nature are often placed in a simple setting. The term pastoral is also used to classify dramas, elegies, and lyrics that exhibit the use of country settings and shepherd characters. Percy Bysshe Shelley's "Adonais" and John Milton's "Lycidas" are two famous examples of pastorals.

Pastorela: The Spanish name for the shepherds play, a folk drama reenacted during the Christmas season. Examples of *pastorelas* include Gomez

Manrique's *Representacion del nacimiento* and the dramas of Lucas Fernandez and Juan del Encina.

Pathetic Fallacy: A term coined by English critic John Ruskin to identify writing that falsely endows nonhuman things with human intentions and feelings, such as "angry clouds" and "sad trees." The pathetic fallacy is a required convention in the classical poetic form of the pastoral elegy, and it is used in the modern poetry of T. S. Eliot, Ezra Pound, and the Imagists. Also known as Poetic Fallacy.

Pelado: Literally the "skinned one" or shirtless one, he was the stock underdog, sharp-witted picaresque character of Mexican vaudeville and tent shows. The *pelado* is found in such works as Don Catarino's *Los effectos de la crisis* and *Regreso a mi tierra.*

Pen Name: See *Pseudonym*

Pentameter: See *Meter*

Persona: A Latin term meaning "mask." *Personae* are the characters in a fictional work of literature. The *persona* generally functions as a mask through which the author tells a story in a voice other than his or her own. A *persona* is usually either a character in a story who acts as a narrator or an "implied author," a voice created by the author to act as the narrator for himself or herself. *Personae* include the narrator of Geoffrey Chaucer's *Canterbury Tales* and Marlow in Joseph Conrad's *Heart of Darkness.*

Personae: See *Persona*

Personal Point of View: See *Point of View*

Personification: A figure of speech that gives human qualities to abstract ideas, animals, and inanimate objects. William Shakespeare used personification in *Romeo and Juliet* in the lines "Arise, fair sun, and kill the envious moon,/ Who is already sick and pale with grief." Here, the moon is portrayed as being envious, sick, and pale with grief— all markedly human qualities. Also known as *Prosopopoeia.*

Petrarchan Sonnet: See *Sonnet*

Phenomenology: A method of literary criticism based on the belief that things have no existence outside of human consciousness or awareness. Proponents of this theory believe that art is a process that takes place in the mind of the observer as he or she contemplates an object rather than a quality of the object itself. Among phenomenological critics

are Edmund Husserl, George Poulet, Marcel Raymond, and Roman Ingarden.

Picaresque Novel: Episodic fiction depicting the adventures of a roguish central character ("picaro" is Spanish for "rogue"). The picaresque hero is commonly a low-born but clever individual who wanders into and out of various affairs of love, danger, and farcical intrigue. These involvements may take place at all social levels and typically present a humorous and wide-ranging satire of a given society. Prominent examples of the picaresque novel are *Don Quixote* by Miguel de Cervantes, *Tom Jones* by Henry Fielding, and *Moll Flanders* by Daniel Defoe.

Plagiarism: Claiming another person's written material as one's own. Plagiarism can take the form of direct, word-for- word copying or the theft of the substance or idea of the work. A student who copies an encyclopedia entry and turns it in as a report for school is guilty of plagiarism.

Platonic Criticism: A form of criticism that stresses an artistic work's usefulness as an agent of social engineering rather than any quality or value of the work itself. Platonic criticism takes as its starting point the ancient Greek philosopher Plato's comments on art in his *Republic.*

Platonism: The embracing of the doctrines of the philosopher Plato, popular among the poets of the Renaissance and the Romantic period. Platonism is more flexible than Aristotelian Criticism and places more emphasis on the supernatural and unknown aspects of life. Platonism is expressed in the love poetry of the Renaissance, the fourth book of Baldassare Castiglione's *The Book of the Courtier,* and the poetry of William Blake, William Wordsworth, Percy Bysshe Shelley, Friedrich Holderlin, William Butler Yeats, and Wallace Stevens.

Play: See *Drama*

Plot: In literary criticism, this term refers to the pattern of events in a narrative or drama. In its simplest sense, the plot guides the author in composing the work and helps the reader follow the work. Typically, plots exhibit causality and unity and have a beginning, a middle, and an end. Sometimes, however, a plot may consist of a series of disconnected events, in which case it is known as an "episodic plot." In his *Aspects of the Novel,* E. M. Forster distinguishes between a story, defined as a "narrative of events arranged in their time- sequence," and plot, which organizes the events to a "sense of causality." This definition closely mirrors Aristotle's discussion of plot in his *Poetics.*

Poem: In its broadest sense, a composition utilizing rhyme, meter, concrete detail, and expressive language to create a literary experience with emotional and aesthetic appeal. Typical poems include sonnets, odes, elegies, *haiku,* ballads, and free verse.

Poet: An author who writes poetry or verse. The term is also used to refer to an artist or writer who has an exceptional gift for expression, imagination, and energy in the making of art in any form. Well-known poets include Horace, Basho, Sir Philip Sidney, Sir Edmund Spenser, John Donne, Andrew Marvell, Alexander Pope, Jonathan Swift, George Gordon, Lord Byron, John Keats, Christina Rossetti, W. H. Auden, Stevie Smith, and Sylvia Plath.

Poetic Fallacy: See *Pathetic Fallacy*

Poetic Justice: An outcome in a literary work, not necessarily a poem, in which the good are rewarded and the evil are punished, especially in ways that particularly fit their virtues or crimes. For example, a murderer may himself be murdered, or a thief will find himself penniless.

Poetic License: Distortions of fact and literary convention made by a writer—not always a poet—for the sake of the effect gained. Poetic license is closely related to the concept of "artistic freedom." An author exercises poetic license by saying that a pile of money "reaches as high as a mountain" when the pile is actually only a foot or two high.

Poetics: This term has two closely related meanings. It denotes (1) an aesthetic theory in literary criticism about the essence of poetry or (2) rules prescribing the proper methods, content, style, or diction of poetry. The term poetics may also refer to theories about literature in general, not just poetry.

Poetry: In its broadest sense, writing that aims to present ideas and evoke an emotional experience in the reader through the use of meter, imagery, connotative and concrete words, and a carefully constructed structure based on rhythmic patterns. Poetry typically relies on words and expressions that have several layers of meaning. It also makes use of the effects of regular rhythm on the ear and may make a strong appeal to the senses through the use of imagery. Edgar Allan Poe's "Annabel Lee" and Walt Whitman's *Leaves of Grass* are famous examples of poetry.

Point of View: The narrative perspective from which a literary work is presented to the reader.

There are four traditional points of view. The "third person omniscient" gives the reader a "godlike" perspective, unrestricted by time or place, from which to see actions and look into the minds of characters. This allows the author to comment openly on characters and events in the work. The "third person" point of view presents the events of the story from outside of any single character's perception, much like the omniscient point of view, but the reader must understand the action as it takes place and without any special insight into characters' minds or motivations. The "first person" or "personal" point of view relates events as they are perceived by a single character. The main character "tells" the story and may offer opinions about the action and characters which differ from those of the author. Much less common than omniscient, third person, and first person is the "second person" point of view, wherein the author tells the story as if it is happening to the reader. James Thurber employs the omniscient point of view in his short story "The Secret Life of Walter Mitty." Ernest Hemingway's "A Clean, Well-Lighted Place" is a short story told from the third person point of view. Mark Twain's novel *Huck Finn* is presented from the first person viewpoint. Jay McInerney's *Bright Lights, Big City* is an example of a novel which uses the second person point of view.

Polemic: A work in which the author takes a stand on a controversial subject, such as abortion or religion. Such works are often extremely argumentative or provocative. Classic examples of polemics include John Milton's *Aeropagitica* and Thomas Paine's *The American Crisis.*

Pornography: Writing intended to provoke feelings of lust in the reader. Such works are often condemned by critics and teachers, but those which can be shown to have literary value are viewed less harshly. Literary works that have been described as pornographic include Ovid's *The Art of Love,* Margaret of Angouleme's *Heptameron,* John Cleland's *Memoirs of a Woman of Pleasure; or, the Life of Fanny Hill,* the anonymous *My Secret Life,* D. H. Lawrence's *Lady Chatterley's Lover,* and Vladimir Nabokov's *Lolita.*

Post-Aesthetic Movement: An artistic response made by African Americans to the black aesthetic movement of the 1960s and early '70s. Writers since that time have adopted a somewhat different tone in their work, with less emphasis placed on the disparity between black and white in the United States. In the words of post-aesthetic authors such as Toni Morrison, John Edgar Wideman, and Kristin Hunter, African Americans are portrayed as looking inward for answers to their own questions, rather than always looking to the outside world. Two well-known examples of works produced as part of the post-aesthetic movement are the Pulitzer Prize-winning novels *The Color Purple* by Alice Walker and *Beloved* by Toni Morrison.

Postmodernism: Writing from the 1960s forward characterized by experimentation and continuing to apply some of the fundamentals of modernism, which included existentialism and alienation. Postmodernists have gone a step further in the rejection of tradition begun with the modernists by also rejecting traditional forms, preferring the anti-novel over the novel and the anti-hero over the hero. Postmodern writers include Alain Robbe-Grillet, Thomas Pynchon, Margaret Drabble, John Fowles, Adolfo Bioy-Casares, and Gabriel Garcia Marquez.

Pre-Raphaelites: A circle of writers and artists in mid nineteenth-century England. Valuing the pre-Renaissance artistic qualities of religious symbolism, lavish pictorialism, and natural sensuousness, the Pre-Raphaelites cultivated a sense of mystery and melancholy that influenced later writers associated with the Symbolist and Decadent movements. The major members of the group include Dante Gabriel Rossetti, Christina Rossetti, Algernon Swinburne, and Walter Pater.

Primitivism: The belief that primitive peoples were nobler and less flawed than civilized peoples because they had not been subjected to the tainting influence of society. Examples of literature espousing primitivism include Aphra Behn's *Oroonoko: Or, The History of the Royal Slave,* Jean-Jacques Rousseau's *Julie ou la Nouvelle Heloise,* Oliver Goldsmith's *The Deserted Village,* the poems of Robert Burns, Herman Melville's stories *Typee, Omoo,* and *Mardi,* many poems of William Butler Yeats and Robert Frost, and William Golding's novel *Lord of the Flies.*

Projective Verse: A form of free verse in which the poet's breathing pattern determines the lines of the poem. Poets who advocate projective verse are against all formal structures in writing, including meter and form. Besides its creators, Robert Creeley, Robert Duncan, and Charles Olson, two other well-known projective verse poets are Denise Levertov and LeRoi Jones (Amiri Baraka). Also known as Breath Verse.

Prologue: An introductory section of a literary work. It often contains information establishing the situation of the characters or presents information about the setting, time period, or action. In drama, the prologue is spoken by a chorus or by one of the principal characters. In the ''General Prologue'' of *The Canterbury Tales,* Geoffrey Chaucer describes the main characters and establishes the setting and purpose of the work.

Prose: A literary medium that attempts to mirror the language of everyday speech. It is distinguished from poetry by its use of unmetered, unrhymed language consisting of logically related sentences. Prose is usually grouped into paragraphs that form a cohesive whole such as an essay or a novel. Recognized masters of English prose writing include Sir Thomas Malory, William Caxton, Raphael Holinshed, Joseph Addison, Mark Twain, and Ernest Hemingway.

Prosopopoeia: See *Personification*

Protagonist: The central character of a story who serves as a focus for its themes and incidents and as the principal rationale for its development. The protagonist is sometimes referred to in discussions of modern literature as the hero or anti-hero. Well-known protagonists are Hamlet in William Shakespeare's *Hamlet* and Jay Gatsby in F. Scott Fitzgerald's *The Great Gatsby.*

Protest Fiction: Protest fiction has as its primary purpose the protesting of some social injustice, such as racism or discrimination. One example of protest fiction is a series of five novels by Chester Himes, beginning in 1945 with *If He Hollers Let Him Go* and ending in 1955 with *The Primitive.* These works depict the destructive effects of race and gender stereotyping in the context of interracial relationships. Another African American author whose works often revolve around themes of social protest is John Oliver Killens. James Baldwin's essay ''Everybody's Protest Novel'' generated controversy by attacking the authors of protest fiction.

Proverb: A brief, sage saying that expresses a truth about life in a striking manner. ''They are not all cooks who carry long knives'' is an example of a proverb.

Pseudonym: A name assumed by a writer, most often intended to prevent his or her identification as the author of a work. Two or more authors may work together under one pseudonym, or an author may use a different name for each genre he or she publishes in. Some publishing companies maintain ''house pseudonyms,'' under which any number of authors may write installations in a series. Some authors also choose a pseudonym over their real names the way an actor may use a stage name. Examples of pseudonyms (with the author's real name in parentheses) include Voltaire (Francois-Marie Arouet), Novalis (Friedrich von Hardenberg), Currer Bell (Charlotte Bronte), Ellis Bell (Emily Bronte), George Eliot (Maryann Evans), Honorio Bustos Donmecq (Adolfo Bioy-Casares and Jorge Luis Borges), and Richard Bachman (Stephen King).

Pun: A play on words that have similar sounds but different meanings. A serious example of the pun is from John Donne's ''A Hymne to God the Father'': Sweare by thyself, that at my death thy sonne Shall shine as he shines now, and hereto fore; And, having done that, Thou haste done; I fear no more.

Pure Poetry: poetry written without instructional intent or moral purpose that aims only to please a reader by its imagery or musical flow. The term pure poetry is used as the antonym of the term ''didacticism.'' The poetry of Edgar Allan Poe, Stephane Mallarme, Paul Verlaine, Paul Valery, Juan Ramoz Jimenez, and Jorge Guillen offer examples of pure poetry.

Q

Quatrain: A four-line stanza of a poem or an entire poem consisting of four lines. The following quatrain is from Robert Herrick's ''To Live Merrily, and to Trust to Good Verses'': Round, round, the root do's run; And being ravisht thus, Come, I will drink a Tun To my *Propertius*.

R

Raisonneur: A character in a drama who functions as a spokesperson for the dramatist's views. The *raisonneur* typically observes the play without becoming central to its action. *Raisonneurs* were very common in plays of the nineteenth century.

Realism: A nineteenth-century European literary movement that sought to portray familiar characters, situations, and settings in a realistic manner. This was done primarily by using an objective narrative point of view and through the buildup of accurate detail. The standard for success of any realistic work depends on how faithfully it transfers common experience into fictional forms. The realistic method may be altered or extended, as in stream of consciousness writing, to record highly subjective experience. Seminal authors in the tradition of Realism include Honore de Balzac, Gustave Flaubert, and Henry James.

Refrain: A phrase repeated at intervals throughout a poem. A refrain may appear at the end of each stanza or at less regular intervals. It may be altered slightly at each appearance. Some refrains are nonsense expressions—as with ''Nevermore'' in Edgar Allan Poe's ''The Raven''—that seem to take on a different significance with each use.

Renaissance: The period in European history that marked the end of the Middle Ages. It began in Italy in the late fourteenth century. In broad terms, it is usually seen as spanning the fourteenth, fifteenth, and sixteenth centuries, although it did not reach Great Britain, for example, until the 1480s or so. The Renaissance saw an awakening in almost every sphere of human activity, especially science, philosophy, and the arts. The period is best defined by the emergence of a general philosophy that emphasized the importance of the intellect, the individual, and world affairs. It contrasts strongly with the medieval worldview, characterized by the dominant concerns of faith, the social collective, and spiritual salvation. Prominent writers during the Renaissance include Niccolo Machiavelli and Baldassare Castiglione in Italy, Miguel de Cervantes and Lope de Vega in Spain, Jean Froissart and Francois Rabelais in France, Sir Thomas More and Sir Philip Sidney in England, and Desiderius Erasmus in Holland.

Repartee: Conversation featuring snappy retorts and witticisms. Masters of *repartee* include Sydney Smith, Charles Lamb, and Oscar Wilde. An example is recorded in the meeting of ''Beau'' Nash and John Wesley: Nash said, ''I never make way for a fool,'' to which Wesley responded, ''Don't you? I always do,'' and stepped aside.

Resolution: The portion of a story following the climax, in which the conflict is resolved. The resolution of Jane Austen's *Northanger Abbey* is neatly summed up in the following sentence: ''Henry and Catherine were married, the bells rang and every body smiled.''

Restoration: See *Restoration Age*

Restoration Age: A period in English literature beginning with the crowning of Charles II in 1660 and running to about 1700. The era, which was characterized by a reaction against Puritanism, was the first great age of the comedy of manners. The finest literature of the era is typically witty and urbane, and often lewd. Prominent Restoration Age writers include William Congreve, Samuel Pepys, John Dryden, and John Milton.

Revenge Tragedy: A dramatic form popular during the Elizabethan Age, in which the protagonist, directed by the ghost of his murdered father or son, inflicts retaliation upon a powerful villain. Notable features of the revenge tragedy include violence, bizarre criminal acts, intrigue, insanity, a hesitant protagonist, and the use of soliloquy. Thomas Kyd's *Spanish Tragedy* is the first example of revenge tragedy in English, and William Shakespeare's *Hamlet* is perhaps the best. Extreme examples of revenge tragedy, such as John Webster's *The Duchess of Malfi,* are labeled "tragedies of blood." Also known as Tragedy of Blood.

Revista: The Spanish term for a vaudeville musical revue. Examples of *revistas* include Antonio Guzman Aguilera's *Mexico para los mexicanos,* Daniel Vanegas's *Maldito jazz,* and Don Catarino's *Whiskey, morfina y marihuana* and *El desterrado.*

Rhetoric: In literary criticism, this term denotes the art of ethical persuasion. In its strictest sense, rhetoric adheres to various principles developed since classical times for arranging facts and ideas in a clear, persuasive, appealing manner. The term is also used to refer to effective prose in general and theories of or methods for composing effective prose. Classical examples of rhetorics include *The Rhetoric of Aristotle,* Quintillian's *Institutio Oratoria,* and Cicero's *Ad Herennium.*

Rhetorical Question: A question intended to provoke thought, but not an expressed answer, in the reader. It is most commonly used in oratory and other persuasive genres. The following lines from Thomas Gray's "Elegy Written in a Country Churchyard" ask rhetorical questions: Can storied urn or animated bust Back to its mansion call the fleeting breath? Can Honour's voice provoke the silent dust, Or Flattery soothe the dull cold ear of Death?

Rhyme: When used as a noun in literary criticism, this term generally refers to a poem in which words sound identical or very similar and appear in parallel positions in two or more lines. Rhymes are classified into different types according to where they fall in a line or stanza or according to the degree of similarity they exhibit in their spellings and sounds. Some major types of rhyme are "masculine" rhyme, "feminine" rhyme, and "triple" rhyme. In a masculine rhyme, the rhyming sound falls in a single accented syllable, as with "heat" and "eat." Feminine rhyme is a rhyme of two syllables, one stressed and one unstressed, as with "merry" and "tarry." Triple rhyme matches the sound of the accented syllable and the two unaccented syllables that follow: "narrative" and "declarative." Robert Browning alternates feminine and masculine rhymes in his "Soliloquy of the Spanish Cloister": Gr-r-r—there go, my heart's abhorrence! Water your damned flower-pots, do! If hate killed men, Brother Lawrence, God's blood, would not mine kill you! What? Your myrtle-bush wants trimming? Oh, that rose has prior claims— Needs its leaden vase filled brimming? Hell dry you up with flames! Triple rhymes can be found in Thomas Hood's "Bridge of Sighs," George Gordon Byron's satirical verse, and Ogden Nash's comic poems.

Rhyme Royal: A stanza of seven lines composed in iambic pentameter and rhymed *ababbcc.* The name is said to be a tribute to King James I of Scotland, who made much use of the form in his poetry. Examples of rhyme royal include Geoffrey Chaucer's *The Parlement of Foules,* William Shakespeare's *The Rape of Lucrece,* William Morris's *The Early Paradise,* and John Masefield's *The Widow in the Bye Street.*

Rhyme Scheme: See *Rhyme*

Rhythm: A regular pattern of sound, time intervals, or events occurring in writing, most often and most discernably in poetry. Regular, reliable rhythm is known to be soothing to humans, while interrupted, unpredictable, or rapidly changing rhythm is disturbing. These effects are known to authors, who use them to produce a desired reaction in the reader. An example of a form of irregular rhythm is sprung rhythm poetry; quantitative verse, on the other hand, is very regular in its rhythm.

Rising Action: The part of a drama where the plot becomes increasingly complicated. Rising action leads up to the climax, or turning point, of a drama. The final "chase scene" of an action film is generally the rising action which culminates in the film's climax.

Rococo: A style of European architecture that flourished in the eighteenth century, especially in France. The most notable features of *rococo* are its extensive use of ornamentation and its themes of lightness, gaiety, and intimacy. In literary criticism, the term is often used disparagingly to refer to a decadent or over-ornamental style. Alexander Pope's "The Rape of the Lock" is an example of literary *rococo.*

Roman a clef: A French phrase meaning "novel with a key." It refers to a narrative in which real persons are portrayed under fictitious names. Jack Kerouac, for example, portrayed various real-life beat generation figures under fictitious names in his *On the Road.*

Romance: A broad term, usually denoting a narrative with exotic, exaggerated, often idealized characters, scenes, and themes. Nathaniel Hawthorne called his *The House of the Seven Gables* and *The Marble Faun* romances in order to distinguish them from clearly realistic works.

Romantic Age: See *Romanticism*

Romanticism: This term has two widely accepted meanings. In historical criticism, it refers to a European intellectual and artistic movement of the late eighteenth and early nineteenth centuries that sought greater freedom of personal expression than that allowed by the strict rules of literary form and logic of the eighteenth-century neoclassicists. The Romantics preferred emotional and imaginative expression to rational analysis. They considered the individual to be at the center of all experience and so placed him or her at the center of their art. The Romantics believed that the creative imagination reveals nobler truths—unique feelings and attitudes— than those that could be discovered by logic or by scientific examination. Both the natural world and the state of childhood were important sources for revelations of "eternal truths." "Romanticism" is also used as a general term to refer to a type of sensibility found in all periods of literary history and usually considered to be in opposition to the principles of classicism. In this sense, Romanticism signifies any work or philosophy in which the exotic or dreamlike figure strongly, or that is devoted to individualistic expression, self-analysis, or a pursuit of a higher realm of knowledge than can be discovered by human reason. Prominent Romantics include Jean-Jacques Rousseau, William Wordsworth, John Keats, Lord Byron, and Johann Wolfgang von Goethe.

Romantics: See *Romanticism*

Russian Symbolism: A Russian poetic movement, derived from French symbolism, that flourished between 1894 and 1910. While some Russian Symbolists continued in the French tradition, stressing aestheticism and the importance of suggestion above didactic intent, others saw their craft as a form of mystical worship, and themselves as mediators between the supernatural and the mundane. Russian symbolists include Aleksandr Blok, Vyacheslav Ivanovich Ivanov, Fyodor Sologub, Andrey Bely, Nikolay Gumilyov, and Vladimir Sergeyevich Solovyov.

S

Satire: A work that uses ridicule, humor, and wit to criticize and provoke change in human nature and institutions. There are two major types of satire: "formal" or "direct" satire speaks directly to the reader or to a character in the work; "indirect" satire relies upon the ridiculous behavior of its characters to make its point. Formal satire is further divided into two manners: the "Horatian," which ridicules gently, and the "Juvenalian," which derides its subjects harshly and bitterly. Voltaire's novella *Candide* is an indirect satire. Jonathan Swift's essay "A Modest Proposal" is a Juvenalian satire.

Scansion: The analysis or "scanning" of a poem to determine its meter and often its rhyme scheme. The most common system of scansion uses accents (slanted lines drawn above syllables) to show stressed syllables, breves (curved lines drawn above syllables) to show unstressed syllables, and vertical lines to separate each foot. In the first line of John Keats's *Endymion,* "A thing of beauty is a joy forever:" the word "thing," the first syllable of "beauty," the word "joy," and the second syllable of "forever" are stressed, while the words "A" and "of," the second syllable of "beauty," the word "a," and the first and third syllables of "forever" are unstressed. In the second line: "Its loveliness increases; it will never" a pair of vertical lines separate the foot ending with "increases" and the one beginning with "it."

Scene: A subdivision of an act of a drama, consisting of continuous action taking place at a single time and in a single location. The beginnings and endings of scenes may be indicated by clearing the stage of actors and props or by the entrances and exits of important characters. The first act of William Shakespeare's *Winter's Tale* is comprised of two scenes.

Science Fiction: A type of narrative about or based upon real or imagined scientific theories and technology. Science fiction is often peopled with alien creatures and set on other planets or in different dimensions. Karel Capek's *R.U.R.* is a major work of science fiction.

Second Person: See *Point of View*

Semiotics: The study of how literary forms and conventions affect the meaning of language. Semioticians include Ferdinand de Saussure, Charles Sanders Pierce, Claude Levi-Strauss, Jacques Lacan, Michel Foucault, Jacques Derrida, Roland Barthes, and Julia Kristeva.

Sestet: Any six-line poem or stanza. Examples of the sestet include the last six lines of the Petrarchan sonnet form, the stanza form of Robert Burns's ''A Poet's Welcome to his love-begotten Daughter,'' and the sestina form in W. H. Auden's ''Paysage Moralise.''

Setting: The time, place, and culture in which the action of a narrative takes place. The elements of setting may include geographic location, characters' physical and mental environments, prevailing cultural attitudes, or the historical time in which the action takes place. Examples of settings include the romanticized Scotland in Sir Walter Scott's ''Waverley'' novels, the French provincial setting in Gustave Flaubert's *Madame Bovary,* the fictional Wessex country of Thomas Hardy's novels, and the small towns of southern Ontario in Alice Munro's short stories.

Shakespearean Sonnet: See *Sonnet*

Signifying Monkey: A popular trickster figure in black folklore, with hundreds of tales about this character documented since the 19th century. Henry Louis Gates Jr. examines the history of the signifying monkey in *The Signifying Monkey: Towards a Theory of Afro-American Literary Criticism,* published in 1988.

Simile: A comparison, usually using ''like'' or ''as'', of two essentially dissimilar things, as in ''coffee as cold as ice'' or ''He sounded like a broken record.'' The title of Ernest Hemingway's ''Hills Like White Elephants'' contains a simile.

Slang: A type of informal verbal communication that is generally unacceptable for formal writing. Slang words and phrases are often colorful exaggerations used to emphasize the speaker's point; they may also be shortened versions of an often-used word or phrase. Examples of American slang from the 1990s include ''yuppie'' (an acronym for Young Urban Professional), ''awesome'' (for ''excellent''), wired (for ''nervous'' or ''excited''), and ''chill out'' (for relax).

Slant Rhyme: See *Consonance*

Slave Narrative: Autobiographical accounts of American slave life as told by escaped slaves. These works first appeared during the abolition movement of the 1830s through the 1850s. Olaudah Equiano's *The Interesting Narrative of Olaudah Equiano, or Gustavus Vassa, The African* and Harriet Ann Jacobs's *Incidents in the Life of a Slave Girl* are examples of the slave narrative.

Social Realism: See *Socialist Realism*

Socialist Realism: The Socialist Realism school of literary theory was proposed by Maxim Gorky and established as a dogma by the first Soviet Congress of Writers. It demanded adherence to a communist worldview in works of literature. Its doctrines required an objective viewpoint comprehensible to the working classes and themes of social struggle featuring strong proletarian heroes. A successful work of socialist realism is Nikolay Ostrovsky's *Kak zakalyalas stal (How the Steel Was Tempered*). Also known as Social Realism.

Soliloquy: A monologue in a drama used to give the audience information and to develop the speaker's character. It is typically a projection of the speaker's innermost thoughts. Usually delivered while the speaker is alone on stage, a soliloquy is intended to present an illusion of unspoken reflection. A celebrated soliloquy is Hamlet's ''To be or not to be'' speech in William Shakespeare's *Hamlet.*

Sonnet: A fourteen-line poem, usually composed in iambic pentameter, employing one of several rhyme schemes. There are three major types of sonnets, upon which all other variations of the form are based: the ''Petrarchan'' or ''Italian'' sonnet, the ''Shakespearean'' or ''English'' sonnet, and the ''Spenserian'' sonnet. A Petrarchan sonnet consists of an octave rhymed *abbaabba* and a ''sestet'' rhymed either *cdecde, cdccdc,* or *cdedce.* The octave poses a question or problem, relates a narrative, or puts forth a proposition; the sestet presents a solution to the problem, comments upon the narrative, or applies the proposition put forth in the octave. The Shakespearean sonnet is divided into three quatrains and a couplet rhymed *abab cdcd efef gg.* The couplet provides an epigrammatic comment on the narrative or problem put forth in the quatrains. The Spenserian sonnet uses three quatrains and a couplet like the Shakespearean, but links their three rhyme schemes in this way: *abab bcbc cdcd ee.* The Spenserian sonnet develops its theme in two parts like the Petrarchan, its final six lines resolving a problem, analyzing a narrative, or applying a proposition put forth in its first eight lines. Examples of sonnets can be found in Petrarch's *Canzoniere,* Edmund Spenser's *Amoretti,* Elizabeth Barrett

Browning's *Sonnets from the Portuguese,* Rainer Maria Rilke's *Sonnets to Orpheus,* and Adrienne Rich's poem "The Insusceptibles."

Spenserian Sonnet: See *Sonnet*

Spenserian Stanza: A nine-line stanza having eight verses in iambic pentameter, its ninth verse in iambic hexameter, and the rhyme scheme ababbcbcc. This stanza form was first used by Edmund Spenser in his allegorical poem *The Faerie Queene.*

Spondee: In poetry meter, a foot consisting of two long or stressed syllables occurring together. This form is quite rare in English verse, and is usually composed of two monosyllabic words. The first foot in the following line from Robert Burns's "Green Grow the Rashes" is an example of a spondee: Green grow the rashes, O

Sprung Rhythm: Versification using a specific number of accented syllables per line but disregarding the number of unaccented syllables that fall in each line, producing an irregular rhythm in the poem. Gerard Manley Hopkins, who coined the term "sprung rhythm," is the most notable practitioner of this technique.

Stanza: A subdivision of a poem consisting of lines grouped together, often in recurring patterns of rhyme, line length, and meter. Stanzas may also serve as units of thought in a poem much like paragraphs in prose. Examples of stanza forms include the quatrain, *terza rima, ottava rima,* Spenserian, and the so-called *In Memoriam* stanza from Alfred, Lord Tennyson's poem by that title. The following is an example of the latter form: Love is and was my lord and king, And in his presence I attend To hear the tidings of my friend, Which every hour his couriers bring.

Stereotype: A stereotype was originally the name for a duplication made during the printing process; this led to its modern definition as a person or thing that is (or is assumed to be) the same as all others of its type. Common stereotypical characters include the absent- minded professor, the nagging wife, the troublemaking teenager, and the kindhearted grandmother.

Stream of Consciousness: A narrative technique for rendering the inward experience of a character. This technique is designed to give the impression of an ever-changing series of thoughts, emotions, images, and memories in the spontaneous and seemingly illogical order that they occur in life. The textbook example of stream of consciousness is the last section of James Joyce's *Ulysses.*

Structuralism: A twentieth-century movement in literary criticism that examines how literary texts arrive at their meanings, rather than the meanings themselves. There are two major types of structuralist analysis: one examines the way patterns of linguistic structures unify a specific text and emphasize certain elements of that text, and the other interprets the way literary forms and conventions affect the meaning of language itself. Prominent structuralists include Michel Foucault, Roman Jakobson, and Roland Barthes.

Structure: The form taken by a piece of literature. The structure may be made obvious for ease of understanding, as in nonfiction works, or may obscured for artistic purposes, as in some poetry or seemingly "unstructured" prose. Examples of common literary structures include the plot of a narrative, the acts and scenes of a drama, and such poetic forms as the Shakespearean sonnet and the Pindaric ode.

Sturm und Drang: A German term meaning "storm and stress." It refers to a German literary movement of the 1770s and 1780s that reacted against the order and rationalism of the enlightenment, focusing instead on the intense experience of extraordinary individuals. Highly romantic, works of this movement, such as Johann Wolfgang von Goethe's *Gotz von Berlichingen,* are typified by realism, rebelliousness, and intense emotionalism.

Style: A writer's distinctive manner of arranging words to suit his or her ideas and purpose in writing. The unique imprint of the author's personality upon his or her writing, style is the product of an author's way of arranging ideas and his or her use of diction, different sentence structures, rhythm, figures of speech, rhetorical principles, and other elements of composition. Styles may be classified according to period (Metaphysical, Augustan, Georgian), individual authors (Chaucerian, Miltonic, Jamesian), level (grand, middle, low, plain), or language (scientific, expository, poetic, journalistic).

Subject: The person, event, or theme at the center of a work of literature. A work may have one or more subjects of each type, with shorter works tending to have fewer and longer works tending to have more. The subjects of James Baldwin's novel *Go Tell It on the Mountain* include the themes of father-son relationships, religious conversion, black life, and sexuality. The subjects of Anne Frank's

Diary of a Young Girl include Anne and her family members as well as World War II, the Holocaust, and the themes of war, isolation, injustice, and racism.

Subjectivity: Writing that expresses the author's personal feelings about his subject, and which may or may not include factual information about the subject. Subjectivity is demonstrated in James Joyce's *Portrait of the Artist as a Young Man,* Samuel Butler's *The Way of All Flesh,* and Thomas Wolfe's *Look Homeward, Angel.*

Subplot: A secondary story in a narrative. A subplot may serve as a motivating or complicating force for the main plot of the work, or it may provide emphasis for, or relief from, the main plot. The conflict between the Capulets and the Montagues in William Shakespeare's *Romeo and Juliet* is an example of a subplot.

Surrealism: A term introduced to criticism by Guillaume Apollinaire and later adopted by Andre Breton. It refers to a French literary and artistic movement founded in the 1920s. The Surrealists sought to express unconscious thoughts and feelings in their works. The best-known technique used for achieving this aim was automatic writing—transcriptions of spontaneous outpourings from the unconscious. The Surrealists proposed to unify the contrary levels of conscious and unconscious, dream and reality, objectivity and subjectivity into a new level of "super-realism." Surrealism can be found in the poetry of Paul Eluard, Pierre Reverdy, and Louis Aragon, among others.

Suspense: A literary device in which the author maintains the audience's attention through the build-up of events, the outcome of which will soon be revealed. Suspense in William Shakespeare's *Hamlet* is sustained throughout by the question of whether or not the Prince will achieve what he has been instructed to do and of what he intends to do.

Syllogism: A method of presenting a logical argument. In its most basic form, the syllogism consists of a major premise, a minor premise, and a conclusion. An example of a syllogism is: Major premise: When it snows, the streets get wet. Minor premise: It is snowing. Conclusion: The streets are wet.

Symbol: Something that suggests or stands for something else without losing its original identity. In literature, symbols combine their literal meaning with the suggestion of an abstract concept. Literary symbols are of two types: those that carry complex associations of meaning no matter what their con-

texts, and those that derive their suggestive meaning from their functions in specific literary works. Examples of symbols are sunshine suggesting happiness, rain suggesting sorrow, and storm clouds suggesting despair.

Symbolism: This term has two widely accepted meanings. In historical criticism, it denotes an early modernist literary movement initiated in France during the nineteenth century that reacted against the prevailing standards of realism. Writers in this movement aimed to evoke, indirectly and symbolically, an order of being beyond the material world of the five senses. Poetic expression of personal emotion figured strongly in the movement, typically by means of a private set of symbols uniquely identifiable with the individual poet. The principal aim of the Symbolists was to express in words the highly complex feelings that grew out of everyday contact with the world. In a broader sense, the term "symbolism" refers to the use of one object to represent another. Early members of the Symbolist movement included the French authors Charles Baudelaire and Arthur Rimbaud; William Butler Yeats, James Joyce, and T. S. Eliot were influenced as the movement moved to Ireland, England, and the United States. Examples of the concept of symbolism include a flag that stands for a nation or movement, or an empty cupboard used to suggest hopelessness, poverty, and despair.

Symbolist: See *Symbolism*

Symbolist Movement: See *Symbolism*

Sympathetic Fallacy: See *Affective Fallacy*

T

Tale: A story told by a narrator with a simple plot and little character development. Tales are usually relatively short and often carry a simple message. Examples of tales can be found in the work of Rudyard Kipling, Somerset Maugham, Saki, Anton Chekhov, Guy de Maupassant, and Armistead Maupin.

Tall Tale: A humorous tale told in a straightforward, credible tone but relating absolutely impossible events or feats of the characters. Such tales were commonly told of frontier adventures during the settlement of the west in the United States. Tall tales have been spun around such legendary heroes as Mike Fink, Paul Bunyan, Davy Crockett, Johnny Appleseed, and Captain Stormalong as well as the real-life William F. Cody and Annie Oakley. Literary use of tall tales can be found in Washington Irving's *History of New York,* Mark Twain's *Life on the Mississippi,* and in the German R. F. Raspe's *Baron Munchausen's Narratives of His Marvellous Travels and Campaigns in Russia.*

Tanka: A form of Japanese poetry similar to *haiku.* A *tanka* is five lines long, with the lines containing five, seven, five, seven, and seven syllables respectively. Skilled *tanka* authors include Ishikawa Takuboku, Masaoka Shiki, Amy Lowell, and Adelaide Crapsey.

Teatro Grottesco: See *Theater of the Grotesque*

Terza Rima: A three-line stanza form in poetry in which the rhymes are made on the last word of each line in the following manner: the first and third lines of the first stanza, then the second line of the first stanza and the first and third lines of the second stanza, and so on with the middle line of any stanza rhyming with the first and third lines of the following stanza. An example of *terza rima* is Percy Bysshe Shelley's ''The Triumph of Love'': As in that trance of wondrous thought I lay This was the tenour of my waking dream. Methought I sate beside a public way Thick strewn with summer dust, and a great stream Of people there was hurrying to and fro Numerous as gnats upon the evening gleam,. . .

Tetrameter: See *Meter*

Textual Criticism: A branch of literary criticism that seeks to establish the authoritative text of a literary work. Textual critics typically compare all known manuscripts or printings of a single work in order to assess the meanings of differences and revisions. This procedure allows them to arrive at a definitive version that (supposedly) corresponds to the author's original intention. Textual criticism was applied during the Renaissance to salvage the classical texts of Greece and Rome, and modern works have been studied, for instance, to undo deliberate correction or censorship, as in the case of novels by Stephen Crane and Theodore Dreiser.

Theater of Cruelty: Term used to denote a group of theatrical techniques designed to eliminate the psychological and emotional distance between actors and audience. This concept, introduced in the 1930s in France, was intended to inspire a more intense theatrical experience than conventional theater allowed. The ''cruelty'' of this dramatic theory signified not sadism but heightened actor/audience involvement in the dramatic event. The theater of cruelty was theorized by Antonin Artaud in his *Le Theatre et son double* (*The Theatre and Its Double*), and also appears in the work of Jerzy Grotowski, Jean Genet, Jean Vilar, and Arthur Adamov, among others.

Theater of the Absurd: A post-World War II dramatic trend characterized by radical theatrical innovations. In works influenced by the Theater of the absurd, nontraditional, sometimes grotesque characterizations, plots, and stage sets reveal a meaningless universe in which human values are irrelevant. Existentialist themes of estrangement, absurdity, and futility link many of the works of this movement. The principal writers of the Theater of the Absurd are Samuel Beckett, Eugene Ionesco, Jean Genet, and Harold Pinter.

Theater of the Grotesque: An Italian theatrical movement characterized by plays written around the ironic and macabre aspects of daily life in the World War I era. Theater of the Grotesque was named after the play *The Mask and the Face* by Luigi Chiarelli, which was described as ''a grotesque in three acts.'' The movement influenced the work of Italian dramatist Luigi Pirandello, author of *Right You Are, If You Think You Are.* Also known as *Teatro Grottesco.*

Theme: The main point of a work of literature. The term is used interchangeably with thesis. The theme of William Shakespeare's *Othello*—jealousy—is a common one.

Thesis: A thesis is both an essay and the point argued in the essay. Thesis novels and thesis plays share the quality of containing a thesis which is supported through the action of the story. A master's thesis and a doctoral dissertation are two theses required of graduate students.

Thesis Play: See *Thesis*

Three Unities: See *Unities*

Tone: The author's attitude toward his or her audience may be deduced from the tone of the work. A formal tone may create distance or convey politeness, while an informal tone may encourage a friendly, intimate, or intrusive feeling in the reader. The author's attitude toward his or her subject matter may also be deduced from the tone of the words he or she uses in discussing it. The tone of John F. Kennedy's speech which included the appeal to ''ask not what your country can do for you'' was intended to instill feelings of camaraderie and national pride in listeners.

Tragedy: A drama in prose or poetry about a noble, courageous hero of excellent character who, because of some tragic character flaw or *hamartia*, brings ruin upon him- or herself. Tragedy treats its subjects in a dignified and serious manner, using poetic language to help evoke pity and fear and bring about catharsis, a purging of these emotions. The tragic form was practiced extensively by the ancient Greeks. In the Middle Ages, when classical works were virtually unknown, tragedy came to denote any works about the fall of persons from exalted to low conditions due to any reason: fate, vice, weakness, etc. According to the classical definition of tragedy, such works present the ''pathetic''—that which evokes pity—rather than the tragic. The classical form of tragedy was revived in the sixteenth century; it flourished especially on the Elizabethan stage. In modern times, dramatists have attempted to adapt the form to the needs of modern society by drawing their heroes from the ranks of ordinary men and women and defining the nobility of these heroes in terms of spirit rather than exalted social standing. The greatest classical example of tragedy is Sophocles' *Oedipus Rex*. The ''pathetic'' derivation is exemplified in ''The Monk's Tale'' in Geoffrey Chaucer's *Canterbury Tales*. Notable works produced during the sixteenth century revival include William Shakespeare's *Hamlet, Othello,* and *King Lear*. Modern dramatists working in the tragic tradition include Henrik Ibsen, Arthur Miller, and Eugene O'Neill.

Tragedy of Blood: See *Revenge Tragedy*

Tragic Flaw: In a tragedy, the quality within the hero or heroine which leads to his or her downfall. Examples of the tragic flaw include Othello's jealousy and Hamlet's indecisiveness, although most great tragedies defy such simple interpretation.

Transcendentalism: An American philosophical and religious movement, based in New England from around 1835 until the Civil War. Transcendentalism was a form of American romanticism that had its roots abroad in the works of Thomas Carlyle, Samuel Coleridge, and Johann Wolfgang von Goethe. The Transcendentalists stressed the importance of intuition and subjective experience in communication with God. They rejected religious dogma and texts in favor of mysticism and scientific naturalism. They pursued truths that lie beyond the ''colorless'' realms perceived by reason and the senses and were active social reformers in public education, women's rights, and the abolition of slavery. Prominent members of the group include Ralph Waldo Emerson and Henry David Thoreau.

Trickster: A character or figure common in Native American and African literature who uses his ingenuity to defeat enemies and escape difficult situations. Tricksters are most often animals, such as the spider, hare, or coyote, although they may take the form of humans as well. Examples of trickster tales include Thomas King's *A Coyote Columbus Story,* Ashley F. Bryan's *The Dancing Granny* and Ishmael Reed's *The Last Days of Louisiana Red.*

Trimeter: See *Meter*

Triple Rhyme: See *Rhyme*

Trochee: See *Foot*

U

Understatement: See *Irony*

Unities: Strict rules of dramatic structure, formulated by Italian and French critics of the Renaissance and based loosely on the principles of drama discussed by Aristotle in his *Poetics*. Foremost among these rules were the three unities of action, time, and place that compelled a dramatist to: (1) construct a single plot with a beginning, middle, and end that details the causal relationships of action and character; (2) restrict the action to the events of a single day; and (3) limit the scene to a single place or city. The unities were observed faithfully by continental European writers until the Romantic Age, but they were never regularly observed in English drama. Modern dramatists are typically more concerned with a unity of impression or emotional effect than with any of the classical unities. The unities are observed in Pierre Corneille's tragedy *Polyeuctes* and Jean-Baptiste Racine's *Phedre.* Also known as Three Unities.

Urban Realism: A branch of realist writing that attempts to accurately reflect the often harsh facts of modern urban existence. Some works by Stephen Crane, Theodore Dreiser, Charles Dickens, Fyodor Dostoyevsky, Emile Zola, Abraham Cahan, and Henry Fuller feature urban realism. Modern examples include Claude Brown's *Manchild in the Promised Land* and Ron Milner's *What the Wine Sellers Buy.*

Utopia: A fictional perfect place, such as ''paradise'' or ''heaven.'' Early literary utopias were included in Plato's *Republic* and Sir Thomas More's

Utopia, while more modern utopias can be found in Samuel Butler's *Erewhon,* Theodor Herzka's *A Visit to Freeland,* and H. G. Wells' *A Modern Utopia.*

Utopian: See *Utopia*

Utopianism: See *Utopia*

V

Verisimilitude: Literally, the appearance of truth. In literary criticism, the term refers to aspects of a work of literature that seem true to the reader. Verisimilitude is achieved in the work of Honore de Balzac, Gustave Flaubert, and Henry James, among other late nineteenth-century realist writers.

Vers de societe: See *Occasional Verse*

Vers libre: See *Free Verse*

Verse: A line of metered language, a line of a poem, or any work written in verse. The following line of verse is from the epic poem *Don Juan* by Lord Byron: ''My way is to begin with the beginning.''

Versification: The writing of verse. Versification may also refer to the meter, rhyme, and other mechanical components of a poem. Composition of a ''Roses are red, violets are blue'' poem to suit an occasion is a common form of versification practiced by students.

Victorian: Refers broadly to the reign of Queen Victoria of England (1837-1901) and to anything with qualities typical of that era. For example, the qualities of smug narrowmindedness, bourgeois materialism, faith in social progress, and priggish morality are often considered Victorian. This stereotype is contradicted by such dramatic intellectual developments as the theories of Charles Darwin, Karl Marx, and Sigmund Freud (which stirred strong debates in England) and the critical attitudes of serious Victorian writers like Charles Dickens and George Eliot. In literature, the Victorian Period was the great age of the English novel, and the latter part of the era saw the rise of movements such as decadence and symbolism. Works of Victorian lit-

erature include the poetry of Robert Browning and Alfred, Lord Tennyson, the criticism of Matthew Arnold and John Ruskin, and the novels of Emily Bronte, William Makepeace Thackeray, and Thomas Hardy. Also known as Victorian Age and Victorian Period.

Victorian Age: See *Victorian*

Victorian Period: See *Victorian*

W

Weltanschauung: A German term referring to a person's worldview or philosophy. Examples of *weltanschauung* include Thomas Hardy's view of the human being as the victim of fate, destiny, or impersonal forces and circumstances, and the disillusioned and laconic cynicism expressed by such poets of the 1930s as W. H. Auden, Sir Stephen Spender, and Sir William Empson.

Weltschmerz: A German term meaning ''world pain.'' It describes a sense of anguish about the nature of existence, usually associated with a melancholy, pessimistic attitude. *Weltschmerz* was expressed in England by George Gordon, Lord Byron in his *Manfred* and *Childe Harold's Pilgrimage,* in France by Viscount de Chateaubriand, Alfred de Vigny, and Alfred de Musset, in Russia by Aleksandr Pushkin and Mikhail Lermontov, in Poland by Juliusz Slowacki, and in America by Nathaniel Hawthorne.

Z

Zarzuela: A type of Spanish operetta. Writers of *zarzuelas* include Lope de Vega and Pedro Calderon.

Zeitgeist: A German term meaning ''spirit of the time.'' It refers to the moral and intellectual trends of a given era. Examples of *zeitgeist* include the preoccupation with the more morbid aspects of dying and death in some Jacobean literature, especially in the works of dramatists Cyril Tourneur and John Webster, and the decadence of the French Symbolists.

Cumulative
Author/Title Index

Nationality/Ethnicity Index

Subject/Theme Index